PRIMARY SOURCE
DOCUMENTS IN GLOBAL HISTORY
VOLUME I: TO 1650

Upper Saddle River, New Jersey 07458

© 2008 by PEARSON EDUCATION, INC.
Upper Saddle River, New Jersey 07458

V036 10 9 8 7 6 5 4 3

ISBN-13: 978-0-13-243203-0
ISBN-10:   0-13-243203-X

Printed in the United States of America

Contents

DOCUMENTS BY TIMELINE

HUMAN BEGINNINGS (1.5 MILLION BP–5,000 BCE)

Chapter 1 - Human Origins   **1**
Margaret Meade, from "Warfare is Only an Invention—Not a Biological Necessity"   1
Jane Goodall, from "The Challenge Lies in All of Us"   5
Marshall Sahlins, "The Original Affluent Society," from *Stone Age Economics*   8

Chapter 2 - Agriculture   **13**
Charles Darwin, "Cultivated Plants: Cereal and Culinary Plants,"   13
    from *The Variation of Animals and Plants under Domestication*
David Rindos, from "Symbiosis, Instability, and the Origins and   17
    Spread of Agriculture: A New Model"
Jack Harlan, from *Crops and Man*   26
James Cook, from *Captain Cook's Journal During his First Voyage Round the World*   28

EARLY STATE BUILDINGS (5,000 BCE–500 BCE)

Chapter 3 - Kings and Priests   **35**
Egyptian Diplomatic Correspondence: Excerpts from *The Amarna Letters*   35
Sumerian Law Code: *The Code of Lipit-Ishtar*   39
The Code of Hammurabi   40
Excerpts from *The Epic of Gilgamesh*   44
Hou-Ji, from *The Shih-Ching*   47
Hittite Law Code: Excerpts from *The Code of the Nesilim*   49
Ancient Egyptian and Hittite Voices: (a) letter from the Pharoah   52
    to Harkhuf the explorer; (b) Ramses III, "The War Against the
    Sea Peoples;" (c) Hittite Soldiers' Oath
Liu and Tan-Fu the Duke, from *The Shih-Ching*   56
Mission to Byblos: *The Report of Wenamun*   61
The Book of Job and Jewish Literature   66
The Babylonian Chronicles, "The Fall of Nineveh Chronicle"   69

Chapter 4 - Farmer and Traders   **72**
Ptahhotep, from the *Egyptian Book of Instructions*   72
Syrian Government Documents: *The Archives of Ebla*   78
Hittite Land Deed   89
Hesiod, Excerpt from *Works and Days*   89

Aristophanes, Excerpt from *The Birds*   93
Early Criminal Justice: The Nippur Murder Trial and the "Silent Wife"   96
Praise of the Scribe's Profession: Egyptian Letter   97
Workings of Ma'at: "The Tale of the Eloquent Peasant"   99
Ancestor Worship: from *The Shih-Ching*   109

THE GREAT IDEAS (1000 BCE–300 BCE)

Chapter 5 - Hinduism and Buddhism   111
Excerpt from the Upanishads   111
Selections from the *Rig Veda*   115
Vardhamana Mahavira, Selections from *Akaranga-sutra*,   118
    "Jain Doctrines and Practices of Nonviolence"
Siddhartha Gautama: "Identity and Nonidentity"   119
Buddhism: Excerpts from the *Dhammapada*   127

Chapter 6 - The Great Thinkers   139
Laozi, from *Tao Te Ching*, "The Unvarying Way"   139
Confucius, Selections from the *Analects*   140
Plato, *The Republic*, "The Philosopher-King"   146
Plato, *The Republic*, "On Shadows and Realities in Education"   149
Aristotle, Excerpts from *Physics and Posterior Analytics*   152
The Nyaya School: "Explanation of the Sutra"   159
Liu An: Excerpt from *Huan Nan Tzu*   161
Confucian Political Philosophy: An Excerpt from Mencius   162
Legalism: Selections from *The Writings of Han Fei*   166

EMPIRES AND BARBARIANS (500 BCE–900 CE)

Chapter 7 - The Idea of Empire   168
Agatharchides of Kindos Describes Saba   168
Zhang Quian, *Han Shu*, "Descriptions of the Western Regions"   169
Pliny the Elder, from *The Natural History*   171
Greece and Persia: The Treaty of Antalcides, 387 BCE   173
Horace, "Dulce et Decorum est Pro Patria Mori"   173
Kautilya, from *Arthashastra*, "The Duties of Government Superintendents"   174
Sima Qian, *The Life of Meng Tian, Builder of the Great Wall*   177
Emperor Asoka, from *The Edicts of Asoka*   180
Excerpts from *The Questions of King Milinda*   183

Chapter 8 - The Collapse of Empires   187
Treaty between Tibet and China, 821–822 CE   187
Excerpts from the *Hildebrandslied*   188
Jordanes, *Deeds of the Goths*, Book Twenty-six   190
Faxien, *Record of Buddhist Countries*, Chapter Sixteen   192
Arabic Poetry: "The Poem of Antar"   194
Excerpts from the *Taika Reform Edicts*   199
Chinese Description of the Tibetans   207
Sidonius Appollinaris: Rome's Decay, and a Glimpse of the New Order   208
Indian Land Grants, 753 CE   212

CHRISTIANITY AND ISLAM (100 CE–1200 CE)

Chapter 9 - Christianity **213**
The Acts of the Apostles, Paul Pronounces the "Good News" in Greece   213
St. Augustine of Hippo: Theory of the "Just War"   215
Pope Leo I on Bishop Hilary of Aries   217
Pliny the Younger, "Epistulae" Letters   218
Paulus Orosius, from *Seven Books of History Against the Pagans*   222
Bishop Synesius of Cyrene: Letter to his Brother   223

Chapter 10 - Islam **226**
A Selection from Muhammad's Orations   226
Rabia al-Adawiyya, "Brothers, My Peace is in my Aloneness"   228
Harun al-Rashid and the Zenith of the Caliphate   228
Excerpts from the Quran   231
Ali: Instructions to Malik al-Ashtar, Governor of Egypt   241
Al-Tabari: Muhammad's Call to Prophesy   244
Al-Tabari and Ibn Hisham, from "The Founding of the Caliphate"   245
Al-Farabi, from *Al-Farabi on the Perfect State*   248
Science and Mathematics: (a) Al-Ghazzali, "On the Separation of Mathematics   253
    and Religion;" (b) Al-Razi, "On the Causes of Smallpox"

CONSOLIDATION AND INTERACTION OF STATES AND IDEAS (800 CE–1500 CE)

Chapter 11 - States, Old and New **255**
Winada Prapanca, *Nagara Kertagama*   255
Anna Comnena, from *The Alexaid*   256
Eusebius of Caesarea, Selections from *The Life of Constantine*   257
Buddhism in Japan: *The Taika Reform Edicts*   259
Excerpts from the *Taika Reform Edicts*   260
Abi Yaqubi, Excerpt from *Tarikh*   267
Selection from *Nihongi*, "The Age of the Gods"   268
Nineteenth-century European Descriptions of the Pacific Island of Lelu   273
Nestor, *The Russian Primary Chronicle*   275
Einhard, Preface to *The Life of Charlemagne*   276
Tang Daizong on *The Art of Government*   277
An Essay Question from the Chinese Imperial Examination System   278
Nineteenth-century Description of Cahokia   280
The Magna Carta 1215   282

Chapter 12 - Eurasian Contacts and Encounters before 1450 **284**
The Mongols: An Excerpt from the *Novgorod Chronicle*, 1315   284
Excerpt from William of Rubruck's Account of the Mongols   285
Behâ-ed-Din: Richard I Massacres Prisoners after Taking Acre, 1191   289
The Book of Dede Korkut, "The Story of Bugach Khan"   291
al-Tha'alibi, *Recollections of Bukhara*   299
Liutprand of Cremona, Excerpt from *Report of his Mission to Constantinople*   299
Benjamin of Tudela, Selection from *Book of Travels*   301
Lu You, Excerpt from *Diary of a Journey to Sichuan*   304
Marco Polo, Excerpt from *Travels*   306
A Fourteenth-century Italian Guide for Merchants   307

Excerpts from The History of the Life and Travels of Rabban Bar Sawma   312
Marchione di Coppo Stefani, *The Florentine Chronicle*, "Concerning a Mortality   317
    in the City of Florence in which Many People Died"
Ibn Battuta, *The Travels of Ibn Battuta*, "Ibn Battuta in Mali"   320
Selection from *Narrative of the Journey of Abd-er Razzak*   322
Ma Huan, Excerpt from *The Overall Survey of the Ocean's Shores*   328
Al'Umari Describes Mansa Musa of Mali   333
Anonymous Descriptions of the Cities of Zanj   338
Ibn Wahab: An Arab Merchant Visits Tang China   340

Chapter 13 - Medieval and Early Modern Thought   342

Jean Bodin, *Six Books of the Commonwealth*, "The True Attributes of Sovereignty"   342
Kino Tsurayaki, Excerpt from *The Tosa Diary*   344
Speculum Principi, "The Animal Life of Greenland and the   350
    Character of the Land in Those Regions"
Murasaki Shikibu, Selections from *The Tale of Genji*   352
Peter Abelard, "Sic et Non"   371
Al Ghazali, Excerpt from *Confessions*   373
Roger Bacon on Experimental Science, 1268   374
Saint Francis of Assisi, Selection from his *Admonitions*   379
University of Paris Medical Faculty, Writings on the Plague   381
John Ball Sermon   389
Ibn Battuta, Selections from the *Rihla*   391
Hugo Grotius, Selections from *On the Law of War and Peace*   396
Niccolo Machiavelli, Excerpts from *The Prince*   398
Thomas Aquinas, *Summa Theologica*, "Of Human Law"   401

CONVERGENCE AND DIVERGENCE (1500–1800)

Chapter 14 - Islamic Empires   405

Excerpts from the Biography of Emperor Akbar of India   405
Abu'l-Fazl Allami's Ain-i-Akbari   409
Sunni versus Shi'ite: Letter from Selim I to Ismail I   410
Ogier Ghiselin de Busbecq, "Süleyman the Lawgiver"   412
Ogier Ghiselin de Busbecq, Excerpt from "Women in Ottoman Society"   414
Paul Rycaut, on the State of the Ottoman Empire, 1668   415
Fathers Simon and Vincent Report on Shah Abbas I, the Safavid Ruler of Persia   417
Excerpts from the Biography of Shah Abbas I   420

Chapter 1

Human Origins

Margaret Mead, from "Warfare is Only an Invention—Not a Biological Necessity"

Margaret Mead (1901–1978 CE) was an American anthropologist who made her fame studying cultures in the South Pacific. Her work compares child-rearing practices in different societies. In her classic books Coming of Age in Samoa *(1928) and* Growing Up in New Guinea *(1930) Mead concludes that children learn the values of their culture, so that experiences of childhood and adolescence (and other values in general) vary considerably across societies. Her 1940 essay "Warfare is Only an Invention—Not a Biological Necessity" was written while German and Japanese fascists were overrunning large parts of Eurasia.*

Source: *Mead, Margaret. "Warfare is Only an Invention—Not a Biological Necessity," ASIA, XL 1940.*

Focus Questions:
1. According to Mead, what are the causes and types of violence?
2. What is the difference between violence and war?
3. Why war?

Is war a biological necessity, a sociological inevitability, or just a bad invention? Those who argue for the first view endow man with such pugnacious instincts that some outlet in aggressive behavior is necessary if man is to reach full human stature. It was this point of view which lay behind William James's famous essay, 'The Moral Equivalent of War', in which he tried to retain the warlike virtues and channel them in new directions. A similar point of view has lain behind the Soviet Union's attempt to make competition between groups rather than between individuals. A basic, competitive, aggressive, warring human nature is assumed, and those who wish to outlaw war or outlaw competitiveness merely try to find new and less socially destructive ways in which these biologically given aspects of man's nature can find expression. Then there are those who take the second view: warfare is the inevitable concomitant of the development of the state, the struggle for land and natural resources, of class societies springing not from the nature of man, but, from the nature of history. War is nevertheless inevitable unless we change our social system and outlaw classes, the struggle for power, and possessions; and in the event of our success warfare would disappear, as a symptom vanishes when the disease is cured.

One may hold a sort of compromise position between these two extremes; one may claim that all aggression springs from the frustration of man's biologically determined drives and that, since all forms of culture are frustrating, it is certain each new generation will be aggressive and the aggression will find its natural and inevitable expression in race war, class war, nationalistic war, and so on. All three of these positions are very popular today among those who think seriously about the problems of war and its possible prevention, but I wish to urge another point of view, less defeatist, perhaps, than the first and third and more accurate than the second: that is, that warfare, by which I mean recognised conflict between two groups as groups, in which each group puts an army (even if the army is only fifteen pygmies) into the field to fight and kill, if possible, some of the members of the army of the other group—that warfare of this sort is an invention like any other of the inventions in terms of which we order our lives, such as writing, marriage, cooking our food instead of eating it raw, trial by jury, or burial of the dead, and so on. Some of this list anyone will grant are inventions: trial by jury is confined to very limited portions of the globe; we know that there are tribes that do not bury their dead but instead expose or cremate them; and we know that only part of the human race has had the knowledge of writing as its cultural inheritance. But, whenever a way of doing things is found universally, such as the use of fire or the practice of some form of marriage, we tend to think at once that it is not an invention at all but an attribute of humanity itself. And yet even such universals as marriage and the use of fire are inventions like the rest, very basic ones, inventions which were, perhaps, necessary if human history was to take the turn that it has taken, but nevertheless inventions. At some point in his social development man was undoubtedly without the institution of marriage or the knowledge of the use of fire.

The case for warfare is much clearer because there are peoples even today who have no warfare. Of these the Eskimos are perhaps the most conspicuous examples, but the Lepchas of Sikkim described by Geoffrey Gorer in Himalayan Village are as good. Neither of these peoples understands war, not even defensive warfare. The idea of warfare is lacking, and this idea is as essential to really carrying on war as an alphabet or a syllabary is to writing. But, whereas the Lepchas are a gentle, unquarrelsome people, and the advocates of other points of view might argue that they are not full human beings or that they had never been frustrated and so had no aggression to expand in warfare, the Eskimo case gives no such possibility of interpretation. The Eskimos are not a mild and meek people; many of them are turbulent and troublesome. Fights, theft of wives, murder, cannibalism, occur among them—all outbursts of passionate men goaded by desire or intolerable circumstance. Here are men faced with hunger, men faced with loss of their wives, men faced with the threat of extermination by other men, and here are orphan children, growing up miserably with no one to care for them, mocked and neglected by those about them. The personality necessary for war, the circumstances necessary to goad men to desperation are present, but there is no war. When a travelling Eskimo entered a settlement, he might have to fight the strongest man in the settlement to establish his position among them, but this was a test of strength and bravery, not war. The idea of warfare, of one group organising against another group to maim and wound and kill them was absent. And, without that idea, passions might rage but there was no war.

But, it may be argued, is not this because the Eskimos have such a low and undeveloped form of social organisation? They own no land, they move from place to place, camping, it is true, season after season on the same site, but this is not something to fight for as the modern nations of the world fight for land and raw materials. They have no permanent possessions that can be looted, no towns that can be burned. They have no social classes to produce stress and strains within the society which might force it to go to war outside. Does not the absence of war among the Eskimos, while disproving the biological necessity of war, just go to confirm the point that it is the state of development of the society which accounts for war and nothing else?

We find the answer among the pygmy peoples of the Andaman Islands in the Bay of Bengal. The Andamans also represent an exceedingly low level of society; they are a hunting and food-gathering people; they live in tiny hordes without any class stratification; their houses are simpler than the snow houses of the Eskimo. But they knew about warfare. The army might contain only fifteen determined pygmies marching in a straight line, but it was the real thing none the less. Tiny army met tiny army in open battle, blows were exchanged, casualties suffered, and the state of warfare could only be concluded by a peacemaking ceremony.

Similarly, among the Australian aborigines, who built no permanent dwellings but wandered from water hole to water hole over their almost desert country, warfare—and rules of 'international law'—were highly developed. The student of social evolution will seek in vain for his obvious causes of war, struggle for lands, struggle for power of one group over another, expansion of population, need to divert the minds of a populace restive under tyranny, or even the ambition of a successful leader to enhance his own prestige. All are absent, but warfare as a practice remained, and men engaged in it and killed one another in the course of a war because killing is what is done in wars.

From instances like these it becomes apparent that an inquiry into the causes of war misses the fundamental point as completely as does an insistence upon the biological necessity of war. If a people have an idea of going to war and the idea that war is the way in which certain situations, defined within their society, are to be handled, they will sometimes go to war. If they are a mild and unaggressive people, like the Pueblo Indians, they may limit themselves to defensive warfare, but they will be forced to think in terms of war because there are peoples near them who have warfare as a pattern, and offensive, raiding, pillaging warfare at that. When the pattern of warfare is known, people like the Pueblo Indians will defend themselves, taking advantage of their natural defences, the mesa village site, and people like the Lepchas, having no natural defences and no idea of warfare, will merely submit to the invader. But the essential point remains the same. There is a way of behaving which is known to a given people and labelled as an appropriate form of behaviour; a bold and warlike people like the Sioux or the Maori may label warfare as desirable as well as possible, a mild people like the Pueblo Indians may label warfare as undesirable, but to the minds of both peoples the possibility of warfare is present. Their thoughts, their hopes, their plans are oriented about this idea—that warfare may be selected as the way to meet some situation.

So simple peoples and civilised peoples, mild peoples and violent, assertive peoples, will all go to war if they have the invention, just as those peoples who have the custom of duelling will have duels and peoples who have the pattern of vendetta will indulge in vendetta. And, conversely, peoples who do not know of duelling will not fight duels, even though their wives are seduced and their daughters ravished; they may on occasion commit murder but they will not fight duels. Cultures which lack the idea of the vendetta will not meet every quarrel in this way. A people can use only the forms it has. So the Balinese have their special way of dealing with a quarrel between two individuals: if the two feel that the causes of quarrel are heavy, they may go and register their quarrel in the temple before the gods, and, making offerings, they may swear never to have anything to do with each other again...But in other societies, although individuals might feel as full of animosity and as unwilling to have any further contact as do the Balinese, they cannot register their quarrel with the gods and go on quietly about their business because registering quarrels with the gods is not an invention of which they know.

Yet, if it be granted that warfare is, after all, an invention, it may nevertheless be an invention that lends itself to certain types of personality, to the exigent needs of autocrats, to the expansionist desires of crowded peoples, to the desire for plunder and rape and loot which is engendered by a dull and frustrating life. What, then, can we say of this congruence between warfare and its uses? If it is a form which fits so well, is not this congruence the essential point? But even here the primitive material causes us to wonder, because there are tribes who go to war merely for glory, having no quarrel with the enemy, suffering from no tyrant within their boundaries, anxious neither for land nor loot nor women, but merely anxious to win prestige which within that tribe has been declared obtainable only by war and without which no young man can hope to win his sweetheart's smile of approval. But if, as was the case with the Bush Negroes of Dutch Guiana, it is artistic ability which is necessary to win a girl's approval, the same young man would have to be carving rather than going out on a war party.

In many parts of the world, war is a game in which the individual can win counters—counters which bring him prestige in the eyes of his own sex or of the opposite sex; he plays for these counters as he might, in our society, strive for a tennis championship. Warfare is a frame for such prestige-seeking merely because it calls for the display of certain skills and certain virtues; all of these skills—riding straight, shooting straight, dodging the missiles of the enemy and sending one's own straight to the mark—can be equally well exercised in some other framework and, equally, the virtues endurance, bravery, loyalty, steadfast-ness—can be displayed in other contexts. The tie-up between proving oneself a man and proving this by a success in organised killing is due to a definition which many societies have made of manliness. And often, even in those societies which counted success in warfare a proof of human worth, strange turns were given to the idea, as when the plains Indians gave their highest awards to the man who touched a live enemy rather than to the man who brought in a scalp—from a dead enemy—because the latter was less risky. Warfare is just an invention known to the majority of human societies by which they permit their young men either to accumulate prestige or avenge their honour or acquire loot or wives or slaves or sago lands or cattle or appease the blood lust of their gods or the restless souls of the recently dead. It is just an inven-tion, older and more widespread than the jury system, but none the less an invention. But, once we have said this, have we said anything at all? Despite a few stances, dear to the instances of controversialist, of the loss of the useful arts, once an invention is made which proves congruent with human needs or social forms, it tends to persist. Grant that war is an invention, that it is not a biological necessity nor the out-come of certain special types of social forms, still once the invention is made, what are we to do about it?

The Indian who had been subsisting on the buffalo for generations because with his primitive weapons he could slaughter only a limited number of buffalo did not return to his primitive weapons when he saw that the white man's more efficient weapons were exterminating the buffalo. A desire for the white man's cloth may mortgage the South Sea Islander to the white man's plantation, but he does not return to mak-ing bark cloth, which would have left him free. Once an invention is known and accepted, men do not easily relinquish it. The skilled workers may smash the first steam looms which they feel are to be their undoing, but they accept them in the end, and no movement which has insisted upon the mere abandon-ment of usable inventions has ever had much success. Warfare is here, as part of our thought; the deeds of warriors are immortalised in the words of our poets, the toys of our children are modelled upon the weapons of the soldier, the frame of reference within which our statesmen and our diplomats work always contains war. If we know that it is not inevitable, that it is due to historical accident that warfare is one of the ways in which we think of behaving, are we given any hope by that? What hope is there of per-suading nations to abandon war, nations so thoroughly imbued with the idea that resort to war is, if not actually desirable and noble, at least inevitable whenever certain defined circumstances arise?

In answer to this question I think we might turn to the history of other social inventions, and inventions which must once have seemed as finally entrenched as warfare. Take the methods of trial which preceded the jury system: ordeal and trial by combat. Unfair, capricious, alien as they are to our feeling today, they were once the only methods open to individuals accused of some offense. The invention of trial by jury gradually replaced these methods until only witches, and finally not even witches, had to resort to the ordeal. And for a long time the jury system seemed the best and finest method of settling legal disputes, but today new inventions, trial before judges only or before commissions, are replacing the jury system. In each case the old method was replaced by a new social invention. The ordeal did not go out because people thought it unjust or wrong; it went out because a method more congruent with the institutions and feel-ings of the period was invented. And, if we despair over the way in which war seems such an ingrained habit of most of the human race, we can take comfort from the fact that a poor invention will usually give place to a better invention.

For this, two conditions, at least, are necessary. The people must recognise the defects of the old inven-tion, and someone must make a new one. Propaganda against warfare, documentation of its terrible cost in human suffering and social waste, these prepare the ground by teaching people to feel that warfare is a defective social institution. There is further needed a belief that social invention is possible and the invention of new methods which will render warfare as out of date as the tractor is making the plough, or the motor car the horse and buggy. A form of behaviour becomes out of date only when something else takes its place, and, in order to invent forms of behaviour which will make war obsolete, it is a first requirement to believe that an invention is possible.

Jane Goodall, from "The Challenge Lies in All of Us"

Jane Goodall (b. 1934 CE) is the scientific director of the Gombe Research Center and an outspoken worldwide advocate of chimpanzee and wildlife conservation. She is one of three researchers (Jane Goodall, Dian Fossey, and Birute Galdikas) originally dispatched by famous anthropologist Louis Leakey to research primates, man's closest relatives. Goodall has been studying chimpanzees in Africa since 1960. She has reported on tool use by chimpanzees and on variations in chimpanzee culture, that is tool making and communication techniques, among chimpanzee populations. Her most unsettling observation of chimpanzee behavior was of the four-year war when the Kasakela group wiped out the neighboring Kahama group. Her book The Chimpanzees of Gombe: Patterns of Behavior *(1986) is considered the definitive work on chimpanzees.*

Source: *Dangers to the Environment, "The Challenge Lies in All of Us," delivered to the Commonwealth Club of California, San Francisco, California. October 10, 2003.*

Focus Questions:
1. How does Goodall characterize violence and aggression in people and primates?
2. How does she compare human and chimpanzee emotions and communications?

Good evening everyone, and thank you for a wonderful welcome. I think that that deserves in return a welcome from Gombe, (the sound of the chimpanzee): Ah-Whoo! Ah-Whoo!

Sometimes I think, how did the little girl who was born in England to a family with very little money—started off my life in the middle of a city, in London—how did that little girl come to be traveling around and getting these honors and getting a wonderful greeting such as you just gave me? It makes me think of a fable my mother used to read to me and my sister when we were little, about the birds coming together to have a competition: who could fly the highest? The mighty eagle is sure he will win, and majestically with those great, strong wings he flies higher and higher, and gradually the other birds get tired and start drifting back to the ground. Finally, even the eagle can go no higher, but that's all right, because he looks down and sees all the other birds below him. That's what he thinks, but hiding in the feathers on his back is a little wren, and she takes off and flies highest of all.

The reason that I love this story is because, as you will learn, I have a passion for symbols, and this is a very symbolic story to me, because if we think of our life as an effort to fly always just a little bit higher and reach a goal that's just a little bit beyond our reach, how high can any of us go by ourselves? We all need our eagle, and when I look back at my life and I think of all the amazing people who have helped me on my flight, I imagine them as the feathers on my eagle—big strong feathers, small feathers, every feather playing its role in keeping me aloft or helping me to get up when I have a tumble. I think of all the field staff at Gombe, the students who over the years have helped to collect the data. Then I think of the amazing friends, the staff and volunteers and supporters of the Jane Goodall Institute—a relatively small institute, but we do an awful lot of things around the world, and that's because the people who work for us and with us are so committed and work so hard and over and above the call of duty, I imagine them as the feathers on my eagle—big strong feathers, small feathers, every feather playing its role in keeping me aloft or helping me to get up when I have a tumble. I think of all the field staff at Gombe, the students who over the years have helped to collect the data. Then I think of the amazing friends, the staff and volunteers and supporters of the Jane Goodall Institute—a relatively small institute, but we do an awful lot of things around the world, and that's because the people who work for us and with us are so committed and work so hard and over and above the call of duty.

The person, though, that I want to pay the most tribute to is my mother. She died three years ago, but I still feel her very much around, and throughout my entire life she was my greatest inspiration and support. Of course, I miss her terribly. Nevertheless, all the values that she imbued in me as a child—she and her mother—have served me in such good stead ever since. I grew up in a family of women, my father fighting in the war, with my mother and her two sisters and my grandmother and my sister—what a house of women. It was towards the end of World War II. When I was eight years old, I found a book about Dr. Doolittle—many of you will remember Dr. Doolittle—and the book I read was describing how he took circus animals back to their native Africa, this doctor who could speak with animals. I was a child who had been passionate about animals all her life and had my passion supported by my mother, who didn't even freak out when I took a whole handful of earthworms to bed with me. She just gently said, "Jane, if you leave them here they'll die. They need the earth." So I was only one and a half and I toddled back with them into the garden. And she supported all these childhood escapades to do with animals.

Well, I found the books by Edgar Rice Burroughs about Tarzan of the Apes, and it was my imagination that created the Tarzan with whom I fell passionately in love, age ten—there was no television in those days. Johnny Weissmuller hadn't appeared in Hollywood. So I felt that I would have been a much better mate for Tarzan than that wimpy Jane of his; I was terribly jealous of Jane, and that was when I got this dream: when I grew up, I would go to Africa, live with animals and write books about them.

Well, end of World War II, we couldn't afford a bicycle, let alone a motorcar. Africa was still thought of as the "Dark Continent," there were no 747s going back and forth with tourists, and we just heard rumors of poisoned arrows and cannibals and things like that. So it wasn't surprising that everybody laughed at me. They said, "Jane, why don't you dream about something you can achieve? Stop thinking about this stupid idea of going to Africa." Except my mother—my whole family actually. She used to say, "Jane, if you really want something and work hard and you take advantage of opportunity and you never, ever give up, you will find a way." So that was how I grew up. And when I left school—I didn't go to university because we couldn't afford it—and I did her bidding, what she suggested was to become a secretary so I could get a job in Africa.

That was how I met the late Louis Leakey, and that was what led to this amazing opportunity to go to Gombe National Park on the romantic-sounding shores of Lake Tanganyika and try to learn about our closest living relatives. He had spent his life searching for human fossils, the fossils of our earliest known Stone Age ancestors. He had this idea, which was way ahead of his time—he was a giant of a man, a genius—and he had the idea that if we found behavior that was similar or the same in human beings today and chimpanzees today, then possibly that behavior would have existed in our ape-like, human-like common ancestors 6 or 7 million years ago, then, perhaps, in the Stone Age ancestors' bones he was uncovering. He wanted to have a better feeling as to how those early humans behaved.

If you read anthropological textbooks today, if you read about people speculating as to the behavior of early humans, you typically will read about chimpanzee behavior and how this may well be a model for understanding our early ancestors. So Louis was vindicated. But when he made that offer to me—first of all, he was going to give money; I didn't have a degree, I'd just come out from England, and I was a female. Back then in 1957, a female going to live in Africa on her own in the bush? Eventually, a wealthy American businessman said, "All right, Louis, here's money for six months." Then, a second problem: at that time, what is Tanzania today was Taganyika—a British protectorate. The British authority had the same reaction: A girl on her own in the forest? They even thought Louis was amoral to suggest it. They denied permission for nearly two months or three months, but finally they said, "Well, all right, but she must have a companion." So who volunteered to come? That same remarkable mother.

She was there for me when I got done in the evening after those early frustrating days when the chimpanzees would run away from me even if I was as far away as way back over in the gallery. They'd never seen a white ape before. They are very conservative.

I was having an amazing time out in the forest. I'd felt I'd come home but, at the same time, I knew that if I didn't see something exciting before that first six months' money came to an end, then the whole thing would be deemed a failure, there certainly would be no more money, and I would have let Louis down. Everyone would say, "Well, we told you so." So I was becoming increasingly agitated, and having my mother there to give me support at that time was great. But even more than that, she started a little clinic. She handed out aspirins and Band-Aids and simple things of that sort, not being a doctor or a nurse. She established a wonderful relationship with all the local people which stood me in good stead ever since, and the students have followed me.

So that was how it all began, and now, 43 years later, we can look back over the results from this longest field study of any group of non-human animals in the world and realize how significant some of the findings from Gombe have been, how some of these findings have changed the way we think about ourselves in relation to the rest of the animal kingdom. Chimpanzees are so like us that it makes it very clear even to hard-nosed scientists, even to people of different religious persuasions that, after all, there isn't a sharp line dividing us from the rest of the animal kingdom. It's a very blurry line, and the chimpanzees, along with the other great apes more than anything, have helped us to realize this. The chimpanzees are like us in the fact that there is a long childhood during which the child is dependent on learning just as our children are, five years of riding the mother's back, suckling and sleeping with her at night, continued dependence on the mother even after the next baby is born and the older child is five or six, because the youngster still has a lot to learn. We find that they have an incredibly complex society, and we find that their nonverbal communication involves many postures and gestures that are very familiar to us: kissing, embracing, holding hands, patting on the back, swaggering, shaking the fist. These are seen in the same kind of context that they are seen in our own species, and they clearly mean the same kind of thing. So if you move around the world you are likely to greet by kissing, embracing, holding hands and patting on the back, and so are chimpanzees. Humans around the world have a begging gesture; so, too, do chimpanzees. Humans around the world shake their fist when they're mad; so do the chimps. And we could continue.

Chimpanzees, unfortunately, have a dark side to their nature. They're capable of extreme brutality and a kind of primitive warfare, which we see between neighboring social groups. There is an intense hatred of strangers, and this reminds us of human behavior, unfortunately. But at the same time, the chimpanzees also show very clear examples of love, compassion and altruism, particularly between family members. So, there I've been criticized, or I was originally when I published the information about inter-community, territorial, aggressive warfare, because people said, certain scientists will seize upon this, certain populists will seize upon this and say, If you're saying there's a common ancestor then clearly we've inherited aggressive tendencies from our ancient primate past, and war and violence in our own species is inevitable. Well, we obviously have inherited aggressive tendencies; you can't really study human behavior around the world and not realize that we are a species which tends to show aggression in many contexts. But at the same time we equally inherited love, compassion and altruism from our ancient primate ancestors. In one way, we differ from the chimpanzees and from all other animals: We have developed a sophisticated, spoken language, a language with which we can discuss ideas, we can discuss the distant past, we can make plans for the distant future. The great apes have an amazing intellect. Their brain is more like ours than ever was thought possible, and, as a result, they are capable of intellectual performances we used to think unique to ourselves. Some of the great apes, orangutans, gorillas and chimpanzees have been taught American Sign Language.

It's very clear that these apes, when they use these signs, are using them in a way that makes it very clear that they understand what the signs are. They can communicate with each other as well as with their teachers, but as far as we know in the wild, they haven't actually developed a way of discussing ideas and are planning for the distant future, and perhaps most importantly, are teaching their young about things that are not present.

So in this way, we stand slightly apart, but we all share emotions like happiness, sadness, fear and despair. We and the apes and other sentient sapien beings can suffer mentally as well as physically. What these studies show us is that, as I said, the line between us and them is very blurred. It makes us rethink our relationship with the rest of the animal kingdom. We're not separate from it; we're a part of it. This is, for me, tremendously exciting. If you think about the world of the animals, think of some of the ways they communicate with each other, some of their senses. Many of you must have dogs; wouldn't you love for just a few minutes to feel what it's like to live in a world of smell, of scents? What is the dog reading when his little nose twitches out of the car window? What is he reading as he walks along the side of the road sniffing those signs that tell him exactly what's been going on? I get so mad when owners yank at the collar or drag the dog away; it's like taking somebody who's window gazing or having fun looking in the shop window. Wouldn't it be amazing to know what it's like to be a whale or a dolphin with that sonic click language that is capable of traveling miles through the currents of the great oceans? Wouldn't it be incredible for a little while to be a bat flying through the darkness with echo location? And how would it feel, I often wonder, to be one of these great birds setting out on a migration for thousands of miles, or a fish or even a butterfly? There is so much that's magic out in this wonderful world of animals, and the chimpanzees and the other apes lead us into that world and welcome us as part of it.

Marshall Sahlins, "The Original Affluent Society"

Marshall Sahlins (b. 1930 CE) is an American anthropologist who began his studies in Polynesia and Hawaii. Sahlins compares Western and non-Western thought in order to question so-called Western rationalism. In How 'Natives' Think: About Captain Cook, For Example *(1995), Sahlins triggered a debate on whether Westerners can fully understand other cultures. His* Stone Age Economics *(1971) challenges assumptions of superiority of modern and rational agricultural societies over allegedly primitive hunter-gatherer societies.*

Source: *Sahlins, Marshall David.* Stone Age Economics. *Chicago: Aldine-Atherton, 1972.*

Focus Questions:
1. What are the difference in mentalities and lifestyles between modern and Paleolithic societies?
2. How do you think hunter-gatherers fared when in places other than deserts?
3. Thinking of Meade's and Goodall's essays on war, how would they apply here?

Hunter-gatherers consume less energy per capita per year than any other group of human beings. Yet when you come to examine it, the original affluent society was none other than the hunter's—in which all the people's material wants were easily satisfied. To accept that hunters are affluent is therefore to recognise that the present human condition of man slaving to bridge the gap between his unlimited wants and his insufficient means is a tragedy of modern times.

There are two possible courses to affluence. Wants may be "easily satisfied" either by producing much or desiring little. The familiar conception, the Galbraithean way—based on the concept of market economies—states that man's wants are great, not to say infinite, whereas his means are limited, although they can be improved. Thus, the gap between means and ends can be narrowed by industrial productivity, at least to the point that "urgent goods" become plentiful. But there is also a Zen road to affluence, which states that human material wants are finite and few, and technical means unchanging but on the whole adequate. Adopting the Zen strategy, a people can enjoy an unparalleled material plenty—with a low standard of living. That, I think, describes the hunters. And it helps explain some of their more curious economic behaviour: their "prodigality" for example—the inclination to consume at once all stocks on hand, as if they had it made. Free from market obsessions of scarcity, hunters' economic propensities may be more consistently predicated on abundance than our own.

Destutt de Tracy, "fish-blooded bourgeois doctrinaire" though he might have been, at least forced Marx to agree that "in poor nations the people are comfortable," whereas in rich nations, "they are generally poor."

"A Kind of Material Plenty"

Considering the poverty in which hunters and gatherers live in theory, it comes as a surprise that Bushmen who live in the Kalahari enjoy "a kind of material plenty," at least in the realm of everyday useful things, apart from food and water:

> "As the !Kung come into more contact with Europeans and this is already happening—they will feel sharply the lack of our things and will need and want more. It makes them feel inferior to be without clothes when they stand among strangers who are clothed. But in their own life and with their own artifacts they were free from material pressures. Except for food and water (important exceptions!) of which the Nyae Nyae !Kung have a sufficiency—but barely so, judging from the fact that all are thin though not emaciated—they all had what they needed or could make what they needed, for every man can and does make the things that men make and every woman the things that women make...

> "They lived in a kind of material plenty because they adapted the tools of their living to materials which lay in abundance around them and which were free for anyone to take (wood, reeds, bone for weapons and implements, fibres for cordage, grass for shelters), or to materials which were at least sufficient for the needs of the population...The !Kung could always use more ostrich egg shells for beads to wear or trade with, but, as it is, enough are found for every woman to have a dozen or more shells for water containers all she can carry—and a goodly number of bead ornaments.

> "In their nomadic hunting-gathering life, travelling from one source of food to another through the seasons, always going back and forth between food and water, they carry their young children and their belongings. With plenty of most materials at hand to replace artifacts as required, the !Kung have not developed means of permanent storage and have not needed or wanted to encumber themselves with surpluses or duplicates. They do not even want to carry one of everything. They borrow what they do not own. With this ease, they have not hoarded, and the accumulation of objects has not become associated with status."[9]

In the non-subsistence sphere, the people's wants are generally easily satisfied. Such "material plenty" depends partly upon the simplicity of technology and democracy of property. Products are homespun: of stone, bone, wood, skin-materials such as "lay in abundance around them." As a rule, neither extraction of the raw material nor its working up take strenuous effort. Access to natural resources is typically direct—"free for anyone to take"—even as possession of the necessary tools is general and knowledge of the required skills common. The division of labour is likewise simple, predominantly a division of labour by sex. Add in the liberal customs of sharing, for which hunters are properly famous, and all the people can usually participate in the going prosperity, such as it is.

For most hunters, such affluence without abundance in the non-subsistence sphere need not be long debated. A more interesting question is why they are content with so few possessions, for it is with them a policy, a "matter of principle" as Gusinde[10] says, and not a misfortune.

---

[9] Marshall, Lorna. 1961. "Sharing, Talking, and Giving: Relief of Social Tensions Among !Kung Bushmen," *Africa* 31:23,149.
[10] Gusinde, Martin. 1961. *The Yamana.* 5 vols. New Haven, Conn.: Human Relations Area Files. (German edition, 1931)

But are hunters so undemanding of material goods because they are themselves enslaved by a food quest "demanding maximum energy from a maximum number of people," so that no time or effort remains for the provision of other comforts? Some ethnographers testify to the contrary that the food quest is so successful that half the time the people seem not to know what to do with themselves. On the other hand, movement is a condition of this success, more movement in some cases than others, but always enough to rapidly depreciate the satisfactions of property. Of the hunter it is truly said that his wealth is a burden. In his condition of life, goods can become "grievously oppressive," as Gusinde observes, and the more so the longer they are carried around. Certain food collectors do have canoes and a few have dog sleds, but most must carry themselves all the comforts they possess, and so only possess what they can comfortably carry themselves. Or perhaps only what the women can carry: the men are often left free to reach to the sudden opportunity of the chase or the sudden necessity of defence. As Owen Lattimore wrote in a not too different context, "the pure nomad is the poor nomad." Mobility and property are in contradiction. That wealth quickly becomes more of an encumbrance than a good thing is apparent even to the outsider. Laurens van der Post[11] was caught in the contradiction as he prepared to make farewells to his wild Bushmen friends:

> "This matter of presents gave us many an anxious moment. We were humiliated by the realisation of how little there was we could give to the Bushmen. Almost everything seemed likely to make life more difficult for them by adding to the litter and weight of their daily round. They themselves had practically no possessions: a loin strap, a skin blanket and a leather satchel. There was nothing that they could not assemble in one minute, wrap up in their blankets and carry on their shoulders for a journey of a thousand miles. They had no sense of possession."

Here then is another economic "peculiarity"—some hunters at least, display a notable tendency to be sloppy about their possessions. They have the kind of nonchalance that would be appropriate to a people who have mastered the problems of production.

> "They do not know how to take care of their belongings. No one dreams of putting them in order, folding them, drying or cleaning them, hanging them up, or putting them in a neat pile. If they are looking for some particular thing, they rummage carelessly through the hodgepodge of trifles in the little baskets. Larger objects that are piled up in a heap in the hut are dragged hither and thither with no regard for the damage that might be done them.

> "The European observer has the impression that these (Yahgan) Indians place no value whatever on their utensils and that they have completely forgotten the effort it took to make them. Actually, no one clings to his few goods and chattels which, as it is, are often and easily lost, but just as easily replaced...The Indian does not even exercise care when he could conveniently do so. A European is likely to shake his head at the boundless indifference of these people who drag brand-new objects, precious clothing, fresh provisions and valuable items through thick mud, or abandon them to their swift destruction by children and dogs...Expensive things that are given them are treasured for a few hours, out of curiosity; after that they thoughtlessly let everything deteriorate in the mud and wet. The less they own, the more comfortable they can travel, and what is ruined they occasionally replace. Hence, they are completely indifferent to any material possessions."

The hunter, one is tempted to say, is "uneconomic man." At least as concerns non-subsistence goods, he is the reverse of that standard caricature immortalised in any General Principles of Economics, page one. His wants are scarce and his means (in relation) plentiful. Consequently he is "comparatively free of material pressures," has "no sense of possession," shows "an undeveloped sense of property," is "completely indifferent to any material pressures," manifests a "lack of interest" in developing his technological equipment.

---

[11] Laurens van der Post: *The Heart of the Hunter.*

In this relation of hunters to worldly goods there is a neat and important point. From the internal perspective of the economy, it seems wrong to say that wants are "restricted," desires "restrained," or even that the notion of wealth is "limited." Such phrasings imply in advance an Economic Man and a struggle of the hunter against his own worse nature, which is finally then subdued by a cultural vow of poverty. The words imply the renunciation of an acquisitiveness that in reality was never developed, a suppression of desires that were never broached. Economic Man is a bourgeois construction—as Marcel Mauss said, "not behind us, but before, like the moral man."

It is not that hunters and gatherers have curbed their materialistic "impulses"; they simply never made an institution of them. "Moreover, if it is a great blessing to be free from a great evil, our (Montagnais) Savages are happy; for the two tyrants who provide hell and torture for many of our Europeans, do not reign in their great forests, I mean ambition and avarice...as they are contented with a mere living, not one of them gives himself to the Devil to acquire wealth."[12]

Three to Five Hour Working Day

Reports on hunters and gatherers of the ethnological present—specifically on those in marginal environments—suggest a mean of three to five hours per adult worker per day in food production. Hunters keep banker's hours, notably less than modern industrial workers (unionised), who would surely settle for a 21–35 hour week. An interesting comparison is also posed by recent studies of labour costs among agriculturalists of neolithic type. For example, the average adult Hanunoo, man or woman, spends 1,200 hours per year in swidden cultivation;[21] which is to say, a mean of three hours twenty minutes per day. Yet this figure does not include food gathering, animal raising, cooking and other direct subsistence efforts of these Philippine tribesmen. Comparable data are beginning to appear in reports on other primitive agriculturalists from many parts of the world.

There is nothing either to the convention that hunters and gatherers can enjoy little leisure from tasks of sheer survival. By this, the evolutionary inadequacies of the palaeolithic are customarily explained, while for the provision of leisure the neolithic is roundly congratulated. But the traditional formulas might be truer if reversed: the amount of work (per capita) increases with the evolution of culture, and the amount of leisure decreases. Hunters' subsistence labours are characteristically intermittent, a day on and a day off, and modern hunters at least tend to employ their time off in such activities as daytime sleep. In the tropical habitats occupied by many of these existing hunters, plant collecting is more reliable than hunting itself. Therefore, the women, who do the collecting, work rather more regularly than the men, and provide the greater part of the food supply.

In alleging this is an affluent economy, therefore, I do not deny that certain hunters have moments of difficulty. Some do find it "almost inconceivable" for a man to die of hunger, or even to fail to satisfy his hunger for more than a day or two. But others, especially certain very peripheral hunters spread out in small groups across an environment of extremes, are exposed periodically to the kind of inclemency that interdicts travel or access to game. They suffer, although perhaps only fractionally, the shortage affecting particular immobilised families rather than the society as a whole.

Still, granting this vulnerability, and allowing the most poorly situated modern hunters into comparison, it would be difficult to prove that privation is distinctly characteristic of the hunter-gatherers. Food shortage is not the indicative property of this mode of production as opposed to others; it does not mark off hunters and gatherers as a class or a general evolutionary stage. Lowie[22] asks:

---

[12] Le Jeune, le Pere Paul. 1897. "Relation of What Occurred in New France in the Year 1634," in R. G. Thwaites (ed.), *The Jesuit Relations and Allied Documents*. Vol. 6. Cleveland: Burrows. (First French edition, 1635)
[21] Conklin, Harold C. 1957. *Hanunoo Agriculture*. Rome: Food and Agricultural Organisation of the United Nations.
[22] Lowie, Robert H. 1938. "Subsistence," in F. Boas (ed.), *General Anthropology*. (2nd ed.) New York: Rinehart.

"But what of the herders on a simple plane whose maintenance is periodically jeopardised by plagues—who, like some Lapp bands of the nineteenth century, were obliged to fall back on fishing? What of the primitive peasants who clear and till without compensation of the soil, exhaust one plot and pass on to the next, and are threatened with famine at every drought? Are they any more in control of misfortune caused by natural conditions than the hunter-gatherer?"

Above all, what about the world today? One-third to one-half of humanity are said to go to bed hungry every night. In the Old Stone Age the fraction must have been much smaller. This is the era of hunger unprecedented. Now, in the time of the greatest technical power, is starvation an increasing situation. Reverse another venerable formula: the amount of hunger increases relatively and absolutely with the evolution of culture. This paradox is my whole point. Hunters and gatherers have by force of circumstances an objectively low standard of living. But taken as their objective, and given their adequate means of production, all the people's material wants usually can be easily satisfied.

The world's most primitive people have few possessions, but they are not poor. Poverty is not a certain small amount of goods, nor is it just a relation between means and ends; above all it is a relation between people. Poverty is a social status. As such it is the invention of civilisation. It has grown with civilisation, at once as an invidious distinction between classes and more importantly as a tributary relation that can render agrarian peasants more susceptible to natural catastrophes than any winter camp of Alaskan Eskimo.

Chapter 2

Agriculture

Charles Darwin, "Cultivated Plants: Cereal and Culinary Plants"

Charles Darwin (1809–1882 CE) was an English naturalist who remains famous for his theory of evolution and natural selection. His revolutionary ideas concerning evolution stemmed from his participation in an 1831–36 science voyage around the world. His conclusions were published many years later in The Origin of Species *(1859). Darwin's theory is based on the premise that variation occurs randomly in nature though most variations are not viable. However, in some circumstances success occurs based on an improved ability to adapt to the environment, in other words natural selection. In terms of crops, according to Darwin selective pressure is applied by man, who favors certain variations over others.*

Source: *Darwin, Charles. "The variation of animals and plants under domestication." 2 vols. 2ⁿᵈ ed. New York: D. Appleton and Co., 1883 [first published London, John Murray, 1868].*

Focus Questions:
1. How does Darwin describe the development of cultivation?
2. How does his attitude to savages and barbarians compared to civilized people affect his viewpoint?
3. What is the selection process of desirable crops?

CHAPTER IX

Cultivated Plants: Cereal and Culinary Plants.

Preliminary remarks on the number and parentage of cultivated plants—first steps in cultivation—geographical distribution of cultivated plants.

Cerealia. Doubts on the number of species—**Wheat:** varieties of—individual variability—changed habits—selection—ancient history of the varieties—**Maize:** great variation of—direct action of climate on.

Culinary Plants.—Cabbages: varieties of, in foliage and stems, but not in other parts—parentage of—other species of brassica—**Peas:** amount of difference in the several kinds, chiefly in the pods and seed—

some varieties constant, some highly variable—do not intercross—**Beans**—Potatoes: numerous varieties of—differing little except in the tubers—characters inherited.

I shall not enter into so much detail on the variability of cultivated plants, as in the case of domesticated animals. The subject is involved in much difficulty. Botanists have generally neglected cultivated varieties, as beneath their notice. In several cases the wild prototype is unknown or doubtfully known; and in other cases it is hardly possible to distinguish between escaped seedlings and truly wild plants, so that there is no safe standard of comparison by which to judge of any supposed amount of change. Not a few botanists believe that several of our anciently cultivated plants have become so profoundly modified that it is not possible now to recognise their aboriginal parent-forms. Equally perplexing are the doubts whether some of them are descended from one species, or from several inextricably commingled by crossing and variation. Variations often pass into, and cannot be distinguished from, monstrosities; and monstrosities are of little significance for our purpose. Many varieties are propagated solely by grafts, buds, layers, bulbs, etc., and frequently it is not known how far their peculiarities can be transmitted by seminal generation. Nevertheless, some facts of value can be gleaned: and other facts will hereafter be incidentally given. One chief object in the two following chapters is to show how many characters in our cultivated plants have become variable.

Before entering on details a few general remarks on the origin of cultivated plants may be introduced M. Alph. De Candolle[1] in an admirable discussion on this subject, in which he displays a wonderful amount of knowledge, gives a list of 157 of the most useful cultivated plants. Of these he believes that 85 are almost certainly known in their wild state; but on this head other competent judges[2] entertain great doubts. Of 40 of them, the origin is admitted by M. De Candolle to be doubtful, either from a certain amount of dissimilarity which they present when compared with their nearest allies in a wild state, or from the probability of the latter not being truly wild plants, but seedlings escaped from culture. Of the entire 157, 32 alone are ranked by M. De Candolle as quite unknown in their aboriginal condition. But it should be observed that he does not include in his list several plants which present ill-defined characters, namely, the various forms of pumpkins, millet, sorghum, kidney-bean, dolichos, capsicum, and indigo. Nor does he include flowers; and several of the more anciently cultivated flowers, such as certain roses, the common Imperial lily, the tuberose, and even the lilac, are said[3] not to be known in the wild state.

From the relative numbers above given, and from other arguments of much weight, M. De Candolle concludes that plants have rarely been so much modified by culture that they cannot be identified with their wild prototypes. But on this view, considering that savages probably would not have chosen rare plants for cultivation, that useful plants are generally conspicuous, and that they could not have been the inhabitants of deserts or of remote and recently discovered islands, it appears strange to me that so many of our cultivated plants should be still unknown or only doubtfully known in the wild state. If, on the other hand, many of these plants have been profoundly modified by culture, the difficulty disappears. The difficulty would also be removed if they have been exterminated during the progress of civilization; but M. De Candolle has shown that this probably has seldom occurred. As soon as a plant was cultivated in any country, the half-civilized inhabitants would no longer have need to search the whole surface of the land for it, and thus lead to its extirpation; and even if this did occur during a famine, dormant seeds would be left in the ground. In tropical countries the wild luxuriance of nature, as was long ago remarked by Humboldt, overpowers the feeble efforts of man. In anciently civilized temperate countries, where the whole face of the land has been greatly changed, it can hardly be doubted that some plants have become extinct; nevertheless De Candolle has shown that all the plants historically known to have been first cultivated in Europe still exist here in the wild state.

---

[1] 'Geographie botanique raisonnée,' 1855, pp. 810–991.
[2] Review by Mr. Bentham in 'Hort. Journal,' vol. ix 1855, p. 133, entitled, 'Historical Notes on Cultivated Plants,' by Dr. A. Targioni-Tozzetti. See also 'Edinburgh Review,' 1866, p. 510.
[3] Hist. Notes, as above by Targioni-Tozzetti.

MM. Loiseleur-Deslongchamps[4] and De Candolle have remarked that our cultivated plants, more especially the cereals, must originally have existed in nearly their present state: for otherwise they would not have been noticed and valued as objects of food. But these authors apparently have not considered the many accounts given by travelers of the wretched food collected by savages. I have read an account of the savages of Australia cooking, during a dearth, many vegetables in various ways, in the hopes of rendering them innocuous and more nutritious. Dr. Hooker found the half-starved inhabitants of a village in Sikhim suffering greatly from having eaten arum-roots,[5] which they had pounded and left for several days to ferment, so as partially to destroy their poisonous nature; and he adds that they cooked and ate many other deleterious plants. Sir Andrew Smith informs me that in South Africa a large number of fruits and succulent leaves, and especially roots, are used in times of scarcity. The natives, indeed, know the properties of a long catalogue of plants, some having been found during famines to be eatable, others injurious to health, or even destructive to life. He met a party of Baquanas who, having been expelled by the conquering Zulus, had lived for years on any roots or leaves which afforded some little nutriment and distended their stomachs, so as to relieve the pangs of hunger. They looked like walking skeletons, and suffered fearfully from constipation. Sir Andrew Smith also informs me that on such occasions the natives observe as a guide for themselves, what the wild animals, especially baboons and monkeys, eat.

From innumerable experiments made through dire necessity by the savages of every land, with the results handed down by tradition, the nutritious, stimulating, and medicinal properties of the most unpromising plants were probably first discovered. It appears, for instance, at first an inexplicable fact that untutored man, in three distant quarters of the world, should have discovered, amongst a host of native plants, that the leaves of the tea-plant and mattee, and the berries of the coffee, all included a stimulating and nutritious essence, now known to be chemically the same. We can also see that savages suffering from severe constipation would naturally observe whether any of the roots which they devoured acted as aperients. We probably owe our knowledge of the uses of almost all plants to man having originally existed in a barbarous state, and having been often compelled by severe want to try as food almost everything which he could chew and swallow.

From what we know of the habits of savages in many quarters of the world, there is no reason to suppose that our cereal plants originally existed in their present state so valuable to man. Let us look to one continent alone, namely, Africa: Barth[6] states that the slaves over a large part of the central region regularly collect the seeds of a wild grass, the *Pennisetum distichum*; in another district he saw women collecting the seeds of a Poa by swinging a sort of basket through the rich meadowland. Near Tete, Livingstone observed the natives collecting the seeds of a wild grass, and farther south, as Andersson informs me, the natives largely use the seed of a grass of about the size of canary-seed, which they boil in water. They eat also the roots of certain reeds, and everyone has read of the Bushmen prowling about and digging up with a fire-hardened stake various roots. Similar facts with respect to the collection of seeds of wild grasses in other parts of the world could be given.[7]

Accustomed as we are to our excellent vegetables and luscious fruits, we can hardly persuade ourselves that the stringy roots of the wild carrot and parsnip, or the little shoots of the wild asparagus, or crabs, sloes, etc., should ever have been valued; yet, from what we know of the habits of Australian and South African savages, we need feel no doubt on this head. The inhabitants of Switzerland during the Stone-

---

[4] 'Considérations sur les Uréales,' 1842, p. 37. 'Géographie Bot.,' 1855, p. 930. "Plus on suppose l'agriculture ancienne et remontant a une époque d'ignorance, plus il est probable que les cultivateurs avaient choisi des especes offrant a l'origine meme un avantage incontestable."

[5] Dr. Hooker has given me this information. *See also* his 'Himalayan Journals,' 1854, vol. ii. p. 49.

[6] 'Travels in Central Africa,' Eng. translat. vol. i. pp. 529 and 390; vol. ii., pp. 29, 265, 270. Livingstone's 'Travels,' p. 551.

[7] For instance, in both North and South America. Mr. Edgeworth ('Journal Proc. Linn. Soc.,' vol. vi., Bot., 1862, p. 181) states that in the deserts of the Punjab poor women sweep up, "by a whisk into straw baskets," the seeds of four genera of grasses, namely, of Agrostis, Panicum, Cenchrus, and Pennisetum, as well as the seeds of four other genera belonging to distinct families.

period largely collected wild crabs, sloes, bullaces, hips of roses, elderberries, beechmast, and other wild berries and fruit.[8] Jemmy Button, a Fuegian on board the 'Beagle,' remarked to me that the poor and acid black currants of Tierra del Fuego were too sweet for his taste.

The savage inhabitants of each land, having found out by many and hard trials what plants were useful, or could be rendered useful by various cooking processes, would after a time take the first step in cultivation by planting them near their usual abodes. Livingstone[9] states that the savage Batokas sometimes left wild fruit-trees standing in their gardens, and occasionally even planted them, "a practice seen nowhere else amongst the natives." But Du Chaillu saw a palm and some other wild fruit-trees which had been planted; and these trees were considered private property. The next step in cultivation, and this would require but little forethought, would be to sow the seeds of useful plants; and as the soil near the hovels of the natives[10] would often be in some degree manured, improved varieties would sooner or later arise. Or a wild and unusually good variety of a native plant might attract the attention of some wise old savage; and he would transplant it, or sow its seed. That superior varieties of wild fruit-trees occasionally are found is certain, as in the case of the American species of hawthorns, plums, cherries, grapes, and hickories, specified by Professor Asa Gray. Downing also refers to certain wild varieties of the hickory, as being "of much larger size and finer flavour than the common species." I have referred to American fruit-trees, because we are not in this case troubled with doubts whether or not the varieties are seedlings which have escaped from cultivation. Transplanting any superior variety, or sowing its seeds, hardly implies more forethought than might be expected at an early and rude period of civilisation. Even the Australian barbarians "have a law that no plant bearing seeds is to be dug up after it has flowered;" and Sir G. Grey[12] never saw this law, evidently framed for the preservation of the plant, violated. We see the same spirit in the superstitious belief of the Fuegians, that killing water-fowl whilst very young will be followed by "much rain, snow, blow much."[13] I may add, as showing forethought in the lowest barbarians, that the Fuegians when they find a stranded whale bury large portions in the sand, and during the often-recurrent famines travel from great distances for the remnants of the half-putrid mass. It has often been remarked[14] that we do not owe a single useful plant to Australia or the Cape of Good Hope, countries abounding to an unparalleled degree with endemic species—or to New Zealand, or to America south of the Plata; and, according to some authors, not to America northward of Mexico. I do not believe that any edible or valuable plant, except the canary-grass, has been derived from an oceanic or uninhabited island. If nearly all our useful plants, natives of Europe, Asia, and South America, had originally existed in their present condition, the complete absence of similarly useful plants in the great countries just named would be indeed a surprising fact. But if these plants have been so greatly modified and improved by culture as no longer closely to resemble any natural species, we can understand why the above-named countries have given us no useful plants, for they were either inhabited by men who did not cultivate the ground at all, as in Australia and the Cape of Good Hope, or who cultivated it very imperfectly, as in some parts of America. These countries do yield plants which are useful to savage man; and Dr. Hooker enumerates no less than 107 such species in Australia alone; but these plants have not been improved, and consequently cannot compete with those which have been cultivated and improved during thousands of years in the civilized world.

---

[8] Prof. O. Heer, 'Die Pflanzen der Pfahlbauten, 1866, aus dem Neujahr. Naturforsch. Geselschaft,' 1866; and Dr. H. Christ in Rutimeyer's 'Die Fauna der Pfahlbauten,' 1861, p. 226.

[9] 'Travels,' p. 535. Du Chaillu, 'Adventures in Equatorial Africa,' 1861, p. 445.

[10] In Tierra del Fuego the spot where wigwams had formerly stood could be distinguished at a great distance by the bright green tint of the native vegetation.

[11] 'American Acad. of Arts and Sciences,' April 10th, 1860, p. 413. Downing, 'The Fruits of America,' 1845, p. 261.

[12] 'Journals of Expeditions in Australia,' 1841, vol. ii., p. 292.

[13] Darwin's 'Journal of Researches,' 1845, p. 215.

[14] De Candolle has tabulated the facts in the most interesting manner in his 'Geographie Bot.,' p. 986.

David Rindos, from "Symbiosis, Instability, and the Origins and Spread of Agriculture: A New Model"

David Rindos (1947–1996 CE) was an American biologist whose specialty was evolutionary relationships between plants and animals. His ideas culminated in his book The Origins of Agriculture *(1984) wherein he tackled the problem of human intent in the development of agriculture. His idea was to bypass the model on human planning used by most anthropologists and, instead, focus on a biological model of mutual selection between plants and the animals (including humans) that eat them.*

Source: *Rindos, David. "Symbiosis, Instability, and the Origins and Spread of Agriculture: A New Model." Current Anthropology, 21, no. 6, December, 1980.*

Focus Questions:
1. What is the difference between domestication and cultivation?
2. Compare Rindos to Darwin in terms of how domestication occurs.
3. Did cultivation bring all benefits or were problems also attached?

AGRICULTURAL ORIGINS AND DISPERSALS

Introduction to the Model

Domestication, as viewed here, is an evolutionary process that is the result of predator/prey interactions. Domestication changes the morphology, physiology, and distribution of organisms. It results in a mutualism—a relationship which benefits genetically unrelated organisms. It is, however, neither inevitable nor orthogenetic. The treatment that follows is prone to a fatal error in interpretation. I shall be providing a model for a certain change in subsistence pattern. The model is a dynamic one and places great emphasis on feedback processes, but it should not be read to condone the view that the process, once begun, must proceed inexorably to certain ends. There are numerous ways in which the processes leading to domestication and agriculture may be subverted.

Likewise, this model does not pretend to be all inclusive. In a sense, I am trying to follow a particular thread of cultural developments backward in time; I am not attempting to describe the fabric. Thus, much of the variation which may occur in human cultures must be excluded from consideration. Little attention can be given to societies which were agricultural or domesticatory at certain times but later abandoned the behavior. Clearly, it would be extremely useful and interesting to deal with such phenomena, but it would go far beyond the bounds of this essay.

Finally, we must begin to refine the concept of domestication advanced earlier. I have attempted to provide an understanding of why domestication occurs, but the view of domestication so far presented is so broad as to be, in the final analysis, uninteresting. Coevolutionary domestication is a process that has occurred in almost all cultures at most periods of human existence. It gains its significance from its interrelationship with agricultural origins.

In order to appreciate the role of domestication in agricultural origins, it is necessary to anticipate some of the later arguments and first present a definition for agriculture: agriculture is characterized by an integrated set of activities which affect the environment inhabited by the domesticated plant throughout its life cycle. As we shall see, the major effect of agriculture is to increase the carrying capacity of the environment for the domesticated plant, and this increase in plants and thus plant productivity has major effects upon human populations.

Agriculture is a level or type of behavior. Like many other phenomena, it is frequently easier to recognize than to define. To attempt to define it solely on the basis of a certain technique, such as plowing or weeding, tends to create a false impression of the importance of any particular technique within the integrated schedule of activities comprising agricultural subsistence. Frequently this leads us into believing that cultures sharing a particular technique, such as the use of a digging stick, or even particular plants, such as wheat, must therefore have had a common origin.

Agriculture is an outgrowth of domestication. Thus it is impossible rigorously to define a moment of transition. At an early stage in the development of agriculture, it would be impossible confidently to identify the protoagricultural society. The interactions with domesticated plants of the early agricultural society would be indistinguishable from those of the domesticatory society. The significant techniques of environmental manipulation might not be being performed for consciously agricultural ends. Fires encouraging the growth of domesticated plants might be being set to drive game; forests might be being cleared to furnish building materials. We could only be sure that we were indeed dealing with a protoagricultural society if we knew how the relationship would develop in the future. If we need to define, for any particular society, the moment of transition from a domesticatory to an agricultural way of life, I would suggest that it is the point at which agricultural interactions became more important to the society than domesticatory interactions with plants. "Importance" may be read in two ways. We may consider it to represent the relative significance of agricultural behavior to the future development of the society. We may also view it as the contribution that each form of behavior makes to the overall subsistence of the society at any given moment, This latter interpretation is of critical importance in understanding the evolution and subsequent spread of agricultural behavior.

Domesticatory Relationships

Predator/prey interaction. Mutualistic relationships such as domestication have the potential to change the relationship which exists between predator and prey. In the typical predator/prey relationship, as the total number of predators increases both the total and relative amounts of food available to the predator decrease.

In a mutualistic relationship between predator and prey, as the number of predators increases the total amount of available food also increases. The energetic cost to the prey inherent in providing subsistence to the predator is compensated for by actions of the predator that provide increased opportunities for the survival or dispersal of the prey. Seen in other terms, mutualisms serve to increase the carrying capacity of the environment for both the predator and the prey. The actions of the predator which tend to increase the number of the prey indirectly permit a greater number of predators.

Domestication tends to increase the yield of prey within the area inhabited by the predator. Of course, this tendency will not continue indefinitely. Numerous factors may act to limit the number of prey and thus of predator. Eventually the compensatory behavior of the predator will become ineffective or all available regions favorable to the growth of the prey will become filled; thus the yield will level off or even assume a negative slope. Yet this stabilization in yield, and thus in predator numbers, is also subject to change. Most of the factors limiting the success of the prey species are environmental variables and are thus external to the mutualistic relationship between predator and prey. Since few, if any, species are naturally limited in numbers by their intrinsic rates of increase, any "relaxation" of the environment will permit increases in the numbers of the prey species. Changes in the environment directly increase the carrying capacity of the environment for the prey and thus indirectly permit greater numbers of predators.

The change that leads to proliferation of the prey species may be a change in the morphology of the prey or a modification of the behavior of its coevolved agent, including change in the way the agent relates to the environment. At a time before agricultural behaviors were well established, changes in the morphology of plants were probably of major importance for the further development of the human/plant relationship. Traits such as indehiscence, gigantism, and aggregation could exclude previously effective dispersal agents and thus allow for a greater available yield to humans. This change in the plants' morphology would enhance the development of the human/plant mutualism.

Domesticates, yield, and instability. As we have just seen, the major effect of the mutualism between man and plant is greater productivity of the environment for man. This increase is not, however, based on equal increases in productivity of all components of the environment (all potential or actual prey species). Rather, a very small subset of potential food sources provides all of the increase in productivity. As domestication proceeds, so does man's reliance upon an ever smaller subset of potential food sources. Increase in the availability of a resource is accompanied by a corresponding increase in its utilization. The effect of this dietary shift is a reduction in the importance of nondomesticates. This simplification of the subsistence pattern has major effects upon its stability.

To understand the relationship between yield and instability in yield, we may first consider the relationship between man and any one domesticated plant. The increase in yield that results from domestication is only the average increase over time, that is, as the mutualistic relationship develops. Any given plant grows in an environment which is subject to periodic and normal fluctuation, and its yield will vary about the mean from year to year because of this fluctuation. Thus the contribution of any particular species of plant to the total plant food available to man will vary in response to environmental factors. While average yield is increasing over time because of the elaboration of coevolutionary domestication relationships, the absolute yield at any given moment is a function of specific environmental conditions.

During the early stages of domestication, before the development of agricultural systems, this fluctuation in yield should have little effect on the total yield available to man. The contribution of any given domesticated plant to the total subsistence pattern will be relatively small. Members of any given domesticated species are likely to be growing in any and all of the locations which are conducive to their growth. Also, the various species of plants with which man has established mutualistic relationships are likely to be fairly uniformly distributed throughout the environment, no particular niche having established itself as the principal one for all domesticated plants. Thus, while environmental fluctuation will have adverse effects on the yield of any particular species, the overall yield will tend to remain reasonably constant. A bad year for one plant is likely to be a good year for another plant growing in a different habitat; a bad year for one species is likely to be a good year for another species with differing edaphic and physiological requirements. This compensation in yield will permit productivity to remain relatively stable from year to year, much as it does in any nondomesticated ecology. As we shall see, this stands in stark contrast to the interaction of yield and environment which occurs in the agricultural setting.

Agricultural Origins

Evolutionary tendencies. The primary effect of agriculture on a society is an intensification of the dependence of that society on domesticated plants. Highly developed agricultural systems are based upon a limited number of cultivated plants which provide the bulk of the society's food. From the preceding discussion it should be clear that this tendency towards a decrease in the number of plants providing subsistence is an outgrowth of the dynamics of the mutualistic relationship. There is a tendency towards increase in yield and concomitant decrease in the number of species of domesticated plants providing that yield. It has also been noted that the environment places the major limitation upon the development of this relationship.

Any environment is composed of various niches for plant colonization. These niches are well defined and relatively stable. Thus the potential number of places in which any given plant might grow is determined by the characteristics of the environment. Clearly, any behavior by man that transcends these environmental limitations on plant growth will be accompanied by increases in yield proportional to the amount of "new" niche space. At the same time, any behavior increasing niche size available for plant colonization will cause a corresponding increase in the carrying capacity of the environment for man.

Any human behavior causing environmental changes which increase the probable reproductive success of the domesticated plant, and thus its yield, will have important effects on the further evolution of the domesticated plant. Within any locality, several tendencies will guide the evolution of the cultivated crop, among them (1) a reduction in diversity, both genetic and phenotypic, (2) a tendency towards increased productivity, and (3) autecological convergence. At the same time, a series of tendencies will become manifest within the total set of crops comprising the domesticated ecology, among them (1) a tendency towards reduction in the number of species on which man relies for his subsistence, (2) increase in total crop yields, and (3) autecological convergence. As we shall see, these interrelated tendencies will form the basis for the elaboration and dispersal of agricultural systems.

Systems, diversity, and yield. Changes in the direction of plant evolution within the early agriculturally modified ecology are based on one rather simple factor: human agricultural technology creates an environment for plant growth and reproduction which, unlike the overall environment, is structurally homogeneous and temporally stable.

As numerous authors have observed, agricultural systems may be described as simplified ecologies: typically the agricultural plant is a "weedy heliophyte," that is, a colonizer of disturbed habitats, and the agricultural field or garden is an environment in which the earliest stages of ecological successions are maintained. The predominance of this colonizer system for agriculture is based upon the fact that there are numerous ways in which a disturbed habitat can be created by human behavior. Fires, disturbance of the soil, the clearing of forests or the ringing of trees, and the creation of dump heaps are all routes by which a disturbed, and thus open, habitat may be created. Early domesticated plants preadapted to this niche will thus be favored in their further evolution into agricultural plants.

Various agricultural behaviors serve to reduce the intensity of natural selection for characteristics of plants that are necessary for survival in the wild. Irrigation reduces the necessity for plants to maintain mechanisms for survival during periodically recurring droughts. Clearing of the land and weeding decrease the importance of competitive mechanisms. Planting encourages specific and uniform germination and seedling physiologies. The techniques of agriculture ultimately reduce the variation to be found in a species of domesticated plant. Both the wild and the early domesticated plant had to maintain pleiotropic responses in the face of an unpredictable environment. With a reduction in overall environmental unpredictability within agricultural systems, this variability is no longer being maintained by natural selection. Physiological and autecological convergence also occurs in all agricultural plants within any given locality. As we shall see, this decrease in variability ultimately yields an increase in vulnerability.

At the same time, the selection for higher yields just discussed will continue and even increase. Plants yielding the greatest number of propagules—those plants best adapted to the agricultural environment—will be most likely to survive and spread. The relaxation of selection pressures for traits such as competitiveness will also bring about a new way for plants to increase their yield. Energy that was previously diverted to such tasks as protection, the manufacture of long internodes, perenniating structures, and the like may now be utilized for further increases in yield. Released from the requirement to possess such structures, the plant which puts energy into the production of propagules will be the most fit within an agricultural system.

Processes analogous to those occurring at the intraspecific level will also occur at the interspecific level. Those plants best adapted to survival and reproduction within the agricultural ecology will come to dominate the system. Given the homogeneity and stability introduced into the environment by agricultural behavior, it is not unreasonable to expect a reduction in species diversity—an increasing reliance upon fewer and fewer species to provide the basis for human subsistence.

Another factor will also reinforce this tendency towards uniformity and simplification of developing agricultural systems. As a food source becomes more common, feeding on it will increase. At first this will be merely a function of availability, but as time passes techniques of production and consumption will tend to improve. Availability and efficiency interact in a positive feedback manner, and further specialization is likely.

Specialization will also be encouraged by the localization of agricultural production. Reduction of usage will decrease the probability of the establishment of co-evolutionary relationships between humans and new species of plants. As more time is spent in the agricultural environment, man will come into contact with fewer species of alternative food sources. These changes in time allocation, generally known as scheduling changes, decrease the importance of enterprises competing with agriculture. Thus the establishment of agriculture within a society will intensify and direct tendencies already existing under the domesticatory way of life.

The development of agricultural ecologies. Agriculture creates a new type of climax formation. The agricultural flora tends towards stability as long as human behavior is interfering with other successional processes. Many of the species which inhabit the agricultural climax are derived from plants adapted to the earliest, colonizing, stage of ecological succession. Agricultural staples are frequently derived from "weedy" plants that tend to exist only in newly disturbed ground. Another characteristic of many of the staple crops of agriculture is that they are descended from plants that did not already have mutualistic dispersal systems with any animal other than man. The agricultural flora is a climax formation composed of highly specialized colonizer species. Many of the plants are descended from ancestors having geophysical modes of dispersal; secondary modifications are adaptations to human mediated dispersal. This striking combination of genetic heritage and evolutionary setting goes far in helping us to understand both the productivity and the limited species diversity typical of agricultural systems.

While the agricultural ecology is both stable and simple compared with the overall ecology, it nevertheless will show change over time. Probably the most important long term change that occurs in agricultural ecologies is the creation of new niches within the ecology. As time passes and plants respond to the options presented by the existence of agricultural areas, subdivision of the existing space will occur. This will permit the entry of new, not necessarily domesticated, plants into the ecology. For example, weeds may evolve to utilize agricultural fields during fallow periods and then begin to be subject to many of the same selective forces experienced by the domesticates.

The changes that occur in agricultural ecologies over time also allow us to understand the evolution of weediness and the entry of "secondary" domesticates into the system. Weeds are colonizers of this new agricultural habitat just like agricultural plants. The only difference between them is in the attitude man has towards them. Vavilov (1926), among others, has pointed out that the distinction between weed and domesticate is at best a tenuous one. Secondary domesticates are plants that are capable of establishing themselves, like weeds, in the agricultural ecology but that provide man with useful products. Prime among these are plants whose utility is found in their vegetative parts. Edible plants which can establish themselves in the disturbed agricultural ecology need not develop special coevolved means of distribution in order to survive. They need only scatter their seed. However, since they are growing in the same environment with other early agricultural plants, they will be subject to the same selection for high propagule yield. They will also exhibit the same tendency towards edaphic and autecological convergence as any other agricultural crop. The secondary domesticate will evolve subject to the same selective pressures as the primary domesticate: it is evolving in the same environment.

The development of the agricultural ecology will, because of the interaction between it and the general ecology, have major effects on the divergence of the cultivated plant from its progenitor species. While diversity within the ecological niche is likely to be, at least initially, less than that outside of it, the result will nevertheless be an increase in the heterogeneity of the entire region. This will permit more opportunities for disruptive selection (Thoday 1958) and intensify the divergence of the agricultural plant from the early domesticated plant. Human interaction with the originally domesticated taxon will decrease as the interaction with the agricultural plant develops. Relaxation of the amount of interaction between man and his earliest domesticated crops will, in the presence of highly developed agricultural systems, leave the early domesticate "stranded." The human agent with which it had developed a coevolved dispersal or protection system will no longer be functioning as dispersal agent or protector, and its extinction is almost inevitable. It is not surprising that it is so difficult to identify the "progenitor species" for so many of our important agricultural plants. Two major opportunities for extinction have occurred in the history of all primary domesticates: (1) The wild, uncoevolved portion of the ancestral gene pool may have become extinct during the long time period during which co-evolutionary domestication occurred. (2) The portion of the gene pool which evolved under the conditions of early domestication may have become extinct during the period of intensified evolution which led to the development of the agricultural plant.

Dispersal of Agricultural Systems

Agriculture and environmental instability. We have already noted that increasing human reliance on cultivated plants brings with it a relative decrease over time in the absolute number of taxa producing the major portion of the society's subsistence; that many domesticated taxa vary in productivity from year to year; that convergence occurs among agricultural crops; and that, by removing certain environmental limitations upon the carrying capacity of the environment for domesticated plants, agricultural behavior permits a tremendous increase in potential yield and thus in potential human population. I would now like to explore the interaction of a contracting subsistence base, increase in carrying capacity, and variation in productivity, an interaction whose demographic effects have led to the spread of agriculture as a mode of human subsistence.

We have discussed some of the consequences of the development of agriculture as a temporally stable niche: the divergence of agricultural domesticates from their progenitors, the evolution of secondary domesticates, and the evolution of agricultural concentration of agricultural plants in limited regions increases yields by allowing a more complete harvest. At the same time, it intensifies the potential instability of the system, and this has major effects upon the demography of the human population dependent upon agricultural production. Locational stability intensifies instability in several ways. Prime among them are the effects of microenvironmental and microclimatic variation. A garden area that optimizes drainage during average years will be too wet during periods of high precipitation and too dry during periods of drought. Other locational effects to be considered later include concentration of resources and predation and edaphic effects.

Domesticated and agricultural plants bring about an increase in the carrying capacity of the environment contributed by domesticated plants, hereafter referred to as K_{dom}. While K_{dom} tends to increase greatly over time, for reasons outlined above, the change in K_{dom} is not always positive from one moment to another. The components of the environment show seasonal and longer term variation. Climate, for example, is not uniform from year to year, and over relatively short periods of time differing average climatic conditions will prevail. Thus, yield will vary in response to these conditions.

In the later phases of nonagricultural domestication, there will be some variation in productivity over time, but variability is restrained by several factors. As we have already noted, the early domesticated plant is growing in a variety of microenvironments. Thus any climatic change need not affect all of the microenvironments in the same way. For example, domesticates growing in sites that are wetter than optimal will prosper during a period of reduced precipitation. Nonagricultural domesticatory societies also tend to have a larger number of species contributing to K_{dom} than do agricultural societies. Thus any given change in the environment is not likely to affect all species of domesticates equally. Both of these intrinsic factors will tend to reduce the effects of changes in the environment on the productivity of the domesticated ecology. Perhaps the most important factor limiting the effects of changes in K_{dom}, however, is external to the domestication symbiosis. The nonagricultural society is relying upon domesticated plants for only part of its total food supply. Thus it is possible to compensate for declines in K_{dom} by increased reliance upon other components of the total carrying capacity (K). The failure of one domesticated plant, or of one domesticated species of plants, will be compensated for by increased reliance upon other plants, both wild and domesticated.

In a period of early agriculture, the variance of K_{dom} will be greater because of the evolution of agricultural ecologies. The evolution of the cultivated plant in the agricultural environment increases not only yield, but also the susceptibility of that yield to environmentally induced crop failure. The autecological convergence brought about by agricultural selection brings with it an increased uniformity in the response of agricultural plants to environmental parameters. Thus a bad year for any given member of a cultivated species is likely to be bad for all members of that species. And since the convergence is also occurring between, as well as amongst, plant species, bad years for any given agricultural staple are likely to be bad for other staples also. Increase in productivity has been bought at the price of uniformity in response to the environment.

Contributing to and intensifying the effects of autecological convergence is the greater locational stability of agricultural ecologies. Localization intensifies the effects of microclimatic effects upon total yield. To take an extreme example, a hailstorm just before the harvest season will have vastly different effects upon a society if it falls upon the cultivated fields than if it falls in the woods. Since hail is frequently a highly localized phenomenon, the effect of hailstorms upon the total available yield will be far greater for agriculturalists than it will be for either a domesticatory or a totally nondomesticatory society. Thus localization of resources in agricultural ecologies increases the possibility that all of the resource may be lost to a catastrophe.

Agricultural subsistence is also accompanied by a growing specialization in diet. Thus a decrease in the yield from a staple crop will have major effects on the total *perceived* food supply, as well as the absolute food supply. Food preferences and techniques of preparation will have placed certain food sources in positions of prominence. Information concerning the edibility and processing of alternative food supplies may be lost. Thus decreases in yield from cultivated plants may create the appearance of food shortage even though the total available food supply in the region may not have fallen to the point where it is actually limiting survival of the population. Animals respond to the perceived food supply, not to some "objective" measure of total available calories.

The basis for instability. The increased susceptibility of the agricultural ecology to the extremes of normal climatic variation may be viewed as an effect of environmental manipulation itself. Many of the simpler forms of environmental manipulation control relatively constant, predictable parameters of the environment. They increase K_{dom} by mitigating the effects of the fundamental restrictions on the carrying capacity of the environment for the plant. Increasing control over any limiting aspect of the environment brings with it, however, an increase in the vulnerability of the newly heightened K_{dom} to those aspects of the environment left unaffected by control behaviors. As we have seen, for example, localization of production increases K_{dom} and thus allows for a larger number of human beings, but it also increases the susceptibility of the system to negative microclimatic and microenvironmental effects. The removal of any given limit on yield allows other, uncontrolled limits to become evident.

Agriculture permits previously nonlimiting factors in the growth and productivity of plants to express themselves. For example, a plant suffering from drought will not have major limitation placed upon its productivity by minor insect infestation. Correction of the drought condition by irrigation will allow for the expression of the limitation on productivity contributed by the insect predation. Thus techniques of environmental manipulation *allow the environment to affect yield adversely in new ways.* At any given time, techniques of environmental control increase the negative effects of conditions that cannot be controlled by the system.

Agriculture also *creates entirely new opportunities for limitations on productivity.* The increasing genetic uniformity of a crop, reduction in species diversity, edaphic and ecological changes created by agricultural practices, and the concentration of resources in a limited area all contribute to new potential instabilities in productivity.

Increasing genetic uniformity increases the susceptibility of the crop to attacks by pathogens. Polymorphisms in the production of secondary metabolites acting as biochemical defenses discourage the evolution of specialized pathogens. A reduction in this defense strategy encourages the evolution of pathogens which may seriously damage a plant species (Feeny 1973). This potential source of damage is especially clear when we consider crops in which secondary metabolites distasteful to man also serve to protect the plant from attack by other animals.

Reduction in species diversity within the agricultural ecology may in and of itself have important effects upon the susceptibility of the crop plant to pathogen attack. Escape from predation may be aided in many plant communities by the association of many different plants; the plants "hide" from potential predators by being hard to find in the mosaic of diverse plant species (Tahvanainen and Root 1972). As noted by Feeny (1973:14), "It is interesting to speculate as to whether the vulnerability of crops to insect herbivores...may result from planting in monoculture species which have evolved chemical defenses appropriate to communities in which the optimum strategy is being hard to find." Competition between agricultural crops which results in tendencies towards both increased yield and reduction in species diversity thus may work to counteract defenses acquired during the evolution of the plant in the wild.

The negative effects of agricultural practices on the land, among them erosion and changes in soil structure and drainage patterns, are well documented and will not be given further consideration here. Less well studied are the effects of agricultural systems on the feeding patterns of animals other than man. Agriculture, especially in its later phases, may significantly alter the local ecology simply by the replacement of areas of wild vegetation with cultivated fields. This destruction of wild habitats creates food shortages for animals that require plants growing in these habitats. Thus they may turn, out of necessity, to feeding upon agricultural crops, even though these plants may not provide favored sources of food.

Finally, the increasing concentration of resources encourages predation. The same concentration of resources which facilitates harvest of the crop by humans will facilitate its harvest by nonhuman predators. And while man may delay consumption of the plant to optimize harvest, most of these predators will not be under the same restraints. Thus they may attack the field before the crop ripens. They may also be capable of utilizing a crop at a period during its life cycle when it cannot be consumed by man, for example, during early seedling or vegetative stages. Thus loss of the total crop may occur before any yield has been given to man.

The fundamental cause of agricultural instability is agriculture itself. All of the new adverse effects which the environment may have on agricultural productivity are induced by agricultural practices. Yet at the same time agriculture is responsible for greatly increased average yield and thus permits greatly elevated human population levels. Over the long term, it would seem justified to say that, despite the greater instability of agricultural production, this increase in population levels is evidence of "progress."

However, the increases in population which accompany increases in K_{dom} over long periods of time are "successes" for the system *only at the moment of change*. The agriculturally enhanced population levels now require continually elevated levels of production for their maintenance. Further, over relatively short periods of time, the enhanced population level becomes nothing more than the "normal" population level. Thus the increases in productivity brought about by agriculture are absorbed by a growing population. Increasingly sophisticated techniques of environmental manipulation are required for the maintenance of the same rate of growth and, because of increasing instability, often for maintenance of the same level of population. Human populations grow in proportion to the effectiveness of agriculture in raising the carrying capacity of the environment for man. Yet, the more effective agricultural procedures are in reducing environmental limitations upon the productivity of the agricultural ecology, the more likely they are to create new opportunities for failures of the system. And as agriculture creates higher and higher population levels, the effect on the society of the failures of the system will become increasingly tragic. Successful agricultural systems require increasingly successful techniques of environmental manipulation merely to maintain the status quo.

Instability and dispersal. The interaction of increase in productivity and increase in instability of productivity has been responsible for the tremendous spread of agricultural techniques. To understand this somewhat paradoxical situation, it is necessary to understand how any animal population responds to changes in the carrying capacity of an environment. No population of animals is capable of instantaneous change in numbers in response to change in the carrying capacity. Instead, the potential population must "track" the changes in the carrying capacity. It will be somewhat out of phase with those changes because of lags in reproduction or behavioral response to perceived changes in the environment. Changes over time in K_{dom} will be responded to, in a delayed manner, by changes in the potential population. The average population over long periods of time, however, will tend to correspond to the effective minimal carrying capacity (K_{dom}). Part of the potential human population produced by recurring increases in K_{dom}. cannot be maintained during periods when K_{dom} drops to its lowest levels. We may view this component of the population as agriculturally induced "excess production" of people, hereafter referred to as P_d. The amplitude of P_d is clearly determined by the interaction of a large number of factors, including the length of a generation, the amplitude of K_{dom}, the rate of change of K_{dom}, the availability of alternative food sources, and the way in which changes in K_{dom} are tracked. Nevertheless, for our purposes treating Pd as determined by the interaction of K_{dom}. and K_{dom} has considerable heuristic value.

Figure 3 is an interpretation of the demographic effects of agricultural instability taking into account the tracking behavior of human populations. The hypothetical productivity and resultant demographic changes represented by this graph represent conditions such as might have existed in an early pristine agricultural society. Here we may note an average increase in K_{dom} the potential populations, and the effective minimal K_{dom} (K_{dom}). The graph also shows three points (*a*, *b*, and *c*) at which the actual population is greater than can be maintained. We must consider the fate of this temporarily excess production of human beings. In essence, we are seeking to identify the factor which acts to reduce the population in a particular locality when an environmental crisis causes a sudden decline in K_{dom}.

The most frequent response of any animal population to a drop in the carrying capacity is emigration. Emigration (rather than starvation or decline in per capita consumption) is especially likely if only one component of the carrying capacity is suddenly reduced. Part of the animal population will leave the area in search of a place where the limiting resource is more abundant.

Humans experiencing a decline in food supply may be expected to respond in the same manner. A drop in K_{dom} will encourage part of the population to leave and establish itself in a new area. A slow decline in relative productivity such as that occurring at Point *a* may be due to ecological or edaphic degradation occurring because of agricultural practices. While large changes in population will not necessarily occur, groups may leave in search of "better" environments in which to farm. Sudden and drastic declines in relative productivity such as are shown at Points *b* and *c* will also cause emigration. In these cases we may assume that emigration will be encouraged by another factor in addition to the search for a "better" agricultural environment. If a drastic drop in production (a famine or a sudden great scarcity of cultivated foods) occurs, it is likely that the population will return to the exploitation of nondomesticated food sources. We have already noted that the famine need not be an "objective" lack of potential calories in order to be perceived as one by the population. However, since an agricultural economy can support higher population levels than a gathering economy, and since at least certain nonagricultural domesticates have been lost, part of the population will be forced into new areas in search of wild resources. Thus a decline in K_{dom} will be especially noticeable to an agricultural population because of several interrelated factors: higher population levels in any given area, losses of wild food sources and nonagricultural domesticates, and changes in the perception of what constitutes food scarcity.

The only other likely and effective response of a society to a drop in K_{dom} is increased demand for environmental control. If this occurs, however, it may simply be incorporated into the graph by increasing the amplitude of the K_{dom} curve. In this model increases in productivity already incorporate techniques of environmental control; thus they cannot be reentered as a new variable. Also, as has been stressed, environmental control is intimately tied up with instability in yield; decreases in K_{dom} are inevitable effects of an agricultural system existing in a variable and evolving environment. At best, environmental manipulation will delay the need of the society to find a solution to the problem of the excess population induced by the periods of "successful" agricultural production.

It is important to recognize that these emigrant groups will probably take with them an agricultural tradition; the instability created by agricultural subsistence will bring about the spread of the system. Besides the conservatism inherent in any society, another factor facilitates the emigration of agricultural populations without loss of agricultural technology. The environmental controls inherent in agricultural behavior permit easy colonization of new regions. Emigrant groups from most nonagricultural societies require a definable set of preexisting conditions if they are to maintain their mode of subsistence. Of course, agricultural societies require definite ecological conditions also, but the relatively slow spread of agricultural societies, such as posited here, will allow time for adaptation by crops to gradients in the environment. Secondary domestication will permit colonization of the fields and gardens by new, better adapted plants, and eventually a whole new ecological zone may open up to the agriculturalist. We might also briefly note that while the activities of most nonagricultural peoples do not interfere with subsequent utilization of the land by agriculturalists, the converse is far from true.

Jack Harlan, from *Crops and Man*

Jack Harlan (1917–1998 CE) was an American botanist specializing in crop breeding and genetics. He believed plant domestication resulted from long-term co-evolution of man and plants in many different areas and under widely different circumstances around the world. He later acted for protecting the world-wide genetic diversity of crops.

Source: Harlan, Jack. Crops and Man. *Wisconsin: American Society of Agronomy, 1975.*

> **Focus Questions:**
> 1. How does Harlan's view of hunter-gatherers differ from Darwin? From Rindos ?
> 2. Why develop agriculture if it consumes so much work and energy?
> 3. How efficient is modern agriculture?

AGRICULTURE AS AN EXTENSION OF GATHERING

In Chapter 1 it became clear that gatherers of today know all they need to know to develop agriculture. While much of this information may have been recently derived through contact with cultivators, the Australian aborigine at the time of European contact also had ample information. He did not need to discover the concepts of planting; he already had them. We have asked, "Why farm?" We could also ask the question, "Why not farm if you are equipped with all the materials and information to do so?" One approach is to ask a gatherer. During his study of the Bushmen Richard Lee did exactly that, and he received the celebrated reply, "Why should I farm when there are so many mongongo nuts?" (Lee and DeVore, 1968). The aborigines put it in almost the same terms:

> You people go to all that trouble, working and planting seeds, but we don't have to do that. All these things are there for us, the Ancestral Beings left them for us. In the end, you depend on the sun and the rain just the same as we do, but the difference is that we just have to go and collect the food when it is ripe. We don't have all this other trouble.

Berndt and Berndt, 1920

We are now beginning to obtain some data to show that the aboriginal opinion is correct. Black (1971) reported on a series of input-output studies of different agricultural systems. For subsistence agriculture where human labor only is expended, he assigned a generalized, arbitrary figure of 150 kilocalories (kcal) of energy expended per hour. The average for 13 systems analyzed showed a return of 17 kcal for each kcal invested although the range was from 3 to 34. Draft animals did not improve the situation and if the energy for maintaining the animals was included, the results would have been negative. However, the by-products of the draft animals (calves, milk, hides, etc.) were also not included. Mechanized societies produce energy deficits. If the energy of gasoline consumed by a tractor is used for the input side of the budget, outputs are within the range of human labor, but the moment one begins to calculate the energy required to mine ore, make steel, manufacture tractors, transport fuel, etc., the system uses far more energy than it produces. Our vaunted, efficient, modern, mechanized agriculture is *not*, in fact, a renewable resource; rather, it consumes energy.

Using the same conversion figure that Black used, my wild wheat harvest in Turkey netted about 50 kcal for every kcal expended, far more efficient than any form of agriculture for which we have input-output data. I am indebted to Lloyd Evans, CSIRO, Australia, for calling this to my attention.

More studies and better data are needed, but we have ample anthropological and ethnographical evidence to show that increasing the food supply through cultivation means an increase in work. In general, the more intensive the agricultural system, the more work is required for a unit of food. Thus, if we are to understand the origins of agriculture, we must visualize situations in which man is willing to expend more energy to obtain food. In this respect, farming is not so attractive that gatherers are likely to take it up on sight or on first contact. Some rather compelling reasons would seem to be required.

In preagricultural times the human population was not regulated by the food supply. If this were the case, Binford (1968) has pointed out that two corollaries would follow: "1) Man would be continually seeking means of increasing his food supply," and "2) It is only when man is freed from preoccupation with the food quest that he has time to elaborate culture." From what we have seen, both are patently false. Populations of hunter-gatherers are regulated well below the carrying capacity of the range, and the environment does not exert pressure on man to change his food procurement systems. Neither agricultural nor industrial man has anything like the leisure time of hunters and gatherers. Therefore, we must look elsewhere for the motivation to carry on agriculture.

What, then, might generate the motives that caused man to domesticate plants (and animals)? A much-cited model in current literature is one based on proposals put forth by Lewis Binford (1968) and Kent Flannery (1968). It attempts to integrate ethnographic and archaeological information, and suggests not only reasons for but places where the initiative toward food production might have been taken. Explicit in the Binford-Flannery model is the recognition that gatherers are sophisticated, applied botanists who know their material and how to exploit it. They are prepared to grow plants if and when they think it would be worth the effort. Furthermore, the difference between intensive gathering and cultivation is minimal; recall the square kilometers of Australian landscape pitted by aborigines digging yams.

Binford, in particular, emphasized the fact that one of the general post-Pleistocene adaptations of man was a fuller exploitation of aquatic resources. This is one of the most characteristic features of the so-called "Mesolithic" wherever it can be identified. Canoes, boats, and rafts were developed, and there was a great proliferation of archaeological sites that suggested fairly permanent residence and subsistence by fishing, fowling, and gathering. The sedentary fisher-folk referred to by Sauer and Anderson did appear in many parts of the world; however, Binford suggests that it was not they who began domestication, but groups that budded off from them and migrated into regions already occupied by hunter-gatherers. The argument goes that long before there was a food resource crisis among the fisherfolk, groups would move out and migrate into less well-endowed regions and ecological zones. The fisherfolk population remained stable, but the migrants precipitated a crisis along the interface between the sedentary peoples and the nomadic hunter-gatherers. It was in response to this crisis that people were willing to go to the effort of cultivation.

The Binford model was spelled out in sufficient detail that he could make some predictions to be tested:

1. The initial activities of domestication in the Near East will appear adjacent to areas occupied by sedentary forager-fisher-folk (evidence for this fairly firm at the time of the prediction).

2. Evidence will be found of independent domestications in European Russia and south-central Europe (suggestions are coming in that this may be true).

3. Evidence will be found of similar events widely separated over Europe, Asia, and the Americas. (Flannery has provided some evidence from Mesoamerica and the African evidence is compatible with the prediction.)

There may be biological and ecological reasons as well for proposing that cultivation would begin adjacent to the best foraging ranges rather than in them. In the Near East massive stands of wild wheats cover many square kilometers. Harlan and Zohary (1966) have asked, "Why should anyone cultivate a cereal where natural stands are as dense as a cultivated field? If wild cereal grasses can be harvested in unlimited quantities, why should anyone bother to till the soil and plant the seed?" The same arguments could well apply to the African savanna or California, where wild food resources were abundant.

A major implication of the model is that the activities of plant domestication are likely to have taken place independently and probably simultaneously in many areas all over the world. The space-time pattern that would emerge would be almost the opposite of that of the Sauer-Anderson model. It would appear that the differences are testable by archaeological means and that even botanical and genetical evidence could come to bear on the problem.

James Cook, from *Captain Cook's Journal During His First Voyage Round the World*

James Cook (1728–1771 CE) was a British naval officer and explorer who completed two global circumnavigations and was killed while on his third. Cook's seamanship on his long voyages of exploration was outstanding. In addition Cook has a reputation for his reasonable treatment of the people he met. Many of the encounters resulted in friendship, trade, and exchanges of information, but others involved fear, misunderstanding, and even conflict. In other words, they ran the gamut of human interactions. What is noticeable about European views of others is the judgment of cultures by their technology and use of agriculture.

Source: Captain Cook's Journal During His First Voyage Round the World, *1768–1771.*

Focus Questions:
1. By what criteria does Cook evaluate the land, plants, and animals?
2. Compare Cook's opinion of the aborigine lifestyle with that of Marshall Sahlins.
3. What are the technologies used by the native Australians? How effective are they?

SOME ACCOUNT OF NEW WALES.*

(*Called in Admiralty and the Queen's Copy New South Wales. It would appear that for this part of the voyage Mr. Corner's copy was the first written, and that Cook's first idea was to christen the country New Wales.)

In the Course of this Journal I have at different times made mention of the Appearance or Aspect of the face of the Country, the Nature of the Soil, its produce, etc. By the first it will appear that to the Southward of 33 or 34 degrees the land in general is low and level, with very few Hills or Mountains; further to the Northward it may in some places be called a Hilly, but hardly anywhere can be called a Mountainous, Country, for the Hills and Mountains put together take up but a small part of the Surface in Comparison to what the Planes and Valleys do which intersect or divide these Hills and Mountains. It is indifferently well water'd, even in the dry Seasons, with small brooks and Springs, but no great Rivers, unless it be in the Wet Season, when the low lands and Values near the Sea, I do suppose, are mostly laid under Water. The Small Brooks may then become large Rivers; but this can only happen with the Tropick. It was only in Thirsty Sound that we could find no fresh Water, and that no doubt was owing to the Country being there very much intersected with Salt Creeks and Mangrove land.

The low land by the Sea, and even as far in land as we were, is for the most part friable, loose, sandy Soil yet indifferently fertile, and Cloathed with woods, long grass, shrubs, plants, etc. The Mountains or Hills are checquer'd with woods and Lawns; some of the Hills are wholy cover'd with Flourishing Trees; others but thinly, and the few that are upon them are small, and the spot of Lawns or Savannahs are rocky and barren, especially to the Northward, where the Country did not afford or produce near the Vegetation that it does to the Southward, nor were the Trees in the Woods half so tall and stout. The Woods do not produce any great variety of Trees; there are only 2 or 3 sorts that can be called Timber. The largest is the gum Tree, which grows all over the country; the wood of this Tree is too hard and ponderous for most common uses. The Tree which resembles our Pines I saw nowhere in perfection but in Botany Bay; this wood, as I have before observed, is something of the same Nature as American Live Oak; in short, most of the large Trees in this Country are of a hard and ponderous nature, and could not be applied to many purposes. Here are several sorts of the Palm kind, Mangrove, and several other sorts of small Trees and Shrubs quite unknown to me, besides a very great number of Plants hitherto unknown; but these things are wholy out of my way to describe, nor will this be of any loss, since not only plants, but every thing that can be of use to the Learned World will be very accurately described by Mr. Banks and Dr. Solander. The Land naturally produces hardly anything fit for Man to eat, and the Natives know nothing of Cultivation. There are, indeed, growing wild in the wood a few sorts of Fruit (the most of them unknown to us), which when ripe do not eat amiss, one sort especially, which we called Apples, being about the size of a Crab Apple it is black and pulpey when ripe, and tastes like a Damson; it hath a large hard stone or Kernel, and grows on Trees or Shrubs.*

(* The Black Apple, or Sapota Australis.)
In the Northern parts of the Country, as about Endeavour River, and probably in many other places, the Boggy or watery Lands produce Taara or Cocos,* (*A species of Taro, Colocasia macrorhiza.) which, when properly cultivated, are very good roots, without which they are hardly eatable; the Tops, however, make very good greens.

Land Animals are scarce, so far as we know confin'd to a very few species; all that we saw I have before mentioned. The sort which is in the greatest Plenty is the Kangooroo or Kanguru, so called by the Natives; we saw a good many of them about Endeavour River, but kill'd only 3, which we found very good Eating. Here are likewise Lizards, Snakes, Scorpions, Centapees, etc., but not in any plenty. Tame Animals they have none but Dogs, and of these we saw but one, and therefore must be very scarce, probably they eat them faster than they breed them; we should not have seen this one had he not made us frequent Visits while we lay in Endeavour River.

The land Fowls are Bustards, Eagles, Hawks, Crows, such as we have in England, Cockatoes of 2 sorts, White and Brown, very beautiful Birds of the Parrot kind, such as Lorryquets, etc., Pidgeons, Doves, Quails, and several sorts of smaller birds. The Sea and Water Fowls are Herons, Boobies, Noddies, Guls, Curlews, Ducks, Pelicans, etc., and when Mr. Banks and Mr. Gore where in the Country, at the head of Endeavour River, they saw and heard in the Night great numbers of Geese. The Sea is indifferently well stocked with fish of Various sorts, such as Sharks, Dog-fish, Rockfish, Mullets, Breams, Cavallies, Mack'rel, old wives, Leather Jackets, Five Fingers,* (*Old wives are Enoploxus Armatus; Leather jackets, Monacanthus; Five fingers, Chilodactylus.) Sting rays, Whip rays, etc., all excellent in their kind. The Shell fish are Oysters of 3 or 4 sorts, viz., Rock Oysters and Mangrove Oysters, which are small, Pearl Oysters and Mud Oysters; these last are the best and Largest I ever saw. Cockles and Clams of several sorts, many of those that are found upon the Reefs are of a prodigious size, Craw fish, Crabs, Muscles, and a variety of other sorts. Here are also upon the Shoals and Reefs great Numbers of the finest Green Turtle in the world, and in the River and Salt Creeks are some Alligators.

[Australian Natives.]

The Natives of this Country are of a middle Stature, streight Bodied and Slender limb'd; their Skins the Colour of Wood soot, their Hair mostly black, some Lank and others curled; they all wear it Cropt Short; their Beards, which are generally black, they likewise crop short, or Singe off. There features are far from being disagreeable, and their Voices are soft and Tunable. They go quite Naked, both Men and Women, without any manner of Cloathing whatever; even the Women do not so much as cover their privities, altho' None of us was ever very near any of their Women, one Gentleman excepted, yet we are all of us as well satisfied of this as if we had lived among them. Notwithstanding we had several interviews with the Men while we lay in Endeavour River, yet, wether through Jealousy or disregard, they never brought any of their women along with them to the Ship, but always left them on the Opposite side of the River, where we had frequent Opportunities viewing them thro' our Glasses. They wear as Ornaments, Necklaces made of Shells, Bracelets, or Hoops, about their Arms, made mostly of Hair Twisted and made like a Cord Hoop; these they wear tight about the upper parts of their Arms, and some have Girdles made in the same manner. The Men wear a bone, about 3 or 4 Inches long and a finger's thick, run thro' the Bridge* (*The cartilage of the nostril. Banks mentions that the bluejackets called this queer ornament the "spritsail yard.") of their Nose; they likewise have holes in their Ears for Ear Rings, but we never saw them wear any; neither are all the other Ornaments wore in Common, for we have seen as many without as with them. Some of these we saw on Possession Island wore breast plates, which we supposed were made of Mother of Pearl Shells. Many of them paint their Bodies and faces with a Sort of White paste or Pigment; this they apply different ways, each according to his fancy.

Their offensive weapons are Darts; some are only pointed at one end, others are barb'd, some with wood, others with Stings of rays, and some with Sharks' Teeth, etc.; these last are stuck fast on with Gum. They throw the Darts with only one hand, in the doing of which they make use of a piece of wood about 3 feet long, made thin like the blade of a Cutlass, with a little hook at one End to take hold of the End of the dart, and at the other end is fix'd a thin piece of bone about 3 or 4 Inches long; the use of this is, I believe, to keep the dart steady, and to make it quit the hand in a proper direction. By the helps of these throwing sticks, as we call them, they will hit a mark at the Distance of 40 or 50 yards, with almost, if not as much, Certainty as we can do with a Musquet, and much more so than with a ball.* (*The invention of these throwing sticks, and of the Boomerang, is sufficient to prove the intelligence of the Australian aborigines.) These throwing sticks we at first took for wooden swords, and perhaps on some occasions they may use them as such; that is, when all their darts are expended. Be this as it may, they never Travel without both them and their Darts, not for fear of Enemies, but for killing of Game, etc., as I shall show hereafter. There defensive weapons are Targets, made of wood; but these we never saw used but once in Botany Bay.

I do not look upon them to be a warlike people; on the contrary, I think them a Timerous and inoffensive race, no ways inclined to Cruelty, as appear'd from their behaviour to one of our people in

Endeavour River, which I have before mentioned, neither are they very numerous. They live in small parties along by the Sea Coast, the banks of Lakes, Rivers, Creeks, etc. They seem to have no fixed habitation, but move about from place to place like wild beasts in search of Food, and, I believe, depend wholy upon the Success of the present day for their Subsistance. They have wooden fish Gigs, with 2, 3, or 4 prongs, each very ingeniously made, with which they strike fish. We have also seen them strike both fish and birds with their Darts. With these they likewise kill other Animals; they have also wooden Harpoons for striking Turtle, but of these I believe they get but few, except at the seasons they come ashore to lay. In short, these people live wholy by fishing and hunting, but mostly by the former, for we never saw one Inch of Cultivated land in the whole Country. They know, however, the use of Taara, and sometimes eat them; we do not know that they Eat anything raw, but roast or broil all they eat on slow small fires. Their Houses are mean, small Hovels, not much bigger than an Oven, made of Peices of Sticks, Bark, Grass, etc., and even these are seldom used but in the Wet seasons, for in the daytimes we know they as often sleep in the Open Air as anywhere else. We have seen many of their Sleeping places, where there has been only some branches or peices of Bark, grass, etc., about a foot high on the Windward side.

[Australian Canoes.]

Their Canoes are as mean as can be conceived, especially to the Southward, where all we saw were made of one peice of the Bark of Trees about 12 or 14 feet long, drawn or Tied together at one end. As I have before made mention, these Canoes will not Carry above 2 people, in general there is never more than one in them; but, bad as they are, they do very well for the purpose they apply them to, better than if they were larger, for as they draw but little water they go in them upon the Mud banks, and pick up Shell fish, etc., without going out of the Canoe. The few Canoes we saw to the Northward were made out of a Log of wood hollow'd out, about 14 feet long and very narrow, with outriggers; these will carry 4 people. During our whole stay in Endeavour River we saw but one Canoe, and had great reason to think that the few people that resided about that place had no more; this one served them to cross the River and to go a Fishing in, etc. They attend the Shoals, and flatts, one where or another, every day at low water to gather Shell fish, or whatever they can find to eat, and have each a little bag to put what they get in; this bag is made of net work. They have not the least knowledge of Iron or any other Metal that we know of; their working Tools must be made of Stone, bone, and Shells; those made of the former are very bad, if I may judge from one of their Adzes I have seen.

Bad and mean as their Canoes are, they at Certain seasons of the Year (so far as we know) go in them to the most distant Islands which lay upon the Coast, for we never landed upon one but what we saw signs of People having been there before. We were surprized to find Houses, etc., upon Lizard Island, which lies 5 Leagues from the nearest part of the Main; a distance we before thought they could not have gone in their Canoes.

The Coast of this Country, at least so much of it as lays to the Northward of 25 degrees of Latitude, abounds with a great Number of fine bays and Harbours, which are Shelter'd from all winds; but the Country itself, so far as we know, doth not produce any one thing that can become an Article in Trade to invite Europeans to fix a settlement upon it. However, this Eastern side is not that barren and miserable country that Dampier and others have described the Western side to be. We are to consider that we see this country in the pure state of nature; the Industry of Man has had nothing to do with any part of it, and yet we find all such things as nature hath bestow'd upon it in a flourishing state. In this Extensive Country it can never be doubted but what most sorts of Grain, Fruit, roots, etc., of every kind would flourish here were they once brought hither, planted and Cultivated by the hands of Industry; and here are Provender for more Cattle, at all seasons of the Year, than ever can be brought into the Country.* (*It says a good deal for Cook's penetration that he wrote like this, for the coast of Australia is not promising, especially in the dry season; and coming as he did from the more apparently fertile countries of Tahiti and New Zealand, Australia must have appeared but a barren land.) When one considers the Proximity of this Country with New Guinea, New Britain, and several other Islands which produce Cocoa Nutts and many other fruits proper for the support of man, it seems strange that they should not long ago be Transplanted here; by its not being done it should seem that the Natives of this Country have no commerce with their Neighbours, the New Guineans.* (*The climate is too dry for the cocoanut palm.) It is very probable that they are a different people, and speak a different Language. For the advantage of such as want to Clear up this point I shall add a small Vocabulary of a few Words in the New Holland Language which we learnt when in Endeavour River.*

(*The languages of the different tribes differ very much. This results from the continual state of war in which they live, as they have no communication the one with the other.)

ENGLISH.	NEW HOLLAND.
The Head	Whageegee.
The Hair of the head	Morye or More.
The Eyes	Meul.
The Ears	Melea.
The Lips	Yembe or Jembi.
The Teeth	Mulere or Moile.
The Chinn	Jaeal.
The Beard	Waller.
The Tongue	Unjar.
The Nose	Bonjoo.
The Naval	Toolpoor or Julpur.
The Penis	Keveil or Kerrial.
The Scrotum	Coonal or Kunnol.
The Arms	Aw or Awl.
The Hand	Marigal.
The Thumb	Eboorbalga.
The Fore, Middle and Ring fingers	Egalbaiga.
Little Finger	Nakil or Eboonakil.
The Thighs	Coman.
The Knees	Ponga.
The Legs	Peegoorgo.
The Feet	Edamal.
The Nails	Kolke or Kulke.
A Stone	Walba.
Sand	Joo'wal, Yowall, or Joralba.
A Rope or Line	Goorgo or Gurka.
Fire	Maianang or Meanang.
The Sun	Galan or Gallan.
The Sky	Kere or Kearre.
A Father	Dunjo.
A Son	Jumurre.
A Man	Bamma or Ba ma.
A Dog	Cotta or Kota.
A Lorryquet	Perpere or Pier-pier.
A Cocatoo	Wanda.
Male Turtle	Poonja or Poinja.
Female	Mamingo.
A great Cockle	Moenjo or Moingo.
Cocos Yams	Maracotu (?).
A Canoe	Maragan.

[Australian Natives.]

From what I have said of the Natives of New Holland they may appear to some to be the most wretched People upon Earth; but in reality they are far more happier than we Europeans, being wholly unacquainted not only with the Superfluous, but with the necessary Conveniences so much sought after in Europe; they are happy in not knowing the use of them. They live in a Tranquility which is not disturbed by the Inequality of Condition. The earth and Sea of their own accord furnishes them with all things necessary for Life. They covet not Magnificient Houses, Household-stuff, etc.; they live in a Warm and fine Climate, and enjoy every wholesome Air, so that they have very little need of Cloathing; and this they seem to be fully sencible of, for many to whom we gave Cloth, etc., left it carelessly upon the Sea beach and in the Woods, as a thing they had no manner of use for; in short, they seem'd to set no Value upon anything we gave them, nor would they ever part with anything of their own for any one Article we could offer them. This, in my opinion, Argues that they think themselves provided with all the necessarys of Life, and that they have no Superfluities.*

(*The native Australians may be happy in their condition, but they are without doubt among the lowest of mankind. Confirmed cannibals, they lose no opportunity of gratifying their love of human flesh. Mothers will kill and eat their own children, and the women again are often mercilessly ill treated by their lords and masters. There are no chiefs, and the land is divided into sections, occupied by families, who consider everything in their district as their own. Internecine war exists between the different tribes, which are very small. Their treachery, which is unsurpassed, is simply an outcome of their savage ideas, and in their eyes is a form of independence which resents any intrusion on THEIR land, THEIR wild animals, and THEIR rights generally. In their untutored state they therefore consider that any method of getting rid of the invader is proper. Both sexes, as Cook observed, are absolutely nude, and lead a wandering life, with no fixed abode, subsisting on roots, fruits, and such living things as they can catch. Nevertheless, although treated by the coarser order of colonists as wild beasts to be extirpated, those who have studied them have formed favorable opinions of their intelligence. The more savage side of their disposition being, however, so very apparent, it is not astonishing that, brought into contact with white settlers, who equally consider that they have a right to settle, the aborigines are rapidly disappearing.)

I shall conclude the account of this Country with a few observations on the Currents and Tides upon the Coast, because I have mentioned in the Course of this Journal that the latter hath sometimes set one way and sometimes another, which I shall Endeavour to account for in the best manner I can. From the Latitude of 32 degrees, or above downwards to Sandy Cape in the Latitude of 24 degrees 46 minutes, we constantly found a Current setting to the Southward at the rate of 10 or 15 Miles per Day, more or less, according to the distance we were from the land, for it runs stronger in shore than in the Offing. All this time I had not been able to satisfy myself whether the flood-tide came from the Southward, Eastward, or Northward, but judged it to come from the South-East; but the first time we anchor'd upon the coast, which was in the Latitude of 24 degrees 30 minutes, and about 10 Leagues to the South-East of Bustard Bay, we found there the flood to come from the North-West. On the Contrary, 30 Leagues further to the North-West, on the South side of Keppel Bay, we found the Flood to come from the East, and at the Northern part of the said Bay we found it come from the Northward, but with a much Slower Motion than the Easterly Tide. Again, on the East side of the Bay of Inlets we found the flood to set strong to the Westward as far as the Op'ning of Broad sound, but on the North side of that sound the flood come with a Slow motion from the North-West; and when at Anchor before Repulse bay we found the flood to come from the northward. We need only admit the flood tide to come from the East or South-East, and then all these seeming Contradictions will be found to be conformable to reason and experience. It is well known that where there are deep Inlets, large Creeks, etc., into low lands, that it is not occasioned by fresh water Rivers; there is a very great indraught of the Flood Tide, the direction of which will be determin'd according to the position or direction of the Coast which forms the Entrance into such Inlets; and this direction the Tide must follow, let it be ever so contrary to their general Course out at Sea, and where the Tides are weak, as they are in general upon this Coast, a large Inlet will, if I may so call it, attract the Flood tide for many Leagues. Any one need only cast an Eye over the Chart to be made sencible of what I have advanced. To the Northward of Whitsundays Passage there are few or no large Inlets, and consequently the Flood sets to the Northward or North-West, according to the direction of the Coast, and Ebb the Contrary; but this is to be understood at a little distance from land, or where there is no Creeks or Inlets, for where such are, be they ever so small, they draw the flood from the Southward, Eastward, and Northward, and, as I found by experience, while we lay in Endeavour River.* (*Cook's reasoning on the course of the flood stream is quite sound.) Another thing I have observed upon the tides which ought to be remarked, which is that there is only one high Tide in 24 Hours, and that is the night Tide. On the Spring Tides the difference between the perpendicular rise of the night and day Tides is not less than 3 feet, which is a great deal where the Tides are so inconsiderable, as they are here.* (*This difference in the heights of consecutive tides is termed the diurnal inequality. It results from the tide wave being made up of a large number of undulations, some caused by the moon, some by the sun; some occurring twice a day, others only once. It occurs in all parts of the world, but is inconspicuous on the coasts of Europe. In Australia it is very marked, and occasions the night tides to be the highest at one time of the year, when the Endeavour was on the coast, and the day tides at the other. There are places on the east coast of Australia where the range of the tide is very great, but Cook did not anchor at any of them.) This inequality of the Tide I did not observe till we run ashore; perhaps it is much more so to the Northward than to the Southward. After we had got within the Reefs the second time we found the Tides more considerable than at any time before, except in the Bay of Inlets. It may be owing to the water being confin'd in Channels between the Shoals, but the flood always set to the North-West to the extremity of New Wales, from thence West and South-West into the India Seas.

Chapter 3

Kings and Priests

Egyptian Diplomatic Correspondence: Excerpts from *The Amarna Letters*

The 250 or so tablets now called The Amarna Letters *were discovered by Egyptian farmers in 1887. The tablets consist of diplomatic correspondence between the pharaohs and their representatives in Canaan, Mesopotamia, and elsewhere. Most of the tablets belong to the reigns of Amenhotep III and Akhnaten (the monotheist) between the years 1386 and 1321 BCE. Written in cuneiform, the language of diplomacy, the letters help us understand the relationships amongst the various kingdoms of the area, including Egypt, Babylon, Assyria, the Hittites, and a number of smaller vassal kingdoms.*

Source: *Pritchard, J.B. ed.,* The Ancient Near East: An Anthology of Texts and Pictures. *New Jersey: Princeton University Press, 1958.*

Focus Questions:
1. What is the relationship between local governors or rulers and the king (pharaoh)?
2. What are the relationships of local rulers with one another? How do they relate their disputes to the king?
3. How would you describe the political situation in the Levant in the fourteenth century BCE?

EA, NO. 234[1]

To the king, my lord, the Sun-god from heaven: Thus Zatatna, prince of Accho, thy servant, the servant of the king, and (5) the dirt (under) his two feet, the ground which he treads. At the two feet of the king, my lord, the Sun-god from heaven, seven times, seven times I fall, both prone and supine. (10) Let the king, my lord, hear the word of his servant! [Zir]damyashda has withdrawn from Biryawaza. [He was] with Shuta, the s[ervant] of the (15) king in the city of [...] He did not say anything to him. The army of the king, my lord, has departed. He was with it in Megiddo. (20) I said nothing to him, but he deserted to me,

---

[1] This letter comes from the time of Akh-en-Aton. Shuta (pronounce *Suta*) was an Egyptian officer, probably the great-grandfather of Ramses II; Biryawaza (whose name was formerly read erroneously *Namyawaza*) was prince of Damascus under Egyptian suzerainty. All personal names (except Shuta) are Indo-Aryan.

and now Shuta has written to me: "Give (25) Zirdamyashda to Biryawaza!" But I did not consent to give him up. Behold, Accho is (as Egyptian) as Magdal (30) in, Egypt, but the king, my lord, has not heard that [Shut]a has turned against me. Now let the king, my lord, send (35) his commissioner and fetch him.

EA, NO. 244[2]

To the king, my lord, and my Sun-god, say: Thus Biridiya, the faithful servant of the (5) king. At the two feet of the king, my lord, and my Sun-god, seven and seven times I fall. Let the king know that (10) ever since the archers returned (to Egypt ?), Lab'ayu has carried on hostilities against me, and we are not able to pluck the wool, and we are not able to go outside the gate in the presence of Lab'ayu, since he learned that thou hast not given (20) archers; and now his face is set to take Megiddo, (25) but let the king protect his city, lest Lab'ayu seize it. (30) Verily, the city is destroyed by death from pestilence and *disease*. Let the king give (35) one hundred garrison troops to guard the city lest Lab'ayu seize it. Verily, there is no other purpose in (41) Lab'ayu. He seeks to destroy Megiddo.

EA, NO. 245[3]

Further, I said to my brethren, "If the gods, of the king, our lord, grant (5) that we capture Lab'ayu, then we will bring him alive to the king, our lord"; but my mare was felled by an arrow, and I alighted (io) afterwards and rode with Yashdata, but before my arrival, they had slain him. (i5) Verily, Yashdata is thy servant, and he entered the battle with me. And verily, [...] (20) the life of the king, m[y lord] [and] [...] all in [...] of the king, [my] lord, [...], and Zurata (25) removed Lab'ayu from Megiddo, saying to me: "I will send him by ship (30) to the king," and Zurata took him and sent him home from Hannathon, for Zurata had received his ransom money (35) in his hand.

Further, what have I done to the king, my lord, that he should despise me and honor (40) my younger brothers? Zurata has sent Lab'ayu, and Zurata has sent Balu-mihir to their homes, and let the king, my lord, be informed!

RA, XIX, P. 97[4]

To the king, my lord, and my Sun-god say: Thus Biridiya, the true servant of the king. (5) At the feet of the king, my lord, and my Sun-god, seven times and seven times I fall. Let the king be informed concerning his servant and concerning his city. (10) Behold, I am working in the town of Shunama, and I bring men of the corvée, (15) but behold, the governors who are with me do not as I (do): they do not (20) work in the town of Shunama, and they do not bring men for the corvée, but I alone (25) bring men for the corvee from the town of Yapu. They come from Shu[nama], and likewise from the town of Nuribda. (30) So let the king be informed concerning his city!

---

[2] Biridiya was prince of Megiddo at the end of the reign of Amen-hotep III and the beginning of the reign of Akh-en-Aton; his name is Indo-Aryan like most other princely names of northern Palestine at that time. Lab'ayu (whose name meant approximately "lion-like" in Canaanite) was prince of Shechem in the central hill-country and was constantly raiding. The territory and caravans of his neighbors on all sides.

[3] This is the latter part (all that is preserved) of a continued letter from Biridiya of Megiddo. Zurata, whom Biridiya accuses of treachery, was prince of Acre (biblical Accho).

[4] This letter from the prince of Megiddo is very instructive because of the light it throws on forced labor for the king in the Plain of Esdraelon, several of whose towns and villages are mentioned. The word for "corvée" is the Hebrew *mas*, which is employed a little later of the tribe of Issachar in this very region.

EA, NO. 250[5]

[To] the king, my lord, say: Thus Ba'lu-UR.SAG, thy servant. At the feet of the king, my lord, seven times, seven times, I fall. Let the king, my lord, know that (5) the two sons of a rebel against the king my lord, the two sons of Lab'ayu, have determined to destroy the land of the king, my lord, after their father's death. And let the king, my lord, know that for many days the two sons of Lab'ayu have accused me (saying): "Why hast thou given the town of Giti-padalla into the hand of the king, thy lord—the city which Lab'ayu, our father, captured?" (15) So thus the two sons of Lab'ayu spoke to me: "Declare war against the people of the land of Qena, because they slew our father; and if you do not declare war, then we are hostile to you."

But I answered them: (20) "May the god of the king, my lord, preserve me from making war against the people of the land of Qena, the servants of the king, my lord!" Now may it be agreeable to the king, my lord, to send one of his officers to Biryawaza (25) and let him say to him: "Wilt thou march against the two sons of Lab'ayu, or art thou a rebel against the king?" And after him, let the king, my lord, send to me the deed (30) [of the king], thy [lord], against the two sons of Lab'ayu […] Milkilu has gone in to *them*[? …] (35) … [land of the king, my lord, with them after Milkilu and Lab'ayu died]. (40) And thus the two sons of Lab'ayu spoke: "Be hostile to the king, thy lord, like our father, when he attacked Shunama and Burquna and Harabu, and (45) destroyed them/smote them. And he took Giti-rimuni, and he betrayed the helpers of the king, thy lord."

But I answered them: "The god of the king, my lord, preserve me from making (50) war against the king, my lord. The king, my lord, I serve, and my brothers who hearken to me." But the courier of Milkilu does not move from the two sons of Lab'ayu (55) a (*single*) day. Behold, Milkilu seeks to destroy the land of the king, my lord. But there is no other intention with me—I serve the king, my lord, and the word which the king, my lord, speaks do I hear.

EA, NO. 252[6]

To the king, my lord, say: Thus Lab'ayu, thy servant. At the feet of my lord I fall. (5) As for what thou hast written, "Are the people strong who have captured the town? How can the men be arrested?" (I reply) "By fighting was the town captured, (10) in spite of the fact that I had taken an oath of conciliation and that, when I took the oath, an (Egyptian) officer took the oath with me! The city as well as my god are captured. I am slandered/blamed (15) before the king, my lord."

Further, when (even) ants are smitten, they do not accept it (passively), but they bite the hand of the man who smites them. (20) How could I hesitate this day when two of my towns are taken?

Further, even if thou shouldst say: "(25) Fall beneath them, and let them smite thee," I should still repel my foe, the men who seized the town and (30) my god, the despoilers of my father, (yea) I would repel them.

---

[5] The prince from whom this letter comes was in control of a district in the northern coastal plain of Palestine, south of Carmel. Here Lab'ayu's sons are described as continuing their father's activities. Biryawaza, whose help is wanted to subdue the recalcitrants, was prince of Damascus. Milkilu was prince of Gezer, whose territory adjoined the territory of Ba'lu-UR.SAG ("Baal is a warrior") on the south.

[6] This letter is written in almost pure Canaanite and was not understood until very recently. Lab'ayu virtuously protests that he was only repelling aggressors who had attacked his native town (not Shechem, which was his capital) in spite of a previous treaty sworn in the presence of an Egyptian official.

EA, NO. 254[7]

To the king, my lord and my Sun-god: Thus Lab'ayu, thy servant, and the dirt on which thou dost tread. At the feet of the king, my lord, (5) and my Sun-god, seven times and seven times I fall.

I have heard the words which the king wrote to me, and who am I that the king should lose his land (10) because of me? Behold, I am a faithful servant of the king, and I have not rebelled and I have not sinned, and I do not withhold my tribute, and I do not refuse (15) the requests of my commissioner. Now they wickedly slander me, but let the king, my lord, not impute rebellion to me!

Further, (20) my crime is namely that I entered Gezer and said publicly: (25) "Shall the king take my property, and not likewise the property of Milkilu?" I know the deeds which. Milkilu has done against me.

(30) Further, the king wrote concerning my son. I did not know that my son associates with the 'Apiru (36), and I have verily delivered him into the hand of Addaya.

Further, if the king should write for my wife, (40) how could I withhold her? If the king should write to me, "Plunge a bronze dagger into thy heart and (45) die!", how could I refuse to carry out the command of the king?

EA, NO. 256[8]

To Yanhamu, my lord say: Thus Mut-ba'lu, thy servant. At the two feet of my lord I fall. How is it said (5) before thee, "Mut-ba'lu has fled, Ayab has hidden himself?" How can the prince of Pella flee from the face of the commissioner (10) of the king, his lord? As the king my lord lives, as the king my lord lives, Ayab is not in Pella. Behold, he has not been (here) for two months(?). (15) Indeed, ask Ben-ilima, ask Taduwa, ask Yashuya. Again, *at the instance of* (20) the house of Shulum-Marduk, the city of Ashtartu came to (my) help, when all the cities of the land of Garu were hostile, (namely) Udumu, Aduru, (25) Araru, Meshqu, Magdalu, Eni-anabu and Zarqu, and when Hayanu and Yabilima were captured.

Further, behold—after (30) thy writing a tablet to me, I wrote to him. Before thou dost arrive with thy caravan, behold, he will have reached Pella, and he will hear (thy) words.

EA, NO. 270[9]

To the king, my lord, my pantheon, my Sun-god, say: Thus Milkilu, thy servant, (5) the dirt (under) thy feet. At the feet of the king, my lord, my pantheon, my Sun-god, seven times, seven times I fall. Let the king, my lord; know (10) the deed which Yanhamu did to me after I left the presence of the king, my lord. Now he seeks (is) two thousand (shekels) of silver from my hand, saying to me: "Give me thy wife and (20) thy children, or I will smite!" Let the king know this deed, and let my lord send to me (26) chariots, and let him take me to himself lest I perish!

---

[7] In this letter Lab'ayu protests his innocence of all charges against him and assures the king (Amen-hotep III) that he is more loyal than the neighbors who complain against him.

[8] Mut-ba'lu (literally "Man of Baal") was prince of Pella in the northern Jordan Valley, opposite Beth-Shan; Ayab (Ayyab, Hebrew Job) was prince of Ashtartu (biblical Ashtaroth) in Bashan. The land of Garu lay in southern Golan between Pella and Ashtartu. Yanhamu, to whom the letter is addressed, was a high Egyptian official of Canaanite (possibly of Hebrew) origin, who seems to have been the Egyptian governor of Palestine at the beginning of the reign of Akh-en-Aton.

[9] Milkilu (Heb. Malchiel) was prince of Gezer. For Yanhamu see the previous letter.

EA, NO. 271[10]

To the king, my lord, my pantheon, my Sun-god, say: Thus Milkilu, thy servant, (5) the dirt (under) thy feet. At the feet of the king, my lord, my pantheon, my Sun-god, seven times, seven times, I fall. Let the king know (10) that powerful is the hostility against me and against Shuwardata. Let the king, my lord, protect his land (15) from the hand of the 'Apiru. If not, (then) let the king, my lord, send chariots (20) to fetch us, lest our servants smite us.

Sumerian Law Code: *The Code of Lipit-Ishtar*

The Code of Lipit-Ishtar *is one of several extant Sumerian law codes. It predates the Code of Hammurabi, which had been considered the oldest for much of the twentieth century. The code is attributed to Lipit-Ishtar the ruler of Isin around 1900 BCE, who was powerful enough to proclaim himself king of Sumer and Akkad. Law codes such as these were often prominently displayed on large stones (stele) for all to see.*

Focus Questions:
1. Compare the prologue to the preamble of the U.S. Constitution; what are the similarities?
2. What does having a law code say about a society and its rulers?
3. What are the types of punishments given?
4. What can you discern about the status of women?

When Anu and Enlil had called Lipit-Ishtar, Lipit-Ishtar the wise shephard whose name had been pronounced by Nunamnir, to the princeship of the land in order to establish justice in the land, to banish complaints, to turn back enmity and rebellion by force of arms, and to bring well-being to the Sumerians and Akkadians, then I, Lipit-Ishtar, the humble shephard of Nippur, the stalwart farmer of Ur, who abandons not Eridu, the suitable lord of Erech, king of Isin, king of Sumer and Akkad, who am fit for the heart of Manna, established justice in Sumer and Akkad in accordance with the word of Enlil.

CODE OF LIPIT-ISHTAR: CIRCA 1868 B.C.

1. If a man entered the orchard of another man and was seized there for stealing, he shall pay ten shekels of silver.
2. If a man cut down a tree in the garden of another man, he shall pay one-half mina of silver.
3. If a man married his wife and she bore him children and those children are living, and a slave also bore children for her master but the father granted freedom to the slave and her children, the children of the slave shall not divide the estate with the children of their former master.
4. If a man's wife has not borne him children but a harlot from the public square has borne him children, he shall provide grain, oil, and clothing for that harlot. The children which the harlot has borne him shall be his heirs, and as long as his wife lives the harlot shall not live in the house with the wife. (*This is the earliest known codified provision for child support.*)

---

[10] For Milkilu see the previous letter. Shuwardata (with an Indo-Aryan name) was prince of the Hebron region in the southern hill-country, and frequently appears in association with Milkilu. The 'Apiru (formerly called Habiru) were a strong semi-nomadic people, or rather class of population in Syria and Palestine. While there is much reason to identify them with the Hebrews of the Patriarchal Age, the combination still remains uncertain and cannot be made the basis for any historical inferences.

5. If adjacent to the house of a man the bare ground of another man has been neglected and the owner of the house has said to the owner of the bare ground, "Because your ground has been neglected someone may break into my house: strengthen your house," and this agreement has been confirmed by him, the owner of the bare ground shall restore to the owner of the house any of his property that is lost.
6. If a man rented an ox and damaged its eye, he shall pay one-half its price.
7. If a man rented an ox and injured the flesh at the nose ring, he shall pay one-third of its price.
8. If a man rented an ox and broke its horn, he shall pay one-fourth its price.
9. If a man rented an ox and damaged its tail, he shall pay one-fourth its price.

The Code of Hammurabi

In order to "establish law and justice in the language of the land" and to "promote the welfare of the people," the Amorite King Hammurabi (c. 1728–1686 BCE), who had made Babylon his capital and conquered Mesopotamia, issued a comprehensive code of laws. He caused them to be inscribed on stones that were erected at crossroads and in marketplaces throughout his kingdom, so that all his subjects would understand the penalties that their actions might incur. This document survives on one of these stones, topped by an illustration showing Hammurabi receiving the order to write the laws from the sun-god Shamash. The stone was discovered by French archaeologists in 1901–1902, and it remains one of the treasures of the Louvre in Paris.

Source: *Robert Francis Harper, trans.,* The Code of Hammurabi, King of Babylon, *Chicago: University of Chicago Press, 1904.*

Focus Questions:
1. What general principles inform the laws stated here?
2. When was a financial punishment appropriate, and when a capital punishment? Is the principle applied consistently?
3. What does the document reveal about the status of women in this society?

When the lofty Anu, king of the Anunnaki, and Bel, lord of heaven and earth; he who determines the destiny of the land, committed the rule of all mankind to Marduk, the chief son of Ea; when they pronounced the lofty name of Babylon: when they made it famous among the quarters of the world and in its midst established an everlasting kingdom whose foundations were firm as heaven and earth—at that time, Ann and Bel called me, Hummurabi, the exalted prince, the worshiper of the gods, to cause justice to prevail in the land, to destroy the wicked and the evil, to prevent the strong from oppressing the weak...to enlighten the land and to further the welfare of the people. Hammurabi, the governor named by Bel, am I, who brought about plenty and abundance...

...the ancient seed of royalty, the powerful king, the Sun of Babylon, who caused light to go forth over the lands of Sumer and Akkad; the king, who caused the four quarters of the world to render obedience; the favorite of Nana, am I. When Marduk sent me to rule the people and to bring help to the country, I established law and justice in the land and promoted the welfare of the people.

1.

If a man bring an accusation against a man, and charge him with a (capital) crime, but cannot prove it, he, the accuser, shall be put to death.

2.

If a man charge a man with sorcery, and cannot prove it, he who is charged with sorcery shall go to the river, into the river he shall throw himself and if the river overcome him, his accuser shall take to himself his house (estate). If the river show that man to be innocent and he come forth unharmed, he who charged him with sorcery shall be put to death. He who threw himself into the river shall take to himself the house of his accuser.

If a man has come forward to bear witness to a felony and then has not proved the statement he has made, if that case (is) a capital one, that man shall be put to death.

If a man aid a male or female slave of the palace, or a male or female slave of a freeman to escape from the city gate, he shall be put to death.

If a man seize a male or female slave, a fugitive, in the field and bring that (slave) back to his owner, the owner of the slave shall pay him two shekels of silver.

23.

If the brigand be not captured, the man who has been robbed, shall, in the presence of god, make an itemized statement of his loss, and the city and the governor, in whose province and jurisdiction the robbery was committed, shall compensate him for whatever was lost.

24.

If it be a life (that is lost), the city and governor shall pay one mana of silver to his heirs.

26.

If either an officer or a constable, who is ordered to go on an errand of the king, do not go but hire a substitute and dispatch him in his stead, that officer or constable shall be put to death; his hired substitute shall take to himself his (the officer's) house.

53.

If a man neglect to strengthen his dyke and do not strengthen it, and a break be made in his dyke and the water carry away the farm-land, the man in whose dyke the break has been made shall restore the grain which he has damaged.

127.

If a man point the finger at a priestess or the wife of another and cannot justify it, they shall drag that man before the judges and they shall brand his forehead.

128.

If a man take a wife and do not arrange with her the (proper) contracts, that woman is not a (legal) wife.

129.

If the wife of a man be taken in lying with another man, they shall bind them and throw them into the water. If the husband of the woman would save his wife, or if the king would save his male servant (he may).

130.

If a man force the (betrothed) wife of another who has not known a male and is living in her father's house, and he lie in her bosom and they take him, that man shall be put to death and that woman shall go free.

131.

If a man accuse his wife and she has not been taken in lying with another man, she shall take an oath in the name of god and she shall return to her house.

132.

If the finger have been pointed at the wife of a man because of another man, and she have not been taken in lying with another man, for her husband's sake she shall throw herself into the river.

142.

If a woman hate her husband, and say: "Thou shalt not have me," they shall inquire into her antecedents for her defects; and if she have been a careful mistress and be without reproach and her husband have been going about and greatly belittling her, that woman has no blame. She shall receive her dowry and shall go to her father's house.

143.

If she have not been a careful mistress, have gadded about, have neglected her house and have belittled her husband, they shall throw that woman into the water.

144.

If a man take a wife and that wife give a maid servant to her husband and she bear children; if that man set his face to take a concubine, they shall not countenance him. He may not take a concubine.

145.

If a man take a wife and she do not present him with children and he set his face to take a concubine, that man may take a concubine and bring her into his house. That concubine shall not rank with his wife.

146.

If a man take a wife and she give a maid servant to her husband, and that maid servant bear children and afterwards would take rank with her mistress; because she has borne children, her mistress may not sell her for money, but she may reduce her to bondage and count her among the maid servants.

196.

If a man destroy the eye of another freeman [i.e., a man in the upper class], they shall destroy his eye.

197.

If one break a man's bone, they shall break his bone.

198.

If one destroy the eye of a villein [a dependent laborer] or break the bone of a freeman, he shall pay one mana of silver.

199.

If one destroy the eye of a man's slave or break a bone of a man's slave he shall pay one-half his price.

200.

If a man knock out a tooth of a man of his own rank, they shall knock out his tooth.

201.

If one knock out a tooth of a villein, he shall pay one-third mana of silver.

203.

If a man strike another man of his own rank, he shall pay one mana of silver.

204.

If a villein strike a villein, he shall pay ten shekels of silver.

205.

If a man's slave strike a man's son, they shall cut off his ear.

253.

If a man hire a man to oversee his farm and furnish him the seed-grain and intrust him with oxen and contract with him to cultivate the field, and that man steal either the seed or the crop and it be found in his possession, they shall cut off his fingers.

254.

If he take the seed-grain and overwork the oxen, he shall restore the quantity of grain which he has hoed.

257.

If a man hire a field-laborer, he shall pay him 8 GUR of grain per year.

258.

If a man hire a herdsman, he shall pay him 6 GUR of grain per year.

The righteous laws, which Hammurabi, the wise king, established and (by which) he gave the land stable support and pure government. Hammurabi, the *perfect king, am I...*

The great gods proclaimed me and I am the guardian governor, whose scepter is righteous and whose beneficent protection is spread over my city...

The king, who is pre-eminent among city kings, am I. My words are precious, my wisdom is unrivaled. By the command of Shamash, the great judge of heaven and earth, may I make righteousness to shine forth on the land. By the order of [the god] Marduk, my lord, may no one efface my statues...

...Let any oppressed man, who has a cause, come before my image as king of righteousness!...

...Let him read the code and pray with a full heart before Marduk, my lord, and Zarpanit, my lady, and may the protecting deities...look with favor on his wishes (plans) in the presence of Marduk, my lord, and Zarpanit, my lady!...

If that man pay attention to my words which I have written upon my monument, do not efface my judgments, do not overrule my words, and do not alter my statues, then will Shamash prolong that man's reign, as he has mine, who am king of righteousness, that he may rule his people in righteousness.

If that man do not pay attention to my words which I have written upon my monument: if he forget my curse and do not fear the curse of god: if he abolish the judgments which I have formulated, overrule my words, alter my statues, efface my name written thereon and write his own name: on account of these curses, commission another to do so—as for that man, be he king or lord, or priest-king or commoner, whoever he may be, may the great god, the father of the gods, who has ordained my reign, take from him the glory of his sovereignty, may be break his scepter, and curse his fate!

May Ea, the great prince, whose decrees take precedence, the leader of the gods, who knows everything, who prolongs the days of my life, deprive him of knowledge and wisdom! May he bring him to oblivion, and dam up his rivers at their sources! May he not permit corn, which *is* the life of the people, to grow in his land!

Excerpts from *The Epic of Gilgamesh*

First written down around 2000 BCE, the story of Gilgamesh is one of the oldest surviving works of world literature. Based on an actual historical figure, King Gilgamesh of Uruk (reigned c. 2700 BCE), it recounts Gilgamesh's travels, adventures, and his search for immortality. In the process, it provides evidence of ancient Mesopotamian ideas about death, the place of humanity in the universe, and societal organization. The work survives in multiple copies, and it seems to have been a compilation of several hero narratives associated with Gilgamesh, his rival-turned-friend Enkidu, and the gods and men they encountered throughout their travels. This selection draws on multiple sections of the "Epic," and it gives a flavor of the whole.

Source: N.K. Sandars., trans. The Epic of Gilgamesh. *(London: Penguin Books Ltd., 1978), pp. 61, 62–3, 69, 87–8, 102, 116–7, 118.*

Focus Questions:
1. What does the document suggest about ancient Mesopotamian beliefs about the gods and their effects on men?
2. What is the reaction of Gilgamesh to death, and how does this motivate his behavior?
3. Is any of this document familiar to you from other sources?

I will proclaim to the world the deeds of Gilgamesh. This was the man to whom all things were known; this was the king who knew the countries of the world. He was wise, he saw mysteries and knew secret things, he brought us a tale of the days before the flood. He went on a long journey, was weary, worn-out with labour, returning he rested, he engraved on a stone the whole story.

When the gods created Gilgamesh they gave him a perfect body. Shamash the glorious sun endowed him with beauty, Adad the god of the storm endowed him with courage, the great gods made his beauty perfect, surpassing all others, terrifying like a great wild bull. Two thirds they made him god and one third man.

Gilgamesh went abroad in the world, but he met with none who could withstand his arms till he came to Uruk. But the men of Uruk muttered in their houses, 'Gilgamesh sounds the tocsin for his amusement, his arrogance has no bounds by day or night. No son is left with his father, for Gilgamesh takes them all, even the children; yet the king would be a shepherd to his people. His lust leaves no virgin to her lover, neither the warrior's daughter nor the wife of the noble; yet this is the shepherd of the city, wise, comely, and resolute.'

The gods heard their lament, the gods in heaven cried to the Lord of Uruk, to Anu the god of Uruk: 'A goddess made him, strong as a savage bull, none can withstand his arms. No son is left with his father, for Gilgamesh takes them all; and is this the king, the shepherd of his people? His lust leaves no virgin to her lover, neither the warrior's daughter nor the wife of the noble.' When Anu had heard their lamentation the gods cried to Aruru, the goddess of creation, 'You made him, O Aruru, now create his equal; let it be as like him as his own reflection, his second self, stormy heart for stormy heart. Let them contend together and leave Uruk in quiet.'

So the goddess conceived an image in her mind, and it was of the stuff of Anu of the firmament. She dipped her hands in water and pinched off clay, she let it fall in the wilderness, and noble Enkidu was created. There was virtue in him of the god of war, of Ninurta himself. His body was rough, he had long hair like a woman's; it waved like the hair of Nisaba, the goddess of the corn. His body was covered with matted hair like Samuquan's, the god of cattle.

In Uruk the bridal bed was made, fit for the goddess of love. The bride waited for the bridegroom, but in the night Gilgamesh got up and came to the house. Then Enkidu stepped out, he stood in the street and blocked the way. Mighty Gilgamesh came on and Enkidu met him at the gate. He put out his foot and prevented Gilgamesh from entering the house, so they grappled, holding each other like bulls. They broke the doorposts and the walls shook, they snorted like bulls locked together. They shattered the doorposts and the walls shook. Gilgamesh bent his knee with his foot planted on the ground and with a turn Enkidu was thrown. Then immediately his fury died. When Enkidu was thrown he said to Gilgamesh, 'There is not another like you in the world. Ninsun, who is as strong as a wild ox in the byre, she was the mother who bore you, and now you are raised above all men, and Enlil has given you the kingship, for your strength surpasses the strength of men.' So Enkidu and Gilgamesh embraced and their friendship was sealed.

[Gilgamesh and Enkidu become great friends. Together they set out on a long journey to the Cedar Forest in the North. They slay a fire-breathing monster called Humbaba who is the guardian of the forest. After their return, Ishtar, the goddess of love, becomes infatuated with Gilgamesh and offers to marry him. Gilgamesh, citing Ishtar's fickle nature in matters of love, refuses. Ishtar becomes incensed.]

Ishtar opened her mouth and said again, 'My father, give me the Bull of Heaven to destroy Gilgamesh. Fill Gilgamesh, I say, with arrogance to his destruction; but if you refuse to give me the Bull of Heaven I will break in the doors of hell and smash the bolts; there will be confusion of people, those above with those from the lower depths. I shall bring up the dead to eat food like the living; and the hosts of dead will outnumber the living'....

When Anu heard what Ishtar had said he gave her the Bull of Heaven to lead by the halter down to Uruk. When they reached the gates of Uruk the Bull went to the river; with his first snort cracks opened in the earth and a hundred young men fell down to death. With his second snort cracks opened and two hundred fell down to death.

With his third snort cracks opened, Enkidu doubled over but instantly recovered, he dodged aside and leapt on the Bull and seized it by the horns. The Bull of Heaven foamed in his face, it brushed him with the thick of its tail. Enkidu cried to Gilgamesh, 'My friend, we boasted that we would leave enduring names behind us. Now thrust the sword between the nape and the horns.' So Gilgamesh followed the Bull, he seized the thick of its tail, he thrust the sword between the nape and the horns and slew the Bull. When they had killed the Bull of Heaven they cut out its heart and gave it to Shamash, and the brothers rested.

[The death of the Bull of Heaven offends the gods. As compensation, they decree that one of the two heroes must die. After an ominous dream, Enkidu passes away. Gilgamesh greatly mourns for his friend and for the fate of all mortal men. He decides to seek the secret of immortality from Utnapishtim, the Mesopotamian Noah to whom the gods granted everlasting life.]

Bitterly Gilgamesh wept for his friend Enkidu; he wandered over the wilderness as a hunter, he roamed over the plains; in his bitterness he cried, 'How can I rest, how can I be at peace? Despair is in my heart. What my brother is now, that shall I be when I am dead. Because I am afraid of death I will go as best I can to find Utnapishtim whom they call the Faraway, for he has entered the assembly of the gods.' So Gilgamesh traveled over the wilderness, he wandered over the grasslands, a long journey, in search of Utnapishtim, whom the gods took after the deluge; and they set him to live in the land of Dilmun, in the garden of the sun; and to him alone of men they gave everlasting life.

[Gilgamesh then encounters Siduri, "the woman of the vine, the maker of wine." She offers him sage advice concerning his quest.]

She answered, 'Gilgamesh, where are you hurrying to? You will never find that life for which you are looking. When the gods created man they allotted to him death, but life they retained in their own keeping. As for you, Gilgamesh, fill your belly with good things; day and night, night and day, dance and be merry, feast and rejoice. Let your clothes be fresh, bathe yourself in water, cherish the little child that holds your hand, and make your wife happy in your embrace; for this too is the lot of man.'

[After an arduous journey, Gilgamesh finds Utnapishtim. Utnapishtim tells the hero the story of the flood: mankind's incessant activity had disturbed the rest of the gods, who thus decided to destroy the humans by flooding the earth. Ea, the god of the waters, warned Utnapishtim of the coming deluge. By building a strong ship, Utnapishtim and his family survive. The gods then repented of their action and granted immortality to the survivor. Utnapishtim also reveals another important secret to Gilgamesh.]

'Gilgamesh, I shall reveal a secret thing, it is a mystery of the gods that I am telling you. There is a plant that grows under the water, it has a prickle like a thorn, like a rose; it will wound your hands, but if you succeed in taking it, then your hands will hold that which restores his lost youth to a man.'

When Gilgamesh heard this he opened the sluices so that a sweet-water current might carry him out to the deepest channel; he tied heavy stones to his feet and they dragged him down to the water-bed. There he saw the plant growing; although it pricked him he took it in his hands; then he cut the heavy stones from his feet, and the sea carried him and threw him on to the shore. Gilgamesh said to Urshanabi the ferryman, 'Come here, and see the marvelous plant. By its virtue a man may win back all his former strength. I will take it to Uruk of the strong walls; there I will give it to the old men to eat. Its name shall be "The Old Men Are Young Again"; and at last I shall eat it myself and have back all my lost youth.'

So Gilgamesh returned by the gate through which he had come, Gilgamesh and Urshanabi went together. They traveled their twenty leagues and then they broke their fast; after thirty leagues they stopped for the night.

Gilgamesh saw a well of cool water and he went down and bathed; but deep in the pool there was lying a serpent, and the serpent sensed the sweetness of the flower. It rose out of the water and snatched it away, and immediately it sloughed its skin and returned to the well. Then Gilgamesh sat down and wept, the tears ran down his face, and he took the hand of Urshanabi; 'O Urshanabi, was it for this that I toiled with my hands, is it for this I have wrung out my heart's blood? For myself I have gained nothing; not I, but the beast of the earth has joy of it now. Already the stream has carried it twenty leagues back to the channels where I found it. I found a sign and now I have lost it. Let us leave the boat on the bank and go.'

The destiny was fulfilled which the father of the gods, Enlil of the mountain, had decreed for Gilgamesh: 'In nether-earth the darkness will show him a light: of mankind, all that are known, none will leave a monument for generations to come to compare with his. The heroes, the wise men, like the new moon have their waxing and waning. Men will say, "Who has ever ruled with might and with power like him?" As in the dark month, the month of shadows, so without him there is no light. O Gilgamesh, this was the meaning of your dream. You were given the kingship, such was your destiny, everlasting life was not your destiny. Because of this do not be sad at heart, do not be grieved or oppressed; he has given you power to bid and to loose, to be the darkness and the light of mankind. He has given unexampled supremacy over the people, victory in battle from which no fugitive returns, in forays and assaults from which there is no going back. But do not abuse this power, deal justly with your servants in the palace, deal justly before the face of the Sun.'

Hou-Shih, from *The Shih-Ching*

The Book of Songs, or Shih-Ching, *consists of the earliest collection of Chinese poems. The 305 songs and poems contain a mix of folk, courtly, and religious elements. The reading consists of a poem about the birth of Hou-Shih, who was a deity also called the "Lord of Millet Grains." His birth fits the frequently used barren or virgin mother story, and the attempt to kill the baby is also a feature common with hero myths. Hou-Shih was acknowledged to produce plentiful harvests and his agricultural bounty provides part of the foundation myth for settled Chinese civilization.*

Source: *Arthur Waley.* The Book of Songs *(London: Allen & Unwin, 1937), pp. 239–243.*

Focus Questions:
1. What other myths or folk tales contain similar stories of barren birth, child abandonment, and survival?
2. Comparing Hou-Shih to Gilgamesh, consider what is a hero.
3. What does the story tell us about natural resources and agriculture of the time?

She who in the beginning gave birth to the people,
This was Chiang Yüan.
How did she give birth to the people?
Well she sacrificed and prayed
That she might no longer be childless.
She trod on the big toe of God's footprint,
Was accepted and got what she desired.
Then in reverence, then in awe

She gave birth, she nurtured;
And this was Hou Chi[1]

Indeed, she had fulfilled her months,
And her first-born came like a lamb
With no bursting or rending,
With no hurt or harm.
To make manifest His magic power
God on high gave her ease.
So blessed were her sacrifice and prayer
That easily she bore her child.

Indeed, they put it in a narrow lane;
But oxen and sheep tenderly cherished it.
Indeed, they[2] put it in a far-off wood;
But it chanced that woodcutters came to
this wood.
Indeed, they put it on the cold ice;
But the birds covered it with their wings.
The birds at last went away,
And Hou Chi began to wail.

Truly far and wide
His voice was very loud.
Then sure enough he began to crawl;
Well he straddled, well he reared,
To reach food for his mouth.
He planted large beans;
His beans grew fat and tall.
His paddy-lines were dose set,
His hemp and wheat grew thick,
His young gourds teemed.

Truly Hou Chi's husbandry
Followed the way that had been shown.[3]
He cleared away the thick grass,
He planted the yellow crop.
It failed nowhere, it grew thick,
It was heavy, it was tall,
It sprouted, it eared,
It was firm and good,
It nodded, it hung—
He made house and home in T'ai.[4]

Indeed, the lucky grains were sent down to us,
The black millet, the double-kernelled;
Millet pink-sprouted and white.
Far and wide the black and the double-kernelled

---

[1]'Lord Millet.'
[2]The ballad does not tell us who exposed the child. According to one version it was the mother herself; according to another, her husband.
[3] By God. Compare No. 153, line 6.
[4] South-west of Wu-kung Hsien, west of Sianfu. Said to where his mother came from.

He reaped and acted;[5]
Far and wide the millet pink and white
He carried in his arms, he bore on his back,
Brought them home, and created the sacrifice.
Indeed, what are they, our sacrifices?
We pound the grain, we bale it out,
We sift, we tread,
We wash it—soak, soak;

We boil it all steamy.
Then with due care, due thought
We gather southernwood, make offering of fat,
Take lambs for the rite of expiation,
We roast, we broil,
To give a start to the corning year.

High we load the stands,
The stands of wood and of earthenware.
As soon as the smell rises
God on high is very pleased:
'What smell is this, so strong and good?'
Hou-chi founded the sacrifices,
And without blemish or flaw
They have gone on till now.

Hittite Law Code: Excerpts from *The Code of the Nesilim*

The Hittites emerged as a major power in the Near East around 1520 BCE, when King Telipinus seized the throne and unified his people. In time, Hittite power grew to rival that of Egypt, and their wars and treaties have been preserved in a remarkable series of documents. Like most ancient peoples, the Hittites also enshrined their beliefs in law codes, expressing their society's values, structure, and priorities. This document is translated from two surviving tablets of a series called "If anyone." Notice the tone of the text, and the sliding scales of punishment.

Source: Ancient History Sourcebook: The Code of the Nesilim, *c. 1650–1500 BCE*

Focus Questions:
1. What general principles inform the laws stated here?
2. When was a financial punishment appropriate and when a capital punishment?
3. Is the principle applied consistently?

1. If anyone slay a man or woman in a quarrel, he shall bring this one. He shall also give four persons, either men or women, he shall let them go to his home.
2. If anyone slay a male or female slave in a quarrel, he shall bring this one and give two persons, either men or women, he shall let them go to his home.
3. If anyone smite a free man or woman and this one die, he shall bring this one and give two persons, he shall let them go to his home.

---

[5] The yield was reckoned per acre (100 ft. square).

4. If anyone smite a male or female slave, he shall bring this one also and give one person, he shall let him or her go to his home.

5. If anyone slay a merchant of Hatti, he shall give one and a half pounds of silver, he shall let it go to his home.

6. If anyone blind a free man or knock out his teeth, formerly they would give one pound of silver, now he shall give twenty half-shekels of silver.

8. If anyone blind a male or female slave or knock out their teeth, he shall give ten half-shekels of silver, he shall let it go to his home.

10. If anyone injure a man so that he cause him suffering, he shall take care of him. Yet he shall give him a man in his place, who shall work for him in his house until he recovers. But if he recover, he shall give him six half-shekels of silver. And to the physician this one shall also give the fee.

17. If anyone cause a free woman to miscarry, if it be the tenth month, he shall give ten half-shekels of silver, if it be the fifth month, he shall give five half-shekels of silver.

18. If anyone cause a female slave to miscarry, if it be the tenth month, he shall give five half-shekels of silver.

20. If any man of Hatti steal a Nesian slave and lead him here to the land of Hatti, and his master discover him, he shall give him twelve half-shekels of silver, he shall let it go to his home.

21. If anyone steal a slave of a Luwian from the land of Luwia, and lead him here to the land of Hatti, and his master discover him, he shall take his slave only.

24. If a male or female slave run away, he at whose hearth his master finds him or her, shall give fifty half-shekels of silver a year.

31. If a free man and a female slave be fond of each other and come together and he take her for his wife and they set up house and get children, and afterward they either become hostile or come to close quarters, and they divide the house between them, the man shall take the children, only one child shall the woman take.

32. If a slave take a woman as his wife, their case is the same. The majority of the children to the wife and one child to the slave.

33. If a slave take a female slave their case is the same. The majority of children to the female slave and one child to the slave.

34. If a slave convey the bride price to a free son and take him as husband for his daughter, nobody dare surrender him to slavery.

36. If a slave convey the bride price to a free son and take him as husband for his daughter, nobody dare surrender him to slavery.

40. If a soldier disappear, and a vassal arise and the vassal say, "This is my military holding, but this other one is my tenancy," and lay hands upon the fields of the soldier, he may both hold the military holding and perform the tenancy duties. If he refuse the military service, then he forfeits the vacant fields of the soldier. The men of the village shall cultivate them. If the king give a captive, they shall give the fields to him, and he becomes a soldier.

98. If a free man set a house ablaze, he shall build the house, again. And whatever is inside the house, be it a man, an ox, or a sheep that perishes, nothing of these he need compensate.

99. If a slave set a house ablaze, his master shall compensate for him. The nose of the slave and his ears they shall cut off, and give him back to his master. But if he do not compensate, then he shall give up this one.

158. If a man go for wages, bind sheaves, load it into carts, spread it on the straw barn and so forth "till they clear the threshing floor, for three months his wages are thirty pecks of barley. If a woman go for wages in the harvest, for two months he shall give twelve pecks of barley.

159. If anyone harness a yoke of oxen, his wages are one-half peck of barley.

160. If a smith make a copper box, his wages are one hundred pecks of barley. He who makes a copper dish of two-pound weight, his wages are one peck of emmer.

164. If anyone come for borrowing, then make a quarrel and throw down either bread or wine jug, then he shall give one sheep, ten loaves, and one jug of beer. Then he cleanses his house by the offering. Not until the year has elapsed may he salute again the other's house.

170. If a free man kill a serpent and speak the name of another, he shall give one pound of silver; if a slave, this one shall die.

173. If anyone oppose the judgment of the king, his house shall become a ruin. If anyone oppose the judgment of a lord, his head shall be cut off. If a slave rise against his master, he shall go into the pit.

176. If anyone buy an artisan's apprentice, buy either a potter, a smith, a carpenter, a leatherworker, a tailor, a weaver, or a lace-maker, he shall give ten half-shekels.

178. A plow-ox costs fifteen half-shekels of silver, a bull costs ten half-shekels of silver, a great cow costs seven half-shekels of silver, a sheep one half-shekel of silver, a draft horse twenty half-shekels of silver, a mule one pound of silver, a horse fourteen half-shekels of silver.

181-182. Four pounds of copper cost one half-shekel of silver; one tub of lard, one half-shekel of silver; two cheese one half-shekel of silver; a gown twelve half-shekels of silver; one blue woolen garment costs twenty half-shekels of silver; breeches cost ten half-shekels of silver...

187. If a man have intercourse with a cow, it is a capital crime, he shall die. They shall lead him to the king's hall. But the king may kill him, the king may grant him his life. But he shall not approach the king.

188. If a man have intercourse with his own mother, it is a capital crime, he shall die. If a man have intercourse with a daughter, it is a capital crime, he shall die. If a man have intercourse with a son, it is a capital crime, he shall die.

190. If a man and a woman come willingly, as men and women, and have intercourse, there shall be no punishment. And if a man have intercourse with his stepmother, there shall be no punishment; except if his father is living, it is a capital crime, the son shall die.

191. If a free man picks up now this woman, now that one, now in this country, then in that country, there shall be no punishment if they came together sexually willingly.

192. If the husband of a woman die, his wife may take her husband's patrimony.

194. If a free man pick up female slaves, now one, now another, there is no punishment for intercourse. If brothers sleep with a free woman, together, or one after the other, there is no punishment. If father and son sleep with a female slave or harlot, together, or one after the other, there is no punishment.

195. If a man sleep with the wife of his brother, while his brother is living, it is a capital crime, he shall die. If a man have taken a free woman, then have intercourse also with her daughter, it is a capital crime, he shall die. If he have taken her daughter, then have intercourse with her mother or her sister, it is a capital crime, he shall die.

197. If a man rape a woman in the mountain, it is the man's wrong, he shall die. But if he rape her in the house, it is the woman's fault, the woman shall die. If the husband find them and then kill them, there is no punishing the husband.

199. If anyone have intercourse with a pig or a dog, he shall die. If a man have intercourse with a horse or a mule, there is no punishment. But he shall not approach the king, and shall not become a priest. If an ox spring upon a man for intercourse, the ox shall die but the man shall not die. One sheep shall be fetched as a substitute for the man, and they shall kill it. If a pig spring upon a man for intercourse, there is no punishment. If any man have intercourse with a foreign woman and pick up this one, now that one, there is no punishment.

200. If anyone give a son for instruction, be it a carpenter, or a potter, or a weaver, or a tailor, or a smith, he shall give six half-shekels of silver for the instruction.

Ancient Egyptian and Hittite Voices: (a) Letter from the Pharoah to Harkhuf the Explorer; (b) Ramses III, "The War Against the Sea Peoples;" (c) Hittite Soldiers' Oath

These Egyptian and Hittite sources all reflect on aspects of power in the ancient world. Around 2200 BCE Harkhuf was sent by the Pharaoh on several diplomatic trips to Nubia, Egypt's powerful southern neighbor. Centuries later, Ramses III (1187-1156 BCE) claimed a great victory over the invading tribes who would however soon overrun Egypt and Mesopotamia. Finally, The Hittite soldiers' oath from about 1400 BCE describes the ritual and oaths sworn by the king's army before battle.

Focus Questions:
1. In what terms are rulers portrayed? How about their followers?
2. In what manner are rewards and punishment described?
3. How would you describe the morale and quality of Hittite and Egyptian soldiers?

LETTER FROM THE PHAROAH TO HARKHUF THE EXPLORER

Harkhuf the explorer reads a letter from the king Old Kingdom (c. 2575–2150 BC).

King's personal seal, year 2, third month of inundation, day 15. Royal decree to the Sole Companion, lector-priest and chief of desert rangers, Harkhuf.

The matter of your letter has been noted, which you sent to the king at the Palace, to the effect that you have returned safely from Iyam together with the army that was with you.

You said in this letter of yours that you have brought all sorts of great and beautiful gifts, which Hathor, the mistress of Nubia, has granted to the spirit of my throne name, who lives for ever.

You said in this letter of yours that you have brought a pygmy, of divine dances, from the land of the horizon-dwellers, like the one that the seal-bearer Bawerdjed brought from Punt in the time of king Isesi, and you said the like of him has never been brought back by any one who did Iyam in the past.

It is true that you know how to do what your lord loves and praises, and it is true that you spend day and night planning to do what your lord loves and praises and commands. His Majesty will provide many splendid rewards, so as to benefit your son's sons for all time, so that people will say when they hear what my Majesty has done for you, "Can anything equal what was done for Harkhuf when he returned from Iyam?"

Come north to the Palace at once! Drop everything—hurry and bring that pygmy you have brought, alive, happy and well, for the divine dances, to gladden the heart, to delight the heart of the king who lives for ever! When he goes down with you the boat, get trusty men to stand around him on the gangplank—don't let him fall in the water! When he goes to bed at night, get trusty men to lie all round him in his hammock. Inspect ten times a night! My Majesty longs to see this pygmy more than all the treasures of Sinai and Punt! If you arrive at the Palace and that pygmy is with you, alive, happy and well, my Majesty will do greater things for you than was done for the seal-bearer Bawerdjed in the time of Isesi, because my Majesty so wishes to see that pygmy. Orders have been given to the chiefs of the New Towns and the overseer of priests to furnish supplies from every depot and every temple under their charge. No exception has been made for this.

"The War Against the Peoples of the Sea"

Source: *Pritchard, J.B., ed. The Ancient Near East: An Anthology of Texts and Pictures (Oxford: Oxford University Press, 1958), pp. 185–187.*

In the latter half of the second millennium B.C. there were extensive movements in the eastern Mediterranean area. Masses of homeless peoples moved, slowly across the sea and its coast-lands, displacing or merging with the older populations. These migrations ended the Minoan civilization in Crete, contributed to the historical populations of Greece and Italy, wiped out the Hittite Empire, thrust the Philistines into Canaan, and washed up on the shores of Egypt. In Ramses III's eighth year (about 1188 B.C.) the pharaoh met and checked their attempt to push into the rich lands of the Nile. The victory was only a check, because the Egyptian Empire in Asia ended shortly after. The following accounts of this war come from Ramses III's temple of Medinet Habu at Thebes.

(1) Year 8 under the majesty of (Ramses III)...

(16)...The foreign countries made a *conspiracy* in their islands. All at once the lands were removed and scattered in the fray. No land could stand before their arms, from Hatti, Kode, Carchemish, Arzawa, and Alashiya on,[1] being cut off *at* [*one time*]. A camp [was set up] in one place in Amor.[2] They desolated its people, and its land was like that which has never come into being. They were coming forward toward Egypt, while the flame was prepared before them. Their confederation was the Philistines, Tjeker, Shekelesh, Denye(n), and Weshesh[3] lands united. They laid their hands upon the lands as far as the circuit of the earth, their hearts confident and trusting: "Our plans will succeed!"

Now the heart of this god, the Lord of the Gods, was prepared and ready to ensnare them like birds... I organized my frontier in Djahi,[4] prepared before them:—princes, commanders of garrisons, (20) and *maryanu*. I have the river-mouths[5] prepared like a strong wall, with warships, galleys and coasters, *(fully) equipped*, for they were manned completely from bow to stern with valiant warriors carrying their weapons. The troops consisted of every picked man of Egypt. They were like lions roaring upon the mountain tops. The chariotry consisted of runners, of *picked men*, of every good and capable chariot-warrior. The horses were quivering in every part of their bodies, prepared to crush the foreign countries under their hoofs. I was the valiant Montu,[6] standing fast at their head, so that they might gaze upon the capturing of my hands...

Those who reached my frontier, their seed is not, their heart and their soul are finished forever and ever. Those who came forward together on the sea, the full flame was in front of them at the river-mouths, while a stockade of lances surrounded them on the shore.[7] They were dragged in, enclosed, and prostrated on the beach, killed, and made into heaps from tail to head. Their ships and their goods were as if fallen into the water.

---

[1] Hatti was the Hittite Empire, Kode the coast of Cilicia and noithern Syria, Carchemish the city on the Euphrates, Arzawa somewhere in or near Cilicia, and Alashiya probably Cypius.

[2] Perhaps in the north Syrian plain or in Code-Syria.

[3] Except for the Philistines (Peleset), these names are rendered close to the Egyptian writings. For the Tjeker, cf. the Wen-Amon story. The Shekelesh might be the Siculi, the Denyen (cuneifoim Danuna) might be the Danaoi. The Weshesh cannot easily be related to any later people.

[4] The Phoenician coast, running down into Palestine. From what little we know of Ramses III, his defensive frontier was not north of Palestine. It is possible that the land battle against the Peoples of the Sea was in Asia, whereas the sea battle was on the coast of Egypt.

[5] Normally used for the mouths of the branches of the Nile in the Delta. Hence probably the line of defense in Egypt. Just possibly, the word might have been extended to harborages on the Asiatic coast.

[6] The god of war.

[7] One body had to be met on land (in Djahi?), whereas another body had to be met on sea (in the Delta?). The scenes show the boats of the Peoples of the Sea and also a movement by land in oxcarts, with women, children, and goods.

I have made the lands turn back from (even) mentioning Egypt; for when they pronounce my name in their land, then (25) they are burned up. Since I sat upon the throne of Har-akhti and the Great-of-Magic[8] was fixed upon my head like Re, I have not let foreign countries behold the frontier of Egypt, to boast thereof to the Nine Bows[9] I have taken away their land, their frontiers being added to mine. Their princes and their tribes people are mine with praise, for I am on the ways of the plans of the All-Lord, my august, divine father, the Lord of the Gods.

Hittites Soldiers' Oath

Source: *Pritchard, J.B., ed.* Ancient Near Eastern Texts Relating to the Old Testament *(Oxford: Oxford University Press, 1950): 353–354.*

Text: KBo, *vi, 34 and its duplicate* KUB, *vii, 59. Literature: J. Friedrich, ZA, NF 1 (1924), 161–192, reprinted with additions in the same author's* Hethitische Studien *(1924). Excerpts are also found in Zimmern's contribution to Lehmann-Haas,* Textbuch zur Religionsgeschichte, *2nd ed. (1922), 335 f. and in J. Friedrich,* Aus dem hethitischen Schrifttum, 2 (AO, xxv/2 [1925]), 16 ff. The tablet in question is marked as the second of a series entitled "When they lead the troops to the (ceremony of taking the) oath." At the beginning about 17 lines are missing.*

[He[1] …]s and says: "[Just as this…cou]ld [see] and was able to find [(its) food], and (as) they have now blinded it at the place of the oath,—(15) whoever breaks these oaths, betrays the king of the Hatti land, and turns his eyes in hostile fashion upon the Hatti land, let these oaths seize him! Let them blind this man's army (20) and make it deaf! Let them not see each other, let them not hear each other! Let them make a cruel fate their lot! Below let them paralyze their feet, and above let them bind their hands! (25) Just as the gods of the oath bound the hands and feet of the army of the Arzawa country[2] and made them unable to move, even so let them bind that man's army and make them unable to move!"

He places yeast in their hands, they *squeeze it* (30) and he says: "Is not this that you have here yeast? Just as they take this little piece of yeast, mix it (into the dough) in the kneading bowl and let the bowl stand for a day (so that) it can ferment—whoever breaks these oaths, (35) shows disrespect to the king of the Hatti land, and turns his eyes in hostile fashion upon the Hatti land, let these oaths seize him! Let him be ridden with disease! Make a cruel fate their lot!" The men (40) declare: "So be it!"

Then he places wax and mutton fat in their hands. He throws them *on a pan* and says: "Just as this wax melts, and just as the mutton fat dissolves,—(45) whoever breaks these oaths, (ii) [shows disrespect to the king] of the Hatti [land], let [him] melt lik[e wax], let him dissolve like[mutton fat] !" [The me]n declare: "So be it!"

(5) He places sinews (and) salt in their hands. He throws them on a pan and speaks as follows: "Just as these sinews split into fragments on the hearth, and just as the salt (10) is scattered on the hearth—whoever breaks these oaths, shows disrespect to the king of the Hatti land, and turns his eyes in hostile fashion upon the Hatti land, let these oaths seize him! (15) Let him split into fragments like the sinews, let him be scattered like the salt! Just as salt has no seed, even so let that man's name, seed, house, cattle (and) sheep perish!"

---

[8] The uraeus-serpent, symbol of kingship.
[9] Traditional enemies of Egypt.
[1] The officiating priest.
[2] The most important group of countries in the southern part of Anatolia bordering on the Mediterranean Sea.

He places malt (and) malt loaf in their hands, (20) they *crush* them and he speaks as follows: "Just as they grind this malt loaf between mill stones, mix it with water, bake it and break it up—whoever breaks these oaths and does evil to the king (and) the queen, (25) the princes (and) to the Hatti land, let these oaths seize him! Let them grind their bones in the same way! Let him *soak* in the same way! Let him be broken up in the same way! Let a cruel fate be his lot!" The men declare: "So be it!"

"Just as this malt no (longer) has the power of growth, (as) one cannot take it to a field and use it as seed, (as) one cannot use it as bread or store it in the storehouse—whoever (35) breaks these oaths and does evil to the king (and) the queen and the princes, even so let the gods of the oath also destroy that man's future! Let not his wife bear sons and daughters! Let his land (and) his fields have no crop, (40) and his pastures no grass! Let not his cattle (and) sheep bear calves (and) lambs!"

They bring the garments of a woman, a distaff and a mirror, they break an arrow and you speak as follows: "Is not this that you see here (45) garments of a woman? We have them here for (the ceremony of taking) the oath. Whoever breaks these oaths and does evil to the king (and) the queen (and) the princes, let these oaths change him from a man into a woman! Let them change his troops into women, (50) let them dress them in the fashion of women and cover their heads with a length of cloth! Let them break the bows, arrows (and) clubs in their hands and (iii) [let them put] in their hands distaff and mirror!"

They parade in front of them a [blind woman] and a deaf man and you speak] as follows: "See! here is a blind woman (5) and a deaf man. Whoever does evil to the king (and) the queen, let the oaths seize him! Let them make him blind! Let them [ma]ke him [deaf]! Let them [blind] him like a blind man! Let them [deafen] him like a deaf man! Let them [annihilate him], the man (himself) (10) together with his wife, [his children] (and) his kin!"

He places an *old* stone image [of a man] in their hands and speaks as follows: "Did not this man whom you see here take the oath? (15) [At some other time] he was sworn in before the gods and then broke his oath. The oaths seized him and his inner parts are sagging out in front, he has to hold his entrails in his hands. Whoever (20) breaks these oaths, let these oaths seize him! Let his inner parts sag out in front! Let "Ishara sons"[3] [live] in his inner parts and eat him up!"

He presents to them [a…]. Before their eyes (25) he [throws] it on the ground; they trample it under foot and he speaks as follows: "Whoever breaks these oaths, even so let the Hatti people come and trample that man's town under foot! Let them make it bare of people!"

(30) They light [a *fire*]brand and trample it under foot so that it scatters here and there and he says: "Just as this one flies apart—whoever breaks these oaths, even so let this man's house be robbed of men, (35) cattle (and) sheep!"

You will place before them an oven. Also a plow, a cart (and) a chariot you will place before the congregation. These things they break and he speaks as follows: "Whoever breaks these oaths, let the Storm-god break his plow! Just as grass does not come rout of] the oven, let not spelt (and) barley (45) [come out] of his field, let *sahlu*[4] come forth!"

(iv) He pours water on the fire (5) and speaks to them as follows: "Just as this burning fire is snuffed out—whoever breaks these oaths, even so let these oaths seize him! Let this man's vitality, vigor (10) and future happiness be snuffed out together with (that of) his wife and his children! Let the oaths put an evil curse upon him! Let no offspring thrive in his corral, his fold (15) (and) his barnyard! From his field let grass not come forth, not even from (one) furrow!"

---

[3] Apparently some kind of worms.
[4] A weed commonly found on ruins.

Liu and Tan-Fu the Duke, from *The Shih-Ching*

Liu and Tan-Fu the Duke were considered foundational figures for the Zhou dynasty. The Zhou dynastic poems highlight the tradition of providing godly ancestors and great heroes as ancestors to show the might and legitimacy of the present dynasty. Liu is credited with settling the people of Zhou into Pin, while Tan-Fu later led the people into migration farther west to escape barbarian attacks.

Source: *Arthur Waley.* The Book of Songs *(London: Allen & Unwin, 1937), pp. 244–251.*

Focus Questions:
1. What are deemed the essentials of good rulership in these poems?
2. What is built and for what purposes?
3. What are the modes of religious worship?

Stalwart was Liu the Duke,
Not one to sit down or take his ease.
He made borders, made balks,
He stacked, he stored,
He tied up dried meat and grain
In knapsacks, in bags;
Far and wide he gathered his stores.
The bows and arrows he tested,
Shield and dagger, halberd and battle-axe;
And then began his march.

Stalwart was Liu the Duke;
He surveyed the people,
They were numerous and flourishing,
He made his royal progress, proclaimed his rule;
There were no complaints, no murmurings
Either high up in the hills
Or down in the plains.
What did they carve for him?
Jade and greenstone
As pairs[1] and ends for his sheath.

Stalwart was Liu the Duke.
He reached the Hundred Springs
And gazed at the wide plain,
Climbed the southern ridge,
Looked upon the citadel,
the lands for the citadel's army.
Here he made his home,
Here he lodged his hosts,
Here they were at peace with one another,
Here they lived happily with one another.

Stalwart was Liu the Duke
In his citadel so safe.

---

[1] Stones that hung in pairs

Walking deftly and in due order
The people supplied mats, supplied stools.
He went up to the dais and leant upon a stool.
Then to make the pig-sacrifice
They took a swine from the sty;
He poured out libation from a gourd,
Gave them food, gave them drink;
And they acknowledged him as their prince
and founder.

Stalwart was Liu the Duke.
In his lands broad and long
He noted the shadows and the height of the hills,
Which parts were in the shade, which in the sun,
Viewed the streams and the springs.
To his army in three divisions
He allotted the low lands and the high,
Tithed the fields that there might be due provision,
Reckoning the evening sunlight,
And took possession of his home in Pin.

Stalwart was Liu the Duke.
He made his lodging in Pin,
But across the Wei River he made a ford,
Taking whetstones and pounding-stones.
He fixed his settlement and set its boundaries;
His people were many and prosperous
On both sides of the Huang Valley,
And upstream along the Kuo Valley.
The multitudes that he had settled there grew dense;
They went on to the bend of the Jui.[2]

A large part of the human race believes that mankind is descended from melon seeds. Dr. Alfred Kuhn, in his excellent book on the origin-myths of Indo-China,[3] mentions some twenty peoples who in one form or another hold this belief. A quite superficial search supplied me with two African examples.[4] I am told that the same belief existed in North America. The general form of the story in Indo-China is summarized by N. Matsumoto in his *Mythologie Japonaise* as follows: 'The human race is destroyed by a flood. The only survivors are a brother and sister, miraculously saved in a pumpkin. Very reluctantly the brother and sister marry, and have as their offspring sometimes a pumpkin, whose seeds sown in mountain and plain give birth to the different races of man, sometimes a mass of flesh, which the man divides into 360 parts...'

In ancient China, as in modern Indo-China, gourds were commonly used as lifebelts, and it is clear that in all these stories the gourd is merely a primitive equivalent to Noah's Ark.

The first line of the song which follows has always been taken as a simile, and no doubt it functions as one to-day. But in view of the facts mentioned above, it is most likely that imbedded in this line is an

[2] The modern Black Water River, which flows into the Ching from the west.
[3] *Berichte über den Weltanfang bei den Indochinesen*, Leipzig, 1935.
[4] Among the Shilluk of the Sudan and the Songo tribe of the Congo. See H. Baumann, *Schopfung and Urzeit des Menschen in; Mythus der Afrikanischen Volker his Mythologie.*

allusion to a forgotten belief that 'the people when they were first brought into being' were gourd seeds or young gourds. One has the impression, when reading the opening of this poem, that Tan-fu is an independent culture-hero, a rival, in fact, to Hou Chi. But tradition makes him a descendant of Hou Chi. He leads the people away from Pin, where their security is menaced by savage tribes, to Mount Ch'i, farther west.

The 'as yet they had no houses' of verse 1 does not mean that they were incapable of making houses, but that till their houses were ready they lived in loess-pits, as many inhabitants of Shensi still do permanently. Compare No. 294, last verse, where a migration is also referred to.

The young gourds spread and spread.
The people after they were first brought into being
From the River Tu[5] went to the Ch'i.[6]
Of old Tan-fu the duke
Scraped shelters, scraped holes;
As yet they had no houses.

Of old Tan-fu the duke
At coming of day galloped his horses,
Going west along the river[7] bank
Till he came to the foot of Mount Ch'i.[8]
Where with the lady Chiang
He came to look for a home.

The plain of Chou was very fertile,
Its celery and sowthistle sweet as rice-cakes.
"Here we will make a start; here take counsel,
Here notch our tortoise."[9]
It says, "Stop," it says, "Halt.
Build houses here."

So he halted, so he stopped.
And left and right
He drew the boundaries of big plots and little,
He opened up the ground, he counted the acres
From west to east;
Everywhere he took his task in hand.

Then he summoned his Master of Works,
Then he summoned his Master of Lands
And made them build houses.
Dead straight was the plumb-line,
The planks were lashed to hold the earth;
They made the Hall of Ancestors, very venerable.

---

[5] i.e. the Wei.
[6] Not the Ch'i of No. 223, but another Lacquer River in western Shensi.
[7] The Wei.
[8] See No. 218.
[9] For taking omens with the tortoise, see W. Perceval Yetts: 'The Shang-Yin Dynasty and the An-yang Finds,' *Journal of the Royal Asiatic Society*, July 1933.

They tilted in the earth with a rattling,
They pounded it with a dull thud,
They beat the walls with a loud clang,
They pared and chiselled them with a faint *p'ing, p'ing*;
The hundred cubits all rose;
The drummers could not hold out[10]

They raised the outer gate;
The outer gate soared high.
They raised the inner gate;
The inner gate was very strong.
They raised the great earth-mound,
Whence excursions of war might start.[11]

And in the time that followed they did not
abate their sacrifices,
Did not let fall their high renown;
The oak forests were laid low,
Roads were opened up.
The K'un[12] tribes scampered away;
Oh, how they panted!

The peoples of Yu and Jui[13] broke faith,
And King Wên harried their lives.
This I will say, the rebels were brought to allegiance,
Those that were first were made last.
This I will say, there were men zealous in their tasks,
There were those that kept the insolent at bay.

King Wên is on high;
Oh, he shines in Heaven!
Chou is an old people,
But its charge is new.
The land of Chou became illustrious,
Blessed by God's charge.
King Wên ascends and descends
On God's left hand, on His right.

Very diligent was King Wên,
His high fame does not cease;
He spread his bounties in Chou,
And now in his grandsons and sons,
In his grandsons and sons
The stem has branched
Into manifold generations,
And all the knights of Chou

---

[10] The drummers were there to set a rhythm for the workmen. But they tired more quickly than the indefatigable builders.
[11] The shrine where the soldiers were 'sworn in' for the combat, just as the Spanish rebels took vows at the tomb of the Cid before marching upon Madrid.
[12] The same as the Dog Barbarians?
[13] In western Shensi.

Are glorious in their generation.
Glorious in their generation,
And their counsels well pondered.
Mighty were the many knights
That brought this kingdom to its birth.
This kingdom well they bore;
They were the prop of Chou.
Splendid were those many knights
Who gave comfort to Wên the king.

August is Wên the king;
Oh, to be reverenced in his glittering light!
Mighty the charge that Heaven gave him.
The grandsons and sons of the Shang,[14]
Shang's grandsons and sons,
Their hosts were innumerable.
But God on high gave His command,
And by Chou they were subdued.

By Chou they were subdued;
Heaven's charge is not for ever.
The knights of Yin, big and little,
Made libations and offerings at the capital;
What they did was to make libations
Dressed in skirted robe and close cap.
O chosen servants of the king,
May you never thus shame your ancestors!

May you never shame your ancestors,
But rather tend their inward power,
That for ever you may be linked to Heaven's charge
And bring to yourselves many blessings.
Before Yin[15] lost its army
It was well linked to God above.
In Yin you should see as in a mirror
That Heaven's high charge is hard to keep.

The charge is not easy to keep.
Do not bring ruin on yourselves.
Send forth everywhere the light of your good fame;
Consider what Heaven did to the Yin.
High Heaven does its business
Without sound, without smell.
Make King Wên your example,
In whom all the peoples put their trust.

---

[14] The people overthrown by the Chou.
[15] Another name for the Shang.

Mission to Byblos: *The Report of Wenamun*

The Report of Wenamun, *discovered in 1891, was a document dating about 1070 BCE. It was written on papyrus in hieratic (Late Egyptian). According to the report, Wenumun was sent by Pharaoh to negotiate trade with Byblos, a wealthy Phoenician city. Bringing valuable gods from Egypt, Wenamun sought to purchase large amounts of wood to be used for making ships and some building construction. Lebanese wood was highly valued in much of the tree-scarce Eastern Mediterranean.*

Source: The Report of Wenamun

Focus Questions:
1. Compare the relationship between Egypt and Byblos in this negotiation with those of earlier readings. What has happened?
2. What are the resources and quantities involved in trade? Who is in charge?
3. Look at sections XIV, XVI, and XXVIII. What do they tell us about maritime trade and technology?

I. Departure from Thebes and journey to Tanis
[1,1] "Year 5, fourth month of the Third Season, day 16: The day on which the Elder of the Portal Wenamun of the Temple of Amun, [1,2] [Lord of the Thrones] of the Two Lands, departed in order to obtain the lumber contract for the great and august [river] bark of Amun King of Gods, [1,3] [whose name is] 'Amun, strong of leadership.' The day I arrived at Tanis [1,4] (at the place where Smendes and Tanetamun were, I gave to [1,5] them the dispatches of Amun-Rec, King of Gods, and they had them read before them. They said 'Yes!!' to the saying of Amun-Rec, King of Gods, [1,6] our [Lord]."

II. Departure from Tanis
"I began the fourth month, while I was in the Residence of Tanis, when Smendes and [1,7] Tanetamun dispatched me with the ship's master Mengebet, and I embarked for [1,8] the Great Syrian Sea."

III. Arrival and larceny at Dor
"Within the month I reached Dor, a harbor of [1,9] Zeker. Beder, its chief, had brought to me 50 loaves (of bread), 1 flagon of wine, [1,10] 1 hunch of beef. One man of my ship ran away stealing [1,11] ... vessels of gold worth 5 deben, 4 jars of silver worth 20 deben, bagged silver 11 deben. [1,12] [Total of what he stole]: 5 deben gold, 31 deben silver."

IV. Wenamun's complaint to the ruler of Dor
"When I got up on that morning, I went [1,13] to the place where the chief was. I said to him: 'I was robbed in your harbor and since you are the ruler of this land and since [1,14] you are its (investigating) judge—retrieve my money! Indeed, as for the money, it belongs to Amun-Rec, [1,15] King of Gods, the Lord of those of the Two Lands; it belongs to Smendes, it belongs to Herihor, my lord and <to> other [1,16] great ones of Egypt. Yours it is. It is for *W-r-t*, it is for *M-k-m-r*. It is [1,17] <for> Zeker-bacl, the ruler of Byblos!"

V. The reply of the ruler of Dor
"He said to me: 'To your importance! To your excellence! But look, I do not [1,18] understand that statement you said to me! If the thief belongs to my country, who boarded [1,19] your ship and stole your money—then I will replace it to you from my storeroom until one [1,20] has found your thief with his name. Alas—as for the thief who robbed you—yours is he, (as) he belongs [1,21] to your ship! Spend some days here and visit me! I will search for him!'"

VI. Wenamun's remonstration

"I spent 9 days, while being moored ||[1,22] in his harbor. And then I went and visited him. And I said to him: 'Lo, you have not found my money!' |[1,23] [O, that I could contend] with the ship captains and with the seafarers!"

VII. Beder's advice

"But he said to me: 'Calm down! |[1,24] [If you wish to f]ind yo[ur money, hea]rken to my [words! Do what I tell] you and do not |[1,25] [do... When you are,] where you want to be, then take possession of their bundles and take possession of [their contents |[1,26]...] and they will set out and search for their thief, who [stole your money]. |[1,27]... [And after you leave] the harbor, lo, you should [sail into open water and avoid] |[1,28] Tyre!'"

VIII. Wenamun's journey to and arrival at Byblos

"And I went clear of Tyre by taking the light [of the stars as the |[1,29] only guidance until reaching the realm of] Zeker-bacl, the ruler of Byblos. [And after we had moored, I searched] the ship, and I found |[30] deben of silver in it. I took possession of it. [When I had disembarked from the boat, I said to its owners: 'Lo, as for] |[1,31] your silver, it will remain with me until you have found [my silver and also |[1,32] the thief], who stole it. Although you have not stolen, I shall confiscate it, except you (yourself compensate) me concerning the money!'|[1,33] And when they had finally gone, I got myself shelter in a tavern at the shore of the harbor [of the Sea] of Byblos, and [I set up a shrine |[1,34] for] Amun-of-the-road and placed his things inside it."

IX. The reception at Byblos

"The ruler of Byblos sent to me saying: 'Get [out of |[1,31] my] harbor!' And I sent to him saying: 'Where [shall I go?]...go |[1,36] to...If (you find a ship] to transport me, let me be taken |[1,37] to Egypt again!' And I spent 29 days in his [harbor and he spent] the time to send to me daily saying: 'Get |[1,38] out of my harbor!'"

X. The miracle in Wenamun's favor

"And while he offered to his gods, the god seized a page of |[1,39] his pages and he put him in ecstasy. And he said to him: 'Bring [the] image up! Bring the envoy who is carrying it! |[1,40] It is Amun who sent it! It is he who caused it to come!'"

XI. Wenamun gets ready for departure

"While the ecstatic carried on the ecstasy until that night, I had |[1,41] found a ship which was bound for Egypt, and I readied all my belongings for it. And while I was looking |[1,42] for complete darkness, so that when it descends, I shall transport the god in order not to allow that |[1,43] another eye see him, the harbor master came to me and said: 'Stay until morning, says he, the ruler!' And I said to him: Aren't you the one |[1,44] who always spent his time coming to me daily saying, 'Get out of my harbor!'? Aren't you saying, 'Stay the night!' |[1,45] in order to let the ship, which I found, depart? And then you shall come and say |[1,46] again, 'Move on!' And he went and told it to the ruler. And the ruler sent to the captain of the vessel, saying: 'Stay until morning', |[1,47] says he, the ruler!'"

XII. Wenamun's audience with Zeker-bacl: The opening

"And when morning came about, he sent <for me> and had me taken up while the god rested in the tavern, |[1,48] in which he had been (already) at the edge of the Sea. And I found him squatting <in> his loft and when he turned his back |[1,49] against the window, the waves of the great Sea of Syria were breaking against the rear |[1,50] of his head. And I said to him: 'Amun will be merciful!' And he said to me: 'How long is it until today, since you came from where |[1,51] Amun is?' And I said to him: '5 months exactly until now!'"

XIII. The request for Wenamun's credentials

"And he said to me: 'Granted that you are right, but where is the |[1,52] edict of Amun, which should be in your hand? And where is the letter of the First High Priest of Amun, which should also be in your hand?'

And I said |^1,53 to him: 'I gave them to Smendes and Tanetamun!' He was really irate and said to me: 'Indeed, edict |^1,54 or letter you have not! Where is the ship for the fir wood, which Smendes assigned to you? Where is |^1,55 its Syrian crew? Did he assign you to that captain and the barbarians in order that he have you killed |^1,56 and that they throw the you into the Sea? Because of whom has one desired the god or you? |^1,57 Because of whom has one desired you?'—so he spoke to me.''

XIV. Who has maritime power?
"And I said to him: 'Isn't an Egyptian ship and an Egyptian crew those who sail |^1,58 under Smendes? So can he hire Syrian crews?' And he said to me: 'Aren't there 20 liners |^1,59 there, belonging to this my harbor, which are in charter with Smendes? And for this, |^2,1 Sidon is another, concerning which you are experienced, aren't there another 50 liners there, which are in charter |^2,2 with *W-r-k-t-l*, which have hauled for his (i.e., Smendes') house! And I was silent to this a long |^2,3 time.''

XV. Getting down to business
"And then he proceeded and said to me: 'For what commission did you come?' And I said to him: 'I have come |^2,4 after the lumber contract for the great and august bark of Amun-Rec, King of Gods. As your father did |^2,5 and as your father's father did (it), you should also do (it)!'—so I said to him. And he said to me: 'They did it in trade! |^2,6 When you pay me for doing it, I shall do it! Yea, my forefathers performed this commission, when the |^2,7 Pharaoh, l.p.h., had sent 6 ships and they were loaded with Egyptian goods and they emptied them into their |^2,8 storehouses. But you, what is it that you have brought for me, myself?'''

XVI. Zeker-bacl's objections to the present deal
"He had brought records of the time of his ancestors |^2,9 and had them read before me. And 1,000 deben of silver were tallied up for all in his records. |^2,10 And he said to me: 'As for the ruler of Egypt, the master of mine—for I am also his servant—|^2,11 is it possible that he actually did send silver and gold while saying "Do the commission for Amun!"? Is it the delivery |^2,12 of coronation gifts, as they used to exist, when he acted for my father? As for me—indeed—am I your |^2,13 servant, am I the servant of the one who sent you? (Assumed) I will call loudly to the |^2,14 'Lebanon, which makes the heaven open, and the wood is delivered there at the shore of the Sea—produce |^2,15 for me the sails you have brought to tackle your ships, which are carrying your wood to <Egypt> |^2,16 (or) produce for me the ropes you have brought [to tie the firwood,] which I shall cut, to supply it to you |^2,17 ...(Assuming) I supply it to you and the sails <for> |^2,18 your ships—(and then) the main yards might be overloaded and might break—and you yourself might die at Sea— |^2,19 lo, Amun could make a thunder in the heaven and appoint Seth for his time!'''

XVII. Zeker-bacl praises the traditional order and decries the present
"Indeed, Amun takes |^2,20 care of all those belonging to the Two Countries; (but) he takes care of them, (after) having taken care of the land of Egypt, from which you come, |^2,21 previously! Indeed, reward came forth from it as far as the place where I am! And punishment came forth |^2,22 from it as far as the place where I am. What is this unsupported travel which you are caused to make?''

XVIII. Wenamun's reply and his praise of Amun
"And I said to him: |^2,23 'Wrong! It is not an unsupported journey that I am on. There is not any ship on the river which |^2,24 does not belong to Amun! His is (also) the Sea! And his is the Lebanon which you think "It is mine!" He makes |^2,25 the growth (there) for (the ship) Amun-woser-hat, the queen of all ships. Aye! he said, namely Amun-Rec, King of Gods, in speaking to |^2,26 Herihor, my lord, who dispatched me. And he sent me bearing this mighty god. Now look, you caused that |^2,27 this mighty god spent 29 days moored <in> your harbor, while you did not find out whether he is there and whether he is the one |^2,28 he used a to be. You dally to empty the Lebanon on behalf of its lord!

As for your saying, that |^2,29 former kings used to send silver and gold—if they could have given life and health, they would not have sent those things! |^2,30 They had to send those (material) things instead of life and health <to> your ancestors. Now as for Amun-Rec, King of Gods, he is the [2.31] lord of the life and health! And he was the lord of your ancestors. They spent their time of life offering [2.32] to Amun. You as well, you are a servant of Amun! If you say 'Yes!' to Amun and carry out his [2.33] commission— while you live you shall be well and prosperous and successful for your entire country and your people. Do not desire [2.34] for yourself anything else from Amun-Rec, <King> of Gods!'"

XIX. Wenamun requests funds from Smendes
"'Truly a lion loves his things! Let your scribe be brought to me, that [2.35] I may send him to Smendes and Tanetamun, those organizers of the land, whom Amun appointed for the North of his country, [2.36] and they will have brought the wherewithall. And I will send him to them, saying: "Let it be brought before I can actually go back South!" And I shall [2.37] bring to you any shortcomings as well!'—so I said to him."

XX. The arrival of funds sent by Smendes
"And he put my letter in the hand of his messenger. And he readied the mud-guard, [2.38] the top of the bow, and the top of the stern together with 4 hewn timbers—total 7. And he sent them to Egypt.[2.39] And his messenger went to Egypt and came back to me to Syria within the first month of the *prt*-season. And Smendes and Tanetamun sent: [2.40] of gold: 4 jars, 1 *k3.k-mn* vessel; of silver: 5 jars; clothing of byssus: 10 pieces; Upper Egyptian linen: 10 veils; smooth material: 500 doublets; [2.41] 500 ox-hides; 500 ropes; lentils: 20 sacks; fish: 30 baskets. And she sent to me clothing [2.42] of upper Egyptian linen: 5 pieces; Upper Egyptian linen: 5 veils; 1 sack of lentils; 5 baskets of fish."

XXI. Zeker-bacl procures the lumber
"And the ruler was pleased and he supplied [2.43] 300 men and 300 oxen, and he appointed supervisors in charge of them, to have them fell the lumber.

And they felled it. And they spent the winter at it [2.44] isolated until the third month of the *smw*-season, when they hauled them to the shore of the Sea."

XXII. Another audience with Zeker-bacl: An incident
And when(ever) the ruler came out, he stopped at them. And then he sent to me, [2.45] saying: 'Come!' And then when I approached him, the shadow of his lotus-fan fell on me. And Penamun, [2.46] a cupbearer who was with him, intercepted me, saying: 'The shadow of Pharaoh, l.p.h., your lord, has fallen on you!' And he became angry [2.47] at him, saying: 'Leave him alone!'

XXIII. Zeker-bacl's request
"And I approached him (again). And he was responding and said to me: "Look! The commission which [2.48] my ancestors used to do previously, I have done it (too). But you, namely yourself, have not done for me that which your forebears would have done for me.

Look! [2.49] The end of your wood donation has arrived and it is stacked up. Do me a favor when you intend to transport it—then could it be denied to you? [2.50] Do not intend to see the tenor of the Sea! In case you want [2.51] to see the tenor of the Sea, you shall also see my own!'

"'Truly, I have not done to you what was done <to> the messengers of Khacemwese, because they spent 17 years [2.52] in this country and they (actually) died in their positions!' And he said to his servant: 'Take him! Let him see their tomb [2.53] in which they lie!'"

XXV. Wenamun's claim of special status
"And I said to him: 'Do not let me see it! As for Khacemwese, humans were those whom he sent to you as messengers. While human [2.54] of body, you don't have one of his envoys here that you could say: "You go and look at your colleagues!"

XXVI. Wenamun proposes the wording for a commemorative inscription

"'Do you not enjoy |[2,55] when you cause that one makes for you a stela and that you (can) say on it: "Amun-Rec, King of Gods, sent to me Amun-of-the-road (as) his envoy, |[2,56] l.p.h., together with Wenamun, his human envoy, in quest of the lumber-donation for the great and august bark of Amun-Rec King of Gods. I cut it, |[2,57] I transported it, and I paid for it and my ships and my crews. I let them reach Egypt to request for me |[2,58] 50 years of life from Amun in addition to my fate. And it happened!" And when afterward in another time an envoy comes. | [2,59] from the land of Egypt and he knows writing; and when he reads your name on the stela, you will receive water <in> the West in the way of the gods who are |[2,60] there.'"

XXVII. Zeker-bacl accepts and Wenamun promises further spiritual benefits

"And he said to me: 'An important instruction for the wording is this, you said to me!' And I said to him: 'As for those many things which you have said to me—if I reach |[2,61] the place where the First High Priest of Amun is and when he sees your commission—it is your commission which will draw |[2,62] profit for you!'

XXVIII. Wenamun attempts to find transportation

"And I went by myself to the shore of the Sea to the place where the |[2,61] lumber was stacked up. And I looked at 11 vessels; |[2,63] they had come in from the Sea and they belonged to the Zeker (ports?)...saying: 'Restrain him! Do not send ships |[2,64] with him to the land of Egypt!'

XXIX. Wenamun's despair

"And I was ready to sit down and cry. And the letter writer of the ruler came out to me |[2,65] and he said to me: 'What is the matter with you?' And I said to him: 'Have you not seen those migratory birds which are going down to Egypt for the second time? |[2,66] Look at them, they are able to move to the northern Delta! Until what has to arrive that I, who have been abandoned, am there? Have you not seen those who came |[2,67] to restrain me a new?'"

XXX. Zeker-bacl sends consolation to Wenamun

"And he went and he told it to the ruler. And the ruler was ready |[2,68] to cry because of the words which were quoted to him and which were sickening. And he let come out to me his letter-scribe bringing to me 2 flagons of wine and a sheep. And he sent |[2,69] to me Tanetne, a songstress from Egypt who was with him, saying: 'Sing for him! Don't let him be desperate!' And he sent to me, |[2,70] saying: 'Eat and drink! Do not despair! You shall hear what is to be said during the morning!'

XXXI. Wenamun's case is settled and he departs

"And when morning |[2,71] came, he had his assembly called together. And when he stood in their midst, he said to the Zeker: 'How about your journey?' |[2,72] And they said to him: 'Assign to us who comes for those ships, (but) beat the one whom you are sending to Egypt as our enemy!' |[2,73] And he said to them: 'I would not know (how) to restrain the envoy of Amun within my country! Let me dispatch him and you pursue him |[2,74] to restrain him!' And he loaded me and came with me as far as the harbor of the Sea."

XXXII. The adventure at Cyprus

"And the winds threw me to the land of |[2,75] Alasiya. And the inhabitants of the landing place charged against me to kill me. And I forced my way through them to the place where *H3-ti-b3*, |[2,76] the princess of the town, was. And I met her, because she was going forth from her one house and was entering into another (house). And I |[2,77] greeted her and I said to the people who were standing around her: 'Isn't there one among you who can understand Egyptian words?' And one |[2,78] of them said: 'I understand!' And I said to him: 'Say to my lady that I have heard as far away as Thebes, the place where Amun is, the following: "Even so |[2,79] evil is done in all towns, but right is done in the land of Alasiya!" Or is evil committed there, too, every day?' And she said: 'Truly, what is it |[2,80] that you talk (about)' And I said to her:

"As the sea raged and the winds blew me to the land in which you are—[2,81] are you allowing that they accept my bow line in order to kill me? As I am an envoy of Amun, look, one should welcome me [2,82] at any time! As for the crew of the ruler of Byblos, whom they wish to kill—couldn't their lord find [2,83] 10 crews of yours and kill them, namely he?' And she let call to the people and one arranged them. And she said to me: 'Be at rest! ...'"

The Book of Job and Jewish Literature

This is one of the most renowned and eloquent portions of the Hebrew Scriptures, and one that deals with one of the most profound questions to be posed to any religious system, that of God's justice in the face of human suffering. As any people of the past, present, or future, the Hebrews wondered whether a just and almighty deity could permit the suffering of the innocent. If one considered a hypothetical situation, for example a man who had exemplary character and who was now suffering as a result of God's test, would this person "curse God and die" or find some way to resolve his suffering at God's hands? This text was written at some point in the 1ˢᵗ millennium BCE, and it purports to describe the words and experiences of a man in Mesopotamia who was also an influential worshipper of Yahweh. These segments are taken from the beginning and end of the Book, in which God sets the conditions of Job's sufferings, and then answers Job's questions, "out of the whirlwind."

Source: *Job 1:1–22; 40:1-14; 42:1–17, NIV*

Focus Questions:
1. What does this document suggest about Hebrew beliefs concerning God and divine justice?
2. In what terms does God justify his treatment of Job?
3. Relate this text to the Laws quoted above. What might both documents tell us about Hebrew society?

JOB 1

Prologue

1 In the land of Uz there lived a man whose name was Job. This man was blameless and upright; he feared God and shunned evil. 2 He had seven sons and three daughters, 3 and he owned seven thousand sheep, three thousand camels, five hundred yoke of oxen and five hundred donkeys, and had a large number of servants. He was the greatest man among all the people of the East.

4 His sons used to take turns holding feasts in their homes, and they would invite their three sisters to eat and drink with them. 5 When a period of feasting had run its course, Job would send and have them purified. Early in the morning he would sacrifice a burnt offering for each of them, thinking, "Perhaps my children have sinned and cursed God in their hearts." This was Job's regular custom.

Job's First Test

6 One day the angels came to present themselves before the LORD, and Satan also came with them. 7 The LORD said to Satan, "Where have you come from?" Satan answered the LORD, "From roaming through the earth and going back and forth in it."

8 Then the LORD said to Satan, "Have you considered my servant Job? There is no one on earth like him; he is blameless and upright, a man who fears God and shuns evil."

9 "Does Job fear God for nothing?" Satan replied. 10 "Have you not put a hedge around him and his household and everything he has? You have blessed the work of his hands, so that his flocks and herds are spread throughout the land. 11 But stretch out your hand and strike everything he has, and he will surely curse you to your face."

12 The LORD said to Satan, "Very well, then, everything he has is in your hands, but on the man himself do not lay a finger." Then Satan went out from the presence of the LORD.

13 One day when Job's sons and daughters were feasting and drinking wine at the oldest brother's house, 14 a messenger came to Job and said, "The oxen were plowing and the donkeys were grazing nearby, 15 and the Sabeans attacked and carried them off. They put the servants to the sword, and I am the only one who has escaped to tell you!"

16 While he was still speaking, another messenger came and said, "The fire of God fell from the sky and burned up the sheep and the servants, and I am the only one who has escaped to tell you!"

17 While he was still speaking, another messenger came and said, "The Chaldeans formed three raiding parties and swept down on your camels and carried them off. They put the servants to the sword, and I am the only one who has escaped to tell you!"

18 While he was still speaking, yet another messenger came and said, "Your sons and daughters were feasting and drinking wine at the oldest brother's house, 19 when suddenly a mighty wind swept in from the desert and struck the four corners of the house. It collapsed on them and they are dead, and I am the only one who has escaped to tell you!"

20 At this, Job got up and tore his robe and shaved his head. Then he fell to the ground in worship 21 and said: "Naked I came from my mother's womb, and naked I will depart. The LORD gave and the LORD has taken away; may the name of the LORD be praised."

22 In all this, Job did not sin by charging God with wrongdoing.

JOB 40

1 The LORD said to Job:

2 "Will the one who contends with the Almighty correct him? Let him who accuses God answer him!"

3 Then Job answered the LORD :

4 "I am unworthy—how can I reply to you? I put my hand over my mouth.

5 I spoke once, but I have no answer—twice, but I will say no more."

6 Then the LORD spoke to Job out of the storm:

7 "Brace yourself like a man; I will question you, and you shall answer me.

8 "Would you discredit my justice? Would you condemn me to justify yourself?

9 Do you have an arm like God's, and can your voice thunder like his?

10 Then adorn yourself with glory and splendor, and clothe yourself in honor and majesty.

11 Unleash the fury of your wrath, look at every proud man and bring him low,

12 look at every proud man and humble him, crush the wicked where they stand.

13 Bury them all in the dust together; shroud their faces in the grave.

14 Then I myself will admit to you that your own right hand can save you.

JOB 42 (New International Version)

1 Then Job replied to the LORD:

2 "I know that you can do all things; no plan of yours can be thwarted.

3 You asked, 'Who is this that obscures my counsel without knowledge?' Surely I spoke of things I did not understand, things too wonderful for me to know.

4 "You said, 'Listen now, and I will speak; I will question you, and you shall answer me.'

5 My ears had heard of you but now my eyes have seen you.

6 Therefore I despise myself and repent in dust and ashes."

EPILOGUE

7 After the LORD had said these things to Job, he said to Eliphaz the Temanite, "I am angry with you and your two friends, because you have not spoken of me what is right, as my servant Job has. 8 So now take seven bulls and seven rams and go to my servant Job and sacrifice a burnt offering for yourselves. My servant Job will pray for you, and I will accept his prayer and not deal with you according to your folly. You have not spoken of me what is right, as my servant Job has." 9 So Eliphaz the Temanite, Bildad the Shuhite and Zophar the Naamathite did what the LORD told them; and the LORD accepted Job's prayer.

10 After Job had prayed for his friends, the LORD made him prosperous again and gave him twice as much as he had before. 11 All his brothers and sisters and everyone who had known him before came and ate with him in his house. They comforted and consoled him over all the trouble the LORD had brought upon him, and each one gave him a piece of silver and a gold ring.

12 The LORD blessed the latter part of Job's life more than the first. He had fourteen thousand sheep, six thousand camels, a thousand yoke of oxen and a thousand donkeys. 13 And he also had seven sons and three daughters. 14 The first daughter he named Jemimah, the second Keziah and the third Keren-Happuch. 15 Nowhere in all the land were there found women as beautiful as Job's daughters, and their father granted them an inheritance along with their brothers.

16 After this, Job lived a hundred and forty years; he saw his children and their children to the fourth generation. 17 And so he died, old and full of years.

The Babylonian Chronicles, "The Fall of Nineveh Chronicle"

The Babylonian Chronicles is a series of tablets written in cuneiform that provide a year-by-year synopsis of Babylonian history from about 705 BCE to 280 BCE. They are an extremely useful source for the period, and supplement the Old Testament writings. The section given here covers part of the reign of Nabopolassar (625–605 BCE) when the Babylonians revive and defeat the Assyrian empire. A series of successful campaigns were capped by the capture of the Assyrian capital, Nineveh, in 612 BCE. Essentially the chronicle describes the military defeat of a military empire.

Source: *Grayson, A.K., trans.,* Assyrian and Babylonian Chronicles, *1975.*

Focus Questions:
1. What are the strategies, tactics, and weapons of the era?
2. What role do towns play? What are their various fates?
3. Are there any rules of war? How does Babylonian warfare reflect on the readings from chapter one?

The tenth year of Nabopolassar [*616–615 BCE*]: In the month Ajaru he mustered the army of Babylonia and marched along the bank of the Euphrates. The Suheans and Hindaneans [*people living south of Harran*] did not do battle against him but placed their tribute before him.

In the month Âbu the army of Assyria prepared for battle in Gablini and Nabopolassar went up against them. On the twelfth of the month Âbu [*24 July 616*] he did battle against the army of Assyria and the army of Assyria retreated before him. He inflicted a major defeat upon Assyria and plundered them extensively. He captured the Manneans, who had come to the Assyrians' aid, and the Assyrian officers. On the same day he captured Gablini.

In the month Âbu the king of Babylonia and his army went upstream to Mane, Sahiri and Bali-hu. He plundered them, sacked them extensively and abducted their gods.

In the month Ulûlu the king of Babylonia and his army returned and on his way he took the people of Hindanu and its gods to Babylon.

In the month Tašrîtu the army of Egypt and the army of Assyria went after the king of Babylonia as far as Gablini but they did not overtake the king of Babylonia. So they withdrew.

In the month Addaru the army of Assyria and the army of Babylonia did battle against one another at Madanu, a suburb of Arraphu [*modern Kirkuk*], and the army of Assyria retreated before the army of Babylonia. The army of Babylonia inflicted a major defeat upon the Assyrian army and drove them back to the Zab river. They captured their chariots and horses and plundered them extensively. They took many [*lacuna*] with them across the Tigris and brought them into Babylon.

The eleventh year [*615–614*]: The king of Babylonia mustered his army, marched along the bank of the Tigris, and in the month Ajaru he encamped against Aššur. On the [*lacuna*] day of the month Simanu he did battle against the city but he did not capture it. The king of Assyria mustered his army, pushed the king of Babylonia back from Aššur and marched after him as far as Takrit, a city on the bank of the Tigris. The king of Babylonia stationed his army in the fortress of Takrit. The king of Assyria and his army encamped against the army of the king of Babylonia, which was stationed in Takrit, and did battle against them for ten days. But the king of Assyria did not capture the city. Instead, the army of the king of Babylonia, which had been stationed in the fortress, inflicted a major defeat upon Assyria. The king of Assyria and his army turned and went home. In the month Arahsamna the Medes went down to Arraphu [*modern Kirkuk*] and [*lacuna*].

The twelfth year [614–613]: In the month Âbu [*July/August*] the Medes, after they had matched against Nineveh [*lacuna*], hastened and they captured Tarbisu, a city in the district of Nineveh. They went along the Tigris and encamped against Assur. They did battle against the city and destroyed it. They inflicted a terrible defeat upon a great people, plundered and sacked them. The king of Babylonia and his army, who had gone to help the Medes, did not reach the battle in time. The city [*lacuna*] The king of Babylonia and Cyaxares the king of the Medes met one another by the city and together they made an entente cordiale. [*lacuna*] Cyaxares and his army went home. The king of Babylonia and his army went home.

The thirteenth year [613–612]: In the month Ajaru the Subeans rebelled against the king of Babylonia and became belligerent. The king of Babylonia mustered his army and marched to Suhu. On the fourth day of the month Simanu [*11 May 613*] he did battle against Rahilu, a city which is on an island in the middle of the Euphrates and at that time he captured the city. He built his [*lacuna*]. The men who live on the bank of the Euphrates came down to him. [*lacuna*] he encamped against Anat and the siege engines he brought over from the western side [*lacuna*] he brought the siege engine up to the wall. He did battle against the city and captured it. [*lacuna*] the king of Assyria and his army came down and [*lacuna*] the king of Babylonia and his army. The king of Babylonia went home.

The fourteenth year [612–611]: The king of Babylonia mustered his army and marched to [*lacuna*]. The king of the Medes marched towards the king of Babylonia. [*lacuna*] they met one another. The king of Babylonia [*lacuna*] Cyaxares [*lacuna*] brought across and they marched along the bank of the Tigris. [lacuna] they encamped against Nineveh.

From the month Simanu [*June*] until the month Âbu [*August*]—for three months—they subjected the city to a heavy siege. On the [*lacuna*] day of the month Âbu they inflicted a major defeat upon a great people. At that time Sin-šar-iškun, king of Assyria, died. [*lacuna*] They carried off the vast booty of the city and the temple and turned the city into a ruin heap [*lacuna*] of Assyria escaped from the enemy and [lacuna] the king of Babylonia [*lacuna*].

On the twentieth day of the month Ulûlu [*15 August 612*] Cyaxares and his army went home. After he had gone, the king of Babylonia dispatched his army and they marched to Nasibin. Plunder and exiles [*lacuna*] and they brought the people of Rusapu [*modern Kirkuk*] to the king of Babylonia at Nineveh. On the [*lacuna*] of the month [*lacuna*] Aššur-uballit ascended to the throne in Harran to rule Assyria. Up until the [*lacuna*] day of the month [*lacuna*] the king of [*lacuna*] set out and in [*lacuna*].

The fifteenth year [611–610]: In the month Du'ûzu [*June/July*] the king of Babylonia mustered his army and [*lacuna*] marched to Assyria victoriously. He marched about of [*lacuna*] and he captured Shu [*lacuna*], plundered it and carried of its vast booty.

In the month Arahsamna [*November/December*] the king of Babylonia took the lead of his army personally and marched against Ruggulitu. He did battle against the city and on the twenty-eighth day of the month Arahsamnu [*8 December 611*] he captured it. [*lacuna*] He did not leave a single man alive. [*lacuna*] He went home.

The sixteenth year [610–609]: In the month Ajaru [*May*] the king of Babylonia mustered his army and marched to Assyria. From the month [*lacuna*] until the month Arahsamna [*November*] he marched about victoriously in Assyria. In the month Arahsamnu the Medes, who had come to the help of the king of Babylonia, put their armies together and marched to Harran against Aššur-uballit, who had ascended to the throne in Assyria. Fear of the enemy overcame Aššur-uballit and the army of Egypt which had come to help him, and they abandoned the city. [*lacuna*] they crossed. The king of Babylonia reached Harran and [*lacuna*] he captured the city. He carried off the vast booty of the city and the temple. In the month Addaru the king of Babylonia left their [*lacuna*]. He went home. The Medes, who had come to help the king of Babylonia, withdrew.

The seventeenth year [*609-608*]: In the month Du'ûzu [*July*] Aššur-uballit, king of Assyria, with a large army from Egypt crossed the river Euphrates and marched against Harran to conquer it. [*lacuna*] They captured [*a town on the road to Harran*]. They defeated the garrison which the king of Babylonia had stationed inside. When they had defeated it they encamped against Harran. Until the month Ulûlu [*September*] they did battle against the city but achieved nothing. However, they did not withdraw. The king of Babylonia went to help his army and [*lacuna*] he went up to Izalla and the numerous cities in the mountains [*lacuna*] he set fire to their [*lacuna*].

At that time the army of [*lacuna*] march as far as the district of Urartu. In the land [*lacuna*] they plundered their [*lacuna*]. The garrison which the king of [*lacuna*] had stationed in it set out. They went up to [*lacuna*]. The king of Babylonia went home.

In the eighteenth year [*608-607*]: In the month Ulûlu [*August/September*] the king of Babylonia mustered his army. [*lacuna*].

Let the one who loves [*the gods*] Nabû and Marduk keep this tablet and not let it stray into other hands.

Chapter 4

Farmers and Traders

Ptahhotep, Excerpt from the Egyptian *Book of Instructions*

Written around 2300 BCE and attributed to Ptahhotep, a member of the royal court. These maxims form a part of a tradition of literature tending advice and wisdom in daily life that has persisted throughout history. The Book of Instructions *is written in the form of a letter from a father to his son, another popular format. These successful and popular maxims were copied and read over many centuries in Egypt.*

Source: *Lichtheim, Miriam.* Ancient Egyptian Literature—A Book of Readings Volume I: The Old and Middle Kingdome. *Berkley, CA: University of California Press, 1973.*

Focus Questions:
1. Which of the advice and values given in the instructions would be acceptable today, and which would not? Why?
2. What does the reading reveal about Egyptian society, especially social classes and women?
3. What deductions can you glean from the phrase in line 34, "Yet [good speech] may be found among maids at the grindstones"?

Follow Your Heart
1 Follow your heart as long as you live,
Do no more than is required...
Don't waste time on daily cares
Beyond providing for your household;
When wealth has come, follow your heart,
Wealth does no good if one is glum!

Conduct
2 If you want a perfect conduct,
To be free from every evil,
Guard against the vice of greed:
A grievous sickness without cure,
There is no treatment for it.
It embroils fathers, mothers,
And the brothers of the mother,

It parts wife from husband;
It is a compound of all evils,
A bundle of all hateful things.
That man endures whose rule is rightness,
Who walks a straight line;
He will make a will by it,
The greedy has no tomb…

3 Be generous as long as you live,
What leaves the storehouse does not return;
It is the food to be shared which is coveted,
One whose belly is empty is an accuser;
One deprived becomes an opponent
Don't have him for a neighbor.
Kindness is a man's memorial
For the years after the action.

4 Don't be proud of your knowledge,
Consult the ignorant and the wise;
The limits of art are not reached,
No artist's skills are perfect;
Good speech is more hidden than greenstone,
Yet may be found among maids at the grindstones.

5 Do not repeat calumny,
 Nor should you listen to it,
It is the spouting of the hot-bellied.
Report a thing observed, not heard,
If it is negligible, don't say anything,
He who is before you recognizes worth.
If a seizure is ordered and carried out,
Hatred will arise against him who seizes;
Calumny is like a dream against which one covers the face.

6 Do not plunder a neighbor's house,
Do not steal the goods of one near you,
Lest he denounce you before you are heard.
A quarreler is a mindless person,
If he is known as an aggressor
The hostile man will have trouble in the neighborhood.

Trust

7 If you are among the people,
Gain supporters through being trusted;
The trusted man who does not vent his belly's speech,
He will himself become a leader.
A man of means—what is he like?
Your name is good, you are not maligned,
Your body is sleek, your face benign,
One praises you without your knowing.
He whose heart obeys his belly
Puts contempt of himself in place of love,
His heart is bald, his body unanointed;

8 If you are a man of trust,
Sent by one great man to another,
Adhere to the nature of him who sent you,
Give his message as he said it.
Guard against reviling speech,
Which embroils one great with another;
Keep to the truth, don't exceed it,
But an outburst should not be repeated.

9 Report your commission without faltering,
Give your advice in your master's council...
If he is fluent in his speech,
It will not be hard for the envoy to report,
Nor will he be answered, "Who is he to know it?"
As to the master, his affairs will fail
If he plans to punish him for it,
He should be silent upon hearing: "I have told."

In Public
10 He who uses elbows is not helped.

11 If you are one among guests
At the table of one greater than you,
Take what he gives as it is set before you;
Look at what is before you,
Don't shoot many glances at him,

12 Don't speak to him until he summons,
One does not know what may displease;
Speak when he has addressed you,
Then your words will please the heart.

13 If you are in the antechamber,
Stand and sit as fits your rank,
Which was assigned you the first day.
Do not trespass—you will be turned back,
Keen is the face to him who enters announced,
Spacious the seat of him who has been called.
The antechamber has a rule,
All behavior is by measure;

Humility
14 Do not boast at your neighbors' side,
One has great respect for the silent man:
A man of character is man of wealth.
If he robs he is like a crocodile in court.
Don't impose on one who is childless,
Neither decry nor boast of it;
There is many a father who has grief,
And a mother of children less content than another;

15 If you are poor, serve a man of worth...
Do not recall if he once was poor,

Don't be arrogant toward him
For knowing his former state;
Respect him for what has accrued to him,
For wealth does not come by itself.
It is their law for him whom they love,
His gain, he gathered it himself.

Friendship

16 As ill will comes from opposition,
So goodwill increases love...

17 Know your helpers, then you prosper,
Don't be mean toward your friends,
They are one's watered field,
And greater then one's riches,
For what belongs to one belongs to another.
The character of a son of man is profit to him;
Good nature is a memorial.

18 If you probe the character of a friend,
Don't inquire, but approach him,
Deal with him alone,
So as not to suffer from his manner.
Dispute with him after a time,
Test his heart in conversation;
If what he has seen escapes him,
If he does a thing that annoys you,
Be yet friendly with him, don't attack;
Be restrained, don't let fly,
Don't answer with hostility,
Neither part from him nor attack him;
His time does not fail to come,
One does not escape what is fated.

19 If you want friendship to endure
In the house you enter
As master, brother, or friend,
In whatever place you enter,
Beware of approaching the women!
Unhappy is the place where it is done,
Unwelcome is he who intrudes on them.
A thousand men are turned away from their good:
A short moment like a dream,
Then death comes for having known them...

Family

20 When you prosper and found your house,
And love your wife with ardor,
Fill her belly, clothe her back,
Ointment soothes her body.
Gladden her heart as long as you live,
She is a fertile field for her lord.
Do not contend with her in court,

Keep her from power, restrain her—
Her eye is her storm when she gazes—
Thus will you make her stay in your house...

21 If you are a man of worth
And produce a son by the grace of god,
If he is straight, takes after you,
Takes good care of your possessions,
Do for him all that is good,
He is your son, your spirit begot him,
Don't withdraw your heart from him.
But an offspring can make trouble:
If he strays, neglects your counsel,
Disobeys all that is said,
His mouth spouting evil speech,
Punish him for all his talk...

Leadership
22 If you are a man who leads,
Who controls the affairs of the many,
Seek out every beneficent deed,
That your conduct may be blameless.
Great is justice, lasting in effect,
Unchallenged since the time of Osiris.
One punishes the transgressor of laws,
Though the greedy overlooks this;
Baseness may seize riches,
Yet crime never lands its wares;
In the end it is justice that lasts,
Man says: "It is my father's ground."

23 If you are mighty, gain respect through knowledge
And through gentleness of speech.
Don't command except as is fitting,
He who provokes gets into trouble.
Don't be haughty, lest you be humbled,
Don't be mute, lest you be chided.
When you answer one who is fuming,
Avert your face, control yourself.
The flame of the hot-heart sweeps across,
He who steps gently, his path is paved.
He who frets all day has no happy moment,
He who's gay all day can't keep house.

24 If you are a man who leads,
Listen calmly to the speech of one who pleads;
Don't stop him from purging his body
Of that which he planned to tell.
A man in distress wants to pour out his heart
More than that his case be won.
About him who stops a plea
One says: "Why does he reject it?"

Not all one pleads for can be granted,
But a good hearing soothes the heart.

²⁵ Punish firmly, chastise soundly,
Then repression of crime becomes an example;
Punishment except for crime
Turns the complainer into an enemy.

Superiors

²⁶ If you are a man of worth
Who sits in his master's council,
Concentrate on excellence,
Your silence is better than chatter.
Speak when you know you have a solution,
It is the skilled who should speak in council;
Speaking is harder than all other work,
He who understands it makes it serve.

²⁷ Don't oppose a great man's action,
Don't vex the heart of one who is burdened;

²⁸ Bend your back to your superior,
Your overseer from the palace;
Then your house will endure in its wealth,
Your rewards in their right place.
Wretched is he who opposes a superior,
One lives as long as he is mild,
Baring the arm does not hurt it.

Disputes

²⁹ If you meet a disputant in action,
A powerful man, superior to you,
Fold your arms, bend your back,
To flout him will not make him agree with you.
Make little of the evil speech
By not opposing him while he's in action;
He will be called an ignoramus,
Your self-control will match his pile of words.

³⁰ If you meet a disputant in action
Who is your equal, on your level,
You will make your worth exceed his by silence,
While he is speaking evilly,
There will be much talk by the hearers,
Your name will be good in the minds of the magistrates.

³¹ If you meet a disputant in action,
A poor man, not your equal,
Do not attack him because he is weak,
Let him alone, he will confute himself.
Do not answer him to relieve your heart,
Do not vent yourself against your opponent,
Wretched is he who injures a poor man,

One will wish to do what you desire,
You will beat him through the magistrates' reproof.

The Worth of Precepts

[32] If you listen to my sayings,
All your affairs will go forward;
In their truth resides their value,
Their memory goes on in the speech of men,
Because of the worth of their precepts...

Syrian Government Documents: *The Archives of Ebla*

The city of Ebla in Syria was a wealthy center of the textile and metallurgy trades during the 3ʳᵈ millennium BCE, until its destruction by Akkadians. Excavations have produced thousands of clay tablets written in Cuneiform revealing the nature of Ebla's economy, government, and religion. Though extremely useful, the records for Ebla remind us that most surviving historical documents are governmental rather than private, thus providing a partial and incomplete record that must be carefully interpreted.

Source: *Pettinato, G. The Archives of Ebla. Garden City, NY: Doubleday, 1981.*

Focus Questions:
1. What are the types and levels of resources in Ebla?
2. If you extrapolate the Eblan economic base all around the Fertile Crescent, how does this affect your opinion of civilization of the period?
3. What skills and knowledge do the Eblans have?

1.1. AGRICULTURE

The geographical situation of Ebla renders agriculture not only possible but also highly profitable. The countryside around Tell Mardikh is flat and abundantly watered, and the data emerging from the tablets show that the Eblaites appreciated the natural potential of their territory.

The metropolitan area was, as a matter of fact, completely encircled by countless towns and villages dedicated to agriculture. When we learn that 17 kinds of wheat were raised, then we understand how rationally they exploited the soil. But before passing on to the various crops, one question should be raised: What area was utilized by agriculture?

A reply to this query will become possible only when all the tablets dealing with work in the field have been studied together, but even now one can safely assert that a vast area was available for farming purposes.

One cadastral text dealing with the farming territory of but 10 villages mentions an area of more than 57 kilometers squared; hence to infer that the farming area of Ebla must have covered hundreds, if not actually thousands, of kilometers squared would not be unwarranted.

The principal crop was that of grains, especially barley and wheat. Numerous are the tablets which describe both the surface and the annual harvest. To give an example, TM.76.G.188 records in the first part the amount of barley needed for sowing, and in the second mentions the agricultural terrain of the 10 villages mentioned above.

obverse

I	1)	[ ] + 26 še-numun	[x +] 26 (Gubar) of barley for sowing
	2)	1 m[i] 30 [ ]	130. . .
	3)	al na-si₁₁ na-si₁₁	due to the people
	4)	da-guᵏⁱ	of the village Dagu;
	5)	66 še-mumum	66 (Gubar) of barley for sowing
	6)	[ˣ²] gú-bar mugᵓ-šim	[x] Gubar . . . šim

II	1)	ša-gúᵏⁱ	of the village Šagu
	2)	26 še-numun	26 (Gubar) of barley for sowing
	3)	za-ba-tùᵏⁱ	of the village Zabatu;
	4)	30 še-numun	30 (Gubar) of barley for sowing
	5)	30 še KAxX-ᵈmul	30 (Gubar) of barley . . .
	6)	ur-lumᵏⁱ	of the village Urlum;
	7)	70 še-numun	70 (Gubar) of barley for sowing

III	1)	1 m[i] 26 [ ]ᵈ mul	126 [Gubar] . . .
	2)	i-ti-ᵈᵓà-da	for Iti-Hada;
	3)	20 še-numun	20 (Gubar) of barley for sowing
	4)	gu-wa-luᵏⁱ	of the village Guwalu;
	5)	20 še-numun	20 (Gubar) of barley for sowing

IV	1)	a-a-daᵏⁱ	of the village A'ada;
	2)	20 lá-3 še-numun	17 (Gubar) of barley for sowing
	3)	gi-duᵏⁱ	of the village Gidu;
	4)	15 še-numun	15 Gubar of barley for sowing
	5)	ì-zuᵏⁱ	of the village Izu;

After a short list of large and small cattle present in these villages, the tablet continues with the indication of the agricultural acreage:

reverse

II	2)	3 li ki	3 thousand iku
	3)	ša-guᵏⁱ	of the village Šagu;
	4)	3 li ki	3 thousand iku
	5)	da-gúᵏⁱ	of the village Dagu;
	6)	1 li ki	a thousand iku
	7)	a-a-daᵏⁱ	of the village A'ada.
	8)	gi-duᵏⁱ	and Gidu
	9)	7 mi ki	7 hundred iku
	10)	gú-wa-luᵏⁱ	of the village Guwalu.

The text continues with the list of the acreage of the five other villages to conclude with the sum of 16,000 iku, corresponding exactly to the 57 kilometers squared mentioned above.

But cereals were not the only crops raised by the inhabitants of Ebla. From the ration lists and from the agricultural texts themselves it is evident that they also cultivated the vine.

Thus text 1847 mentions 300 tuns of wine which the man in charge of viticulture consigned to the governor of the kingdom. Though this is a sporadic bit of information, one may assume that, like the cereals, the vintage must have been abundant.

In the third position belongs the cultivation of olives for the production of olive oil. TM.76.G.281 registers the casks of olive oil delivered by eight villages; it specifies 341 casks of oil described as "of the hillside."' Text TM.75.G.1767 records the acreage and the number of olive trees thereon. These olive groves are located in various villages, and the scope of the text is to indicate those charged with their care:

obverse

I	1)	2 *li* 2 *mi* 60 gána-kešda^(ki)	2,260 iku of cultivated ground
	2)	1 *li* giš-ì-giš	1,000 olive trees
	3)	lú-al-KU	in charge of

II	1)	*zú-ba-lum*	Zubalum
	2)	lú-*hu-ba-ra*	the man of Hubara
	3)	šu-ba₄-ti	has received;
	4)	1 *li* 1 *mi* gána-kešda^(ki)	1,100 iku of cultivated ground
	5)	5 *mi* giš-ì-giš	500 olive trees
	6)	al-KU	in charge of

III	1)	*ip-tù-[la]*	Iptula
	2)	lú-*en-na-il*	the man of Enna-Il
	3)	šu-ba₄-ti	has received;
	4)	6 *mi* gána-kešda^(ki)	600 iku of cultivated ground,
	5)	5 *mi* giš-ì-giš diri-diri	500 olive trees. . .

IV	1)	ga-sa^(ki)	from the town of Gasa.

Then follow the areas of various other villages which have Gasa as the chief town, without, however, any indications of the olive trees. The oil of Ebla was surely much sought after if it constitutes an article of export, as witnessed by several texts, of which one may be quoted:

obverse

I	1)	3 sìla ì-giš-du₁₀	3 sila of excellent oil
	2)	*ha-ra-yà*	Hara-Ya
	3)	šu-ba₄-ti	has received
	4)	4 sìla ì-giš-du₁₀	4 sila of excellent oil
	5)	*ši-in*	for
	6)	*du-bù-hu-ma-lik*	Dubuhu-Malik;

II	1)	2 sìla	2 sila
	2)	*ra-é-ak*^(ki)	(for the city of) Raeak
	3)	2 sìla	2 sila
	4)	*ì-mar*^(ki)	(for the city of) Emar,
	5)	2 sìla	2 sila
	6)	*tù-ub*^(ki)	(for the city of) Tub,
	7)	1 sìla	1 sila
	8)	*bur-ma-an*^(ki)	(for the city of) Burman,

reverse

I	1)	1 sìla	1 sila
	2)	*gàr-mu*^(ki)	(for the city of) Garmu,
	3)	1 sìla	1 sila
	4)	*lum-na-nu*^(ki)	(for the city of) Lumnanu,

	5) 1 sìla	1 sila	
	6) *i*-NE-*bu-ni*ᵏ ⁱ	(for the city of) Inebuni,	
II	1) 1 sìla	1 sila	
	2) *gú-da-da-núm*ᵏ ⁱ	(for the city of) Gudadanum,	
	3) 2 sìla	2 sila	
	4) *ur-sá-um*ᵏ ⁱ	(for the city of) Ursa'um.	

Not all of the nine cities mentioned here are identifiable, but the appearance among them of Emar, present-day Meskene on the Euphrates, suggests that Ebla's olive oil reached other kingdoms.

In addition to the growing of cereals, grapes, and olives, which doubtless form the nucleus of the agricultural wealth of Ebla's kingdom, the texts point to the existence of a very diversified production.

Malt, for instance, was intensely cultivated for brewing beer, surely the most common drink at Ebla as well as in the entire ancient Near East. Among the fruits figure the fig and the pomegranate, together with other species which have not yet been identified.

From this brief catalogue it appears that the crops raised are those proper to the Mediterranean regions. This accords with the westward extension of its kingdom, nor does the almost complete lack of date palms, so characteristic of the Mesopotamian belt, engender surprise.

This discussion would be incomplete without mention of plants raised for industrial purposes, such as the flax used by the highly developed textile industry of Ebla; linen was doubtless the number one article of export.

1.2. CATTLE BREEDING

When speaking of the royal table in Chapter V and of the old calendar in Chapter VI, we had occasion to mention quantities of small cattle. What is more, Ebla had need for small cattle, especially sheep, not only to feed its population, but also for the wool, a basic element of the textile industry.

The breeding of cattle, whether large or small, was intensely developed throughout the kingdom and the figures given by the texts are truly impressive. In three homogeneous texts, for example, the numbers of sheep destined as offerings to the gods and for other purposes are 10,796, 12,354, and 36,892.

Even more impressive are the figures gathered from those tablets dealing with the period inspection of cattle in the kingdom. TM.75.G.1846 registers 79,300 sheep of the king of Ebla, while TM.75.G.1582 records more than 80,000 sheep.

The following tablet records the number of sheep counted during the inspection carried out in the month of Iši as 72,240.

obverse

I	1) [2] *rí-ba*ₓ 2 *li-im* 1 *mi-at* 60 udu-udu igi-du₈	1) 22,160 sheep inspected,
II	1) [3] *rí-ba*ₓ 1 *li-im* 1 *mi-at* 40 sila₄-sila₄	1) 31,140 lambs
	2) 3 *li-im* udu-udu	2) 3,000 sheep
	3) šu-du₈	3) tax

III   1) kur^{ki}   1) of the mountain town
      2) *i-ḫuš-zi-nu*   2) Ihušzinu,
      3) 2 *mi-at* udu-udu-niga 3) 200 fat sheep
      4) 2 *mi-at* udu-udu   4) 200 sheep
      5) PA.USAN   5) superin-
         PA.USAN   tendent. . .

IV   1) 1 *mi-at* 50 udu-udu   1) 150 sheep
      2) *iš-tá-al*   2) Išta'al,
      3) 1 *mi-at* 50 udu-udu   3) 150 sheep

reverse

I   1) mu-túm   1) mutum taxes
      2) 1 *rí-ba*ₓ 3 *li-im* 2 *mi-at*   2) 13,200
         udu-udu igi-du₈   sheep inspected,
      3) *dar-mi-a*   3) Darmia,

II   1) 1 *li-im* 6 *mi-at* 10 udu-udu   1) 1,610 sheep
      2) PA.USAN   2) superin-
         PA.USAN   tendent...
      3) 4 *mi-at* 30 udu-udu   3) 430 sheep
      4) GIBIL.ZA-*il*   4) GIBIL.ZA-*il*,

III   1) en   1) for the king
      2) 2 mu   2) second year,

IV   1) an-še-gú 7 *rí-ba*ₓ 2 *li-im* 2 *mi-at* 40   1) total: 72,240
         udu-udu igi-du₈   sheep inspected,
      2) [it] u *i-ši*   2) month of Iši

This text proves all the more interesting when mentioning Ihušzinu and Darmia, two provincial governors of the kingdom, whose administrative role becomes so evident. Besides sheep, rams, and ewes, it explicitly lists 31,140 lambs, thus giving a good idea of the amount of sheep breeding practiced.

Other tablets are more explicit in distinguishing various species of small livestock; the following records goats and pigs alongside the sheep:

16 u₈   16 sheep
14 udu-nita   14 rams
23 megida   23 pigs
81 ùz-sal máš-sal   81 she-goats with he-goats
   máš-nita ti-la   and kids.

For the destination of the small livestock, see the Table on p. 91, where for 12,354 sheep there are seven precise assignments corresponding to their current uses.

But if the small livestock is preponderant, the large cattle are surely not lacking; text TM.75.G.2033, which lists 417 bull calves, proves the existence of large herds of oxen. Another tablet mentions 273 cattle coming from various districts of the kingdom.

Greater numbers of large livestock are documented as imports, such as that from the city Luatim:

1 *li-im* 3 *mi-at* gu₄-gu₄	1,300 oxen
en	of the king,
gàr-ra	(delivered by) Garra
*lu-a-tim*ᵏ ⁱ	of the city Luatim.

Another document yields information about the delivery of heads of large cattle to the palace from some villages situated around Ebla:

1 áb	1 cow
*ri-du*ᵏ ⁱ	from the village Ridu,
2 áb	2 cows
*za-ba-tù*ᵏ ⁱ	from the village Zabatu,
2 gu₄ 2 áb	2 oxen, 2 cows
*ur-lum*ᵏ ⁱ	from the village Urlum,
1 gu₄	1 ox
*gú-wa-lu*ᵏ ⁱ	from the village Guwalu,
2 áb	2 cows
*ni-zi-mu*ᵏ ⁱ	from the village Nizimu,
2 gu₄	2 oxen
*da-'à-wa*ᵏ ⁱ	from the village Da'awa,
2 gu₄ [ ] áb	2 oxen [ ] cows
*zu-ra-mu*ᵏ ⁱ	from the village Zuramu.

Some bovids were destined for slaughter or as offerings to the gods, but for the most part they served for work in the fields, an activity which, curiously enough, has found no documentation in the archives. Equally surprising is the lack of references to beasts of burden. The tablets frequently talk about messengers traversing the whole Near East and we know they traveled on carts, but thus far no mention of beasts of burden has come to our knowledge.

1.3. INDUSTRY

The third source of wealth for the state of Ebla was the industry which may be considered the chief activity of this newly discovered people. To be sure, it was more a question of transforming raw materials imported from outside the country, but once exported through the complex commercial network, these transformed materials formed the true wealth of Ebla.

The textile industry must be mentioned first. This consisted of working the wool and the flax to produce fabrics in the state spinning mills. Since the most significant texts will be quoted in connection with commerce (section 4), it will suffice here to cite some brief pieces which will give an idea of the extraordinary production of cloths in Ebla:

2 *li-im* 4 *mi-at* 50 lá-3 túg-túg	2,447 fabrics;
30 *é-da-um-* túg-2	30 Edaum fabrics of second quality,
2 *mi-at* 30 lá-3 íb-túg-ša₆-dar	227 Ib fabrics of top quality and multicolored;
61 íb-túg-dar	61 multicolored Ib fabrics
al-gál	present
é-síg	in the spinning mill.

This brief but clear inventory tablet confirms the existence in the city of a spinning mill called "house of wool," where materials of various colors and qualities were produced. Very similar to the preceding is this tablet, which reports more substantial quantities of fabrics:

5 *li* 8 *mi* 91 túg-túg	5,891 fabrics;
70 lá-1 *é-da-um*-túg-2	69 Edaum fabrics of second quality;
4 *mi-at* 80 íb-túg-ša₆-dar	480 fabrics of top quality and multicolored;
2 *li* 2 *mi* 34 íb-túg-dar	2,234 Ib fabrics, multicolored,
al-gál	present.

The different quantities documented in the examples previously cited confirm the character of simple inventory of the material existing at a given moment, which does not mean to include the entire production or to detail all the kinds of cloth manufactured in Ebla.

As a matter of fact, the series of kinds of cloth that Ebla exported to all the world is much more variegated, and one must note with satisfaction that medieval and contemporary Syria has kept alive a millennia-old tradition.

Among the kinds of material produced in Ebla is damask. Linen or woolen fabrics intertwined with threads of gold, these have become so famous that they take their name from the present capital of Syria, Damascus. This tradition is ancient indeed, and though its populations have changed, Syria has faithfully preserved and transmitted for several millennia some techniques of workmanship that may have originated with Ebla.

Though the textile industry employed the largest percentage of workers, it was not the only enterprise at Ebla. The metal industry was no less impressive. When a tiny tablet reads "1,740 *ma-na* guškin al-gál," that is, "1,740 minas of gold present" (= circa 870 kilograms), then one begins to form an idea of Ebla's wealth and the modernity of its concepts.

The gold was not only crafted and re-exported but also served, as will be shown presently, as a commodity of international exchange. The first notice of this practice in the third millennium comes from these archives.

The texts mention not only enormous quantities of gold and numberless precious objects made from this metal but also indicate that the Eblaites appreciated diverse kinds of gold, more or less pure, which we today classify by carats. An example may be cited from TM.75.G.1479:

an-še-gú 1 *mi* 22 *ma-na* guškin-4	total: 122 minas of gold at 4
1 *li* 3 *mi* 36 *ma-na* 5 guškin 1-1/2	1,136 minas and 5 shekels of gold at 1-1/2,
bù-la-ù	Bulau.

It is still too early to determine the grade of purification of the gold and the signification of "at 4" and "one and a half," but it would appear that carats are intended.

Gold was the most precious metal, but silver was the most common among the precious metals; tons of it were on hand in Ebla. The reader may well suspect exaggeration, but the texts speak for themselves. After its defeat Mari had to pay Ebla tribute amounting to 2,193 minas of silver and 134 minas and 26 shekels of gold, which correspond to a ton of silver and 60 kilograms of gold. Someone might ironically reply that this is typical Oriental rhetoric, but similar data crop up in economic texts where falsification cannot readily be admitted.

Moreover, Ebla must have been very rich in silver if it could afford "annual outlays" approaching tons as may be gathered from TM.75.G.1841 dealing with three years of King Ebrium's reign:

3 *li-im* 7 *mi-at* 96 *ma-na* 10 (gín) kù:babbar	3,796 minas and 10 shekels of silver
è	outlay
3 mu	of the third year;
1 *li-im* 7 *mi-at* 80 *ma-na* 50 (gín) kù:babbar	1,780 minas and 50 shekels of silver
2 mu	(outlay) of the second year;
2 *li* 6 *mi* 36 *ma-na* kù:babbar	2,636 minas of silver
wa	and
1 *mi-at* 1 *ma-na* kù:babbar	101 minas of silver
kaskal	(for) the voyage;
10 *ma-na* kù:babbar	101 minas of silver
bar-za-ma-ù	(for) Barzamau;
6 *ma-na* kù:babbar	6 minas of silver
*du-bù-hu*ᵈ*à-da*	(for) Dubuhu-Hada
an-šè-gu 2 *li* 8 *mi-at* 6 *ma-na* kù:babbar	Sum: 2,806 minas of silver
è	outlay
1 mu	of the first year.
šu-nigín 8 *li* 3 *mi* 90 lá-1 kù:babbar	Total: 8,389 minas of silver.

On the strength of this text alone, Ebla's outlays in just three years exceeded four tons of silver subdivided thus:

3rd year	3,796 minas 10 shekels	= circa 2,000 kg.
2nd year	1,780 minas 50 shekels	= circa 900 kg.
1st year	2,806 minas	= circa 1,400 kg.

We do not know if the text furnishes information about all the outlays of silver by the state of Ebla or whether it treats of some specific budgets of only one department, but even then the wealth of this state exceeds all expectations. The same text goes on to list the expenditures of gold for six years of the reign, and it will serve a purpose to cite the second part of the document so that a comparison of the two outlays may permit a verification of how much the Eblaites appreciated gold:

10 lá-1 *ma-na* 30 (gín) guškin	9 minas and 30 shekels of gold (at 4)
10 lá -1 *ma-na* 10 (gín) guškin-2-1/2	9 minas and 10 shekels of gold at 2-1/2, outlay
è	outlay
6 mu	of the sixth year;
30 *ma-na* guškin-4	30 minas of gold at 4,
[65 *ma*]-*na* 50 (gín) guškin	65 minas and 50 shekels of gold (at 2-1/2),
5 mu	(outlay) of the fifth year;
1 *ma-na* 5 (gín) guškin-4	1 mina and 5 shekels of gold at 4,
70 lá-1 *ma-na* *ša-pi* guškin-2-1/2	69 minas and 40 shekels of gold at 2-1/2
4 mu	(outlay) of the fourth year,
1 *ma-na* 52 (gín) guškin-4	1 mina and 52 shekels of gold at 4,
46 *ma-na* 35 (gín) guškin	46 minas and 35 shekels of gold (at 2-1/2),

3 mu	(outlay) of the third year;
56 *ma-na*	56 minas and
25 (gin) guškin-4	25 shekels of gold at 4,
1 *mi-at* 64 *ma-na*	164 minas and
30 (gín) guškin-2-1/2	30 shekels of gold at 2-1/2,
è	outlay
2 mu	of the second year;
an-šè-gú 96 *ma-na*	sum: 96 minas and
5 (gín) guškin-4	5 shekels of gold at 4,
4 *mi* 5 *ma-na ša-pi*	405 minas and
7 (gín) guškin-2-1/2	47 shekels of gold at 2-1/2,
è	outlay.

From this text it appears that the outlays of silver with respect to gold are, for the same stretch of time, 16 times superior; this shows that gold was certainly considered more valuable than silver. This tablet is also important for revealing a degree of purity of gold unknown till now, namely, 2-1/2.

Among the other precious metals, copper, tin, lead, and bronze also figure. Text 1656 mentions 209 minas of bronze received by the "metal worker."

The third type of industry deals with precious stones. Two kinds deserve attention, as they are frequently encountered in the texts: carnelian and lapis lazuli. The discovery at Ebla of an undressed block of lapis lazuli brings to mind TM.75.G.1599 which reads:

obverse

I	1)	1 *ma-na* 10 (gín) za:gìn	1 mina and 10 shekels of lapis lazuli
	2)	*a-du-lum*	Adulum
	3)	nagar	the smith
	4)	šu-ba₄-ti	has received;
II	1)	13-1/2 (gín) za:gìn	13 and a half shekels of lapis lazuli
	2)	*a-bù-ma-lik*	Abu-Malik
	3)	šu-ba₄-ti	has received.

The very small quantities received by the two smiths underline how precious must have been this stone which, according to current opinion, was imported from Afghanistan.

Before concluding this discussion, it may be instructive to cite a text dealing with silver and gold and their utilization. Only thus will a clearer idea of the Eblaites and their activities take shape. As the final clause reveals, 56 minas and 50 shekels of silver were used as purchase and sale, exchange, donation, and taxes of governors.

obverse

I	1)	8 *ma-na* kù:babbar	8 minas of silver
	2)	UNKEN-aka	to make
	3)	an-dùl	a statue;
	4)	15 *ma-na* kù:babbar	15 minas of silver
	5)	šu-bala-aka	to be converted
	6)	3 *ma-na* guškin	into 3 minas of gold
	7)	UNKEN-aka	to make
II	1)	an-dùl	a statue,
	2)	ni-du8	a gift
	3)	en	of the king

	4) é	for the temple
	5) ᵈ'à-da	of Hada;
	6) 1 *ma-na* kù:babbar	1 mina of silver
	7) šu-bala-aka	to be converted
	8) 6 2-NI gín-dilmun guškin	into 6 and 2/3 shekels of gold
	9) 2 *gú-li-lum*	(for) two bracelets
III	1) ᵈ*ku-ra*	of the god Kura,
	2) 5 3-NI gín-dilmun guškin	(and) into 5 and 1/3 shekels of gold
	3) UNKEN-aka	to make
	4) gír-gír-dingir	daggers of the divinity
	5) 1 *ma-na ša-pi* gín-dilmun kù:babbar	1 mina and 40 shekels of silver
	6) ní-šam$_x$	price
	7) 1 *mi-at* na$_4$:síg-ša$_6$	of 100 "threads" of fine wool
	8) 6 gín-dilmun kù:babbar	6 shekels of silver
IV	1) šu-bala-aka	to be converted
	2) 3 gín-dilmun MI + ŠITA$_x$-gul za:gín-si$_4$-si$_4$	into 2 shekels of ...clear reddish lapis lazuli;
	3) 4 *ma-na* kù:babbar	4 minas of silver
	4) nì-sam$_x$	price
	5) 10 zára-túg	of 10 Zar fabrics
	2 aktum-túg	2 Aktum fabrics
	2 íb + 3-babbar-túg	of white Ib,
	1 nì-lá-sag	and 10 foulards;
	6) 10 gín-dilmun kù:babbar	10 shekels of silver,
	7) nì-šam$_x$	price
V	1) udu:nita:ša$_6$	of excellent rams
	2) *áš-ti*	from
	3) *kab-lu$_5$-ul*ᵏⁱ	the city of Kablul;
	4) 4 *ma-na* 50 gín-dilmun kù:babbar	4 minas and 50 shekels of silver
	5) nì-šam$_x$	price
	6) 1 *mi-at* 45 sal-túg	of 145 fine fabrics
	7) *iš$_x$-ki*	for
	8) *ìr-ra-ku*ᵏⁱ	the city of Irraku;
VI	1) 2(+x) *ma-na* 7 gín-dilmun kù:babbar	2(+x) minas and 7 shekels of silver,
	2) ní-šam$_x$	price
	3) 1 gír-mar-tu guškin-sa$_6$	of one Martu dagger of fine gold;
	4) ku$_5$ 6 gín-dilmun kù:babbar	36 shekels of silver
	5) UNKEN-aka	to make
	6) ᵍⁱˢban-ᵍⁱˢban	bows
	7) guruš-guruš	of the officials;
VII	1) 5 gín-dilmun kù:babbar	5 shekels of silver
	2) kešda	"alloy"
	3) gr-mar-tu zu-ᵈa-ama	of point of Martu dagger of A'ama

4) nin-uš-bu   Ninushu
5) šu-ba₄-ti   has received
6) 3 gín-dilmun kù:babbar   3 shekels of silver;
7) 1 šu ba₄-ti   first receipt
8) 3 gín-dilmun kù:babbar   3 shekels of silver;

VIII 1) 2 šu-ba₄-ti   second receipt
   2) 1 gín-dilmun kù:babbar   one shekel of silver;
   3) 3 šu ba₄ti   third receipt
   4) *a-na-ma-lik*   Ana-Malik
   5) šu-ba₄-ti   has received
   6) 5 gín-dilmun kù:babbar   5 shekels of silver;
   7) *ít-tá-gàr*   Iltagar
   8) l ú *i-gi*   the man of Tgi.

reverse

I   1) šu ba₄-ti   has received
   2) [3] gín-dilmun kù:babbar   3 shekels of silver;
   3) 2 BU.DI   2 Budi pins
   4) [x]-ti   ...-ti
   5) ExPAP   house...
   6) ama   the mother
   7) *i-[ti]-da-ši-[in]*   of Iti-Dašin,
   8) 15 *ma-na* kù:babbar   15 minas of silver
   9) 1 nì-gú   1 Nigu object

II   1) al-gál   present
   2) é   in the palace
   3) en   of the king;
   4) 5 *ma-na* kù:babbar   5 minas of silver
   5) šu-bala-aka   to be converted
   6) ku₅ guškin   into 30 shekels of gold
   7) 2 *gú-li-lum*   for 2 bracelets
   8) *zàr-i-iq-da-mu*   of Zariq-Damu;

III   1) gur₈ 4 gín-dilmun guškin   24 shekels of gold
   2) giš-PI-lá   for...
   3) *ir_x-kab-du-lum*   of Irkab-Dulum;

IV   1) an-še-gu 56 *ma-na* 50 gín-   total: 56 minas,
    -dilmun kù:babbar   50 shekels of silver;
   2) dub-gar   tablet concerning
   3) nì-šam_x   purchase sale,
   4) šu-bala-aka   exchange,
   5) nì-ba   gift
   6) mul   for the divinity;
   7) mu-túm   tax

V   1) lugal-lugal   of the governors,
   2) 2 mu   second year,
   3) itu *M Axganatenû*-sag   month: M Axganatenû-sag.

Hittite Land Deed

Besides law codes, few other sources survive for the Hittites. Fortunately, a number of title deeds and estate inventories have been found which provide information on Hittite society and economy. It is worth considering the Hittite land deed in comparison to the archive for Ebla.

Source: *Gurney, O.R. The Hittites (United Kingdom: Penguin, 1960), 66–67.*

Focus Questions:
1. What does the estate of Tiwataparas tell us about property and wealth for individuals?
2. Where on the social scale do you think he is?
3. In what order are the people ranked? Why?

Estate of Tiwataparas: 1 man, Tiwataparas; 1 boy, Hartuwandulis; 1 woman, Azzias; 2 girls, Anittis and Hantawiyas; (total) 5 persons; 2 oxen, 22 sheep, 6 draught-oxen...; [18] ewes, and with the ewes 2 female lambs, and with the rams 2 male lambs; 18 goats, and with the goats 4 kids, and with the he-goat 1 kid; (total) 36 small cattle: 1 house. As pasture for oxen, 1 acre of meadow in the town Parkalla. 3 1/2 acres of vineyard, and in it 40 apple-trees, 42 pomegranate-trees, in the town Hanzusra, belonging to the estate of Hantapis.

Hesiod, Excerpt from *Works and Days*

Hesiod was a Greek poet living around 700 BCE; he was in fact a rough contemporary of Homer. Hesiod's poem reflected more on the mundane subjects of daily life as opposed to Homer's grand epics. In Works and Days, *Hesiod submits that labor is the fate of all men, but he feels that hard work is rewarded and idleness punished. The poem also contains bits of folklore and common wisdom. His other work,* Theogony, *is more mythological in tone as it concerns the origins of the world and of the Gods.*

Source: *Translated by Hugh G. Evelyn-White, 1914.*

Focus Questions:
1. How does Hesiod's description of ships and sailing differ from our sources referencing Phoenicia?
2. What is Hesiod's opinion of sea-trading? Why?
3. In regard to farming, has anything changed compared to our earlier sources?

(ll. 571-581) But when the House-carrier (26) climbs up the plants from the earth to escape the Pleiades, then it is no longer the season for digging vineyards, but to whet your sickles and rouse up your slaves. Avoid shady seats and sleeping until dawn in the harvest season, when the sun scorches the body. Then be busy, and bring home your fruits, getting up early to make your livelihood sure. For dawn takes away a third part of your work, dawn advances a man on his journey and advances him in his work—dawn which appears and sets many men on their road, and puts yokes on many oxen.

(ll. 582-596) But when the artichoke flowers (27), and the chirping grass-hopper sits in a tree and pours down his shrill song continually from under his wings in the season of wearisome heat, then goats are plumpest and wine sweetest; women are most wanton, but men are feeblest, because Sirius parches head and knees and the skin is dry through heat. But at that time let me have a shady rock and wine of Biblis, a clot of curds and milk of drained goats with the flesh of an heifer fed in the woods, that has never calved, and of firstling kids; then also let me drink bright wine, sitting in the shade, when my heart is satisfied with food, and so, turning my head to face the fresh Zephyr, from the everflowing spring which pours down unfouled thrice pour an offering of water, but make a fourth libation of wine.

(ll. 597-608) Set your slaves to winnow Demeter's holy grain, when strong Orion (28) first appears, on a smooth threshing-floor in an airy place. Then measure it and store it in jars. And so soon as you have safely stored all your stuff indoors, I bid you put your bondman out of doors and look out for a servant-girl with no children—for a servant with a child to nurse is troublesome. And look after the dog with jagged teeth; do not grudge him his food, or some time the Day-sleeper (29) may take your stuff. Bring in fodder and litter so as to have enough for your oxen and mules. After that, let your men rest their poor knees and unyoke your pair of oxen.

(ll. 609-617) But when Orion and Sirius are come into mid-heaven, and rosy-fingered Dawn sees Arcturus (30), then cut off all the grape-clusters, Perses, and bring them home. Show them to the sun ten days and ten nights: then cover them over for five, and on the sixth day draw off into vessels the gifts of joyful Dionysus. But when the Pleiades and Hyades and strong Orion begin to set (31), then remember to plough in season: and so the completed year (32) will fitly pass beneath the earth.

(ll. 618-640) But if desire for uncomfortable sea-faring seize you; when the Pleiades plunge into the misty sea (33) to escape Orions rude strength, then truly gales of all kinds rage. Then keep ships no longer on the sparkling sea, but bethink you to till the land as I bid you. Haul up your ship upon the land and pack it closely with stones all round to keep off the power of the winds which blow damply, and draw out the bilge-plug so that the rain of heaven may not rot it. Put away all the tackle and fittings in your house, and stow the wings of the sea-going ship neatly, and hang up the well-shaped rudder over the smoke. You yourself wait until the season for sailing is come, and then haul your swift ship down to the sea and stow a convenient cargo in it, so that you may bring home profit, even as your father and mine, foolish Perses, used to sail on shipboard because he lacked sufficient livelihood. And one day he came to this very place crossing over a great stretch of sea; he left Aeolian Cyme and fled, not from riches and substance, but from wretched poverty which Zeus lays upon men, and he settled near Helicon in a miserable hamlet, Ascra, which is bad in winter, sultry in summer, and good at no time.

(ll. 641-645) But you, Perses, remember all works in their season but sailing especially. Admire a small ship, but put your freight in a large one; for the greater the lading, the greater will be your piled gain, if only the winds will keep back their harmful gales.

(ll. 646-662) If ever you turn your misguided heart to trading and with to escape from debt and joyless hunger, I will show you the measures of the loud-roaring sea, though I have no skill in sea-faring nor in ships; for never yet have I sailed by ship over the wide sea, but only to Euboea from Aulis where the Achaeans once stayed through much storm when they had gathered a great host from divine Hellas for Troy, the land of fair women. Then I crossed over to Chalcis, to the games of wise Amphidamas where the sons of the great-hearted hero proclaimed and appointed prizes. And there I boast that I gained the victory with a song and carried off an handled tripod which I dedicated to the Muses of Helicon, in the place where they first set me in the way of clear song. Such is all my experience of many-pegged ships; nevertheless I will tell you the will of Zeus who holds the aegis; for the Muses have taught me to sing in marvellous song.

(ll. 663-677) Fifty days after the solstice (34), when the season of wearisome heat is come to an end, is the right time for me to go sailing. Then you will not wreck your ship, nor will the sea destroy the sailors, unless Poseidon the Earth-Shaker be set upon it, or Zeus, the king of the deathless gods, wish to slay them; for the issues of good and evil alike are with them. At that time the winds are steady, and the sea is harmless. Then trust in the winds without care, and haul your swift ship down to the sea and put all the freight no board; but make all haste you can to return home again and do not wait till the time of the new wine and autumn rain and oncoming storms with the fierce gales of Notus who accompanies the heavy autumn rain of Zeus and stirs up the sea and makes the deep dangerous.

(ll. 678-694) Another time for men to go sailing is in spring when a man first sees leaves on the topmost shoot of a fig-tree as large as the foot-print that a cow makes; then the sea is passable, and this is the spring sailing time. For my part I do not praise it, for my heart does not like it. Such a sailing is snatched, and you will hardly avoid mischief. Yet in their ignorance men do even this, for wealth means life to poor mortals; but it is fearful to die among the waves. But I bid you consider all these things in your heart as I say. Do not put all your goods in hallow ships; leave the greater part behind, and put the lesser part on board; for it is a bad business to meet with disaster among the waves of the sea, as it is bad if you put too great a load on your waggon and break the axle, and your goods are spoiled. Observe due measure: and proportion is best in all things.

(ll. 695-705) Bring home a wife to your house when you are of the right age, while you are not far short of thirty years nor much above; this is the right age for marriage. Let your wife have been grown up four years, and marry her in the fifth. Marry a maiden, so that you can teach her careful ways, and especially marry one who lives near you, but look well about you and see that your marriage will not be a joke to your neighbours. For a man wins nothing better than a good wife, and, again, nothing worse than a bad one, a greedy soul who roasts her man without fire, strong though he may be, and brings him to a raw (35) old age.

(ll. 706-714) Be careful to avoid the anger of the deathless gods. Do not make a friend equal to a brother; but if you do, do not wrong him first, and do not lie to please the tongue. But if he wrongs you first, offending either in word or in deed, remember to repay him double; but if he ask you to be his friend again and be ready to give you satisfaction, welcome him. He is a worthless man who makes now one and now another his friend; but as for you, do not let your face put your heart to shame (36).

(ll. 715-716) Do not get a name either as lavish or as churlish; as a friend of rogues or as a slanderer of good men.

(ll. 717-721) Never dare to taunt a man with deadly poverty which eats out the heart; it is sent by the deathless gods. The best treasure a man can have is a sparing tongue, and the greatest pleasure, one that moves orderly; for if you speak evil, you yourself will soon be worse spoken of.

(ll. 722-723) Do not be boorish at a common feast where there are many guests; the pleasure is greatest and the expense is least (37).

(ll. 724-726) Never pour a libation of sparkling wine to Zeus after dawn with unwashed hands, nor to others of the deathless gods; else they do not hear your prayers but spit them back.

(ll. 727-732) Do not stand upright facing the sun when you make water, but remember to do this when he has set towards his rising. And do not make water as you go, whether on the road or off the road, and do not uncover yourself: the nights belong to the blessed gods. A scrupulous man who has a wise heart sits down or goes to the wall of an enclosed court.

(ll. 733-736) Do not expose yourself befouled by the fireside in your house, but avoid this. Do not beget children when you are come back from ill-omened burial, but after a festival of the gods.

(ll. 737-741) Never cross the sweet-flowing water of ever-rolling rivers afoot until you have prayed, gazing into the soft flood, and washed your hands in the clear, lovely water. Whoever crosses a river with hands unwashed of wickedness, the gods are angry with him and bring trouble upon him afterwards.

(ll. 742-743) At a cheerful festival of the gods do not cut the withered from the quick upon that which has five branches (38) with bright steel.

(ll. 744-745) Never put the ladle upon the mixing-bowl at a wine party, for malignant ill-luck is attached to that.

(ll. 746-747) When you are building a house, do not leave it rough-hewn, or a cawing crow may settle on it and croak.

(ll. 748-749) Take nothing to eat or to wash with from uncharmed pots, for in them there is mischief.

(ll. 750-759) Do not let a boy of twelve years sit on things which may not be moved (39), for that is bad, and makes a man unmanly; nor yet a child of twelve months, for that has the same effect. A man should not clean his body with water in which a woman has washed, for there is bitter mischief in that also for a time. When you come upon a burning sacrifice, do not make a mock of mysteries, for Heaven is angry at this also. Never make water in the mouths of rivers which flow to the sea, nor yet in springs; but be careful to avoid this. And do not ease yourself in them: it is not well to do this.

(ll. 760-763) So do: and avoid the talk of men. For Talk is mischievous, light, and easily raised, but hard to bear and difficult to be rid of. Talk never wholly dies away when many people voice her: even Talk is in some ways divine.

(ll. 765-767) Mark the days which come from Zeus, duly telling your slaves of them, and that the thirtieth day of the month is best for one to look over the work and to deal out supplies.

(ll. 769-768) (40) For these are days which come from Zeus the all-wise, when men discern aright.

(ll. 770-779) To begin with, the first, the fourth, and the seventh—on which Leto bare Apollo with the blade of gold—each is a holy day. The eighth and the ninth, two days at least of the waxing month (41), are specially good for the works of man. Also the eleventh and twelfth are both excellent, alike for shearing sheep and for reaping the kindly fruits; but the twelfth is much better than the eleventh, for on it the airy-swinging spider spins its web in full day, and then the Wise One (42), gathers her pile. On that day woman should set up her loom and get forward with her work.

(ll. 780-781) Avoid the thirteenth of the waxing month for beginning to sow: yet it is the best day for setting plants.

(ll. 782-789) The sixth of the mid-month is very unfavourable for plants, but is good for the birth of males, though unfavourable for a girl either to be born at all or to be married. Nor is the first sixth a fit day for a girl to be born, but a kindly for gelding kids and sheep and for fencing in a sheep-cote. It is favourable for the birth of a boy, but such will be fond of sharp speech, lies, and cunning words, and stealthy converse.

(ll. 790-791) On the eighth of the month geld the boar and loud-bellowing bull, but hard-working mules on the twelfth.

(ll. 792-799) On the great twentieth, in full day, a wise man should be born. Such an one is very sound-witted. The tenth is favourable for a male to be born; but, for a girl, the fourth day of the mid-month. On that day tame sheep and shambling, horned oxen, and the sharp-fanged dog and hardy mules to the touch of the hand. But take care to avoid troubles which eat out the heart on the fourth of the beginning and ending of the month; it is a day very fraught with fate.

(ll. 800-801) On the fourth of the month bring home your bride, but choose the omens which are best for this business.

(ll. 802-804) Avoid fifth days: they are unkindly and terrible. On a fifth day, they say, the Erinyes assisted at the birth of Horcus (Oath) whom Eris (Strife) bare to trouble the forsworn.

(ll. 805-809) Look about you very carefully and throw out Demeter's holy grain upon the well-rolled (43) threshing floor on the seventh of the mid-month. Let the woodman cut beams for house building and plenty of ships' timbers, such as are suitable for ships. On the fourth day begin to build narrow ships.

(ll. 810-813) The ninth of the mid-month improves towards evening; but the first ninth of all is quite harmless for men. It is a good day on which to beget or to be born both for a male and a female: it is never an wholly evil day.

(ll. 814-818) Again, few know that the twenty-seventh of the month is best for opening a wine-jar, and putting yokes on the necks of oxen and mules and swift-footed horses, and for hauling a swift ship of many thwarts down to the sparkling sea; few call it by its right name.

(ll. 819-821) On the fourth day open a jar. The fourth of the mid-month is a day holy above all. And again, few men know that the fourth day after the twentieth is best while it is morning: towards evening it is less good.

(ll. 822-828) These days are a great blessing to men on earth; but the rest are changeable, luckless, and bring nothing. Everyone praises a different day but few know their nature. Sometimes a day is a stepmother, sometimes a mother. That man is happy and lucky in them who knows all these things and does his work without offending the deathless gods, who discerns the omens of birds and avoids transgressions.

Aristophanes, Excerpt from *The Birds*

Aristophanes (circa 448–380 BCE) was a Greek comic playwright. Writing in Athens during the long war with Sparta, his political satires reflected the often pessimistic mood of the times. He wrote about 40 plays of which 11 have survived including the classic anti-war piece Lysistrata, *and satires such as* The Clouds *(poking fun at Socrates) and* The Frogs *(satirizing several great tragic playwrights). The* Birds *was written in 414 BCE during the war and concerns the attempts of two men to leave busy Athens and seek a quiet and peaceful life elsewhere.*

Source: The Birds: The Complete Greek Drama, volume 2, *trans. by Eugene O'Neill, Jr. (New York, 1938).*

Focus Questions:
1. What is significant about the term citizen?
2. Why do the men want to leave Athens?
3. How do Aristophanes' values compare to Hesiod's?

Dramatis Personae

EUELPIDES
PITHETAERUS
TROCHILUS, Servant to Epops
Epops (the Hoopoe)
A BIRD
A HERALD
A PRIEST
A POET
AN ORACLE-MONGER
METON, a Geometrician
AN INSPECTOR
A DEALER IN DECREES
IRIS
A PARRICIDE
CINESIAS, a Dithyrambic Poet
AN INFORMER
PROMETHEUS
POSIDON
TRIBALLUS
HERACLES
SLAVES OF PITHETAERUS
MESSENGERS

CHORUS OF BIRDS
Scene

A wild and desolate region; only thickets, rocks, and a single tree are seen. EUELPIDES and PITHETAERUS enter, each with a bird in his hand.

EUELPIDES *to his jay*
Do you think I should walk straight for yon tree?

PITHETAERUS *to his crow*
Cursed beast, what are you croaking to me?...to retrace my steps?

EUELPIDES
Why, you wretch, we are wandering at random, we are exerting ourselves only to return to the same spot; we're wasting our time.

PITHETAERUS
To think that I should trust to this crow, which has made me cover more than a thousand furlongs!

EUELPIDES
And that I, in obedience to this jay, should have worn my toes down to the nails!

PITHETAERUS
If only I knew where we were...

EUELPIDES
Could you find your country again from here?

PITHETAERUS
No, I feel quite sure I could not, any more than could Execestides find his.

EUELPIDES
Alas!

PITHETAERUS
Aye, aye, my friend, it's surely the road of "alases" we are following.

EUELPIDES
That Philocrates, the bird-seller, played us a scurvy trick, when he pretended these two guides could help us to find Tereus, the Epops, who is a bird, without being born of one. He has indeed sold us this jay, a true son of Tharrhelides, for an obolus, and this crow for three, but what can they do? Why, nothing whatever but bite and scratch!

To his jay

What's the matter with you then, that you keep opening your beak? Do you want us to fling ourselves headlong down these rocks? There is no road that way.

PITHETAERUS
Not even the vestige of a trail in any direction

EUELPIDES
And what does the crow say about the road to follow?

PITHETAERUS
By Zeus, it no longer croaks the same thing it did.

EUELPIDES
And which way does it tell us to go now?

PITHETAERUS
It says that, by dint of gnawing, it will devour my fingers.

EUELPIDES
What misfortune is ours! We strain every nerve to get to the crows, do everything we can to that end, and we cannot find our way! Yes, spectators, our madness is quite different from that of Sacas. He is not a citizen, and would fain be one at any cost; we, on the contrary, born of an honorable tribe and family and living in the midst of our fellow-citizens, we have fled from our country as hard as ever we could go. It's not that we hate it; we recognize it to be great and rich, likewise that everyone has the right to ruin himself paying taxes; but the crickets only chirrup among the fig-trees for a month or two, whereas the Athenians spend their whole lives in chanting forth judgments from their law-courts. That is why we started off with a basket, a stew-pot and some myrtle boughs! And have come to seek a quiet country in which to settle. We are going to Tereus, the Epops, to learn from him, whether, in his aerial flights, he has noticed some town of this kind.

Early Criminal Justice: The Nippur Murder Trial and the "Silent Wife"

One of the earliest known examples of a criminal justice proceeding was the trial of men accused of murdering a temple servant (nishakku) at Nippur. The Assembly of Nippur, whose responsibility it was to render a verdict, also had to make a ruling on the situation of the victim's wife, who had been informed of the murder (by the murderers) after the crime had been committed, but had chosen to remain silent on the matter, and was therefore prosecuted as an accessory to murder.

Source: *Kramer, Samuel Noah.* From the Tablets of Sumer. *Indian Hills, Co: Falcon's Wing Press, 1956, pp. 53–54.*

Focus Questions:
1. What possible motive is suggested for the wife's "silence"?
2. Summarize briefly the argument presented, and accepted by the Assembly, for sparing the wife's life.
3. What appears to have been the standard legal procedure in Sumerian criminal cases, and how might it compare/contrast to contemporary procedure in the U.S. legal system?

Nanna-sig, the son of Lu-Sin, Ku-Enlil, the son of Ku-Nanna, the barber, and Enlil-ennam, the slave of Adda-kalla, the gardener, killed Lu-lnanna, the son of Lugal-apindu, the nishakku-official.

After Lu-Inanna, the son of Lugal-apindu, had been put to death, they told Nin-dada, the daughter of Lu-Ninurta, the wife of Lu-Inanna, that her husband Lu-Inanna had been killed.

Nin-dada, the daughter of Lu-Ninurta, opened not her mouth, (her) lips remained sealed.

Their case was (then) brought to (the city) Isin before the king, (and) the King Ur-Ninurta ordered their case to be taken up in the Assembly of Nippur.

(There) Ur-gula, son of Lugal-.., Dudu, the bird-hunter, Ali-ellati, the dependent, Buzu, the son of Lu-Sin, Eluti, the son of..-Ea, Shesh-Kalla, the porter (?), Lugal-Kan, the gardener, Lugal-azida, the son of Sin-andul, (and) Shesh-kalla, the son of Shara-.., faced (the Assembly) and said:

"They who have killed a man are not (worthy) of life. Those three males and that woman should be killed in front of the chair of Lu-Inanna, the son of Lugal-apindu, the nishakku-official."

(Then) Shu..-lilum, the..-official of Ninurta, (and) Ubar-Sin, the gardener, faced (the Assembly) and said:

"Granted that the husband of Nin-dada, the daughter of Lu-Ninurta, had been killed, (but) what had (?) the woman done (?) that she should be killed?"

(Then) the (members of the) Assembly of Nippur faced (them) and said:

"A woman whose husband did not support (?) her—granted that she knew her husband's enemies, and that (after) her husband had been killed she heard that her husband had been killed—why should she not remain silent (?) about (?) him? Is it she (?) who killed her husband? The punishment of those (?) who (actually) killed should suffice."

In accordance with the decision (?) of the Assembly of Nippur, Nanna-sig, the son of Lu-Sin, Ku-Enlil, the son of Ku-Nanna, the barber, and Enlil-ennam, the slave of Adda-kalla, the gardener, were handed over (to the executioner) to be killed.

(This is) a case taken up by the Assembly of Nippur.

Praise of the Scribe's Profession: Egyptian Letter

A scribe was typically a royal or temple official, one of the few literate, and so ranked higher than the illiterate masses. This document is a letter of advice from a high-level government official to his son, exhorting him to learn the skills of a scribe. This document gives us insight into the demanding and perilous existence of the majority of the ancient Egyptian population, as well as the attitude of Egyptian elites toward various types of work.

Source: *Lichtheim, Miriam.* Ancient Egyptian Literature: A Book of Readings. Volume 2: The New Kingdom. *Berkeley, CA: University of California Press, 1976.*

Focus Questions:
1. What sorts of class distinctions are described in this document?
2. What daily pleasures and activities are described?
3. Why describe the life of the peasant and the soldier so bleakly?

PAPYRUS LANSING

Title

[Beginning of the instruction in letter-writing made by the royal scribe and chief overseer of the cattle of Amen-Re, King of Gods, Nebmare-nakht.] For his apprentice, the scribe Wenemdiamun.

Praise of the Scribe's Profession

[The royal scribe] and chief overseer of the cattle of Amen-[Re, King of Gods. Nebmare-nakht speaks to the scribe Wenemdiamun]. [Apply yourself to this] noble profession... You will find it useful... You will be advanced by your superiors. You will be sent on a mission... Love writing, shun dancing; then you become a worthy official. Do not long for the marsh thicket. Turn your back on throw stick and chase. By day write with your fingers; recite by night. Befriend the scroll, the palette. It pleases more than wine. Writing for him who knows it is better than all other professions. It pleases more than bread and beer, more than clothing and ointment. It is worth more than an inheritance in Egypt, than a tomb in the west.

Advice to the Unwilling Pupil

Young fellow, how conceited you are! You do not listen when I speak. Your heart is denser than a great obelisk, a hundred cubits high, ten cubits thick. When it is finished and ready for loading, many work gangs draw it. It hears the words of men; it is loaded on a barge. Departing from Yebu it is conveyed, until it comes to rest on its place in Thebes.

So also a cow is bought this year, and it plows the following year. It learns to listen to the herdsman; it only lacks words. Horses brought from the fields, they forget their mothers. Yoked they go up and down in all his majesty's errand. They become like those that bore them, that stand in the stable. They do their utmost for fear of a beating.

But although I beat you with every kind of stick, you do not listen. If I knew another way of doing it, I would do it for you, that you might listen. You are a person fit for writing, through you have not yet known a woman. Your heart discerns. Your fingers are skilled, your mouth is apt for reciting.

Writing is more enjoyable than enjoying a basket of...and beans; more enjoyable than a mother's giving birth, when her heart knows no distaste. She is constant in nursing her son; her breast is in his mouth every day. Happy is the heart [of] him who writes; he is young each day.

All Occupations Are Bad Except That of the Scribe

See for yourself with your own eye. The occupations lie before you.

The washer man's day is going up, going down. All his limbs are weak, [from] whitening his neighbors' clothes every day, from washing their linen.

The maker of pots is smeared with soil, like one whose relations have died. His hands, his feet are full of clay, he is like one who lives in the bog.

The cobbler mingles with vats. His odor is penetrating. His hands are red with madder, like one who is smeared with blood. He looks behind him for the kite, like one whose flesh is exposed.

The watchman prepares garlands and polishes vase-stands. He spends a night of toil just as one on whom the sun shines.

The merchants travel downstream and upstream. They are as busy as can be, carrying goods from one town to another. They supply him who has wants. But the tax collectors carry off the gold, that most precious of metals.

The ships' crews from every house (of commerce), they receive their loads. They depart from Egypt for Syria, and each man's god is with him. (But) not one of them says: "We shall see Egypt again!"

The carpenter who is in the shipyard carries the timber and stacks it. If he gives today the Output of yesterday, woe to his limbs! The shipwright stands behind him to tell him evil things.

His outworker who is in the fields, his is the toughest of all the jobs. He spends the day loaded with his tools, tied to his tool box. When he returns home at night, he is loaded with the tool box and the timbers, his drinking mug, and his whet-stones.

The scribe, he alone, records the output of all of them. Take note of it!

The Misfortunes of the Peasant

Let me also expound to you the situation of the peasant, that other tough occupation. [Comes] the inundation and soaks him...he attends to his equipment. By day he cuts his farming tools; by night he twists rope. Even his midday hour he spends on farm labor. He equips himself to go to the field as if he were a warrior. The dried field lies before him; he goes out to get his team. When he has been after the herdsman for many days, he gets his team and comes back with it. He makes for it a place in the field. Comes dawn, he goes to make a start and does not find it in its place. He spends three days searching for it; he finds it in the bog. He finds no hides on them; the jackals have chewed them. He comes out, his garment in his hand, to beg for himself a team.

When he reaches his field he finds [it] broken up. He spends time cultivating, and the snake is after him. It finishes off the seed as it is cast to the ground. He does not see a green blade. He does three plowings with borrowed grain. His wife has gone down to the merchants and found nothing for barter. Now the scribe lands on the shore. He surveys the harvest. Attendants are behind him with staffs, Nubians with clubs. One says (to him): "Give grain." "There is none." He is beaten savagely. He is bound, thrown in the well, submerged head down. His wife is bound in his presence. His children are in fetters. His neighbors abandon them and flee. When it's over, there is no grain.

If you have any sense, be a scribe. If you have learned about the peasant, you will not be able to be one. Take note of it!...

The Scribe Does Not Suffer Like the Soldier

Furthermore, look, I instruct you to make you sound; to make you hold the palette freely. To make you become one whom the king trusts; to make you gain entrance to treasury and granary. To make you receive the ship-load at the gate of the granary. To make you issue the offerings on feast days. You are dressed in fine clothes; you own horses. Your boat is on the river; you are supplied with attendants. You stride about inspecting. A mansion is built in your town. You have a powerful office, given you by the king. Male and female slaves are about you. Those who are in the fields grasp your hand, on plots that you have made. Look, I make you into a staff of life! Put the writings in your heart, and you will be protected from all kinds of toil. You will become a worthy official.

Do you not recall the (fate of) the unskilled man? His name is not known. He is ever burdened [like an ass carrying] in front of the scribe who knows what he is about.

Come, [let me tell] you the woes of the soldier, and how many are his supervisors; the general, the troop-commander, the officer who leads, the standard-bearer, the lieutenant, the scribe, the commander of fifty, and the garrison captain. They go in and out in the halls of the palace, saying: "Get laborers!" He is awakened at any hour. One is after his as (after) a donkey. He toils until the Aten (sun) sets in his darkness of night. He is hungry, his belly hurts; he is dead while yet alive. When he receives the grain-ration, having been released from duty, it is not good for grinding.

He is called up for Syria. He may not rest. There are no clothes, no sandals. The weapons of war are assembled at the fortress of Sile. His march is uphill through mountains. He drinks water every third day: it is smelly and tastes of salt. His body is ravaged by illness. The enemy comes, surrounds him with missiles, and life recedes from him. He is told: "Quick, forward, valiant soldier! Win for yourself a good name!" He does not know what he is about. His body is weak, his legs fail him. When victory is won, the captives are handed over to his majesty, to be taken to Egypt. The foreign woman faints on the march; she hangs herself [on] the soldier's neck. His knapsack drops, another grabs it while he is burdened with the woman. His wife and children are in their village; he dies and does not reach it. If he comes out alive, he is worn out from marching. Be he at large, be he detained, the soldier suffers. If he leaps and joins the deserters, all his people are imprisoned. He dies on the edge of the desert, and there is none to perpetuate his name. He suffers in death as in life. A big sack is brought for him; he does not know his resting place.

Be a scribe, and be spared from soldiering! You call and one says: "Here I am." You are safe from torments. Every man seeks to raise himself up. Take note of it!

Workings of Ma'at: "The Tale of the Eloquent Peasant"

The "Tale of the Eloquent Peasant" is among the most accomplished works of the Middle Kingdom, and underscores the basic concept of Ma'at (roughly translated as "the spirit of truth and righteousness") and the role of pharaoh as the paternal judge who sits at the court of last resort. The work also pays tribute to the power and beauty of the spoken word, even from such an unlikely source as the lips of the lowly peasant Khun-Anup.

Source: *Lichtheim, Miriam,* Ancient Egyptian Literature. *Berkeley, CA: University of California Press, 1975.*

Focus Questions:
1. What products did Khun-Aup bring with him on his journey to Egypt to trade for food?
2. What legal pretext/ruse did Nemtynakht employ to confiscate Khun-Anup's donkey?
3. What "appeals process" did Khun-Anup have to go through in order to receive pharaoh's ruling?
4. What does the story of Khun-Anup reveal about the Egyptian concept of justice and legality?

There was a man named Khun-Anup, a peasant of Salt-Field. He had a wife whose name was [Ma]rye. This peasant said to his wife: "Look here, I am going down to Egypt to bring food from there for my children. Go, measure for me the barley which is in the barn, what is left of [last year's] barley." Then she measured for him [twenty-six] gallons of barley. This peasant said to his wife: "Look, you have twenty gallons of barley as food for you and your children. Now make for me these six gallons of barley into bread and beer for every day in which [I shall travel]."

This peasant went down to Egypt. He had loaded his donkeys with rushes, rdmt-grass, natron, salt, sticks of ——, staves from Cattle-Country, leopard skins, wolf skins, ns3-plants, 'nw-stones, tnm-plants, hprwr-plants, s3hwt, s3skwt, miswt-plants, snt-stones, 'b3w-stones, ibs3-plants, inbi-plants, pidgeons, n'rw-birds, wgs-birds, wbn-plants, tbsw-plants, gngnt, earth-hair, and inst; in sum, all the good products of Salt-Field. This peasant went south toward Hnes. He arrived in the district of Perfefi, north of Medenyt. There he met a man standing on the riverbank whose name was Nemtynakht. He was the son of a man named Isri and a subordinate of the high steward Rensi, the son of Meru.

This Nemtynakht said, when he saw this peasant's donkeys which tempted his heart: "If only I had a potent divine image through which I could seize this peasant's goods!" Now the house of this Nemtynakht was at the beginning of a path which was narrow, not so wide as to exceed the width of a shawl. And one side of it was under water, the other under barley. This Nemtynakht said to his servant: "Go, bring me a sheet from my house." It was brought to him straightway. He spread it out on the beginning of the path, so that its fringe touched the water, its hem the barley.

Now this peasant came along the public road. Then this Nemtynakht said: "Be careful, peasant; don't step on my clothes!" This peasant said: "I'll do as you wish, my course is a good one." So he went up higher. This Nemtynakht said: "Will you have my barley for a path?" This peasant said: "My course is a good one. The riverbank is steep and our way is under barley, for you block the path with your clothes. Will you then not let us pass on the road?"

Just then one of the donkeys filled its mouth with a wisp of barley. This Nemtynakht said: "Now I shall seize your donkey, peasant, for eating my barley. It shall tread out grain for its offense!" This peasant said: "My course is a good one. Only one (wisp) is destroyed. Could I buy my donkey for its value, if you seize it for filling its mouth with a wisp of barley? But I know the lord of this domain; it belongs to the high steward Rensi, the son of Meru. He punishes every robber in this whole land. Shall I be robbed in his domain?" This Nemtynakht said: "Is this the saying people say: 'A poor man's name is pronounced for his master's sake.' It is I who speak to you, and you invoke the high steward!"

Then he took a stick of green tamarisk to him and thrashed all his limbs with it, seized his donkeys, drove them to his domain. Then this peasant wept very loudly for the pain of that which was done to him. This Nemtynakht said: "Don't raise your voice, peasant. Look, you are bound for the abode of the Lord of Silence!" This peasant said: "You beat me, you steal my goods, and now you take the complaint from my mouth! O Lord of Silence, give me back my things, so that I can stop crying to your dreadedness!"

This peasant spent the time of ten days appealing to this Nemtynakht who paid no attention to it. So this peasant proceeded southward to Hnes, in order to appeal to the high steward Rensi, the son of Meru. He found him coming out of the door of his house, to go down to his courthouse barge. This peasant said: "May I be allowed to acquaint you with this complaint? Might a servant of your choice be sent to me, through whom I could inform you of it?" So the high steward Rensi, the son of Meru, sent a servant of his choice ahead of him, and this peasant informed him of the matter in all its aspects.

Then the high steward Rensi, the son of Meru, denounced this Nemtynakht to the magistrates who were with him. Then they said to him: "Surely it is a peasant of his who has gone to someone else beside him. That is what they do to peasants of theirs who go to others beside them. That is what they do. Is there cause for punishing this Nemtynakht for a trifle of natron and a trifle of salt? If he is ordered to replace it, he will replace it." Then the high steward Rensi, the son of Meru, fell silent. He did not reply to these magistrates, nor did he reply to this peasant.

Now this peasant came to appeal to the high steward Rensi, the son of Meru. He said: "O high steward, my lord, greatest of the great, leader of all!

When you go down to the sea of justice
And sail on it with a fair wind,
No squall shall strip away your sail,
Nor will your boat be idle.
No accident will affect your mast,
Your yards will not break.
You will not founder when you touch land,
No flood will carry you away.
You will not taste the river's evils,
You will not see a frightened face.
Fish will come darting to you,
Fatted fowl surround you.
For you are father to the orphan,
Husband to the widow,
Brother to the rejected woman,
Apron to the motherless.

Let me make your name in this land according to all the good rules:

Leader free of greed,
Great man free of baseness,
Destroyer of falsehood,
Creator of rightness,
Who comes at the voice of the caller!
When I speak, may you hear!
Do justice, O praised one,
Who is praised by the praised;
Remove my grief, I am burdened,
Examine me, I am in need!

Now this peasant made this speech in the time of the majesty of King Nebkaure, the justified. Then the high steward Rensi, the son of Meru, went before his majesty and said: "My lord, I have found one among those peasants whose speech is truly beautiful. Robbed of his goods by a man who is in my service, he has come to petition me about it." Said his majesty: "As truly as you wish to see me in health, you shall detain him here, without answering whatever he says. In order to keep him talking, be silent. Then have it brought to us in writing, that we may hear it. But provide for his wife and his children. For one of those peasants comes here (only) just before his house is empty. Provide also for this peasant himself. You shall let food be given him without letting him know that it is you who gives it to him."

So they gave him ten loaves of bread and two jugs of beer every day. It was the high steward Rensi, the son of Meru, who gave it. He gave it to a friend of his, and he gave it to him. Then the high steward Rensi, the son of Meru, wrote to the mayor of Salt-Field about providing food for this peasant's wife, a total of three bushels of grain every day.

...

Now this peasant came to petition him a second time. He said: "O high steward, my lord, greatest of the great, richest of the rich, truly greater that his great ones, richer than his rich ones!

Rudder of heaven, beam of earth,
Plumb-line that carries the weight!
Rudder, drift not,
Beam, tilt not,
Plumb-line, swing not awry!

A great lord taking a share of that which is (now) ownerless; stealing from a lonely man? Your portion is in your house: a jug of beer and three loaves. What is that you expend to satisfy your clients? A mortal man dies along with his underlings; shall you be a man of eternity?

Is it not wrong, a balance that tilts,
A plummet that strays,
The straight becoming crooked?
Lo, justice flees from you,
Expelled from its seat!
The magistrates do wrong,
Right-dealing is bent sideways,
The judges snatch what has been stolen.
He who trims a matter's rightness makes it swing awry:
The breath-giver chokes him who is down,
He who should refresh makes pant.
The arbitrator is a robber,
The remover of need orders its creation.
The town is a floodwater,
The punisher of evil commits crimes!"

Said the high steward Rensi, the son of Meru: "Are your belongings a greater concern to you than that my servant might seize you?" This peasant said:

"The measurer of grain-heaps trims for himself,
He who fills for another shaves the other's share;
He who should rule by law commands theft,
Who then will punish crime?
The straightener of another's crookedness
Supports another's crime.
Do you find here something for you?
Redress is short, misfortune long,
A good deed is remembered.
This is the precept:
Do to the doer to make him do.
It is thanking a man for what he does,
Parrying a blow before it strikes,
Giving a commission to one who is skillful."

Oh for a moment of destruction, havoc in your vineyard, loss among your birds, damage to your water birds!

A man who saw has turned blind,
A hearer deaf,
A leader now leads astray!

…You are strong and mighty. Your arm is active, your heart greedy, mercy has passed you by. How miserable is the wretch whom you have destroyed! You are like a messenger of the Crocodile; you surpass the Lady of Pestilence! If you have nothing, she has nothing. If there's nothing against her, there's nothing against you. If you don't act, she does not act. The wealthy should be merciful; violence is for the criminal; robbing suits him who has nothing. The stealing done by the robber is the misdeed of one who is poor. One can't reproach him; he merely seeks for himself. But you are sated with your bread, drunken with your beer, rich in all kinds of [treasures].

Though the face of the steersman is forward, the boat drifts as it pleases. Though the king is in the palace, though the rudder is in your hand, wrong is done around you. Long is my plea, heavy my task. "What is the matter with him?" people ask.

Be a shelter, make safe your shore,
See how your quay is infested with crocodiles!
Straighten your tongue, let it not stray,
A serpent is this limb of man.
Don't tell lies, warn the magistrates,
Greasy baskets are the judges,
Telling lies is their herbage,
It weighs lightly on them.
Knower of all men's ways:
Do you ignore my case?
Savior from all water's harm:
See I have a course without a ship!
Guider to port of all who founder:
Rescue the drowning!
……"

Then this peasant came to petition him a third time; he said:

"High steward, my lord,
You are Re, lord of sky, with your courtiers,
Men's sustenance is from you as from the flood,
You are Hapy who makes green the fields,
Revives the wastelands.
Punish the robber, save the sufferer,
Be not a flood against the pleader!
Heed eternity's coming,
Desire to last, as is said:
Doing justice is breath for the nose.
Punish him who should be punished,
And none will equal your rectitude.
Does the hand-balance deflect?
Does the stand-balance tilt?
Does Thoth show favor

So that you may do wrong?
Be the equal of these three:
If the three show favor,
Then may you show favor!
Answer not good with evil,
Put not one in place of another!

My speech grows more than snmyt-weed, to assault the smell with its answers. Misfortune pours water till cloth will grow! Three times now to make him act!

By the sail-wind should you steer,
Control the waves to sail aright;
Guard from landing by the helm-rope,
Earth's rightness lies in justice!
Speak not falsely—you are great,
Act not lightly—you are weighty;
Speak not falsely—you are the balance,
Do not swerve—you are the norm!
You are one with the balance,
If it tilts you may tilt.
Do not drift, steer, hold the helm-rope!
Rob not, act against the robber,
Not great is one who is great in greed.
Your tongue is the plummet,
Your heart the weight,
Your two lips are its arms.
If you avert your face from violence,
Who then shall punish wrongdoing?
Lo, you are a wretch of a washerman,
A greedy one who harms a friend,
One who forsakes his friend for his client,
His brother is he who comes with gifts.
Lo, you are a ferryman who ferries him who pays,
A straight one whose straightness is splintered,
A storekeeper who does not let a poor man pass,
Lo, you are a hawk to the little people,
One who lives on the poorest of the birds.
Lo, you are a butcher whose joy is slaughter,
The carnage is nothing to him.
You are a herdsman...

"Hearer, you hear not! Why do you not hear? Now I have subdued the savage; the crocodile retreats! What is your gain? When the secret of truth is found, falsehood is thrown on its back on the ground. Trust not the morrow before it has come; none knows the trouble in it."

Now this peasant had made this speech to the high steward Rensi, the son of Meru, at the entrance to the courthouse. Then he had two guards go to him with whips, and they thrashed all his limbs.

This peasant said: "The son of Meru goes on erring. His face is blind to what he sees, deaf to what he hears; his heart strays from what is recalled to him.

You are like a town without a mayor,
Like a troop without a leader,

Like a ship without a captain,
A company without a chief.
You are a sheriff who steals,
A mayor who pockets,
A district prosecutor of crime
Who is the model for the (evil)-doer!"

...

Now this peasant came to petition him a fourth time. Finding him coming out of the gate of the temple of Harsaphes, he said: "O praised one, may Harsaphes praise you, from whose temple you have come!

Goodness is destroyed, none adhere to it,
To fling falsehood's back to the ground.
If the ferry is grounded, wherewith does one
cross?...

Is crossing the river on sandals a good crossing? No! Who now sleeps till daybreak? Gone is walking by night, travel by day, and letting a man defend his own good cause. But it is no use to tell you this; mercy has passed you by. How miserable is the wretch whom you have destroyed!

Lo, you are a hunter who takes his fill,
Bent on doing what he pleases;
Spearing hippopotami, shooting bulls,
Catching fish, snaring birds.
(But) none quick to speak is free from haste,
None light of heart is weighty in conduct.
Be patient so as to learn justice,
Restrain your [anger] for the good of the humble seeker.
No hasty man attains excellence,
No impatient man is leaned upon.

Let the eyes see, let the heart take notice. Be not harsh in your power lest trouble befall you. Pass over a matter, it becomes two. He who eats tastes; one addressed answers. It is the sleeper who sees the dream; and a judge who deserves punishment is a model for the (evil)doer. Fool, you are attacked! Ignorant man, you are questioned! Spouter of water, you are attained!

Steersman, let not drift your boat,
Life-sustainer, let not die,
Provider, let not perish,
Shade, let one not dry out,
Shelter, let not the crocodile snatch!
The fourth time I petition you!
Shall I go on all day?"

Now this peasant came to petition him a fifth time; he said:

"O high steward, my lord! The fisher of hwdw-fish, ------, the --- slays the iy-fish; the spearer of fish pierces the `wbb-fish; the ḏ3hbw-fisher attacks the p`kr-fish; and the catcher of wh`-fish ravages the river. Now you are like them! Rob not a poor man of his goods, a humble man whom you know! Breath to the poor are his belongings; he who takes them stops up his nose. It is to hear cases that you were installed, to judge between two, to punish the robber. But what you do is to uphold the thief! One puts one's trust in you, but you have become a transgressor! You were placed as a dam for the poor lest he drown, but you have become a swift current to him!

Now this peasant came to petition him a sixth time; he said: "O high steward my lord!

He who lessens falsehood fosters truth,
He who fosters the good reduces evil,
As satiety's coming removes hunger,
Clothing removes nakedness;
As the sky is serene after a storm,
Warming all who shiver;
As fire cooks what is raw,
As water quenches thirst.
Now see for yourself:
The arbitrator is a robber,
The peacemaker makes grief,
He who should soothe makes sore.
But he who cheats diminishes justice!
Rightly filled justice either falls short nor brims over.

If you acquire, give to your fellow; gobbling up is dishonest. But my grief will lead to parting; my accusation brings departure. The heart's intent cannot be known. Don't delay! Act on the charge! If you sever, who shall join? The sounding pole is in your hand; sound! The water is shallow! If the boat enters and is grounded, its cargo perishes on the shore.

You are learned, skilled, accomplished,
But not in order to plunder!
You should be the model for all men,
But your affairs are crooked!
The standard for all men cheats the whole land!
The vintner of evil waters his plot with crimes,
Until his plot sprouts falsehood,
His estate flows with crimes!"

Now this peasant came to petition him a seventh time; he said: "O high steward, my lord!

You are the whole land's rudder,
The land sails by your bidding;
You are the peer of Thoth,
The judge who is not partial.

My lord, be patient, so that a man may invoke you about his rightful cause. Don't be angry; it is not for you. The long-faced becomes short-tempered. Don't brood on what has not yet come, nor rejoice at what has not yet happened. The patient man prolongs friendship; he who destroys a case will not be trusted. If law is laid waste and order destroyed, no poor man can survive: when he is robbed, justice does not address him.

My body was full, my heart burdened. Now therefore it has come from my body. As a dam is breached and water escapes, so my mouth opened to speak. I plied my sounding pole, I bailed out my water; I have emptied what was in my body; I have washed my soiled linen. My speech is done. My grief is all before you. What do you want? But your laziness leads you astray; your greed makes you dumb; your gluttony makes enemies for you. But will you find another peasant like me? Is there an idler at whose house door a petitioner will stand?

...

There is no silent man whom you gave speech,
No sleeper whom you have wakened,
None downcast whom you have roused,
None whose shut mouth you have opened,
None ignorant whom you gave knowledge,
None foolish whom you have taught.
(Yet) magistrates are dispellers of evil,
Masters of the good,
Craftsmen who create what is,
Joiners of the severed head!"

Now this peasant came to petition him an eighth time; he said: "O high steward, my lord! Men fall low through greed. The rapacious man lacks success; his success is loss. Though you are greedy it does nothing for you. Though you steal you do not profit. Let a man defend his rightful cause!

Your portion is in your house; your belly is full. The grain-bin brims over; shake it, its overflow spoils on the ground. Thief, robber, plunderer! Magistrates are appointed to suppress crime. Magistrates are shelters against the aggressor. Magistrates are appointed to fight falsehood!

No fear of you makes me petition you; you do not know my heart. A humble man who comes back to reproach you is not afraid of him with whom he pleads. The like of him will not be brought you from the street!

You have your plot of ground in the country, your estate in the district, your income in the storehouse. Yet the magistrates give to you and you take! Are you then a robber? Does one give to you and the troop with you at the division of plots?

Do justice for the Lord of Justice
The justice of whose justice is real!
Pen, papyrus, palette of Thoth,
Keep away from wrongdoing!
When goodness is good it is truly good,
For justice is for eternity:
It enters the graveyard with its doer.
When he is buried and earth enfolds him,
His name does not pass from the earth;
He is remembered because of goodness,
That is the rule of god's command.

The hand-balance—it tilts not; the stand-balance—it leans not to one side. Whether I come, whether another comes, speak! Do not answer with the answer of silence! Do not attack one who does not attack you. You have no pity, you are not troubled, you are not disturbed! You do not repay my good speech which comes from the mouth of Re himself!

Speak justice, do justice,
For it is mighty;
It is great, it endures,
Its worth is tried,
It leads one to reveredness.

Does the hand-balance tilt? Then it is its scales which carry things. The standard has no fault. Crime does not attain its goal; he who is helpful reaches land."

...

Now this peasant came to petition him a ninth time; he said: "O high steward, my lord! The tongue is men's stand-balance. It is the balance that detects deficiency. Punish him who should be punished, and none shall equal your rectitude.—...When falsehood walks it goes astray. It does not cross in the ferry; it does not progress. He who is enriched by it has no children, has no heirs on earth. He who sails with it does not reach land; his boat does not moor at its landing place.

Be not heavy, nor yet light,
Do not tarry, nor yet hurry,
Be not partial, nor listen to desire.
Do not avert your face from one you know,
Be not blind to one you have seen,
Do not rebuff one who beseeches you.
Abandon this slackness,
Let your speech be heard.
Act for him who would act for you,
Do not listen to everyone,
Summon a man to his rightful cause!

A sluggard has no yesterday, one deaf to justice has no friend; the greedy has no holiday. When the accuser is a wretch, and the wretch becomes a pleader, his opponent is a killer. Here I have been pleading with you, and you have not listened to it. I shall go and plead about you to Anubis!"

...

Then the high steward Rensi, the son of Meru, sent two guards to bring him back. Then this peasant was fearful, thinking it was done so as to punish him for this speech he had made. This peasant said: "A thirsty man's approach to water, an infant's mouth reaching for milk, thus is a longed-for death seen coming, thus does his death arrive at last." Said the high steward Rensi, the son of Meru: "Don't be afraid, peasant; be ready to deal with me!" Said this peasant: "By my life! Shall I eat your bread and drink your beer forever?" Said the high steward Rensi, the son of Meru: "Now wait here and hear your petitions!" Then he had them read from a new papyrus roll, each petition in its turn. The high steward Rensi, the son of Meru, presented them to the majesty of King Nebkaure, the justified. They pleased his majesty's heart more than anything in the whole land. His majesty said: "Give judgment yourself, son of Meru!"

Then the high steward Rensi, the son of Meru, sent two guards [to bring Nemtynakht]. He was brought and a report was made of [all his property] ------ his wheat, his barley, his donkeys, ---, his pigs, his small cattle ------. --- of this Nemtynakht [was given] to this peasant ------.

Colophon: It is finished ------.

Ancestor Worship: from *The Shih-Ching*

During the Zhou period, families, both noble and common, sacrificed to their ancestors. These sacrifices were of the utmost importance and any neglect would bring about misfortune and calamity, for ancestors had the power to aid or punish their descendants.

Human sacrifice was practiced extensively during the Shang dynasty and to a lesser extent down to the third century BCE. The third selection decries the practice that "takes all our good men" in following the king in death. Duke Mu of Qin died in 621 BCE. The last selection is a conversation between a Zhou king and his minister and demonstrates the Chinese belief in the close interaction between the spirit world and the political environment. The king could not afford to lose the favor and protection of Heaven.

Source: *Arthur Waley,* The Book of Songs, *1937. Used by permission of Grove/Atlantic, Inc.*

Focus Questions:
1. What role did spirits play in the lives of the Chinese?
2. Why was it important to placate them?
3. How was human sacrifice regarded by the Chinese?

ABUNDANT IS THE YEAR

Abundant is the year, with much millet, much rice;
But we have tall granaries,
To hold myriads, many myriads and millions of grain.
We make wine, make sweet liquor,
We offer it to ancestor, to ancestress,
We use it to fulfill all the rites,
To bring down blessings upon each and all.

GLORIOUS ANCESTORS

Ah, the glorious ancestors
Endless, their blessings,
Boundless their gifts are extended;
To you, too, they needs must reach.
We have brought them clear wine;
They will give victory.
Here, too, is soup well seasoned,
Well prepared, well mixed.
Because we come in silence,
Setting all quarrels aside,
They make safe for us a ripe old age,
We shall reach the withered cheek, we shall go on and on.
With our leather-bound naves, our bronzeclad yokes,
With eight bells a-jangle
We come to make offering.
The charge put upon us is vast and mighty,
From Heaven dropped our prosperity,
Good harvests, great abundance.
They come [the ancestors], they accept,

They send down blessings numberless.
They regard the paddy-offerings, the offerings of first-fruits
That Tang's descendant brings.

HUMAN SACRIFICE

"Kio" sings the oriole
As it lights on the thorn-bush.
Who went with Duke Mu to the grave?
Yanxi of the clan Ziju.
Now this Yanxi
Was the pick of all our men;
But as he drew near the tomb-hole
His limbs shook with dread.
That blue one, Heaven,
Takes all our good men.
Could we but ransom him
There are a hundred would give their lives.

"Kio" sings the oriole
As it lights on the thorn-bush.
Who went with Duke Mu to the grave?
Zhonghang of the clan Ziju. Now this Zhonghang
Was the sturdiest of all our men;
But as he drew near the tomb-hole
His limbs shook with dread.
That blue one, Heaven,
Takes all our good men.
Could we but ransom him
There are a hundred would give their lives.

"Kio" sings the oriole
As it lights on the thorn-bush.
Who went with Duke
Mu to the grave?
Zhenhu of the clan Ziju.
Now this Quan-hu
Was the strongest of all our men;
But as he drew near the tomb-hole
His limbs shook with dread.
That blue one, Heaven,
Takes all our good men.
Could we but ransom him
There are a hundred would give their lives.

Chapter 5

Hinduism and Buddhism

Excerpt from the Upanishads

The Upanishads *(ninth to fifth centuries BCE) follow the* Rig Vedas *as the foundational literature for Indian spirituality. A significant transformation has occurred between the two. The Vedas consist of rituals to placate the gods who represent natural forces. The* Upanishads *renounce worldly matters for the inner spirit which seeks unity with the universal. There are several Upanishads each written at different times. The Kena Upanishad attempts to grasp ideas of the Brahma, who is the universal or absolute being. Brahma is typically conceptualized as a Trinity, Brahma the Creator, Vishnu the Preserver, and Siva the Transformer.*

Source: *Paramanada, Swami.* Upanishads.

Focus Questions:
1. According to the *Upanishads*, how does the universe work?
2. What are the differences between the *Upanishads* and pagan polytheistic religions?
3. What are the similarities to the later Monotheistic religions?

PART THIRD

I

The Brahman once won a victory for the Devas. Through that victory of the Brahman, the Devas became elated. They thought, "This victory is ours. This glory is ours." Brahman here does not mean a personal Deity. There is a Brahma, the first person of the Hindu Trinity; but Brahman is the Absolute, the One without a second, the essence of all. There are different names and forms which represent certain personal aspects of Divinity, such as Brahma the Creator, Vishnu the Preserver and Siva the Transformer; but no one of these can fully represent the Whole. Brahman is the vast ocean of being, on which rise numberless ripples and waves of manifestation. From the smallest atomic form to a Deva or an angel, all spring from that limitless ocean of Brahman, the inexhaustible Source of life. No manifested form of life can be independent of its source, just as no wave, however mighty, can be independent of the ocean. Nothing moves without that Power. He is the only Doer. But the Devas thought: "This victory is ours, this glory is ours."

II

The Brahman perceived this and appeared before them. They did not know what mysterious form it was.

III

They said to Fire: "O Jataveda (All–knowing)! Find out what mysterious spirit this is." He said: "Yes."

IV

He ran towards it and He (Brahman) said to him: "Who art thou?" "I am Agni, I am Jataveda," he (the Fire–god) replied.

V

Brahman asked: "What power resides in thee?" Agni replied: "I can burn up all whatsoever exists on earth."

VI

Brahman placed a straw before him and said: "Burn this." He (Agni) rushed towards it with all speed, but was not able to burn it. So he returned from there and said (to the Devas): "I was not able to find out what this great mystery is."

VII

Then they said to Vayu (the Air–god): "Vayu! Find out what this mystery is." He said: "Yes."

VIII

He ran towards it and He (Brahman) said to him: "Who art thou?" "I am Vayu, I am Matarisva (traveller of Heaven)," he (Vayu) said.

IX

Then the Brahman said: "What power is in thee?" Vayu replied: "I can blow away all whatsoever exists on earth."

X

Brahman placed a straw before him and said: "Blow this away." He (Vayu) rushed towards it with all speed, but was not able to blow it away. So he returned from there and said (to the Devas): "I was not able to find out what this great mystery is."

XI

Then they said to Indra: "O Maghavan (Worshipful One)! Find out what this mystery is." He said: "Yes"; and ran towards it, but it disappeared before him.

XII

Then he saw in that very space a woman beautifully adorned, Uma of golden hue, daughter of Haimavat (Himalaya). He asked: "What is this great mystery?" Here we see how the Absolute assumes concrete form to give knowledge of Himself to the earnest seeker. Brahman, the impenetrable mystery, disappeared and in His place appeared a personal form to represent Him. This is a subtle way of showing the difference between the Absolute and the personal aspects of Deity. The Absolute is declared to be unknowable and unthinkable, but He assumes deified personal aspects to make Himself known to His devotees. Thus Uma, daughter of the Himalaya, represents that personal aspect as the offspring of the Infinite Being; while the Himalaya stands as the symbol of the Eternal, Unchangeable One.

PART FOURTH

I

She (Uma) said: "It is Brahman. It is through the victory of Brahman that ye are victorious." Then from her words, he (Indra) knew that it (that mysterious form) was Brahman. Uma replied to Indra, "It is to Brahman that you owe your victory. It is through His power that you live and act. He is the agent and you are all only instruments in His hands. Therefore your idea that 'This victory is ours, this glory is ours,' is based on ignorance." At once Indra saw their mistake. The Devas, being puffed up with vanity, had thought they themselves had achieved the victory, whereas it was Brahman; for not even a blade of grass can move without His command.

II

Therefore these Devas,—Agni, Vayu and Indra—excel other Devas, because they came nearer to Brahman. It was they who first knew this spirit as Brahman.

III

Therefore Indra excels all other Devas, because he came nearest to Brahman, and because he first (before all others) knew this spirit as Brahman. Agni, Vayu and Indra were superior to the other Devas because they gained a closer vision; and they were able to do this because they were purer; while Indra stands as the head of the Devas, because he realized the Truth directly, he reached Brahman. The significance of this is that whoever comes in direct touch with Brahman or the Supreme is glorified.

IV

Thus the teaching of Brahman is here illustrated in regard to the Devas. He dashed like lightning, and appeared and disappeared just as the eye winks. The teaching as regards the Devas was that Brahman is the only Doer. He had appeared before them in a mysterious form; but the whole of the unfathomable Brahman could not be seen in any definite form; so at the moment of vanishing, He manifested more of His immeasurable glory and fleetness of action by a sudden dazzling flash of light.

V

Next (the teaching) is regarding Adhyatman (the embodied Soul). The mind seems to approach Him (Brahman). By this mind (the seeker) again and again remembers and thinks about Brahman. Only by the mind can the seeker after knowledge approach Brahman, whose nature in glory and speed has been described as like unto a flash of lightning. Mind alone can picture the indescribable Brahman; and mind alone, being swift in its nature, can follow Him. It is through the help of this mind that we can think and meditate on Brahman; and when by constant thought of Him the mind becomes purified, then like a polished mirror it can reflect His Divine Glory.

VI

That Brahman is called Tadvanam (object of adoration). He is to be worshipped by the name Tadvanam. He who knows Brahman thus, is loved by all beings. Brahman is the object of adoration and the goal of all beings. For this reason he should be worshipped and meditated upon as Tadvanam. Whoever knows Him in this aspect becomes one with Him, and serves as a clear channel through which the blessings of Brahman flow out to others. The knower of God partakes of all His lovable qualities and is therefore loved by all true devotees.

VII

The disciple asked: O Master, teach me the Upanishad. (The teacher replied:) The Upanishad has been taught thee. We have certainly taught thee the Upanishad about Brahman.

VIII

The Upanishad is based on tapas (practice of the control of body, mind and senses), dama (subjugation of the senses), karma (right performance of prescribed actions). The Vedas are its limbs. Truth is its support.

IX

He who knows this (wisdom of the Upanishad), having been cleansed of all sin, becomes established in the blissful, eternal and highest abode of Brahman, in the highest abode of Brahman.

Here ends this Upanishad.

This Upanishad is called Kena, because it begins with the inquiry: "By whom" (Kena) willed or directed does the mind go towards its object? From whom comes life? What enables man to speak, to hear and see? And the teacher in reply gives him the definition of Brahman, the Source and Basis of existence. The spirit of the Upanishads is always to show that no matter where we look or what we see or feel in the visible world, it all proceeds from one Source.

The prevailing note of all Vedic teaching is this: One tremendous Whole becoming the world, and again the world merging in that Whole. It also strives in various ways to define that Source, knowing which all else is known and without which no knowledge can be well established. So here the teacher replies: That which is the eye of the eye, the ear of the ear, that is the inexhaustible river of being which flows on eternally; while bubbles of creation rise on the surface, live for a time, then burst.

The teacher, however, warns the disciple that this eye, ear, mind, can never perceive It; for It is that which illumines speech and mind, which enables eye and ear and all sense—faculties to perform their tasks. "It is distinct from the known and also It is beyond the unknown." He who thinks he knows It, knows It not; because It is never known by those who believe that It can be grasped by the intellect or by the senses; but It can be known by him who knows It as the basis of all consciousness.

The knower of Truth says, "I know It not," because he realizes the unbounded, infinite nature of the Supreme. "Thou art this (the visible), Thou art That (the invisible), and Thou art all that is beyond," he declares. The ordinary idea of knowledge is that which is based on sense preceptions; but the knowledge of an illumined Sage is not confined to his senses. He has all the knowledge that comes from the senses and all that comes from Spirit.

The special purpose of this Upanishad is to give us the knowledge of the Real, that we may not come under the dominion of the ego by identifying ourselves with our body, mind and senses. Mortals become mortals because they fall under the sway of ego and depend on their own limited physical and mental strength. The lesson of the parable of the Devas and Brahman is that there is no real power, no real doer except God. He is the eye of the eye, the ear of the ear; and eyes, ears, and all our faculties have no power independent of Him. When we thus realize Him as the underlying Reality of our being, we transcend death and become immortal.

OM! PEACE! PEACE! PEACE!

Selections from the *Rig Veda*

The Rig Veda *is the foundational document of Indian civilization, dating probably around 1000 BCE. It consists of a set of creation myths and sacrificial rites and chants. Although written after the Harappan civilization, the scattered references to Harappa are evidence the oral traditions of the Vedas go back a long time. The verses address the natural forces of the world, which are often personified in the form of deities, such as Indra in the example given.*

Source: *Ralph T.H. Griffith, Translator [1896].*

Focus Questions:
1. How do the attributes of Indra reflect on the attributes of kingship?
2. What do the verse writers ask Indra to do or provide for them?
3. What force does Indra personify?

BOOK THE EIGHTH

HYMN LXXXVII. Indra.
1. To Indra sing a Sama hymn, a lofty song to Lofty Sage,
   To him who guards the Law, inspired, and fain for praise.
2. Thou, Indra, art the Conqueror: thou gavest splendour to the Sun.
   Maker of all things, thou art Mighty and All-God.
3. Radiant with light thou wentest to the sky, the luminous realm of heaven.
   ne Deities, Indra strove to win thee for their Friend.
4. Come unto us, O Indra, dear, still conquering, unconcealable,
   Vast as a mountain spread on all sides, Lord of Heaven.
5. O truthful Soma-drinker, thou art mightier than both the worlds.
   Thou strengthenest him who pours libation, Lord of Heaven.
6. For thou art he, O Indra, who stormeth all castles of the foe,
   Slayer of Dasyus, man's Supporter, Lord of Heaven.
7. Now have we, Indra, Friend of Song, sent our great wishes forth to thee,
   Coming like floods that follow floods.
8. As rivers swell the ocean, so, Hero, our prayers increase thy might,
   Though of thyself, O Thunderer, waxing day by day.
9. With holy song may bind to the broad wide-yoked car the Bay Steeds of the rapid God,
   Bearers of Indra, yoked by word.
10. O Indra, bring great strength to us, bring valour, Satakratu, thou most active, bring
    A hero conquering in war.
11. For, gracious Satakratu, thou hast ever been a Mother and a Sire to us,
    So now for bliss we pray to thee.
12. To thee, Strong, Much-invoked, who showest forth thy strength, O Satakratu, do I speak:
    So grant thou us heroic strength.

HYMN LXXXVIII. Indra.
1. O THUNDERER, zealous worshippers gave thee drink this time yesterday.
   So, Indra, listen here to those who bring the laud: come near unto our dwelling place.
2. Lord of Bay Steeds, fair-helmed, rejoice thee: this we crave. Here the disposers wait on thee.
   Thy loftiest glories claim our lauds beside the juice, O Indra, Lover of the Song.
3. Turning, as 'twere, to meet the Sun, enjoy from Indra all good things.
   When he who will be born is born with power we look to treasures as our heritage.

4. Praise him who sends us wealth, whose bounties injure none: good are the gifts which Indra. grants. He is not worth with one who satisfies his wish: he turns his mind to giving boons.

5. Thou in thy battles, Indra, art subduer of all hostile bands. Father art thou, all-conquering, canceling the curse, thou victor of the vanquisher.

6. The Earth and Heaven clung close to thy victorious might as to their calf two mother-cows. When thou attackest Vrtra all the hostile bands shrink and faint, Indra, at thy wrath.

7. Bring to your aid the Eternal One, who shoots and none may shoot at him, Inciter, swift, victorious, best of Charioteers. Tugrya's unvanquished Strengthener;

8. Arranger of things unarranged, e'en Satakratu, source of might, Indra, the Friend of all, for succour we invoke, Guardian of treasure, sending wealth.

HYMN LXXXIX Indra. Vak.

1. I MOVE before thee here present in person, and all the Deities follow behind me. When, Indra, thou securest me my portion, with me thou shalt perform heroic actions.

2. The food of meath in foremost place I give thee, thy Soma shall be pressed, thy share appointed. Thou on my right shalt be my friend and comrade; then shall we two smite dead full many a foeman.

3. Striving for strength bring forth a laud to Indra, a truthful hymn if he in truth existeth. One and another say, There is no Indra. Who hath beheld him? Whom then shall we honour?

4. Here am I, look upon me here, O singer. All that existeth I surpass in greatness. The Holy Law's commandments make me mighty. Rending with strength I rend the worlds asunder.

5. When the Law's lovers mounted and approached me as I sat alone upon the dear sky's summit. Then spake my spirit to the heart within me, My friends have cried unto me with their children.

6. All these thy deeds must be declared at Soma-feasts, wrought, Indra, Bounteous Lord, for him who sheds the juice, When thou didst open wealth heaped up by many, brought from far away to Sarablia, the Rsi's kin.

7. Now run ye forth your several ways; he is not here who kept you back. For hath not Indra sunk his bolt deep down in Vrtra's vital part?

8. On-rushing with the speed of thought within the iron fort he pressed; The Falcon went to heaven and brought the Soma to the Thunderer.

9. Deep in the ocean lies the bolt with waters compassed round about, And in continuous onward flow the floods their tribute bring to it.

10. When, uttering words which no one comprehended, Vak, Queen of Gods, the Gladdener, was seated, The heaven's four regions drew forth drink and vigour; now whither hath her noblest portion vanished?

11. The Deities generated Vak the Goddess, and animals of every figure speak her. May she, the Gladdener, yielding food and vigour, the Milch-cow Vak, approach us meetly lauded.

12. Step forth with wider stride, my comrade Visnu; make room, Dyaus, for the leaping of the lightning. Let us slay Vrtra, let us free the rivers let them flow loosed at the command of Indra.

7 - soma pavamana

1. FORTH on their way the glorious drops have flowed for maintenance of Law, Knowing this sacrifice's course.

2. Down in the mighty waters sinks the stream of meath, most excellent, Oblation best of all in worth.

3. About the holy place, the Steer true, guileless, noblest, hath sent forth Continuous voices in the wood.

4. When, clothed in manly strength, the Sage flows in celestial wisdom round,
    The Strong would win the light of heaven.
5. When purified, he sits as King above the hosts, among his folk,
    What time the sages bring him nigh.
6. Dear, golden-coloured, in the fleece he sinks and settles in the wood;
    The Singer shows his zeal in hymns.
7. He goes to Indra, Vayu, to the Asvins, as his custom is,
    With gladdening juice which gives them joy.
8. The streams of pleasant Soma flow to Bhaga, Mitra-Varuna,
    Well-knowing through his mighty powers.
    Heaven and Earth, riches of meath to win us wealth;
    Gain for us treasures and renown.

8 - soma pavamana

1. OBEYING Indra's dear desire these Soma juices have flowed forth,
    Increasing his heroic might.
2. Laid in the bowl, pure-flowing on to Vayu and the Asvins, may
    These give us great heroic strength.
3. Soma, as thou art purified, incite to bounty Indra's heart,
    To sit in place of sacrifice.
4. The ten swift fingers deck thee forth, seven ministers impel thee on;
    The sages have rejoiced in thee.
5. When through the filter thou art poured, we clothe thee with a robe of milk
    To be a gladdening draught for Gods.
6. When purified within the jars, Soma, bright red and golden-hued,
    Hath clothed him with a robe of milk.
7. Flow on to us and make us rich. Drive all our enemies away.
    O Indu, flow into thy Friend.
8. Send down the rain from heaven, a stream of opulence from earth. Give us,
    O Soma, victory in war.
9. May we obtain thee, Indra's drink, who viewest men and findest light,
    Gain thee, and progeny and food.

9 - soma pavamana

1. THE Sage of Heaven whose heart is wise, when laid between both hands and pressed,
    Sends us delightful powers of life.
2. On, onward to a glorious home; dear to the people void of guile,
    With excellent enjoyment, flow.
3. He, the bright Son, when born illumed his Parents who had sprung to life,
    Great Son great Strengtheners of Law.
4. Urged by the seven devotions he hath stirred the guileless rivers which
    Have magnified the Single Eye.
5. These helped to might the Youthful One, high over all, invincible,
    Even Indu, Indra! in thy law.
6. The immortal Courser, good to draw, looks down upon the Seven; the fount
    Hath satisfied the Goddesses
7. Aid us in holy rites, O Man: O Pavamana, drive away
    Dark shades that must be met in fight.
8. Make the paths ready for a hymn newer and newer evermore;
    Make the lights shine as erst they shone.
9. Give, Pavamana, high renown, give kine and steeds and hero sons;
    Win for us wisdom, win the light.

Vardhamana Mahavira, Selections from *Akaranga-sutra*, "Jain Doctrines and Practices of Nonviolence"

India has an ancient tradition of wandering ascetics and teachers preaching compassion and poverty. In the case of Mahavira (circa 560-490 BCE), his teachings became the central tenets for Jainism. Mahavira had been a wealthy prince who at age 30 renounced his property and family and all worldly pleasures to lead an ascetic life. He spent many years as a beggar and loner. After many hardships he began his own community and developed more fixed rules based on the five vows of nonviolence, truthfulness, no stealing, chastity, and no possessions.

Source: *Translation from Prakit by Herman Jacobi,* Jaina Sutras, *part I, in* The Sacred Books of the East. *New York: Dover Publications, 1968.*

Focus Questions:
1. According to Mahavira, what is sin?
2. What are his attitudes towards the body and the senses?
3. What is his attitude towards women? Why?

I. 3. For a year and a month he did not leave off his robe. Since that time the Venerable One, giving up his robe, was a naked, world-relinquishing, houseless (sage).

4. Then he meditated (walking) with his eye fixed on a square space before him of the length of a man. Many people assembled, shocked at the sight; they struck him and cried.

5. Knowing (and renouncing) the female sex in mixed gathering places, he meditated, finding his way himself: I do not lead a worldly life.

6. Giving up the company of all householders whomsoever, he meditated. Asked, he gave no answer; he went and did not transgress the right path.

7. For some it is not easy (to do what he did), not to answer those who salute; he was beaten with sticks, and struck by sinful people.

10. For more than a couple of years he led a religious life without using cold water; he realized singleness, guarded his body, had got intuition, and was calm.

11. Thoroughly knowing the earth-bodies and water-bodies and fire-bodies and wind-bodies, the lichens, seeds and sprouts,

12. He comprehended that they are, if narrowly inspected, imbued with life, and avoided to injure them; he, the Great Hero.

13. The immovable (beings) are changed to movable ones, and the movable beings to immovable ones; beings which are born in all states become individually sinners by their actions.

14. The Venerable One understands thus: he who is under the conditions (of existence), that fool suffers pain. Thoroughly knowing (karma), the Venerable One avoids sin.

15. The sage, perceiving the double (karma), proclaims the incomparable activity, he, knowing one; knowing the current of worldliness, the current of sinfulness, and the impulse.

16. Practicing the sinless abstinence from killing, he did no acts, neither himself nor with the assistance of others; he to whom women were known as the causes of all sinful acts, he saw (the true state of the world).

III. 7. Ceasing to use the stick (i.e. cruelty) against living beings, abandoning the care of the body, the houseless (Mahavira), the Venerable One, endures the thorns of the villages (i.e. the abusive language of the peasants), (being) perfectly enlightened.

8. As an elephant at the head of the battle, so was Mahavira there victorious. Sometimes he did not reach a village there in Ladha.

9. When he who is free from desires approached the village, the inhabitants met him on the outside, and attacked him, saying, 'Get away from here.'

10. He was struck with a stick, the fist, a lance, hit with a fruit, a clod, a potsherd. Beating him again and again, many cried.
11. When he once (sat) without moving his body, they cut his flesh, tore his hair under pains, or covered him with dust.
12. Throwing him up, they let him fall, or disturbed him in his religious postures; abandoning the care of his body, the Venerable One humbled himself and bore pain, free from desire.
13. As a hero at the head of the battle is surrounded on all sides, so was there Mahavira. Bearing all hardships, the Venerable One, undisturbed, proceeded (on the road to Nirvana)...

IV. 1. The Venerable One was able to abstain from indulgence of the flesh, though never attacked by diseases. Whether wounded or not wounded, he desired not medical treatment.
2. Purgatives and emetics, anointing of the body and bathing, shampooing and cleaning of the teeth do not behove him, after he learned (that the body is something unclean).
3. Being averse from the impressions of the senses, the Brahmana wandered about, speaking but little. Sometimes in the cold season the Venerable One was meditating in the shade.
4. In summer he exposes himself to the heat, he sits squatting in the sun; he lives on rough (food): rice, pounded jujube, and beans.
5. Using these three, the Venerable One sustained himself eight months. Sometimes the Venerable One did not drink for half a month or even for a month.
6. Or he did not drink for more than two months, or even six months, day and night, without desire (for drink). Sometimes he ate stale food.
7. Sometimes he ate only the sixth meal, or the eighth, the tenth, the twelfth; without desires, persevering in meditation.
8. Having wisdom, Mahavira committed no sin himself, nor did he induce others to do so, nor did he consent to the sins of others.

Siddhartha Gautama: "Identity and Non-identity"

Siddhartha Gautama (623–543 BCE) was also a prince who renounced property at age 30. After five years of seeking truth he meditated under the Bodhi tree and achieved enlightenment. Calling himself Buddha (the enlightened one) he then traveled around India teaching. After his death, Buddha's followers wrote down many of his teachings for posterity and to help others achieve enlightenment. Buddhist beliefs are based on the Four Noble Truths: life is suffering, the origin of suffering is attachment, cessation of suffering is achievable, and enlightenment may be achieved by the eightfold path. The alleviation of suffering, according to Buddha, is through detachment and moderation, not in hedonism or asceticism.

Source: Carua, Paul. The Gospel of Buddha, According to Old Records. *Chicago: The Open Court Publishing Company, 1894.*

Focus Questions:
1. How does Buddha compare law and belief?
2. How are the universal and the individual defined?
3. How would you interpret verse 25?

Kutadanta, the head of the Brahmans in the village of Danamati having approached the Blessed One respectfully, greeted him and said:

"I am told, O samana, that thou art the Buddha,
the Holy One, the All-knowing, the Lord of the World.

But if thou wert the Buddha,
wouldst thou not come like a king
in all thy glory and power?" [1]

Said the Blessed One:
"Thine eyes are holden.
If the eye of thy mind were undimmed
thou couldst see the glory and the power of truth." [2]

Said Kutadanta:
"Show me the truth and I shall see it.
But thy doctrine is without consistency.
If it were consistent, it would stand;
but as it is not, it will pass away." [3]

The Blessed One replied: *"The truth will never pass away."* [4]

Kutadanta said:
"I am told that thou teachest the law,
yet thou tearest down religion.
Thy disciples despise rites and abandon immolation,
but reverence for the gods can be shown only by sacrifices.
The very nature of religion consists in worship and sacrifice." [5]

Said the Buddha:
"Greater than the immolation of bullocks is the sacrifice of self.
He who offers to the gods his evil desires
will see the uselessness of slaughtering animals at the altar.
Blood has no cleansing power,
but the eradication of lust will make the heart pure.
Better than worshipping gods
is obedience to the laws of righteousness." [6]
Kutadanta, being of religious disposition
and anxious about his fate after death,
had sacrificed countless victims.
Now he saw the folly of atonement by blood.
Not yet satisfied, however, with the teachings of the Tathagata,

Kutadanta continued:
"Thou believest, O Master, that beings are reborn;
that they migrate in the evolution of life;
and that subject to the law of karma we must reap what we sow.
Yet thou teachest the non-existence of the soul!
Thy disciples praise utter self-extinction
as the highest bliss of Nirvana.
If I am merely a combination of the sankharas,
my existence will cease when I die.
If I am merely a compound of sensations and ideas and desires,
whither can I go at the dissolution of the body?" [7]

Said the Blessed One:
"O Brahman, thou art religious and earnest.

Thou art seriously concerned about thy soul.
Yet is thy work in vain because thou art lacking
in the one thing that is needful. [8]

"There is rebirth of character,
but no transmigration of a self
Thy thought-forms reappear,
but there is no egoentity transferred.
The stanza uttered by a teacher
is reborn in the scholar who repeats the words. [9]

"Only through ignorance and delusion do men indulge in the dream
that their souls are separate and self-existent entities. [10]

"Thy heart, O Brahman, is cleaving still to self;
thou art anxious about heaven
but thou seekest the pleasures of self in heaven,
and thus thou canst not see the bliss of truth
and the immortality of truth. [11]

"Verily I say unto thee:
The Blessed One has not come to teach death, but to teach life,
and thou discernest not the nature of living and dying. [12]

"This body will be dissolved
and no amount of sacrifice will save it.
Therefore, seek thou the life that is of the mind.
Where self is, truth cannot be;
yet when truth comes, self will disappear.
Therefore, let thy mind rest in the truth;
propagate the truth, put thy whole will in it, and let it spread.
In the truth thou shalt live for ever. [13]

"Self is death and truth is life.
The cleaving to self is a perpetual dying,
while moving in the truth
is partaking of Nirvana
which is life everlasting." [14]

Kutadanta said: *"Where, O venerable Master, is Nirvana?"* [15]

"Nirvana is wherever the precepts are obeyed,"
replied the Blessed One. [16]

"Do I understand thee aright," rejoined the Brahman,
"that Nirvana is not a place,
and being nowhere it is without reality?" [17]

"Thou dost not understand me aright," said the Blessed One,
"Now listen and answer these questions:
Where does the wind dwell?" [18]

"Nowhere," was the reply. [19]

Buddha retorted: *"Then, sir,*
there is no such thing as wind." [20]

Kutadanta made no reply;
and the Blessed One asked again:
"Answer me, O Brahman,
where does wisdom dwell?
Is wisdom a locality?" [21]

"Wisdom has no allotted dwelling-place," replied Kutadanta. [22]

Said the Blessed One:
"Meanest thou that there is no wisdom,
no enlightenment, no righteousness, and no salvation,
because Nirvana is not a locality?
As a great and mighty wind
which passeth over the world
in the heat of the day,
so the Tathagata comes to blow
over the minds of mankind
with the breath of his love,
so cool, so sweet, so calm, so delicate;
and those tormented by fever assuage their suffering
and rejoice at the refreshing breeze." [23]

Said Kutadanta:
"I feel, O Lord,
that thou proclaimest a great doctrine,
but I cannot grasp it.
Forbear with me that I ask again:
Tell me, O Lord, if there be no atman,
how can there be immortality?
The activity of the mind passeth,
and our thoughts are gone
when we have done thinking." [24]

Buddha replied:
"Our thinking is gone,
but our thoughts continue.
Reasoning ceases,
but knowledge remains." *[25]*

Said Kutadanta: *"How is that?*
Is not reasoning and knowledge the same?" [26]

The Blessed One explained the distinction by an illustration:
"It is as when a man wants,
during the night, to send a letter,
and, after having his clerk called,
has a lamp lit, and gets the letter written.
Then, when that has been done, he extinguishes the lamp.
But though the writing has been finished
and the light has been put out the letter is still there.

Thus does reasoning cease and knowledge remain;
and in the same way mental activity ceases,
but experience, wisdom, and all the fruits of our acts
endure." [27]

Kutadanta continued:
"Tell me, O Lord, pray tell me,
where, if the sankharas are dissolved, is the identity of my self?
If my thoughts are propagated, and if my soul migrates,
my thoughts cease to be my thoughts
and my soul ceases to be my soul.
Give me an illustration, but pray, O Lord,
tell me, where is the identity of my self?" [28]

Said the Blessed One:
"Suppose a man were to light a lamp;
would it burn the night through?" [29]

"Yes, it might do so," was the reply. [30]

"Now, is it the same flame that burns
in the first watch of the night as in the second?" [31]

Kutadanta hesitated.
He thought, *"Yes, it is the same flame,"*
but fearing the complications of a hidden meaning,
and trying to be exact, he said:
"No, it is not." [32]

"Then," continued the Blessed One,
"there are flames, one in the first watch
and the other in the second watch." [33]

"No, sir," said Kutadanta.
"In one sense it is not the same flame,
but in another sense it is the same flame.
It burns the same kind of oil,
it emits the same kind of light,
and it serves the same purpose." [34]

"Very well," said the Buddha,
"and would you call those flames
the same that have burned yesterday
and are burning now in the same lamp,
filled with the same kind of oil,
illuminating the same room?" [35]

"They may have been extinguished during the day," suggested Kutadanta. [36]

Said the Blessed One:
"Suppose the flame of the first watch
had been extinguished during the second watch,
would you call it the same if it burns again in the third watch?" [37]

Replied Kutadanta:
"In one sense it is a different flame,
in another it is not." [38]

The Tathagata asked again:
"Has the time that elapsed during the extinction of the flame
anything to do with its identity or non-identity?" [39]

"No, sir," said the Brahman, *"it has not.*
There is a difference and an identity,
whether many years elapsed or only one second,
and also whether the lamp
has been extinguished in the meantime or not." [40]

"Well, then, we agree that the flame of to-day
is in a certain sense the same as the flame of yesterday,
and in another sense it is different at every moment.
Moreover, the flames of the same kind,
illuminating with equal power the same kind of rooms
are in a certain sense the same." [41]

"Yes, sir," replied Kutadanta. [42]

The Blessed One continued:
"Now, suppose there is a man
who feels like thyself,
thinks like thyself,
and acts like thyself,
is he not the same man as thou?" [43]

"No, sir," interrupted Kutadanta. [44]

Said the Buddha:
"Dost thou deny that the same logic holds good for thyself
that holds good for the things of the world" [45]

Kutadanta bethought himself
and rejoined slowly: *"No, I do not.*
The same logic holds good universally;
but there is a peculiarity about my self
which renders it altogether different
from everything else and also from other selves.
There may be another man who feels exactly like me,
thinks like me, and acts like me;
suppose even he had the same name
and the same kind of possessions
he would not be myself." [46]

"True, Kutadanta," answered Buddha,
"he would not be thyself.
Now, tell me, is the person who goes to school one,
and that same person when he has finished his schooling another?

*Is it one who commits a crime, another
who is punished by having his hands and feet cut off?"* [47]

"They are the same," was the reply. [48]

"Then sameness is constituted by continuity only?" asked the Tathagata. [49]

"Not only by continuity," said Kutadanta,
"but also and mainly by identity of character." [50]

"Very well," concluded the Buddha,
*"then thou agreest that persons can be the same, in the same sense
as two flames of the same kind are called the same;
and thou must recognize that in this sense
another man of the same character
and product of the same karma
is the same as thou."* [51]

"Well, I do." said the Brahman. [52]

The Buddha continued:
*"And in this same sense alone art thou the same to-day as yesterday.
Thy nature is not constituted by the matter of which thy body consists
but by thy sankharas, the forms of the body, of sensations, of thoughts.
Thy person is the combination of the sankharas.
Wherever they are, thou art.
Whithersoever they go, thou goest.
Thus thou wilt recognize in a certain sense
an identity of thy self, and in another sense a difference.
But he who does not recognize the identity should deny all identity,
and should say that the questioner is no longer the same person
as he who a minute after receives the answer.
Now consider the continuation of thy personality,
which is preserved in thy karma.
Dost thou call it death and annihilation,
or life and continued life?"* [53]

"I call it life and continued life," rejoined Kutadanta,
*"for it is the continuation of my existence,
but I do not care for that kind of continuation.
All I care for is the continuation of self
in the other sense which makes of every man,
whether identical with me or not,
an altogether different person."* [54]

"Very well," said Buddha.
*"This is what thou desirest
and this is the cleaving to self.
This is thy error.
All compound things are transitory:
they grow and they decay.
All compound things are subject to pain:
they will be separated from what they love*

and be joined to what they abhor.
All compound things lack a self, an atman, an ego." [55]

"How is that?" asked Kutadanta. [56]

"Where is thy self?" asked the Buddha.
And when Kutadanta made no reply, he continued:
"Thy self to which thou cleavest is a constant change.
Years ago thou wast a small babe;
then, thou wast a boy;
then a youth, and now, thou art a man.
Is there any identity of the babe and the man?
There is an identity in a certain sense only.
Indeed there is more identity between the flames
of the first watch and the third watch,
even though the lamp might have been extinguished during the second watch.
Now which is thy true self,
that of yesterday, that of to-day, or that of to-morrow,
for the preservation of which thou clamourest?" [57]

Kutadanta was bewildered.

"Lord of the world," he said,
"I see my error, but I am still confused." [58]

The Tathagata continued:
"It is by a process of evolution that sankharas come to be.
There is no sankhara which has sprung into being without a gradual becoming.
Thy sankharas are the product of thy deeds in former existences.
The combination of thy sankharas is thy self.
Wheresoever they are impressed thither thy self migrates.
In thy sankharas thou wilt continue to live
and thou wilt reap in future existences
the harvest sown now and in the past." [59]

"Verily, O Lord," rejoined Kutadanta,
"this is not a fair retribution.
I cannot recognize the justice
that others after me will reap
what I am sowing now." [60]

The Blessed One waited a moment and then replied:
"Is all teaching in vain?
Dost thou not understand that those others are thou thyself?
Thou thyself wilt reap what thou sowest, not others. [61]

"Think of a man who is ill-bred and destitute,
suffering from the wretchedness of his condition.
As a boy he was slothful and indolent, and when he grew up
he had not learned a craft to earn a living.
Wouldst thou say his misery
is not the product of his own action,
because the adult is no longer the same person as was the boy? [62]

"Verily, I say unto thee:
Not in the heavens,
not in the midst of the sea,
not if thou hidest thyself away in the clefts of the mountains,
wilt thou find a place where thou canst escape the fruit of thine evil actions. [63]

"At the same time thou art sure
to receive the blessings of thy good actions. [64]

"The man who has long been travelling and who returns home in safety,
the welcome of kinsfold, friends, and acquaintances awaits.
So, the fruits of his good works bid him welcome
who has walked in the path of righteousness,
when he passes over from the present life into the hereafter." [65]

Kutadanta said:
"I have faith in the glory and excellency of thy doctrines.
My eye cannot as yet endure the light;
but I now understand that there is no self,
and the truth dawns upon me.
Sacrifices cannot save, and invocations are idle talk.
But how shall I find the path to life everlasting?
I know all the Vedas by heart and have not found the truth." [66]

Said the Buddha:
"Learning is a good thing; but it availeth not.
True wisdom can be acquired by practice only.
Practise the truth that thy brother is the same as thou.
Walk in the noble path of righteousness
and thou wilt understand that while there is death in self,
there is immortality in truth." [67]

Said Kutadanta:
"Let me take my refuge in the Blessed One,
in the Dharma, and in the brotherhood.
Accept me as thy disciple
and let me partake of the bliss of immortality." [68]

Buddhism: Excerpts from the *Dhammapada*

The Dhammapada contains over 400 verses spoken at various times by the Buddha compiled into a single book by his followers. The title may be translated in a variety of ways; a good rendition is The Path of Virtue. *The work itself consists mainly of a discussion of Buddhist morality; its main goal is to draw distinctions between an evil and a good way of life. More particularly, the author instructs novices in the requirements they must fulfill to become worthy Buddhist monks, wearing "the yellow gown."*

Source: *Trans. F. Max Müller.*

Focus Questions:
1. What traits do the good and evildoer share? Do these similar traits lead to similar results?
2. According to Buddha, What is the most beneficial type of companionship? The least?
3. Who is a fool's worst enemy?

THE TWIN VERSES

All that we are is the result of what we have thought: it is founded on our thoughts, it is made up of our thoughts. If a man speaks or acts with an evil thought..., pain follows him, as the wheel follows the foot of the ox that draws the carriage.

All that we are is the result of what we have thought: it is founded on our thoughts, it is made up of our thoughts. If a man speaks or acts with a pure thought, happiness follows him, like a shadow that never leaves him.

'He abused me, he beat me, he defeated me, he robbed me,'—in those who harbour such thoughts hatred will never cease.

'He abused me, he beat me, he defeated me, he robbed me,'—in those who do not harbour such thoughts hatred will cease.

For hatred does not cease by hatred at any time: hatred ceases by love, this is an old rule.

The world does not know that we must all come to an end here;—but those who know it, their quarrels cease at once.

He who lives looking for pleasures only, his senses uncontrolled, immoderate in his food, idle, and weak, Mâra (the tempter) will certainly overthrow him, as the wind throws down a weak tree.

He who lives without looking for pleasures, his senses well controlled, moderate in his food, faithful and strong, him Mâra will certainly not overthrow, any more than the wind throws down a rocky mountain.

He who wishes to put on the yellow dress without having cleansed himself from sin, who disregards also temperance and truth, is unworthy of the yellow dress.

But he who has cleansed himself from sin, is well grounded in all virtues, and regards also temperance and truth, he is indeed worthy of the yellow dress.

They who imagine truth in untruth, and see untruth in truth, never arrive at truth, but follow vain desires.

They who know truth in truth, and untruth in untruth, arrive at truth, and follow true desires.

As rain breaks through an ill-thatched house, passion will break through an unreflecting mind.

As rain does not break through a well thatched house, passion will not break through a well reflecting mind.

The evildoer mourns in this world, and he mourns in the next; he mourns in both. He mourns and suffers when he sees the evil of his own work.

The virtuous man delights in this world, and he delights in the next; he delights in both. He delights and rejoices when he sees the purity of his own work.

The evildoer suffers in this world, and he suffers in the next; he suffers in both. He suffers when he thinks of the evil he has done; he suffers more when going on the evil path.

The virtuous man is happy in this world, and he is happy in the next; he is happy in both. He is happy when he thinks of the good he has done; he is still more happy when going on the good path.

The thoughtless man, even if he can recite a large portion (of the law), but is not a doer of it, has no share in the priesthood, but is like a cowherd counting the cows of others.

The follower of the law, even if he can recite only a small portion (of the law), but, having forsaken passion and hatred and foolishness, possesses true knowledge and serenity of mind, he, caring for nothing in this world or that to come, has indeed a share in the priesthood.

CHAPTER III

Thought

As a fletcher makes straight his arrow, a wise man makes straight his trembling and unsteady thought, which is difficult to guard, difficult to hold back.

As a fish taken from his watery home and thrown on the dry ground, our thought trembles all over in order to escape the dominion of Mâra (the tempter).

It is good to tame the mind, which is difficult to hold in and flighty, rushing wherever it listeth; a tamed mind brings happiness.

Let the wise man guard his thoughts, for they are difficult to perceive, very artful, and they rush wherever they list; thoughts well guarded bring happiness.

Those who bridle their mind which travels far, moves about alone, is without a body, and hides in the chamber (of the heart), will be free from the bonds of Mâra (the tempter).

If a man's thoughts are unsteady, if he does not know the true law, if his peace of mind is troubled, his knowledge will never be perfect.

If a man's thoughts are not dissipated, if his mind is not perplexed, if he has ceased to think of good or evil, then there is no fear for him while he is watchful.

Knowing that this body is (fragile) like a jar, and making this thought firm like a fortress, one should attack Mâra (the tempter) with the weapon of knowledge, one should watch him when conquered, and should never rest.

Before long, alas! this body will lie on the earth, despised, without understanding, like a useless log.

Whatever a hater may do to a hater, or an enemy to an enemy, a wrongly directed mind will do us greater mischief.

Not a mother, not a father will do so much, nor any other relative; a well directed mind will do us greater service.

CHAPTER V

The Fool

Long is the night to him who is awake; long is a mile to him who is tired; long is life to the foolish who do not know the true law.

If a traveller does not meet with one who is his better, or his equal, let him firmly keep to his solitary journey; there is no companionship with a fool.

'These sons belong to me, and this wealth belongs to me,' with such thoughts a fool is tormented. He himself does not belong to himself; how much less sons and wealth?

The fool who knows his foolishness is wise at least so far. But a fool who thinks himself wise, he is called a fool indeed.

If a fool be associated with a wise man even all his life, he will perceive the truth as little as a spoon perceives the taste of soup.

If an intelligent man be associated for one minute only with a wise man, he will soon perceive the truth as the tongue perceives the taste of soup.

Fools of little understanding have themselves for their greatest enemies, for they do evil deeds which must bear bitter fruits.

That deed is not well done of which a man must repent, and the reward of which he receives crying and with a tearful face.

No, that deed is well done of which a man does not repent, and the reward of which he receives gladly and cheerfully.

As long as the evil deed done does not bear fruit, the fool thinks it is like honey; but when it ripens, then the fool suffers grief.

Let a fool month after month eat his food (like an ascetic) with the tip of a blade of Kusa grass, yet is he not worth the sixteenth particle of those who have well weighed the law?

An evil deed, like newly drawn milk, does not turn (suddenly); smouldering, like fire covered by ashes, it follows the fool.

CHAPTER VI

The Wise Man

If you see an intelligent man who tells you where true treasures are to be found, who shows what is to be avoided, and administers reproofs, follow that wise man; it will be better, not worse, for those who follow him.

Let him admonish, let him teach, let him forbid what is improper!—he will be beloved of the good, by the bad he will be hated.

Do not have evildoers for friends, do not have low people for friends; have virtuous people for friends, have for friends the best of men.

He who drinks in the law lives happily with a serene mind; the sage rejoices always in the law, as preached by the elect (Ariyas).

Well makers lead the water (wherever they like); fletchers bend the arrow; carpenters bend a log of wood; wise people fashion themselves.

As a solid rock is not shaken by the wind, wise people falter not amidst blame and praise.

Wise people, after they have listened to the laws, become serene, like a deep, smooth, and still lake.

Good people walk on whatever befalls, the good do not prattle, longing for pleasure; whether touched by happiness or sorrow wise people never appear elated or depressed.

If, whether for his own sake, or for the sake of others, a man wishes neither for a son, nor for wealth, nor for lordship, and if he does not wish for his own success by unfair means, then he is good, wise, and virtuous.

CHAPTER IX

Evil

If a man would hasten towards the good, he should keep his thought away from evil; if a man does what is good slothfully, his mind delights in evil.

If a man commits a sin, let him not do it again; let him not delight in sin; pain is the outcome of evil.

If a man does what is good, let him do it again; let him delight in it; happiness is the outcome of good.

Even an evildoer sees happiness as long as his evil deed has not ripened; but when his evil deed has ripened, then does the evildoer see evil.

Even a good man sees evil days, as long as his good deed has not ripened; but when his good deed has ripened, then does the good man see happy days.

Let no man think lightly of evil, saying in his heart, It will not come nigh unto me. Even by the falling of water—drops a water—pot is filled; the fool becomes full of evil, even if he gathers it little by little.

Let no man think lightly of good, saying in his heart. It will not come nigh unto me. Even by the falling of water—drops a water—pot is filled; the wise man becomes full of good, even if he gathers it little by little.

Let a man avoid evil deeds, as a merchant, if he has few companions and carries much wealth, avoids a dangerous road; as a man who loves life avoids poison.

He who has no wound on his hand, may touch poison with his hand; poison does not affect one who has no wound; nor is there evil for one who does not commit evil.

If a man offend a harmless, pure, and innocent person, the evil falls back upon that fool, like light dust thrown up against the wind.

Some people are born again; evildoers go to hell; righteous people go to heaven; those who are free from all worldly desires attain Nirvana.

CHAPTER XIII

The World

Do not follow the evil law! Do not live on in thoughtlessness! Do not follow false doctrine! Be not a friend of the world.

Rouse thyself! Do not be idle! Follow the law of virtue! The virtuous rest in bliss in this world and in the next.

Follow the law of virtue; do not follow that of sin. The virtuous rests in bliss in this world and in the next.

Look upon the world as a bubble, look upon it as a mirage; the king of death does not see him who thus looks down upon the world.

Come, look at this glittering world, like unto a royal chariot; the foolish are immersed in it, but the wise do not touch it.

He who formerly was reckless and afterwards became sober, brightens up this world, like the moon when freed from clouds.

He whose evil deeds are covered by good deeds, brightens up this world, like the moon when freed from clouds.

This world is dark, few only can see here; a few only go to heaven, like birds escaped from the net.

The swans go on the path of the sun, they go through the ether by means of their miraculous power; the wise are led out of this world, when they have conquered Mâra and his train.

If a man has transgressed one law, and speaks lies, and scoffs at another world, there is no evil he will not do.

The uncharitable do not go to the world of the gods; fools only do not praise liberality; a wise man rejoices in liberality, and through it becomes blessed in the other world.

Better than sovereignty over the earth, better than going to heaven, better than lordship over all worlds, is the reward of the first step in holiness.

CHAPTER XIV

The Buddha

He whose conquest is not conquered again, into whose conquest no one in this world enters, by what track can you lead him, the Awakened, the Omniscient, the trackless?

He whom no desire with its snares and poisons can lead astray, by what track can you lead him, the Awakened, the Omniscient, the trackless?

Even the gods envy those who are awakened and not forgetful, who are given to meditation, who are wise, and who delight in the repose of retirement (from the world).

Difficult (to obtain) is the conception of men, difficult is the life of mortals, difficult is the hearing of the True Law, difficult is the birth of the Awakened (the attainment of Buddhahood).

Not to commit any sin, to do good, and to purify one's mind, that is the teaching of (all) the Awakened.

The Awakened call patience the highest penance, longsuffering the highest Nirvana; for he is not an anchorite who strikes others, he is not an ascetic who insults others.

Not to blame, not to strike, to live restrained under the law, to be moderate in eating, to sleep and sit alone, and to dwell on the highest thoughts,—this is the teaching of the Awakened.

There is no satisfying lusts, even by a shower of gold pieces; he who knows that lusts have a short taste and cause pain, he is wise.

Even in heavenly pleasures he finds no satisfaction, the disciple who is fully awakened delights only in the destruction of all desires.

Men, driven by fear, go to many a refuge, to mountains and forests, to groves and sacred trees.

But that is not a safe refuge, that is not the best refuge; a man is not delivered from all pains after having gone to that refuge.

He who takes refuge with Buddha, the Law, and the Church; he who, with clear understanding, sees the four holy truths.

Viz, pain, the origin of pain, the destruction of pain, and the eightfold holy way that leads to the quieting of pain.

That is the safe refuge, that is the best refuge; having gone to that refuge, a man is delivered from all pain.

A supernatural person (a Buddha) is not easily found, he is not born everywhere. Wherever such a sage is born, that race prospers.

Happy is the arising of the awakened, happy is the teaching of the True Law, happy is peace in the church, happy is the devotion of those who are at peace.

He who pays homage to those who deserve homage, whether the awakened (Buddha) or their disciples, those who have overcome the host (of evils), and crossed the flood of sorrow, he who pays homage to such as have found deliverance and know no fear, his merit can never be measured by anybody.

CHAPTER XVI

Pleasure

He who gives himself to vanity, and does not give himself to meditation, forgetting the real aim (of life) and grasping at pleasure, will in time envy him who has exerted himself in meditation.

Let no man ever look for what is pleasant, or what is unpleasant. Not to see what is pleasant is pain, and it is pain to see what is unpleasant.

Let, therefore, no man love anything; loss of the beloved is evil. Those who love nothing, and hate nothing, have no fetters.

From pleasure comes grief, from pleasure comes fear; he who is free from pleasure knows neither grief nor fear.

From affection comes grief, from affection comes fear; he who is free from affection knows neither grief nor fear.

From lust comes grief, from lust comes fear; he who is free from lust knows neither grief nor fear.

From love comes grief, from love comes fear; he who is free from love knows neither grief nor fear.

From greed comes grief, from greed comes fear; he who is free from greed knows neither grief nor fear.

He who possesses virtue and intelligence, who is just, speaks the truth, and does what is his own business, him the world will hold dear.

CHAPTER XVII

Anger

Let a man leave anger, let him forsake pride, let him overcome all bondage! No sufferings befall the man who is not attached to name and form, and who calls nothing his own.

He who holds back rising anger like a rolling chariot, him I call a real driver; other people are but holding the reins.

Let a man overcome anger by love, let him overcome evil by good; let him overcome the greedy by liberality, the liar by truth!

Speak the truth, do not yield to anger; give, if thou art asked for little; by these three steps thou wilt go near the gods.

The sages who injure nobody, and who always control their body, they will go to the unchangeable place (Nirvana), where, if they have gone, they will suffer no more.

Those who are ever watchful, who study day and night, and who strive after Nirvana their passions will come to an end.

This is an old saying, O Atula, this is not only of today: 'They blame him who sits silent, they blame him who speaks much, they also blame him who says little; there is no one on earth who is not blamed.'

There never was, there never will be, nor is there now, a man who is always blamed, or a man who is always praised.

But he whom those who discriminate praise continually day after day, as without blemish, wise, rich in knowledge and virtue, who would dare to blame him like a coin made of gold from the Gambû river? Even the gods praise him, he is praised even by Brahman.

Beware of bodily anger, and control thy body! Leave the sins of the body, and with thy body practice virtue!

Beware of the anger of the tongue, and control thy tongue! Leave the sins of the tongue, and practice virtue with thy tongue!

Beware of the anger of the mind, and control thy mind! Leave the sins of the mind, and practice virtue with they mind!

The wise who control their body, who control their tongue, the wise who control their mind, are indeed well controlled.

CHAPTER XVIII

Impurity

Thou art now like a sere leaf, the messengers of death have come near to thee; thou standest at the door of thy departure, and thou hast no provision for thy journey.

Make thyself an island, work hard, be wise! When thy impurities are blown away, and thou art free from guilt, thou wilt enter into the heavenly world of the elect.

Thy life has come to an end, thou art come near to death, there is no resting place for thee on the road, and thou hast no provision for thy journey.

Make thyself an island, work hard, be wise! When thy impurities are blown away, and thou art free from guilt, thou wilt not enter again into birth and decay.

Let a wise man blow off the impurities of his self, as a smith blows off the impurities of silver, one by one, little by little, and from time to time.

As the impurity which springs from the iron, when it springs from it, destroys it; thus do a transgressor's own works lead him to the evil path.

The taint of prayers is non-repetition; the taint of houses, non-repair; the taint of the body is sloth; the taint of a watchman, thoughtlessness.

Bad conduct is the taint of woman, greediness the taint of a benefactor; tainted are all evil ways, in this world and in the next.

But there is a taint worse than all taints,—ignorance is the greatest taint. O mendicants! throw off that taint, and become taintless!

Life is easy to live for a man who is without shame, a crow hero, a mischief-maker, an insulting, bold, and wretched fellow.

But life is hard to live for a modest man, who always looks for what is pure, who is disinterested, quiet, spotless, and intelligent.

He who destroys life, who speaks untruth, who in this world takes what is not given him, who goes to another man's wife.

And the man who gives himself to drinking intoxicating liquors, he, even in this world, digs up his own root.

O man, know this, that the unrestrained are in a bad state; take care that greediness and vice do not bring thee to grief for a long time!

The world gives according to their faith or according to their pleasure; if a man frets about the food and the drink given to others, he will find no rest either by day or by night.

He in whom that feeling is destroyed, and taken out with the very root, finds rest by day and by night.

There is no fire like passion, there is no shark like hatred, there is no snare like folly, there is no torrent like greed.

The fault of others is easily perceived, but that of oneself is difficult to perceive; a man winnows his neighbour's faults like chaff, but his own fault he hides, as a cheat hides the bad die from the gambler.

CHAPTER XXII

The Downward Course

He who says what is not, goes to hell; he also who, having done a thing, says I have not done it. After death both are equal, they are men with evil deeds in the next world.

Many men whose shoulders are covered with the yellow gown are ill-conditioned and unrestrained; such evildoers by their evil deeds go to hell.

Better it would be to swallow a heated iron ball, like flaring fire, than that a bad unrestrained fellow should live on the charity of the land.

Four things does a reckless man gain who covets his neighbour's wife,—a bad reputation, an uncomfortable bed, thirdly, punishment, and lastly, hell.

There is bad reputation, and the evil way (to hell), there is the short pleasure of the frightened in the arms of the frightened, and the king imposes heavy punishment; therefore let no man think of his neighbour's wife.

As a grass blade, if badly grasped, cuts the arm, badly—practised asceticism leads to hell.

An act carelessly performed, a broken vow, and hesitating obedience to discipline, all this brings no great reward.

If anything is to be done, let a man do it, let him attack it vigorously! A careless pilgrim only scatters the dust of his passions more widely.

An evil deed is better left undone, for a man repents of it afterwards; a good deed is better done, for having done it, one does not repent.

Like a well guarded frontier fort, with defences within and without, so let a man guard himself. Not a moment should escape, for they who allow the right moment to pass, suffer pain when they are in hell.

They who are ashamed of what they ought not to be ashamed of, and are not ashamed of what they ought to be ashamed of, such men, embracing false doctrines, enter the evil path.

They who fear when they ought not to fear, and fear not when they ought to fear, such men, embracing false doctrines, enter the evil path.

They who forbid when there is nothing to be forbidden, and forbid not when there is something to be forbidden, such men, embracing false doctrines, enter the evil path.

They who know what is forbidden as forbidden, and what is not forbidden as not forbidden, such men, embracing the true doctrine, enter the good path.

CHAPTER XXIV

Thirst

The thirst of a thoughtless man grows like a creeper; he runs from life to life, like a monkey seeking fruit in the forest.

Whomsoever this fierce thirst overcomes, full of poison, in this world, his sufferings increase like the abounding Bîrana grass.

He who overcomes this fierce thirst, difficult to be conquered in this world, sufferings fall off from him, like water drops from a lotus leaf.

This salutary word I tell you, 'Do ye, as many as are here assembled, dig up the root of thirst, as he who wants the sweet-scented Usîra root must dig up the Bîrana grass, that Mâra (the tempter) may not crush you again and again, as the stream crushes the reeds.'

As a tree, even though it has been cut down, is firm so long as its root is safe, and grows again, thus, unless the feeders of thirst are destroyed, this pain (of life) will return again and again.

He whose thirst running towards pleasure is exceeding strong in the thirty-six channels, the waves will carry away that misguided man, viz, his desires which are set on passion.

The channels run everywhere, the creeper (of passion) stands sprouting; if you see the creeper springing up, cut its root by means of knowledge.

A creature's pleasures are extravagant and luxurious; sunk in lust and looking for pleasure, men undergo (again and again) birth and decay.

Men, driven on by thirst, run about like a snared hare; held in fetters and bonds, they undergo pain for a long time, again and again.

Men, driven on by thirst, run about like a snared hare; let therefore the mendicant drive out thirst, by striving after passionlessness for himself.

He who having got rid of the forest (of lust) (i.e. after having reached Nirvana) gives himself over to forest life (i.e. to lust), and who, when removed from the forest (i.e. from lust), runs to the forest (i.e. to lust), look at that man! Though free, he runs into bondage.

Wise people do not call that a strong fetter which is made of iron, wood, or hemp; far stronger is the care for precious stones and rings, for sons and a wife.

That fetter wise people call strong which drags down, yields, but is difficult to undo; after having cut this at last, people leave the world, free from cares, and leaving desires and pleasures behind.

Those who are slaves to passions, run down with the stream (of desires), as a spider runs down the web which he has made himself; when they have cut this, at last, wise people leave the world, free from cares, leaving all affection behind.

Give up what is before, give up what is behind, give up what is in the middle, when thou goest to the other shore of existence; if thy mind is altogether free, thou wilt not again enter into birth and decay.

If a man is tossed about by doubts, full of strong passions, and yearning only for what is delightful, his thirst will grow more and more, and he will indeed make his fetters strong. If a man delights in quieting doubts, and, always reflecting, dwells on what is not delightful (the impurity of the body, etc.), he certainly will remove, nay, he will cut the fetter of Mâra.

He who has reached the consummation, who does not tremble, who is without thirst and without sin, he has broken all the thorns of life; this will be his last body.

Chapter 6

The Great Thinkers

Laozi, Excerpt from *Tao Te Ching*, "The Unvarying Way"

Following the wandering ascetic tradition, Lao Tzu is alleged to have taught in the sixth century BCE.
The essential book on Taoism, the Tao Te Ching *(The Way and Its Power), is attributed to him. The*
book contains about 5,000 characters providing brief poetic statements on how to follow the Way (Tao).
Since the Way is a universal absolute, resisting or forcing it creates friction and suffering. Taoism recom-
mends spontaneous action (Wu Wei) and an emphasis on the free and carefree individual. Taoism has a
rational impulse also, as it is argued a better understanding of the natural world helps individuals know
the Way.

Source: *Lao Tzu. "The Unvarying Way."* Tao Te Ching, *trans. by Arthur Waley, 1934.*

Focus Questions:
1. In Taoism, how are the universal and the individual defined?
2. How do Taoist values compare with Christianity?
3. Also, how does the Way compare to God and Nirvana?

THE UNVARYING WAY

The unvarying way that can be preached is not the enduring and unchanging way. The name that can be named is not the enduring and unchanging name.

We look at it, and we do not see it, and we name it 'the invisible.' We listen to it, and we do not hear it, and we name it 'the inaudible.' We try to grasp it, and do not get hold of it, and we name it 'the intangible.' With these three qualities, it cannot be made the subject of description; blended together they are a unity.

The unvarying way is all pervading, it may be found on the left or the right.

The unvarying way is hidden, and has no name; but it is the way things are, which is skillful at imparting to all things what they need to make them complete.

All things depend on it and it does not desert them. Ambitionless, it may be found in the smallest things. It clothes all things, but does not act as a master. Always without desire, it may be called insignificant. All things return to it; it may be named great.

Heaven and earth under its guidance unite together and send down the sweet dew, which, without the directions of men, reaches equally everywhere as of its own accord.

Likewise, the relation of the unvarying way to all the world is like that of the great rivers and seas to the streams from the valleys.

There is nothing in the world more soft and weak than water, and yet there is nothing better for attacking things that are firm and strong. There is nothing so effectual for causing change.

Water has the highest excellence. It benefits all things, and occupies without striving the low place which all men dislike. Hence it is close to the way things are.

The unvarying way relies on non-action, and so there is nothing which it does not do.

The way things are is to act without thinking of acting; to conduct affairs without feeling the trouble of them; to taste without consuming; it considers what is small as great, and a few as many; and it recompenses injury with kindness.

The unvarying way moves by contraries, and weakness marks the course of its action.

As soon as the way is expressed in a creative act, it has a name. When it once has that name, men can know how to come into equilibrium with it. When they know how to come to equilibrium, they can be free from risk of failure and error.

Confucius, Selections from the *Analects*

To many of us, the words "Confucius say" are the preamble to a witticism, but to billions of Chinese people over thousands of years the sayings of the master have been words of highest wisdom, to be received with respect, if not with reverence. As a result, Confucius has molded the Chinese mind and character in a manner and to an extent that has hardly been equaled by any other single figure in the history of a major civilization.

Although it is difficult to summarize briefly the teachings of Confucius, certain of their basic features are apparent. He was an optimistic moralist; believing people to be fundamentally good, he thought that with proper education and leadership they could realize their potential and achieve the form of life which he described as that of "the superior man." A social order composed of such individuals, including particularly its political leaders, would constitute the ideal society. Although he also believed that such a society is in harmony with the will of heaven, Confucius, unlike many early social philosophers, did not found his ideal society on principles derived from theology. On the contrary, he is well described as a humanist.

Many of the details of the moral and social ideals of Confucius appear in his Analects, or "Collection" (of sayings). This collection, which is rambling, ill-arranged, and repetitious, contains twenty "Books," which include the master's sayings, descriptions of contemporary Chinese society, excursions into past history, and stories about various political leaders.

Confucius (551–479 B.C.) was born of a poor family that apparently had ancestors of substance. Early in life he decided to become a scholar and teacher. He soon gathered a group of disciples about him, and, because he believed that society could be reformed only if those who were properly educated held the reins of government, he sought public office and encouraged his students to do so as well. During his career he held a number of government posts, some of consequence. But practical politicians were suspicious of his lofty ideals and he was finally dismissed. He spent the twilight of his career wandering about China while still teaching.

Near the end of his life he wrote the following succinct autobiography: "At fifteen, I set my heart on learning. At thirty, I was firmly established. At forty, I had no more doubts. At fifty, I knew the will of Heaven. At sixty, I was ready to listen to it. At seventy, I could follow my heart's desire without transgressing what was right."

The moral teachings of the Analects, which Confucius did not actually originate but which he edited and molded to reflect his own ideals, were gathered together, mainly after his death, by his admirers. The selection that follows includes some of his central sayings. These have been rearranged to give them greater coherency, and the topic headings have been added.

Source: *Legge, James, trans.* The Chinese Classics; with a translation, critical and exegetical notes, prolegomena, and copious indexes. *Hong Kong: Hong Kong University Press, 1960.*

Focus Questions:
1   According to Confucius, what is the basis for a stable society?
2. What behaviors or attitudes does Confucius consider virtuous?
3. What is the purpose of being virtuous?

ANALECTS

The Master said, "Is it not pleasant to learn with a constant perseverance and application? Is it not delightful to have friends coming from distant quarters? Is he not a man of complete virtue who feels no discomposure though men may take no note of him?"

FILIAL PIETY

The Master said, "A youth, when at home, should be filial, and, abroad, respectful to his elders. He should be earnest and truthful. He should overflow in love to all, and cultivate the friendship of the good. When he has time and opportunity, after the performance of these things, he should employ them in polite studies."

Mang I asked what filial piety was. The Master said, "It is not being disobedient." Soon after, as Fan Chi was driving him, the Master told him, saying, "Mangsun asked me what filial piety was, and I answered him,—'not being disobedient.'" Fan Chi said, "What did you mean?" The Master replied, "That parents, when alive, should be served according to propriety; that, when dead, they should be buried according to propriety; and that they should be sacrificed to according to propriety."

The Master said, "In serving his parents, a son may remonstrate with them, but gently; when he sees that they do not incline to follow his advice, he shows an increased degree of reverence, but does not abandon his purpose; and should they punish him, he does not allow himself to murmur."

EDUCATION

The Master said, "If the scholar be not grave, he will not call forth any veneration, and his learning will not be solid."

The Master said, "If a man keeps cherishing his old knowledge, so as continually to be acquiring new, he may be a teacher of others."

The Master said, "The accomplished scholar is not a utensil."

The Master said, "Learning without thought is labor lost; thought without learning is perilous."

The Master said, "Yu, shall I teach you what knowledge is? When you know a thing, to hold that you know it; and when you do not know a thing, to allow that you do not know it; this is knowledge."

The Master said, "They who know the truth are not equal to those who love it, and they who love it are not equal to those who delight in it."

The Master said, "The scholar who cherishes the love of comfort is not fit to be deemed a scholar."

When the Master went to Wei, Zan Yu acted as driver of his carriage. The Master observed, "How numerous are the people!" Yu said, "Since they are so numerous, what more shall be done for them?" "Enrich them," was the reply. "And when they have been enriched, what more shall be done?" The Master said, "Teach them."

GOVERNMENT

The Master said, "To rule a country of a thousand chariots, there must be reverent attention to business, and sincerity; economy in expenditure, and love for men; and the employment of the people at the proper seasons."

The Master said, "He who exercises government by means of his virtue may be compared to the north polar star, which keeps its place and all the stars turn towards it."

The Master said, "If the people be led by laws, and uniformity sought to be given them by punishment, they will try to avoid the punishment, but have no sense of shame. If they be led by virtue, and uniformity sought to be given them by the rules of propriety, they will have the sense of shame, and moreover will become good."

Ji Kang asked how to cause the people to reverence their ruler, to be faithful to him, and to go on to nerve themselves to virtue. The Master said, "Let him preside over them with gravity; then they will reverence him. Let him be filial and kind to all; then they will be faithful to him. Let him advance the good and teach the incompetent; then they will eagerly seek to be virtuous."

Zigong asked about government. The Master said, "The requisites of government are that there be sufficiency of food, sufficiency of military equipment, and the confidence of the people in their ruler." Zigong said, "If it cannot be helped, and one of these must be dispensed with, which of the three should be foregone first?" "The military equipment," said the Master. Zigong again asked, "If it cannot be helped, and one of the remaining two must be dispensed with, which of them should be foregone?" The Master answered, "Part with the food. From of old, death has been the lot of all men; but if the people have no faith in their rulers, there is no standing for the State."

Ji Kang asked Confucius about government, saying, "What do you say to killing the unprincipled for the good of the principled?" Confucius replied, "Sir, in carrying on your government, why should you use killing at all? Let your evinced desires be for what is good, and the people will be good. The relation between superiors and inferiors is like that between the wind and the grass. The grass must bend, when the wind blows across it."

The Master said, "When a prince's personal conduct is correct, the government is effective without the issuing of orders. If his personal conduct is not correct, he may issue orders, but they will not be followed."

Zizhang asked Confucius, saying, "In what way should a person in authority act in order that he may conduct government properly?" The Master replied, "Let him honor the five excellent, and banish away the four bad, things; then may he conduct government properly." Zizhang said, "What are meant by the five excellent things?" The Master said, "When the person in authority is beneficent without great expenditure; when he lays tasks on the people without their repining; when he pursues what he desires without being covetous; when he maintains a dignified ease without being proud; when he is majestic without being fierce."...

Zizhang then asked, "What are meant by the four bad things?" The Master said, "To put the people to death without having instructed them; this is called cruelty. To require from them, suddenly, the full tale of work, without having given them warning; this is called oppression. To issue orders as if without urgency, at first, and, when the time comes, to insist on them with severity; this is called injury. And, generally, in the giving pay or rewards to men, to do it in a stingy way; this is called acting the part of a mere official."

RELIGION

The Master said, "He who offends against Heaven has none to whom he can pray."

Ji Lu asked about serving the spirits of the dead. The Master said, "While you are not able to serve men, how can you serve their spirits?" Ji Lu added, "I venture to ask about death." He was answered, "While you do not know life, how can you know about death?"

The Master said, "Alas! there is no one that knows me." Zi Gong said, "What do you mean by thus saying—that no one knows you?" The Master replied, "I do not murmur against Heaven. I do not grumble against men. My studies lie low, and my penetration rises high. But there is Heaven; that knows me!"

The Master said, "I would prefer not speaking." Zi Gong said, "If you, Master, do not speak, what shall we, your disciples, have to record?" The Master said, "Does Heaven speak? The four seasons pursue their courses, and all things are continually being produced, but does Heaven say anything?"

The Master said, "Without recognizing the ordinances of Heaven, it is impossible to be a superior man."

VIRTUE AND GOODNESS

The Master said, "Fine words and an insinuating appearance are seldom associated with true virtue."

The Master said, "See what a man does. Mark his motives. Examine in what things he rests. How can a man conceal his character?"

The Master said, "I do not know how a man without truthfulness is to get on. How can a large carriage be made to go without the cross-bar for yoking the oxen to, or a small carriage without the arrangement for yoking the horses?"

The Master said, "To see what is right and not to do it is want of courage."

The Master said, "If the will be set on virtue, there will be no practice of wickedness."

The Master said, "Riches and honors are what men desire. If virtue cannot be obtained in the proper way, they should not be held. Poverty and meanness are what men dislike. If virtue cannot be obtained in the proper way, they should be avoided."

The Master said, "I have not seen a person who loved virtue, or one who hated what was not virtuous. He who loved virtue, would esteem nothing above it. He who hated what is not virtuous, would practice virtue in such a way that he would not allow anything that is not virtuous to approach his person. Is any one able for one day to apply his strength to virtue? I have not seen the case in which his strength would be insufficient."

The Master said, "A man should say, I am not concerned that I have no place, I am concerned how I may fit myself for one. I am not concerned that I am not known, I seek to be worthy to be known."

The Master said, "When we see men of worth, we should think of equaling them; when we see men of a contrary character, we should turn inwards and examine ourselves."

The Master said, "Virtue is not left to stand alone. He who practices it will have neighbors."

The Master said, "Let the will be set on the path of duty. Let every attainment in what is good be firmly grasped. Let perfect virtue be accorded with. Let relaxation and enjoyment be found in the polite arts."

The Master said, "With coarse rice to eat, with water to drink, and my bended arm for a pillow; I have still joy in the midst of these things. Riches and honors acquired by unrighteousness are to me as a floating cloud."

The Master said, "Is virtue a thing remote? I wish to be virtuous, and lo! virtue is at hand."

The Master said, "Respectfulness, without the rules of propriety, becomes laborious bustle; carefulness, without the rules of propriety, becomes timidity; boldness, without the rules of propriety, becomes insubordination; straightforwardness, without the rules of propriety, becomes rudeness."

The Master said, "Can men refuse to assent to the words of strict admonition? But it is reforming the conduct because of them which is valuable. Can men refuse to be pleased with words of gentle advice? But it is unfolding their aim which is valuable. If a man be pleased with these words, but does not unfold their aim, and assents to those, but does not reform his conduct, I can really do nothing with him."

The Master said, "Hold faithfulness and sincerity as first principles. Have no friends not equal to yourself. When you have faults, do not fear to abandon them."

The Master said, "The commander of the forces of a large State may be carried off, but the will of even a common man cannot be taken from him."

The Master said, "The wise are free from perplexities; the virtuous from anxiety; and the bold from fear."

The Master said, "To go beyond is as wrong as to fall short."

Zhong Gong asked about perfect virtue. The Master said, "It is, when you go abroad, to behave to every one as if you were receiving a great guest; to employ the people as if you were assisting at a great sacrifice; not to do to others as you would not wish done to yourself to have no murmuring against you in the country, and none in the family."

Fan Chi asked about benevolence. The Master said, "It is to love all men." He asked about knowledge. The Master said, "It is to know all men."

Fan Chi asked about perfect virtue. The Master said, "It is, in retirement, to be sedately grave; in the management of business, to be reverently attentive; in intercourse with others, to be strictly sincere. Though a man go among rude, uncultivated tribes, these qualities may not be neglected."

Zigong asked, saying, "What do you say of a man who is loved by all the people of his neighborhood?" The Master replied, "We may not for that accord our approval of him." "And what do you say of him who is hated by all the people of his neighborhood?" The Master said, "We may not for that conclude that he is bad. It is better than either of these cases that the good in the neighborhood love him, and the bad hate him."

The Master said, "He who speaks without modesty will find it difficult to make his words good."

Someone said, "What do you say concerning the principle that injury should be recompensed with kindness?" The Master said, "With what then will you recompense kindness? Recompense injury with justice, and recompense kindness with kindness."

Zigong asked, saying, "Is there one word which may serve as a rule of practice for all one's life?" The Master said, "Is not RECIPROCITY such a word? What you do not want done to yourself, do not do to others."

The Master said, "Virtue is more to man than either water or fire. I have seen men die from treading on water and fire, but I have never seen a man die from treading the course of virtue."

Confucius said, "There are three friendships which are advantageous, and three which are injurious. Friendship with the upright; friendship with the sincere; and friendship with the man of much observation; these are advantageous. Friendship with the man of specious airs; friendship with the insinuatingly soft; and friendship with the glib-tongued; these are injurious."

Confucius said, "There are three things men find enjoyment in which are advantageous, and three things they find enjoyment in which are injurious. To find enjoyment in the discriminating study of ceremonies and music; to find enjoyment in speaking of the goodness of others; to find enjoyment in having many worthy friends; these are advantageous. To find enjoyment in extravagant pleasures; to find enjoyment in idleness and sauntering; to find enjoyment in the pleasures of feasting; these are injurious."

Zigong asked Confucius about perfect virtue. Confucius said, "To be able to practice five things everywhere under Heaven constitutes perfect virtue." He begged to ask what they were, and was told, "Gravity, generosity of soul, sincerity, earnestness, and kindness. If you are grave, you will not be treated with disrespect. If you are generous, you will win all. If you are sincere, people will repose trust in you. If you are earnest, you will accomplish much. If you are kind, this will enable you to employ the services of others."

Plato, *The Republic*, "The Philosopher-King"

Plato (427–347 BCE) was an Athenian philosopher and student of Socrates who eventually founded a school of his own in Athens. The dialogues of Socrates were actually written by Plato, who greatly admired his teacher. Plato later developed his own philosophies concerning ethics and knowledge. His book, The Republic, *discusses the virtues of justice, wisdom, and moderation. He then evaluates how these virtues are developed or hindered in society by comparing different forms of government. Plato's conclusion is that a philosopher is most fit to rule.*

Source: The Republic, *translated by Benjamin Jowett, New York: P.F. Collier & Son. 1901. The Colonial Press.*

Focus Questions:
1. How does Plato's philosopher king compare in values with the great religious thinkers?
2. What are the strengths of Plato's idea of rule by philosopher kings?
3. What are the weaknesses?

Inasmuch as philosophers only are able to grasp the eternal and unchangeable, and those who wander in the region of the many and variable are not philosophers, I must ask you which of the two classes should be the rulers of our State?

And how can we rightly answer that question?

Whichever of the two are best able to guard the laws and institutions of our State—let them be our guardians.

Very good.

Neither, I said, can there be any question that the guardian who is to keep anything should have eyes rather than no eyes?

There can be no question of that.

And are not those who are verily and indeed wanting in the knowledge of the true being of each thing, and who have in their souls no clear pattern, and are unable as with a painter's eye to look at the absolute truth and to that original to repair, and having perfect vision of the other world to order the laws about beauty, goodness, justice in this, if not already ordered, and to guard and preserve the order of them—are not such persons, I ask, simply blind?

Truly, he replied, they are much in that condition.

And shall they be our guardians when there are others who, besides being their equals in experience and falling short of them in no particular of virtue, also know the very truth of each thing?

There can be no reason, he said, for rejecting those who have this greatest of all great qualities; they must always have the first place unless they fail in some other respect. Suppose, then, I said, that we determine how far they can unite this and the other excellences.

By all means.

In the first place, as we began by observing, the nature of the philosopher has to be ascertained. We must come to an understanding about him, and, when we have done so, then, if I am not mistaken, we shall also acknowledge that such a union of qualities is possible, and that those in whom they are united, and those only, should be rulers in the State.

What do you mean?

Let us suppose that philosophical minds always love knowledge of a sort which shows them the eternal nature not varying from generation and corruption.

Agreed.

And further, I said, let us agree that they are lovers of all true being; there is no part whether greater or less, or more or less honorable, which they are willing to renounce; as we said before of the lover and the man of ambition.

True.

And if they are to be what we were describing, is there not another quality which they should also possess?

What quality?

Truthfulness: they will never intentionally receive into their minds falsehood, which is their detestation, and they will love the truth.

Yes, that may be safely affirmed of them.

"May be" my friend, I replied, is not the word; say rather, "must be affirmed," for he whose nature is amorous of anything cannot help loving all that belongs or is akin to the object of his affections.

Right, he said.

And is there anything more akin to wisdom than truth?

How can there be?

Can the same nature be a lover of wisdom and a lover of falsehood?

Never.

The true lover of learning then must from his earliest youth, as far as in him lies, desire all truth?

Assuredly.

But then again, as we know by experience, he whose desires are strong in one direction will have them weaker in others; they will be like a stream which has been drawn off into another channel.

True.

He whose desires are drawn toward knowledge in every form will be absorbed in the pleasures of the soul, and will hardly feel bodily pleasure—I mean, if he be a true philosopher and not a sham one.

That is most certain.

Such a one is sure to be temperate and the reverse of covetous; for the motives which make another man desirous of having and spending, have no place in his character.

Very true.

Another criterion of the philosophical nature has also to be considered.

What is that?

There should be no secret corner of illiberality; nothing can be more antagonistic than meanness to a soul which is ever longing after the whole of things both divine and human.

Most true, he replied.

Then how can he who has magnificence of mind and is the spectator of all time and all existence, think much of human life?

He cannot.

Or can such a one account death fearful?

No, indeed.

Then the cowardly and mean nature has no part in true philosophy?

Certainly not.

Or again: can he who is harmoniously constituted, who is not covetous or mean, or a boaster, or a coward—can he, I say, ever be unjust or hard in his dealings?

Impossible.

Then you will soon observe whether a man is just and gentle, or rude and unsociable; these are the signs which distinguish even in youth the philosophical nature from the un-philosophical.

True.

There is another point which should be remarked.

What point?

Whether he has or has not a pleasure in learning; for no one will love that which gives him pain, and in which after much toil he makes little progress.

Certainly not.

And again, if he is forgetful and retains nothing of what he learns, will he not be an empty vessel?

That is certain.

Laboring in vain, he must end in hating himself and his fruitless occupation?

Yes.

Then a soul which forgets cannot be ranked among genuine philosophic natures; we must insist that the philosopher should have a good memory?

Certainly.

And once more, the inharmonious and unseemly nature can only tend to disproportion?

Undoubtedly.

And do you consider truth to be akin to proportion or to disproportion?

To proportion.

Then, besides other qualities, we must try to find a naturally well-proportioned and gracious mind, which will move spontaneously toward the true being of everything.

Certainly.

Well, and do not all these qualities, which we have been enumerating, go together, and are they not, in a manner, necessary to a soul, which is to have a full and perfect participation of being?

They are absolutely necessary, he replied.

And must not that be a blameless study which he only can pursue who has the gift of a good memory, and is quick to learn—noble, gracious, the friend of truth, justice, courage, temperance, who are his kindred?

The god of jealousy himself, he said, could find no fault with such a study.

And to men like him, I said, when perfected by years and education, and to these only you will entrust the State.

Plato, *The Republic*, "On Shadows and Realities in Education"

Plato (427–347 BCE) followed his teacher Socrates in using the Socratic method in seeking truth. This method required carefully defining all basic principles or concepts before making conclusions, a surprisingly difficult proposition. Plato goes so far as to state that the concepts or Ideas (nous) are actually real and that the world is simply a reflection of these Ideas. These Ideas are expressed by an ultimate being and then impressed upon matter to create beings. The later Christian Neo-Platonics devised the belief that God originates the nous and the soul is the part of the nous impressed on matter to form men. From the fifth century CE onwards Neo-Platonism became a fundamental part of Christian theology.

Source: The Republic, *translated by Benjamin Jowett, New York: P.F. Collier & Son. 1901, The Colonial Press.*

Focus Questions:
1. How is a prophet described? How is he treated by people?
2. What are we seeing in the world?
3. How would you compare the concept of nous with logos?

BOOK VII: ON SHADOWS AND REALITIES IN EDUCATION

SOCRATES - GLAUCON

AND now, I said, let me show in a figure how far our nature is enlightened or unenlightened:—Behold! human beings living in an underground den, which has a mouth open towards the light and reaching all along the den; here they have been from their childhood, and have their legs and necks chained so that they cannot move, and can only see before them, being prevented by the chains from turning round their heads. Above and behind them a fire is blazing at a distance, and between the fire and the prisoners there is a raised way; and you will see, if you look, a low wall built along the way, like the screen which marionette players have in front of them, over which they show the puppets.

I see.

And do you see, I said, men passing along the wall carrying all sorts of vessels, and statues and figures of animals made of wood and stone and various materials, which appear over the wall? Some of them are talking, others silent.

You have shown me a strange image, and they are strange prisoners.

Like ourselves, I replied; and they see only their own shadows, or the shadows of one another, which the fire throws on the opposite wall of the cave?

True, he said; how could they see anything but the shadows if they were never allowed to move their heads?

And of the objects which are being carried in like manner they would only see the shadows?

Yes, he said.

And if they were able to converse with one another, would they not suppose that they were naming what was actually before them?

Very true.

And suppose further that the prison had an echo which came from the other side, would they not be sure to fancy when one of the passers-by spoke that the voice which they heard came from the passing shadow?

No question, he replied.

To them, I said, the truth would be literally nothing but the shadows of the images.

That is certain.

And now look again, and see what will naturally follow if the prisoners are released and disabused of their error. At first, when any of them is liberated and compelled suddenly to stand up and turn his neck round and walk and look towards the light, he will suffer sharp pains; the glare will distress him, and he will be unable to see the realities of which in his former state he had seen the shadows; and then conceive some one saying to him, that what he saw before was an illusion, but that now, when he is approaching nearer to being and his eye is turned towards more real existence, he has a clearer vision,— what will be his reply? And you may further imagine that his instructor is pointing to the objects as they pass and requiring him to name them,—will he not be perplexed? Will he not fancy that the shadows which he formerly saw are truer than the objects which are now shown to him?

Far truer.

And if he is compelled to look straight at the light, will he not have a pain in his eyes which will make him turn away to take and take in the objects of vision which he can see, and which he will conceive to be in reality clearer than the things which are now being shown to him?

True, he said.

And suppose once more, that he is reluctantly dragged up a steep and rugged ascent, and held fast until he's forced into the presence of the sun himself, is he not likely to be pained and irritated? When he approaches the light his eyes will be dazzled, and he will not be able to see anything at all of what are now called realities.

Not all in a moment, he said.

He will require to grow accustomed to the sight of the upper world. And first he will see the shadows best, next the reflections of men and other objects in the water, and then the objects themselves; then he will gaze upon the light of the moon and the stars and the spangled heaven; and he will see the sky and the stars by night better than the sun or the light of the sun by day?

Certainly.

Last of all he will be able to see the sun, and not mere reflections of him in the water, but he will see him in his own proper place, and not in another; and he will contemplate him as he is.

Certainly.

He will then proceed to argue that this is he who gives the season and the years, and is the guardian of all that is in the visible world, and in a certain way the cause of all things which he and his fellows have been accustomed to behold?

Clearly, he said, he would first see the sun and then reason about him.

And when he remembered his old habitation, and the wisdom of the den and his fellow-prisoners, do you not suppose that he would felicitate himself on the change, and pity them?

Certainly, he would.

And if they were in the habit of conferring honors among themselves on those who were quickest to observe the passing shadows and to remark which of them went before, and which followed after, and which were together; and who were therefore best able to draw conclusions as to the future, do you think that he would care for such honors and glories, or envy the possessors of them? Would he not say with Homer,

"Better to be the poor servant of a poor master, and to endure anything, rather than think as they do and live after their manner?"

Yes, he said, I think that he would rather suffer anything than entertain these false notions and live in this miserable manner.

Imagine once more, I said, such an one coming suddenly out of the sun to be replaced in his old situation; would he not be certain to have his eyes full of darkness?

To be sure, he said.

And if there were a contest, and he had to compete in measuring the shadows with the prisoners who had never moved out of the den, while his sight was still weak, and before his eyes had become steady (and the time which would be needed to acquire this new habit of sight might be very considerable) would he not be ridiculous? Men would say of him that up he went and down he came without his eyes; and that it was better not even to think of ascending; and if any one tried to loose another and lead him up to the light, let them only catch the offender, and they would put him to death.

No question, he said.

This entire allegory, I said, you may now append, dear Glaucon, to the previous argument; the prison-house is the world of sight, the light of the fire is the sun, and you will not misapprehend me if you interpret the journey upwards to be the ascent of the soul into the intellectual world according to my poor belief, which, at your desire, I have expressed whether rightly or wrongly God knows. But, whether true or false, my opinion is that in the world of knowledge the idea of good appears last of all, and is seen only with an effort; and, when seen, is also inferred to be the universal author of all things beautiful and right, parent of light and of the lord of light in this visible world, and the immediate source of reason and truth in the intellectual; and that this is the power upon which he who would act rationally, either in public or private life must have his eye fixed.

Aristotle, Excerpts from *Physics and Posterior Analytics*

Aristotle (384–322 BCE) was a philosopher from Macedonia who studied at Plato's academy. He later acted as the tutor for Alexander the Great before returning to Athens and founding his own school. Aristotle is famous for four groups of works on logic, physics, natural history, and ethics. The approach in all these works is more empirical and materialist than in Plato. The ethics is considered very subtle and moderate, while his physics and logic would form the foundations of much subsequent western and Islamic philosophy and science. Aristotle's thought and methods eventually evolved in the seventeenth and eighteenth centuries CE into scientific experimentalism and the modern concept of a mechanical rather than teleological concept of nature.

Source: Analytica Posteriora Books I & II, *trans. G.R.G. Mure, ed., in* The Works of Aristotle, *Ross Oxford, 1924.*

Focus Questions:
1. How does Aristotle refute Zeno's paradoxes?
2. How can Aristotle's logic be used?
3. According to Aristotle, what is physics?

PHYSICS

Zeno's reasoning, however, is fallacious, when he says that if everything when it occupies an equal space is at rest, and if that which is in locomotion is always occupying such a space at any moment, the flying arrow is therefore motionless. This is false, for time is not composed of indivisible moments any more than any other magnitude is composed of indivisibles.

Zeno's arguments about motion, which cause so much disquietude to those who try to solve the problems that they present, are four in number. The first asserts the nonexistence of motion on the ground that that which is in locomotion must arrive at the half-way stage before it arrives at the goal. This we have discussed above.

The second is the so-called 'Achilles', and it amounts to this, that in a race the quickest runner can never overtake the slowest, since the pursuer must first reach the point whence the pursued started, so that the slower must always hold a lead. This argument is the same in principle as that which depends on bisection, though it differs from it in that the spaces with which we successively have to deal are not divided into halves. The result of the argument is that the slower is not overtaken: but it proceeds along the same lines as the bisection-argument (for in both a division of the space in a certain way leads to the result that the goal is not reached, though the 'Achilles' goes further in that it affirms that even the quickest runner in legendary tradition must fail in his pursuit of the slowest), so that the solution must be the same. And the axiom that that which holds a lead is never overtaken is false: it is not overtaken, it is true, while it holds a lead: but it is overtaken nevertheless if it is granted that it traverses the finite distance prescribed. These then are two of his arguments.

The third is that already given above, to the effect that the flying arrow is at rest, which result follows from the assumption that time is composed of moments: if this assumption is not granted, the conclusion will not follow.

The fourth argument is that concerning the two rows of bodies, each row being composed of an equal number of bodies of equal size, passing each other on a race-course as they proceed with equal velocity in opposite directions, the one row originally occupying the space between the goal and the middle point of the course and the other that between the middle point and the starting-post. This, he thinks, involves the conclusion that half a given time is equal to double that time. The fallacy of the reasoning lies in the assumption that a body occupies an equal time in passing with equal velocity a body that is in motion and a body of equal size that is at rest; which is false. For instance (so runs the argument), let A, A...be the stationary bodies of equal size, B, B...the bodies, equal in number and in size to A, A..., originally occupying the half of the course from the starting-post to the middle of the A's, and G, G...those originally occupying the other half from the goal to the middle of the A's, equal in number, size, and velocity to B, B...Then three consequences follow:

First, as the B's and the G's pass one another, the first B reaches the last G at the same moment as the first G reaches the last B. Secondly at this moment the first G has passed all the A's, whereas the first B has passed only half the A's, and has consequently occupied only half the time occupied by the first G, since each of the two occupies an equal time in passing each A. Thirdly, at the same moment all the B's have passed all the G's: for the first G and the first B will simultaneously reach the opposite ends of the course, since (so says Zeno) the time occupied by the first G in passing each of the B's is equal to that occupied by it in passing each of the A's, because an equal time is occupied by both the first B and the first G in passing all the A's. This is the argument, but it presupposed the aforesaid fallacious assumption.

Nor in reference to contradictory change shall we find anything unanswerable in the argument that if a thing is changing from not-white, say, to white, and is in neither condition, then it will be neither white nor not-white: for the fact that it is not wholly in either condition will not preclude us from calling it white or not-white. We call a thing white or not-white not necessarily because it is be one or the other, but cause most of its parts or the most essential parts of it are so: not being in a certain condition is different from not being wholly in that condition. So, too, in the case of being and not-being and all other conditions which stand in a contradictory relation: while the changing thing must of necessity be in one of the two opposites, it is never wholly in either.

Again, in the case of circles and spheres and everything whose motion is confined within the space that it occupies, it is not true to say the motion can be nothing but rest, on the ground that such things in motion, themselves and their parts, will occupy the same position for a period of time, and that therefore they will be at once at rest and in motion. For in the first place the parts do not occupy the same position for any period of time: and in the second place the whole also is always changing to a different position: for if we take the orbit as described from a point A on a circumference, it will not be the same as the orbit as described from B or G or any other point on the same circumference except in an accidental sense, the sense that is to say in which a musical man is the same as a man. Thus one orbit is always changing into another, and the thing will never be at rest. And it is the same with the sphere and everything else whose motion is confined within the space that it occupies.

Our next point is that that which is without parts cannot be in motion except accidentally: i.e., it can be in motion only in so far as the body or the magnitude is in motion and the partless is in motion by inclusion therein, just as that which is in a boat may be in motion in consequence of the locomotion of the boat, or a part may be in motion in virtue of the motion of the whole. (It must be remembered, however, that by 'that which is without parts' I mean that which is quantitatively indivisible (and that the case of the motion of a part is not exactly parallel): for parts have motions belonging essentially and severally to themselves distinct from the motion of the whole. The distinction may be seen most clearly in the case of a revolving sphere, in which the velocities of the parts near the centre and of those on the surface are different from one another and from that of the whole; this implies that there is not one motion but many). As we have said, then, that which is without parts can be in motion in the sense in which a man sitting in a boat is in motion when the boat is traveling, but it cannot be in motion of itself. For suppose that it is changing from AB to BG—either from one magnitude to another, or from one form to another, or from some state to its contradictory—and let D be the primary time in which it undergoes the change. Then in the time in which it is changing it must be either in AB or in BG or partly in one and partly in the other: for this, as we saw, is true of everything that is changing. Now it cannot be partly in each of the two: for then it would be divisible into parts. Nor again can it be in BG: for then it will have completed the change, whereas the assumption is that the change is in process. It remains, then, that in the time in which it is changing, it is in AB. That being so, it will be at rest: for, as we saw, to be in the same condition for a period of time is to be at rest. So it is not possible for that which has no parts to be in motion or to change in any way: for only one condition could have made it possible for it to have motion, viz. that time should be composed of moments, in which case at any moment it would have completed a motion or a change, so that it would never be in motion, but would always have been in motion. But this we have already shown above to be impossible: time is not composed of moments, just as a line is not composed of points, and motion is not composed of starts: for this theory simply makes motion consist of indivisibles in exactly the same way as time is made to consist of moments or a length of points.

Again, it may be shown in the following way that there can be no motion of a point or of any other indivisible. That which is in motion can never traverse a space greater than itself without first traversing a space equal to or less than itself. That being so, it is evident that the point also must first traverse a space equal to or less than itself. But since it is indivisible, there can be no space less than itself for it to traverse first: so it will have to traverse a distance equal to itself. Thus the line will be composed of points, for the point, as it continually traverses a distance equal to itself, will be a measure of the whole line. But since this is impossible, it is likewise impossible for the indivisible to be in motion.

Again, since motion is always in a period of time and never in a moment, and all time is divisible, for everything that is in motion there must be a time less than that in which it traverses a distance as great as itself. For that in which it is in motion will be a time, because all motion is in a period of time; and all time has been shown above to be divisible. Therefore, if a point is in motion, there must be a time less than that in which it has itself traversed any distance. But this is impossible, for in less time it must traverse less distance, and thus the indivisible will be divisible into something less than itself, just as the time is so divisible: the fact being that the only condition under which that which is without parts and indivisible could be in motion would have been the possibility of the infinitely small being in motion in a moment: for in the two questions—that of motion in a moment and that of motion of something indivisible—the same principle is involved.

Our next point is that no process of change is infinite: for every change, whether between contradictories or between contraries, is a change from something to something. Thus in contradictory changes the positive or the negative, as the case may be, is the limit, e.g. being is the limit of coming to be and not-being is the limit of ceasing to be: and in contrary changes the particular contraries are the limits, since these are the extreme points of any such process of change, and consequently of every process of alteration: for alteration is always dependent upon some contraries. Similarly contraries are the extreme points of processes of increase and decrease: the limit of increase is to be found in the complete magnitude proper to the peculiar nature of the thing that is increasing, while the limit of decrease is the complete loss of such magnitude. Locomotion, it is true, we cannot show to be finite in this way, since it is not always between contraries. But since that which cannot be cut (in the sense that it is inconceivable that it should be cut, the term 'cannot' being used in several senses)—since it is inconceivable that that which in this sense cannot be cut should be in process of being cut, and generally that that which cannot come to be should be in process of coming to be, it follows that it is inconceivable that that which cannot complete a change should be in process of changing to that to which it cannot complete a change. If, then, it is to be assumed that that which is in locomotion is in process of changing, it must be capable of completing the change. Consequently its motion is not infinite, and it will not be in locomotion over an infinite distance, for it cannot traverse such a distance.

It is evident, then, that a process of change cannot be infinite in the sense that it is not defined by limits. But it remains to be considered whether it is possible in the sense that one and the same process of change may be infinite in respect of the time which it occupies. If it is not one process, it would seem that there is nothing to prevent its being infinite in this sense; e.g. if a process of locomotion be succeeded by a process of alteration and that by a process of increase and that again by a process of coming to be: in this way there may be motion for ever so far as the time is concerned, but it will not be one motion, because all these motions do not compose one. If it is to be one process, no motion can be infinite in respect of the time that it occupies, with the single exception of rotatory locomotion.

POSTERIOR ANALYTICS

Part 1

The kinds of question we ask are as many as the kinds of things which we know. They are in fact four:- (1) whether the connexion of an attribute with a thing is a fact, (2) what is the reason of the connexion, (3) whether a thing exists, (4) what is the nature of the thing. Thus, when our question concerns a complex of thing and attribute and we ask whether the thing is thus or otherwise qualified—whether, e.g. the sun suffers eclipse or not—then we are asking as to the fact of a connexion. That our inquiry ceases with the discovery that the sun does suffer eclipse is an indication of this; and if we know from the start that the sun suffers eclipse, we do not inquire whether it does so or not. On the other hand, when we know the fact we ask the reason; as, for example, when we know that the sun is being eclipsed and that an earthquake is in progress, it is the reason of eclipse or earthquake into which we inquire.

Where a complex is concerned, then, those are the two questions we ask; but for some objects of inquiry we have a different kind of question to ask, such as whether there is or is not a centaur or a God. (By 'is or is not' I mean 'is or is not, without further qualification'; as opposed to 'is or is not [e.g.] white'.) On the other hand, when we have ascertained the thing's existence, we inquire as to its nature, asking, for instance, 'what, then, is God?' or 'what is man?'.

Part 2

These, then, are the four kinds of question we ask, and it is in the answers to these questions that our knowledge consists.

Now when we ask whether a connexion is a fact, or whether a thing without qualification is, we are really asking whether the connexion or the thing has a 'middle'; and when we have ascertained either that the connexion is a fact or that the thing is—i.e. ascertained either the partial or the unqualified being of the thing—and are proceeding to ask the reason of the connexion or the nature of the thing, then we are asking what the 'middle' is.

(By distinguishing the fact of the connexion and the existence of the thing as respectively the partial and the unqualified being of the thing, I mean that if we ask 'does the moon suffer eclipse?', or 'does the moon wax?', the question concerns a part of the thing's being; for what we are asking in such questions is whether a thing is this or that, i.e. has or has not this or that attribute: whereas, if we ask whether the moon or night exists, the question concerns the unqualified being of a thing.)

We conclude that in all our inquiries we are asking either whether there is a 'middle' or what the 'middle' is: for the 'middle' here is precisely the cause, and it is the cause that we seek in all our inquiries. Thus, 'Does the moon suffer eclipse?' means 'Is there or is there not a cause producing eclipse of the moon?', and when we have learnt that there is, our next question is, 'What, then, is this cause? for the cause through which a thing is—not is this or that, i.e. has this or that attribute, but without qualification is—and the cause through which it is—not is without qualification, but is this or that as having some essential attribute or some accident—are both alike the middle'. By that which is without qualification I mean the subject, e.g. moon or earth or sun or triangle; by that which a subject is (in the partial sense) I mean a property, e.g. eclipse, equality or inequality, interposition or non-interposition. For in all these examples it is clear that the nature of the thing and the reason of the fact are identical: the question 'What is eclipse?' and its answer 'The privation of the moon's light by the interposition of the earth' are identical with the question 'What is the reason of eclipse?' or 'Why does the moon suffer eclipse?' and the reply 'Because of the failure of light through the earth's shutting it out'. Again, for 'What is a concord? A commensurate numerical ratio of a high and a low note', we may substitute 'What ratio makes a high and a low note concordant? Their relation according to a commensurate numerical ratio.' 'Are the high and the low note concordant?' is equivalent to 'Is their ratio commensurate?'; and when we find that it is commensurate, we ask 'What, then, is their ratio?'.

Cases in which the 'middle' is sensible show that the object of our inquiry is always the 'middle': we inquire, because we have not perceived it, whether there is or is not a 'middle' causing, e.g. an eclipse. On the other hand, if we were on the moon we should not be inquiring either as to the fact or the reason, but both fact and reason would be obvious simultaneously. For the act of perception would have enabled us to know the universal too; since, the present fact of an eclipse being evident, perception would then at the same time give us the present fact of the earth's screening the sun's light, and from this would arise the universal.

Thus, as we maintain, to know a thing's nature is to know the reason why it is; and this is equally true of things in so far as they are said without qualification to he as opposed to being possessed of some attribute, and in so far as they are said to be possessed of some attribute such as equal to right angles, or greater or less.

Part 3

It is clear, then, that all questions are a search for a 'middle'. Let us now state how essential nature is revealed and in what way it can be reduced to demonstration; what definition is, and what things are definable. And let us first discuss certain difficulties which these questions raise, beginning what we have to say with a point most intimately connected with our immediately preceding remarks, namely the doubt that might be felt as to whether or not it is possible to know the same thing in the same relation, both by definition and by demonstration. It might, I mean, be urged that definition is held to concern essential nature and is in every case universal and affirmative; whereas, on the other hand, some conclusions are negative and some are not universal; e.g. all in the second figure are negative, none in the third are universal. And again, not even all affirmative conclusions in the first figure are definable, e.g. 'every triangle has its angles equal to two right angles'. An argument proving this difference between demonstration and definition is that to have scientific knowledge of the demonstrable is identical with possessing a demonstration of it: hence if demonstration of such conclusions as these is possible, there clearly cannot also be definition of them. If there could, one might know such a conclusion also in virtue of its definition without possessing the demonstration of it; for there is nothing to stop our having the one without the other.

Induction too will sufficiently convince us of this difference; for never yet by defining anything—essential attribute or accident—did we get knowledge of it. Again, if to define is to acquire knowledge of a substance, at any rate such attributes are not substances.

It is evident, then, that not everything demonstrable can be defined. What then? Can everything definable be demonstrated, or not? There is one of our previous arguments which covers this too. Of a single thing qua single there is a single scientific knowledge. Hence, since to know the demonstrable scientifically is to possess the demonstration of it, an impossible consequence will follow: possession of its definition without its demonstration will give knowledge of the demonstrable.

Moreover, the basic premises of demonstrations are definitions, and it has already been shown that these will be found indemonstrable; either the basic premises will be demonstrable and will depend on prior premises, and the regress will be endless; or the primary truths will be indemonstrable definitions.

But if the definable and the demonstrable are not wholly the same, may they yet be partially the same? Or is that impossible, because there can be no demonstration of the definable? There can be none, because definition is of the essential nature or being of something, and all demonstrations evidently posit and assume the essential nature—mathematical demonstrations, for example, the nature of unity and the odd, and all the other sciences likewise. Moreover, every demonstration proves a predicate of a subject as attaching or as not attaching to it, but in definition one thing is not predicated of another; we do not, e.g. predicate animal of biped nor biped of animal, nor yet figure of plane—plane not being figure nor figure plane. Again, to prove essential nature is not the same as to prove the fact of a connexion. Now definition reveals essential nature, demonstration reveals that a given attribute attaches or does not attach to a given subject; but different things require different demonstrations—unless the one demonstration is related to the other as part to whole. I add this because if all triangles have been proved to possess angles equal to two right angles, then this attribute has been proved to attach to isosceles; for isosceles is a part of which all triangles constitute the whole. But in the case before us the fact and the essential nature are not so related to one another, since the one is not a part of the other.

So it emerges that not all the definable is demonstrable nor all the demonstrable definable; and we may draw the general conclusion that there is no identical object of which it is possible to possess both a definition and a demonstration. It follows obviously that definition and demonstration are neither identical nor contained either within the other: if they were, their objects would be related either as identical or as whole and part.

Part 4

So much, then, for the first stage of our problem. The next step is to raise the question whether syllogism—i.e. demonstration—of the definable nature is possible or, as our recent argument assumed, impossible.

We might argue it impossible on the following grounds:—(a) syllogism proves an attribute of a subject through the middle term; on the other hand (b) its definable nature is both 'peculiar' to a subject and predicated of it as belonging to its essence. But in that case (1) the subject, its definition, and the middle term connecting them must be reciprocally predicable of one another; for if A is to C, obviously A is 'peculiar' to B and B to C—in fact all three terms are 'peculiar' to one another: and further (2) if A inheres in the essence of all B and B is predicated universally of all C as belonging to C's essence, A also must be predicated of C as belonging to its essence.

If one does not take this relation as thus duplicated—if, that is, A is predicated as being of the essence of B, but B is not of the essence of the subjects of which it is predicated—A will not necessarily be predicated of C as belonging to its essence. So both premises will predicate essence, and consequently B also will be predicated of C as its essence. Since, therefore, both premises do predicate essence—i.e. definable form-C's definable form will appear in the middle term before the conclusion is drawn.

We may generalize by supposing that it is possible to prove the essential nature of man. Let C be man, A man's essential nature—two-footed animal, or aught else it may be. Then, if we are to syllogize, A must be predicated of all B. But this premise will be mediated by a fresh definition, which consequently will also be the essential nature of man. Therefore the argument assumes what it has to prove, since B too is the essential nature of man. It is, however, the case in which there are only the two premises—i.e. in which the premises are primary and immediate—which we ought to investigate, because it best illustrates the point under discussion.

Thus they who prove the essential nature of soul or man or anything else through reciprocating terms beg the question. It would be begging the question, for example, to contend that the soul is that which causes its own life, and that what causes its own life is a self-moving number; for one would have to postulate that the soul is a self-moving number in the sense of being identical with it. For if A is predicable as a mere consequent of B and B of C, A will not on that account be the definable form of C: A will merely be what it was true to say of C. Even if A is predicated of all B inasmuch as B is identical with a species of A, still it will not follow: being an animal is predicated of being a man—since it is true that in all instances to be human is to be animal, just as it is also true that every man is an animal—but not as identical with being man.

We conclude, then, that unless one takes both the premises as predicating essence, one cannot infer that A is the definable form and essence of C: but if one does so take them, in assuming B one will have assumed, before drawing the conclusion, what the definable form of C is; so that there has been no inference, for one has begged the question.

The Nyaya School: "Explanation of the Sutra"

The Nyaya Sutras were written in the 2ⁿᵈ century BCE in India. The Nayaya is a school of Hindu philosophy that addresses issues of knowledge and truth. In order to better seek truth, the school brought about advances in philosophical methods, especially in the use of logic. Their main approaches were through the methods of perception, inference, analogy, and reference to authority. Since wrong ideas could lead people away from Nirvana, the Nyaya believed that right knowledge of the universe could help bring enlightenment.

Source: *Ganganatha Jha.* The Nyaya Sutras of Gautama. *New Delhi: Motilal Banarsidass Publishers Pvt. Ltd, 1998.*

Focus Questions:
1. What are the logical steps of thought in the Sutra?
2. What happens as a result of wrong notions compared to true knowledge?
3. How do the methods and values of the Nyaya compare to Plato?

EXPLANATION OF SŪTRA (2).

BHĀYSA
[*P.* 7, *l.* 13 to *P.* 9, *l.* 9.]

(A.) Of 'Wrong Notion' (mentioned in the *Sūtra* as the first to cease after the attainment of true knowledge), there are various kinds, pertaining as it does to the several objects of cognition, beginning with 'Soul' and ending with 'Final Release.' (*a*) With reference to the *Soul*, the 'Wrong Notion' is in the form 'there is no such thing as Soul';—(*b*) with regard to the *Not-Soul*, people have 'Wrong Notion' when it is regarded as the 'Soul';—(*c*) when *pain* is regarded as pleasure, we have the 'Wrong Notion' of pain; and so on; (*d*) when the *non-eternal* is regarded as eternal; (*e*) when *non-safety* is regarded as *safety*; (*f*) when the *fearful* is regarded as *free from fear*;—(*g*) when the *disgusting* is regarded as *agreeable*;—(*h*) when that which deserves to be *rejected* is regarded as worthy of *not being rejected*; (*i*) when with regard to *activity*, we have such notions as 'there is no such thing as *Karma*, nor any result of *Karma*'; (*j*) when with regard to *Defects* we have the notion that metempsychosis is not due to 'defects';—(*k*) with regard to *Death and Birth* (i.e., Transmigration) we have such *wrong notions* as—'there is no such thing as an animal or a living being, or a being or soul, who could die, or, having died, could be born again,' 'the transmigration of living beings is without cause,' 'the cessation of birth is without cause,' 'Transmigration has beginning, but no end,' 'even though caused, Transmigration is not caused by Karma,' 'Transmigration can have no relation to the soul, it consists only in the disruption (at death) and restoration (at rebirth) of the continuous connection of such things as the body, the sense-organs, the intellect and the sensations';—(*l*) with regard to *Final Release* we have such *wrong notions* as 'it is something terrible, involving as it does the cessation of all activity,' 'in Final Release which consists in separation from, all things, we lose much that is desirable,' 'how can any intelligent person have any longing for Final Release, in which there is neither pleasure nor pain, nor any consciousness (or sensation) at all?'

(B.) From the above-described *Wrong Notion* proceeds attachment to the agreeable and aversion for the disagreeable; and under the influence of this attachment and aversion, there appear the *Defects*,—such as untruthfulness, jealousy, deceit, avarice and the like.

(C.) Urged by these *Defects*, when the man acts, he commits such misdeeds as,—(*a*) killing, stealing, illicit intercourse, and such other acts pertaining to the body; (*b*) lying, rude talking and incoherent babbling, these pertaining to speech; (c) malice, desire for things belonging to others, and atheism, these pertaining to the mind; such misdeeds constitute the Wrong or Sinful Activity which tends to *Adharma* (Vice, demerit). The right sort of *Activity* consists in the following actions—(a) with the body, charity, supporting and service; (b) with speech, telling the truth, saying what is beneficial and agreeable, studying the Veda; (c) with the mind, mercy, entertaining no desire for the belongings of other people, and faith; this right Activity tends to *Dharma* (virtue, merit). What are meant by 'activity' ('*pravritti*') in this connection (in the sūtra) are the *results* of activity, in the form of Merit and Demerit; just as life, being the result of food, we speak of the life of living beings as 'food'.

(D.) The 'Activity' described above (in the form of Merit and Demerit) becomes the cause of disreputable and respectable *birth* (respectively); and *Birth* consists in the collective appearance (in one congregated group) of the Body, the Sense-organs and the Intellect (*Buddhi*).

(E) When there is *birth*, there is *Pain*; it is that which is felt as disagreeable, and is also known by such names as '*bādhanā*' (harassment), *pīdā* (suffering) and '*tāpa*' (affliction).

The above five qualities (or principles), beginning with *Wrong Notion* and ending with *Pain*,* when functioning contiguously (without break) constitute Metempsychosis.

When 'true knowledge' is attained, 'wrong notions' disappear; on the disappearance of 'wrong notions' the 'defects' disappear; the disappearance of 'defects' is followed by the disappearance 'activity' (merit and demerit); when there is no activity there is no 'birth'; on the cessation of birth there is cessation of 'pain'; and the cessation of pain is followed by Final Release, which is the 'highest good'.

What is 'true knowledge' is explained by the contrary of the 'wrong notion' indicated above. For instance, (a) the 'true knowledge' with regard to the *Soul* is in the form 'there is such a thing as Soul;'—(b) That with regard to: the '*not-Soul*' is in the form 'the not-soul is not the Soul;'—similarly with regard to (c) pain, (d) the *eternal*, (e) *safety*, (f) the *fearful*, (g) the *disgusting*, and (h) the *rejectable*, we have 'true knowledge' when each is known in its real character ;—(i) with regard to *activity* it is in the form 'there is such a thing as *karma*, and it is effective in bringing about results'; (j) with regard to *defects* it is in the form 'metempsychosis is due to defects';—(k) with regard to *transmigration* it is in the form 'there is such a thing as an animal, a living being, a being, a soul which, having died, is reborn,—birth a definite cause,— the cessation of birth has a definite cause,—transmigration is without beginning, but ends in Final Release,—transmigration, having a cause, is caused by activity (merit and demerit)—transmigration is connected with the soul and operates through disruption and restoration of the continuous connection of such things as the body, the sense-organs, the intellect and the sensations; '—(l) with regard to Final Release, it is in the form Final Release, involving separation from all things and cessation from all activity, is extremely peaceful,—much that is painful, frightful and sinful disappears on Final Release,—and how can any intelligent person fail to have a longing for it, being, as it is, free from all pain and, entirely devoid of all consciousness of pain? Final Release must be free not only from pain, but from *pleasure* also; because all pleasure is invariably connected with some *pain*, and as such should be avoided, in the same manner as food mixed with honey and poison is avoided.

---

*The order of these as given in the Sutra has been altered here.

Liu An, Excerpt from *Huan Nan Tzu*

Sometime before 122 BCE Liu An, a prince of Nan, patronized eight eminent scholars to write a book of Taoist learning. The same Liu An is also claimed as the inventor of Tofu. The book, Huan Nan Tzu, replicates earlier Taoist principles but additionally emphasizes a rationalist approach to ethics and knowledge. Old traditions and rituals are discarded in favor of the practical, while magic and alchemy are rejected for logic and following the Way.

Source: *LeBlanc, C.* Huan Nan Tzu. *China: Hong Kong University Press, 1985.*

Focus Questions:
1. How are knowledge and theory compared and used?
2. What function does the use of examples serve?
3. How is truth found?

SECTION IX

15a .4   Coming to the present time, the Son of

.5   Heaven reigns supreme, sustaining [all] with *Tao* and *Te*, assisting [all] with human-heart-edness (*jen*) and equity (*yi*). Those close [to him] offer their

.6   wisdom, and those far removed cherish his *Te*. [Simply] by clasping his hands on his breast and stretching them forward, the Four Seas pay obeisance and in spring and autumn, winter and

.7   summer offer their tribute. The whole world coalesces and becomes one, sons and grandsons succeeding one another. Such was the way in which the Five Emperors greeted the *Te* of Heaven.

.8   Even the sage ruler cannot create the time. The time comes along, and he does not miss it. He promotes the competent and dismisses those who show the slightest penchant for slander and flattery,

.9   cuts short clever disputations and does away with mutilating laws, brushes aside petty and trouble

.10   some affairs and obliterates the first traces of rumors, shuts the door to cabals and cliques, gets rid of [conventional] knowledge and ability, and enhances the office of Minister of Ceremonies.

.11   He (the Sage) dissolves his limbs and body, casts out [sense] knowledge, merges with form-less obscurity, unloosens his mind, sloughs off his spirit and becomes blank as if soulless, causing the Ten

15b .1   Thousand Things one by one to return to their Root. This, then, is how to follow in the footsteps of Fu Hsi and revert to the *Tao* of the Five Emperors. How explain that Ch'ien Ch'ieh and Ta Ping

.2   used neither rein nor bit and were nevertheless renowned throughout the whole world for their excellent driving? How explain that Fu Hsi and Nil Kua did not set up laws and measures and were nevertheless treasured by later generations for their perfect virtue? They reached empty non-being and pure unity, and did not peck at vexatious

15b .3   affairs. The Book of Chou says: "[When] he who

.4   nets ringed pheasants fails to catch any, he changes [his techniques] to accord with their (the pheasants') habits."

.5   Now, let us take the manner in which Shen [Puhai], Han [Fei-tzu] and Shang Yang managed

.6   government. They plucked up the stem [of good government] and weeded out its roots, without investigating wherefrom it grew. How did they

.7   get to this? They forcibly created the Five Punishments and practiced cutting and slicing, thus turning their back on the root of Tao and Te and fighting over the tip of an awl. They mowed down

.8   the Hundred Surnames (the people) like grass and

.9   exterminated more than half of them. Then, inflated with self-satisfaction, they prided themselves on having performed [the tasks of] Government. This is...like adding fuel wood in order to put out a fire,

.10 or boring holes to stop water.

16a .1   Now, stump shoots may grow on the wooden

.2   casing of a well, obstructing the bucket from reaching the bottom; and branches may grow on the side beams of a canal, obstructing the passage of

.7   boats. But three months will not pass before they (the growths) will surely be dead. Why is it so? [Because] these [growths] were all born hap-

.8   hazardly, lacking their own roots. That the Yellow River makes nine turns to flow into the sea without being stopped [by any obstacle] is due to its being carried forward by

.10 the K'un-lun [Mountains]. That flood waters, however, do not flow but spread out to the limit of one's gaze—if it does not rain for a full month, their waters dry up and leave a stagnant swamp—

.11 is due to their being the result of mere accumulation and lacking a source [of their own].

16b .3   This may be compared to Yi requesting the drug of immortality from the Queen Mother of the

.4   West. Heng O stole it and fled to the moon.

.8   [Yi] was dejected and forlorn, having no way to perpetuate it (the drug). Why was this, then?

.9   [Because] he did not know wherefrom the drug of

.10 immortality grew. Therefore, to beg for fire is not

.11 as good as to obtain a fire-maker. To depend on [other people's] water is not as good as to dig a well [of one's own].

Confucian Political Philosophy: An Excerpt from Mencius

Mencius (372–289 BCE) was considered the second sage of Confucianism after Confucius himself. Like Confucius, Mencius moved from court to court during a very unsettled period. At the same time, he organized and developed the basic tenets and political theories of Confucianism. Mencius based his political philosophy on the concepts of humaneness and on duty. His society in true Confucian pattern was based on a set of social relations and obligations between social classes that operated in both directions. Relationships should be based on decorous behavior and trusting in the innate goodness of people.

Source: *Legge, James, trans.,* Chinese Classics, v.2 [1895].

Focus Questions:
1. What, according to Mencius, is righteous?
2. Compare Mencius's values to those of Plato.
3. Compare Mencius with the religious thinkers in terms of Heaven and the Way.

MENCIUS CHAPTER 18

1. Wan Chang said, 'Was it the case that Yâo gave the throne to Shun?' Mencius said, 'No. The sovereign cannot give the throne to another.'

2. 'Yes;— but Shun had the throne. Who gave it to him?' 'Heaven gave it to him,' was the answer.

3. '"Heaven gave it to him:"— did Heaven confer its appointment on him with specific injunctions?'

4. Mencius replied, 'No. Heaven does not speak. It simply showed its will by his personal conduct and his conduct of affairs.'

5. '"It showed its will by his personal conduct and his conduct of affairs:"— how was this?' Mencius's answer was, 'The sovereign can present a man to Heaven, but he cannot make Heaven give that man the throne. A prince can present a man to the sovereign, but he cannot cause the sovereign to make that man a prince. A great officer can present a man to his prince, but he cannot cause the prince to make that man a great officer. Yâo presented Shun to Heaven, and Heaven accepted him. He presented him to the people, and the people accepted him. Therefore I say, "Heaven does not speak. It simply indicated its will by his personal conduct and his conduct of affairs."'

6. Chang said, 'I presume to ask how it was that Yâo presented Shun to Heaven, and Heaven accepted him; and that he exhibited him to the people, and the people accepted him.' Mencius replied, 'He caused him to preside over the sacrifices, and all the spirits were well pleased with them;—thus Heaven accepted him. He caused him to preside over the conduct of affairs, and affairs were well administered, so that the people reposed under him;—thus the people accepted him. Heaven gave the throne to him. The people gave it to him. Therefore I said, "The sovereign cannot give the throne to another."'

7. 'Shun assisted Yâo in the government for twenty and eight years;—this was more than man could have done, and was from Heaven. After the death of Yâo, when the three years' mourning was completed, Shun withdrew from the son of Yâo to the south of South River. The princes of the kingdom, however, repairing to court, went not to the son of Yâo, but they went to Shun. Litigants went not to the son of Yâo, but they went to Shun. Singers sang not the son of Yâo, but they sang to Shun. Therefore I said, "Heaven gave him the throne." It was after these things that he went to the Middle Kingdom, and occupied the seat of the Son of Heaven. If he had, before these things, taken up his residence in the palace of Yâo, and had applied pressure to the son of Yâo, it would have been an act of usurpation, and not the gift of Heaven.

8. 'This sentiment is expressed in the words of The Great Declaration,—"Heaven sees according as my people see; Heaven hears according as my people hear."'

1. Wan Chang asked Mencius, saying, 'People say, "When the disposal of the kingdom came to Yü, his virtue was inferior to that of Yâo and Shun, and he transmitted it not to the worthiest but to his son." Was it so?' Mencius replied, 'No, it was not so. When Heaven gave the kingdom to the worthiest, it was given to the worthiest. When Heaven gave it to the son of the preceding sovereign, it was given to him. Shun presented Yü to Heaven. Seventeen years elapsed, and Shun died. When the three years' mourning was expired, Yü withdrew from the son of Shun to Yang-ch'ang. The people of the kingdom followed him just as after the death of Yâo, instead of following his son, they had followed Shun. Yü presented Yî to Heaven. Seven years elapsed, and Yü died. When the three years' mourning was expired, Yî withdrew from the son of Yü to the north of mount Ch'î. The princes, repairing to court, went not to Yî, but they went to Ch'î. Litigants did not go to Yî but they went to Ch'î, saying, "He is the son of our sovereign;" the singers did not sing Yî, but they sang Ch'î, saying, "He is the son of our sovereign."

2. 'That Tan-chû was not equal to his father, and Shun's son not equal to his; that Shun assisted Yâo, and Yü assisted Shun, for many years, conferring benefits on the people for a long time;

that thus the length of time during which Shun, Yü, and Yî assisted in the government was so different; that Ch'î was able, as a man of talents and virtue, reverently to pursue the same course as Yü; that Yî assisted Yü only for a few years, and had not long conferred benefits on the people; that the periods of service of the three were so different; and that the sons were one superior, and the other superior:—all this was from Heaven, and what could not be brought about by man. That which is done without man's doing is from Heaven. That which happens without man's causing is from the ordinance of Heaven.

3. 'In the case of a private individual obtaining the throne, there Must be in him virtue equal to that of Shun or Yü; and moreover there Must be the presenting of him to Heaven by the preceding sovereign. It was on this account that Confucius did not obtain the throne.

4. 'When the kingdom is possessed by natural succession, the sovereign who is displaced by Heaven Must be like Chieh or Châu. It was on this account that Yî, Î Yin, and Châu-kung did not obtain the throne.

5. 'Î Yin assisted T'ang so that he became sovereign over the kingdom. After the demise of T'ang, T'âi-ting having died before he could be appointed sovereign, Wâ'i-ping reigned two years, and Chung-zin four. T'âi-chiâ was then turning upside down the statutes of T'ang, when Î Yin placed him in T'ung for three years. There Tâi-chiâ repented of his errors, was contrite, and reformed himself. In T'ung he came to dwell in benevolence and walk in righteousness, during those three years, listening to the lessons given to him by Î Yin. Then Î Yin again returned with him to Po.

6. 'Châu-kung not getting the throne was like the case of Yî and the throne of Hsiâ, or like that of Î Yin and the throne of Yîn.

7. 'Confucius said, "T'ang and Yü resigned the throne to their worthy ministers. The sovereign of Hsiâ and those of Yîn and Châu transmitted it to their sons. The principle of righteousness was the same in all the cases."'

1. Wan Chang asked Mencius, saying, 'People say that Î Yin sought an introduction to T'ang by his knowledge of cookery. Was it so?'

2. Mencius replied, 'No, it was not so. Î Yin was a farmer in the lands of the prince of Hsin, delighting in the principles of Yâo and Shun. In any matter contrary to the righteousness which they prescribed, or contrary to their principles, though he had been offered the throne, he would not have regarded it; though there had been yoked for him a thousand teams of horses, he would not have looked at them. In any matter contrary to the righteousness which they prescribed, or contrary to their principles, he would neither have given nor taken a single straw.

3. 'T'ang sent persons with presents of silk to entreat him to enter his service. With an air of indifference and self-satisfaction he said, "What can I do with those silks with which T'ang invites me? Is it not best for me to abide in the channeled fields, and so delight myself with the principles of Yâo and Shun?"

4. "T'ang thrice sent messengers to invite him. After this, with the change of resolution displayed in his countenance, he spoke in a different style,—"Instead of abiding in the channeled fields and thereby delighting myself with the principles of Yâo and Shun, had I not better make this prince a prince like Yâo or Shun, and this people like the people of Yâo or Shun ? Had I not better in my own person see these things for myself?

5. '"Heaven's plan in the production of mankind is this:—that they who are first informed should instruct those who are later in being informed, and they who first apprehend principles should instruct those who are slower to do so. I am one of Heaven's people who have first apprehended;—I will take these principles and instruct this people in them. If I do not instruct them, who will do so?"

6. 'He thought that among all the people of the kingdom, even the private men and women, if there were any who did not enjoy such benefits as Yâo and Shun conferred, it was as if he himself pushed them into a ditch. He took upon himself the heavy charge of the kingdom in this way, and therefore he went to T'ang, and pressed upon him the subject of attacking Hsiâ and saving the people.

7. 'I have not heard of one who bent himself, and at the same time made others straight;—how Mûch less could one disgrace himself, and thereby rectify the whole kingdom? The actions of the sages have been different. Some have kept remote from court, and some have drawn near to it; some have left their offices, and some have not done so;—that to which those different courses all agree is simply the keeping of their persons pure.

8. 'I have heard that Î Yin sought an introduction to T'ang by the doctrines of Yâo and Shun. I have not heard that he did so by his knowledge of cookery.

9. 'In the "Instructions of I," it is said, "Heaven destroying Chieh commenced attacking him in the palace of Mû. I commenced in Po."'

1. Wan Chang asked Mencius, saying, 'Some say that Confucius, when he was in Wei, lived with the ulcer-doctor, and when he was in Chî, with the attendant, Ch'î Hwan;—was it so?' Mencius replied, 'No, it was not so. Those are the inventions of men fond of strange things.

2. 'When he was in Wei, he lived with Yen Ch'âu-Yû. The wives of the officer Mî and Tsze-lû were sisters, and Mî told Tsze-lû, "If Confucius will lodge with me, he may attain to the dignity of a high noble of Wei." Tsze-lû informed Confucius of this, and he said, "That is as ordered by Heaven." Confucius went into office according to propriety, and retired from it according to righteousness. In regard to his obtaining office or not obtaining it, he said, "That is as ordered." But if he had lodged with the attendant Chî Hwan, that would neither have been according to righteousness, nor any ordering of Heaven.

3. 'When Confucius, being dissatisfied in Lû and Wei, had left those States, he met with the attempt of Hwan, the Master of the Horse, of Sung, to intercept and kill him. He assumed, however, the dress of a common man, and passed by Sung. At that time, though he was in circumstances of distress, he lodged with the city-master Ch'ang, who was then a minister of Châu, the marquis of Ch'an.

4. 'I have heard that the characters of ministers about court may be discerned from those whom they entertain, and those of stranger officers, from those with whom they lodge. If Confucius had lodged with the ulcer-doctor, and with the attendant Chî Hwan, how could he have been Confucius?'

1. Wan Chang asked Mencius, 'Some say that Pâi-lî Hsî sold himself to a cattle-keeper of Ch'in for the skins of five rams, and fed his oxen, in order to find an introduction to the duke Mû of Ch'in;—was this the case?' Mencius said, 'No; it was not so. This story was invented by men fond of strange things.

2. 'Pâi-lî Hsî was a man of Yü. The people of Tsin, by the inducement of a round piece of jade from and four horses of the Ch"ü breed, borrowed a passage through Yü to attack Kwo. On that occasion, Kung Chih-ch'î remonstrated against granting their request, and Pâi-lî Hsî did not remonstrate.

3. 'When he knew that the duke of Yü was not to be remonstrated with, and, leaving that State, went to Ch'in, he had reached the age of seventy. If by that time he did not know that it would be a mean thing to seek an introduction to the duke Mû of Ch'in by feeding oxen, could he be called wise? But not remonstrating where it was of no use to remonstrate, could he be said not to be wise? Knowing that the duke of Yü would be ruined, and leaving him before that event, he cannot be said not to have been wise. Being then advanced in Ch'in, he knew that the duke Mû was one with whom he would enjoy a field for action, and became minister to him;—could he, acting thus, be said not to be wise? Having become chief minister of Ch'in, he made his prince distinguished throughout the kingdom, and worthy of being handed down to future ages;—could he have done this, if he had not been a man of talents and virtue? As to selling himself in order to accomplish all the aims of his prince, even a villager who had a regard for himself would not do such a thing; and shall we say that a man of talents and virtue did it?'

Legalism: Selections from *The Writings of Han Fei*

Han Fei (280–233 BCE) was a lesser member of the Han royal family. He apparently suffered from a severe stutter, so he concentrated more on writing rather than success at court. He became one of the founders of the Legalist school. During a period of intense political upheaval in China, the legalists argued for firm control of the state by the ruler and for strict rule of law and order to bring about peace. The legalist approach helped the Qin achieve power and unify China. Afterwards, their ideas were vilified until Mao Zedong revived them in the twentieth century. Han Fei himself was ultimately forced to commit suicide in 233 as the result of a palace conspiracy.

Source: The Writings of the Han Fei, *from the Chinese Text Project.*

Focus Questions:
1. What are the two "handles" for the ruler?
2. Under what circumstances are the two "handles" useful?

HAVING REGULATIONS

No country is permanently strong. Nor is any country permanently weak. If conformers to law are strong, the country is strong; if conformers to law are weak, the country is weak...

Any ruler able to expel private crookedness and uphold public law finds the people safe and the state in order; and any ruler able to expunge private action and act on public law finds his army strong and his enemy weak. So, find out men following the discipline of laws and regulations, and place them above the body of officials. Then the sovereign cannot be deceived by anybody with fraud and falsehood...

Therefore, the intelligent sovereign makes the law select men and makes no arbitrary promotion himself. He makes the law measure merits and makes no arbitrary regulation himself. In consequence, able men cannot be obscured, bad characters cannot be disguised, falsely praised fellows cannot be advanced, wrongly defamed people cannot be degraded. To govern the state by law is to praise the right and blame the wrong.

The law does not fawn on the noble...Whatever the law applies to, the wise cannot reject nor can the brave defy. Punishment for fault never skips ministers, reward for good never misses commoners. Therefore, to correct the faults of the high, to rebuke the vices of the low, to suppress disorders, to decide against mistakes, to subdue the arrogant, to straighten the crooked, and to unify the folkways of the masses, nothing could match the law. To warn the officials and overawe the people, to rebuke obscenity and danger, and to forbid falsehood and deceit, nothing could match penalty. If penalty is severe, the noble cannot discriminate against the humble. If law is definite, the superiors are esteemed and not violated. If the superiors are not violated, the sovereign will become strong and able to maintain the proper course of government. Such was the reason why the early kings esteemed Legalism and handed it down to posterity. Should the lord of men discard law and practice selfishness, high and law would have no distinction.

THE TWO HANDLES

The means whereby the intelligent ruler controls his ministers are two handles only. The two handles are chastisement and commendation. What are meant by chastisement and commendation? To inflict death or torture upon culprits is called chastisement; to bestow encouragements or rewards on men of merit is called commendation.

Ministers are afraid of censure and punishment but fond of encouragement and reward. Therefore, if the lord of men uses the handles of chastisement and commendation, all ministers will dread his severity and turn to his liberality. The villainous ministers of the age are different. To men they hate they would by securing the handle of chastisement from the sovereign ascribe crimes; on men they love they would by securing the handle of commendation. From the sovereign bestow rewards. Now supposing the lord of men placed the authority of punishment and the profit of reward not in his hands but let the ministers administer the affairs of reward and punishment instead, then everybody in the country would fear the ministers and slight the ruler and turn to the ministers and away from the ruler. This is the calamity of the ruler's loss of the handles of chastisement and commendation.

Chapter 7

The Idea of Empire

Agatharchides of Kindos Describes Saba

Saba was located in modern Yemen at the bottom of the Arabian Peninsula. It is often known through the Hebrew name of Sheba. For several centuries the Sabeans controlled much of the lucrative trade between the Indian Ocean and the Mediterranean via the Red Sea. They benefited especially from their monopoly on frankincense and myrrh (the components of incense) which created tremendous wealth for the region. Saba finally fell through division and war in 115 BCE.

Source: *Agatharcides of Kindos.*

Focus Questions:
1. Trace the land and sea routes from India to the Mediterranean; where are the choke points?
2. How are the Sabean towns and lifestyle described?
3. Why are they described that way?

"No people appear to be wealthier than the Sabeans and Gerrheans (in NE Arabia and in the Arab Gulf), for they have piled up in their treasuries all the riches that they have gained from Europe and Asia. They are the ones that have made Ptolemy's Syria rich. It is they who have, amongst many other things, made it possible for the Phoenicians to make lucrative deals. Their luxury is not only displayed in marvelous embossed and engraved metal work and in the variety of their drinking vessels but in their beds and tripods, which are also unusually large. This luxury reaches its climax in the many house-hold objects which are known to us well. Many of these people own royal riches. It is said that they have numerous gold and silver columns, and the doors of their houses are decked with ornaments and jewels. Even the walls between the columns are said to be magnificently decorated."

Zhang Qian, *Han Shu*, "Descriptions of the Western Regions"

Zhang Qian was an official in the emperor's employ tasked in 138 BCE as an ambassador to find allies among the western tribes. He was captured by the Xiongnu and held for ten years before escaping. Upon escaping, he continued his mission west, still seeking allies. Finally, in 125 BCE he returned to the emperor and reported on all he had found. As a result of this report, the emperor began a series of campaigns to the West which opened trade routes on what would become known as the Silk Road.

Source: *Qian, Zhang. "Descriptions of the Western Regions," from the* Journal of the Anthropological Institute of Great Britain and Ireland *(1874), A. Wylie, translator.*

Focus Questions:
1. What types of societies are encountered?
2. What products are traded and where?
3. What do you think of the emperor's analysis and conclusions?

Ferghana [Ta-yuan] is to the southwest of the Xiongnu and due west of China, at a distance of about 10,000 li. The people are permanent dwellers and given to agriculture; and in their fields they grow rice and wheat. They have wine made of grapes (pu tau) and many good horses. The horses sweat blood and come from the stock of the *tian ma* [heavenly horse, perhaps the wild horse]. They have walled cities and houses; the large and small cities belonging to them, fully seventy in number, contain an aggregate population of several hundreds of thousands. Their arms consist of bows and halberds, and they shoot arrows while on horseback. North of this country is Sogdiana; in the west are [the] Yue-chi; in the southwest is Bactria; in the northeast are the Wu-sun; and in the east Han-mi and Khotan [Yu-tien]. All the rivers west of Khotan flow in a westerly direction and feed the Western Sea; all the rivers east of it flow east and feed the Salt Lake [Lopnor]. The Salt Lake flows underground. To the south of it [Khotan] is the source from which the Ho [Yellow River] arises. The country contains much jadestone. The river flows through China; and the towns of Loulan and Kushi with their city walls closely border on the Salt Lake. The Salt Lake is possibly 5000 *li* distant from Changan. The right [i.e. western] part of the Xiongnu live to the east of the Salt Lake as far as the great wall in Lungsi. To the south they are bounded by the Tanguts, where they bar the road [to China]. *Wu-sun* may be 2000 *li* northeast of Ferghana; its people are nomads [following their flocks of cattle], and have the same customs as the Xiongnu. Of archers they have several tens of thousands, all daring warriors. Formerly they were subject to the Xiongnu, but they became so strong that, while maintaining nominal vassalage, they refused to attend the meetings of the court.

Sogdiana is to the northwest of Ferghana perhaps 2000 *li* distant. It also is a country of nomads with manners and customs very much the same as those of the Yue-chi. They have eighty or ninety thousand archers. The country is coterminous with Ferghana. It is small. In the south it is under the political influence of the Yue-chi; in the east, under that of the Xiongnu.

An-ts'ai [Aorsi] lies to the northwest of Sogdiana, perhaps at a distance of 2000 *li*. It is a nomad state, and its manners and customs in the main identical with those of Sogdiana. It has fully a hundred thousand archers. The country lies close to a great sea [*ta-tso*, lit. 'great marsh,' the Palus Maeotis, i.e. the Sea of Azov] which has no limit, for it is the Northern Sea.

The *Ta-yue-chi* [Indoscythians] are perhaps two or three thousand *li* to the west of Ferghana. They live to the north of the K'ui-shui [Oxus]. South of them is Bactria [Ta-hia]; in the west is An-si [Parthia]; in the north, Sogdiana. They are a nomad nation, following their flocks and changing their abodes. Their customs are the same as those of the Xiongnu. They may have one to two hundred thousand archers. In olden times they relied on their strength, and thought lightly of the Xiongnu, but when Mau-tun ascended the throne he attacked and defeated the Yue-chi. Up to the time when Lau-shang, Shan-yu of the Xiongnu, killed the king of the Yue-chi and made a drinking vessel out of his skull, the Yue-chi had lived between Dunhuang [now Sha-chou] and the K'i-lien [a hill southwest of Kan-chou-fu]. But when they were beaten by the Xiongnu, they fled to a distant country and crossed to the west of Yuan [Ferghana], attacked Bactria [Ta-hia], and conquered it. Subsequently they had their capital in the north of the K'ui-shui [Oxus] and made it the court of their king. The minority, which were left behind and were not able to follow them, took refuge among the Tanguts of the Nan-shan, and were called *Siau Yue-chi* (Small Yue-chi).

An-si [Parthia] may be several thousand *li* west of the Ta-yue-chi. The people live in fixed abodes and are given to agriculture; their fields yield rice and wheat; and they make wine of grapes. Their cities and towns are like those of Ferghana. Several hundred small and large cities belong to it. The territory is several thousand li square; it is a very large country and is close to the K'ui-shui [Oxus]. Their market folk and merchants travel in carts and boats to the neighboring countries perhaps several thousand *li* distant. They make coins of silver; the coins resemble their king's face. Upon the death of a king the coins are changed for others on which the new king's face is represented. They paint [rows of characters] running sideways on [stiff] leather, to serve as records. West of this country is T'iau-chi; north is Ants'ai.

Li-kan [Syria] and *T'iau-chi* [Chaldea] are several thousand *li* west of An-si and close to the Western Sea. It [referring to T'iau-ch'i] is hot and damp. The inhabitants plow their fields, in which they grow rice. There is a big bird with eggs like jars. The number of its inhabitants is very large and they have in many places their own petty chiefs; but An-si [Parthia], while having added it to its dependencies, considers it a foreign country. They have clever jugglers. Although the old people in An-si maintain the tradition that the Jo-shui and the Si-wang-mu are in T'iau-chi, they have not been seen there.

Bactria [Ta-hia] is more than 2000 *li* to the southwest of Ferghana, on the south bank of the K'ui-shui [Oxus]. The people have fixed abodes and live in walled cities and regular houses like the people of Ferghana. They have no great king or chief, but everywhere the cities and towns have their own petty chiefs. While the people are shrewd traders, their soldiers are weak and afraid to fight, so that, when the Ta-yue-chi migrated westward, they made war on the Bactria, who became subject to them. The population of Bactria may amount to more than a million. Their capital is called Lan-shi, and it has markets for the sale of all sorts of merchandise. To the southeast of it is the country of *Shon-tu* [India]. Zhang Qian says [in his report to the Emperor]: 'When I was in Bactria, I saw there a stick of bamboo of Kiung [Kiung-chou in Ssi-ch'uan] and some cloth of Shu [Ssi-ch'uan]. When I asked the inhabitants of Bactria how they had obtained possession of these, they replied: "The inhabitant of our country buy them in Shon-tu [India]." Shon-tu may be several thousand *li* to the southeast of Bactria. The people there have fixed abodes, and their customs are very much like those of Bactria; but the country is low, damp, and hot. The people ride eliphants to fight in battle. The country is close to a great river. According to my calculation, Bactria must be 12,000 *li* distant from China and to the southwest of the latter. Now the country of Shon-tu being several thousand li the southeast of Bactria, and the produce of Shu [Ssi-ch'uan] being found there, that country cannot be far from Shu. Suppose we send ambassadors to Bactria through the country of the Tanguts, there is the danger that the Tanguts will object; if we send them but slightly farther north, they will be captured by the Xiongnu; but by going by way of Shu [Ssi-ch'uan] they may proceed direct and will be unmolested by robbers.'

The Son of Heaven on hearing all this reasoned thus: Ferghana and the possessions of Bactria and An-si are large countries, full of rare things, with a population living in fixed abodes and given to occupations somewhat identical with those of the Chinese people, but with weak armies, and placing great value on the rich produce of China; in the north the possessions of the Ta-yue-chi and Sogdiana, being of military strength, might be made subservient to the interests of the court by bribes and thus gained over by the mere force of persuasion. In this way a territory 10,000 *li* in extent would be available for the spread among the four seas of Chinese superior civilization by communicating through many interpreters with the nations holding widely different customs. As a result the Son of Heaven was pleased to approve Zhang Qian's proposal. He thereupon gave orders that, in accordance with Cliang K'ien's suggestions, exploring expeditions be sent out from Kien-wei of the Shu kingdom [the present Su-chou-fu on the Upper Yangtzi] by four different routes at the same time: one to start by way of Mang; one by way of Jan [both names referring to barbarous hill tribes on the southwestern frontier]; one by way of Ssi [or Si]; and one by way of Kiung [Kiung-chou in Ssi-ch'uan] and P'o [the present Ya-chou]. These several missions had each traveled but one or two thousand *li* when those in the north were prevented from proceeding farther by the Ti and Tso tribes, and those in the south by the Sui and K'un-ming tribes [placed by the commentators in the southwest of Si-chou-fu], who had no chiefs, and, being given to robbery, would have killed or captured the Chinese envoys. The result was that the expeditions could not proceed farther. They heard, however, that about a thousand li or more to the west there was the 'elephant-riding country' called *Tien-yue* [possibly meaning 'the Tien,' or Yunnan, part of Yue or South China], whither the traders of Shu [Ssi-ch'uan] were wont to proceed, exporting produce surreptitiously. Thus it was that by trying to find the road to Bactria [Ta-hia] the Chinese obtained their first knowledge of the Tien country (Yun-nan).

Pliny the Elder, from *The Natural History*

Caius Plinius Secundus (24–79 CE), anglicized as Pliny the Elder, was a wealthy Roman landowner, soldier, administrator, and writer. Pliny served as a military tribune in Gaul between 45 and 59 CE. He next served as a provincial administrator, also mostly in Gaul, until 75 CE. Then he became an administrator of the navy. He died in 79 during the eruption of Vesuvius while launching galleys in a rescue effort. Although he wrote several books during his career, including the History of the Germanic Wars, *his only surviving work is his* Natural History, *an encyclopedia on just about everything geographical and natural. Pliny's book was in continuous use throughout the Roman and medieval periods.*

Source: *Pliny the Elder,* The Natural History, *trans. by John Bostock and H. T. Riley, 1855.*

> **Focus Questions:**
> 1. What is the technology and infrastructure for trade?
> 2. What products are named? What types of goods are they?
> 3. What does the west have to offer?

BOOK VI

In later times it has been considered a well-ascertained fact that the voyage from *Syagrus*, the Promontory of *Arabia*, to Patale, reckoned at thirteen hundred and thirty-five miles, can be performed most advantageously with the aid of a westerly wind, which is there known by the name of Hippalus.

The age that followed pointed out a shorter route, and a safer one, to those who might happen to sail from the same promontory for Sigerus, a port of India; and for a long time this route was followed, until at last a still shorter cut was discovered by a merchant, and the thirst for gain brought India even still nearer to us. At the present day voyages are made to India every year, and companies of archers are carried on board the vessels, as those seas are greatly infested with pirates.

It will not be amiss too, on the present occasion, to set forth the whole of the route from *Egypt*, which has been stated to us of late, upon information on which reliance may be placed, and is here published for the first time. The subject is one well worthy of our notice, seeing that in no year does India drain our empire of less than five hundred and fifty millions of sesterces, giving back her own wares in exchange, which are sold among us at fully one hundred times their prime cost.

Two miles distant from *Alexandria* is the town of *Juliopolis*. The distance thence to *Coptos*, up the *Nile*, is three hundred and eight miles; the voyage is performed, when the Etesian winds are blowing, in twelve days. From *Coptos* the journey is made with the aid of camels, stations being arranged at intervals for the supply of fresh water. The first of these stations is called Hydreuma, and is distant twenty-two miles; the second is situate on a mountain, at a distance of one day's journey from the last; the third is at a second Hydreuma, distant from *Coptos* ninety-five miles; the fourth is on a mountain; the next to that is at another Hydreuma, that of *Apollo*, and is distant from *Coptos* one hundred and eighty-four miles; after which, there is another on a mountain. There is then another station at a place called the New Hydreuma, distant from *Coptos* two hundred and thirty miles: and next to it there is another, called the Old Hydreuma, or the Troglodytic, where a detachment is always on guard, with a caravansary that affords lodging for two thousand persons. This last is distant from the New Hydreuma seven miles. After leaving it we come to the city of *Berenice*, situate upon a harbour of the Red Sea, and distant from *Coptos* two hundred and fifty-seven miles. The greater part of this distance is generally traveled by night, on account of the extreme heat, the day being spent at the stations; in consequence of which it takes twelve days to perform the whole journey from *Coptos* to *Berenice*.

Passengers generally set sail at midsummer, before the rising of the Dog-star, or else immediately after, and in about thirty days arrive at *Ocelis* in *Arabia*, or else at Cane, in the region which bears *frankincense*. There is also a third port of *Arabia*, *Muza* by name; it is not, however, used by persons on their passage to India, as only those touch at it who deal in incense and the perfumes of *Arabia*. More in the interior there is a city; the residence of the king there is called Sapphar, and there is another city known by the name of Save. To those who are bound for India, *Ocelis* is the best place for embarkation. If the wind, called Hippalus, happens to be blowing, it is possible to arrive in forty days at the nearest mart of India, *Muziris* by name. This, however, is not a very desirable place for disembarkation, on account of the pirates which frequent its vicinity, where they occupy a place called Nitrias; nor, in fact, is it very rich in articles of merchandize. Besides, the road-stead for shipping is a considerable distance from the shore, and the cargoes have to be conveyed in boats, either for loading or discharging. At the moment that I am writing these pages, the name of the king of this place is Calobothras. Another port, and a much more convenient one, is that which lies in the territory of the people called Neacyndi, *Barace* by name. Here king *Pandion* used to reign, dwelling at a considerable distance from the mart in the interior, at a city known as Modiera. The district from which pepper is carried down to *Barace* in boats hollowed out of a single tree, is known as Cottonara. None of these names of nations, ports, and cities are to be found in any of the former writers, from which circumstance it would appear that the localities have since changed their names. Travellers set sail from India on their return to *Europe*, at the beginning of the Egyptian month Tybis, which is our December, or at all events before the sixth day of the Egyptian month Mechir, the same as our ides of *January*: if they do this, they can go and return in the same year. They set sail from India with a southeast wind, and upon entering the Red Sea, catch the southwest or south. We will now return to our main subject.

Greece and Persia: The Treaty of Antalcides, 387 BCE

Artaxerxes II of Persia (404–358 BCE) ruled the Persian-dominated lands from India to Egypt. However, on the western flank, the Persian Empire had waged intermittent war with the Greeks for over a century. Although the Greeks were no threat, the Persians were irritated by their constant interference with the affairs of Asia Minor. The Persians developed a policy of "divide and conquer" by giving help to weaker city states fighting against other more powerful states; typically Athens or Sparta. In the case of Artaxerxes II, he helped Sparta against Athens, bringing about a peace settlement in the Treaty of Antalcides in the year 387 BCE.

Source: *Treaty of Antaclides (387).*

> **Focus Questions:**
> 1. Why is the treaty so short?
> 2. How does the length relate to its tone?
> 3. Is the dividing line between Asia and Greece geographical or political?

"The king, Artaxerxes, deems it just that the cities in Asia, with the islands of Clazomenae and Cyprus, should belong to himself; the rest of the Hellenic cities he thinks it just to leave independent, both small and great, with the exception of Lemnos, Imbros, and Scyros, which three are to belong to Athens as of yore. Should any of the parties concerned not accept this peace, I, Artaxerxes, will war against him or them with those who share my views. This will I do by land and by sea, with ships and with money."

Horace, "Dulce et Decorum est Pro Patria Mori"

Quintus Horatius Flaccus (65–8 BCE), anglicized to Horace, was of a modest farming family, and was barely able to afford an education in both Athens and Rome. He later fought for Brutus and the republicans against Caesar, and returned home after the war to find his family gone and his lands confiscated. Fortunately Horace found wealthy patronage and was given an estate in Tivoli, which permitted him to concentrate on writing. His opus includes odes, satires, and epistles. He also wrote the Carmen Saeculare, *a hymn written for the emperor Augustus. Horace's odes are considered brilliant art, while his satires and epistles are thought very personal and intimate.*

Source: *John Conington, trans. and ed., Horatius Flaccus, Odes.*

> **Focus Questions:**
> 1. How does the poem reflect on Roman values?
> 2. How would the knowledge that Horace ran away from the only battle in which he fought affect your reading?
> 3. Which Roman value is found in the title (it is repeated in line 13)? How does it compare or contrast with modern attitudes?

To suffer hardness with good cheer,
In sternest school of warfare bred,
Our youth should learn; let steed and spear
Make him one day the *Parthian's* dread;
Cold skies, keen perils, brace his life.

Methinks I see from rampired town
Some battling tyrant's matron wife,
Some maiden, look in terror down,—
Ah, my dear lord, untrain'd in war!
O tempt not the infuriate mood
Of that fell lion I see! from far
He plunges through a tide of blood!
What joy, for fatherland to die!
Death's darts e'en flying feet o'ertake,
Nor spare a recreant chivalry,
A back that cowers, or loins that quake.
True Virtue never knows defeat:
Her robes she keeps unsullied still,
Nor takes, nor quits, *her* curule seat
To please a people's veering will.
True Virtue opens heaven to worth:
She makes the way she does not find:
The vulgar crowd, the humid earth,
Her soaring pinion leaves behind.
Seal'd lips have blessings sure to come:
Who drags *Eleusis'* rite today,
That man shall never share my home,
Or join my voyage: roofs give way
And boats are wreck'd: true men and thieves
Neglected Justice oft confounds:
Though Vengeance halt, she seldom leaves
The wretch whose flying steps she hounds.

Kautilya, from *Arthashastra*, "The Duties of Government Superintendents"

Around 300 BCE Kautilya, the chief minister for the emperor Chandragupta Maurya, wrote this treatise on government. Kautilya had helped Maurya build up the new empire that would peak in the reign of Asoka. Pragmatic realpolitik is very evident in the Arthashatra. In fact the book is often compared to Machiavelli's The Prince in its claim that the ruler should use any means to achieve his ends. However, the importance of maintaining a solid economy and secure peasantry is given emphasis. Kautilya's work was influential in the Mauryan empire, probably influencing Asoka himself.

Source: *Translated by R. Shamasastry, 1915.*

> **Focus Questions:**
> 1. What are the main types of responsibilities for the king?
> 2. What obligations do the people have?
> 3. What is the extent of infrastructure?

BOOK II, "THE DUTIES OF GOVERNMENT SUPERINTENDENTS"

CHAPTER I. FORMATION OF VILLAGES.

EITHER by inducing foreigners to immigrate (paradesapraváhanena) or by causing the thickly-populated centres of his own kingdom to send forth the excessive population (svadésábhishyandavámanéna vá), the king may construct villages either on new sites or on old ruins (bhútapúrvama vá).

Villages consisting each of not less than a hundred families and of not more than five-hundred families of agricultural people of sudra caste, with boundaries extending as far as a krósa (2250 yds.) or two, and capable of protecting each other shall be formed. Boundaries shall be denoted by a river, a mountain, forests, bulbous plants (grishti), caves, artificial buildings (sétubandha), or by trees such as sálmali (silk cotton tree), samí (Acacia Suma), and kshíravriksha (milky trees).

There shall be set up a stháníya (a fortress of that name) in the centre of eight-hundred villages, a drónamukha in the centre of four-hundred villages, a khárvátika in the centre of two-hundred villages and sangrahana in the midst of a collection of ten villages.

There shall be constructed in the extremities of the kingdom forts manned by boundary-guards (antapála) whose duty shall be to guard the entrances into the kingdom. The interior of the kingdom shall be watched by trap-keepers (vágurika), archers (sábara), hunters (pulinda), chandálas, and wild tribes (aranyachára).

Those who perform sacrifices (ritvik), spiritual guides, priests, and those learned in the Vedas shall be granted Brahmadaya lands yielding sufficient produce and exempted from taxes and fines (adandkaráni).

Superintendents, Accountants, Gopas, Sthánikas, Veterinary Surgeons (Aníkastha), physicians, horse-trainers, and messengers shall also be endowed with lands which they shall have no right to alienate by sale or mortgage.

Lands prepared for cultivation shall be given to tax-payers (karada) only for life (ekapurushikáni).

Unprepared lands shall not be taken away from those who are preparing them for cultivation.

Lands may be confiscated from those who do not cultivate them; and given to others; or they may be cultivated by village labourers (grámabhritaka) and traders (vaidehaka), lest those owners who do not properly cultivate them might pay less (to the government). If cultivators pay their taxes easily, they may be favourably supplied with grains, cattle, and money.

The king shall bestow on cultivators only such favour and remission (anugrahaparihárau) as will tend to swell the treasury, and shall avoid such as will deplete it.

A king with depleted treasury will eat into the very vitality of both citizens and country people. Either on the occasion of opening new settlements or on any other emergent occasions, remission of taxes shall be made.

He shall regard with fatherly kindness those who have passed the period of remission of taxes.

He shall carry on mining operations and manufactures, exploit timber and elephant forests, offer facilities for cattlebreeding and commerce, construct roads for traffic both by land and water, and set up market towns (panyapattana).

He shall also construct reservoirs (sétu) filled with water either perennial or drawn from some other source. Or he may provide with sites, roads, timber, and other necessary things those who construct reservoirs of their own accord. Likewise in the construction of places of pilgrimage (punyasthána) and of groves.

Whoever stays away from any kind of cooperative construction (sambhúya setubhandhát) shall send his servants and bullocks to carry on his work, shall have a share in the expenditure, but shall have no claim to the profit.

The king shall exercise his right of ownership (swámyam) with regard to fishing, ferrying and trading in vegetables (haritapanya) in reservoirs or lakes (sétushu).

Those who do not heed the claims of their slaves (dása), hirelings (áhitaka), and relatives shall be taught their duty.

The king shall provide the orphans, (bála), the aged, the infirm, the afflicted, and the helpless with maintenance. He shall also provide subsistence to helpless women when they are carrying and also to the children they give birth to.

Elders among the villagers shall improve the property of bereaved minors till the latter attain their age; so also the property of Gods.

When a capable person other than an apostate (patita) or mother neglects to maintain his or her child, wife, mother, father, minor brothers, sisters, or widowed girls (kanyá vidhaváscha), he or she shall be punished with a fine of twelve panas.

When, without making provision for the maintenance of his wife and sons, any person embraces asceticism, he shall be punished with the first amercement; likewise any person who converts a woman to asceticism (pravrájayatah).

Whoever has passed the age of copulation may become an ascetic after distributing the properties of his own acquisition (among his sons); otherwise, he will be punished.

No ascetic other than a vánaprastha (forest-hermit), no company other than the one of local birth (sájátadanyassanghah), and no guilds of any kind other than local cooperative guilds (sámutthávika danyassamayánubandhah) shall find entrance into the villages of the kingdom. Nor shall there be in villages buildings (sáláh) intended for sports and plays. Nor, in view of procuring money, free labour, commodities, grains, and liquids in plenty, shall actors, dancers, singers, drummers, buffoons (vágjívana), and bards (kusílava) make any disturbance to the work of the villagers; for helpless villagers are always dependent and bent upon their fields.

The king shall avoid taking possession of any country which is liable to the inroads of enemies and wild tribes and which is harassed by frequent visitations of famine and pestilence. He shall also keep away from expensive sports.

He shall protect agriculture from the molestation of oppressive fines, free labour, and taxes (dandavishtikarábádhaih); herds of cattle from thieves, tigers, poisonous creatures and cattle-disease.

He shall not only clear roads of traffic from the molestations of courtiers (vallabha), of workmen (kár-mika), of robbers, and of boundary-guards, but also keep them from being destroyed by herds of cattle.

Thus the king shall not only keep in good repair timber and elephant forests, buildings, and mines created in the past, but also set up new ones.

[Thus ends Chapter I, "Formation of Villages" in Book II, "The Duties of Government Superintendents," of the Arthasástra of Kautilya. End of twenty-second chapter from the beginning.]

Sima Qian, *The Life of Meng Tian*, Builder of the Great Wall

Sima Qian (145–86 BCE) was China's first scientific historian. As the official court historian for the Han Dynasty, he developed a definitive history of China by pioneering methods of reconstructing the past through primary sources, finishing towards the end of his life the "Records of the Grand Historian." So devoted (some might say obsessed) was he to the historian's craft that, when given the choice between death and castration for transgressing the will of the Emperor, he opted for castration on the sole basis of at least being able to complete his book. Here he relates the life of Meng Tian, designer of the Great Wall.

Source: *Raymond Dawson, trans.,* Sima Qian: Historical Records *(Oxford & N.Y.: Oxford University Press, 1994), pp. 55–61.*

Focus Questions:
1. To which professions were Meng Tian's ancestors and relatives appointed?
2. Under what circumstances did Meng Tian build the Wall and how long was he engaged in this task?
3. For what crime—in Meng's own words—did he commit suicide?
4. What is Sima's assessment of Meng Tian's life and character?

As for Meng Tian, his forebears were men of Qi. Tian's paternal grandfather, Meng Ao, came from Qi to serve King Zhaoxiang of Qin, and attained the office of senior minister. In the first year of King Zhuangxiang of Qin, Meng Ao became general of Qin, made an assault on Han and took Chenggao and Xingyang, and established the Sichuan province. In the second year Meng Ao attacked Zhao and took thirty-seven cities. In the third year of the First Emperor, Meng Ao attacked Han and took thirteen cities. In the fifth year Meng Ao attacked Wei, took twenty cities, and established Dong province. In the seventh year of the First Emperor, Meng Ao died. Ao's son was called Wu and Wu's son was called Tian. Tian at one time kept legal records and was in charge of the relevant literature. In the twenty-third year of the First Emperor, Meng Wu became an assistant general of Qin and, together with Wang Jian, made an attack on Chu and inflicted a major defeat upon it and killed Xiang Yan. In the twenty-fourth year Meng Wu attacked Chu and took the King of Chu prisoner. Meng Tian's younger brother was Meng Yi.

In the twenty-sixth year of the First Emperor, Meng Tian was able to become a general of Qin on account of the long-term service given by his family. He attacked Qi and inflicted a major defeat upon it, and was appointed Prefect of the Capital. When Qin had unified all under Heaven, Meng Tian was consequently given command of a host of 300,000 to go north and drive out the Rong and Di barbarians and take over the territory to the south of the Yellow River. He built the Great Wall, taking advantage of the lie of the land and making use of the passes. It started from Lintao and went as far as Liaodong, extending more than 10,000 li. Crossing the Yellow River, it followed the Yang Mountains and wriggled northwards. His army was exposed to the elements in the field for more than ten years when they were stationed in Shang province, and at this time Meng Tian filled the Xiongnu with terror.

The First Emperor held the Meng family in the highest esteem. Having confidence in them and so entrusting them with responsibility, he regarded them as men of quality. He allowed Meng Yi to be on terms of close intimacy, and he reached the position of senior minister. When he went out, he took him with him in his carriage, and within the palace he was constantly in the imperial presence. Tian was given responsibility for matters outside the capital, but Yi was constantly made to take part in internal planning. They were reputed to be loyal and trustworthy, so that none even of the generals or leading ministers dared to take issue with them in these matters.

Zhao Gao was a distant connection of the various Zhaos. He had several brothers, and all of them were born in the hidden part of the palace. His mother had been condemned to death, and her descendants were to be of low station for generations to come. When the King of Qin heard that Zhao Gao was forceful and well acquainted with the law, he promoted him and made him Director of Palace Coach-houses. Thereupon Gao privately served Prince Huhai and gave him instruction in judicial decisions. When Zhao Gao committed a major crime, the King of Qin ordered Meng Yi to try him at law. Yi did not dare to show partiality, so he condemned Gao to death and removed him from the register of officials, but because of Gao's estimable performance in the conduct of affairs, the Emperor pardoned him and restored his office and rank.

The First Emperor intended to travel throughout the Empire and go via Jiuyuan directly to Ganquan, so he made Meng Tian open up a road from Jiuyuan straight to Ganquan, hollowing out mountains and filling in valleys for 1,800 li. The road had not yet been completed when the First Emperor in the winter of the thirty-seventh year went forth on his journey and travelled to Kuaiji. Going along the sea coast, he went north to Langye. When he fell ill on the way, he made Meng Yi return to offer prayers to the mountains and streams. He had not yet got back when the First Emperor passed away on reaching Shaqiu. It was kept a secret, and none of the officials knew. At this time Chief Minister Li Si, Prince Huhai, and Director of Palace Coach-houses Zhao Gao were in constant attendance. Gao had regularly obtained favours from Huhai and wanted him to be set on the throne. He was also resentful that when Meng Yi had tried him at law he had not been in favour of letting him off. Consequently he felt like doing him harm, and so he secretly plotted together with Chief Minister Li Si and Prince Huhai to establish Huhai as crown prince. When the Crown Prince had been established, messengers were sent to bestow death on Prince Fusu and Meng Tian because of their alleged crimes. Even after Fusu was dead, Meng Tian felt suspicious and requested confirmation of it. The messengers handed Meng Tian over to the law officers and replaced him.

The messengers returned and made their report, and when Huhai heard that Fusu was dead he intended to free Meng Tian. But Zhao Gao, fearing that the Meng family would again be treated with honour and be employed on affairs, felt resentful about this.

So when Meng Yi got back, Zhao Gao, making his plans on the pretext of loyalty towards Huhai, intended on this account to wipe out the Meng family. 'Your servant hears that the previous Emperor had long intended to promote a man of quality and set up a crown prince,' he therefore said, 'but Meng Yi had remonstrated and said that this would be improper. But if he was aware that you were a man of quality and yet insisted that you should not be set up, this would be acting disloyally and deluding one's sovereign. In your servant's foolish opinion, the best thing would be to put him to death.' Paying heed, Huhai had Meng Yi put in bonds at Dai. (Previously he had taken Meng Tian prisoner at Yangzhou.) When the announcement of mourning reached Xianyang and the funeral had taken place, the Crown Prince was set up as Second Generation Emperor and Zhao Gao, being admitted to terms of close intimacy; slandered the Meng family day and night, seeking out their crimes and mistakes so as to recommend their impeachment.

Ziying came forward to remonstrate, saying: 'I hear that in ancient times King Qian of Zhao killed his good minister Li Mu and employed Yan Ju, and King Xi of Yan secretly employed the stratagems of Jing Ke and ignored the pact with Qin, and King Jian of Qi killed loyal ministers from ancient families which had given long-standing service and made use of the counsels of Hou Sheng. Each of these three rulers lost their states through changing ancient ways so that disaster befell them. Now the Meng family are [sic] important officials and counsellors of Qin and yet our sovereign intends to get rid of them all in a single morning, but your servant humbly considers this to be improper. Your servant hears that it is impossible for one who plans frivolously to govern a state and it is impossible for one who exercises wisdom on his own to preserve his ruler. If you put to death loyal servants and set up people who have nothing to do with integrity, then within the palace this will cause all your servants to lose confidence in each other, and in the field it will cause the purposes of your fighting men to lose their cohesion. Your servant humbly considers this to be improper.'

Huhai did not take any notice, but dispatched the imperial scribe Qu Gong to ride relay and go to Dai and instruct Meng Yi as follows: 'You, minister, made things difficult when our previous sovereign wanted to set up a crown prince. Now the Chief Minister considers that you are disloyal, and that your whole clan is implicated in the crime. But in the kindness of Our heart We bestow death upon you, minister, which is surely extremely gracious. It is for you to give this your consideration!'

'If it is thought that your servant was incapable of grasping the wishes of our previous sovereign,' replied Meng Yi, 'then when he was young he was in his service and obediently received his patronage until he passed away, so it may be said that he knew what he wanted. Or if it is thought that your servant was unaware of the abilities of the Crown Prince, then he went all over the Empire with the Crown Prince in sole attendance, and left all the other princes far behind, so your servant had no doubts. Our previous sovereign's proposal to employ him as crown prince had been building up over several years, so what words would your servant have dared to utter in remonstrance, and what plan would he dare to have devised! It is not that I dare to produce showy verbiage for the purpose of avoiding death and implicate the reputation of our previous sovereign by creating an embarrassment, but I would like you, sir, to devote your thoughts to this, and make sure that the circumstances which cause your servant to be put to death are true. Moreover, perfect obedience is what the Way honours, and killing as a punishment is what the Way puts an end to. In former times Duke Mu of Qin died having killed three good men, and charged Baili Xi with a crime although it was not his. Therefore he was given the title of "False." King Zhaoxiang killed Bai Qi, Lord Wan. King Ping of Chu killed Wu She. Fucha King of Wu killed Wu Zixu. These four rulers all made major mistakes and so all under Heaven regarded them as wrong and thought such rulers were unenlightened, and as such they were recorded by the feudal lords. Therefore it is said that "Those who govern in accordance with the Way do not kill the guiltless and punishment is not inflicted on the innocent." It is up to you, my lord, to take notice!' But the messengers were aware of what Huhai wanted, so they took no notice of Meng Yin's words, and killed him forthwith.

Second Generation also dispatched messengers to go to Yangzhou, with the following instructions for Meng Tian: 'Your errors, my lord, have become numerous, and your younger brother Yi bears a great burden of guilt, so the law has caught up with you.' 'From my grandfather right down to his sons and grandsons,' said Meng Tian, 'their achievements and trustworthiness have been built up in Qin over three generations. Now your servant has been in command of more than 300,000 soldiers, and although he personally is a prisoner, his influence is sufficient to instigate a revolt. But as one who safeguards righteousness although he is aware he is bound to die, he does not dare to disgrace the teachings of his forbears, and in this way does not forget his former sovereign. In former times when King Cheng of Zhou was first set on the throne and had not yet left his swaddling clothes, Dan Duke of Zhou carried the King on his back to go to court, and ultimately restored order in all under Heaven. When King Cheng had an illness and was in extreme danger, Duke Dan personally cut his finger-nails and sank the parings in the Yellow River. "The King does not yet possess understanding and it is I who handle affairs," he said. "If there is a crime-engendered disaster, I accept the unfortunate consequences of it."

Accordingly he made an account and stored it away in the repository of records, and he may be said to have behaved with good faith. When the time came when the King was able to govern the country, there was a malicious official who said: "Dan Duke of Zhou has long intended to make a rebellion, and if the King is not prepared, there is bound to be a major crisis." The King was consequently furious and Dan Duke of Zhou ran away and fled to Chu. When King Cheng looked at the repository of records, he got hold of the account of the sinking, and so he said, with tears streaming down his face: "Who said that Dan Duke of Zhou intended to make a rebellion?" He killed the one who had said this and restored Dan Duke of Zhou. Thus the Book Zhou says: "One must put them in threes and fives." Now for generations my family has avoided duplicity, so if our affairs are finally in such straits, this is bound to be due to the methods of a wicked minister rebelliously stirring up trouble. That King Cheng made a mistake, but when he restored the situation, he ultimately flourished; but Jie killed Guan Longfeng and Zhou killed Prince Bi Gan, and they did not repent, and when they died their country was destroyed. Your servant therefore says that errors can be remedied and remonstrance can be understood. To examine into threes and fives is the method of supreme sages. All in all, your servant's words have not been for the purpose of seeking to escape from blame. He is about to die because he is making a remonstrance, and he wishes Your Majesty would think about following the Way for the sake of the myriad people.' 'Your servants have received an imperial decree to carry out the law on you, general,' said the messengers, 'and they do not dare to report your words to the Supreme One.' Meng Tian sighed deeply. 'For what am I being blamed by Heaven,' he cried, 'that I should die although I have avoided error?' After a good long while he solemnly said: 'There is a crime for which I certainly ought to die. I built a wall stretching more than 10,000 li from Lintao as far as Liaodong, and so in the course of this I surely could not avoid cutting through the earth's arteries. This then is my crime.' And so he swallowed poison and killed himself.

The Grand Historiographer says: 'I have been to the northern border and returned via the direct road. On my journey I observed the ramparts of the Great Wall which Meng Tian built for Qin. He hollowed out the mountains and filled in the valleys and opened up a direct road. To be sure, he showed little concern for the efforts of the people. Qin had only just destroyed the feudal states and the hearts of the people of all under Heaven had not yet been restored to order, and the wounded had not yet been healed; but Tian, although he had become a famous general, did not use this occasion to remonstrate strongly and remedy the distresses of the people, minister to the old and enable the orphans to survive, and strive to cultivate harmony among the masses. Instead he embarked on great enterprises to pander to imperial ambition, so was it not therefore reasonable that both he and his brother should suffer the death penalty? Why in that case should cutting the arteries of the earth be made a crime?'

Emperor Asoka, Excerpt from *The Edicts* of Asoka

Emperor Asoka (c. 274–232 BCE) was the grandson of the Maurya Dynasty's founder, Chandragupta I and, in his early days, acted in the conventional manner of potentates, always seeking to enlarge his personal power and expand his domains through conquest. The sight of the horrendous slaughter and devastation caused by the Battle of Kalinga, however, brought about a spiritual crisis and a change of heart; thereafter Asoka never waged war and tried to atone for his past actions by governing his subjects in as moral and benevolent a manner as possible. A convert to Buddhism, Asoka has been, on up to this day, considered the role model for successive Indian rulers (kings, prime ministers, etc.). His decrees, sometimes inscribed on stone pillars and rocks, set forth his philosophy of government.

Source: *N.A. Nikam & Richard McKeon, trans.,* The Edicts of Asoka *(Chicago: University of Chicago Press, 1959), pp. 27–30, 51–52. Quoted in Mircea Eliade, From Medicine Men to Muhammad (N.Y.: Harper & Row, 1974), pp. 142–145.*

Focus Questions:
1. What reasons does Asoka (Priyadarshi-) give for his repentence? How does he propose to deal with the forest peoples?
2. Taking an overview based on reading all the edicts presented here, precisely what does Asoka's concept of Dharma seem to entail?
3. What rationale does Asoka give for his policy of religious tolerance? What benefits does he see in following such a course?

('ROCK EDICT' XIII)

The Kalinga country was conquered by King Priyadarshi-, Beloved of the Gods, in the eighth year of his reign. One hundred and fifty thousand persons were carried away captive, one hundred thousand were slain, and many times that number died.

Immediately after the Kalingas had been conquered, King Priyadarshi- became intensely devoted to the study of Dharma, to the love of Dharma, and to the inculcation of Dharma.

The Beloved of the Gods, conqueror of the Kalingas, is moved to remorse now. For he has felt profound sorrow and regret because the conquest of a people previously unconquered involves slaughter, death, and deportation.

But there is a more important reason for the King's remorse. The Brahmanas and Shramanas [the priestly and ascetic orders] as well as the followers of other religions and the householders—who all practiced obedience to superiors, parents, and teachers, and proper courtesy and firm devotion to friends, acquaintances, companions, relatives, slaves, and servants—all suffer from the injury, slaughter and deportation inflicted on their loved ones. Even those who escaped calamity themselves are deeply afflicted by the misfortunes suffered by those friends, acquaintances, companions, and relatives for whom they feel an undiminished affection. Thus all men share in the misfortune, and this weighs on King Priyadarshi-'s mind.

[Moreover, there is no country except that of the Yo-nas (that the Greeks) where Brahmin and Buddhist ascetics do not exist] there is no place where men are not attached to one faith or another.

Therefore, even if the number of people who were killed died or who were carried away in the Kalinga war had been only one one-hundredth or one one-thousandth of what it actually was, this would still have weighed on the King's mind.

King Priyadarshi- now thinks that even a person who wrongs him must be forgiven for wrongs that can be forgiven.

King Priyadarshi- seeks to induce even the forest peoples who have come under his dominion [that is, primitive peoples in the sections of the conquered territory] to adopt this way of life and this ideal. He reminds them, however, that he exercises the power to punish, despite his repentance, in order to induce them to desist from their crimes and escape execution.

For King Priyadarshi- desires security, self-control, impartiality, and cheerfulness for all living creatures.

King Priyadarshi- considers moral conquest [that is, conquest by Dharma, Dharma vijaya] the most important conquest. He has achieved this moral conquest repeatedly both here and among the peoples living beyond the borders of his kingdom, even as far away as six hundred yojanas [about three thousand miles], where the Yo-na [Greek] king Antiyoka rules, and even beyond Antiyoka in the realm of the four kings named Turamaya, Antikini, Maka, and Alikasudara and to the south among the Cholas and Pandyas [in the southern tip of the Indian peninsula] as far as Ceylon.

Here in the King's dominion also, among the Yo-nas [inhabitants a northwest frontier province, probably Greeks] and the Kambo-jas [neighbours of the Yo-nas], among the Na-bhakas and Na-bhapanktis [who probably lived along the Himalayan frontier], among the Bhojas and Paitryanikas, among the Andhras and Paulindas [all peoples of the Indian peninsula], everywhere people heed his instructions in Dharma.

Even in countries which King Priyadarshi-'s envoys have not reached, people have heard about Dharma and about his Majesty's ordinances and instructions in Dharma, and they themselves conform to Dharma and will continue to do so.

Wherever conquest is achieved by Dharma, it produces satisfaction. Satisfaction is firmly established by conquest by Dharma [since it generates no opposition of conquered and conqueror]. Even satisfaction, however, is of little importance. King Priyadarshi- attaches value ultimately to consequences of action in the other world.

This edict on Dharma has been inscribed so that my sons and great-grandsons who may come after me should not think new conquests worth achieving. If they do conquer, let them take pleasure in moderation and mild punishments. Let them consider moral conquest the only true conquest.

That is good, here and hereafter. Let their pleasure be pleasure in [Dharma-rati]. For this alone is good, here and hereafter.

('ROCK EDICT' XII)

King Priyadarshi- honours men of all faith, members of religious orders and laymen alike, with gifts and various marks of esteem. Yet he does not value either gifts or honours as much as growth in the qualities essential to religion in men of all faiths.

This growth may take many forms, but its root is in guarding one's speech to avoid extolling one's own faith and disparaging the faith of others improperly or, when the occasion is appropriate, immoderately.

The faiths of others all deserve to be honoured for one reason or another. By honouring them, one exalts one's own faith and at the same time performs a service to the faith of others. By acting otherwise, one injures one's own faith and also does disservice to that of others. For if a man extols his own faith and disparages another because of devotion to his own and because he wants to glorify it, he seriously injures his own faith.

Therefore concord alone is commendable, for through concord men may learn and respect the conception of Dharma accepted by others.

King Priyadarshi- desires men of all faiths to know each other's doctrines and to acquire sound doctrines. Those who are attached to their particular faiths should be told that King Priyadarshi- does not value gifts or honours as much as growth in the qualities essential to religion in men of all faiths.

Many officials are assigned to tasks bearing on this purpose—the officers in charge of spreading Dharma, the superintendents of women the royal households, the inspectors of cattle and pasture lands, and other officials.

The objective of these measures is the promotion of each man's particular faith and the glorification of Dharma.

('KALINGA EDICT' II)

King Priyadarshi- says:

I command that the following instructions be communicated to my official at Sama-pa:

Whenever something right comes to my attention, I want it put into practice and I want effective means devised to achieve it. My principal means to do this is to transmit my instructions to you.

All men are my children. Just as I seek the welfare and happiness of my own children in this world and the next, I seek the same things for all men.

Unconquered peoples along the borders of my dominions may wonder what my disposition is towards them. My only wish with respect to them is that they should not fear me, but trust me; that they should expect only happiness from me, not misery; that they should understand further that I will forgive them for offences which can be forgiven; that they should be induced by my example to practice Dharma; and that they should attain happiness in this world and the next.

I transmit these instructions to you in order to discharge my debt [to them] by instructing you and making known to you my will and my unshakable resolution and commitment. You must perform your duties in this way and establish their confidence in the King, assuring them that he is like a father to them, that he loves them as he loves himself, and that they are like his own children.

Having instructed you and informed you of my will and my unshakable resolution and commitment, I will appoint officials to carry out this programme in all the provinces. You are able to inspire the border peoples with confidence in me and to advance their welfare and happiness in this world and the next. By doing so, you will also attain heaven and help me discharge my debts to the people.

This edict has been inscribed here so that my officials will work at all times to inspire the peoples of neighbouring countries with confidence in me and to induce them to practice Dharma.

Excerpts from *The Questions of King Milinda*

The "King Milinda" of the revered Buddhist scripture "The Questions of King Milinda" was based on the historical Greek King Menender of Bactria (c. 160–135 B.C.E.), whose realm was one of the successor-states to the empire of Alexander the Great. Buddhist tradition asserts that Menander converted to Buddhism after exchanging thought and insights with the monk Negasena.

Source: *T. W. Rhys Davids, trans.,* The Questions of King Milinda *(Delhi, India: Motiles Banarsidass, 1965; first published by Oxford University Press, 1894) pp. 1–10.*

Focus Questions:
1. What can be gleaned from the description of Sagala that sheds light on the city's economic/commercial life?
2. What references might tend to bear out Milinda's Greek education and upbringing, and what traits does Milinda demonstrate that might confirm this?
3. In what manner does the author tie in Buddhist spiritual ideas to the story?

THE SECULAR NARRATIVE

1. King Milinda, at Sâgala the famous town of yore,
To Nâgasena, the world famous sage, repaired.
(So the deep Ganges to the deeper ocean flows.)
To him, the eloquent, the bearer of the torch
Of Truth, dispeller of the darkness of men's minds,
Subtle and knotty questions did he put, many,
Turning on many points. Then were solutions given
Profound in meaning, gaining access to the heart,
Sweet to the ear, and passing wonderful and strange.
For Nâgasena's talk plunged to the hidden depths
Of Vinaya and of Abhidhamma (Law and Thought)
Unravelling all the meshes of the Suttas' net,
Glittering the while with metaphors and reasoning high.
Come then! Apply your minds, and let your hearts rejoice,
And hearken to these subtle questionings, all grounds
Of doubt well fitted to resolve.

2. Thus hath it, been handed down by tradition—There is in the country of the Yonakasa a great centre of trade, a city that is called Sâgala, situate in a delightful country well watered and hilly, abounding in parks and gardens and groves and lakes and tanks a paradise of rivers and mountains and woods. Wise architects have laid it out, and its people know of no oppression, since all their enemies and adversaries have been put down. Brave is its defence, with many and various strong towers and ramparts, with superb gates and entrance archways; and with the royal citadel in its midst, white walled and deeply moated. Well laid out are its streets, squares, cross roads, and market places. Well displayed are the innumerable sorts of costly merchandise with which its shops are filled. It is richly adorned with hundreds of alms-halls of various kinds; and splendid with hundreds of thousands of magnificent mansions, which rise aloft like the mountain peaks of the Himalayas. Its streets are filled with elephants, horses, carriages, and foot-passengers, frequented by groups of handsome men and beautiful women, and crowded by men of all sorts and conditions, Brahmans, nobles, artificers, and servants. They resound with cries of welcome to the teachers of every creed, and the city is the resort of the leading men of each of the differing sects. Shops are there for the sale of Benares muslin, of Kotumbara stuffs, and of other cloths of various kinds; and sweet odours are exhaled from the bazaars, where all sorts of flowers and perfumes are tastefully set out. Jewels are there in plenty, such as men's hearts desire, and guilds of traders in all sorts of finery display their goods in the bazaars that face all quarters of the sky. So full is the city of money, and of gold and silver ware, of copper and stone ware, that it is a very mine of dazzling treasures. And there is laid up there much store of property and corn and things of value in warehouses—foods and drinks of every sort, syrups and sweetmeats of every kind. In wealth it rivals Uttara-kuru, and in glory it is as Âlakamandâ, the city of the gods.

3. Having said thus much we must now relate the previous birth history of these two persons (Milinda and Nâgasena) and the various sorts of puzzles. This we shall do under six heads:—

1. Their previous history (Pubba-yoga).
2. The Milinda problems.
3. Questions as to distinguishing characteristics.
4. Puzzles arising out of contradictory statements.
5. Puzzles arising out of ambiguity.
6. Discussions turning on metaphor.

And of these the Milinda problems are in divisions—questions as to distinctive characteristics; and questions aiming at the dispelling of doubt; and the puzzles arising out of contradictory statements are in two divisions—the long chapter, and the problems in the life of the recluse.

THEIR PREVIOUS HISTORY (PUBBA-YOGA)

4. By Pubba-yoga is meant their past Karma (their doings in this or previous lives). Long ago, they say, when Kassapa the Buddha was promulgating the faith, there dwelt in one community near the Ganges a great company of members of the Order. There the brethren, true to established rules and duties, rose early in the morning, and taking the long-handled brooms, would sweep out the courtyard and collect the rubbish into a heap, meditating the while on the virtues of the Buddha.

5. One day a brother told a novice to remove the heap of dust. But he, as if he heard not, went about his business; and on being called a second time, and a third, still went his way as if he had not heard. Then the brother, angry with so intractable a novice, dealt him a blow with the broom stick. This time, not daring to refuse, he set about the task crying; and as he did so he muttered to himself this first aspiration: 'May I, by reason of this meritorious act of throwing out the rubbish, in each successive condition in which I may be born up to the time when I attain Nirvâna, be powerful and glorious as the midday sun!'

6. When he had finished his work he went to the river side to bathe, and on beholding the mighty billows of the Ganges seething and surging, he uttered this second aspiration: 'May I, in each successive condition in which I may be born till I attain Nirvâna, possess the power of saying the right thing, and saying it instantly, under any circumstance that may arise, carrying all before me like this mighty surge!'

7. Now that brother, after he had put the broom away in the broom closet, had likewise wandered down to the river side to bathe, and as he walked he happened to overhear what the novice had said. Then thinking: 'If this fellow, on the ground of such an act of merit, which after all was instigated by me, can harbour hopes like this, what may not I attain to?' he too made his wish, and it was thus: 'In each successive condition in which I may be born till I attain Nirvâna, may I too be ready in saying the right thing at once, and more especially may I have the power of unravelling and of solving each problem and each puzzling question this young man may put—carrying all before me like this mighty surge!'

8. Then for the whole period between one Buddha and the next these two people wandered from existence to existence among gods and men. And our Buddha saw them too, and just as he did to the son of Moggall and to Tissa the Elder, so to them also did he foretell their future fate, saying: 'Five hundred years after I have passed away with these two reappear, and the subtle Law and Doctrine taught by me will they two explain, unravelling and disentangling its difficulties by questions put and metaphors adduced.'

9. Of the two the novice became the king of the city of Sâgala in India, Milinda by name, learned eloquent, wise, and able; and a faithful observer, and that at the right time, of all the various acts of devotion and ceremony enjoined by his own sacred hymns concerning things past, present, and to come. Many were the arts and sciences he knew—holy tradition and secular law; the Sânkhya, Yoga, Nyâya, and Vaiseshika systems of philosophy; arithmetic; music; medicine; the four Vedas, the Purânas, and the Itihâsas; astronomy, magic, causation, and spells; the art of war; poetry; conveyancing—in a word, the whole nineteen.

As a disputant he was hard to equal, harder still to overcome; acknowledged superior of all the founders of the schools of thought. And as in wisdom so in strength of body, swiftness, and valour there was none equal to Milinda in all India. He was rich too, mighty in wealth and prosperity, and the number of his armed hosts knew no end.

10. Now one day Milinda the king proceeded forth out of the city to pass in review the innumerable host of his mighty army in its fourfold array (of elephants, cavalry, bowmen, and soldiers on foot). And when the numbering of the forces was over, the king, who was fond of wordy disputation, and eager for discussion with casuists, sophists, and gentry of that sort, looked at the sun (to ascertain the time), and then said to his ministers: 'The day is yet young. What would be the use of getting back to town so early? Is there no learned person, whether wandering teacher or Brahman, the head of some school or order, or the master of some band of pupils (even though he profess faith in the Arahat, the Supreme Buddha), who would be able to talk with me, and resolve my doubts?'

11. Thereupon the five hundred Yonakas said to Milinda the king: 'There are the six Masters, O king!— Pûrana Kassapa, Makkhali of the cowshed, the Nigantha of the Nâta clan, Sañgaya the son of the Belattha woman, Agita of the garment of hair, and Pakudha Kakkâyana. These are well known as famous founders of schools, followed by bands of disciples and hearers, and highly honoured by the people. Go, great king! put to them your problems, and have your doubts resolved.

12. So king Milinda, attended by the five hundred Yonakas, mounted the royal car with its splendid equipage, and went out to the dwelling-place of Pûrana Kassapa, exchanged with him the compliments of friendly greeting, and took his seat courteously apart. And thus sitting he said to him: 'Who is it, venerable Kassapa, who rules the world?'

'The Earth, great king, rules the world!'

'But, venerable Kassapa, if it be the Earth that rules the world, how comes it that some men go to the Avîki hell, thus getting outside the sphere of the Earth?'

When he had thus spoken, neither could Pûrana Kassapa swallow the puzzle, nor could he bring it up; crestfallen, driven to silence, and moody, there he sat.

13. Then Milinda the king said to Makkhali of the cowshed: 'Are there, venerable Gosâla, good and evil acts? Is there such a thing as fruit, ultimate result, of good and evil acts?'

'There are no such acts, O king; and no such fruit, or ultimate result. Those who here in the world are nobles, they, O king, when they go to the other world, will become nobles once more. And those who are Brahmans, or of the middle class, or workpeople, or outcasts here, will in the next world become the same. What then is the use of good or evil acts?'

'If, venerable Gosâla, it be as you say then, by parity of reasoning, those who, here in this world have a hand cut off, must in the next world become persons with a hand cut off, and in like manner those who have had a foot cut off or an ear or their nose!'

And at this saying Makkhali was silenced.

14. Then thought Milinda the king within himself: 'All India is an empty thing, it is verily like chaff! There is no one, either recluse or Brahman capable of discussing things with me, and dispelling my doubts.' And he said to his ministers: 'Beautiful is the night and pleasant! Who is the recluse or Brahman we can visit to-night to question him who will be able to converse with us and dispel our doubts?' And at that saying the counsellors remained silent, and stood there gazing upon the face of the king.

Chapter 8

The Collapse of Empires

Treaty between Tibet and China, 821–822

Tibet entered into a period of aggressive expansionism in the eighth century that brought it into conflict with Tang China, which was already on the defensive in central Asia after its defeat at the hands of an Arab army at the Talas River in 751. But Tibetan expansionism coincided with the spread of Buddhism in the kingdom, and both religious contacts and marriage politics made peace negotiations possible. A peace treaty was signed in 783 establishing the boundaries of the two lands. In 821, that treaty was renewed and reaffirmed with Buddhist rituals and the carving of the treaty onto three stone pillars. One was placed in the Chinese capital Chang-an, one at the border, and one in the Tibetan capital Lhasa. The last still survives and provides the text translated below.

Source: *Treaty between Tibet and China, 821–822, Tibetan Parliamentary and Policy Research Center.*

Focus Questions:
1. What factors appear to have influenced both sides to make peace? How does the language of the treaty reinforce the ties that bind the two powers?
2. What does the text of the treaty tell us about diplomatic procedures and government record-keeping in the two kingdoms during this period?
3. What does the treaty tell us about the sorts of everyday activities that took place along the border of the two kingdoms? What sorts of regulations does the treaty impose on such activities?

The Great King of Tibet, the Miraculous Divine Lord, and the Great King of China, the Chinese Ruler Hwang-ti, being in the relationship of nephew and uncle, have conferred together for the alliance of their kingdoms. They have made and ratified a great agreement. Gods and men all know it and bear witness so that it may never be changed; and an account of the agreement has been engraved on this stone pillar to inform future ages and generations.

The Miraculous Divine Lord Tri-tsug De-tseji and the Chinese King Wen Wu Hsiao-te Wang-ti, nephew and uncle, seeking in their far-reaching wisdom to prevent all causes of harm to the welfare of their countries now or in the future, have extended their benevolence impartially over all. With the single desire of acting for the peace and benefit of all their subjects they have agreed on high purpose of ensuring lasting good; and they have made this great treaty in order to full fill their decision to restore the former ancient friendship and mutual regard and the old relationship of friendly neighborliness.

Between the two countries no smoke nor dust shall be seen. There shall be no sudden alarms and the very word 'enemy' shall not be spoken. Even the frontier guards shall have no anxiety nor fear and shall enjoy land and bed at their ease. All shall live in peace and share the blessing of happiness for ten thousand years. The fame of this shall extend to all places reached by the sun and the moon.

This solemn agreement has established a great epoch when Tibetans shall be happy in the land of Tibet, and Chinese in the land of China. So that it may never be changed, the Three Precious Jewels of Religion, the Assembly of Saints, the Sun and Moon, Planets and Stars have been invoked as witnesses. An oath bas been taken with solemn words and with the sacrifice of animals; and the agreement has been ratified.

If the parties do not act in accordance with this agreement or if they violate it, whichever it be, Tibet or China, nothing that the other party may do by way of retaliation shall be considered a breach of the treaty on their part.

The Kings and Ministers of Tibet and China have taken the prescribed oath to this effect and the agreement has been written in detail. The two Kings have affixed their seals. The Ministers specially empowered to execute the agreement have inscribed their signatures and copies have been deposited in the royal records of each party.

Tibet and China shall abide by the frontiers of which they are now in occupation. All to the east is the country of Great China; and all to the west is, without question, the country of Great Tibet. Henceforth on neither side shall there be waging of war nor seizing of territory. If any person incurs suspicion he shall be arrested; his business shall be inquired into and he shall be escorted back.

Now that the two kingdoms have been allied by this great treaty it is necessary that messengers should once again be sent by the old route to maintain communications and carry the exchange of friendly messages regarding the harmonious relations between the Nephew and Uncle. According to the old custom, horses shall be changed at the foot of the Chiang Chun pass, the frontier between Tibet and China. At the Suiyung barrier the Chinese shall meet Tibetan envoys and provide them with all facilities from there onwards. At Ch'ing-shui the Tibetans shall meet Chinese envoys and provide all facilities. On both sides they shall be treated with customary honor and respect in conformity with the friendly relations between Nephew and Uncle.

Excerpts from the *Hildebrandslied*

The Hildebrandslied only survives in a single 68-line fragment that had been copied onto the flyleaves of a religious book in about 830 CE. It is a good example of the Germanic tradition of heroic verse, a form that is well known to us in the shape of great epics such as Beowulf and the Nebelungenlied. The events of the Hildebrandslied take place during the early fifth century amidst the epoch-marking encounters amongst the Huns, Germans, and Romans.

Source: *Freely translated by D. L. Ashliman (1997).*

Focus Questions:
1. Where do the character's loyalties lay?
2. How do their values compare with the Romans?
3. What groups and leaders are mentioned, and in what tone?

I have heard tell,
that two chosen warriors, Hildebrand and Hadubrand,
met one another, between two armies.
Father and son, the champions examined their gear,
prepared their armor, and buckled their swords
over their chain mail, before riding out to battle.
Hildebrand, the older and more experienced man, spoke first,
asking, with few words who his father was
and from which family he came.
"Tell me the one, young man, and I'll know the other,
for I know all great people in this kingdom."
Hadubrand, the son of Hildebrand, replied:
"Old and wise people who lived long ago
told me that my father's name was Hildebrand.
My name is Hadubrand.
Long ago he road off into the East with Dietrich,
and his many warriors, fleeing Otacher's wrath.
He rode off into the East, leaving his wife at home
with a small child, deprived of his inheritance.
Dietrich, a man with but few friends,
came to rely upon my father.
His feud with Otacher grew more intense,
and my father became his best-loved warrior.
He was at the front of every battle, wanting to be in every duel.

.....

Brave men knew him well."

.....

"With Almighty God in Heaven for a witness,
may you never go to battle against your next of kin."
And he took from his arm a band of rings,
braided from the emperor's gold,
which the King of the Huns had given to him.
"I give you this in friendship."
Hadubrand, the son of Hildebrand, replied:
"A gift should be received with a spear,
point against point.
You are a cunning old Hun,
leading me into a trap with your words,
only to throw your spear at me.
You have grown old by practicing such treachery.
Sailors traveling westward across the Mediterranean Sea
told me that he fell in battle.
Hildebrand, the son of Heribrand, is dead."
Hildebrand, the son of Heribrand, replied:
"I see from your battle gear that you have a good master at home,
and that you have never been banished by your prince.

.....

Alas, Lord God, fate has struck.
Sixty times I have seen summer turn to winter
and winter to summer in a foreign land.
I was always placed on the front lines;
I was never killed while storming a fortress,
and now my own child should strike me with his sword
and hit me with his ax, if I don't kill him first.
But if you have the courage, you can easily
win the armor from an old man like me,
and take away the spoils, if you have any right to them.

.....

Not even the worst of the men from the East
would turn down the the chance to fight with you,
with your desire to duel. Cost what it may,
let us see who will boast of this gear and who will lay claim to these two suits of chain mail."
Then they let sail their ashen spears,
Sharp showers, sticking in their shields.
They came closer on foot, splitting each other's bright boards,
striking fiercely until their weapons shattered their shields.

Jordanes, *Deeds of the Goths*, Book Twenty-six

At least part Goth himself, Jordanes wrote his history around 550 while the Byzantines were at war with the Goths in Italy. Jordanes' idea was to present the Goths as a classical and civilized nation in order to legitimize their claim to become part of Rome. Jordanes is therefore sympathetic in general to both Byzantines and Goths. In this reading of events occurring in 378 CE, the Goths have just arrived in the empire as refugees and are rebelling against corrupt Roman officials.

Source: *Jordanes*. Deeds of the Goths, *Book XXVI, trans. by Charles Christopher Mierow, 1915.*

Focus Questions:
1. How are the Romans and Goths contrasted?
2. What is so treacherous about the trick at the banquet?
3. What do you think the Romans should do next?

134

Quibus evenit, ut assolet genti necdum bene loco fundatae, penuria famis, coeperuntque primates eorum et duces, qui regum vice illis praeerant—id est Fritigernus, Alatheus et Safrac exercitus inopiae condolere negotiationemque a Lupicino Maximoque, Romanorum ducibus, expetere.

Soon famine and want came upon them, as often happens to a people not yet well settled in a country. Their princes and the leaders who ruled them in place of kings, that is Fripi-gairn {"Peace-yearning"}, {"General-minister," lit. "All-servant"} and Saba-rak {(perhaps) "Clearsighted narrator"}, began to lament the plight of their army and begged Lupicinus and Maximus, the Roman commanders, to open a market.

Verum quid non "auri sacra fames" (Virgilius, Aeneidis 3,56) compellit acquiescere? Coeperunt duces, avaritia compellente, non solum ovium boumque carnes, verum etiam canum et immundorum animalium morticina eis pro magno contradere, adeo, ut quodlibet mancipium uno pane aut decem libris carnis mercarentur.

But to what will not the "cursed lust for gold" (Vergil, Aeneid 3,56) compel men to assent? The generals, swayed by avarice, sold them at a high price not only the flesh of sheep and oxen, but even the carcasses of dogs and unclean animals, to the point that a slave would be bartered for a loaf of bread or ten pounds of meat.

135

Sed jam mancipiis et supellectile deficientibus, filios eorum avarus mercator victus necessitate exposcit. Haut enim secus parentes faciunt, saluti suorum pignorum providentes—faciliusque deliberant ingenuitatem perire quam vitam, dum misericorditer alendus quis venditur quam moriturus servatur.

When the Goths ran out of slaves and household items, the greedy trader demanded their sons in return for the necessities of life. And the parents consented even to this, in order to provide for the safety of their children, arguing that it was better to lose liberty than life; and indeed it is better that one be sold, if he will be mercifully fed, than that he should be kept free only to die.

Contigit etenim illo sub tempore aerumnoso, Lupicinus ut ductor Romanorum Fritigernum Gothorum regulum in convivium invitaret dolumque ei—ut post exitus docuit—moliretur.

Now it came to pass in that troublous time that Lupicinus, the Roman general, invited Fripi-gaírn, a chieftain of the Goths, to a feast and, as the event revealed, devised a plot against him.

136

Sed Fritigernus doli nescius cum paucorum comitatu ad convivium veniens, dum intus in praetorio epularetur, clamorem miserorum morientium audit; nam in alia parte socios ejus clausos dum milites, ducis sui jussu, trucidare conarentur, et vox morientium duriter emissa jam suspectis auribus intonaret, ilico aperte dolum cognoscens, Fritigernus, evaginato gladio, e convivio non sine magna temeritate velocitateque egreditur suosque socios ab imminenti morte ereptos ad necem Romanorum instigat.

But Fripi-gaírn, thinking no evil, came to the feast with a few followers. While he was dining in the praetorium he heard the dying cries of his ill-fated men, for, by order of the general, the soldiers were slaying his companions who were shut up in another part of the house. The loud cries of the dying fell upon ears already suspicious, and Fripi-gaírn at once perceived the treacherous trick. He drew his sword and with great courage dashed quickly from the banqueting-hall, rescued his men from their threatening doom and incited them to slay the Romans.

137

Qui nancti occasionem votivam, elegerunt viri fortissimi in bello magic quam in fame deficere, et ilico in ducum Lupicini et Maximi armantur occisionem.

Thus these valiant men gained the chance they had longed for—to be free to die in battle rather than to perish of hunger—and immediately took arms to kill the generals Lupicinus and Maximus.

Illa namque dies Gothorum famem Romanorumque securitatem ademit, coeperuntque Gothi jam non ut advenae et peregrini, sed ut cives et domini possessoribus imperare totasque partes septentrionales usque ad Danubium suo jure tenere.

Thus that day put an end to the famine of the Goths and the safety of the Romans, for the Goths no longer as strangers and pilgrims, but as citizens and lords, began to rule the inhabitants and to hold in their own right all the northern country as far as the Danube.

138

Quod comperiens in Antiochia Valens Imperator mox, armato exercitu, in Thraciarum partes egreditur; ubi, lacrimabili bello commisso, vincentibus Gothis, in quoddam praedium juxta Hadrianopolim saucius ipse refugiens, ignorantibusque quod Imperator in tam vili casula delitesceret Gothis, igneque, ut assolet saevienti inimico, supposito, cum regali pompa crematus est - haut secus quam Dei prorsus judicio, ut ab ipsis igne combureretur, quos ipse veram fidem petentes in perfidiam declinasset ignemque caritatis ad gehennae ignem detorsisset.

When the Emperor Valens heard of this at Antioch, he made ready an army at once and set out for the country of Thrace. Here a grievous battle took place {378 August 9} and the Goths prevailed. The Emperor himself was wounded and fled to a farm near Adrianople {modern Edirne, northernmost European Turkey}. The Goths, not knowing that an emperor lay hidden in so poor a hut, set fire to it (as an enraged foe commonly does), and thus he was cremated in royal splendor. Plainly it was a direct judgment of God that he should be burned with fire by the very men whom he had perfidiously led astray when they sought the true faith, twisting the flame of love into the fire of hell.

Quo tempore Wisigothae Thracias Daciamque Ripensem post tanti gloriam tropaei tamquam solo genitali potiti coeperunt incolere.

From this time the Visigoths, in consequence of their glorious victory, possessed Thrace and Dacia Ripensis as if it were their native land.

Faxien, *Record of Buddhist Countries*, Chapter Sixteen

Faxien (circa 334–415 CE) was a Chinese monk who, with several companions, traveled the Silk Road to India and returned via the Indian Ocean trade route between 399 and 413 CE. Their quest to find Buddhist knowledge, books, and art was successful, and, after they returned, they helped to spread Buddhism around east Asia. Fortunately, Faxien also recorded his travels, which provide us with a comprehensive geography of central and south Asia of the time.

Source: *Faxien,* A Record of Buddhist Kingdoms: Being an Account by the Chinese Monk Faxien of His Travels in India and Ceylon, *trans. by James Legge, 1886.*

Focus Questions:
1. How do Buddhist beliefs influence attitudes towards the Chandalas?
2. How are rulers described?
3. Compare the life of Buddhist monks to those of Christians.

CHAPTER XVI

ON TO MATHURA OR MUTTRA. CONDITION AND CUSTOMS OF CENTRAL INDIA; OF THE MONKS, VIHARAS, AND MONASTERIES.

From this place they traveled southeast, passing by a succession of very many monasteries, with a multitude of monks, who might be counted by myriads. After passing all these places, they came to a country named Ma-t' aou-lo. They still followed the course of the P'oo-na river, on the banks of which, left and right, there were twenty monasteries, which might contain three thousand monks; and (here) the Law of Buddha was still more flourishing. Everywhere, from the Sandy Desert, in all the countries of India, the kings had been firm believers in that Law. When they make their offerings to a community of monks, they take off their royal caps, and along with their relatives and ministers, supply them with food with their own hands. That done, (the king) has a carpet spread for himself on the ground, and sits down in front of the chairman;—they dare not presume to sit on couches in front of the community. The laws and ways, according to which the kings presented their offerings when Buddha was in the world, have been handed down to the present day.

All south from this is named the Middle Kingdom. In it the cold and heat are finely tempered, and there is neither hoarfrost nor snow. The people are numerous and happy; they have not to register their households, or attend to any magistrates and their rules; only those who cultivate the royal land have to pay (a portion of) the grain from it. If they want to go, they go; if they want to stay on, they stay. The king governs without decapitation or (other) corporal punishments. Criminals are simply fined, lightly or heavily, according to the circumstances (of each case). Even in cases of repeated attempts at wicked rebellion, they only have their right hands cut off. The king's body-guards and attendants all have salaries. Throughout the whole country the people do not kill any living creature, nor drink intoxicating liquor, nor eat onions or garlic. The only exception is that of the Chandalas. That is the name for those who are (held to be) wicked men, and live apart from others. When they enter the gate of a city or a market-place, they strike a piece of wood to make themselves known, so that men know and avoid them, and do not come into contact with them. In that country they do not keep pigs and fowls, and do not sell live cattle; in the markets there are no butchers' shops and no dealers in intoxicating drink. In buying and selling commodities they use cowries. Only the Chandalas are fishermen and hunters, and sell flesh meat.

After Buddha attained to pari-nirvana, the kings of the various countries and the heads of the Vaisyas built viharas for the priests, and endowed them with fields, houses, gardens, and orchards, along with the resident populations and their cattle, the grants being engraved on plates of metal, so that afterwards they were handed down from king to king, without any daring to annul them, and they remain even to the present time.

The regular business of the monks is to perform acts of meritorious virtue, and to recite their Sutras and sit wrapt in meditation. When stranger monks arrive (at any monastery), the old residents meet and receive them, carry for them their clothes and alms-bowl, give them water to wash their feet, oil with which to anoint them, and the liquid food permitted out of the regular hours. When (the stranger) has enjoyed a very brief rest, they further ask the number of years that he has been a monk, after which he receives a sleeping apartment with its appurtenances, according to his regular order, and everything is done for him which the rules prescribe.

Where a community of monks resides, they erect topes to Sariputtra, to Mahamaudgalyayana, and to Ananda, and also topes (in honour) of the Abhidharma, the Vinaya, and the Sutras. A month after the (annual season of) rest, the families which are looking out for blessing stimulate one another to make offerings to the monks, and send round to them the liquid food which may be taken out of the ordinary hours. All the monks come together in a great assembly, and preach the Law; after which offerings are presented at the tope of Sariputtra, with all kinds of flowers and incense. All through the night lamps are kept burning, and skilful musicians are employed to perform.

When Sariputtra was a great Brahman, he went to Buddha, and begged (to be permitted) to quit his family (and become a monk). The great Mugalan and the great Kasyapa also did the same. The bhikshunis for the most part make their offerings at the tope of Ananda, because it was he who requested the World-honoured one to allow females to quit their families (and become nuns). The Sramaneras mostly make their offerings to Rahula. The professors of the Abhidharma make their offerings to it; those of the Vinaya to it. Every year there is one such offering, and each class has its own day for it. Students of the mahayana present offerings to the Prajna-paramita, to Manjusri, and to Kwan-she-yin. When the monks have done receiving their annual tribute (from the harvests), the Heads of the Vaisyas and all the Brahmans bring clothes and other such articles as the monks require for use, and distribute among them. The monks, having received them, also proceed to give portions to one another. From the nirvana of Buddha, the forms of ceremony, laws, and rules, practised by the sacred communities, have been handed down from one generation to another without interruption.

From the place where (the travelers) crossed the Indus to Southern India, and on to the Southern Sea, a distance of forty or fifty thousand li, all is level plain. There are no large hills with streams (among them); there are simply the waters of the rivers.

Arabic Poetry: "The Poem of Antar"

This is a surviving example of pre-Islamic Arabic poetry. Antar is one of seven classical poems that were hung in the Kaaba in Mecca along with various idols. Under Islam the idols were removed, but the "hanged poems" were retained. One of them, Antar the poet, became a heroic figure in Arabic romances. He was the son of an African slave but successfully became a strong warrior. Eventually he met and loved the princess Iblah, and their relationship along with his warrior prowess became the subject of later romances.

Source: *"The Poem of Antar," from* The Diwans of the Six Ancient Poets *(London, 1870).*

Focus Questions:
1. What are Antar's views towards the Princess?
2. How are various animals described in the poem?
3. What is the type of warfare in which Antar partakes?

Have the poets left in the garment a place for a patch to be patched by me; and did you know the abode of your beloved after reflection?

The vestige of the house, which did not speak, confounded thee, until it spoke by means of signs, like one deaf and dumb.

Verily, I kept my she-camel there long grumbling, with a yearning at the blackened stones, keeping and standing firm in their own places.

It is the abode of a friend, languishing in her glance, submissive in the embrace, pleasant of smile.

Oh house of 'Ablah situated at Jiwaa, talk with me about those who resided in you. Good morning to you, O house of 'Ablah, and be safe from ruin.

I halted my she-camel in that place; and it was as though she were a high palace; in order that I might perform the wont of the lingerer.

And 'Ablah takes up her abode at Jiwaa; while our people went to Hazan, then to Mutathallam.

She took up her abode in the land of my enemies; so it became difficult for me to seek you, O daughter of Mahzam.

I was enamored of her unawares, at a time when I was killing her people, desiring her in marriage; but by your father's life I swear, this was not the time for desiring.

And verily you have occupied in my heart the place of the honored loved one, so do not think otherwise than this, that you are my beloved.

And how may be the visiting of her; while her people have taken up their residence in the spring at 'Unaizatain and our people at Ghailam?

I knew that you had intended departing, for, verily, your camels were bridled on a dark night.

Nothing caused me fear of her departure, except that the baggage camels of her people were eating the seeds of the Khimkhim tree throughout the country.

Amongst them were two and forty milk-giving camels, black as the wing-feathers of black crows.

When she captivates you with a mouth possessing sharp, and white teeth, sweet as to its place of kissing, delicious of taste.

As if she sees with the two eyes of a young, grown up gazelle from the deer.

It was as though the musk bag of a merchant in his case of perfumes preceded her teeth toward you from her mouth.

Or as if it is an old wine-skin, from Azri'at, preserved long, such as the kings of Rome preserve;

Or her mouth is as an ungrazed meadow, whose herbage the rain has guaranteed, in which there is but little dung; and which is not marked with the feet of animals.

The first pure showers of every rain-cloud rained upon it, and left every puddle in it bright and round like a dirham;

Sprinkling and pouring; so that the water flows upon it every evening, and is not cut off from it.

The fly enjoyed yet alone, and so it did not cease humming, as is the act of the singing drunkard;

Humming, while he rubs one foreleg against the other, as the striking on the flint of one, bent on the flint, and cut off as to his palm.

She passes her evenings and her mornings on the surface of a well-stuffed couch, while I pass my nights on the back of a bridled black horse.

And my couch is a saddle upon a horse big-boned in the leg, big in his flanks, great of girth.

Would a Shadanian she-camel cause me to arrive at her abode, who is cursed with an udder scanty of milk and cut off?

After traveling all night, she is lashing her sides with her tail, and is strutting proudly, and she breaks up the mounds of earth she passes over with her foot with its sole, treading hard.

As if I in the evening am breaking the mounds of earth by means of an ostrich, very small as to the distance between its two feet, and earless.

The young ostriches flock toward him, as the herds of Yamanian camels flock to a barbarous, unintelligible speaker.

They follow the crest of his head, as though it was a howdah on a large litter, tented for them.

He is small headed, who returns constantly to look after his eggs at Zil-'Ushairah; he is like a slave, with a long fur cloak and without ears.

She drank of the water of Duhruzain and then turned away, being disgusted, from the pools of stagnant water.

And she swerves away with her right side from the fear of one, whistling in the evening, a big ugly-headed one;

From the fear of a cat, led at her side, every time she turned toward him, in anger, he met her with both claws and mouth.

She knelt down at the edge of the pool of Rada', and groaned as though she had knelt on a reed, broken, and emitting a cracking noise.

And the sweat on the back was as though it were oil or thick pitch, with which fire is lighted round the sides of a retort.

Her places of flexure were wetted with it and she lavishly poured of it, on a spreading forelock, short and well-bred.

The length of the journey left her a strong, well-built body, like a high palace, built with cement, and rising high; and feet like the supports of a firmly pitched tent.

And surely I recollected you, even when the lances were drinking my blood, and bright swords of Indian make were dripping with my blood.

I wished to kiss the swords, for verily they shone as bright as the flash of the fore tooth of your smiling mouth.

If you lower your veil over yourself in front of me, of what use will it be? For, verily, I am expert in capturing the mailed horseman.

Praise me for the qualities, which you know I possess, for, verily, when I am not ill-treated, I am gentle to associate with.

And if I am ill-treated, then, verily, my tyranny is severe, very bitter is the taste of it, as the taste of the colocynth.

And, verily, I have drunk wine after the midday heats have subsided, buying it with the bright stamped coin.

From a glass, yellow with the lines of the glass cutter on it, which was accompanied by a white-stoppered bottle on the left-hand side.

And when I have drunk, verily, I am the squanderer of my property, and my honor is great, and is not sullied.

And when I have become sober, I do not diminish in my generosity, and as you know, so are my qualities and my liberality.

And many a husband of a beautiful woman, I have left prostrate on the ground, with his shoulders hissing like the side of the mouth of one with a split lip.

My two hands preceded him with a hasty blow, striking him before he could strike me; and with the drops of blood from a penetrating stroke, red like the color of Brazil wood.

Why did you not ask the horsemen, O daughter Malik! if you were ignorant, concerning what you did not know about my condition,

At a time when I never ceased to be in the saddle of a long striding, wounded, sturdy horse, against whom the warriors came in succession.

At one time he is detached to charge the enemy with the lance, and at another he joins the large host with their bows tightly strung.

He who was present in the battle will inform you that verily I rush into battle, but I abstain at the time of taking the booty.

I see spoils, which, if I want I would win; but my bashfulness and my magnanimity hold me back from them.

And many a fully armed one, whom the warriors shunned fighting with, neither a hastener in flight, nor a surrenderer;

My hands were generous to him by a quick point with a straightened spear, strong in the joints;

Inflicting a wound wide of its two sides, the sound of the flow of blood from it leads at night the prowling wolves, burning with hunger.

I rent his vesture with a rigid spear, for the noble one is not forbidden to the spears.

Then I left him a prey for the wild beasts, who seize him, and gnaw the beauty of his fingers and wrist.

And many a long, closely woven coat of mail, I have split open the links of it, with a sword, off one defending his rights, and renowned for bravery.

Whose hands are ready with gambling arrows when it is winter, a tearer-down of the signs of the wine-sellers, and one reproached for his extravagance.

When he saw that I had descended from my horse and was intending killing him, he showed his teeth, but without smiling.

My meeting with him was when the day spread out, and he was as if his fingers and his head were dyed with indigo.

I pierced him with my spear, and then I set upon him with my Indian sword pure of steel, and keen.

A warrior, so stately in size as if his clothes were on a high tree: soft leather shoes are worn by him and he is not twinned.

Oh, how wonderful is the beauty of the doe of the hunt, to whom is she lawful? To me she is unlawful; would to God that she was not unlawful.

So, I sent my female slave, and said to her, "Go, find out news of her and inform me."

She said, "I saw carelessness on the part of the enemies, and that the doe is possible to him who is shooting."

And it was as though she looked toward me with the neck of a doe, a fawn of the gazelles, pure and with a white upper lip.

I am informed that 'Amru is unthankful for my kindness while ingratitude is a cause of evil to the soul of the giver.

And, verily, I remember the advice of my uncle, in the battle, when the two lips quiver from off the white teeth of the mouth,

In the thick of the battle, of which the warriors do not complain of the rigors, except with an unintelligible noise.

When they (*i.e.*, my people) defended themselves with me against the spears of the enemy, I did not refrain from them (*i.e.*, the spears) through cowardice, but the place of my advance had become too strait.

When I heard the cry of Murrah rise, and saw the two sons of Rabi'ah in the thick dust,

While the tribe of Muhallam were struggling under their banners, and death was under the banners of the tribe of Mulhallam {sic.},

I made sure that at the time of their encounter there would be a blow, which would make the heads fly from the bodies, as the bird flies from off her young ones sitting close.

When I saw the people, while their mass advanced, excite one another to fight, I turned against them without being reproached for any want of bravery.

They were calling 'Antarah, while the spears were as though they were well-ropes in the breast of Adham.

They were calling 'Antarah, while the swords were as though they were the flash of lightnings in a dark cloud.

They were calling 'Antarah, while the arrows were flying, as though they were a flight of locusts, hovering above watering places.

They were calling "O 'Antarah," while the coats of mail shone with close rings, shining as though they were the eyeballs of frogs floating in a wavy pond.

I did not cease charging them, (the enemy) with the prominent part of his (horse's) throat and breast, until he became covered with a shirt of blood.

Then he turned on account of the falling of the spears on his breast, and complained to me with tears and whinnyings.

If he had known what conversation was, he would have complained with words, and verily he would have, had he known speech, talked with me.

And verily the speech of the horsemen, "Woe to you, 'Antarah, advance, and attack the enemy," cured my soul and removed its sickness.

While the horses sternly frowning were charging over the soft soil, being partly the long-bodied mares, and partly the long-bodied, well-bred horses.

My riding-camels are tractable, they go wherever I wish; while my intellect is my helper, and I drive it forward with a firm order.

Verily, it lay beyond my power that I should visit you; so, know what you have known, and some of what you have not known.

The lances of the tribe of Bagheez intercepted you and the perpetrators of the war set aside those who did not perpetrate it.

And, verily, I turned the horse for the attack, while his neck was bleeding, until the horses began to shun me.

And verily I feared that I should die, while there has not yet been a turn for war against the two sons of Zamzam;`

The two revilers of my honor, while I did not revile them, and the threateners of my blood, when I did not see them.

There is no wonder should they do so, for I left their father a prey for the wild beasts and every large old vulture.

Excerpts from the *Taika Reform Edicts*

The edicts of 646 CE mark the creation of strong central government in Japan. The Emperor Kotoku had defeated the rival clans and cemented his control by seizing direct control of the rice producing lands. He then created a government structure based on a sacrosanct emperor rather than the old clan system. The Japanese government was strongly influenced by Chinese Buddhist and Confucian philosophies, in many cases through deliberate acts of copying.

Source: *Richard Hooker. intro and ed., W.G. Aston, trans.,* Nihongi *(London: Kegan, Paul, Trench, Trubner, 1896) pp. 197–227.*

Focus Questions:
1. What is the treatment of various classes and of women?
2. How are law and government organized in comparison to China?
3. How is the military organized?

EMPEROR KOTOKU'S VOW

19th day (645 A.D.).

The Emperor, the Empress Dowager, and the Prince Imperial summoned together the Ministers under the great tsuki tree, and made an oath appealing to the Gods of Heaven and Earth, and said,

"Heaven covers us; Earth upbears us; the Imperial way is one and only one way. But in this last degenerate age, the order of Lord and Vassal was destroyed until Supreme Heaven by Our hands put to death the traitors. Now, from this time forward, both parties shedding their heart's blood, the Lord will not tolerate double methods of government, and the Vassal will avoid duplicity in his service of the sovereign! On him who breaks this oath, Heaven will send a curse and earth a plague, demons will slay them, and men will kill them. This is as manifest as the sun and moon."

REGULATION OF THE PROVINCES

8th month, 5th day.

Governors of the Eastern provinces were appointed. Then the Governors were addressed as follows:

"In accordance with the charge entrusted to Us by the Gods of Heaven, We propose at the present for the first time to regulate the myriad provinces.

When you proceed to your posts, prepare registers of all the free subjects of the State and of the people under the control of others, whether great or small. Take account also of the acreage of cultivated land. As to the profits arising from the gardens and ponds, the water and land, deal with them in common with the people.

In addition, it is not right for the provincial Governors, while in their provinces, to decide criminal cases, nor are they permitted by accepting bribes to bring the people to poverty and misery. When they come up to the capital they must not bring large numbers of the people in their train. They are only allowed to bring with them the Kuni no Miyakko and the district officials. But when they travel on public business they may ride the horses of their department and eat the food of their department. From the rank of Suke upwards, those who obey this law will surely be rewarded, while those who disobey it shall be liable to be reduced in rank. From the rank of Hangwan downwards, all those who accept bribes shall be fined double the amount of the bribe, and they shall eventually be criminally punished according to the greater or less severity of the case.

Nine men are allowed as attendants on a Chief Governor, seven on an assistant, and five on a secretary. If this limit is exceeded, and they are accompanied by a greater number, both chief and followers shall be criminally punished...

In addition, on waste pieces of ground let arsenals be erected, and let the swords and armour, with the bows and arrows of the provinces and districts, be deposited together in them. In the case of the frontier provinces which border close on the Yemishi, let all the weapons be gathered together, and let them remain in the hands of their original owners. In regard to the six districts of the province of Yamato, let the officials who are sent there prepare registers of the population, and also take an account of the acreage of cultivated land. This means to examine the acreage of the cultivated ground, and the numbers, houses, and ages of the people.

You Governors of provinces, take careful note of this and withdraw..."

COMPLAINTS AND BIRTH

The Emperor issued an order, saying:

"If there be a complainant, in case the person in question belongs to a Tomo no Miyakko, let the Tomo no Miyakko first make inquiry and then report to Us. In case the person in question has an elder, let the elder first make inquiry and then report to Us. If, however, the Tomo no Miyakko or the elder does not come to a clear decision respecting the complaint, let a document be received and placed in the box, and punishment will be inflicted according to the offence. The person who receives the document should at dawn take it and make report to the Inner Palace, when We will mark on it the year and month, and communicate it to the Ministers. In case there is any neglect to decide it, or if there are malpractices on the part of intriguing persons, let the complainant strike the bell. This is why the bell is hung and box provided in the Court. Let the people of the Empire know and appreciate Our intention.

Moreover, the law of men and women shall be that the children born of a free man and a free woman shall belong to the father: if a free man takes to wife a slave woman, her children shall belong to the mother; if a free woman marries a slave man, the children of the marriage shall belong to the father; if they are slaves of two houses, the children shall belong to the mother. The children of temple serfs shall follow the rule for freemen. But in regard to others who become slaves, they shall be treated according to the rule for slaves. Publish this well to the people as a beginning of regulations."

BUDDHISM

8th day.

A messenger was sent to the Great Temple to summon together the Buddhist priests and nuns, and to address them on the part of the Emperor, saying,

"In the 13th year of the reign of the Emperor who ruled the world in the Palace of Shikishima, King Myong of Pekche reverently transmitted the Law of Buddha to our great Yamato. At this time the Ministers in a body were opposed to its transmission. Only Soga no Iname no Sukune believed in this Law, and the Emperor accordingly instructed him to receive it with reverence. In the reign of the Emperor who ruled the world in the Palace of Wosada, Soga no Mumako no Sukune, influenced by reverence for his deceased father, continued to prize highly the doctrines of Buddha. But the other Ministers had no faith in it, and its institutes had almost perished when the Emperor instructed Mumako no Sukune reverently to receive this Law. In the reign of the Empress who ruled the world in the Palace of Woharida, Mumako no Sukune, on behalf of the Empress, made an embroidered figure of Buddha sixteen feet high and a copper image of Buddha sixteen feet high. He exalted the doctrine of Buddha and showed honour to its priests and nuns. It is our desire to exalt the pure doctrine and brilliantly to promulgate great principles. We therefore appoint as professors the following ten persons: The S'ramana, Poknyang, Hye-un, Syang-an, Nyong-un, and Hye-chi, Taih-shi of Koma, and Subin, Doto, Yerin, Yemyo and Yeon, chief priests of temples. We separately appoint the Hoshi, Yemyo, chief priest of the Temple of Kudara.

Let these ten professors well instruct the priests in general in the practice of the teachings of Shaka. It is needful that they be made to comply with the Law. If there is a difficulty about repairing Temples built by any from the Emperor down to the Tomo no Miyakko, We will in all cases assist in doing so. We shall also cause Temple Commissioners and Chief Priests to be appointed, who shall make a circuit to all the temples, and having ascertained the actual facts respecting the priests and nuns, their male and female slaves, and the acreage of their cultivated lands, report all the particulars clearly to us."

CORRUPTION OF REGIONAL OFFICIALS

19th day

Commissioners were sent to all the provinces to take a record of the total numbers of the people. The Emperor on this occasion made an edict, as follows:

"In the times of all the Emperors, from antiquity downwards, subjects have been set apart for the purpose of making notable their reigns and handing down their names to posterity. Now the Omi and Muraji, the Tomo no Miyakko and the Kuni no Miyakko, have each one set apart their own vassals, whom they compel to labor at their arbitrary pleasure. Moreover, they cut off the hills and seas, the woods and plains, the ponds and rice-fields belonging to the provinces and districts, and appropriate them to themselves. Their contests are never ceasing. Some engross to themselves many tens of thousands of shiro of rice land, while others possess in all patches of ground too small to stick a needle into. When the time comes for the payment of taxes, the Omi, the Muraji, and the Tomo no Miyakko, first collect them for themselves and then hand over a share. In the case of repairs to palaces or the construction of misasagi, they each bring their own vassals, and do the work according to circumstances. The Book of Changes says, "Diminish that which is above: increase that which is below: if measures are framed according to the regulations, the resources of the State suffer no injury, and the people receive no hurt."

"At the present time, the people are still few. And yet the powerful cut off portions of land and water, and converting them into private ground, sell it to the people, demanding the price yearly. From this time forward the sale of land is not allowed. Let no man without due authority make himself a landlord, engrossing to himself that which belongs to the helpless."

The people rejoiced.

REGULATION OF THE CAPITAL; TAXES; WOMEN

A.D. 646. 2nd year, Spring, 1st month, 1st day.

As soon as the ceremonies of the new years congratulations were over, the Emperor promulgated an edict of reforms, as follows:

"I. Let the people established by the ancient Emperors, etc., as representatives of children be abolished, also the Miyake of various places and the people owned as serfs by the Wake, the Omi, the Muraji, the Tomo no Miyakko, the Kuni no Miyakko and the Mura no Obito. Let the farmsteads in various places be abolished."

Consequently fiefs were granted for their sustenance to those of the rank of Daibu and upwards on a descending scale. Presents of cloth and silk stuffs were given to the officials and people, varying in value.

"Further we say, it is the business of the Daibu to govern the people. If they discharge this duty thoroughly, the people have trust in them, and an increase of their revenue is therefore for the good of the people.

II. The capital is for the first time to be regulated, and Governors appointed for the Home provinces and districts. Let barriers, outposts, guards, and post-horses, both special and ordinary, be provided, bell-tokens made, and mountains and rivers regulated.

For each ward in the capital let there be appointed one alderman, and for four wards one chief alderman, who shall be charged with the superintendence of the population, and the examination of criminal matters. For appointment as chief aldermen of wards let men be taken belonging to the wards, of unblemished character, firm and upright, so that they may fitly sustain the duties of the time. For appointments as aldermen, whether of rural townships or of city wards, let ordinary subjects be taken belonging to the township or ward, of good character and solid capacity. If such men are not to be found in the township or ward in question, it is permitted to select and employ men of the adjoining township or ward.

The Home provinces shall include the region from the River Yokogaha at Nabari on the east, from Mount Senoyama in Kii on the south, from Kushibuchi in Akashi on the west, and from Mount Afusakayama in Sasanami in Afumi on the north. Districts of forty townships are constituted Greater Districts, of from thirty to four townships are constituted Middle Districts, and of three or fewer townships are constituted Lesser Districts. For the district authorities, of whatever class, let there be taken Kuni no Miyakko of unblemished character, such as may fitly sustain the duties of the time, and made Tairei and Shorei. Let men of solid capacity and intelligence who are skilled in writing and arithmetic be appointed assistants and clerks.

The number of special or ordinary post-horses given shall in all cases follow the number of marks on the posting bell-tokens. When bell-tokens are given to (officials of) the provinces and barriers, let them be held in both cases by the chief official, or in his absence by the assistant official.

III. Let there now be provided for the first time registers of population, books of account and a system of the receipt and re-granting of distribution-land.

Let every fifty houses be reckoned a township, and in every township let there be one alderman who shall be charged with the superintendence of the registers of population, the direction of the sowing of crops and the cultivation of mulberry trees, the prevention and examination of offences, and the enforcement of the payment of taxes and of forced labor.

For rice-land, thirty paces in length by twelve paces in breadth shall be reckoned a tan. Ten tan make one cho. For each tan the tax is two sheaves and two bundles (such as can be grasped in the hand) of rice; for each cho the tax is twenty-two sheaves of rice. On mountains or in valleys where the land is precipitous, or in remote places where the population is scanty, such arrangements are to be made as may be convenient.

IV. The old taxes and forced labor are abolished, and a system of commuted taxes instituted. These shall consist of fine silks, coarse silks, raw silk, and floss silk, all in accordance with what is produced in the locality. For each cho of rice land the rate is ten feet of fine silk, or for four cho one piece forty feet in length by two and a half feet in width. For coarse silk the rate is twenty feet (per cho), or one piece for every two cho of the same length and width as the fine silk. For cloth the rate is forty feet of the same dimensions as the fine and coarse silk, i.e. one tan for each cho. Let there be levied separately a commuted house tax. All houses shall pay each twelve feet of cloth. The extra articles of this tax, as well as salt and offerings, will depend on what is produced in the locality.

For horses for the public service, let every hundred houses contribute one horse of medium quality. Or if the horse is of superior quality, let one be contributed by every two hundred houses. If the horses have to be purchased, the price shall be made up by a payment from each house of twelve feet of cloth.

As to weapons, each person shall contribute a sword, armour, bow and arrows, a flag, and a drum.

For servants, the old system, by which one servant was provided by every thirty houses, is altered, and one servant is to be furnished from every fifty houses [one is for employment as a menial servant] for allotment to the various functionaries. Fifty houses shall be allotted to provide rations for one servant, and one house shall contribute twenty two feet of cloth and five masu of rice in lieu of service.

For waiting-women in the Palace, let there be furnished the sisters or daughters of district officials of the rank of Shorei or upwards—good-looking women [with one male and two female servants to attend on them], and let 100 houses be allotted to provide rations for one waiting-woman. The cloth and rice supplied in lieu of service shall, in every case, follow the same rule as for servants."

COMPLAINTS AND JUSTICE

2nd month, 1st day.

The Emperor proceeded to the Eastern Gate of the Palace, where, by Soga, Oho-omi of the Right, he decreed as follows:

"The God Incarnate, the Emperor Yamato-neko, who rules the world, gives command to the Ministers assembled in his presence, to the Omi, Muraji, Kuni no Miyakko, Tomo no Miyakko, and subjects of various classes, saying, 'We are informed that wise rulers of the people hung a bell at their gate, and so took cognizance of the complaints of their subjects; they erected buildings in the thoroughfares, where they listened to the censures of the passers-by. Even the opinions of the grass and firewood gatherers they inquired personally and used for their guidance. We therefore, on a former occasion, made an edict, saying: "In ancient times the Empire was ruled by having at the Court flags of honour for the encouragement of good, and a board of censure, the object being to diffuse principles of Government and to invite remonstrances." All this served widely to ascertain the opinions of those below...

The object of hanging up a bell, of providing a box, and of appointing a man to receive petitions, is to make those who have grievances or remonstrances deposit their petitions in the box. The receivers of petitions are commanded to make their report to Us every morning. When We receive this report We shall draw the attention of the Ministers to it, and cause them to consider it, and We trust that this may be done without delay. But if there should be neglect on the part of the Ministers, and a want of diligence or partisan intrigues, and if We, moreover, should refuse to listen to remonstrance, let the complainant strike the bell. There has been already an Imperial command to this effect. But some time afterwards there was a man of intelligence and uprightness who, cherishing in his heart the spirit of a national patriot, addressed Us a memorial of earnest remonstrance, which he placed in the box prepared for the purpose. We therefore now publish it to the black-haired people here assembled. This memorial runs as follows: "Those subjects who come to the capital in connection with the discharge of their duty to the Government of the Country, are detained by the various public functionaries and put to forced labor of various kinds, etc." We are still moved with strong sympathy by this. How could the people expect that things would come to this? Now no long time has elapsed since the capital was removed, so that so far from being at home, we are, as it were, strangers. It is therefore impossible to avoid employing the people, and they have therefore been, against Our will, compelled to labor. As often as Our minds dwell on this We have never been able to sleep in peace. When We saw this memorial we could not refrain from a joyous exclamation. We have accordingly complied with the language of remonstrance, and have put a stop to the forced services at various places.

In a former edict, we said, "Let the man who remonstrates sign his name." Those who disobey this injunction are doubtless actuated by a wish to serve their country, and not by a desire of personal gain. Whether a man signs his name or not, let him not fail to remonstrate with Us on Our neglect or forgetfulness."

Centralized Government and Social Rules

20th day.

The Prince Imperial said,

"In Heaven there are not two suns: in a country there are not two rulers. It is therefore the Emperor alone who is supreme over all the Empire, and who has a right to the services of the myriad people.

22nd day.

The Emperor made a decree, as follows,

"We are informed that a Prince of the Western Land admonished his people, saying, 'Those who made interments in ancient times resorted to a high ground which they formed into a tomb. They did not pile up a mound, nor did they plant trees. The inner and outer coffin were merely enough to last till the bones decayed, the shroud was merely sufficient to last till the flesh decayed... Deposit not in them gold or silver or copper or iron, and let earthenware objects alone represent the clay chariots and straw figures of antiquity. Let the interstices of the coffin be varnished. Let the offerings consist of rice presented three times, and let not pearls or jewels be placed in the mouth of the deceased. Bestow not jewel-shirts or jade armour. All these things are practices of the unenlightened vulgar...' Of late, the poverty of our people is absolutely owing to the construction of tombs...

When a man dies, there have been cases of people sacrificing themselves by strangulation, or of strangling others by way of sacrifice, or of compelling the dead man's horse to be sacrificed, or of burying valuables in the grave in honour of the dead, or of cutting off the hair, and stabbing the thighs and pronouncing an eulogy on the dead (while in this condition). Let all such old customs be entirely discontinued.

A certain book says, 'No gold or silver, no silk brocades, and no coloured stuffs are to be buried.' Again it is said, 'From the Ministers of all ranks down to the common people, it is not allowed to use gold or silver...'

Again, there are many cases of persons who, having seen, say that they have not seen, or who, having not seen, say that they have seen, or who, having heard, say that they have not heard, or who, having not heard, say that they have heard, being deliberate liars, and devoid of truth in words and in sight.

Again, there have been many cases in which slaves, both male and female, false to their masters in their poverty, betake themselves of their own accord to influential houses in quest of a livelihood, which influential houses forcibly detain and purchase them, and do not send them to their original owners.

Again, there have been very many cases in which wives or concubines, when dismissed by their husbands, have, after the lapse of years, married other husbands, as ordinary morality allows. Then their former husbands, after three or four years, have made greedy demands on the second husband's property, seeking their own gain.

Again, there have been very many cases in which men, relying on their power, have rudely demanded people's daughters in marriage. In the interval, however, before going to his house, the girl has, of her own accord, married another, and the rude suitor has angrily made demands of the property of both families for his own gain.

Again, there have been numerous cases of this kind. Sometimes a wife who has lost her husband marries another man after the lapse of ten or twenty years and becomes his spouse, or an unmarried girl is married for the first time. Upon this, people, out of envy of the married pair, have made them perform purgation.

Again, there are cases in which women, who have become men's wives and who, being put away owing to their husbands' dislike of them, have, in their mortification at this injury, compelled themselves to become blemished slaves.

Again, there are cases in which the husband, having frequent occasion to be jealous of his wife's illicit intercourse with others, voluntarily appeals to the authorities to decide the matter. Let such persons not lay their information until they have obtained, let us say, three credible witnesses to join with them in making a declaration. Why should they bring forward ill-considered plaints?

Again, there have been cases of men employed on forced labour in border lands who, when the work was over and they were returning to their village, have fallen suddenly ill and lain down to die by the roadside. Upon this the (inmates of the) houses by the roadside say, 'Why should people be allowed to die on our road?' And they have accordingly detained the companions of the deceased and compelled them to do purgation. For this reason it often happens that even if an elder brother lies down and dies on the road, his younger brother will refuse to take up his body (for burial).

Again, there are cases of peasants being drowned in a river. The bystanders say, 'Why should we be made to have anything to do with drowned men?' They accordingly detain the drowned man's companions and compel them to do purgation. For this reason it often happens that even when an elder brother is drowned in a river his younger brother will not render assistance.

Again, there are cases of people who, when employed on forced labor, cook their rice by the roadside. Upon this the (inmates of the) houses by the roadside say, 'Why should people cook rice at their own pleasure on our road?' and have compelled them to do purgation.

Again, there are cases when people have applied to others for the loan of pots in which to boil their rice, and the pots have knocked against something and have been upset. Upon this the owner of the pot compels purgation to be made.

All such practices are habitual among the unenlightened vulgar. Let them now be discontinued without exception, and not permitted again...

THE ROLE OF THE EMPEROR

Autumn, 8th month, 14th day.

An edict was issued, saying,

"Going back to the origin of things, we find that it is Heaven and Earth with the male and female principles of nature, which guard the four seasons from mutual confusion. We find, more over, that it is this Heaven and earth which produces the ten thousand things. Amongst these ten thousand things Man is the most miraculously gifted. Among the most miraculously gifted beings, the sage takes the position of ruler. Therefore the Sage Rulers, that is, the Emperors, take Heaven as their model in ruling the World, and never for a moment dismiss from their breasts the thought of how men shall gain their fit place..."

THE MONARCHY AND THE PEOPLE

Summer, 4th month, 29th day.

An edict was issued as follows,

"The Empire was entrusted (by the Sun-Goddess to her descendants, with the words) 'My children, in their capacity as Deities, shall rule it.' For this reason, this country, since Heaven and Earth began, has been a monarchy. From the time that Our Imperial ancestor first ruled the land, there has been great concord in the Empire, and there has never been any factiousness. In recent times, however, the names, first of the Gods, and then of the Emperors, have in some cases been separated (from their proper application) and converted into the Uji of Omi or Muraji, or they have been separated and made the qualifications of Miyakko, etc. In consequence of this, the minds of the people of the whole country take a strong partisan bias, and conceiving a deep sense of the "me" and "you," hold firmly each to their names. Moreover the feeble and incompetent Omi, Muraji, Tomo no Miyakko and Kuni no Miyakko make of such names their family names; and so the names of Gods and the names of sovereigns are applied to persons and places in an unauthorized manner, in accordance with the bent of their own feelings. Now, by using the names of Gods and the names of sovereigns as bribes, they draw to themselves the slaves of others, and so bring dishonor upon unspotted names.

The consequence is that the minds of the people have become unsettled and the government of the country cannot be carried on. The duty has therefore now devolved on Us in Our capacity as Celestial Divinity, to regulate and settle these things. In order to make them understood, and thereby to order the State and to order the people, we shall issue, one after another, a succession of edicts, one earlier, another later, one to-day and another to-morrow. But the people, who have always trusted in the civilizing influence exercised by the Emperors, and who are used to old customs, will certainly find it hard to wait until these edicts are made. We shall therefore remit to all, from Princes and Ministers down to the common people of all classes, the tax in lieu of service."

Chinese Description of the Tibetans

Tibet became unified into a powerful kingdom by the seventh century, adopting Buddhism in the process. The kingdom stretched over large stretches of mountains, rivers, and steppes at its peak, before disintegrating in the mid-ninth century. The Tibetans became actively involved in connections with the Silk Road trade as well as their neighbors in India, China, and Central Asia. Tibet became a center through which traveled ideas, goods, and people from all over Eurasia.

Source: *D. Snellgrove, and H. Richardson,* A Cultural History of Tibet *(London: Weidenfield & Nicholson, 1968) pp. 29–30.*

Focus Questions:
1. What is the Chinese opinion of Tibetans?
2. Which cultures are the Tibetans most like?
3. What have the Chinese possibly left out of the description and why?

We are told that the country has a very cold climate, that oats, barley, wheat and buckwheat grow there, and that there are yaks, excellent horses, and dogs, sheep and pigs. The capital is known as Lhasa where there are city-walls and houses with flat roofs. The king and his nobles live in felt tents, which are joined together as one large one. They sleep in unclean places and they never wash or comb their hair. For the most, part the people lead a pastoral life with their flocks and herds without fixed habitation. They dress in felt and leather. They like to paint themselves with red ochre. The women plait their hair. They worship the heavens and believe in sorcerers and soothsayers. They do not know the seasons, and their year begins when the barley is ripe. Their games are chess and dice, and for music they have conch-shells and drums. They have no writing for official purposes, and they fix arrangements by means of knotted cords and notched tally-sticks. They make vessels by bending round a piece of wood and fitting in a leather bottom, or they make basins of felt. They knead roasted grain (*viz. tsam-pa*) into little cups, and they fill these with broth or curds and eat it all together. They drink their beer in their cupped hands.

There are hundreds of thousands of men ready to bear arms, and in order to levy troops they used a golden arrow (as insignia of authority). In order to give warning of enemy attacks they use fire and smoke signals. There is a watch-post every hundred *li*. Their armor and helmets are excellent. When they put them on their whole body is covered, with holes just for the eyes. Their bow and their sword never leave them. They prize physical strength and despise old age. A mother salutes her son, and a son has precedence over his father. When they go out and in, it is always the young men who go first and the older men afterwards. Military discipline is strict. In battle it is not until the troops in front have been completely wiped out that the troops behind come up into line. They prize death in battle and hate to end their lives by sickness. Those families of whom several generations have died in battle are considered of highest rank. But when someone is defeated in battle or runs away, they fix a foxtail to his head to show that he is cowardly like the fox. A great crowd will assemble and he is certain to be put to death. According to their customs they feel great shame in this matter, and they consider that it is far better to be dead.

As punishments, even for a small fault, they take out the eyes, or cut off the feet or the nose. They give floggings with leather whips just as they see fit and without any regulated number (of lashes). For prisons they dig down into the earth several dozens of feet, and they keep their prisoners there for two or three years.

The king and five or six of his followers are bound in friendship and they are called 'living in common'. When the king dies, they are all killed sacrificially. His garments, his treasure, the horses he has ridden, are interred, and a large chamber is made which is covered with a mound. Trees are planted there, and it is in this place that ancestral sacrifices are performed.

Sidonius Apollinaris, Rome's Decay, and a Glimpse of the New Order

Sidonius Apollinaris (c. 430–485 CE) descended from an aristocratic family that had, by the time of his birth, completely converted to Christianity. Sidonius would witness the final agonizing years of the western Roman Empire, ending his days as Bishop of Clermont in Southern France. Like many people of his rank and position, Sidonius had to come to terms with the half-civilized Germanic invaders (in his case, the Visigoths). He writes admiringly of the Visigothic king, Theodoric II (first letter); and of the wedding of the Frankish prince Sigismer (second letter). All the same, his third letter reflects a pervasive concern over the power of the Germans, and their potential for destruction.

Source: *Finley, Hooper & Matthew Schwartz, ed.,* Roman Letters: History from a Personal Point of View *(Detriot: Wayne State University, 1991), pp. 272–277.*

1

You have often begged a description of Theodoric the Gothic king, whose gentle breeding fame commends to every nation; you want him in his quantity and quality, in his person, and the manner of his existence. I gladly accede, as far as the limits of my page allow, and highly approve so fine and ingenuous a curiosity.

Well, he is a man worth knowing, even by those who cannot enjoy his close acquaintance, so happily have Providence and Nature joined to endow him with the perfect gifts of fortune; his way of life is such that not even the envy which lies in wait for a king can rob him of his proper praise. And first as to his person. He is well set up, in height above the average man, but below the giant. His head is round, with curled hair retreating somewhat from brow to crown. His nervous neck is free from disfiguring knots. The eyebrows are bushy and arched; when the lids droop, the lashes reach almost half-way down the cheeks. The upper ears are buried under overlying locks, after the fashion of his race. The nose is finely aquiline; the lips are thin and not enlarged by undue distention of the mouth. Every day the hair springing from his nostrils is cut back; that on the face springs thick from the hollow of the temples, but the razor has not yet come upon his cheek, and his barber is assiduous in eradicating the rich growth on the lower part of the face. Chin, throat, and neck art full, but not fat, and all of fair complexion; seen close, their colour is fresh as that of youth; they often flush, but from modesty, and not from anger. His shoulders are smooth, the upper- and forearms strong and hard; hands broad, breast prominent; waist receding. The spine dividing the broad expanse of back does not project, and you can see the spring of the ribs; the sides swell with salient muscle, the well-girt flanks are full of vigour. His thighs are like hard horn; the knee-joints firm and masculine; the knees themselves the comeliest and least wrinkled in the world. A full ankle supports the leg, and the foot is small to bear such mighty limbs.

Now for the routine of his public life. Before daybreak he goes with a very small suite to attend the service of his priests. He prays with assiduity, but, if I may speak in confidence, one may suspect more of habit than conviction in this piety. Administrative duties of the kingdom take up the rest of the morning. Armed nobles stand about the royal seat; the mass of guards in their garb of skins are admitted that they may be within call but kept at the threshold for quiet's sake; only a murmur of them comes in from their post at the doors, between the curtain and the outer barrier. And now the foreign envoys are introduced. The king hears them out, and says little; if a thing needs more discussion he puts it off, but accelerates matters ripe for dispatch. The second hour arrives; he rises from the throne to inspect his treasure-chamber or stable. If the chase is the order of the day, he joins it, but never carries his bow at his side, considering this derogatory to royal state. When a bird or beast is marked for him, or happens to cross his path, he puts his hand behind his back and takes the bow from a page with the string all hanging loose; for as he deems it a boy's trick to bear it in a quiver, so he holds it effeminate to receive the weapon ready strung. When it is given him, he sometimes holds it in both hands and bends the extremities towards each other; at others he sets it, knot-end downward, against his lifted heel, and runs his finger up the slack and wavering string. After that, he takes his arrows, adjusts, and lets fly. He will ask you beforehand what you would like him to transfix; you choose, and he hits. If there is a miss through either's error, your vision will mostly be at fault, and not the archer's skill.

On ordinary days, his table resembles that of a private person. The board does not groan beneath a mass of dull and unpolished silver set on by panting servitors; the weight lies rather in the conversation than in the plate; there is either sensible talk or none. The hangings and draperies used on these occasions are sometimes of purple silk, sometimes only of linen; art, not costliness, commends the fare, as spotlessness rather than bulk the silver. Toasts are few, and you will oftener see a thirsty guest impatient, than a full one refusing cup or bowl. In short, you will find elegance of Greece, good cheer of Gaul, Italian nimbleness, the state of public banquets with the attentive service of a private table, and everywhere the discipline of a king's house. What need for me to describe the pomp of his feast days? No man is so unknown as not to know of them. But to my theme again. The siesta after dinner is always slight and sometimes intermitted. When inclined for the board-game, he is quick to gather up the dice, examines them with care, shakes the box with expert hand, throws rapidly, humorously apostrophizes them, and patiently waits the issue. Silent at a good throw, he makes merry over a bad, annoyed by neither fortune, and always the philosopher. He is too proud to ask or to refuse a revenge; he disdains to avail himself of one if offered; and if it is opposed will quietly go on playing. You effect recovery of your man without obstruction on his side; he recovers his without collusion upon yours. You see the strategist when he moves the pieces; his one thought is victory. Yet at play he puts off a little of his kingly rigour, inciting all to good fellowship and the freedom of the game: I think he is afraid of being feared. Vexation in the man whom he beats delights him; he will never believe that his opponents have not let him win unless their annoyance proves him really victor. You would be surprised how often the pleasure born of these little happenings may favour the march of great affairs...I myself am gladly beaten by him when I have a favor to ask, since the loss of my game may mean the gaining of my cause. About the ninth hour, the burden of government begins again. Back come the importunates, back the ushers to remove them; on all sides buzz the voices of petitioners, a sound which lasts till evening, and does not diminish till interrupted by the royal repast; even then they disperse to attend their various patrons among the courtiers, and are astir till bedtime. Sometimes, though this is rare, supper is enlivened by sallies of mimes, but no guest is ever exposed to the wound of a biting tongue. Withal there is no noise of hydraulic organ, or choir with its conductor intoning a set piece; you will hear no players of lyre of flute, no master of the music, no girls with cithara or tabor; the king cares for no strains but those which no less charm the mind with virtue than the ear with melody. When he rises to withdraw, the treasury watch begins its vigil; armed sentries stand on guard during the first hours of slumber. But I am wandering from my subject. I never promised a whole chapter on the kingdom, but a few words about the king. I must stay my pen; you asked for nothing more than one or two facts about the person and the tastes of Theodoric; and my own aim was to write a letter, not a history.

2

You take such pleasure in the sight of arms and those who wear them, that I can imagine your delight if you could have seen the young prince Sigismer on his way to the palace of his father-in-law in the guise of a bridegroom or suitor in all the pomp and bravery of the tribal fashion. His own steed with its caparisons, other steeds laden with flashing gems, paced before and after; but the conspicuous interest in the procession centred in the prince himself as with a charming modesty he went afoot amid his body-guard and footmen, in flame-red mantle, with much glint of ruddy gold, and gleam of snowy silken tunic, his fair hair, red cheeks and white skin according with the three hues of his equipment. But the chiefs and allies who bore him company were dread of aspect, even thus on peace intent. Their feet were laced in boots of bristly hide reaching to the heels; ankles and legs were exposed. They wore high tight tunics of varied colour hardly descending to their bare knees, the sleeves covering only the upper arm. Green mantles they had with crimson borders; baldrics supported swords hung from their shoulders, and pressed on sides covered with cloaks of skin secured by brooches. No small part of their adornment consisted of their arms; in their hands they grasped barbed spears and missile axes; their left sides were guarded by shields, which flashed with tawny golden bosses and snowy silver borders, betraying at once their wealth and their good taste. Though the business in hand was wedlock, Mars was no whit less prominent in all his pomp than Venus. Why need I say more? Only your presence was wanting to the full enjoyment of so fine a spectacle. For when I saw you had missed the things you love to see, I longed to have you with me in all the impatience of your longing soul.

3

Rumour has it that the Goths have occupied Roman soil; our unhappy Auvergne is always their gateway on every such incursion. It is our fate to furnish fuel to the fire of a peculiar hatred, for, by Christ's aid, we are the sole obstacle to the fulfilment of their ambition to extend their frontier to the Rhone, and so hold all the country between that river, the Atlantic, and the Loire. Their menacing power has long pressed us hard; it has already swallowed up whole tracts of territory round us, and threatens to swallow more. We mean to resist with spirit, though we know our peril and the risks which we incur. But our trust is not in our poor walls impaired by fire, or in our rotting palisades, or in our ramparts worn by the breasts of the sentries, as they lean on them in continual watch. Our only present help we find in those Rogations which you introduced; and this is the reason why the people of Clermont refuse to recede, though terror surge about them on every side. By inauguration and institution of these prayers we are already new initiates; and if so far we have effected less than you have, our hearts are affected equally with yours. For it is not unknown to us by what portents and alarms the city entrusted to you by God was laid desolate at the time when first you ordained this form of prayer. Now it was earthquake, shattering the outer palace walls with frequent shocks; now fire, piling mounds of glowing ash upon proud houses fallen in ruin; now, amazing spectacle! wild deer grown ominously tame, making their lairs in the very forum. You saw the city being emptied of its inhabitants, rich and poor taking to flight. But you resorted in our latter day to the example shown of old in Nineveh, that you at least might not discredit the divine warning by the spectacle of your despair. And, indeed, you of all men have been least justified in distrusting the providence of God, after the proof of it vouchsafed to your own virtues. Once, in a sudden conflagration, your faith burned stronger than the flames. In full sight of the trembling crowd you stood forth all alone to stay them, and lo! the fire leapt back before you, a sinuous beaten fugitive. It was miracle, a formidable thing, unseen before and unexampled; the element which naturally shrinks from nothing, retired in awe at your approach. You therefore first enjoined a fast upon a few members of our sacred order, denouncing gross offences, announcing punishment, promising relief. You made it clear that if the penalty of sin was nigh, so also was the pardon; you proclaimed that by frequent prayer the menace of coming desolation might be removed. You taught that it was by water of tears rather than water of rivers that the obstinate and raging fire could best be extinguished, and by firm faith the threatening shock of earthquake stayed. The multitude of the lowly forthwith followed your counsel, and this influenced persons of higher rank, who had not scrupled to abandon the town, and now were not ashamed to return to it. By this devotion God was appeased, who sees into all hearts; your fervent prayers were counted to you for salvation; they became an example for your fellow citizens, and a defence about you all, for after those days there were neither portents to alarm, nor visitations to bring disaster.

We of Clermont know that all these ills befell your people of Vienne before the Rogations, and have not befallen them since; and therefore it is that we are eager to follow the lead of so holy a guide, beseeching your Beatitude from your own pious lips to give us the advocacy of those prayers now known to us by the examples which you have transmitted. Since the Confessor Ambrose discovered the remains of Gervasius and Protasius, it has been granted to you alone in the West to translate the relics of two martyrs—all the holy body of Ferteolus, and the head of our martyr Julian, which once the executioner's gory hand brought to the raging persecutor from the place of testimony. It is only fair, then, in compensation for the loss of this hallowed relic, that some part of your patronage should come to us from Vienne, since a part of our patronal saint has migrated thither. Deign to hold us in remembrance, my Lord Bishop.

Indian Land Grants, 753 CE

This is a series of land grants dated to the reign of Nandivarman II (732–796 CE), ruler of the Pallava empire. The Pallava was one of a number of powerful southern Indian kingdoms making their riches from trade and from farming. These land grants were imprinted onto copper plates, and most were grants from the prince to religious institutions, though some were also for individuals.

Source: *Thapar, R.* Early India: From the Origins to AD 1300 *(London: Penguin, 2002).*

Focus Questions:
1. Why is such attention paid to water?
2. What are the resources of the area?
3. What does the new landlord control, and what does he receive?

INDIAN INSCRIPTIONS ON COPPER–ROYAL LAND GRANTS

The author of the above eulogy was Trivikrama. The above is an order of the king dated in the twenty-second year of his reign. Let the inhabitants of Urrukkattukottam see. Having seen the order which was issued after the king had been pleased to give Kodukalli village of our country—having expropriated the former owners at the request of Brahmayuvaraja, having appointed Ghorasharman as the effector of the grant, having excluded previous grants to temples and grants to brahmans, having excluded the houses of the cultivators to the extent of altogether two *Patti* [a measure of land]—as a *brahmadeya* (grant) to Shettiranga Sonaayajin [Shettiranga, who performs the Soma sacrifice], who belongs to the Bharadvaja *gotra* [a brahman exogamous sept], follows the Chhandogyasutra and resides at Puni, we, the inhabitants went to the boundaries which the headman of the *nadu* [district] pointed out, circumambulated the village from right to left, and planted milk-bushes and placed stones around it. The boundaries of this village are—the eastern boundary is to the west of the boundary of Palaiyur, the southern boundary is to the north of the boundary of Palaiyur, the western boundary is to the east of the boundary of Manarpakkam and of the boundary of Kollipakkam, and the northern boundary is to the south of the boundary of Velimanallur. The donee shall enjoy the wet land and the dry land included within these four boundaries, wherever the iguana runs and the tortoise crawls, and shall be permitted to dig river channels and inundation channels for conducting water from the Seyaru, the Vehka, and the tank of Tiraiyan...Those who take and use the water in these channels by pouring out baskets, by cutting branch channels, or by employing small levers shall pay a fine to be collected by the king. He (the donee) and his descendants shall enjoy the houses, house gardens, and so forth, and shall have the right to build houses and halls of burnt tiles. The land included within these boundaries we have endowed with all exemptions. He himself shall enjoy the exemptions obtaining in this village without paying for the oil-mills and looms, the hire of the well-diggers, the share of the brahmans of the king, the share of *shen-godi* [a plant], the share of the *kallal* [a type of fig tree], the share of *kannittu*, the share of corn-ears, the share of the headman, the share of the potter, the sifting of paddy, the price of ghi, the price of cloth, the share of cloth, the hunters, messengers, dancing-girls, the grass, the best cow and the best bull, the share of the district, cotton threads, servants, palmyra molasses, the fines to the accountant and the minister, the tax on planting water-lilies, the share of the water-lilies, the fourth part of the trunks of old trees of various kinds, including areca palms and coconut trees... The grant was made in the presence of the local authorities, of the ministers, and of the secretaries.

Kasakkudi Plates of Nandivarman, *South Indian Inscriptions*, II. 3, pp. 360 ff.

Chapter 9

Christianity

The Acts of the Apostles: Paul Pronounces the "Good News" in Greece

Written at some point in the late 1st century CE, the Acts of the Apostles *seems to have been joined to the* Gospel of Luke, *and thus the document is often labelled "Luke–Acts." The author claims to have had knowledge of Jesus' ministry and death, as well as of the first generation of his followers or "disciples," as they spread the "evangelion" ("good news") that Jesus had been resurrected from the dead.* Acts *is an especially important document for reconstructing the life of St. Paul, who was born into a Jewish family (but with Roman citizenship) in Tarsus, a city in Cilicia. Upon his "conversion" to Christian belief, Paul began his career as a missionary, sharing the "gospel," first with his fellow Jews throughout the Mediterranean's major cities, but then, and increasingly, with non-Jews, or "Gentiles." The first Christian documents (c. 50s CE) are attributed to him, and he traveled extensively, sailing to Rome and Greece, as well as to a great deal of Asia Minor and Palestine. In this passage of* Acts, *Paul confronts philosophers in Athens, the intellectual heart of the Empire, and he finds little encouragement of his ministry from various quarters.*

Source: *Acts 17:16–18:23, NIV.*

Focus Questions:
1. Why are the Greeks resistant to Paul's message?
2. What does this document suggest about the growing tension between Christians and the Jews, from whose religious experience theirs ultimately sprang?

ACTS OF THE APOSTLES 17:16-18:23

In Athens

16While Paul was waiting for them in Athens, he was greatly distressed to see that the city was full of idols. 17So he reasoned in the synagogue with the Jews and the God-fearing Greeks, as well as in the marketplace day by day with those who happened to be there. 18A group of Epicurean and Stoic philosophers began to dispute with him. Some of them asked, "What is this babbler trying to say?" Others remarked, "He seems to be advocating foreign gods." They said this because Paul was preaching the good news about Jesus and the resurrection. [19]Then they took him and brought him to a meeting of the Areopagus, where they said to him, "May we know what this new teaching is that you are presenting? [20]You are bringing some strange ideas to our ears, and we want to know what they mean." [21](All the Athenians and the foreigners who lived there spent their time doing nothing but talking about and listening to the latest ideas.)

[22]Paul then stood up in the meeting of the Areopagus and said: "Men of Athens! I see that in every way you are very religious. [23]For as I walked around and looked carefully at your objects of worship, I even found an altar with this inscription: TO AN UNKNOWN GOD. Now what you worship as something unknown I am going to proclaim to you.

[24]"The God who made the world and everything in it is the Lord of heaven and earth and does not live in temples built by hands. [25]And he is not served by human hands, as if he needed anything, because he himself gives all men life and breath and everything else. [26]From one man he made every nation of men, that they should inhabit the whole earth; and he determined the times set for them and the exact places where they should live. [27]God did this so that men would seek him and perhaps reach out for him and find him, though he is not far from each one of us. [28]'For in him we live and move and have our being.' As some of your own poets have said, 'We are his offspring.'

[29]"Therefore since we are God's offspring, we should not think that the divine being is like gold or silver or stone—an image made by man's design and skill. [30]In the past God overlooked such ignorance, but now he commands all people everywhere to repent. [31]For he has set a day when he will judge the world with justice by the man he has appointed. He has given proof of this to all men by raising him from the dead."

[32]When they heard about the resurrection of the dead, some of them sneered, but others said, "We want to hear you again on this subject." [33]At that, Paul left the Council. [34]A few men became followers of Paul and believed. Among them was Dionysius, a member of the Areopagus, also a woman named Damaris, and a number of others.

ACTS 18

In Corinth

[1]After this, Paul left Athens and went to Corinth. [2]There he met a Jew named Aquila, a native of Pontus, who had recently come from Italy with his wife Priscilla, because Claudius had ordered all the Jews to leave Rome. Paul went to see them, [3]and because he was a tentmaker as they were, he stayed and worked with them. [4]Every Sabbath he reasoned in the synagogue, trying to persuade Jews and Greeks.

[5]When Silas and Timothy came from Macedonia, Paul devoted himself exclusively to preaching, testifying to the Jews that Jesus was the Christ. [6]But when the Jews opposed Paul and became abusive, he shook out his clothes in protest and said to them, "Your blood be on your own heads! I am clear of my responsibility. From now on I will go to the Gentiles."

[7]Then Paul left the synagogue and went next door to the house of Titius Justus, a worshiper of God. [8]Crispus, the synagogue ruler, and his entire household believed in the Lord; and many of the Corinthians who heard him believed and were baptized.

[9]One night the Lord spoke to Paul in a vision: "Do not be afraid; keep on speaking, do not be silent. [10]For I am with you, and no one is going to attack and harm you, because I have many people in this city." [11]So Paul stayed for a year and a half, teaching them the word of God.

[12]While Gallio was proconsul of Achaia, the Jews made a united attack on Paul and brought him into court. [13]"This man," they charged, "is persuading the people to worship God in ways contrary to the law."

[14]Just as Paul was about to speak, Gallio said to the Jews, "If you Jews were making a complaint about some misdemeanor or serious crime, it would be reasonable for me to listen to you. [15]But since it involves questions about words and names and your own law—settle the matter yourselves. I will not be a judge of such things." [16]So he had them ejected from the court. [17]Then they all turned on Sosthenes the synagogue ruler and beat him in front of the court. But Gallio showed no concern whatever.

Priscilla, Aquila and Apollos
[18]Paul stayed on in Corinth for some time. Then he left the brothers and sailed for Syria, accompanied by Priscilla and Aquila. Before he sailed, he had his hair cut off at Cenchrea because of a vow he had taken. [19]They arrived at Ephesus, where Paul left Priscilla and Aquila. He himself went into the synagogue and reasoned with the Jews. [20]When they asked him to spend more time with them, he declined. [21]But as he left, he promised, "I will come back if it is God's will." Then he set sail from Ephesus. [22]When he landed at Caesarea, he went up and greeted the church and then went down to Antioch.

[23]After spending some time in Antioch, Paul set out from there and traveled from place to place throughout the region of Galatia and Phrygia, strengthening all the disciples.

St. Augustine of Hippo: Theory of "The Just War"

St. Augustine was the first father of the church to develop the theory of the just war. His ideas emerged in response to current events, as Christians were required to cope with increasing threats to the security of the empire. Pieced together from numerous topical writings he completed over the years, his theory can be presented in terms of four characteristics that a just war must have: (1) It must be defensive in nature. (2) It must not do more damage than it prevents. (3) Its aim must be the restoration of peace, rather than the expansion of control. (4) It must be waged only by constituted authority.

Source: From De civitate Dei libri xxii, ed. Emmanuel Hoffman (Vienna: F. Tempsky, 1899–1900), extracts from Books I–V and XIX, passim; and Contra Faustum libri xxxiii, ed. Josephus Zycha (Vienna: F. Tempsky, 1891), extracts from Book XXII, chs. 74–75. Trans. Henry A. Myers.

Focus Questions:
1. Why does St. Augustine view the sack of Rome as a cause for heightened, rather than diminished, respect for Christianity?
2. Why is a temporary peace observable between the City of God and the Earthly City?
3. What are the earthly and heavenly cities? How do they reflect on Christian society and government?

ABOUT THE WAR IN WHICH KING RAGADAIS OF THE GOTHS, A WORSHIPPER OF DEMONS, WAS DEFEATED WITH HIS HUGE ARMY IN A SINGLE DAY

When Radagais, King of the Goths, was already threatening the Romans' very necks with his huge and savage army encamped near the city, he was beaten in one day with such speed and in such a way that not one single Roman was wounded, let alone killed, while well over a hundred thousand of his soldiers were struck down, and he was captured and soon put to a deserved death. For if such a godless man with such equally godless troops had entered Rome, who would have been spared by him? What shrines of the martyrs would he have respected? In dealing with what person would the fear of God have restrained him? Whose blood would he have wanted to leave unshed and whose chastity unravaged?

WHETHER THE SWEEP OF IMPERIAL COMMAND...IS AMONG THINGS OF VALUE FOR WISE AND HAPPY MEN

It makes sense that if the true God is worshipped and served with true rites and good morals, it is a benefit for good men to have long reigns over great territories. This is actually not of so much use to themselves as it is to their subjects, because as far as they themselves are concerned their own true faith and righteousness, which are great gifts from God, are enough to give them the true happiness that lets them live this life well and attain eternal life afterwards. Thus the reign of good men here on earth does not serve their own good so much as it does human concerns.

THE HARSH BRUTALITY IN THE SACK OF ROME CORRESPONDED WITH THE ESTABLISHED CUSTOM OF WAR, WHEREAS THE MERCY SHOWN REVEALED THE POWER OF CHRIST'S NAME

All the destruction, killing, looting, burning, and suffering which took place in the recent sack of Rome happened in accordance with the customs of waging war. What was altogether new and previously unheard of, however, was that the barbarian brutality [of the Goths] was so tamed that they picked the largest of the basilicas and allowed them to remain sanctuaries, where no one could be struck down and from which no one could be dragged away. Many people were led there to freedom and safety by soldiers showing sympathy for them...Anyone who does not see fit to credit this to the name of Christ—yes, to Christian times— is blind. Anyone who sees this new turn of events but fails to praise it is most ungrateful.

THE SAINTS LOSE NOTHING OF VALUE IN LOSING MATERIAL GOODS

In the sack of Rome faithful and godly men..."lost everything they had." How about their faith? How about their godliness? How about the goods of the inner-being which make a person rich before God? Listen to what the Apostle Paul says about the riches of Christianity: "...Godliness with contentment is great gain, for we brought nothing into this world and certainly we can carry nothing out. If we have food and clothing, let us be content with them. People who want to be rich fall into temptations and traps. They fall into foolish and harmful desires which drown men in destruction and perdition."

THE UNIVERSAL PEACE, WHICH THE LAW OF NATURE PRE-SERVES THROUGH ALL DISTURBANCES, AND THE CONDITION WHICH EACH PERSON DESERVES TO FIND HIMSELF IN, ACCORDING TO THE WAY HE HAS USED HIS WILL AND ACCORDING TO THE DECISION OF THE JUST JUDGE

Domestic peace is a harmonious arrangement in matters of command and obedience among those of the same household, and the peace of a [normal] city is a similar one among its citizens. The peace of the Heavenly City is the most perfectly and harmoniously designed communal relationship in the enjoyment of God and in the fellowship resulting from union with God. Peace for all beings is tranquility within order. Order is the arrangement of equal and unequal things, with each assigned its proper place.

And so we see that miserable people [lacking faith and godliness]…in the very fact that they justly deserve their misery are confined to a condition of misery by the principle of order. This keeps them from being united with saved people. When they live without obvious disturbances they adapt to their bondage, and so there is a bit of tranquil order among them, and so they enjoy a peace of sorts. They still remain miserable, however, since, in spite of not suffering constantly from a total lack of security, they are not within that realm where there is no cause to worry about either suffering or security…

WHERE PEACE AND DISCORD BETWEEN THE HEAVENLY AND EARTHLY CITIES COMES FROM

The Earthly City, which does not live by faith, desires an earthly peace, seeking to bring it about through harmony of command and obedience among citizens, even though its scope is limited to uniting people's wills on matters pertaining to this mortal life.

The Heavenly City, however, or, to be more precise, those of its members who are living by faith during their mortal pilgrimages, must make use of this peace, although only until they are through with their transient status on earth, which requires it. For this reason, the Heavenly City sojourning either as a captive or a wandering stranger in the Earthly City does not hesitate to obey earthly authority in matters required by the communal life of mortals. With mortal life common to the people of both Cities, a certain harmony between them may be maintained in relation to its requirements.

While the Heavenly City sojourns on earth, it recruits members from all peoples and forms a pilgrim society of men and women speaking all different languages, which pays no attention to the diversity of customs, laws, and institutions among them, by which earthly peace is established and maintained.

WHETHER WAR IS ALWAYS EVIL OR MAY SOMETIMES BE JUST

Just what is wrong with war? Is it that some people will die in it—people who will die sometime anyway— so that others may live in peace under authority? That is the objection of cowards, not believers. The real evils in war are: a love of inflicting violence, vengeful cruelty, raging and implacable hatred, ferocity in rebelling, lust for power, and similar things. It is normally to punish under law these very things that, at the command of God or some legitimate authority, good men resort to war against violent offenders…Much depends on the reasons for which and the authority by which men commit themselves to waging war. The natural order among mortal men requires the promotion of peace. It justifies the exercise of military force through the authority and direction of the ruler when he decides it is necessary for soldiers to carry out their duties on behalf of the peace and safety of the community. When men wage war in obedience to God, it is not appropriate to doubt that it is waged justly either to deter, or humble, or subdue the pride of men.

Pope Leo I: on Bishop Hilary of Arles

There is no evidence that, during the Church's early years, the Bishop of Rome was held in any greater esteem than his colleagues who shepherded the major cities of the time: Antioch, Alexandria, or Jerusalem. It was only after four centuries had elapsed that the leadership claims of the Bishop of Rome (who assumed the title of Pope), on the basis of Apostolic Succession to St. Peter, and an interpretation of Matthew 16:13–19, were solidified into the Petrine Theory. It was Pope Leo I (440–461 C.E.) who most effectively asserted these claims of supremacy as representative of Christ on earth. In the following instance, he states some of these claims while attacking an opponent, Bishop Hilary of Arles.

Source: *Filey Cooper and Matthew Schwartz. eds.,* Roman Letters: History from a Personal Point of View *(Detroit: Wayne State University, 1991), pp. 291–292.*

Focus Questions:
1. Of what does Leo accuse Bishop Hilary?
2. How does Leo explain his ideas as to why Christ would have placed the Apostle Peter in the position of leadership?
3. What consequences does Leo foresee for what he views as Hilary's insubordinate actions?

Our Lord Jesus Christ, Saviour of the human race, desired to have the observance of divine religion shine out through God's grace unto all nations and races. He established it in such a way that truth, previously contained only in proclamations of the Law and the Prophets, might proceed from the Apostles' trumpet for the salvation of all, as it is written: "Their sound has gone forth unto all the earth: and their words unto the ends of the world." Now, the Lord desired that the dispensing of this gift should be shared as a task by all the Apostles, but in such a way that He put the principal charge on the most blessed Peter, the highest of all the Apostles. He wanted His gifts to flow into the entire body from Peter himself, as it were from the head…But the man who attempts to infringe on its power by furthering his own desires and not following practices received from antiquity is trying with absolutely blasphemous presumption, to destroy this most sacred solidity of that rock, established with God as the builder, as we mentioned. For he believes that he is subject to no law, that he is not restrained by any regulations that the Lord ordained. Being intent on novel assumption of power, he departs from what you and we are accustomed to; he presumes to do what is illegal and neglects traditions that he ought to have maintained…Your Fraternities should, of course, realize with us that the Apostolic See (out of reverence for it) has countless times been reported to in consultation by bishops even in your province. And through the appeal of various cases to it, decisions already made have been either rescinded or confirmed, as dictated by long-standing custom. As a result, with "unity of spirit in the bond of peace" being preserved, with letters being sent and received, what was done in a holy manner has been conducive to abiding charity. For our solicitude, which seeks not its own interests but those of Christ, does not detract from the dignity given by God to the churches and the bishops of the churches. This was the procedure always well observed and profitably maintained by our predecessors. But Hilary has departed from it, aiming to disturb the status of the churches and harmony among the bishops by his novel usurpations of power. He seeks to subject you to his authority while not allowing himself to be under the Jurisdiction of the blessed Apostle Peter. He claims for himself the right to consecrate in all the churches of Gaul and takes as his own the dignity which belongs to the metropolitan bishops. He even lessens the reverence due to the most blessed Peter himself by his quite arrogant statements. And although the power to bind and loose was given to Peter before the others, still, in an even more special way, the pasturing of the sheep was entrusted to him. Anyone who thinks that the primacy should be denied to Peter cannot in any way lessen the Apostle's dignity: inflated with the wind of his own pride, he buries himself in hell.

Pliny the Younger, "Epistulae" Letters

Caius Plinius Caecilius Secundus, or "Pliny the Younger" (62–113 CE), has always stood in the shadow of his illustrious uncle and adoptive father, Pliny the Elder, but grew up to be a competent official in his own right. His letters "Epistulae" provide a significant insight into major events and problems in the early Roman Empire. The first of these describes, for the historian Tacitus, the Mount Vesuvius explosion of 79 CE, and the second is an exchange with the Emperor Trajan over how Pliny, in his capacity as governor of Bithynia, might best deal with members of the illegal sect of Christianity.

Source: *Betty Radice, trans.,* The Letters of the Younger Pliny *(Baltimore: Penguin, 1963), pp. 166–168, 293–295.*

Focus Questions:
1. What traits exhibited by Pliny's uncle during the crisis of the Vesuvius eruption are held up as being the most admirable, and why?
2. From certain comments made by Pliny in his letter to Tacitus, what does he envision as being the historian's task?
3. What dilemma was Pliny faced with regarding people accused of practicing Christianity, and what administrative procedures did he follow?
4. To what extent and in what manner does the Emperor both praise and criticize Pliny in his letter of reply?

PLINY TO CORNELIUS TACITUS

To Cornelius Tacitus

Thank you for asking me to send you a description of my uncle's death so that you can leave an accurate account of it for posterity; I know that immortal fame awaits him if his death is recorded by you. It is true that he perished in a catastrophe which destroyed the loveliest regions of the earth, a fate shared by whole cities and their people, and one so memorable that it is likely to make his name live for ever: and he himself wrote a number of books of lasting value: but you write for all time and can still do much to perpetuate his memory. The fortunate man, in my opinion, is he to whom the gods have granted the power either to do something which is worth recording or to write what is worth reading, and most fortunate of all is the man who can do both. Such a man was my uncle, as his own books and yours will prove. So you set me a task I would choose for myself, and I am more than willing to start on it.

My uncle was stationed at Misenum in active command of the fleet. On 24 August, in the early afternoon, my mother drew attention to a cloud of unusual size and appearance. He had been out in the sun, had taken a cold bath, and lunched while lying down, and was then working at his books. He called for his shoes and climbed up to a place which would give him the best view of the phenomenon. It was not clear at that distance from which mountain the cloud was rising (it was afterwards known to be Vesuvius); its general appearance can best be expressed as being like an umbrella pine, for it rose to a great height on a sort of trunk and then split off into branches, I imagine because it was thrust upwards by the first blast and then left unsupported as the pressure subsided, or else it was borne down by its own weight so that it spread out and gradually dispersed. In places it looked white, elsewhere blotched and dirty, according to the amount of soil and ashes it carried with it. My uncle's scholarly acumen saw at once that it was important enough for a closer inspection, and he ordered a boat to be made ready, telling me I could come with him if I wished. I replied that I preferred to go on with my studies, and as it happened he had himself given me some writing to do.

As he was leaving the house he was handed a message from Rectina, wife of Tascus whose house was at the foot of the mountain, so that escape was impossible except by boat. She was terrified by the danger threatening her and implored him to rescue her from her fate. He changed his plans, and what he had begun in a spirit of inquiry he completed as a hero. He gave orders for the warships to be launched and went on board himself with the intention of bringing help to many more people besides Rectina, for this lovely stretch of coast was thickly populated. He hurried to the place where everyone else was hastily leaving, steering his course straight for the danger zone. He was entirely fearless, describing each new movement and phase of the portent to be noted down exactly as he observed them. Ashes were already falling, hotter and thicker as the ships drew near, followed by bits of pumice and blackened stones, charred and cracked by the flames: then suddenly they were in shallow water, and the shore was blocked by debris from the mountain. For a moment my uncle wondered whether to turn back, but when the helmsman advised this he refused, telling him that Fortune stood by the courageous and that they must make for Pomponianus at Stabiae. He was cut off there by the breadth of the bay (for the shore gradually curves round a basin filled by the sea) so that he was not as yet in danger, though it was clear that this would come nearer as it spread. Pomponianus had therefore already put his belongings on board ship, intending to escape if the contrary wind fell. This wind was of course full in my uncle's favour, and he was able to bring his ship in. He embraced his terrified friend, cheered and encouraged him, and thinking he could calm his fears by showing his own composure, gave orders that he was to be carried to the bathroom. After his bath he lay down and dined; he was quite cheerful, or at any rate he pretended he was, which was no less courageous.

Meanwhile on Mount Vesuvius broad sheets of fire and leaping flames blazed at several points, their bright glare emphasized by the darkness of night. My uncle tried to allay the fears of his companion by repeatedly declaring that these were nothing but bonfires left by the peasants in their terror, or else empty homes on fire in the districts they had abandoned. Then he went to rest and certainly slept, for as he was a stout man his breathing was rather loud and heavy and could be heard by people coming and going outside his door. By this time the courtyard giving access to his room was full of ashes mixed with pumice-stones, so that its level had risen, and if he had stayed in the room any longer he would never have got out. He was wakened, came out and joined Pomponianus and the rest of the household who had sat up all night. They debated whether to stay indoors or take their chance in the open, for the buildings were now shaking with violent shocks, and seemed to be swaying to and fro as if they were torn from their foundations. Outside on the other hand, there was the danger of falling pumice-stones, even though these were light and porous; however, after comparing the risks they chose the latter. In my uncle's case one reason outweighed the other, but for the others it was a choice of fears. As a protection against falling objects they put pillows on their heads tied down with cloths.

Elsewhere there was daylight by this time, but they were still in darkness, blacker and denser than any ordinary night, which they relieved by lighting torches and various kinds of lamp. My uncle decided to go down to the shore and investigate on the spot the possibility of any escape by sea, but he found the waves still wild and dangerous. A sheet was spread on the ground for him to lie down, and he repeatedly asked for cold water to drink. Then the flames and smell of sulphur which gave warning of the approaching fire drove the others to take flight and roused him to stand up. He stood leaning on two slaves and then suddenly collapsed, I imagine because the dense fumes choked his breathing by blocking his windpipe which was constitutionally weak and narrow and often inflamed. When daylight returned on the 26th—two days after the last day he had seen—his body was found intact and uninjured, still fully clothed and looking more like sleep than death.

Meanwhile my mother and I were at Misenum, but this is not of any historic interest, and you only wanted to hear about my uncle's death. I will say no more, except to add that I have described in detail every incident which I either witnessed myself or heard about immediately after the event, when reports were most likely to be accurate. It is for you to select what best suits your purpose, for there is a great difference between a letter to a friend and history written well for all to read.

PLINY TO THE EMPEROR TRAJAN

It is my custom to refer all my difficulties to you, Sir, for no one is better able to resolve my doubts and to inform my ignorance.

I have never been present at an examination of Christians. Consequently, I do not know the nature of the extent of the punishments usually meted out to them, nor the grounds for starting an investigation and how far it should be pressed. Nor am I at all sure whether any distinction should be made between them on the grounds of age, or if young people and adults should be treated alike; whether a pardon ought to be granted to anyone retracting his beliefs, or if he has once professed Christianity, he shall gain nothing by renouncing it; and whether it is the mere name of Christian which is punishable, even if innocent of crime, or rather crimes associated with the name.

For the moment this is the line I have taken with all persons brought before me on the charge of being Christians. I have asked them in person if they are Christians, and if they admit it, I repeat the question a second and a third time, with a warning of punishment awaiting them. If they persist, I order them to be led away for execution; for, whatever the nature of their admission, I am convinced that their stubbornness and unshakeable obstinacy ought not to go unpunished. There have been others similarly fanatical who are Roman citizens. I have entered them on the list of persons to be sent to Rome for trial.

Now that I have begun to deal with this problem, as so often happens, the charges are becoming more widespread and increasing in variety. An anonymous pamphlet has been circulated which contains the names of a number of accused persons. Amongst these I considered that I should dismiss any who denied that they were or had been Christians when they had repeated after me a formula of invocation to the gods and had made offerings of wine and incense to your statue (which I had ordered to be brought into court for this purpose along with the images of the gods), and furthermore had reviled the name of Christ: none of which things, I understand, any genuine Christian can be induced to do.

Others, whose names were given to me by an informer, first admitted the charge and then denied it; they said that they had ceased to be Christiana two or more years previously, and some of them even twenty years ago. They all did reverence to your statue and the images of the gods in the same way as the others, and reviled the name of Christ. They also declared that the sum total of their guilt or error mounted to no more than this: they had met regularly before dawn on a fixed day to chant verses alternately amongst themselves in honour of Christ as if to a god, and also to bind themselves by oath, not for any criminal purpose, but to abstain from theft, robbery, and adultery, to commit no breach of trust and not to deny a deposit when called upon to restore it. After this ceremony it had been their custom to disperse and reassemble later to take food of an ordinary, harmless kind; but they had in fact given up this practice since my edict, issued on your instructions, which banned all political societies. This made me decide it was all the more necessary to extract the truth by torture from two slave-women, whom they call deaconesses. I found nothing but a degenerate sort of cult carried to extravagant lengths.

I have therefore postponed any further examination and hastened to consult you. The question seems to me to be worthy of your consideration, especially in view of the number of persons endangered; for a great many individuals of every age and class, both men and women, are being brought to trial, and this is likely to continue. It is not only the towns, but villages and rural districts too which are infected through contact with this wretched cult. I think though that it is still possible for it to be checked and directed to better ends, for there is no doubt that people have begun to throng the temples which had been almost entirely deserted for a long time; the sacred rites which had been allowed to lapse are being performed again, and flesh of sacrificial victims is on sale everywhere, though up till recently scarcely anyone could be found to buy it. It is easy to infer from this that a great many people could be reformed if they were given an opportunity to repent.

TRAJAN TO PLINY

You have followed the right course of procedure, my dear Pliny, in your examination of the cases of persons charged with being Christians, for it is impossible to lay down a general rule to a fixed formula. These people must not be hunted out; if they are brought before you and the charge against them is proved, they must be punished, but in the case of anyone who denies that he is a Christian, and makes it clear that he is not by offering prayers to our gods, he is to be pardoned as a result of his repentance however suspect his past conduct may be. But pamphlets circulated anonymously must play no part in any accusation. They create the worst sort of precedent and are quite out of keeping with the spirit of our age.

Paulus Orosius, from *Seven Books of History Against the Pagans*

In writing this dissertation for St. Augustine, Orosius became the first Christian graduate student on record. His work, entitled without the slightest pretense of objectivity, Seven Books of History Against the Pagans, *became the Christian textbook of world history, as opposed to plain Church history, from creation to CE 417.*

Source: *Allen C. Myers. Trans., Karl Zangemeister, ed.,* Historiarum Adversum Paganos libri *VII (Vienna: C. Gerold, 1882), excerpts from Books III, pp. viii, 5–8, and V, i, 10–13, ii, 1–8.*

> **Focus Questions:**
> 1. In spite of the great optimism of Orosius, he does give a few hints that the Roman Empire in the West is coming apart at the seams. Can you find one or more of them?
> 2. Comparing the excerpts from St. Augustine and Orosius, what similarities do you find? Where is the emphasis different?

Let us assume there is no doubt about the fact that it was under Augustus Caesar, following the peace treaty with the Parthians, that for the first time the entire world laid down its arms and overcame its disagreements under an all-encompassing peace and new tranquility in obedience of Roman laws. Foreign peoples preferred relying on Roman laws to relying on their own arms. All races, all provinces, innumerable city-states, infinite populations—in fact, the whole world—finally united with a single will in freely and honestly serving the cause of peace, ever mindful of the common good. In earlier days, not even one city-state, nor one group of citizens, nor even (more significantly) one household of brothers could get along with another indefinitely. If we confirm that all this came to pass under Augustus as ruler, it is quite clear that in the same empire of Augustus the birth of our Lord Jesus Christ was beginning to light up the world in a most certain manifestation of His approval.

Although it will be against their will, those driven to blasphemy by jealousy will be forced to admit and acknowledge that this worldwide peace and most tranquil serenity was made possible not by the greatness of Augustus Caesar, but by the Son of God, who appeared at the time of Caesar and who came not just to be the ruler of one city-state but rather as the Creator of the universe, to be recognized by everyone, in order to unite the world. In the same way as the rising sun fills the day with light, upon His arrival he mercifully adorned the world with peace.

We need to take a look at ourselves and the lifestyles we have chosen and gotten used to, in order to get our bearings. Our ancestors waged wars until, exhausted by wars, they sought peace by offering to pay tribute. Tribute is the price of peace: we pay tribute to avoid the suffering of war, and we stop and wait in the same harbor (of tribute-paying) where our ancestors sheltered themselves from storms of evils.

It is in this light that we should judge whether our times are happy ones: surely we find them happier than those of old because we continually enjoy the peace they arrived at only late in their game. We are strangers to the violence of wars which exhausted them. In fact, we are able to enjoy that carefree existence from birth to old age, which they could enjoy only in part after the coming of Augustus Caesar's empire and Christ's birth. What we contribute freely for our defense was simply taken from them earlier, as what they owed in their slave-like status. How different modern times are from past ones can be seen when we compare the way Rome extorted money by force of arms from its subject peoples, in order to support Roman luxury, with the way Rome now allocates funds for the general good of all our communities.

For me my native land is everywhere. I can get away to a safe place at the first hint of any sort of disturbance. Right now Africa has taken me in with a hospitality commensurate with my confidence in approaching her. Now Africa receives me into its own community with its carefree enjoyment of peace under laws common to us all. That same Africa, of which it was said in olden days and truly said,

We dare not ask for refuge on her sand:
The wars they stir up keep us from this land

now opens wide the doors to her hearths for weary bodies and keeps them warm and welcome. The huge expanse of the East, the abundance produced in the North, the expansive diversity of the South, the great and secure strongholds on our large islands now have my law and name because I come to Christians and Romans as a Christian and Roman. I do not fear any gods of my host. I do not fear that his religion will mean my death. I have none of that fear of strange lands where a native gets away with whatever he wants and a traveller cannot tend to his own business in peace or even of lands where the law of foreigners is not mine. One God, loved and feared by all, established this unity of the kingdom at the time He chose to reveal Himself among men: those same laws under one God now rule everywhere. Whenever I arrive unknown, I need not fear sudden violence as if I were alone and deserted. Among Romans, as I was saying, I am a Roman; among Christians, a Christian; among men, a man. I can appeal to the state on the basis of its laws, to the consciences of men on the basis of religion, and to nature on the basis of our common sharing of it. I enjoy time spent in each country, as though it were my own fatherland—keeping in mind that the true fatherland I love most does not have its roots on earth. I have lost nothing where I loved nothing, and I have everything when He whom I do love is with me, particularly since He is the same among all men. He not only gives me an introduction to all men but helps me become a friend of theirs. Nor does He desert me when I am in need, for "The earth is His and the fullness thereof." He instructs that all things from this abundance be made available to all people in common. These are the benefits of our own time, and our ancestors did not enjoy them fully, whether we refer to our present tranquility, or to hope for the future, or to places of refuge for all. Lacking these, they waged wars without end. Since they were not free to move as groups from place to place, they had to cling to their old homes when warfare came and face miserable death or the disgrace of enslavement.

Bishop Synesius of Cyrene: Letter to His Brother

In contrast with the steadfast conduct of the martyrs as described by Eusebius, there were some Christians who would not have carried their zeal for the faith to such lengths. Synesius (c. 365–414 CE), who was born in North Africa, was a worldly-wise, skeptical man who was versed in hermetic studies through the school of Hypatia of Alexandria, and in Neoplatonic philosophy. Though he was named Bishop of Cyrene in 410, he was never that zealous in his faith, as evidenced from this letter to his brother.

Source: *Finley Cooper & Matthew Schwartz, eds.,* Roman Letters: History from a Personal Point of View *(Detroit: Wayne State University, 1991), pp. 264–267.*

Focus Questions:
1. In what ways does Synesius believe that he falls short of the priestly requirements?
2. What important dogmas of church belief does Synesius doubt? And how so?
3. What does Synesius assert that he will not do if he becomes a bishop?
4. What individual is dominant in this letter: Synesius the philosopher or Synesius the Christian? Explain.

I should be altogether lacking in sense, if I did not show myself very grateful to the inhabitants of Ptokmais, who consider me worthy of an honour to which I should never have dared to aspire. At the same time I ought to examine, not the importance of the duties with which they desire to entrust me, but merely my own capacity for fulfillng them. To see oneself called to a vocation which is almost divine, when after all one is only a man, is a great source of joy, if one really deserves it. But if, on the other hand, one is very unworthy of it, the prospects of the future are sombre. It is by no means a recent fear of mine, but a very old one, the fear of winning honour from men at the price of sinning against God.

When I examine myself, I fail to find the capacity necessary to raise me to the sanctity of such a priesthood as this. I will now speak to you of the emotions of my soul: for I cannot speak to any one in preference to you who are so dear to me, and have been brought up with me. It is quite natural that you should share my anxieties, that you should watch with me during the night, and that by day we should search together whatever may bring me joy or turn sorrow away from me. Let me tell you, then, how my circumstances are, although you know in advance most of what I am going to say to you.

I took up a light burden, and up to this moment I think I have borne it well. It is, in a word, philosophy. Inasmuch as I have never fallen too far below the level of the duties which it imposed upon me, people have praised me for my work. And I am regarded as capable of better things still, by those who do not know how to estimate in what directions my talents lie. Now, if I frivolously accept the dignity of the position which has been offered to me, I fear I may fail in both causes, slighting the one, without at the same time raising myself to the high level of the other. Consider the situation. All my days are divided between study and recreation. In my hours of work, above all when I am occupied with divine matters, I withdraw into myself. In my leisure hours I give myself up to my friends. For you know that when I look up from my books, I like to enter into every sort of sport. I do not share in the political turn of mind, either by nature or in my pursuits. [That statement seems to be at variance with his own actions, however.] But the priest should be a man above human weaknesses. He should be a stranger to every sort of diversion, even as God Himself. All eyes are keeping watch on him to see that he justifies his mission. He is of little or no use unless he has made himself austere and unyielding towards any pleasure. In carrying out his holy office he should belong no longer to himself, but to all men. He is a teacher of the law, and must utter that which is approved by law. In addition to all this, he has as many calls upon him as all the rest of the world put together, for the affairs of all he alone must attend to, or incur the reproaches of all.

Now, unless he has a great and noble soul, how can he sustain the weight of so many cares without his intellect being submerged? How can he keep the divine flame alive within him when such varied duties claim him on every side? I know well that there are such men I have every admiration for their character, and I regard them as really divine men, whom intercourse with man's affairs does not separate from God. But I know myself also. I go down to the town, and from the town I come up again, always enveloped in thoughts that drag me down to earth, and covered with more stains than anybody could imagine. In a word, I have so many personal defilements of old date, that the slightest addition fills up my measure. My strength fails me; I have no strength and there is no health in me. I am not equal to confronting what is without me, and I am far from being able to bear the distress of my own conscience. If anybody asks me what my idea of a bishop is, I have no hesitation in saying explicitly that he ought to be spotless, more than spotless, in all things, he to whom is allotted the purification of others.

In writing to you, my brother, I have still another thing to say. You will not be by any means the only one to read this letter. In addressing it to you, I wish above all things to make known to everyone what I feel, so that whatever happens hereafter, no one will have a right to accuse me before God or before man, nor, above all, before the venerable Theophilus [the bishop of Alexandria]. In publishing my thoughts, and in giving myself up entirely to his decision, how can I be in the wrong? God himself, the law of the land, and the blessed hand of Theophilus himself have given me a wife. I, therefore, proclaim to all and call them to witness once for all that I will not be separated from her, nor shall I associate with her surreptitiously like an adulterer; for of these two acts, the one is impious, and the other is unlawful. I shall desire and pray to have many virtuous children. This is what I must inform the man upon whom depends my consecration. Let him learn this from his comrades Paul and Dionysius, for I understand that they have become his deputies by the will of the people.

There is one point, however, which is not new to Theophilus, but of which I must remind him. I must press my point here a little more, for beside his difficulty all the others are as nothing. It is difficult, if not quite impossible, that convictions should be shaken, which have entered the soul through knowledge to the point of demonstration. Now you know that philosophy rejects many of those convictions which are cherished by the common people. For my own part, I can never persuade myself that the soul is of more recent origin than the body. Never would I admit that the world and the parts which make it up must perish. This resurrection, which is an object of common belief, is nothing for me but a sacred and mysterious allegory, and I am far from sharing the views of the vulgar crowd thereon. The philosophic mind, albeit the discerner of truth, admits the employment of falsehood, for light is to truth what the eye is to the mind. Just as the eye would be injured by excess of light, and just as darkness is more helpful to those of weak eyesight, even so do I consider that the false may be beneficial to the populace, and the truth injurious to those not strong enough to gaze steadfastly on the radiance of real being. If the laws of the priesthood that obtain with us permit these views to me, I can take over the holy office on condition that I may prosecute philosophy at home and spread legends abroad, so that if I teach no doctrine, at all events I undo no teaching, and allow men to remain in their already acquired convictions. But if anybody says to me that he must be under this influence, that the bishop must belong to the people in his opinions, I shall betray myself very quickly. What can there be in common between the ordinary man and philosophy? Divine truth should remain hidden, but the vulgar need a different system. I shall never cease repeating that I think the wise man, to the extent that necessity allows, should not force his opinions upon others, nor allow others to force theirs upon him.

No, if I am called to the priesthood, I declare before God and man that I refuse to preach dogmas in which I do not believe. Truth is an attribute of God, and I wish in all things to be blameless before Him. This one thing I will not dissimulate. I feel that I have a good deal of inclination for amusements. Even as a child, I was charged with a mania for arms and horses. I shall be grieved, indeed greatly shall I suffer at seeing my beloved dogs deprived of their hunting, and my bow eaten up by worms. Nevertheless I shall resign myself to this, if it is the will of God. Again, I hate all care; nevertheless, whatever it costs, I will endure lawsuits and quarrels, so long as I can fulfill this mission, heavy though it he, according to God's will; but never will I consent to conceal my beliefs, nor shall my opinions be at war with my tongue. I believe that I am pleasing God in thinking and speaking thus. I do not wish to give anyone the opportunity of saying that I, an unknown man, grasped at the appointment. But let the beloved of God, the right reverend Theophilus, knowing the situation and giving me clear evidence that he understands it, decide on this issue concerning me. He will then either leave me to myself to lead my own life, and to philosophize, or he will not leave himself any grounds on which hereafter to sit in judgment over me, and to turn me out of the ranks of the priesthood. In comparison with these truths, every opinion is insignificant, for I know well that Truth is dearest to God. I swear it by your sacred head, nay, better still, I swear by God the guardian of Truth that I suffer. How can I fail to suffer, when I must, as it were, remove from one life to another? But if after those things have been made clear which I least desire to conceal, if the man who holds this power from Heaven persists in putting me in the hierarchy of bishops I will submit to the inevitable, and I will accept the token as divine. For I reason thus, that if the emperor or some ill-fated Augustal had given an order, I should have been punished if I disobeyed, but that one must obey God with a willing heart. But even at the expense of God's not admitting me to this service, I must nevertheless place first my love for Truth, the most divine thing of all. And I must not slip into His service through ways most opposed to it—such as falsehood. See then that the scholasti [we would say intellectuals of Alexandria] know well my sentiments, and that they inform Theophilus.

Chapter 10

Islam

A Selection from Muhammad's Orations

Muhammad was more than a religious leader; he was a political figure who had, by the time of his death, united most of the Arab peoples into a centralized government based on "Shariah" (Islamic law), and which encompassed both the secular and religious. Church-state separation is a concept that is foreign to Orthodox Islam: the two were originally viewed as inseparable. Collections of Muhammad's "Orations" reveal the Prophet in his role of charismatic messenger. The excerpt is Muhammad's last oration and was delivered, while he was ill, only five days prior to his death.

Source: *Mohammad Ubaidul Akbar,* Orations of Muhammad, the Prophet of Islam *(New Delhi, India: Nusrat Ali Nasri for Kitab Bhanan, 1979), pp. 101–106.*

Focus Questions:
1. In what ways does Muhammad foster solidarity amongst his followers?
2. How does Muhammad attempt to encourage and comfort his people against the eventuality of his death?
3. From this last oration, how does it appear that Muhammad wishes to be remembered?

He praised Allah, thanked Him, sought forgiveness for the martyrs of the battle of Uhad and prayed for them. Then he said: "O people, (draw near) to me." So they gathered round him.

Then he said: "Well, there is a man whose Lord has given him option between living in this world as long as he wishes to live and eating from this world as much as he likes to eat, or meeting his Lord."

(Hearing it) Abu Bakr wept and said: "Nay, may our fathers, mothers and properties be your ransom..."

Then the Apostle of Allah—may Allah send him bliss and peace!—said: "There is none more bountiful to us for his company and wealth than the son of Abu QuhAfa (Abu Bakr). Had I taken any intimate friend except my Lord, I would have taken the son of Abu QuhAfa as my intimate friend. But there is love and brotherhood of Faith"—(He said it twice or thrice).

"The fact is that your companion is the intimate friend of Allah. There should not remain in the mosque any door (open) except the door of Abu Bakr."

"O people, it has reached me that you are afraid of your Prophet's death. Has any previous prophet lived forever among those to whom he was sent: so that I would live forever among you?

"Behold, I am going to my Lord and you will be going to Him. I recommend you to do good to the First Emigrants and I recommend the Emigrants to do good among themselves.

"Lo, Allah, the Exalted, says: 'By the time, Man is in loss'—to the end of the Sura (ciii.).

"Verily the things run with the permission of Allah, the Exalted, and verily delay in a matter should not urge you on its hastening in demand. Allah—the Mighty and the Great—does not hasten for the hastiness of anybody.

"He who contends with Allah, He overcomes him. He who tries to deceive Allah, He outwits him. In a near future if you get the authority then do no mischief on the earth and do not cut off your blood relations.

"I recommend you to do good to the Helpers. They are those who prepared the lodging and faith for you. So you should behave them well.

"Did they not divide with you their fruits equally? Did they not make space for you in their houses? Did they not prefer you to themselves while poverty was with them?'

"Lo, men will increase in number, but the Helpers will decrease to the extent that they will be among men as salt in food. They are my family with whom I took my shelter; they are my sandals; and they are my paunch in which I eat. So observe me in them.

"By Him in Whose hand is my life, verily I love you; verily the Helpers have done what was on them and there remains what is on you.

"So he who from among you gets power in any matter and becomes able to do harm to people therein or to do good to others therein, then he should appreciate one of them who does well and should overlook one of them who does bad. Lo, do not be selfish about them.

"Behold, I shall precede you; I will be your witness and you are to meet me. Lo, the 'Haud' is your meeting place. By Allah, just now, I see my 'Haud' from here.

"Beware, he who likes to come to it along with me to-morrow, should hold back his hand and tongue except from necessary matters."

"Lo, I have, indeed, been given the keys of the treasures of the earth. By Allah, I do not fear for you that you will turn polytheists after me. But I fear for you that you will be entangled in them, then you will fight one another and will perish like those who perished before you.

"O people, verily the sins spoil the blessings and change the lots. When the people are good, their rulers do good to them and when the people are bad, they oppress them."

Then he said: "There may be some rights which I owe to you and I am nothing but a human being. So if there be any man whose honour I have injured a bit, here is my honour; he may retaliate.

"Whosoever he may be if I have wounded a bit of his skin, here is my skin; He may retaliate.

"Whosoever he may be, if I have taken anything from his property, here is my property; so he may take. Know that he, among you, is more loyal to me who has got such a thing and takes it or absolves me; then I meet my Lord while I am absolved.

"Nobody should say, I fear enmity and grudge of the Apostle of Allah. Verily these things are not in my nature and character. He whose passion has overcome him in aught, should seek help from me so that I may pray for him."

Rabia al-Adawiyya, "Brothers, My Peace Is In My Aloneness"

Sufism is the Islamic mystic and spiritual tradition that is defined by a rejection of ritual and the development of a close personal and loving relationship with Allah. The female poet Rabi'a al-'Adawiyya (717-801 C.E.) was a very strict ascetic devotee of Sufism. She lived in Basra her whole life, preaching to locals and disputing with scholars over the meaning of Islam. She is best remembered by her poetry, which is wonderfully descriptive of the Sufi way.

Source: *Rabi'a al-'Adawiyya, "Brothers, My Peace is my Aloneness," from* Love Poems from God: Twelve Sacred Voices from the East and West, *ed. by Daniel Ladinsky (New York, 2002).*

> **Focus Questions:**
> 1. According to Adawiyya, what is love?
> 2. What is sought in the poem?
> 3. What is her relationship with her Beloved?

Rabi'a al-'Adawiyya, "Brothers, My Peace Is My Aloneness"
Brothers, my peace is in my aloneness.
My Beloved is alone with me there, always.
I have found nothing in all the worlds
That could match His love,
This love that harrows the sands of my desert.
If I come to die of desire
And my Beloved is still not satisfied,
I would live in eternal despair.

To abandon all that He has fashioned
And hold in the palm of my hand
Certain proof that He loves me–
That is the name and the goal of my search.

Harun al-Rashid and the Zenith of the Caliphate

The Caliphate endured as a political entity until 1258 CE. After the rule of the first four ("Orthodox") Caliphs, all of whom had been directly associated with Muhammad, the Ummayyad family assumed control and maintained a dynasty from 661–750 CE. They were then overturned by the Abbasid clan, who claimed descent from the Prophet's uncle, Abbas. The Abbasids established the Islamic capital at

Baghdad, and it was there, during the reign of Caliph Harun al-Rashid (786–809), that the Empire attained its peak of power and prestige.

Source: *Bernard Lewis., ed.,* Islam from the Prophet to the Capture of Constantinople, *vol. I (N.Y.: Walker & Co., 1974), pp. 27–30*

Focus Questions:
1. Under what circumstances did Nikephoros become ruler of the (Byzantine) Romans, and how did his attitude to the Caliph differ from his predecessor's?
2. What was Harun's response, and the consequences?
3. Why did no one wish to inform Harun of Nikephoros' treachery and what device was ultimately employed to alert him?

A woman came to rule over the Romans because at the time she was the only one of their royal house who remained. She wrote to the Caliphs al-Mahdi- and al-Ha-di- and to al-Rashi-d at the beginning of his Caliphate with respect and deference and showered him with gifts. When her son [Constantine VI] grew up and came to the throne in her place, he brought trouble and disorder and provoked al-Rashi-d. The empress, who knew al-Rashi-d and feared his power, was afraid lest the kingdom of the Romans pass away and their country be ruined. She therefore overcame her son by cunning and put out his eyes so that the kingdom was taken from him and returned to her. But the people of their kingdom disapproved of this and hated her for it. Therefore Nikephoros, who was her secretary, rose against her, and they helped and supported him so that he seized power and became the ruler of the Romans.

When he was in full control of his kingdom, he wrote to al-Rashi-d, "From Nikephoros, the king of Romans, to al-Rashi-d, the king of the Arabs, as follows: That woman put you and your father and your brother in the place of kings and put herself in the place of a commoner. I put you in a different place and am preparing to invade your lands and attack your cities, unless you repay me what that woman paid you. Farewell!"

When his letter reached al-Rashi-d, he replied, "In the name of God, the Merciful and the Compassionate, from the servant of God, Ha-ru-n, Commander of the Faithful, to Nikephoros, the dog of the Romans, as follows: I have understood your letter, and I have your answer. You will see it with your own eye, not hear it." Then he at once sent an army against the land of the Romans of a size the like of which was never heard before and with commanders unrivaled in courage and skill. When news of this reached Nikephoros, the earth became narrow before him and he took counsel. Al-Rashi-d advanced relentlessly into the land of the Romans, killing, plundering, taking captives, destroying castles, and obliterating traces, until they came to the narrow roads before Constantinople, and when they reached there, they found that Nikephoros had already had trees cut down, thrown across these roads, and set on fire. The first who put on the garments of the naphtha-throwers was Muhammad ibn Yaz-id ibn Mazyad. He plunged boldly through, and then the others followed him.

Nikephoros sent gifts to al-Rashi-d and submitted to him very humbly and paid him the poll tax for himself as well as for his companions.

> On this Abu'l-'Ata-hiya said:
> O Imam of God's guidance, you have become the
> guardian of religion, quenching the thirst of all who
> pray for rain.
> You have two names drawn from righteousness
> [rasha-d] and guidance [huda-], for you are the one
> called Rashi-d and Mahdi-,

Whatever displeases you becomes loathsome; if any
thing pleases you, the people are well pleased with it.
You have stretched out the hand of nobility to us, east
and west, and bestowed bounty on both easterner and westerner.
You have adorned the face of the earth with generosity
and munificence, and the face of the earth is
adorned with generosity.
O, Commander of the Faithful, brave and pious, you
have opened that part of benevolence which was closed!
God has destined that the kingdom should remain to
Ha-ru-n, and, God's destiny is binding on mankind.
The world submits to Ha-ru-n, the favored of God, and
Nikepharos has become the dhimmI of Ha-ru-n.

Then al-Rashi-d went back, because of what Nikephoros had given him, and got as far as Raqqa. When the snow fell and Nikephoros felt safe from attack, he took advantage of the respite and broke the agreement between himself and al-Rashi-d and returned to his previous posture. Yahy-a ibn Kha-lid [the vizier], let alone any other, did not dare to inform al-Rashi-d of the treachery of Nikephoros. Instead, he and his sons offered money to the poets to recite poetry and thereby inform al-Rashi-d of this. But they all held back and refrained, except for one poet from Jedda, called Ab-u Muhammad, who was very proficient, strong of heart and strong of poetry, distinguished in the days of al-Ma'mu-n and of very high standing. He accepted the sum of 100,000 dirhams from Yahy-a and his sons and then went before al-Rashi-d and recited the following verses:

Nikephoros has broken the promise he gave you, and
now death hovers above him.
I bring good tidings to the Commander of the
Faithful, for Almighty God is bringing you a great
victory.
Your subjects hail the messenger who brings the good
news of his treachery
Your right hand craves to hasten to that battle which
will assuage our souls and bring a memorable
punishment.
He paid you his poll tax and bent his cheek in fear of
sharp swords and in dread of destruction.
You protected him from the blow of swords which we
brandished like blazing torches.
You brought all your armies back from him and he to
whom you gave your protection was secure and
happy.
Nikephoros! If you played false because the Imam
was far from you, how ignorant and deluded you
were!
Did you think you could play false and escape? May
your mother mourn you! What you thought is delusion.
Your destiny will throw you into its brimming depths;
seas will envelop you from the Imam.
The Imam has power to overwhelm you, whether your
dwelling be near or far away.
Though we may be neglectful the Imam does not
neglect that which he rules and governs with his

strong will. A king who goes in person to the holy war! His
enemy is always conquered by him.
O you who seek God's approval by your striving,
nothing in your inmost heart is hidden from God.
No counsel can avail him who deceives his Imam, but
counsel from loyal counsellers deserves thanks.
Warning the Imam is a religious duty, an expiation
and a cleansing for those who do it.

When he recited this, al-Rashi-d asked, "Has he done that?" and he learned that the viziers had used this device to inform him of it. He then made war against Nikephoros while the snow still remained and conquered Heraclea at that time.

Excerpts from the Quran

Although of more recent origin than the others, Islam is one of the great world religions; today the number of its adherents is comparable to that of Christianity. The word "Islam" itself means submission or surrender, and a Muslim, or follower of Islam, is one who surrenders or submits himself to the will of Allah (God).

Islam had its beginnings on the Arab peninsula in the seventh century CE. Its founder, Muhammad (c. 571-632), was orphaned in early childhood and grew up in poverty. As he matured he became increasingly estranged from the polytheistic religion of his native city of Mecca, with its worship of idols and its practice of female infanticide. He began to absent himself from Mecca for protracted periods, retiring to a cave in the mountains to meditate. There, one night, he had a vision in which the angel Gabriel appeared before him, telling him he was a messenger, transmitting to him the word of God. On later occasions Gabriel reappeared with more messages, which Muhammad memorized and repeated to his disciples. These were collected together and became the Quran. Opposed by the traditional religious functionaries in Mecca, Muhammad was forced to flee for his life to the city of Medina, where he consolidated his forces, finally returning in triumph to Mecca. By the time of his death in 632, Muhammad and Islam had achieved both religious and political control over Arabia.

The Quran is the sacred book of Islam; it is held by Muslims to be the infallible word of God, directly revealed to Muhammad. Although it was written in part during the prophet's lifetime it was completed and arranged in its present form shortly after his death. The Islamic creed rests on two central articles of faith. The first is "There is no god but God (Allah)." Thus Islam is a strict monotheism; as such it rejects not only the traditional Arabian polytheism that it supplanted but the trinitarianism of Christianity as well. The second article of faith is "Muhammad is the messenger, or prophet, of Allah." Islam recognizes other important prophets, like Abraham, Moses, and Jesus, and frequent references to them appear in the Quran, but it insists that Muhammad is the ultimate, authoritative prophet. Yet he is a human and not a divine being. Although Muslims believe that on one occasion Muhammad actually ascended to the throne of God and conversed with him, he lived and died as an ordinary mortal.

As an elaborated religion the Muslim faith rests on "Five Pillars," which are obligatory on its adherents: (1) Repetition of the creed "There is no god but Allah, and Muhammad is the prophet of Allah"; (2) prayer, normally done five times daily while bowing toward Mecca; (3) alms-giving, for the support of the poor and needy; (4) the fast, for a full day during the sacred month of Ramadan; and (5) the pilgrimage, to Mecca, which every Muslim is expected to make once in a lifetime.

To one outside of the Muslim community the organization of the Quran may appear baffling because it seems to lack any recognizable logical coherence. To give the Quran's message greater structure and con-

tinuity, the contents of the selection that follows have been rearranged. The numbers of the "Suras" or chapters of the Quran from which the excerpts have been taken are given in parentheses at the end of each quotation. Also, headings describing the contents of each of these have been added.

Source: *J.M. Rodwell, trans., the* Quran.

Focus Questions:
1. Summarize the message of the Quran. How is it similar to, or different from, the central message of the Christian Scriptures? The Hebrew Scriptures?
2. What sort of social structures (class, gender, ethnicity, etc.) are assumed in the Quran?

THE QURAN

PREAMBLE
In the Name of God, The
    Compassionate, the Merciful
Praise be to God, Lord of the worlds!
The compassionate, the merciful!
King on the day of reckoning!
Thee only do we worship, and to Thee do we cry for
    help.
Guide Thou us on the straight path,
The path of those to whom Thou hast been gracious;
    with whom thou are not angry, and who go not
    astray. (1)

GOD
He is God alone;
God the eternal!
He begetteth not, and He is not begotten;
And there is none like unto Him. (112)

MUHAMMAD THE PROPHET
Muhammad is not more than an apostle; other apostles have already passed away before him. If he die, therefore, or be slain, will ye turn upon your heels? But he who turneth on his heels shall not injure God at all, and God will certainly reward the thankful! (3)

THE QURAN
This Book is without a doubt a revelation sent down from the Lord of the Worlds.

Will they say, he [Muhammad] hath forged it? Nay, it is the truth from thy Lord that thou mayest warn a people to whom no warner hath come before thee, that haply they may be guided.

God it is who hath created the heavens and the earth and all that is between them in six days, then ascended his throne. Save Him ye have no patron, and none to plead for you. Will ye not then reflect?

From the heaven to the earth He governeth all things; hereafter shall they come up to him on a day, whose length shall be a thousand of such years as ye reckon.

This is He who knoweth the unseen and the seen; the Mighty, the Merciful. Who hath made everything which he hath created most good; and began the creation of man with clay;

Then ordained his progeny from germs of life, from sorry water;

Then shaped him and breathed of His Spirit into him, and gave you hearing and seeing and hearts: What little thanks do ye return? (32)

> By the star when it setteth,
> Your compatriot [Muhammad] erreth not, nor is he led
> astray,
> Neither speaketh he from mere impulse.
> The Qur'an is no other than a revelation revealed to him.
> One terrible in power [Gabriel] taught it him,
> Endued with wisdom. With even balance stood he
> In the highest part of the horizon
> Then came he nearer and approached,
> And was at the distance of two bows, or even closer,—
> And he revealed to his servant what he revealed. (53)

GOD'S CREATION AND CREATURES

Verily God causeth the grain and the date stone to put forth. He bringeth forth the living from the dead, and dead from the living! This is God! Why, then, are ye turned aside from Him?

He causeth the dawn to appear, and hath ordained the night for rest, and the sun and the moon for computing time! The ordinance of the Mighty, the Wise!

And it is He who hath ordained the stars for you that ye may be guided thereby in the darknesses of the land and of the sea! Clear have we made our signs to men of knowledge.

And it is He who hath produced you from one man, and hath provided for you an abode and resting place! Clear have we made our signs for men of insight.

And it is He who sendeth down rain from heaven; and we bring forth by it the buds of all the plants, and from them bring we forth the green foliage, and the close growing grain, and palm trees with sheaths of clustering dates, and gardens of grapes, and the olive and the pomegranate, like and unlike. Look ye on their fruits when they fruit and ripen. Truly herein are signs unto people who believe. (6)

Now of fine clay have we created man;

Then we placed him a moist germ, in a safe abode;

Then made we the moist germ a clot of blood; then made the clotted blood into a piece of flesh; then made the piece of flesh into bones; and we clothed the bones with flesh; then brought forth man of yet another make—Blessed therefore be God, the most excellent of makers—

Then after this ye shall surely die;

Then shall ye be waked up on the day of resurrection.

And we have created over you seven heavens:—and we are not careless of the creation.

And we send down water from the heaven in its due degree, and we cause it to settle on the earth;—and we have power for its withdrawal;—

And by it we cause gardens of palm trees, and vineyards to spring forth for you, in which ye have plenteous fruits, and whereof ye eat;

And the tree that groweth up on Mount Sinai; which yieldeth oil and a juice for those who eat.

And there is a lesson for you in the cattle. We give you to drink of what is in their bellies, and many advantages do ye derive from them, and for food they serve you;

And on them and on ships are ye borne. (23)

> Nay! but it (the Qur'an) is a warning; (And whoso is
> willing beareth it in mind)
> Written on honored pages,
> Exalted, purified,
> By the hands of scribes, honored, righteous.
> Cursed be man! What hath made him unbelieving?
> Of what thing did God create him?
> Out of moist germs,
> He created him and fashioned him,
> Then made him an easy passage from the womb,
> Then causeth him to die and burieth him;
> Then, when he pleaseth, will raise him again to life.
> Aye! but man hath not yet fulfilled the bidding of his Lord.
> Let man look at his food;
> It was We who rained down the copious rains,
> Then cleft the earth with clefts,
> And caused the upgrowth of the grain,
> And grapes and healing herbs,
> And the olive and the palm,
> And enclosed gardens thick with trees,
> And fruits and herbage,
> For the service of yourselves and of your cattle. (80)

GOD'S PROVIDENCE

And with Him are the keys of the secret things; none knoweth them but He. He knoweth whatever is on the land and in the sea; and no leaf falleth but He knoweth it; neither is there a grain in the darknesses of the earth, nor a thing green or sere, but it is noted in a distinct writing.

It is He who taketh your souls at night, and knoweth what ye have merited in the day; then he awaketh any one of you, our messengers take his soul, and fail not.

Then are they returned to God their Lord, the True. Is not judgment His? (6)

Thus unto thee as unto those who preceded thee doth God, the Mighty, the Wise, reveal!

All that is in the heavens and all that is in the earth is His, and He is the High, the Great!

Ready are the heavens to cleave asunder from above for very awe, and the angels celebrate the praise of their Lord, and ask forgiveness for the dwellers on earth. Is not God the Indulgent, the Merciful?

But whoso take aught beside Him as lords—God watcheth them! But thou hast them not in thy charge.

It is thus moreover that we have revealed to thee an Arabic Qur'an, that thou mayest warn the mother city [Mecca] and all around it, and that thou mayest warn them of that day of the Gathering, of which there is no doubt-when part shall be in Paradise and part in the flame.

Had God so pleased, He had made them one people and of one creed, but He bringeth whom He will within His mercy; and as for the doers of evil, no patron, no helper shall there be for them.

Will they take other patrons than Him? But God is man's only Lord. He quickeneth the dead, and He is mighty over all things.

And whatever the subject of your disputes, with God doth its decision rest. This is God, my Lord; in Him do I put my trust, and to Him do I turn in penitence.

Creator of the heavens and of the earth! He giveth with open hand, or sparingly, to whom He will; He knoweth all things.

To you hath He prescribed the faith which He commanded unto Noah, and which we have revealed to thee, and which we commanded unto Abraham and Moses and Jesus, saying, "Observe this faith, and be not divided into sects therein." Intolerable to those who worship idols jointly with God is that faith to which thou dost call them. Whom He pleaseth will God choose for it, and whosoever shall turn to Him in penitence will He guide to it. (42)

ESCHATOLOGY

By the night when she spreads her veil;
By the day when it brightly shineth;
By Him who made male and female;
At different ends truly do ye aim!
But as to him who giveth alms and feareth
    God,
And yieldeth assent to the good,
To him will we make easy the path to
    happiness.
But as to him who is covetous and bent on
    riches,
And calleth the good a lie,
To him will we make easy the path to misery,
And what shall his wealth avail him when he
    goeth down?
Truly man's guidance is with Us,
And ours, the future and the past.
I warn you therefore of the flaming fire;
None shall be cast to it but the most
    wretched,
Who hath called the truth a lie and turned his
    back.
But the God-fearing shall escape it,
Who giveth away his substance that he may
    become pure;
And who offereth not favors to any one for
    the sake of recompense,
But only as seeking the face of his Lord the
    Most High.

And surely in the end he shall be well
   content. (92)

Of what ask they of one another?
Of the great news.
The theme of their disputes.
Nay! they shall certainly know its truth!
Again. Nay! they shall certainly know it.
Have we not made the earth a couch?
And the mountains its tent-stakes?
We have created you of two sexes,
And ordained you sleep for rest,
And ordained the night as a mantle,
And ordained the day for gaining livelihood.
And built above you seven solid heavens,
And placed therein a burning lamp;
And we send down water in abundance from
   the rain-clouds,
That we may bring forth by it corn and herbs,
And gardens thick with trees.
Lo! the day of Severance is fixed;
The day when there shall be a blast on the
   trumpet, and ye shall come in crowds,

And the heaven shall be opened and be
   full of portals,
And the mountains shall be set in motion,
   and melt into thin vapor.
Hell truly shall be a place of snares,
The home of transgressors,
To abide therein ages.
No coolness shall they taste therein nor any
   drink,
Save boiling water and running sores;
Meet recompense!
For they looked not forward to their account;
And they gave the lie to our signs, charging
   them with falsehood.
But we noted and wrote down all.

"Taste this then, and we will give you
   increase of naught but torment."
But for the God-fearing is a blissful abode,
Enclosed gardens and vineyards;
And damsels with swelling breasts, their
   peers in age,
And a full cup.
There shall they hear no vain discourse nor
   any falsehood;
A recompense from thy Lord-sufficing gift!—

Lord of the heavens and of the earth, and of all that between them lieth—the God of Mercy! But not a word shall they obtain from Him.

On the day whereon the Spirit and the Angels shall be ranged in order, they shall not speak; save he whom the God of Mercy shall permit, and who shall say that which is right.

This is the sure day. Whoso then will, let him take the path of return to his Lord.

Verily, we warn you of a chastisement close at hand.

The day on which a man shall see the deeds which his hands have sent before him; and when the unbeliever shall say, "Oh! would I were dust!" (78)

O children of Adam! There shall come to you apostles from among yourselves, rehearsing my signs to you; and whoso shall fear God and do good works, no fear shall be upon them, neither shall they be put to grief.

But they who charge our signs with falsehood, and turn away from them in their pride, shall be inmates of the fire; for ever shall they abide therein. And who is worse than he who deviseth a lie of God, or treateth our signs as lies? To them shall a portion here below be assigned in accordance with the Book of our decrees, until the time when our messengers, as they receive their souls, shall say, "Where are they on whom ye called beside God?" They shall say, "Gone from us." And they shall witness against themselves that they were infidels. He shall say, "Enter ye into the Fire with the generations of Djinn and men who have preceded you. So oft as a fresh generation entereth, it shall curse its sister, until when they have all reached it, the last comers shall say to the former, "O our Lord! these are they who led us astray; assign them therefore a double torment of the fire." He will say, "Ye shall all have double." But of this are ye ignorant.

And the former of them shall say to the latter, "What advantage have ye over us? Taste ye therefore the torment for that which ye have done."

Verily, they who have charged our signs with falsehood and have turned away from them in their pride, heaven's gates shall not be opened to them, nor shall they enter Paradise, until the camel passeth through the eye of the needle. After this manner will we recompense the transgressors.

They shall make their bed in hell, and above them shall be coverings of fire! And this way will we recompense the evil doers.

But as to those who have believed and done the things which are right (we will lay on no one a burden beyond his power)—these shall be inmates of Paradise, for ever shall they abide therein.

And we will remove whatever rancor was in their bosoms; rivers shall roll at their feet, and they shall say, "Praise be to God who hath guided us hither! We had not been guided had not God guided us! Of a surety the apostles of our Lord came to us with truth." And a voice shall cry to them, "This is Paradise, of which, as the meed of your works, ye are made heirs."

And the inmates of Paradise shall cry to the inmates of the fire, "Now have we found what our Lord promised us to be true. Have ye too found what your Lord promised you to be true?" And they shall answer, "Yes." And a herald shall proclaim between them, "The curse of God be upon the evil doers.

"Who turn men aside from the way of God, and seek to make it crooked, and who believe not in the life to come!"

And between them shall be a partition, and on the wall Al Araf [between heaven and hell] shall be men who will know all, by their tokens, and they shall cry to the inmates of Paradise, "Peace be on you!" but they shall not yet enter it, although they long to do so.

And when their eyes are turned towards the inmates of the fire they shall say, "O our Lord! place us not with the offending people."

And they who upon Al Araf shall cry to those whom they shall know by their tokens, "Your amassings and your pride have availed you nothing.

"Are these they on whom ye swore God would not bestow mercy? Enter ye into Paradise! where no fear shall be upon you, neither shall ye be put to grief."

And the inmates of the fire shall cry to the inmates of Paradise, "Pour upon us some water, or of the refreshments God hath given you." They shall say, "Truly God hath forbidden both to unbelievers, who made their religion a sport and pastime, and whom the life of the world hath deceived." This day therefore will we forget them...(71)

MORAL PRECEPTS

Kill not your children for fear of want; for them and for you will we provide. Verily, the killing them is a great wickedness.

Have naught to do with adultery; for it is a foul thing and an evil way.

Neither slay any one whom God hath forbidden you to slay, unless for a just cause; and whosoever shall be slain wrongfully, to his heir have we given powers; but let him not outstep bounds in putting the manslayer to death, for he too, in his turn, will be assisted and avenged.

And touch not the substance of the orphan, unless in an upright way, till he attain his age of strength. And perform your covenant; verily the covenant shall be inquired of.

And give full measure when you measure, and weigh with just balance. This will be better, and fairest for settlement.

And follow not that of which thou hast no knowledge; because the hearing and the sight and the heart-each of these shall be inquired of.

And walk not proudly on the earth, for thou canst not cleave the earth, neither shalt thou reach to the mountains in height. (17)

There is no piety in turning your faces toward the east or the west, but he is pious who believeth in God, and the last day, and the angels, and the scriptures, and the prophets; who for the love of God disburseth his wealth to his kindred, and to the orphans, and the needy, and the wayfarer, and those who ask, and for ransoming; who observeth prayer, and payeth the legal alms, and who is of those who are faithful to their engagements when they have engaged in them, and patient under ills and hardships, and in time of trouble. These are they who are just, and these are they who fear the Lord.

O believers! retaliation for blood-shedding is prescribed to you; the free man for the free, and the slave for the slave, and the woman for the woman. But he to whom his brother shall make any remission is to be dealt with equitably, and to him should he pay a fine with liberality.

This is a relaxation from your Lord and a mercy. For him who after shall transgress a sore punishment!

But in this law of retaliation is your security for life, O men of understanding! to the intent that ye may fear God.

It is prescribed to you, when any one of you is at the point of death, if he leave goods, that he bequeath equitably to his parents and kindred. This is binding on those who fear God. But as for him who after he hath heard the bequest shall change it, surely the wrong of this shall be on those who change it; verily, God heareth, knoweth.

But he who feareth from the testator any mistake or wrong, and shall make a settlement between the parties—that shall be no wrong in him; verily, God is Lenient, Merciful.

O believers! a Fast is prescribed to you as it was prescribed to those before you, that ye may fear God, for certain days.

But he among you who shall be sick, or on a journey shall fast that same number of other days; and as for those who are able to keep it and yet break it, the expiation of this shall be the maintenance of a poor man. And he who of his own accord performeth a good work shall derive good from it, and good shall it be for you to fast if ye knew it.

As to the month Ramadhan in which the Qur'an was sent down to be man's guidance, and an explanation of that guidance, and of that illumination, as soon as any one of you observeth the moon, let him set about the fast; but he who is sick, or upon a journey, shall fast a like number of other days. God wisheth you ease, but wisheth not your discomfort and that you fulfil the number of days, and that you glorify God for his guidance, and that you be thankful.

And when my servants ask thee concerning me, then will I be nigh unto them. I will answer the cry of him that crieth, when he crieth unto me; but let them hearken unto me, and believe in me, that they may proceed aright.

You are allowed on the night of the fast to approach your wives; they are your garment and ye are their garment. God knoweth that ye defraud yourselves therein, so He turneth unto you and forgiveth you! Now, therefore, go in unto them with full desire for that which God hath ordained for you; and eat and drink until ye can discern a white thread from a black thread by the daybreak, then fast strictly till night, and go not in unto them, but rather pass the time in the Mosque.

The likeness of those who expend their wealth for the cause of God is that of a grain of corn which produceth seven ears, and in each ear a hundred grains; and God will multiply to whom He pleaseth. God is Liberal, Knowing!

They who expend their wealth for the cause of God, and never follow what they have laid out with reproaches or harm, shall have their reward with their Lord; no fear shall come upon them, neither shall they be put to grief.

A kind speech and forgiveness is better than alms followed by injury. God is Rich, Clement.

O ye who believe! make not your alms void by reproaches and injury, like him who spendeth his substance to be seen of men, and believeth not in God and in the latter day. The likeness of such an one is that of a rock with a thin soil upon it, on which a heavy rain falleth but leaveth it hard. No profit from their works shall they be able to gain; for God guideth not the unbelieving people.

And the likeness of those who expend their substance from a desire to please God, and for the stablishing of their souls, is as a garden on a hill, on which the heavy rain falleth, and it yieldeth its fruits twofold; and even if a heavy rain fall not on it, yet is there a dew. God beholdeth your actions.

. . .

Ye may divorce your wives twice. Keep them honorably or put them away with kindness. But it is not allowed you to appropriate to yourselves aught of what ye have given to them, unless both fear that they cannot keep within the bounds set up by God. And if ye fear that they cannot observe the ordinances of God, no blame shall attach to either of you for what the wife shall herself give for her redemption. These are the bounds of God; therefore overstep them not, for whoever oversteppeth the bounds of God, they are evildoers.

But if the husband divorce her a third time, it is not lawful for him to take her again, until she shall have married another husband; and if he also divorce her, then shall no blame attach to them if they return to each other, thinking that they can keep within the bounds fixed by God. (2)

O men! fear your Lord, who hath created you of one man (soul), and of him created his wife, and from these twain hath spread abroad so many men and women. And fear ye God, in whose name ye ask mutual favors,—and reverence the wombs that bare you. Verily is God watching over you!

And give to the orphans their property; substitute not worthless things of your own for their valuable ones, and devour not their property after adding it to your own, for this is a great crime.

And if ye are apprehensive that ye shall not deal fairly with orphans, then of other women who seem good in your eyes, marry but two, or three, or four; and if ye still fear that ye shall not act equitably, then one only; or the slaves whom ye have acquired. This will make justice on your part easier. Give women their dowry freely; but if of themselves they give up aught thereof to you, then enjoy it as convenient, and profitable.

And entrust not to the incapable the substance which God hath placed with you for their support; but maintain them therewith, and clothe them, and speak to them with kindly speech.

. . .

And if ye be desirous to exchange one wife for another, and have given one of them a talent, make no deduction from it. Would ye take it by slandering her, and with manifest wrong?

How, moreover, could ye take it, when one of you hath gone in unto the other, and they have received from you a strict bond of union?

And marry not women whom your fathers have married; for this is a shame, and hateful, and an evil way:—though what is past may be allowed.

Forbidden to you are your mothers, and your daughters, and your sisters, and your aunts, both on the father and mother's side, and your nieces on the brother and sister's side, and your foster-mothers, and your foster-sisters, and the mothers of your wives, and your step-daughters who are your wards, born of your wives to whom ye have gone in; (but if ye have not gone in unto them, it shall be no sin in you to marry them); and the wives of your sons who proceed out of your loins; and ye may not have two sisters, except where it is already done. Verily, God is Indulgent, Merciful!

Forbidden to you also are married women, except those who are in your hands as slaves. This is the law of God for you. And it is allowed you, beside this, to seek out wives by means of your wealth, with modest conduct, and without fornication. And give those with whom ye have cohabited their dowry. This is the law. But it shall be no crime in you to make agreements over and above the law.

. . .

Men are superior to women on account of the qualities with which God hath gifted the one above the other, and on account of the outlay they make from their substance for them. Virtuous women are obedient, careful, during the husband's absence, because God hath of them been careful. But chide those for whose refractoriness ye have cause to fear; remove them into beds apart, and scourge them. But if they are obedient to you, then seek not occasion against them. (4)

WARFARE

Fight for the cause of God against those who fight against you; but commit not the injustice of attacking them first. God loveth not such injustice.

And kill them wherever ye shall find them, and eject them from whatever place they have ejected you; for civil discord is worse than carnage. Yet attack them not at the sacred Mosque, unless they attack you therein; but if they attack you, slay them. Such is the reward of the infidels.

But if they desist, then verily God is Gracious, Merciful.

Fight therefore against them until there be no more civil discord, and the only worship be that of God. But if they desist, then let there be no hostility, save against the wicked. (2)

CHRISTIANS AND JEWS

We believe in God, and in what hath been sent down to us, and what hath been sent down to Abraham, and Ismael, and Isaac, and Jacob, and the tribes, and in what was given to Moses, and Jesus, and the Prophets, from their Lord. We make no difference between them. And to Him are we resigned (Muslims).

Whoso desireth any other religion than Islam, that religion shall never be accepted from him, and in the next world he shall be among the lost. (3)

Verily, they who believe (Muslims), and they who follow the Jewish religion, and the Christians, and the Sabeites—whoever of these believeth in God and the last day, and doeth that which is right, shall have their reward with their Lord. Fear shall not come upon them, neither shall they be grieved. (2)

Make war upon such of those to whom the Scriptures have been given as believe not in God, or in the last day, and who forbid not that which God and His Apostle have forbidden, and who profess not the profession of the truth, until they pay tribute out of hand, and they be humbled.

The Jews say, "Ezra is a son of God," and the Christians say, "The Messiah is a son of God." Such the sayings in their mouths! They resemble the saying of the infidels of old! God do battle with them! How are they misguided!

They take their teachers, and their monks, and the Messiah, son of Mary, for Lords beside God, though bidden to worship one God only. There is no God but He! Far from His glory be what they associate with Him! (9)

Ali: Instructions to Malik al-Ashtar, Governor of Egypt

Shiism, the most substantial dissenting denomination within the Islamic faith (as opposed to the Sunni majority), was born out of the issue over who should succeed Muhammad in his leadership over the Muslim world. Shiites demand that true authority must be vested in an Imam, who must be a physical descendent of the Prophet through his daughter Fatima and her husband (Muhammad's nephew), Ali. Within the Shiite community, Ali, who from 656–661 CE was the fourth successor to Muhammad, is mainly considered to have been the sole legitimate Caliph. The following document is excerpted from Ali's instructions to Malik al-Ashtar, whom he had just appointed governor of Egypt.

Source: William C. Chittick, ed., A Shiite Anthology (Albany, N.Y.: State University of New York Press, 1981, copyright: Muhammadi Trust of Great Britain and Northern Ireland), pp. 68–72.

Focus Questions:
1. What advice does Ali give the al-Ashtar about policy towards the proper customs of the subject peoples?
2. What does Ali recommend as a cure for pride generated by power?
3. What five classes does Ali designate whose well-being is essential for conducting a successful administration, and what claims do each of them have on those who govern them?

Have the poets left in the garment a place for a patch to be patched by me; and did you know the abode of your beloved after reflection?

ᶜAli- wrote these instructions to al-Ashtar al-Nakhaʿt when he appointed him governor of Egypt and its provinces at the time the rule of Muhammad ibn Ab-i Bakr was in turmoil. It is the longest set of instructions (in the Nahj al-bal-a-ghah). Among all his letters it embraces the largest number of good qualities.

PART ONE: INTRODUCTION

In the Name of God, the Merciful, the Compassionate

This is that with which ᶜAli-, the servant of God and Commander of the Faithful, charged Malik ibn al-Harith al-Ashtar in his instructions to him when he appointed him governor of Egypt: to collect its land tax, to war against its enemies, to improve the condition of the people and to engender prosperity in its regions. He charged him to fear God, to prefer obedience to Him (over all else) and to follow what He has directed in His Book—both the acts He has made obligatory and those He recommends—for none attains felicity but he who follows His directions, and none is overcome by wretchedness but he who denies them and lets them slip by. (He charged him) to help God—glory be to Him—with his heart, his hand and his tongue, for He—majestic is His Name—has promised to help him who exalts Him. And he charged him to break the passions of his soul and restrain it in its recalcitrance, for the soul incites to evil, except inasmuch as God has mercy.

PART TWO: COMMANDS AND INSTRUCTIONS CONCERNING RIGHTEOUS ACTION IN THE AFFAIRS OF THE STATE

Know, O Ma-lik, that I am sending you to a land where governments, just and unjust, have existed before you. People will look upon your affairs in the same way that you were wont to look upon the affairs of the rulers before you. They will speak about you as you were wont to speak about those rulers. And the righteous are only known by that which God causes to pass concerning them on the tongues of His servants. So let the dearest of your treasuries be the treasury of righteous action. Control your desire and restrain your soul from what is not lawful to you, for restraint of the soul is for it to be equitous in what it likes and dislikes. Infuse your heart with mercy, love and kindness for your subjects. Be not in face of them a voracious animal, counting them as easy prey, for they are of two kinds: either they are your brothers in religion or your equals in creation. Error catches them unaware, deficiencies overcome them, (evil deeds) are committed by them intentionally and by mistake. So grant them your pardon and your forgiveness to the same extent that you hope God will grant you His pardon and His forgiveness. For you are above them, and he who appointed you is above you, and God is above him who appointed you. God has sought from you the fulfillment of their requirements and He is trying you with them.

Set yourself not up to war against God, for you have no power against His vengeance, nor are you able to dispense with His pardon and His mercy. Never be regretful of pardon or rejoice at punishment, and never hasten (to act) upon an impulse if you can find a better course. Never say, "I am invested with authority, I give orders and I am obeyed," for surely that is corruption in the heart, enfeeblement of the religion and an approach to changes (in fortune). If the authority you possess engender in you pride or arrogance, then reflect upon the tremendousness of the dominion of God above you and His power over you in that in which you yourself have no control. This will subdue your recalcitrance, restrain your violence and restore in you what has left you of the power of your reason. Beware of vying with God in His tremendousness and likening yourself to Him in His exclusive power, for God abases every tyrant and humiliates all who are proud.

See that justice is done towards God and justice is done towards the people by yourself, your own family and those whom you favor among your subjects. For if you do not do so, you have worked wrong. And as for him who wrongs the servants of God, God is his adversary, not to speak of His servants. God renders null and void the argument of whosoever contends with Him. Such a one will be God's enemy until he desists or repents. Nothing is more conducive to the removal of God's blessing and the hastening of His vengeance than to continue in wrongdoing, for God harkens to the call of the oppressed and He is ever on the watch against the wrongdoers.

Let the dearest of your affairs be those which are middlemost in rightfulness, most inclusive in justice and most comprehensive in (establishing) the content of the subjects. For the discontent of the common people invalidates the content of favorites, and the discontent of favorites is pardoned at (the achievement of) the content of the masses. Moreover, none of the subjects is more burdensome upon the ruler in ease and less of a help to him in trial than his favorites. (None are) more disgusted by equity, more importunate in demands, less grateful upon bestowal, slower to pardon (the ruler upon his) withholding (favor) and more deficient in patience at the misfortunes of time than the favorites. Whereas the support of religion, the solidarity of Muslims and preparedness in the face of the enemy lie only with the common people of the community, so let your inclination and affection be toward them.

Let the farthest of your subjects from you and the most hateful to you be he who most seeks out the faults of men. For men possess faults, which the ruler more than anyone else should conceal. So do not uncover those of them which are hidden from you, for it is only encumbent upon you to remedy what appears before you. God will judge what is hidden from you. So veil imperfection to the extent you are able; God will veil that of yourself which you would like to have veiled from your subjects. Loose from men the knot of every resentment, sever from yourself the cause of every animosity, and ignore all that which does not become your station. Never hasten to believe the slanderer, for the slanderer is a deceiver, even if he seems to be a sincere advisor.

Bring not into your consultation a miser, who might turn you away from liberality and promise you poverty; nor a coward, who might enfeeble you in your affairs; nor a greedy man, who might in his lust deck out oppression to you as something fair. Miserliness, cowardliness and greed are diverse temperaments which have in common distrust in God.

Truly the worst of your viziers are those who were the viziers of the evil (rulers) before you and shared with them in their sins. Let them not be among your retinue, for they are aides of the sinners and brothers of the wrongdoers. You will find the best of substitutes for them from among those who possess the like of their ideas and effectiveness but are not encumbranced by the like of their sins and crimes; who have not aided a wrongdoer in his wrongs nor a sinner in his sins. These will be a lighter burden upon you, a better aid, more inclined toward you in sympathy and less intimate with people other than you. So choose these men as your special companions in privacy and at assemblies. Then let the most influential among them be he who speaks most to you with the bitterness of the truth and supports you least in activities which God dislikes in His friends, however this strikes your pleasure. Cling to men of piety and veracity. Then accustom them not to lavish praise upon you nor to (try to) gladden you by (attributing to you) a vanity you did not do, for the lavishing of abundant praise causes arrogance and draws (one) close to pride.

Never let the good-doer and the evil-doer possess an equal station before you, for that would cause the good-doer to abstain from his good-doing and habituate the evil-doer to his evil-doing. Impose upon each of them what he has imposed upon himself.

Know that there is nothing more conducive to the ruler's trusting his subjects than that he be kind towards them, lighten their burdens and abandon coercing them in that in which they possess not the ability. So in this respect you should attain a situation in which you can confidently trust your subjects, for trusting (them) will sever from you lasting strain. And surely he who most deserves your trust is he who has done well when you have tested him, and he who most deserves your mistrust is he who has done badly when you have tested him.

Abolish no proper custom (sunnah) which has been acted upon by the leaders of this community, through which harmony has been strengthened and because of which the subjects have prospered. Create no new custom which might in any way prejudice the customs of the past, lest their reward belong to him who originated them, and the burden be upon you to the extent that you have abolished them.

Study much with men of knowledge ('ulama-') and converse much with sages (hukana-') concerning the consolidation of that which causes the state of your land to prosper and the establishment of that by which the people before you remained strong.

PART THREE: CONCERNING THE CLASSES OF MEN

Know that subjects are of various classes, none of which can be set aright without the others and none of which is independent from the others. Among them are (1.) the soldiers of God, (2.) secretaries for the common people and the people of distinction, executors of justice, and administrators of equity and kindness, (3.) payers of jizyah and land tax, namely the people of protective covenants—and the Muslims, (4.) merchants and craftsmen and (5.) the lowest class, the needy and wretched. For each of them God has designated a portion, and commensurate with each portion He has established obligatory acts (fari-dah) in His Book and the Sunnah of His Prophet—may God bless him and his household and give them peace—as a covenant from Him maintained by us.

Now soldiers, by the leave of God, are the fortresses of the subjects, the adornment of rulers, the might of religion and the means to security. The subjects have no support but them, and the soldiers in their turn have no support but the land tax which God has extracted for them, (a tax) by which they are given the power to war against their enemy and upon which they depend for that which puts their situation in order and meets their needs. Then these two classes (soldiers and taxpayers) have no support but the third class, the judges, administrators and secretaries, for they draw up contracts, gather yields, and are entrusted with private and public affairs. And all of these have no support but the merchants and craftsmen, through the goods which they bring together and the markets which they set up. They provide for the needs (of the first three classes) by acquiring with their own hands those (goods) to which the resources of others do not attain. Then there is the lowest class, the needy and wretched, those who have the right to aid and assistance. With God there is plenty for each (of the classes). Each has a claim upon the ruler to the extent that will set it aright. But the ruler will not truly accomplish what God has enjoined upon him in this respect except by resolutely striving, by recourse to God's help, by reconciling himself to what the truth requires and by being patient in the face of it in what is easy for him or burdensome.

Al-Tabari: Muhammad's Call to Prophesy

Though the Quran itself provides hints about Muhammad's past and his personal life, biographies of the Prophet, which drew upon various (usually oral) accounts and recollections, came out shortly after his death in 632 CE. One of the most revered of the early Muslim chroniclers was Al-Tabari, who made it a habit to cite his sources whenever possible. Here he has left us an account of a crucial event: the first call of Muhammad to prophesy (note: Aisha was Muhammad's second wife; Khadija his first).

Source: Arthur Jeffrey, trans., Islam, Muhammad and His Religion *(N.Y.: Liberal Arts Press, 1958), pp. 15–17. Quoted in Mircea Eliade,* From Medicine Men to Muhammad *(N.Y.: Harper & Row, 1974), pp. 63–64.*

Focus Questions:
1. How did Muhammad react to the first visitations from Gabriel?
2. What role did Khadija play?
3. What form of suffering does Muhammad's uncle foresee will occur to the Prophet on account of his visions?

Ahmad b. 'Uthman, who is known as Abu'l-jawza', has related to me on the authority of Wahb b. Jarir, who heard his father say that he had heard from an-Nu'man b. Rashid, on the authority of az-Zuhri from 'Urwa, from 'A'isha, who said: The way revelation (wahy) first began to come to the Apostle of Allah—on whom be Allah's blessing and peace—was by means of true dreams which would come like the morning dawn. Then he came to love solitude, so he used to go off to a cave in Hira where he would practise tahannuth certain nights before returning to his family. Then he would come back to his family and take provisions for the like number [of nights] until unexpectedly the truth came to him.

He (i.e., Gabriel) came to him saying: 'O Muhammad, thou art Allah's Apostle (rasUl).' Said the Apostle of Allah—upon whom be Allah's blessing and peace: 'Thereat I fell to my knees where I had been standing, and then with trembling limbs dragged myself along till I came in to Khadija, saying: "Wrap ye me up! Wrap ye me up!" till the terror passed from me. Then [on another occasion] he came to me again and said: "O Muhammad, thou art Allah's Apostle," [which so disturbed me] that I was about to cast myself down from some high mountain cliff. But he appeared before me as I was about to do this, and said: "O Muhammad, I am Gabriel, and thou art Allah's Apostle." Then he said to me: "Recite!"; but I answered: "What should I recite?"; whereat he seized me and grievously treated me three times, till he wore me out. Then he said: "Recite, in the name of thy Lord who has created" (SUra XCVI, 1). So I recited it and then went to Khadija, to whom I said: "I am worried about myself." Then I told her the whole story. She said: "Rejoice, for by Allah, Allah will never put thee to shame. By Allah, thou art mindful of thy kinsfolk, speakest truthfully, renderest what is given thee in trust, bearest burdens, art ever hospitable to the guest, and dost always uphold the right against any wrong." Then she took me to Waraqua b. Naufal b. Asad [to whom] she said: "Give ear to what the son of thy brother [has to report]." So he questioned me, and I told him [the whole] story. Said he: "This is the nAmUs which was sent down upon Moses the son of Amram. Would that I might be a stalwart youth [again to take part] in it. Would that I might still be alive when your people turn you out." "And will they turn me out?" I asked. "Yes," said he, "never yet has a man come with that with which you come but has been turned away. Should I be there when your day comes I will lend you mighty assistance."'

Al-Tabari and Ibn Hisham, from "The Founding of the Caliphate"

The sudden demise of Muhammad in 632 CE left his state in disarray; he had never specified procedures for designating a successor. How was the Muslim state he had forged to be governed? A debate ensued and its results had far-reaching implications, as related by the respective chroniclers Al-Tabari and Ibn Hisham.

Source: *Bernard Lewis, ed.,* Islam from the Prophet to the Capture of Constantinople, *Vol. I (N.Y.: Walker & Co.,1974), pp. 2–6.*

Focus Questions:
1. What was the nature of the split between the Helpers and the Emigrants after the Prophet's death?
2. What was Abu- Bakr's perspective on the difference in prestige and authority between the two?
3. In his accession speech, how does Abu- Bakr personally set limits on his own authority as Caliph?

THE FOUNDING OF THE CALIPHATE (632)

An account of what happened between the Emigrants and the Helpers concerning the leadership, in the porch of the Banu Sa'ida. Hisha-m ibn Muhammad told me on the authority of Ab-u Mikhnaf, who said: 'Abdalla-h ibn 'Abd al-Rahma-n ibn Abi-'Umra, the Helper, told me:

When the Prophet of God, may God bless and save him, died, the Helpers assembled in the porch of the Banu S-a'ida and said, "Let us confer this authority, after Muhammad, upon him be peace, on Sa'd ibn 'Uba-da." Sa'd, who was ill, was brought to them, and when they assembled Sa'd said to his son or to one of his nephews, "I cannot, because of my sickness, speak so that all the people can hear my words. Therefore, hear what I say and then repeat it to them so that they may hear it." Then he spoke and the man memorized his words and raised his voice so that the others could hear.

He said, after praising God and lauding Him, "O company of the Helpers! You have precedence in religion and merit in Islam which no other Arab tribe has. Muhammad, upon him be peace, stayed for more than ten years amid his people, summoning them to worship the Merciful One and to abandon false gods and idols. But among his own people only a few men believed in him, and they were not able to protect the Prophet of God or to glorify his religion nor to defend themselves against the injustice which beset them. God therefore conferred merit on you and brought honor to you and singled you out for grace and vouchsafed to you faith in Him and in His Prophet and protection for Him and His companions and glorification to Him and His religion and holy war against His enemies. It was you who fought hardest against His enemy and weighed more heavily on His enemy than any other, until the Arabs obeyed the command of God willy-nilly and the distant ones gave obedience, humbly and meekly; until Almighty God, through you, made the world submit to His Prophet, and through your swords the Arabs drew near to him. And when God caused him to die, he was content with you and delighted with you. Therefore, keep this authority for yourselves alone, for it is yours against all others."

They all replied to him, "Your judgment is sound and your words are true. We shall not depart from what you say and we shall confer this authority on you. You satisfy us and you will satisfy the right believer."

Then they discussed it among themselves and some of them said, "What if the Emigrants of Quraysh refuse, and say: 'We are the Emigrants and the first Companions of the Prophet of God; we are his clan and his friends. Why therefore do you dispute the succession to his authority with us?'" Some of them said, "If so, we would reply to them, 'An amir from us and an amir from you! And we shall never be content with less than that.'" Sa'd ibn 'Uba-da, when he heard this, said, "This is the beginning of weakness."

News of this reached 'Umar, and he went to the house of the Prophet, may God bless and save him. He sent to Abu- Bakr, who was in the Prophet's house with 'Ali- ibn Abi- Ta-lib, upon him be peace, preparing the body of the Prophet, may God bless and save him, for burial. He sent asking Abu- Bakr to come to him, and Abu- Bakr sent a message in reply saying that he was busy. Then 'Umar sent saying that something had happened which made his presence necessary, and he went to him and said, "Have you not heard that the Helpers have gathered in the porch of the Banu S-a'ida? They wish to confer this authority on Sa'd ibn 'Ub-ada, and the best they say is, 'an amir from among us and an amir from among Quraysh.'" They made haste toward them, and they met Abu- 'Ubayda ibn al-Jarr-ah. The three of them went on together, and they met 'Asim ibn 'Adi- and 'Uwaym ibn S-a'ida, who both said to them: "Go back, for what you want will not happen." They said, "We shall not go back," and they came to the meeting.

'Umar ibn al-Khatt-ab said: We came to the meeting, and I had prepared a speech which I wished to make to them. We reached them, and I was about to begin my speech when Abu- Bakr said to me, "Gently! Let me speak first, and then afterwards say whatever you wish." He spoke. 'Umar said, "He said all I wanted to say, and more."

'Abdalla-h ibn 'Abd al-Rahma-n said: Abu- Bakr began. He praised and lauded God and then he said, "God sent Muhammad as a Prophet to His creatures and as a witness to His community that they might worship God and God alone, at a time when they were worshipping various gods beside Him and believed that they were intercessors for them with God and could be of help to them, though they were only of hewn stone and carved wood. Then he recited to them, 'And they worship apart from God those who could neither harm them nor help them, and they say these are our intercessors with God' [Qur'a-n x, 19/18]. And they said, 'We worship them only so that they may bring us very near to God' [Qur'-an xxxix, 4/3]. It was a tremendous thing for the Arabs to abandon the religion of their fathers. God distinguished the first Emigrants of his people by allowing them to recognize the truth and believe in him and console him and suffer with him from the harsh persecution of his people when they gave them the lie and all were against them and reviled them. Yet they were not affrighted because their numbers were few and the people stared at them and their tribe was joined against them. They were the first in the land who worshipped God and who believed in God and the Prophet. They are his friends and his clan and the best entitled of all men to this authority after him. Only a wrongdoer would dispute this with them. And as for you, O company of the Helpers, no one can deny your merit in the faith or your great precedence in Islam. God was pleased to make you Helpers to His religion and His Prophet and caused him to migrate to you, and the honor of sheltering his wives and his Companions is still yours, and after the first Emigrants there is no one we hold of equal standing with you. We are the amirs and you are the viziers. We shall not act contrary to your advice and we shall not decide things without you."

Abu- Bakr said, "Here is 'Umar and here is Abu- 'Ubayda. Swear allegiance to whichever of them you choose." The two of them said, "No, by God, we shall not accept this authority above you, for you are the worthiest of the Emigrants and the second of the two who were in the cave and the deputy [khali-fa] of the Prophet of God in prayer, and prayer is the noblest part of the religion of the Muslims. Who then would be fit to take precedence of you or to accept this authority above you? Stretch out your hand so that we may swear allegiance to you."

And when they went forward to swear allegiance to him, Bashi-r ibn Sa'd went ahead of them and swore allegiance to him...and when the tribe of Aws saw what Bashi-r ibn Sa'd had done...they came to him and swore allegiance to him...

Hisha-m said on the authority of Abu- Mikhnaf: 'Abdalla-h ibn 'Abd al-Rahma-n said: People came from every side to swear allegiance to Abu- Bakr.

THE ACCESSION SPEECH OF ABU- BAKR (632)

Then Abu- Bakr spoke and praised and lauded God as is fitting, and then he said: O people, I have been appointed to rule over you, though I am not the best among you. If I do well, help me, and if I do ill, correct me. Truth is loyalty and falsehood is treachery; the weak among you is strong in my eyes until I get justice for him, please God, and the strong among you is weak in my eyes until I exact justice from him, please God. If any people holds back from fighting the holy war for God, God strikes them with degradation. If weakness spreads among a people, God brings disaster upon all of them. Obey me as long as I obey God and His Prophet. And if I disobey God and His Prophet, you do not owe me obedience. Come to prayer, and may God have mercy on you.

Al-Farabi, from *Al-Farabi on the Perfect State*

One of the most important Muslim thinkers during the Golden Age of Islam was Abu Nasr Muhammad al-Farabi (c. 870-950 CE). Of Turkish descent, al-Farabi was born in Turkestan, in the interior of southern Asia. For most of his life he lived in the city of Baghdad, where he became a student of philosophy, taught by Christians steeped in the classical Greek tradition as it had been developed during the Hellenistic age and later in the school of Alexandria in Egypt. Although he was a noted philosopher in his own time, al-Farabi shunned fame and publicity, preferring to live a secluded and austere life.

The influence of classical Greek philosophy on al-Farabi, particularly of Plato, Aristotle, and the neo-Platonists, is evident throughout his writings, including his book The Perfect State. *Although the title of this work indicates its subject to be politics, al-Farabi turns to his description of the ideal state only in Chapter 15, after he has grounded his views in a full theory both of metaphysics (including theology and natural science) and psychology, employing arguments from analogy as the basis for his political conclusions. His use of this kind of philosophical generalization and integration reveals the influence of Aristotle, as does the opening paragraph of the following selection, in which he reiterates the Aristotelian view that "man is a political animal." In his description of the ideal ruler, whom al-Farabi conceives to be a philosopher-king, can be found a strong echo of the central theme of Plato's* Republic.

But al-Farabi's thought was not just derivative from the Greeks. As a Muslim he added a further dimension to the philosopher-king concept. The ideal ruler must also be a prophet. Not only is such a ruler an individual of high intelligence but one of an intellect of "divine quality" who can look into the future and warn "of things to come."

Source: *Richard Walzer, trans.,* Al-Farabi on the Perfect State, *(Oxford: Clarendon Press, 1985). Reprinted by permission of Oxford University Press.*

Focus Questions:
1. To what extent has al-Farabi adopted the philosophy of the Central Mediterranean?
2. To what extent does this selection reflect Islamic ideas and assumptions?

SECTION V

Chapter 15 Perfect Associations and Perfect Ruler; Faulty Associations

1. In order to preserve himself and to attain his highest perfections every human being is by his very nature in need of many things which he cannot provide all by himself, he is indeed in need of people who each supply him with some particular need of his. Everybody finds himself in the same relation to everybody in this respect. Therefore man cannot attain the perfection, for the sake of which his inborn nature has been given to him, unless many (societies of) people who co-operate come together who each supply everybody else with some particular need of his, so that as a result of the contribution of the whole community all the things are brought together which everybody needs in order to preserve himself and to attain perfection. Therefore human individuals have come to exist in great numbers, and have settled in the inhabitable region of the earth, so that human societies have come to exist in it, some of which are perfect, others imperfect.

2. There are three kinds of perfect society, great, medium and small. The great one is the union of all the societies in the inhabitable world; the medium one the union of one nation in one part of the inhabitable world; the small one the union of the people of a city in the territory of any nation whatsoever. Imperfect are the union of people in a village, the union of people in a quarter, then the union in a street, eventually the union in a house, the house being the smallest union of all. Quarter and village exist both

for the sake of the city, but the relation of the village to the city is one of service whereas the quarter is related to the city as a part of it; the street is a part of the quarter, the house a part of the street. The city is a part of the territory of a nation, the nation a part of all the people of the inhabitable world.

3. The most excellent good and the utmost perfection is, in the first instance, attained in a city, not in a society which is less complete than it. But since good in its real sense is such as to be attainable through choice and will, and evils are also due to will and choice only, a city may be established to enable its people to cooperate in attaining some aims that are evil. Hence felicity is not attainable in every city. The city, then, in which people aim through association at co-operating for the things by which felicity in its real and true sense can be attained, is the excellent city, and the society in which there is a co-operation to acquire felicity is the excellent society; and the nation in which all of its cities co-operate for those things through which felicity is attained is the excellent nation. In the same way, the excellent universal state will arise only when all the nations in it co-operate for the purpose of reaching felicity.

4. The excellent city resembles the perfect and healthy body, all of whose limbs co-operate to make the life of the animal perfect and to preserve it in this state. Now the limbs and organs of the body are different and their natural endowments and faculties are unequal in excellence, there being among them one ruling organ, namely the heart, and organs which are close in rank to that ruling organ, each having been given by nature a faculty by which it performs its proper function in conformity with the natural aim of that ruling organ. Other organs have by nature faculties by which they perform their functions according to the aims of those organs which have no intermediary between themselves and the ruling organ; they are in the second rank. Other organs, in turn, perform their functions according to the aim of those which are in the second rank, and so on until eventually organs are reached which only serve and do not rule at all.

The same holds good in the case of the city. Its parts are different by nature, and their natural dispositions are unequal in excellence: there is in it a man who is the ruler, and there are others whose ranks are close to the ruler, each of them with a disposition and a habit through which he performs an action in conformity with the intention of that ruler; these are the holders of the first ranks. Below them are people who perform their actions in accordance with the aims of those people; they are in the second rank. Below them in turn are people who perform their actions according to the aims of the people mentioned in the second instance, and the parts of the city continue to be arranged in this way, until eventually parts are reached which perform their actions according to the aims of others, while there do not exist any people who perform their actions according to their aims; these, then, are the people who serve without being served in turn, and who are hence in the lowest rank and at the bottom of the scale.

But the limbs and organs of the body are natural, and the dispositions which they have are natural faculties, whereas, although the parts of the city are natural, their dispositions and habits, by which they perform their actions in the city, are not natural but voluntary, notwithstanding that the parts of the city are by nature provided with endowments unequal in excellence which enable them to do one thing and not another. But they are not parts of the city by their inborn nature alone but rather by the voluntary habits which they acquire such as the arts and their likes; to the natural faculties which exist in the organs and limbs of the body correspond the voluntary habits and dispositions in the parts of the city.

5. The ruling organ in the body is by nature the most perfect and most complete of the organs in itself and in its specific qualification, and it also has the best of everything of which another organ has a share as well; beneath it, in turn, are other organs which rule over organs inferior to them, their rule being lower in rank than the rule of the first and indeed subordinate to the rule of the first; they rule and are ruled.

In the same way, the ruler of the city is the most perfect part of the city in his specific qualification and has the best of everything which anybody else shares with him; beneath him are people who are ruled by him and rule others.

The heart comes to be first and becomes then the cause of the existence of the other organs and limbs of the body, and the cause of the existence of their faculties in them and of their arrangement in the ranks proper to them, and when one of its organs is out of order, it is the heart which provides the means to remove that disorder. In the same way the ruler of this city must come to be in the first instance, and will subsequently be the cause of the rise of the city and its parts and the cause of the presence of the voluntary habits of its parts and of their arrangement in the ranks proper to them; and when one part is out of order he provides it with the means to remove its disorder.

The parts of the body close to the ruling organ perform of the natural functions, in agreement—by nature—with the aim of the ruler, the most noble ones; the organs beneath them perform those functions which are less noble, and eventually the organs are reached which perform the meanest functions. In the same way the parts of the city which are close in authority to the ruler of the city perform the most noble voluntary actions, and those below them less noble actions, until eventually the parts are reached which perform the most ignoble actions. The inferiority of such actions is sometimes due to the inferiority of their matter, although they may be extremely useful, like the action of the bladder and the action of the lower intestine in the body; sometimes it is due to their being of little use; at other times it is due to their being very easy to perform. This applies equally to the city and equally to every whole which is composed by nature of well ordered coherent parts: they have a ruler whose relation to the other parts is like the one just described.

6. This applies also to all existents. For the relation of the First Cause to the other existents is like the relation of the king of the excellent city to its other parts. For the ranks of the immaterial existents are close to the First. Beneath them are the heavenly bodies, and beneath the heavenly bodies the material bodies. All these existents act in conformity with the First Cause, follow it, take it as their guide and imitate it; but each existent does that according to its capacity, choosing its aim precisely on the strength of its established rank in the universe: that is to say the last follows the aim of that which is slightly above it in rank, equally the second existent, in turn, follows what is above itself in rank, and in the same way the third existent has an aim which is above it. Eventually existents are reached which are linked with the First Cause without any intermediary whatsoever. In accordance with this order of rank all the existents permanently follow the aim of the First Cause. Those which are from the very outset provided with all the essentials of their existence are made to imitate the First (Cause) and its aim from their very outset, and hence enjoy eternal bliss and hold the highest ranks; but those which are not provided from the outset with all the essentials of their existence, are provided with a faculty by which they move towards the expected attainment of those essentials and will then be able to follow the aim of the First (Cause). The excellent city ought to be arranged in the same way: all its parts ought to imitate in their actions the aim of their first ruler according to their rank.

7. The ruler of the excellent city cannot just be any man, because rulership requires two conditions: (a) he should be predisposed for it by his inborn nature, (b) he should have acquired the attitude and habit of will for rulership which will develop in a man whose inborn nature is predisposed for it. Nor is every art suitable for rulership; most of the arts, indeed, are rather suited for service within the city, just as most men are by their very nature born to serve. Some of the arts rule certain (other) arts while serving others at the same time, whereas there are other arts which, not ruling anything at all, only serve. Therefore the art of ruling the excellent city cannot just be any chance art, nor due to any chance habit whatever. For just as the first ruler in a genus cannot be ruled by anything in that genus, (for instance the ruler of the limbs cannot be ruled by any other limb, and this holds good for any ruler of any composite whole), so the art of the ruler in the excellent city of necessity cannot be a serving art at all and cannot be ruled by any other art, but his art must be an art towards the aim of which all the other arts tend, and for which they strive in all the actions of the excellent city.

8. That man is a person over whom nobody has any sovereignty whatsoever. He is a man who has reached his perfection and has become actually intellect and actually being thought (intelligized), his rep-

resentative faculty having by nature reached its utmost perfection in the way stated by us; this faculty of his is predisposed by nature to receive, either in waking life or in sleep, from the Active Intellect the particulars, either as they are or by imitating them, and also the intelligibles, by imitating them. His Passive Intellect will have reached its perfection by [having apprehended] all the intelligibles, so that none of them is kept back from it, and it will have become actually intellect and actually being thought. Indeed any man whose Passive Intellect has thus been perfected by [having apprehended] all the intelligibles and has become actually intellect and actually being thought, so that the intelligible in him has become identical with that which thinks in him, acquires an actual intellect which is superior to the Passive Intellect and more perfect and more separate from matter than the Passive Intellect. It is called the 'Acquired Intellect' and comes to occupy a middle position between the Passive Intellect and the Active Intellect, nothing else being between it and the Active Intellect. The Passive Intellect is thus like matter and substratum for the Acquired Intellect, and the Acquired Intellect like matter and substratum for the Active Intellect, and the rational faculty, which is a natural disposition, is a matter underlying the Passive Intellect which is actually intellect.

9. The first stage, then, through which man becomes man is the coming to be of the receptive natural disposition which is ready to become actually intellect; this disposition is common to all men. Between this disposition and the Active Intellect are two stages, the Passive Intellect which has become actually intellect, and [the rise of] the Acquired Intellect. There are thus two stages between the first stage of being a man and the Active Intellect. When the perfect Passive Intellect and the natural disposition become one thing in the way the compound of matter and form is one-and when the form of the humanity of this man is taken as identical with the Passive Intellect which has become actually intellect, there will be between this man and the Active Intellect only one stage. And when the natural disposition is made the matter of the Passive Intellect which has become actually intellect, and the Passive Intellect the matter of the Acquired Intellect, and the Acquired Intellect the matter of the Active Intellect, and when all this is taken as one and the same thing, then this man is the man on whom the Active Intellect has descended.

10. When this occurs in both parts of his rational faculty, namely the theoretical and the practical rational faculties, and also in his representative faculty, then it is this man who receives Divine Revelation, and God Almighty grants him Revelation through the mediation of the Active Intellect, so that the emanation from God Almighty to the Active Intellect is passed on to his Passive Intellect through the mediation of the Acquired Intellect, and then to the faculty of representation. Thus he is, through the emanation from the Active Intellect to his Passive Intellect, a wise man and a philosopher and an accomplished thinker who employs an intellect of divine quality, and through the emanation from the Active Intellect to his faculty of representation a visionary prophet: who warns of things to come and tells of particular things which exist at present.

11. This man holds the most perfect rank of humanity and has reached the highest degree of felicity. His soul is united as it were with the Active Intellect, in the way stated by us. He is the man who knows every action by which felicity can be reached. This is the first condition for being a ruler. Moreover, he should be a good orator and able to rouse [other people's] imagination by well-chosen words. He should be able to lead people well along the right path to felicity and to the actions by which felicity is reached. He should, in addition, be of tough physique, in order to shoulder the tasks of war.

This is the sovereign over whom no other human being has any sovereignty whatsoever; he is the Imam; he is the first sovereign of the excellent city, he is the sovereign of the excellent nation, and the sovereign of the universal state.

12. But this state can only be reached by a man in whom twelve natural qualities are found together, with which he is endowed by birth. (1) One of them is that he should have limbs and organs which are free from deficiency and strong, and that they will make him fit for the actions which depend on them; when he intends to perform an action with one of them, he accomplishes it with ease. (2) He should by

nature be good at understanding and perceiving everything said to him, and grasp it in his mind according to what the speaker intends and what the thing itself demands. (3) He should be good at retaining what he comes to know and see and hear and apprehend in general, and forget almost nothing. (4) He should be well provided with ready intelligence and very bright; when he sees the slightest indication of a thing, he should grasp it in the way indicated. (5) He should have a fine diction, his tongue enabling him to explain to perfection all that is in the recess of his mind. (6) He should be fond of learning and acquiring knowledge, be devoted to it and grasp things easily, without finding the effort painful, nor feeling discomfort about the toil which it entails. (7) He should by nature be fond of truth and truthful men and hate falsehood and liars. (8) He should by nature not crave for food and drink and sexual intercourse, and have a natural aversion to gambling and hatred of the pleasures which these pursuits provide. (9) He should be proud of spirit and fond of honour, his soul being by his nature above everything ugly and base, and rising naturally to the most lofty things. (10) Dirham and dinar and the other worldly pursuits should be of little amount in his view. (11) He should by nature be fond of justice and of just people, and hate oppression and injustice and those who practice them, giving himself and others their due, and urging people to act justly and showing pity to those who are oppressed by injustice; he should lend his support to what he considers to be beautiful and noble and just; he should not be reluctant to give in nor should he be stubborn and obstinate if he is asked to do justice; but he should be reluctant to give in if he is asked to do injustice and evil altogether. (12) He should be strong in setting his mind firmly upon the thing which, in his view, ought to be done, and daringly and bravely carry it out without fear and weak-mindedness.

13. Now it is difficult to find all these qualities united in one man, and, therefore, men endowed with this nature will be found one at a time only, such men being altogether very rare. Therefore if there exists such a man in the excellent city who, after reaching maturity, fulfils the six aforementioned conditions—or five of them if one excludes the gift of visionary prophecy through the faculty of representation—he will be the sovereign. Now when it happens that, at a given time, no such man is to be found but there was previously an unbroken succession of sovereigns of this kind, the laws and the customs which were introduced will be adopted and eventually firmly established.

The next sovereign, who is the successor of the first sovereigns, will be someone in whom those [twelve] qualities are found together from the time of his birth and his early youth and who will, after reaching his maturity, be distinguished by the following six qualities: (1) He will be a philosopher. (2) He will know and remember the laws and customs (and rules of conduct) with which the first sovereigns had governed the city, conforming in all his actions to all their actions. (3) He will excel in deducing a new law by analogy where no law of his predecessors has been recorded, following for his deductions the principles laid down by the first Imams. (4) He will be good at deliberating and be powerful in his deductions to meet new situations for which the first sovereigns could not have laid down any law; when doing this he will have in mind the good of the city. (5) He will be good at guiding the people by his speech to fulfill the laws of the first sovereigns as well as those laws which he will have deduced in conformity with their principles after their time. (6) He should be of tough physique in order to shoulder the tasks of war, mastering the serving as well as the ruling military art.

14. When one single man who fulfills all these conditions cannot be found but there are two, one of whom is a philosopher and the other fulfils the remaining conditions, the two of them will be the sovereigns of this city.

But when all these six qualities exist separately in different men, philosophy in one man and the second quality in another man and so on, and when these men are all in agreement, they should all together be the excellent sovereigns.

But when it happens, at a given time, that philosophy has no share in the government, though every other condition may be present in it, the excellent city will remain without a king, the ruler actually in charge of this city will not be a king, and the city will be on the verge of destruction; and if it happens that no philosopher can be found who will be attached to the actual ruler of the city, then, after a certain interval, this city will undoubtedly perish.

Science and Mathematics: Al-Ghazzali, "On the Separation of Mathematics and Religion"

The Islamic community during the Middle Ages and beyond was not simply concerned with matters of faith and obedience to doctrine. As Muslim armies covered North Africa and the Middle East, even venturing into Europe, they carried with them some of the great advancements of Islamic civilization. Muslim learning was embraced in such academic centers as Córdoba, Spain, where Jewish scholars were central in establishing a conduit of knowledge to the West by translating Arabic science and medical texts into Spanish and Latin. Many of these ideas in astronomy, medicine, advanced mathematics, law, literature, poetry, philosophy, and history fell on deaf ears in the West because of the fear of doctrinal contamination. Indeed, for Western Christians, the followers of Allah were the "Infidel," to be feared and opposed through Crusades to recapture the Holy Land for the glory of a Christian God.

The sources below are from Abu Hamid al-Ghazzali (1058–1111), one of the greatest Muslim jurists, theologians, and mystics, and Abu Bakr Muhammad ibn Zakariya al-Razi (865–925), a noted Persian physician, philosopher, and scholar.

Source[s]: Claud Field, trans., "On the Separation of Mathematics and Religion" from Al-Ghazzali, The Confession of Al-Ghazzali *(London: John Murray Publishers Ltd., 1908), pp. 33–34.*

William A. Greenhill, trans., "On the Causes of Small-Pox" from Abu Bekr Muhammad Ibn Zacariya Al-Razi, A Treatise on Small-Pox and Measles *(London, 1848), pp. 28–31.*

Focus Questions:
1. What do the selections on mathematics and the scientific description of smallpox tell you about Islamic values?
2. According to Al-Ghazzali, should mathematics and religion be separated? Why or why not?

Mathematics comprises the knowledge of calculation, geometry, and cosmography: it has no connection with the religious sciences, and proves nothing for or against religion; it rests on a foundation of proofs which, once known and understood, cannot be refuted. Mathematics tend, however, to produce two bad results.

The first is this: Whoever studies this science admires the subtlety and clearness of its proofs. His confidence in philosophy increases, and he thinks that all its departments are capable of the same clearness and solidity of proof as mathematics. But when he hears people speak on the unbelief and impiety of mathematicians, of their professed disregard for the Divine Law, which is notorious, it is true that, out of regard for authority, he echoes these accusations, but he says to himself at the same time that, if there was truth in religion, it would not have escaped those who have displayed so much keenness of intellect in the study of mathematics.

Next, when he becomes aware of the unbelief and rejection of religion on the part of these learned men, he concludes that to reject religion is reasonable. How many of such men gone astray I have met whose sole argument was that just mentioned...

It is therefore a great injury to religion to suppose that the defence of Islam involves the condemnation of the exact sciences. The religious law contains nothing which approves them or condemns them, and in their turn they make no attack on religion. The words of the Prophet, "The sun and the moon are two signs of the power of God; they are not eclipsed for the birth or the death of any one; when you see these signs take refuge in prayer and invoke the name of God"—these words, I say, do not in any way condemn the astronomical calculations which define the orbits of these two bodies, their conjunction and opposition according to particular laws.

AL-RAZI, ON THE CAUSES OF SMALL-POX

Although [scholars] have certainly made some mention of the treatment of the Small-Pox (but without much accuracy and distinctness), yet there is not one of them who has mentioned the cause of the existence of the disease, and how it comes to pass that hardly any one escapes it, or who has disposed the modes of treatment in their right places. And for this reason I...have mentioned whatever is necessary for the treatment of this disease, and have arranged and carefully disposed everything in its right place, by god's permission...

I say then that every man, from the time of his birth until he arrives at old age, is continually tending to dryness; and for this reason the blood of children and infants is much moister than the blood of young men, and still more so than that of old men...Now the Small-Pox arises when the blood putrefies and ferments, so that the superfluous vapors are thrown out of it, and it is changed from the blood of infants, which is like must, into the blood of young men, which is like wine perfectly ripened: and the Small-Pox itself may be compared to the fermentation and the hissing noise which takes place in must at that time. And this is the reason why children, especially males, rarely escape being seized with this disease, because it is impossible to prevent the blood's changing from this state into its second state...

As to young men, whereas their blood is already passed into the second state, its maturation is established, and the superfluous particles of moisture which necessarily cause putrefaction are now exhaled; hence it follows that this disease only happens to a few individuals among them, that is, to those whose vascular system abounds with too much moisture, or is corrupt in quality with a violent inflammation...

And as for old men, the Small-Pox seldom happens to them, except in pestilential, putrid, and malignant constitutions of the air, in which this disease is chiefly prevalent. For a putrid air, which has an undue proportion of heat and moisture, and also an inflamed air, promotes the eruption of this disease.

Chapter 11

States, Old and New

Winada Prapanca, *Nagara Kertagama*

The Javanese poem, the Nagara Kertagama, was written in 1365. Its author, Winada Prapanca, was a Buddhist monk and a lifetime confidant of King Hayan Wuruk of Majapahit, in whose praise he wrote. The poem has features in common with other contemporary praise poems addressed to rulers in South and Southeast Asia. The extracts below include the poet's account of lands beyond Java supposedly subject to the king's power.

Source: *Pigeaud, T. The* Nagara Kertagama, *The Hague, 1960–1963.*

Focus Questions:
1. How does the poet show the king's authority over distant lands? The poet is a Buddhist. How, then, does he justify the use of violence?
2. How is the king's realm portrayed? What evidence do we have in these extracts of cultural syncretism?

Canto 16
Then, surely, other lands, anywhere, that are in the guardianship of the Javanese Royal compound are executing any orders of the honored Prince, equally faithful in conduct. Even though there were any commandment-breakers, they are visited by expeditionary forces and annihilated, altogether, by the activity of those (warriors) there who belong to the mandarins, numerous and glorious.

Canto 17
Already has begun the consolidation of the Prince's reign in Yawaland (Java), victorious over the other countries. There in Majapahit town is He, being obeyed, working out the welfare of the world. In great numbers are the buildings, public foundations, and spiritual domains founded by Him, giving pleasure to the minds of common people. Mandarins, Brahmins, ecclesiastical officers, the honored ones who are equally given magnificence, follow having public foundations in the world for the people's benefit.

How great is the manfulness and magnificence that have been attained by the Prince's activity, verily, verily a most excellent king. At ease, there is no anxiety with Him, he realizes his pleasure, all the delight of his heart. Virgins, whoever is beautiful in Janggala and also in Kadiri are chosen when there is a possible case, not to mention surely those who are captured from foreign Royal compounds, whoever is beautiful is brought into the Interior of the Royal Compound.

Canto 92

Thus is His order (of life): enjoying pleasure in the Royal compound attaining all desires of the heart, not selfish at all, not forgetting the care for the welfare of others (especially) for the benefit of the realm. Young to be sure now (and moreover), and burdened is He, but then being Sugata (Buddha) in the body, he is rich in wisdom.　On account of wisdom's paramount power is (to be considered) pure His killing of the rascality of miscreants…

Such is the cause that the Prince's excellence is renowned, praised in the three worlds. All people, middle, excellent, low, equally are uttering songs of praise.　Only this is their prayer:　hereafter lasting with the life of a mountain may He be, the shelter of all the world, that he verily may imitate the great age of the Lords Sun and Moon, shining over the earth-circle.

Anna Comnena, from *The Alexaid*

Scholars have recently shed much light on the important role of Byzantine empresses in shaping the affairs of the state.　Princess Anna Comnena (1083–1153) is considered one of the first female historians.　The extract below is from The Alexiad, *a fifteen-volume which work that she composed when she was fifty-five years old and living in a monastery.　It sheds invaluable light on her royal family, the Comneni, and especially the reign of her father, Alexios I.*

Source: *Comnena, Anna. The Alexiad (London 1928), Volume I: 123–25.*

Focus Questions:
1.　How does Anna Comnena portray her grandmother?
2.　Anna Comnena felt that was born to rule, though she never did.　How much of her description is an expression of frustrated ambition?

One might be amazed that my father accorded his mother such high honor in these matters and that he deferred to her in all respects, as if her were turning over the reins of the empire to her and running alongside her while she drove the imperial chariot, contenting himself simply with the title of emperor. Indeed, he had already passed beyond the period of boyhood, an age especially when lust for power grows in men of such nature [as Alexius]. He took upon himself the wars against the barbarians and whatever battles and combats pertained to them, while he entrusted to his mother the complete management of [civil] affairs: the selection of civil magistrates, the collection of incoming revenues and the expenses of the government. A person who has reached this point in my text may blame my father for entrusting management of the empire to the gynaiconites [women's section of the palace]. But if he had known this woman's spirit, how great she was in virtue and intellect and how extremely vigorous, he would cease his reproach and his criticism would be changed into admiration. For my grandmother was so dextrous in handling affairs of state and so highly skilled in controlling and running the government, that she was not only able to manage the Roman empire but could have handled every empire under the sun. She had a vast amount of experience and understood the internal workings of many things: she knew how each affair began and to what result it might lead, which actions were destructive and which rather were beneficial. She was exceedingly acute in discerning whatever course of action was necessary and in carrying it out safely. She was not only acute in her thought, but was no less proficient in her manner of speech. Indeed, she was a persuasive orator, neither verbose nor stretching her phrases out at great length; nor did she quickly lose the sense of her argument. What she began felicitously she would finish even more so...

But, as I was saying, my father, after he had assumed power, managed by himself the strains and labors of war, while making his mother a spectator to these actions, but in other affairs he set her up as ruler, and as if he were her servant he used to say and do whatever she ordered. The emperor loved her deeply and was dependent upon her advice (so much affection had he for his mother), and he made his right hand the executor of her orders, his ear paid heed to her words, and everything which she accepted or rejected the emperor likewise accepted or rejected. In a word, the situation was thus: Alexius possessed the external formalities of imperial power, but she held the power itself. She used to promulgate laws, to manage and administer everything while he confirmed her arrangements, both written and unwritten, either through his signature or by oral commands, so that he seemed the instrument of her imperial authority and not himself the emperor. Everything which she decided or ordered he found satisfactory. Not only was he very obedient to her as is fitting for a son to his mother, but even more he submitted his spirit to her as to a master in the science [episteme] of ruling. For he felt that she had attained perfection in everything and far surpassed all men of that time in prudence and in comprehension of affairs.

Eusebius of Caesarea, Selections from *The Life of Constantine*

The bishop of Caesarea in Palestine, Eusebius (260-341 CE) wrote volumes on church doctrine and church history. His most famous work is the History of the Church, *which remains critical for our understanding of early Christianity. As a contemporary of the emperor Constantine, Eusebius was witness to the great events around Constantine's accession to control of the empire and his historic action in granting tolerance to Christianity.*

Source: *Medieval Source book: Eusebius of Caesarea,* The Life of the Blessed Emperor Constantine

> **Focus Questions:**
> 1. What is the nature of Constantine's conversion?
> 2. What is his relationship with God?
> 3. What is the fate of pagans, including Maxentius?

CHAPTER XXVII: That after reflecting on the Dawn fall [sic] of those who had worshiped Idols, he made Choice of Christianity.

Being convinced, however, that he needed some more powerful aid than his military forces could afford him, on account of the wicked and magical enchantments which were so diligently practiced by the tyrant, (1) he sought Divine assistance, deeming the possession of arms and a numerous soldiery of secondary importance, but believing the co-operating power of Deity invincible and not to be shaken. He considered, therefore, on what God he might rely for protection and assistance. While engaged in this enquiry, the thought occurred to him, that, of the many emperors who had preceded him, those who had rested their hopes in a multitude of gods, and served them with sacrifices and offerings, had in the first place been deceived by flattering predictions, and oracles which promised them all prosperity, and at last had met with an unhappy end, while not one of their gods had stood by to warn them of the impending wrath of heaven; while one alone who had pursued an entirely opposite course, who had condemned their error, and honored the one Supreme God during his whole life, had found him to be the Saviour and Protector of his empire, and the Giver of every good thing. Reflecting on this, and well weighing the fact that they who had trusted in many gods had also fallen by manifold forms of death, without leaving behind them either family or offspring, stock, name, or memorial among men: while the God of his father had given to him, on the other hand, manifestations of his power and very many tokens: and considering farther that those who had already taken arms against the tyrant, and had marched to the battle-field under the protection of a multitude of gods, had met with a dishonorable end (for one of them (2) had shamefully retreated from the contest without a blow, and the other, (3) being slain in the midst of his own troops, became, as it were, the mere sport of death (4)); reviewing, I say, all these considerations, he judged it to be folly indeed to join in the idle worship of those who were no gods, and, after such convincing evidence, to err from the truth; and therefore felt it incumbent on him to honor his father's God alone.

CHAPTER XXVIII: How, while he was praying, God sent him a Vision of a Cross of Light in the Heavens at Mid-day, with an Inscription admonishing him to conquer by that.

Accordingly he called on him with earnest prayer and supplications that he would reveal to him who he was, and stretch forth his right hand to help him in his present difficulties. And while he was thus praying with fervent entreaty, a most marvelous sign appeared to him from heaven, the account of which it might have been hard to believe had it been related by any other person. But since the victorious emperor himself long afterwards declared it to the writer of this history, (1) when he was honored with his acquaintance and society, and confirmed his statement by an oath, who could hesitate to accredit the relation, especially since the testimony of after-time has established its truth? He said that about noon, when the day was already beginning to decline, he saw with his own eyes the trophy of a cross of light in the heavens, above the sun, and bearing the inscription, CONQUER BY THIS. At this sight he himself was struck with amazement, and his whole army also, which followed him on this expedition, and witnessed the miracle. (2)

CHAPTER XXIX: How the Christ of God appeared to him in his Sleep, and commanded him to use in his Wars a Standard made in the Form of the Cross.

He said, moreover, that he doubted within himself what the import of this apparition could be. And while he continued to ponder and reason on its meaning, night suddenly came on; then in his sleep the Christ of God appeared to him with the same sign which he had seen in the heavens, and commanded him to make a likeness of that sign which he had seen in the heavens, and to use it as a safeguard in all engagements with his enemies.

CHAPTER XXXVII: Defeat of Maxentius's Armies in Italy.

Constantine, however, filled with compassion on account of all these miseries, began to arm himself with all warlike preparation against the tyranny. Assuming therefore the Supreme God as his patron, and invoking His Christ to be his preserver and aid, and setting the victorious trophy, the salutary symbol, in front of his soldiers and body-guard, he marched with his whole forces, trying to obtain again for the Romans the freedom they had inherited from their ancestors.

And whereas, Maxentius, trusting more in his magic arts than in the affection of his subjects, dared not even advance outside the city gates, (1) but had guarded every place and district and city subject to his tyranny, with large bodies of soldiers, (2) the emperor, confiding in the help of God, advanced against the first and second and third divisions of the tyrant's forces, defeated them all with ease at the first assault, (3) and made his way into the very interior of Italy.

Buddhism in Japan: *The Taika Reform Edicts*

Japan was gradually converted to Buddhism in the sixth century by missionaries sent by the Korean emperor. By the seventh century Buddhism was essentially the state religion for Japan, though never supplanting Shintoism. During the eighth century Buddhist scholars founded a number of influential academic schools. In addition, the Taika Reform edict of 645 had set up a central rule by emperor with active royal support of Buddhism.

Source: *The Taika Reform Edicts (645), trans. by W. G. Aston (London, 1896).*

Focus Questions:
1. How is Buddhism disseminated?
2. What are the Buddhist institutions and symbols?
3. How widespread does Buddhism appear at this point?

BUDDHISM

8th Day

A messenger was sent to the Great Temple to summon together the Buddhist priests and nuns, and to address them on the part of the Emperor, saying,

"In the 13th year of the reign of the Emperor who ruled the world in the Palace of Shikishima, King Myong of Pekche reverently transmitted the Law of Buddha to our great Yamato. At this time the Ministers in a body were opposed to its transmission. Only Soga no Iname no Sukune believed in this Law, and the Emperor accordingly instructed him to receive it with reverence. In the reign of the Emperor who ruled the world in the Palace of Wosada, Soga no Mumako no Sukune, influenced by reverence for his deceased father, continued to prize highly the doctrines of Buddha. But the other Ministers had no faith in it, and its institutes had almost perished when the Emperor instructed Mumako no Sukune reverently to receive this Law. In the reign of the Empress who ruled the world in the Palace of Woharida, Mumako no Sukune, on behalf of the Empress, made an embroidered figure of Buddha sixteen feet high and a copper image of Buddha sixteen feet high. He exalted the doctrine of Buddha and showed honour to its priests and nuns. It is Our desire to exalt the pure doctrine and brilliantly to promulgate great principles. We therefore appoint as professors the following ten persons: The S'ramana, Poknyang, Hye-un, Syang-an, Nyong-un, and Hye-chi, Taih-shi of Koma, and Subin, Doto, Yerin, Yemyo and Yeon, chief priests of temples. We separately appoint the Hoshi, Yemyo, chief priest of the Temple of Kudara.

Let these ten professors well instruct the priests in general in the practice of the teachings of Shaka. It is needful that they be made to comply with the Law. If there is a difficulty about repairing Temples built by any from the Emperor down to the Tomo no Miyakko, We will in all cases assist in doing so. We shall also cause Temple Commissioners and Chief Priests to be appointed, who shall make a circuit to all the temples, and having ascertained the actual facts respecting the priests and nuns, their male and female slaves, and the acreage of their cultivated lands, report all the particulars clearly to us."

Excerpts from the *Taika Reform Edicts*

The edicts of 646 CE mark the creation of strong central government in Japan. The Emperor Kotoku had defeated the rival clans and cemented his control by seizing direct control of the rice-producing lands. He then created a government structure based on a sacrosanct emperor rather than the old clan system. The Japanese government was strongly influenced by Chinese Buddhist and Confucian philosophies, in many cases through deliberate acts of copying.

Source: *Richard Hooker. intro and ed., W.G. Aston, trans., Nihongi (London: Kegan, Paul, Trench, Trubner, 1896) pp. 197–227.*

> **Focus Questions:**
> 1. What is the treatment of various classes and of women?
> 2. How are law and government organized in comparison to China?
> 3. How is the military organized?

EMPEROR KOTOKU'S VOW

19th day (645 A.D.).

The Emperor, the Empress Dowager, and the Prince Imperial summoned together the Ministers under the great tsuki tree, and made an oath appealing to the Gods of Heaven and Earth, and said,

"Heaven covers us; Earth upbears us; the Imperial way is one and only one way. But in this last degenerate age, the order of Lord and Vassal was destroyed until Supreme Heaven by Our hands put to death the traitors. Now, from this time forward, both parties shedding their heart's blood, the Lord will not tolerate double methods of government, and the Vassal will avoid duplicity in his service of the sovereign! On him who breaks this oath, Heaven will send a curse and earth a plague, demons will slay them, and men will kill them. This is as manifest as the sun and moon."

REGULATION OF THE PROVINCES

8th month, 5th day.

Governors of the Eastern provinces were appointed. Then the Governors were addressed as follows:

"In accordance with the charge entrusted to Us by the Gods of Heaven, We propose at the present for the first time to regulate the myriad provinces.

When you proceed to your posts, prepare registers of all the free subjects of the State and of the people under the control of others, whether great or small. Take account also of the acreage of cultivated land. As to the profits arising from the gardens and ponds, the water and land, deal with them in common with the people.

In addition, it is not right for the provincial Governors, while in their provinces, to decide criminal cases, nor are they permitted by accepting bribes to bring the people to poverty and misery. When they come up to the capital they must not bring large numbers of the people in their train. They are only allowed to bring with them the Kuni no Miyakko and the district officials. But when they travel on public business they may ride the horses of their department and eat the food of their department. From the rank of Suke upwards, those who obey this law will surely be rewarded, while those who disobey it shall be liable to be reduced in rank. From the rank of Hangwan downwards, all those who accept bribes shall be fined double the amount of the bribe, and they shall eventually be criminally punished according to the greater or less severity of the case.

Nine men are allowed as attendants on a Chief Governor, seven on an assistant, and five on a secretary. If this limit is exceeded, and they are accompanied by a greater number, both chief and followers shall be criminally punished...

In addition, on waste pieces of ground let arsenals be erected, and let the swords and armour, with the bows and arrows of the provinces and districts, be deposited together in them. In the case of the frontier provinces which border close on the Yemishi, let all the weapons be gathered together, and let them remain in the hands of their original owners. In regard to the six districts of the province of Yamato, let the officials who are sent there prepare registers of the population, and also take an account of the acreage of cultivated land. This means to examine the acreage of the cultivated ground, and the numbers, houses, and ages of the people.

You Governors of provinces, take careful note of this and withdraw..."

COMPLAINTS AND BIRTH

The Emperor issued an order, saying:

"If there be a complainant, in case the person in question belongs to a Tomo no Miyakko, let the Tomo no Miyakko first make inquiry and then report to Us. In case the person in question has an elder, let the elder first make inquiry and then report to Us. If, however, the Tomo no Miyakko or the elder does not come to a clear decision respecting the complaint, let a document be received and placed in the box, and punishment will be inflicted according to the offence. The person who receives the document should at dawn take it and make report to the Inner Palace, when We will mark on it the year and month, and communicate it to the Ministers. In case there is any neglect to decide it, or if there are malpractices on the part of intriguing persons, let the complainant strike the bell. This is why the bell is hung and box provided in the Court. Let the people of the Empire know and appreciate Our intention.

Moreover, the law of men and women shall be that the children born of a free man and a free woman shall belong to the father: if a free man takes to wife a slave woman, her children shall belong to the mother; if a free woman marries a slave man, the children of the marriage shall belong to the father; if they are slaves of two houses, the children shall belong to the mother. The children of temple serfs shall follow the rule for freemen. But in regard to others who become slaves, they shall be treated according to the rule for slaves. Publish this well to the people as a beginning of regulations."

BUDDHISM

8th day.

A messenger was sent to the Great Temple to summon together the Buddhist priests and nuns, and to address them on the part of the Emperor, saying,

"In the 13th year of the reign of the Emperor who ruled the world in the Palace of Shikishima, King Myong of Pekche reverently transmitted the Law of Buddha to our great Yamato. At this time the Ministers in a body were opposed to its transmission. Only Soga no Iname no Sukune believed in this Law, and the Emperor accordingly instructed him to receive it with reverence. In the reign of the Emperor who ruled the world in the Palace of Wosada, Soga no Mumako no Sukune, influenced by reverence for his deceased father, continued to prize highly the doctrines of Buddha. But the other Ministers had no faith in it, and its institutes had almost perished when the Emperor instructed Mumako no

Sukune reverently to receive this Law. In the reign of the Empress who ruled the world in the Palace of Woharida, Mumako no Sukune, on behalf of the Empress, made an embroidered figure of Buddha sixteen feet high and a copper image of Buddha sixteen feet high. He exalted the doctrine of Buddha and showed honour to its priests and nuns. It is Our desire to exalt the pure doctrine and brilliantly to promulgate great principles. We therefore appoint as professors the following ten persons: The S'ramana, Poknyang, Hye-un, Syang-an, Nyong-un, and Hye-chi, Taih-shi of Koma, and Subin, Doto, Yerin, Yemyo and Yeon, chief priests of temples. We separately appoint the Hoshi, Yemyo, chief priest of the Temple of Kudara.

Let these ten professors well instruct the priests in general in the practice of the teachings of Shaka. It is needful that they be made to comply with the Law. If there is a difficulty about repairing Temples built by any from the Emperor down to the Tomo no Miyakko, We will in all cases assist in doing so. We shall also cause Temple Commissioners and Chief Priests to be appointed, who shall make a circuit to all the temples, and having ascertained the actual facts respecting the priests and nuns, their male and female slaves, and the acreage of their cultivated lands, report all the particulars clearly to us."

CORRUPTION OF REGIONAL OFFICIALS

19th day

Commissioners were sent to all the provinces to take a record of the total numbers of the people. The Emperor on this occasion made an edict, as follows:

"In the times of all the Emperors, from antiquity downwards, subjects have been set apart for the purpose of making notable their reigns and handing down their names to posterity. Now the Omi and Muraji, the Tomo no Miyakko and the Kuni no Miyakko, have each one set apart their own vassals, whom they compel to labor at their arbitrary pleasure. Moreover, they cut off the hills and seas, the woods and plains, the ponds and rice-fields belonging to the provinces and districts, and appropriate them to themselves. Their contests are never ceasing. Some engross to themselves many tens of thousands of shiro of rice land, while others possess in all patches of ground too small to stick a needle into. When the time comes for the payment of taxes, the Omi, the Muraji, and the Tomo no Miyakko, first collect them for themselves and then hand over a share. In the case of repairs to palaces or the construction of misasagi, they each bring their own vassals, and do the work according to circumstances. The Book of Changes says, 'Diminish that which is above: increase that which is below: if measures are framed according to the regulations, the resources of the State suffer no injury, and the people receive no hurt.'

"At the present time, the people are still few. And yet the powerful cut off portions of land and water, and converting them into private ground, sell it to the people, demanding the price yearly. From this time forward the sale of land is not allowed. Let no man without due authority make himself a landlord, engrossing to himself that which belongs to the helpless."

The people rejoiced.

REGULATION OF THE CAPITAL; TAXES; WOMEN

A.D. 646. 2nd year, Spring, 1st month, 1st day.

As soon as the ceremonies of the new years congratulations were over, the Emperor promulgated an edict of reforms, as follows:

"I. Let the people established by the ancient Emperors, etc., as representatives of children be abolished, also the Miyake of various places and the people owned as serfs by the Wake, the Omi, the Muraji, the Tomo no Miyakko, the Kuni no Miyakko and the Mura no Obito. Let the farmsteads in various places be abolished."

Consequently fiefs were granted for their sustenance to those of the rank of Daibu and upwards on a descending scale. Presents of cloth and silk stuffs were given to the officials and people, varying in value.

"Further We say. It is the business of the Daibu to govern the people. If they discharge this duty thoroughly, the people have trust in them, and an increase of their revenue is therefore for the good of the people.

II. The capital is for the first time to be regulated, and Governors appointed for the Home provinces and districts. Let barriers, outposts, guards, and post-horses, both special and ordinary, be provided, bell-tokens made, and mountains and rivers regulated.

For each ward in the capital let there be appointed one alderman, and for four wards one chief alderman, who shall be charged with the superintendence of the population, and the examination of criminal matters. For appointment as chief aldermen of wards let men be taken belonging to the wards, of unblemished character, firm and upright, so that they may fitly sustain the duties of the time. For appointments as aldermen, whether of rural townships or of city wards, let ordinary subjects be taken belonging to the township or ward, of good character and solid capacity. If such men are not to be found in the township or ward in question, it is permitted to select and employ men of the adjoining township or ward.

The Home provinces shall include the region from the River Yokogaha at Nabari on the east, from Mount Senoyama in Kii on the south, from Kushibuchi in Akashi on the west, and from Mount Afusakayama in Sasanami in Afumi on the north. Districts of forty townships are constituted Greater Districts, of from thirty to four townships are constituted Middle Districts, and of three or fewer townships are constituted Lesser Districts. For the district authorities, of whatever class, let there be taken Kuni no Miyakko of unblemished character, such as may fitly sustain the duties of the time, and made Tairei and Shorei. Let men of solid capacity and intelligence who are skilled in writing and arithmetic be appointed assistants and clerks.

The number of special or ordinary post-horses given shall in all cases follow the number of marks on the posting bell-tokens. When bell-tokens are given to (officials of) the provinces and barriers, let them be held in both cases by the chief official, or in his absence by the assistant official.

III. Let there now be provided for the first time registers of population, books of account and a system of the receipt and re-granting of distribution-land.

Let every fifty houses be reckoned a township, and in every township let there be one alderman who shall be charged with the superintendence of the registers of population, the direction of the sowing of crops and the cultivation of mulberry trees, the prevention and examination of offences, and the enforcement of the payment of taxes and of forced labor.

For rice-land, thirty paces in length by twelve paces in breadth shall be reckoned a tan. Ten tan make one cho. For each tan the tax is two sheaves and two bundles (such as can be grasped in the hand) of rice; for each cho the tax is twenty-two sheaves of rice. On mountains or in valleys where the land is precipitous, or in remote places where the population is scanty, such arrangements are to be made as may be convenient.

IV. The old taxes and forced labor are abolished, and a system of commuted taxes instituted. These shall consist of fine silks, coarse silks, raw silk, and floss silk, all in accordance with what is produced in the locality. For each cho of rice land the rate is ten feet of fine silk, or for four cho one piece forty feet in length by two and a half feet in width. For coarse silk the rate is twenty feet (per cho), or one piece for every two cho of the same length and width as the fine silk. For cloth the rate is forty feet of the same dimensions as the fine and coarse silk, i.e. one tan for each cho. Let there be levied separately a commuted house tax. All houses shall pay each twelve feet of cloth. The extra articles of this tax, as well as salt and offerings, will depend on what is produced in the locality.

For horses for the public service, let every hundred houses contribute one horse of medium quality. Or if the horse is of superior quality, let one be contributed by every two hundred houses. If the horses have to be purchased, the price shall be made up by a payment from each house of twelve feet of cloth.

As to weapons, each person shall contribute a sword, armour, bow and arrows, a flag, and a drum.

For servants, the old system, by which one servant was provided by every thirty houses, is altered, and one servant is to be furnished from every fifty houses [one is for employment as a menial servant] for allotment to the various functionaries. Fifty houses shall be allotted to provide rations for one servant, and one house shall contribute twenty-two feet of cloth and five masu of rice in lieu of service.

For waiting-women in the Palace, let there be furnished the sisters or daughters of district officials of the rank of Shorei or upwards—good-looking women [with one male and two female servants to attend on them], and let 100 houses be allotted to provide rations for one waiting-woman. The cloth and rice supplied in lieu of service shall, in every case, follow the same rule as for servants."

COMPLAINTS AND JUSTICE

2nd month, 1st day.

The Emperor proceeded to the Eastern Gate of the Palace, where, by Soga, Oho-omi of the Right, he decreed as follows:

"The God Incarnate, the Emperor Yamato-neko, who rules the world, gives command to the Ministers assembled in his presence, to the Omi, Muraji, Kuni no Miyakko, Tomo no Miyakko, and subjects of various classes, saying, 'We are informed that wise rulers of the people hung a bell at their gate, and so took cognizance of the complaints of their subjects; they erected buildings in the thoroughfares, where they listened to the censures of the passers-by. Even the opinions of the grass and firewood gatherers they inquired personally and used for their guidance. We therefore, on a former occasion, made an edict, saying: "In ancient times the Empire was ruled by having at the Court flags of honour for the encouragement of good, and a board of censure, the object being to diffuse principles of Government and to invite remonstrances." All this served widely to ascertain the opinions of those below...

The object of hanging up a bell, of providing a box, and of appointing a man to receive petitions, is to make those who have grievances or remonstrances deposit their petitions in the box. The receivers of petitions are commanded to make their report to Us every morning. When We receive this report We shall draw the attention of the Ministers to it, and cause them to consider it, and We trust that this may be done without delay. But if there should be neglect on the part of the Ministers, and a want of diligence or partisan intrigues, and if We, moreover, should refuse to listen to remonstrance, let the complainant strike the bell. There has been already an Imperial command to this effect. But some time afterwards there was a man of intelligence and uprightness who, cherishing in his heart the spirit of a national patriot, addressed Us a memorial of earnest remonstrance, which he placed in the box prepared for the purpose. We therefore now publish it to the black-haired people here assembled. This memorial runs as follows: "Those subjects who come to the capital in connection with the discharge of their duty to the Government of the Country, are detained by the various public functionaries and put to forced labor of various kinds, etc." We are still moved with strong sympathy by this. How could the people expect that things would come to this? Now no long time has elapsed since the capital was removed, so that so far from being at home, we are, as it were, strangers. It is therefore impossible to avoid employing the people, and they have therefore been, against Our will, compelled to labor. As often as

Our minds dwell on this We have never been able to sleep in peace. When We saw this memorial we could not refrain from a joyous exclamation. We have accordingly complied with the language of remonstrance, and have put a stop to the forced services at various places.

In a former edict, we said, "Let the man who remonstrates sign his name." Those who disobey this injunction are doubtless actuated by a wish to serve their country, and not by a desire of personal gain. Whether a man signs his name or not, let him not fail to remonstrate with Us on Our neglect or forgetfulness."

CENTRALIZED GOVERNMENT AND SOCIAL RULES

20th day.

The Prince Imperial said,

"In Heaven there are not two suns: in a country there are not two rulers. It is therefore the Emperor alone who is supreme over all the Empire, and who has a right to the services of the myriad people.

22nd day.

The Emperor made a decree, as follows,

"We are informed that a Prince of the Western Land admonished his people, saying, 'Those who made interments in ancient times resorted to a high ground which they formed into a tomb. They did not pile up a mound, nor did they plant trees. The inner and outer coffin were merely enough to last till the bones decayed, the shroud was merely sufficient to last till the flesh decayed... Deposit not in them gold or silver or copper or iron, and let earthenware objects alone represent the clay chariots and straw figures of antiquity. Let the interstices of the coffin be varnished. Let the offerings consist of rice presented three times, and let not pearls or jewels be placed in the mouth of the deceased. Bestow not jewel-shirts or jade armour. All these things are practices of the unenlightened vulgar...' Of late, the poverty of our people is absolutely owing to the construction of tombs...

When a man dies, there have been cases of people sacrificing themselves by strangulation, or of strangling others by way of sacrifice, or of compelling the dead man's horse to be sacrificed, or of burying valuables in the grave in honour of the dead, or of cutting off the hair, and stabbing the thighs and pronouncing an eulogy on the dead (while in this condition). Let all such old customs be entirely discontinued.

A certain book says, 'No gold or silver, no silk brocades, and no coloured stuffs are to be buried.' Again it is said, 'From the Ministers of all ranks down to the common people, it is not allowed to use gold or silver...'

Again, there are many cases of persons who, having seen, say that they have not seen, or who, having not seen, say that they have seen, or who, having heard, say that they have not heard, or who, having not heard, say that they have heard, being deliberate liars, and devoid of truth in words and in sight.

Again, there have been many cases in which slaves, both male and female, false to their masters in their poverty, betake themselves of their own accord to influential houses in quest of a livelihood, which influential houses forcibly detain and purchase them, and do not send them to their original owners.

Again, there have been very many cases in which wives or concubines, when dismissed by their husbands, have, after the lapse of years, married other husbands, as ordinary morality allows. Then their former husbands, after three or four years, have made greedy demands on the second husband's property, seeking their own gain.

Again, there have been very many cases in which men, relying on their power, have rudely demanded people's daughters in marriage. In the interval, however, before going to his house, the girl has, of her own accord, married another, and the rude suitor has angrily made demands of the property of both families for his own gain.

Again, there have been numerous cases of this kind. Sometimes a wife who has lost her husband marries another man after the lapse of ten or twenty years and becomes his spouse, or an unmarried girl is married for the first time. Upon this, people, out of envy of the married pair, have made them perform purgation.

Again, there are cases in which women, who have become men's wives and who, being put away owing to their husbands' dislike of them, have, in their mortification at this injury, compelled themselves to become blemished slaves.

Again, there are cases in which the husband, having frequent occasion to be jealous of his wife's illicit intercourse with others, voluntarily appeals to the authorities to decide the matter. Let such persons not lay their information until they have obtained, let us say, three credible witnesses to join with them in making a declaration. Why should they bring forward ill-considered plaints?

Again, there have been cases of men employed on forced labour in border lands who, when the work was over and they were returning to their village, have fallen suddenly ill and lain down to die by the roadside. Upon this the (inmates of the) houses by the roadside say, 'Why should people be allowed to die on our road?' And they have accordingly detained the companions of the deceased and compelled them to do purgation. For this reason it often happens that even if an elder brother lies down and dies on the road, his younger brother will refuse to take up his body (for burial).

Again, there are cases of peasants being drowned in a river. The bystanders say, 'Why should we be made to have anything to do with drowned men?' They accordingly detain the drowned man's companions and compel them to do purgation. For this reason it often happens that even when an elder brother is drowned in a river his younger brother will not render assistance.

Again, there are cases of people who, when employed on forced labor, cook their rice by the roadside. Upon this the (inmates of the) houses by the roadside say, 'Why should people cook rice at their own pleasure on our road?' and have compelled them to do purgation.

Again, there are cases when people have applied to others for the loan of pots in which to boil their rice, and the pots have knocked against something and have been upset. Upon this the owner of the pot compels purgation to be made.

All such practices are habitual among the unenlightened vulgar. Let them now be discontinued without exception, and not permitted again...

THE ROLE OF THE EMPEROR

Autumn, 8th month, 14th day.
An edict was issued, saying,

"Going back to the origin of things, we find that it is Heaven and Earth with the male and female principles of nature, which guard the four seasons from mutual confusion. We find, more over, that it is this Heaven and earth which produces the ten thousand things. Amongst these ten thousand things Man is the most miraculously gifted. Among the most miraculously gifted beings, the sage takes the position of ruler. Therefore the Sage Rulers, that is, the Emperors, take Heaven as their model in ruling the World, and never for a moment dismiss from their breasts the thought of how men shall gain their fit place..."

THE MONARCHY AND THE PEOPLE

Summer, 4th month, 29th day.
An edict was issued as follows,

"The Empire was entrusted (by the Sun-Goddess to her descendants, with the words) 'My children, in their capacity as Deities, shall rule it.' For this reason, this country, since Heaven and Earth began, has been a monarchy. From the time that Our Imperial ancestor first ruled the land, there has been great concord in the Empire, and there has never been any factiousness. In recent times, however, the names, first of the Gods, and then of the Emperors, have in some cases been separated (from their proper application) and converted into the Uji of Omi or Muraji, or they have been separated and made the qualifications of Miyakko, etc. In consequence of this, the minds of the people of the whole country take a strong partisan bias, and conceiving a deep sense of the "me" and "you," hold firmly each to their names. Moreover the feeble and incompetent Omi, Muraji, Tomo no Miyakko and Kuni no Miyakko make of such names their family names; and so the names of Gods and the names of sovereigns are applied to persons and places in an unauthorized manner, in accordance with the bent of their own feelings. Now, by using the names of Gods and the names of sovereigns as bribes, they draw to themselves the slaves of others, and so bring dishonor upon unspotted names.

The consequence is that the minds of the people have become unsettled and the government of the country cannot be carried on. The duty has therefore now devolved on Us in Our capacity as Celestial Divinity, to regulate and settle these things. In order to make them understood, and thereby to order the State and to order the people, we shall issue, one after another, a succession of edicts, one earlier, another later, one to-day and another to-morrow. But the people, who have always trusted in the civilizing influence exercised by the Emperors, and who are used to old customs, will certainly find it hard to wait until these edicts are made. We shall therefore remit to all, from Princes and Ministers down to the common people of all classes, the tax in lieu of service."

Abi Yaqubi, excerpt from *Tarikh*

Abi Yaqubi was a ninth-century Arab scholar who wrote the Tarikh *or History of the Countries in 891. He followed the Arabic tradition, which continued throughout the Middle Ages, of producing detailed geographic, political, and historical descriptions of the vast areas of Eurasia touched by Islam. These geographies often also included other areas in contact with the Islamic World, including China, Europe, and Africa.*

Source: *Levtzion, N. and J.P.F. Hopkins.* Corpus of Early Arabic Sources for West African History. *(London: Cambridge University Press, 1981) pp. 20–21.*

> **Focus Questions:**
> 1. What are the religious elements involved in the description?
> 2. What types of cultures are described?
> 3. What products are available?

ARABIC TRAVELER REPORTS ON THE RAGHAWA (329)

When Nuh awoke from his sleep and learnt what had happened he cursed Kan'an b. Ham but he did not curse Ham. Of his posterity are the Qibt, the Habasha, and the Hind. Kan'an was the first of the sons of Nub to revert to the ways of the sons of Qabil (Cain) and indulged in distractions and singing and made flutes (mizmar) and drums and guitars (barbat) and cymbals (sanj) and obeyed Satan in vain amusements.

Nub divided the earth between his sons, assigning to Sam the middle of the earth…and to Ham the land of the west and the coasts (sawābil). The posterity of Kush b. Ham and Kan'an b. Ham are the Nuba, the Zanj, and the Habasha.

THE KINGDOMS OF THE HABASHA AND THE SUDAN

When the progeny of Nub dispersed from the country of Babil (Babylon) the descendants of Ham son of Nub went to the west, and crossed the Furat (Euphrates) towards the setting sun.

After they had crossed the Nile of Egypt the descendants of Kush son of Ham, namely the Habasha and the Sudan, split into two groups. One of these groups proceeded to the south, between the east and the west. These were the Nuba, Buja, Habasha and Zanj. The other group went to the west. These were the Zaghawa, HBSH, Qaqu, Marawiyyun, Maranda, Kawkaw and Ghana.

The Sudan who went to the west traversed several countries and created several kingdoms. The first of their kingdoms is that of the Zaghawa who live in the place called Kanim. Their dwellings are huts made of reeds and they have no towns. Their king is called KAKRH. Among the Zaghawa is a group called al-HWDN who have a king who is from among the Zaghawa. Then [there is] another kingdom [of a people] called Malal, who hate the king of Kānim. Their king is called MYWSY. Then there is the kingdom of al-HBshH, who have a town called ThBYR. The king of this town is called MRH. Adjacent to them are the Qaqu, but they are not independent and their ruler is the king of ThBYR.

Then there is the kingdom of the Kawkaw, which is the greatest of the realms of the Sudan, the most important and powerful. All the kingdoms obey its king. Al-Kawkaw is the name of the town. Besides this there are a number of kingdoms of which the rulers pay allegiance to him and acknowledge his sovereignty, although they are kings in their own lands. Among them is the kingdom of al-MRW, which is an extensive realm. Its king has a town called al-HYA. Also, the kingdom of MuRDBH, the kingdom of al-HRBR, the kingdom of Sanhaja, the kingdom of TDhKRYR, the kingdom of the Zayanir, the kingdom of 'RWR and the kingdom of BQARWT. All these are assigned to the kingdom of the Kawkaw.

Then there is the kingdom of Ghana, whose king is also very powerful. In his country are the gold mines, and under his authority are a number of kings. Among them are the kingdom of 'AM and the kingdom of Sama. Gold is found in the whole of this country.

Selection from *Nihongi,* "The Age of the Gods"

This Japanese chronicle was written around 720 CE in Chinese characters. It describes the ancient age of the gods and the creation of the Japanese imperial line, culminating in the God emperor Jimmu. The chronicle progresses to the historical imperial line, providing especially detailed information on the reigns of emperors between 626 and 702. The Nihongi chronicle was based on traditional Japanese legends but polished and refined by the new Chinese scholarship; in the century preceding, Japan had been transformed through adoption of Buddhist and Chinese ideas and systems.

Source: *Aston, W.G.* Nihongi: Chronicles of Japan from Earliest Times to AD 697. *(London: Kegan Paul, Trench, Trubner & Co., 1896) pp. 19–25.*

Focus Questions:
1. What do the references to natural processes and bodily functions tell us about society?
2. What was the fate of the leech child, and why did it befall him?
3. What other myths are similar to Nihongi? Why?

Their next child was Sosa no wo no Mikoto.[1]

Called in one Writing Kami Sosa no Wo no Mikoto or

Haya Sosa no wo no Mikoto.[2]

This God had a fierce temper and was given to cruel acts. Moreover he made a practice of continually weeping and wailing. So he brought many of the people of the land to an untimely end. Again he caused green mountains to become withered. Therefore the two Gods, his parents, addressed[3] Sosa no wo no Mikoto, saying:—"Thou art exceedingly wicked, and it is not meet that thou shouldst reign over the world. Certainly thou must depart far away to the Nether-Land."[4] So they at length expelled him.

> In one writing it is said:—"Izanagi no Mikoto said: I wish to procreate the precious child Who is to rule the world.' He therefore took in his left hand a White-copper mirror,[5] upon which a Deity was produced from it called Oho-hiru-me no Mikoto. In his right hand he took a white-copper mirror, and forthwith there was produced from it a God who was named Tsuki-yumi no Mikoto. Again, while turning his head and looking askance, a God was produced who was named Sosa no Wo no Mikoto. Now Oho-hirume no Mikoto and Tsuki-yumi no Mikoto were both of a bright and beautiful nature, and were therefore made to shine down upon Heaven and Earth. But Sosa no Wo's character was to love destruction, and he was accordingly sent down to rule the Nether Land."

> In one writing it is said:—"After the sun and moon, the next, child which was born was the leech-child. When this child had completed his third year, he was nevertheless still unable to stand upright. The reason why the leech-child was born was that in the beginning, when Izanagi no Mikoto and Izanami no Mikoto Went round the pillar, the female Deity was the first to utter an exclamation of pleasure, and the law of male and female was therefore broken. They next procreated Sosa no wo no Mikoto. This God was of a wicked nature, and was always fond of wailing and wrath. Many of the people of the land died, and the green moun-

---

[1] This name is written indifferently Sosa no wo and Susa no wo. The accepted derivation refers Susa to Susamu, a verb which means "to be impetuous." Hence the "Impetuous Male" of Chamberlain's and Satow's translations. I am disposed to prefer a derivation suggested by the "Idzumo Fudoki," a very old book, which states:

"Village of Susa. Nineteen ri due west to the Town-house of the district. Kamu-Ssua no wo no Mikotyo said:–'This is only a small country, but it is a Kuni-dokoro (local capital?). Therefore my name shall not be affixed to wood or stone.' This was accordingly the place where he allowed his august spirit to repose. There were, therefore, established by him the Greater Susa rice-lands and the Lesser Susa rice-lands.

Susa no wo is therefore simply the "male of Susa." It will be remembered that by one Japanese tradition, Idzumo is the home of the Gods, and that several of the legends respecting them relate to this locality. It is, however, probable that the older derivation is really a volks-etymologie, which has given colour to the stories told of this deity. Idzumo is a chief home of the worship of Susa no wo at the present day. His wife's mother is called Susa no Yatsu-mimi, but it has not occurred to anybody to make her an "impetuous female." Hirata rejects the modern identification of this God with Godzu Tenno.

[2] Kami, deity; haya, quik.

[3] The character used is that appropriate to a sovereign addressing his subjects.

[4] Ne no kuni, lit. the root-country, by which Hades or Yomi is no doubt meant.

[5] See Index–Copper.

tains withered. Therefore his parents addressed him, saying: "Supposing that thou wert to rule this country, much destruction of life would surely ensue. Thou must govern the far-distant Nether Land.' Their next child was the bird-rock-camphor-wood boat of Heaven. They forthwith took this boat and, placing the leech-child in it, abandoned it to the current. Their next child was Kagu tsuchi."[6]

Now Izanami no Mikoto was burnt by Kagu tsuchi so that she died.[7] When she was lying down to die, she gave birth to the Earth-Goddess, Hani-yama-hime,[8] and the Water-Goddess, Midzu-ha-no-me. Upon this Kagu tsuchi took to Wife Hani-yama-hime, and they had a child named Waka-musubi.[9] On the crown of this Deity's head were produced the silkworm and the mulberry tree, and in her navel the five kinds of grain.[10]

In one writing it is said:—"When Izanami no Mikoto gave birth to Ho-no-musubi,[11] she was burnt by the child, and died.[12] When she was about to die, she brought forth the Water-Goddess, Midzu-ha-no-me, and the Earth-Goddess, Hani-yama-hime. She also brought forth the gourd[13] of Heaven."

In one writing it is said:—"When about to give birth to the Fire-God, Kagu tsuchi, Izanami no Mikoto became feverish and ill. In consequence she vomited, and the vomit became changed into a God, who was called Kana-yama-hiko.[14] Next her urine became changed into a Goddess, who was called Midzu-ha-no-me. Next her excrement was changed into a Goddess, who was called Hani-yama-hime."

In one writing it is said:—"When Izanami no Mikoto gave birth to the Fire-God, she was burnt, and died. She was, therefore, buried at the village of Arima in Kumano, in the province of Kut. In the time of flowers, the inhabitants worship the spirit of this Goddess by offerings of flowers. They also worship her with drums, flutes, flags, singing and dancing."

In one Writing it is said:—"Izanagi no Mikoto and Izanami no Mikoto, having together procreated the Great-eight-island Land, Izanagi no Mikoto said: "Over the country which we have produced there is naught but morning mists which shed a perfume everywhere!' So he puffed them away with a breath, which became changed into a God, named Shina[15] tohe no Mikoto. He is also called Shina tsu hiko no Mikoto. This is the God of the Wind. Moreover, the child which they procreated when they were hungry was called Uka no mi-tama[16] no Mikoto. Again they produced the Sea-Gods, who were called Wata[17] tsu mi no Mikoto, and the Mountain-Gods, Who Were called Yama tsu mi, the Gods of the River-mouths, who were called Haya-aki-[18] tsubi no Mikoto, the Tree-Gods, who were called Ku-ku no chi, and the Earth-Goddess,

---

[6] Kago tsuchi was the God of Fire. Tsu is here probably the genetive particle, and chi that same honorific word as appears in several other names of Gods. He was worshipped at Nagusa in Kii.

[7] Lit. ended.

[8] Clay-mountain-lady.

[9] Young-growth.

[10] Hemp, millet, rice, corn, pulse. This is a Chinese form of speech, and with the mention of the silkworm betrays a recent origin of this tradition.

[11] Fire-growth.

[12] Lit. retired.

[13] The gourd was to hold water to subdue the Fire-God with when he became violent.

[14] Metal-mountain prince. This legend indicates an acquaintance with mining.

[15] Shina is said to be derived from shi, wind or breath, and na, a short form of naga, long. See Chamberlain's "Kojiki," p. 27. The worship of this God is frequently referred to in the last two books of the Nihongi. See also Satow's "Ancient Japanese Rituals," where a prayer to him is given. Tohe means chief.

[16] Food august-spirit. The Chinese characters transliterated Uka mean storehouse rice.

[17] Wata is an old word for sea; mi is probably "body."

[18] Haya-aki means swift-autumn; tsu, of, and bi (or mi) perhaps person or body.

who Was called Hani-yasuno[19] Kami. Thereafter they produced all manner of things whatsoever. When the time came for the Fire-God Kagu tsuchi to be born, his mother Izanami no Mikoto Was burnt, and suffered change and departed[20]. Then Izanagi no Mikoto was wroth, and said: Oh, that I should have given my beloved younger sister[21] in exchange for a single child! So while he crawled at her head, and crawled at her feet, weeping and lamenting, the tears which he shed fell down and became a Deity. It is this Deity who dwells at Unewo no Konomoto, and who is called Naki-saha-me[22] no Mikoto. At length he drew the ten-span sword with which he was girt, and cut Kagu tsuchi into three pieces, each of which became changed into a God. Moreover, the blood which dripped from the edge of the sword[23] became the multitudinous[24] rocks which are in the bed of the Easy-River[25] of Heaven. This God was the father of Futsu-nushi no Kami. Moreover, the blood which dripped from the hilt-ring of the sword spurted out and became deities, whose names Were Mika no Haya-hi[26] no Kami and next Hi no Haya-hi no[27] Kami. This Mika no Haya-hi no Kami was the parent of Take-mika-suchi[28] no Kami."

Another version is:—"Mika no haya-hi no Mikoto, next Hi no haya-hi no Mikoto, and next Take-Mika-tsuchi no Kami."

"Moreover, the blood which dripped from the point of the sword spurted out and became deities, who were called Iha-sakuno Kami[29], after him Ne-saku no Kami,[30] and next Iha-tsut-su-wo[31] no Mikoto. This Iha-saku no Kami was the father of Futsu-nushi[32] no Kami."

One account says:—"Iha-tsutsu-Wo no Mikoto, and next Iha-tsutsu-me no Mikoto."

"Moreover, the blood which dripped from the head of the sword spurted out and became deities, who were called Kura o Kami no Kami,[33] next Kurayamatsumi no Kami,[34] and next Kura-midzu-ha no Kami."[35]

Thereafter, Izanagi no Mikoto went after Izanami no Mikoto, and entered the land of Yomi.[36] When he reached her they conversed together, and Izanami no Mikoto said : My lord and husband, why is thy coming so late? I have already eaten of the cooking-furnace of Yomi.[37]

---

[19] Clay-easy.

[20] i.e. died.

[21] The ancient Japanese word for younger sister was imo, which is also applied to a wife. It may be doubted whether this justifies any adverse inference as to the morals of the Japanese in early times. "Sister" is used as an endearing epithet in the Song of Solomon where the relation is certainly not that of brother and sister. It is true, however, that marriages were allowed between brothers and sisters when of different mothers.

[22] Weep-abundant-female.

[23] Cf. Ch. "Kojiki," p. 32.

[24] Literally, five hundred.

[25] i.e. The Milky Way. Yasu, easy, is probably in error for sa-so, eighty, i.e. manifold, having many reaches.

[26] Jar-swift-sun. So written, but mika is probably a word meaning very or mighty.

[27] Fire-swift-sun. See Ch. "Kojiki," p. 32.

[28] Brave-jar-father.

[29] Rock-splitting-god.

[30] Root-splitting-god.

[31] Rock-elder-male-god.

[32] Futsu is interpreted as "a snapping sound"; nushi is master.

[33] Dark-god.

[34] Dark-mountain-body-god.

[35] Dark-water-goddess.

[36] The original has "yellow springs," a Chinese expression. Yomi or Yomo is Hades. It is no doubt connected with yo or yoru, night.

Nevertheless; I am about to lie down to rest. I pray thee, do not thou look on me. Izanami no Mikoto did not give ear to her, but secretly took his many-toothed comb and, breaking off its end tooth,[38] made of it a torch, and looked at her. Putrefying matter had gushed up, and maggots swarmed. This is why people at the present day avoid using a single light at night, and also avoid throwing away a comb[39] at night. Izanagi no Mikoto was greatly shocked, and said: 'Nay! I have come unawares to a hideous and polluted land.' So he speedily ran away back again. Then Izanami no Mikoto was angry, and said: 'Why didn't thou not observe that which I charged thee? Now am I put to shame.' So she sent the eight Ugly Females of Yomi[40] (*Shikome, called by some Hisame*) to pursue and stay him. Izanagi no Mikoto therefore drew his sword, and, flourishing it behind him, ran away. Then he took his black head-dress and flung it down. It became changed into grapes, which the Ugly Females seeing, took and ate. When they had finished eating them, they again pursued Izanagi no Mikoto. Then he flung down his many-toothed comb, which forthwith became changed into bamboo-shoots. The Ugly Females pulled them up and ate them, and when they had done eating them, again gave chase. Afterwards, Izanami no Mikoto came herself and pursued him.[41] By this time Izanagi no Mikoto had reached the Even Pass of Yomi.

---

[37] This is a feature of many old-world and savage myths. In the legend of the rape of Proserpine by Pluto, as told by Ovid, Jupiter replies to Ceres, who demanded back her daughter–

> "...Repetat Proserpine caelum,
> Lege tamen certâ: si nullos contiget illic
> Ore cibos."

But Proserpine already–

> "Puniceum curva decerpserat arbore pomum
> Sumta que pallenti septem de cortice grana
> Presserat ore suo."

Compare also the story of Nachikétas from Taittiríya Brahmana, and Katha Upanishad:–

> "Three nights within his (Yama's) mansion stay,
> But taste not, though a guest, his food."

Muir's Sanskrit texts, Vol. V, p. 329

The resemblance of the name Yama of the Indian God of the Lower World to the Japanese Yomi has been noted, and also at some points of similarity in the myth of Yami and Yama to that of Izanagi and Izanami. See Lang, "Custom and Myth," p. 171.

[38] End-tooth is in Japanese wo-bashira, i.e. male-pillar, for which see above, note to p. 11.

[39] The "Adzuma Kagami," mentions a superstition that any one who picks up a comb which has been thrown away is transformed into another person.

[40] The "Wamiosho" mentions a statement that these were used as bogeys to frighten children with under the name of Gogo-me.

[41] The student of folklore will at once recognize this pursuit. Cf. Lang's "Custom and Myth," pp. 88 and 92: "A common incident is the throwing behind of a comb, which turns into a thicket."

Nineteenth-century European Descriptions of the Pacific Island of Lelu

Lelu island is connected to Kosrae Island by a causeway. Both form part of the Caroline Islands, an archipelago in the South Pacific, but several centuries ago Kosrae was itself a powerful kingdom. Between about 1200 and 1600 CE, Kosrae, with its capital on Lelu, peaked in size and wealth. Several thousand people dwelled within large walled compounds. The land was controlled by a king and twenty chiefs who divided their compounds amongst their followers into smaller compounds. When European explorers arrived at Kosrae and Lelu in the nineteenth century, they found a much smaller population within the walled compounds, but still found the structures and society quite impressive.

Source: *Cordy, R.* The Lelu Stone Ruins. *(Honolulu: Social Science Research Institute, 1993)*

Focus Questions:
1. What are the available resources?
2. What are the Kosraen attitudes towards property?
3. How does the size of the island affect matters?

THE CITY: GENERAL PHYSICAL DESCRIPTION

The following descriptions give one a general feel for the nature of the city.

1824
Ahead of us, in the midst of the waves, appeared the small island of Lelu, surrounded by the small houses of the islanders, and crowned by a hill of greenery, and at some distance from Lelu, two even smaller islands appeared, covered by beautiful dwellings. (Duperrey in D'Urville 1835, II: 458)

1824
As we approached the shores of Lelu, a new scene presented itself to us: beautiful houses enclosed by high walls, well-paved streets, and on the beach was gathered the entire population of Lelu, at least 800 people, who had come to be present at our disembarkation. (D'Urville 1835, II: 458)

1824
The streets were bordered by enormous walls. (D'Urville 1835, II: 460)

1824
We passed between the two islets of Yenyen and Yenasr, where are established the great fisheries, and we disembarked on the beach.(19) (D'Urville 1835, II: 461 on his departure from Lelu)

1824
We crossed many winding streets, bordered by wide coral stone walls and canals. We observed with total bewilderment a wall, composed of blocks, of truly cyclopean size, and we wondered how and why they had been able to erect such masses to a 15 foot height. The elegant houses of these islanders lined the streets on elevated mounds... (Lesson 1839, II; 480–81)

1824
Lesson also noted that Lelu spread along the bay with coconuts and houses along the shore. He mentioned mangroves and canals, "that are stagnant between the houses built on small mounds. (20) The residence of the chiefs and the king is found at the foot of a high hill." (Lesson 1839, II: 494)

1824

It is in this manner that the village of Lelu is divided into streets and quarters, while the periphery of the island of the same name is encircled by an enclosure of these high walls, built of fragments of very large coral, placed one on top of the other. (Lesson 1839, II: 496)

1824

This island of Lele is but a mile in length from east to west by two thirds of a mile in width. Its eastern part presents a rather high bleak cone: the rest is very flat, and probably would be invaded by the sea if the natives who had chosen this locality as their principal residence had not taken the precaution to raise the level of the soil to fifteen or twenty feet above sea level, and to envelop the entire island with a belt of walls, capable of offering an insurmountable dike against the periodic phenomena of the tides. (Duperrey 1828: 635; Ritter and Ritter 1981: 8)

1824

The village...is crossed, in different directions, by the canals which the canoes travel easily when the tide is high; and the walls which enclose these canals, like those which skirt the island, are built of fragments of basalt, of skillfully cut corals, placed without any cement one on top of the other. (Duperrey 1828: 635)

1827

After walking down a very muddy street, we arrived at his house, which was not distinguished in any way from the others. (This was the Tokosra's compound.) (Lutke 1835, I: 322)

1827

Lutke added that the whole shore, except where there were trees or cliffs, "is enclosed by a wall of stone" about 5 feet high. Also, "...to protect the house and the fields from the assault of the waves. The land belonging to the different chiefs are enclosed by similar walls. These reach a height of 3 fathoms [6 meters]." (Lutke 1835, I: 325)

1827

(Lutke also took "a walk along the street of the grand villas, or houses.") Several of our friends whose houses we happened to pass by, would come to us with coconuts and bananas, and would invite us to rest at their house. (Lutke 1835, I: 330)

1827

The island itself is very small, of longish shape, and formed one side of the spacious shallow enclosed by a coral reef...It is not however, as one should think, merely a coral island; rather it has a not inconsiderable height for its small circumference. The summit is beautifully wooded. All the rest appears covered with houses and gardens and has the appearance of a single town, whose elegant, sometimes imposingly high houses, together with the numerous coconut tree tops waving above, already granted an impressive view from afar, ...(Kittlitz 1858, II: 44-45; Ritter and Ritter 1981: 201-202)

1827

All living places here are surrounded by garden walls built of basalt blocks, ...Narrow, very muddy lanes, (muddy from frequent rains) pass between these walls, which like a labyrinth cover the greater part of the island; ...From within these wall-enclosed compounds loom the high, half-moon shaped, scalloped roofs with their graceful gables of thin poles woven together; the woodwork of these gables, especially on those buildings which serve the chiefs as dwellings, is painted red like the canoes with pleasing white decoration. Thus, a compound forms a miniature city, cut off from the rest of the world by walls. The number of these buildings erected within the small compounds, as well as the number of courtyards, is arranged according to the personal circumstances of the owner. (Kittlitz 1858, I II: 45)

Neston, *The Russian Primary Chronicle*

The primary chronicle is a twelfth-century CE compilation of various older annals and sagas of Norse, Slavic, and Byzantine origin. It documents the foundation of Kiev, supposedly by Norse travelers, and the spread of Christianity by Byzantine missionaries. In format and tone it is typical of many medieval monastic chronicles, and is very useful for determining Christian and Russian attitudes towards their local origins.

Source: *S.H. Cross and O.P Sherbowitz-Wetzor, trans.,* Nestor. The Russian Primary Chronicle, *(Cambridge, MA: The Medieval Academy of America, 1953) pp. 59–60.*

Focus Questions:
1. What is the chronicler's attitude towards the Slavs?
2. What is a more likely explanation for the arrival of the Rus?
3. How does Christianity fit into events?

6367 (859). The Varangians from beyond the sea imposed tribute upon the Cnuds, the Slavs, the Merians, the Ves', and the Krivichians. But the Khazars imposed it upon the Polyanians, the Severians, and the Vyatichians, and collected a white squirrel-skin from each hearth.

6368–6370 (860–862). The tributaries of the Varangians drove them back beyond the sea and, refusing them further tribute, set out to govern themselves. There was no law among them, but tribe rose against tribe. Discord thus ensued among them, and they began to war one against another. They said to themselves, "Let us seek a prince who may rule over us and judge us according to the Law." They accordingly went overseas to the Varangian Russes: these particular Varangians were known as Russes, just as some are called Swedes, and others Normans, English, and Gotlanders, for they were thus named. The Chuds, the Slavs, (20) the Krivichians, and the Ves' then said to the people of Rus', "Our land is great and rich, but there is no order in it. Come to rule and reign over us." They thus selected three brothers, with their kinsfolk, who took with them all the Russes and migrated. The oldest, Rurik, located himself in Novgorod; the second, Sineus, at Beloozero; and the third, Truvor, in Izborsk. On account of these Varangians, the district of Novgorod became known as the land of Rus'. The present inhabitants of Novgorod are descended from the Varangian race, but aforetime they were Slavs.

After two years, Sineus and his brother Truvor died, and Rurik assumed the sole authority. He assigned cities to his followers, Polotsk to one, Rostov to another, and to another Beloozero. In these cities there are thus Varangian colonists, but the first settlers were, in Novgorod, Slavs; in Polotsk, Krivichians; at Beloozero, Ves', in Rostov, Merians; and in Murom, Muromians. Rurik had dominion over all these districts.

With Rurik there were two men who did not belong to his kin, but were boyars. They obtained permission to go to Tsar'grad with their families. They thus sailed down the Dnieper, and in the course of their journey they saw a small city on a hill. Upon their inquiry as to whose town it was, they were informed that (21) three brothers, Kiy, Shchek, and Khoriv, had once built the city, but that since their deaths, their descendants were living there as tributaries of the Khazars. Askold and Dir remained in the city, and after gathering together many Varangians, they established their dominion over the country of the Polyanians at the same time that Rurik was ruling at Novgorod.

6371–6374 (863–866). Askold and Dir attacked the Greeks during the fourteenth year of the reign of the Emperor Michael. When the Emperor had set forth against the infidels and had arrived at the Black River, the eparch sent him word that the Russes were approaching Tsar'grad, and the Emperor turned back. Upon arriving inside the strait, the Russes made a great massacre of the Christian; and attacked Tsar'grad in two hundred boats. The Emperor succeeded with difficulty in entering the city. He straightway hastened with the Patriarch Photius to the Church of Our Lady of the Blachernae, where they prayed all night. They also sang hymns and carried the sacred vestment of the Virgin to dip it in the sea. The weather was still, and the sea was calm, but a storm of wind came up, and when great waves straightway rose, confusing the boats of the godless Russes, it threw them upon the shore (22) and broke them up, so that few escaped such destruction and returned to their native land.

Einhard, Preface to *The Life of Charlemagne*

The ninth-century biography of the Frankish emperor was written by a churchman named Einhard (c. 770–840 CE). Einhard received initial monastic training followed by advanced education at the palace school of Charlemagne, and he became an advisor to the emperor, benefiting through land grants and a good marriage to a bishop's sister. While Einhard based the biography on the classical life of the Roman emperor Augustus by Suetonius, he was able to reveal Charlemagne's personal side through his close connections to the emperor.

Source: *Samuel Epes Turner, trans.,* Einhard, The Life of Charlemagne *(New York: Harper & Brothers, 1880).*

> **Focus Questions:**
> 1. Why does Einhard provide so many classical allusions?
> 2. How is Charlemagne described?
> 3. Is Einhard a barbarian, as he describes himself?

EINHARD'S PREFACE

Since I have taken upon myself to narrate the public and private life, and no small part of the deeds, of my lord and foster-father, the most lent and most justly renowned King Charles, I have condensed the matter into as brief a form as possible. I have been careful not to omit any facts that could come to my knowledge, but at the same time not to offend by a prolix style those minds that despise everything modern, if one can possibly avoid offending by a new work men who seem to despise also the masterpieces of antiquity, the works of most learned and luminous writers. Very many of them, I have no doubt, are men devoted to a life of literary leisure, who feel that the affairs of the present generation ought not to be passed by, and who do not consider everything done today as unworthy of mention and deserving to be given over to silence and oblivion, but are nevertheless seduced by lust of immortality to celebrate the glorious deeds of other times by some sort of composition rather than to deprive posterity of the mention of their own names by not writing at all.

Be this as it may, I see no reason why I should refrain from entering upon a task of this kind, since no man can write with more accuracy than I of events that took place about me, and of facts concerning which I had personal knowledge, ocular demonstration as the saying goes, and I have no means of ascertaining whether or not any one else has the subject in hand.

In any event, I would rather commit my story to writing, and hand it down to posterity in partnership with others, so to speak, than to suffer the most glorious life of this most excellent king, the greatest of all the princes of his day, and his illustrious deeds, hard for men of later times to imitate, to be wrapped in the darkness of oblivion.

But there are still other reasons, neither unwarrantable nor insufficient, in my opinion, that urge me to write on this subject, namely, the care that King Charles bestowed upon me in my childhood, and my constant friendship with himself [sic] and his children after I took up my abode at court. In this way he strongly endeared me to himself, and made me greatly his debtor as well in death as in life, so that were I unmindful of the benefits conferred upon me, to keep silence concerning the most glorious and illustrious deeds of a man who claims so much at my hands, and suffer his life to lack due eulogy and written memorial, as if he had never lived, I should deservedly appear ungrateful, and be so considered, albeit my powers are feeble, scanty, next to nothing indeed, and not at all adapted to write and set forth a life that would tax the eloquence of a Tully [note: *Tully* is Marcus Tullius Cicero].

I submit the book. It contains the history of a very great and distinguished man; but there is nothing in it to wonder at besides his deeds, except the fact that I, who am a barbarian, and very little versed in the Roman language, seem to suppose myself capable of writing gracefully and respectably in Latin, and to carry my presumption so far as to disdain the sentiment that Cicero is said in the first book of the *Tusculan Disputations* to have expressed when speaking of the Latin authors. His words are: "It is an outrageous abuse both of time and literature for a man to commit his thoughts to writing without having the ability either to arrange them or elucidate them, or attract readers by some charm of style." This dictum of the famous orator might have deterred me from writing if I had not made up my mind that it was better to risk the opinions of the world, and put my little talents for composition to the test, than to slight the memory of so great a man for the sake of sparing myself.

Tang Daizong on *The Art of Government*

The Tang Dynasty (618–907 CE) was the high point of Chinese medieval civilization in terms of territory, wealth, technology, and a cultural golden age. In the following document, Tang Taizon, a founder of the Tang dynasty, set the tone for his new administration to his chosen officials. His emphasis on honesty and open communication contrast the single-minded and obsessive rule of the former Sui dynasty.

Source: Reprinted with the permission of Scribner, a Division of Simon & Schuster, Inc., from The Civilization of China, *translated by Dun J. Li. Copyright © 1975 by Dun J. Li.*

Focus Questions:
1. What mistakes did Sui Wendi make?
2. What were the responsibilities of Tang government officials?

TANG DAIZONG

Different people are bound to have different opinions; the important thing is that differences in opinion should not degenerate into personal antagonism. Sometimes to avoid the possibility of creating personal grievances or causing embarrassment to a colleague, an official might decide to go ahead with the implementation of a policy even though he knows that the policy is wrong. Let us remember that preservation of a colleague's prestige, or the avoidance of embarrassment to him, cannot be compared with the welfare of the nation in importance, and to place personal consideration above the well-being of the multitude will lead to defeat for the government as a whole. I want all of you to understand this point and act accordingly.

During the Sui dynasty, all officials, in the central as well as the local governments, adopted an attitude of conformity to the general trend in order to be amiable and agreeable with one another. The result was disaster as all of you well know. Most of them did not understand the importance of dissent and comforted themselves by saying that as long as they did not disagree, they could forestall harm to themselves that might otherwise cross their path. When the government, as well as their families, finally collapsed in a massive upheaval, they were severely but justifiably criticized by their contemporaries for their complacency and inertia, even if they themselves may have been fortunate enough to escape death through a combination of circumstances. This is the reason that I want all of you to place public welfare above private interest and hold steadfastly the principle of righteousness, so that all problems, whatever they are, will be resolved in such a way as to bring about a most beneficial result. Under no circumstances are you allowed to agree with one another for the sake of agreement.

As for Sui Wendi, I would say that he was politically inquisitive, but mentally closed. Being close-minded, he could not see truth even if it were spotlighted for him; being over inquisitive, he was suspicious even when there was no valid reason for his suspicion. He rose to power by trampling on the rights of orphans and widows and was consequently not so sure that he had the unanimous support of his own ministers. Being suspicious of his own ministers, he naturally did not trust them and had to make a decision on every matter himself. He became a hard worker out of necessity and, having overworked, could not make the right decision every time. Knowing the kind of man he was, all his ministers, including the prime minister, did not speak as candidly as they should have and unanimously uttered "Yes, sir" when they should have registered strong dissent.

I want all of you to know that I am different. The empire is large and its population enormous. There are thousands of matters to be taken care of, each of which has to be closely coordinated with the others in order to bring about maximum benefit. Each matter must be thoroughly investigated and thought out before a recommendation is submitted to the prime minister, who, having consulted all the men knowledgeable in this matter, will then present the commendation, modified if necessary, to the emperor for approval and implementation. It is impossible for one person, however intelligent and capable, to be able to make wise decisions by himself...

I want all of you to know that whenever an imperial decree is handed down you should carefully study its content and decide for yourselves whether all or part of it is or is not wise or feasible. If you have any reservations, postpone the enforcement and petition me immediately. You can do no less as my loyal ministers.

Governing a country is like taking care of a patient. The better the patient feels, the more he should be looked after, lest in a moment of complacency and neglect one irrevocably reverse the recovery process and send him to death. Likewise, when a country has only recently recovered from chaos and war, those responsible for running the country should be extremely diligent in their work, for false pride and self-indulgence will inevitably return the country to where it used to be and perhaps make it worse.

I realize that the safety of this nation relies to a great extent on what I can or may do and consequently I have not relaxed for a moment in doing the best I can. But I cannot do it alone. You gentlemen are my eyes and ears, legs and arms, and should do your best to assist me. If anything goes wrong anywhere in the empire, you should let me know immediately. If there is less than total trust between you and me and consequently you and I cannot do the best we can, the nation will suffer enormous damage.

An Essay Question from the Chinese Imperial Examination System

One of the unique features of the imperial government of China was the imperial examination system. Through it, the Chinese government recruited the members of its bureaucracy from the general populace, rather than leaving the imperial administration to the hereditary nobles. This system evolved gradually, starting in the second century BCE. during the former Han dynasty, (206 BCE–8 CE), becoming more elaborate and institutionalized during the early part of the Song dynasty (960–1279 CE), and continuing with only slight modifications down to the early years of last century. The last imperial examinations were held in 1905.

Millions of young men in China during the imperial period invested their time, energy, money, and passion in an effort to pass the examination, since this was the road to power and wealth. Aspirants for imperial bureaucratic posts usually spent ten or more years preparing for the examination, primarily by reading, analyzing, and memorizing the voluminous Confucian classics. During the Sung period, prospective candidates for imperial administrative posts were expected to pass three levels of highly competitive examinations—prefectural, metropolitan, and palace—and attain the Presented Scholar (Jinshi) degree, which was the most coveted degree, roughly comparable to a Ph.D. in the West. The candidates in the palace examination were ranked in order of their achievements in the examination. The higher the rank the candidates achieved, the better the chances were that they would receive more powerful and prestigious imperial appointments. The candidate for the Jinshi degree was required to produce, among other things, poems in various styles, a rhyme prose piece, a policy essay, answers to five policy questions, and answers to ten "written elucidation" questions on Confucian classics such as the Spring and Autumn Annals and the Book of Rites. The following selection is an example of an essay question on policy matters.

Source: *Copyright © 1985 Thomas H.C. Lee. From* Government Education and Examinations in Sung China, *pp. 150–51. Reprinted with permission of St. Martin's Press and The Chinese University Press.*

Focus Questions:
1. What do you think are the merits and demerits of the Chinese imperial examination system?
2. Compare Chinese orders with the contemporary west. What are the similarities and what are the differences?

It is stated in the Book of Guanzi: "the method by which a sage rules the world is this: he does not let the four classes of people live together. Therefore, there are no complaints, and things run smoothly. As a result, scholars know how to spend their leisure, laborers abide with the orders of officials, merchants go to the marketplaces and farmers go to the fields. Everyone goes to his appropriate place and lives there satisfactorily. Young children are sent to study; their wills are satisfied and they do not change their minds when they see strange things." The Guanzi Book further states: "Children of scholars and farmers must always be scholars and farmers and children of merchants and laborers must also always be merchants and laborers, so that a scholar can give instructions and take care of his proper status, and a farmer can work attentively in cultivating his crops to feed the people. Everyone is satisfied with his occupation and does not seek to change. This is truly good! Otherwise, hundreds of laborers might all go to the marketplaces and ten thousand merchants might all try to work in the same [most profitable] business; they would all become cunning, deceitful, eager to play tricks, and they would also become capricious, greedy and seek only profits."

Now, to fit people in their occupations is not to improve morals. To see something better and change— what harm is there in this? Take the example of Duanmu who became a merchant [after being a disciple of Confucius], Jiao Li who became a fisherman [after being an important official] and Wang Meng who went to sell dust-baskets [after being a prime minister]; these men responded to their times and changed in myriad ways, why should they have been restricted to their fixed occupations? Similarly, Huang Xian was originally a lowly veterinarian, Sang Hungyang [Sang Hongyang] a merchant, Sun Shuao a wood-cutter, and yet they all were able to preserve their intelligence and help strengthen their states. How can we accuse them of responding to their times and of going to take up responsibilities other than their own occupations! We now have a regulation keeping the descendants of those in despised occupations from taking the civil service examinations. Although this rule has been in force for some time, I consider that it still is a good time to examine this regulation. You candidates have excelled yourselves in knowledge of the past, and in debating various problems; I would like you to spend time considering the issue I have just outlined above.

Nineteenth-century Description of Cahokia

Europeans were impressed by the ruins of Cahokia when they first encountered them, as seen in this early description of 1810 CE. The original city appears to have thrived between about 700 and 1400 CE before declining, probably due to climate change. It was about six square miles in size and filled with houses and pyramids, amounting to a population of about 20,000. Cahokia formed part of the Mississippi culture which had developed agricultural settlements along the Mississippi and affiliated rivers. Cahokia had been long-abandoned by the time Europeans arrived in the late eighteenth century.

Source: *Henry M. Brackenridge,* Views of Louisiana *(1814).*

Focus Questions:
1. How does the description of the "American bottom" compare to the modern Mississippi?
2. What sort of society does the writer assume existed? What alternatives might have existed?
3. Where were the nearest urban civilizations to Cahokia? How did one get there?

VIEWS OF LOUISIANA (186)

The mounds at Grave creek and Marietta have been minutely described, but in point of magnitude they fall far short of others which I have seen.

To form a more correct idea of these, it will be necessary to give the reader some view of the tract of country in which they are situated. The *American bottom*, is a tract of rich alluvion [sic] land, extending on the Mississippi, from the Kaskaskia to the Cahokia river, about eighty miles in length, and five in breadth; several handsome streams meander through it; the soil of the richest kind, and but little subject to the effects of the Mississippi floods. A number of lakes are interspersed through it, with high and fine banks; these abound in fish, and in the autumn are visited by millions of wild fowl. There is, perhaps, no spot in the western country, capable of being more highly cultivated, or of giving support to a more numerous population than this valley. If any vestige of the ancient population were to be found, this would be the place to search for it—accordingly, this tract, as also the bank of the river on the western side,* exhibits proofs of an immense population. If the city of Philadelphia and its environs, were deserted, there would not be more numerous traces of human existence. The great number of mounds, and the astonishing quantity of human bones, every where dug up, or found on the surface of the ground, with a thousand other appearances, announce that this vicinity was at one period, filled with habitations and villages. The whole face of the bluff, or hill which bounds it to the east, appears to have been a contined [sic] burial ground.

But the most remarkable appearances, are two groups of mounds or pyramids, the one about ten miles above Cahokia, the other nearly the same distance below it, which in all, exceed one hundred and fifty, of various sizes. The western side, also, contains a considerable number.

A more minute description of those above Cahokia, which I visited in the fall of 1811, will give a tolerable idea of them all.

---

* The Saline, below St. Genevieve, cleared out some time ago, and deepened, was found to contain wagon loads of earthen ware, some fragments bespeaking vessels as large as a barrel, and proving that the salines had been worked before they were known to the whites.

ANTIQUITIES – BOOK II (187)

I crossed the Mississippi at St. Louis, and after passing through the wood which borders the river, about half a mile in width, entered an extensive open plain. In 15 minutes, I found myself in the midst of a group of mounds, mostly of a circular shape, and at a distance, resembling enormous haystacks scattered through a meadow. One of the largest which I ascended, was about two hundred paces in circumference at the bottom, the form nearly square, though it had entirely undergone considerable alteration from the washing of the rains. The top was level, with an area sufficient to contain several hundred men.

The prospect from this mound is very beautiful; looking towards the bluffs, which are dimly seen at the distance of six or eight miles, the bottom at this place being very wide, I had a level plain before me, varied by *islets* of wood, and a few solitary trees; to the right, the prairie is bounded by the horizon, to the left, the course of the Cahokia may be distinguished by the margin of wood upon its banks, and crossing the valley diagonally, S. S. W. Around me, I counted forty-five mounds, or pyramids, besides a great number of small artificial elevations; these mounds form something more than a semicircle, about a mile in extent, the open space on the river.

Pursuing my walk along the bank of the Cahokia, I passed eight others in the distance of three miles, before I arrived at the largest assemblage. When I reached the foot of the principal mound, I was struck with a degree of astonishment, not unlike that which is experienced in contemplating the Egyptian pyramids. What a stupendous pile of earth! To heap up such a mass must have required years, and the labors of thousands—It stands immediately on the bank of the Cahokia, and on the side next it, is covered with lofty trees; were it not for the regularity and design which it manifests, the circumstances of its being on alluvial ground, and the other mounds scattered around it, we could scarcely believe it the work of human hands—The shape is that of a parallelogram, standing from north to south; on the south side there is a broad apron or step, about half-way down, and from this, another projection into the plain, (188), about fifteen feet wide, which was probably intended as an ascent to the mound. By stepping round the base, I computed the circumference to be at least eight hundred yards, and the height of the mound about ninety feet. The step, or apron, has been used as a kitchen garden, by the monks of La Trappe, settled near this, and the top is sowed with wheat. Nearly west there is another of a smaller size, and forty others scattered through the plain. Two are also seen on the bluff, at the distance of three miles. Several of these mounds are almost conical. As the sward had been burnt, the earth was perfectly naked, and I could trace with ease, any unevenness of surface, so as to discover whether it was artificial or accidental. I everywhere observed a great number of small elevations of earth, to the height of a few feet, at regular distances from each other, and which appeared to observe some order; near them I also observed pieces of flint, and fragments of earthen vessels. I concluded, that a very populous town had once existed here, similar to those of Mexico, described by the first conquerors. The mounds were sites of temples, or monuments to the great men. It is evident, this could never have been the work of thinly scattered tribes. If the human species had at any time been permitted in this country to have increased freely, and there is every probability of the fact, it must, as in Mexico, have become astonishingly numerous. The same space of ground would have sufficed to maintain fifty times the number of the present inhabitants, with ease; their agriculture having no other object than mere sustenance. Amongst a numerous population, the power of the chief must necessarily be more absolute, and where there are no laws, degeneration into despotism. This was the case in Mexico, and in the nations of South America; a great number of individuals were at the disposal of the chief, who treated them little better than salves. The smaller the society, the greater the consequences of each individual. Hence, there would not be wanting a sufficient number of hands to erect mounds or pyramids.

The Magna Carta, 1215

King John of England (r. 1199–1216) was the younger brother of the Crusader Richard I "the Lionhearted" and the son of Henry II, who had done much to reform the legal system of his realm. John was far less successful than his predecessors in maintaining and exercising royal power, and this was exacerbated by his disastrous failed invasion of France in 1214. The following year, the English barons, disgusted with John's poor performance, forced him to concede certain rights to them, in a document that would have lasting repercussions in the English-speaking world for several hundred years. This "Magna Carta" or "Great Charter" was concluded at Runnymeade, west of London, in 1215, and a few of its provisions are set out below. John had little intention of living up to the letter of this agreement, but the document set England on a course that would ultimately lead to Parliamentary supremacy over the monarchs.

Source: Statutes of the Realm, *(London, 1810).*

Focus Questions:
1. In which passages does John concede that the King can make a mistake?
2. Which measures particularly stress that no one, not even the King, is above the law?
3. What are the stated reasons for John's making concessions on this occasion? Are they the real ones?

John, by the grace of God, king of England, lord of Ireland, duke of Normandy and Aquitaine, and count of Anjou, to the archbishops, bishops, abbots, earls, barons, justiciars, foresters, sheriffs, stewards, servants and to all his bailiffs and loyal persons, greeting. Know that, having regard to God and for the salvation of our souls, and those of all our predecessors and heirs, and unto the honour of God and the advancement of Holy Church, and for the reform of our realm, by the counsel of our venerable fathers...we have granted:

XII. No scutage [tax] or aid shall be imposed on our kingdom, unless by common counsel of our kingdom, except for ransoming our person, for making our eldest son a knight, and for marrying our eldest daughter once; and for them there shall not be levied more than a reasonable aid. In like manner it shall be done concerning aids from the city of London.

XXIX. No constable shall compel any knight to give money in stead of castle guard, when he is willing to perform it in his own person, or (if he himself cannot do it from any reasonable cause) then by another reliable man; and if we have led him or sent him upon military service, he shall be quit of guard, in proportion to the time during which he has been on service because of us.

XXXIX. No freeman shall be taken or imprisoned or disseised or exiled or in anyway destroyed, not will we go upon him nor send upon him, except by the lawful judgement of his peers or by the law of the land.

LV. All fines made by us unjustly and against the law of the land, shall be entirely remitted, or else it shall be done concerning them according to the decision of the five-and-twenty barons of whom mention is made below in (the clause for) securing the peace, or according to the judgement of the majority of the same, along with the aforesaid Stephen, archbishop of Canterbury, if he can be present, and such others as he may wish to bring with him for this purpose; and if he cannot be present the business shall nevertheless proceed without him, provided always that if any one or more of the aforesaid five-and-twenty barons are in a similar suit, they shall be removed as far as shall concern this particular judgement, others being substituted in their places after having been selected by the rest of the five-and-twenty for this purpose only, and after having been sworn.

LXI. Since, moreover, for God and the amendment of our kingdom and for the better allaying of our quarrel that has arisen between us and our barons, we have granted all these concessions, desirous that they should enjoy them in complete and firm stability for ever, we give and grant to them the underwritten security, namely, that the barons choose five-and-twenty barons of the kingdom, whomsoever they will, who shall be obliged, to observe and hold, and cause to be observed, with all their might, the peace and liberties which we have granted and confirmed to them by this our present Charter, so that if we, or our justiciar, or our bailiffs or anyone of our officers, shall in anything be at fault towards anyone, or shall have broken anyone of the articles of the peace or of this security, and the offence be notified to four barons of the aforesaid five-and-twenty, the said four barons shall come to us (or to our justiciar, if we are out of the realm) and, laying the transgression before us, petition to have that transgression redressed without delay. And if we shall not have corrected the transgression (or, in event of our being out of the kingdom, if our justiciar shall not have corrected it) within forty days, reckoning from the time it has been notified to us (or to our justiciar, if we should be out of the kingdom), the four barons and those five-and-twenty barons shall, together with the community of the whole land, distrain and distress us in all possible ways, namely, by seizing our castles, lands, possessions, and in any other way they can, until redress has been obtained as they deem fit, saving our own person and the persons of our queen and children; and when redress has been obtained, they shall resume their former relations toward us.

Chapter 12

Eurasian Contacts and Encounters before 1450

The Mongols: An Excerpt from the *Novgorod Chronicle*, 1315

The Novgorod Chronicle *is one of the most vital documents from postclassical Russia—or what is more properly called Kievan Russia, the first development of a Russian civilization centered in what is now western Russia, Ukraine, and Belarus. Maintained by Orthodox monks and reflecting their fervent religion, the* Chronicle *detailed major events, without much interpretation save that inspired by religious and local loyalties. Novgorod was a trading city of 250,000 people on the route between Scandinavia and Byzantium. As Kievan Rus fell apart in the twelfth century, Novgorod developed an increasingly independent regional government and army. During the mid-thirteenth century (from 1240 to 1263) the city was ruled by Prince Alexander Nevsky, who won important victories over Germans and Swedes but submitted to Mongol—called Tartar in the* Chronicle—*tax gatherers in order to buy his city's independence. Alexander also visited Mongol leaders to negotiate for his city. Mongol incursions occurred, but Novgorod remained the only Russian state to escape full Mongol (Tartar) control. Only in the late fourteenth century did the city begin to lose more of its independence, to the expanding Russian government now based in Moscow.*

Source: *Robert Mitchell and Nevill Forbes, eds.,* The Chronicle of Novgorod (1076–1471) *(London: Royal Historical Society, 1914), pp. 186–88.*

Focus Questions:
1. Why did the Mongols come, and why did they succeed in their conquest?
2. How has the chronicler interpreted this invasion in religious terms? Why?

A.D. 1224. The same year for our sins, unknown tribes came, whom no one exactly knows, who they are, nor whence they came out, nor what their language is, nor of what race they are, nor what their faith is; but they call them Tartars...God alone knows who they are and whence they came out. Very wise men know them exactly, who understand books; but we do not know who they are, but have written of them here for the sake of the memory of the Russian Princes and of the misfortune which came to them from them. For we have heard that they have captured many countries...

A.D. 1238. And the accursed ones having come thence took Moscow, Pereyaslavl, Yurev, Dmitrov, *Volok*, and Tver; there also they killed the son of [King] Yaroslay. And thence the lawless ones came and invested [the city of] Torzhok on the festival of the first Sunday in Lent. They fenced it all round with a fence as they had taken other towns, and here the accursed ones fought with battering rams for two weeks. And the people in the town were exhausted and from Novgorod there was no help for them; but already every man began to be in perplexity and terror. And so the pagans took the town, and slew all from the male sex even to the female, all the priests and the monks, and all stripped and reviled gave up their souls to the Lord in a bitter and a wretched death, on March 5, the day of the commemoration of the holy Martyr Nikon, on Wednesday in Easter week. And there, too, were killed Ivanko the Posadnik of Novi-torg, Yakin Vlunkovich, Gleb Borisovich and Mikhailo Moiseivich. And the accursed godless ones then pushed on from Torzhok by the road of Seregeri right up to Ignati's cross, cutting down everybody like grass, to within 100 *versts* of Novgorod. God, however, and the great and sacred apostolic cathedral Church of St. Sophia, and St. Kyuril, and the prayers of the holy and orthodox archbishop, of the faithful Princess, and of the very reverend monks finally ended the attack...

The same winter the accursed raw-eating Tartars, Berkai and Kasachik, came with their wives, and many others, and there was a great tumult in Novgorod, and they did much evil in the provinces, taking contribution for the accursed Tartars. And the accursed ones began to fear death; they said to [Prince] Alexander: "Give us guards, lest they kill us." And the Prince ordered... all the sons of the *Boyars* to protect them by night. The Tartars said: "Give us your numbers for tribute or we will run away." And the common people would not give their numbers for tribute but said: "Let us die honourably for St. Sophia and for the angelic houses." Then the people were divided: who was good stood by St. Sophia and by the True Faith; and they made opposition; the greater men bade the lesser, be counted for tribute. And the accursed ones wanted to escape, driven by the Holy Spirit, and they devised an evil counsel how to strike at the town at the other side, and the others at this side by the lake; and Christ's power evidently forbade them, and they durst not. And becoming frightened they began to crowd to one point to St. Sophia, saying: "Let us lay our heads by St. Sophia." And it was on the morrow, the Prince rode down...and the accursed Tartars with him, and by the counsel of the evil they numbered themselves for tribute; for the *Boyars* thought it would be easy for themselves, but fall hard on the lesser men. And the accursed ones began to ride through the streets, writing down the Christian houses; because for our sins God has brought wild beasts out of the desert to eat the flesh of the strong, and to drink the blood of the *Boyars*. And having numbered them for tribute and taken it, the accursed ones went away, and Alexander followed them, having set his son Dmitri on the throne.

Excerpt from William of Rubruck's Account of the Mongols

At the behest of King Louis IX of France, friar William of Rubruck embarked in 1253 on a two-year journey that took him to Karakorum, the Mongol capital. His report relates detailed and vivid observations of the Mongols and their customs and is one of the masterpieces of medieval geographical literature.

Source: The Journey of William of Rubruck to the Eastern Parts of the World, 1253–1255, as Narrated by Himself. *Translated by William Woodville Rockhill, London, Hakluyt Society, 1900.*

Focus Questions:
1. What sort of portrayal of nomadic life does William convey?
2. Why would a Christian clergyman like William be concerned with recording details of Mongol customs and practices?

[YURTS AND THEIR FURNISHINGS]

Nowhere have they fixed dwelling-places, nor do they know where their next will be. They have divided among themselves Cithia [Scythia—the ancient kingdom of the western steppes], which extendeth from the Danube to the rising of the sun; and every captain, according as he hath more or less men under him, knows the limits of his pasture land and where to graze in winter and summer, spring and autumn. For in winter they go down to warmer regions in the south: in summer they go up to cooler towards the north. The pasture lands without water they graze over in winter when there is snow there, for the snow serveth them as water. They set up the dwelling in which they sleep on a circular frame of interlaced sticks converging into a little round hoop on the top, from which projects above a collar as a chimney, and this (framework) they cover over with white felt. Frequently they coat the felt with chalk, or white clay, or powdered bone, to make it appear whiter, and sometimes also (they make the felt) black. The felt around this collar on top they decorate with various pretty designs. Before the entry they also suspend felt ornamented with various embroidered designs in color. For they embroider the felt, colored or otherwise, making vines and trees, birds and beasts.

And they make these houses so large that they are sometimes thirty feet in width. I myself once measured the width between the wheel-tracks of a cart twenty feet, and when the house was on the cart it projected beyond the wheels on either side five feet at least. I have myself counted to one cart twenty-two oxen drawing one house, eleven abreast across the width of the cart, and the other eleven before them. The axle of the cart was as large as the mast of a ship, and one man stood in the entry of the house on the cart driving the oxen.

Furthermore they weave light twigs into squares of the size of a large chest, and over it from one end to the other they put a turtle-back also of twigs, and in the front end they make a little doorway; and then they cover this coffer or little house with black felt coated with tallow or ewe's milk, so that the rain cannot penetrate it, and they decorate it likewise with embroidery work. And in such coffers they put all their bedding and valuables, and they tie them tightly on high carts drawn by camels, so that they can cross rivers (without getting wet). Such coffers they never take off the cart.

When they set down their dwelling-houses, they always turn the door to the south and after that they place the carts with coffers on either side near the house at a half stone's throw, so that the dwelling stands between two rows of carts as between two walls. The matrons make for themselves most beautiful (luggage) carts, which I would not know how to describe to you unless by a drawing, and I would depict them all to you if I knew how to paint. A single rich Mo'al or Tartar has quite one hundred or two hundred such carts with coffers. Baatu has twenty-six wives, each of whom has a large dwelling, exclusive of the other little ones which they set up after the big one, and which are like closets, in which the sewing girls live, and to each of these (large) dwellings are attached quite two hundred carts. And when they set up their houses, the first wife places her dwelling on the extreme west side, and after her the others according to their rank, so that the last wife will be in the extreme east; and there will be the distance of a stone's throw between the *iurt* of one wife and that of another. The *ordu* of a rich Mo'al seems like a large town, though there will be very few men in it. One girl will lead twenty or thirty carts, for the country is flat, and they tie the ox or camel carts the one after the other, and a girl will sit on the front one driving the ox, and all the others follow after with the same gait. Should it happen that they come to some bad piece of road, they untie them, and take them across one by one. So they go along slowly, as a sheep or an ox might walk.

When they have fixed their dwelling, the door turned to the south, they set up the couch of the master on the north side. The side for the women is always the east side, that is to say, on the left of the house of the master, he sitting on his couch his face turned to the south. The side for the men is the west side, that is, on the right. Men coming into the house would never hang up their bows on the side of the woman.

[THE MONGOLS' SOCIAL AND RELIGIOUS CUSTOMS AND CELEBRATIONS]

And over the head of the master is always an image of felt, like a doll or statuette, which they call the brother of the master: another similar one is above the head of the mistress, which they call the brother of the mistress, and they are attached to the wall: and higher up between the two of them is a little lank one (*macilenta*), who is, as it were, the guardian of the whole dwelling. The mistress places in her house on her right side, in a conspicuous place at the foot of her couch, a goat-skin full of wool or other stuff, and beside it a very little statuette looking in the direction of attendants and women. Beside the entry on the woman's side is yet another image, with a cow's tit for the women, who milk the cows: for it is part of the duty of the women to milk the cows. On the other side of the entry, toward the men, is another statue with a mare's tit for the men who milk the mares.

And when they have come together to drink, they first sprinkle with liquor this image which is over the master's head, then the other images in order. Then an attendant goes out of the dwelling with a cup and liquor, and sprinkles three times to the south, each time bending the knee, and that to do reverence to the fire; then to the east, and that to do reverence to the air; then to the west to do reverence to the water; to the north they sprinkle for the dead. When the master takes the cup in hand and is about to drink, he first pours a portion on the ground. If he were to drink seated on a horse, he first before he drinks pours a little on the neck or the mane of the horse. Then when the attendant has sprinkled toward the four quarters of the world he goes back into the house, where two attendants are ready, with two cups and platters to carry drink to the master and the wife seated near him upon the couch. And when he hath several wives, she with whom he hath slept that night sits beside him in the day, and it becometh all the others to come to her dwelling that day to drink, and court is held there that day, and the gifts which are brought that day are placed in the treasury of that lady. A bench with a skin of milk, or some other drink, and with cups, stands in the entry.

In winter they make a capital drink of rice, of millet, and of honey; it is clear as wine: and wine is carried to them from remote parts. In summer they care only for *cosmos*. There is always *cosmos* near the house, before the entry door, and beside it stands a guitar-player with his guitar. Lutes and vielles [i.e. guitars] such as we have I did not see there, but many other instruments which are unknown among us. And when the master begins to drink, then one of the attendants cries with a loud voice, "Ha!" and the guitarist strikes his guitar, and when they have a great feast they all clap their hands, and also dance about to the sound of the guitar, the men before the master, the women before the mistress. And when the master has drunken, then the attendant cries as before, and the guitarist stops. Then they drink all around, and sometimes they do drink right shamefully and gluttonly. And when they want to challenge anyone to drink, they take hold of him by the ears, and pull so as to distend his throat, and they clan and dance before him. Likewise, when they want to make a great feasting and jollity with someone, one takes a full cup, and two others are on his right and left, and thus these three come singing and dancing towards him who is to take the cup, and they sing and dance before him; and when he holds out his hand to take the cup, they quickly draw it back, and then again they come back as before, and so they elude him three or four times by drawing away the cup, till he hath become well excited and is in good appetite, and then they give him the cup, and while he drinks they sing and clap their hands and strike with their feet.

[MORE ON FOOD]

Of their food and victuals you must know that they eat all their dead animals without distinction, and with such flocks and herds it cannot be but that many animals die. Nevertheless, in summer, so long as lasts their *cosmos*, that is to say mare's milk, they care not for any other food. So then if it happens that an ox or a horse dies, they dry its flesh by cutting it into narrow strips and hanging it in the sun and the wind, where at once and without salt it becomes dry without any evidence of smell. With the intestines of horses they make sausages better than pork ones, and they eat them fresh. The rest of the flesh they keep for winter. With the hides of oxen they make big jars [J: bags], which they dry in admirable fashion in the smoke. With the hind part of the hide of horses they make most beautiful shoes. With the flesh of a single sheep they give to eat to fifty men or a hundred; for they cut it up very fine in a platter with salt and water, for they make no other sauce; and then with the point of a knife or a fork which they make for the purpose, like that which we used to eat coddled pears or apples, they give to each of the bystanders a mouthful or two according to the number of the guests. Prior to this, before the flesh of the sheep is served, the master takes what pleases him; and furthermore if he gives to anyone a special piece, it is the custom, that he who receives it shall eat it himself, and he may not give it to another; but if he cannot eat it all he carries it off with him, or gives it to his servant if he be present, who keeps it; otherwise he puts it away in his *captargac*, which is a square bag which they carry to put such things in, in which they store away bones when they have not time to gnaw them well, so that they can gnaw them later and that nothing of the food be lost.

[KUMISS (FERMENTED MARE'S MILK, CALLED COSMOS BY RUBRUCK)]

This *cosmos*, which is mare's milk, is made in this wise. They stretch a long rope on the ground fixed to two stakes stuck in the ground, and to this rope they tie toward the third hour the colts of the mares they want to milk. Then the mothers stand near their foal, and allow themselves to be quietly milked; and if one be too wild, then a man takes the colt and brings it to her, allowing it to suck a little; then he takes it away and the milker takes its place. When they have got together a great quantity of milk, which is as sweet as cow's as long as it is fresh, they pour it into a big skin or bottle, and they set to churning it with a stick prepared for that purpose, and which is as big as a man's head at its lower extremity and hollowed out; and when they have beaten it sharply it begins to boil up like new wine and to sour or ferment, and they continue to churn it until they have extracted the butter. Then they taste it, and when it is mildly pungent, they drink it. It is pungent on the tongue like râpé wine [i.e., a wine of inferior quality] when drunk, and when a man has finished drinking, it leaves a taste of milk of almonds on the tongue, and it makes the inner man most joyful and also intoxicates weak heads, and greatly provokes urine. They also make *cara cosmos* that is "black *cosmos*," for the use of the great lords. It is for the following reason that mare's milk curdles not. It is a fact that (the milk) of no animal will curdle in the stomach of whose fetus is not found curdled milk. In the stomach of mares' colts it is not found, so the milk of mares curdles not. They churn then the milk until all the thicker parts go straight to the bottom, like the dregs of wine, and the pure part remains on top, and it is like whey or white must. The dregs are very white, and they are given to the slaves, and they provoke much to sleep. This clear (liquor) the lords drink, and it is assuredly a most agreeable drink and most efficacious. Baatu has thirty men around his camp at a day's distance, each of whom sends him every day such milk of a hundred mares, that is to say every day the milk of three thousand mares, exclusive of the other white milk which they carry to others. As in Syria the peasants give a third of their produce, so it is these (Tartars) must bring to the *ordu* of their lords the milk of every third day. As to cow's milk they first extract the butter, then they boil it down perfectly dry, after which they put it away in sheep paunches which they keep for that purpose; and they put no salt in the butter, for on account of the great boiling down it spoils not. And they keep this for the winter. What remains of the milk after the butter they let sour as much as can be, and they boil it, and it curdles in boiling, and the curd they dry in the sun, and it becomes as hard as iron slag, and they put it away in bags for the winter. In winter time, when milk fails them, they put this sour curd, which they call *gruit*, in a skin and pour water on it, and churn it vigorously till it dissolves in the water, which is made sour by it, and this water they drink instead of milk. They are most careful not to drink pure water.

[ANIMALS IN THE MONGOLS' DIET]

The great lords have villages in the south, from which millet and flour are brought to them for the winter. The poor procure (these things) by trading sheep and pelts. The slaves fill their bellies with dirty water, and with this they are content. They catch also rats, of which many kinds abound here. Rats with long tails they eat not, but give them to their birds. They eat mice and all kinds of rats which have short tails. There are also many marmots, which are called *sogur*, and which congregate in one hole in winter, twenty or thirty together, and sleep for six months; these they catch in great numbers. There are also conies, with a long tail like a cat's, and on the end of the tail they have black and white hairs. They have also many other kinds of small animals good to eat, which they know very well how to distinguish. I saw no deer there. I saw few hares, many gazelles. Wild asses I saw in great numbers, and these are like mules. I saw also another kind of animal which is called *arcali* [a wild sheep], which has quite the body of a sheep, and horns bent like a ram's, but of such size that I could hardly lift the two horns with one hand, and they make of these horns big cups. They have hawks and peregrine falcons in great numbers, which they all carry on their right hand. And they always put a little thong around the hawk's neck, which hangs down to the middle of its breast, by which, when they cast it at its prey, they pull down with the left hand the head and breast of the hawk, so that it be not struck by the wind and carried upward. So it is that they procure a large part of their food by the chase. When they want to chase wild animals, they gather together in a great multitude and surround the district in which they know the game to be, and gradually they come closer to each other till they have shut up the game in among them as in an enclosure, and then they shoot them with their arrows.

Behâ ed-Din: Richard I Massacres Prisoners after Taking Acre

The recapture of Jerusalem by the Muslim leader Salah ed-Din (Saladin) in 1187 triggered a Third Crusade from Western Europe. At the key point in the campaign, King Richard I of England and King Philip II Augustus of France led a successful siege of the Muslim stronghold at Acre, on the Palestinian coast. Both armies suffered outbreaks of disease, a critical shortage of water, and complex negotiations that often broke down. As part of the terms of surrender in August 1191, the Crusaders held 2700 Muslims, men, women, and children, as hostages against Saladin's completion of the remainder of the terms. When Saladin failed, at least in Richard's estimation, to fulfill his part of the bargain, Richard ordered the execution of the hostages. Behâ ed-Din, a member of Saladin's court, was a witness to the massacre, and he describes it in vivid detail.

Source: *T. A. Archer, ed.,* The Crusade of Richard I *(New York: G. P. Putnams, 1885), pp. 127–31.*

Focus Questions:
1. How did religion motivate the behavior of the combatants on both sides?
2. Does this document suggest that Richard I, famed for "chivalry," did not deserve that reputation?

BEHÂ ED-DIN

The same day Hossâm ad-Din Ibn Barîc...brought news that the king of France had set out for Tyre, and that they had come to talk over the matter of the prisoners and to see the true cross of the Crucifixion if it were still in the Muslim camp, or to ascertain if it really had been sent to Bagdad. It was shewn to them, and on beholding it they shewed the profoundest reverence, throwing themselves on the ground till they were covered with dust, and humbling themselves in token of devotion. These envoys told us that the French princes had accepted the Sultan's proposition, viz., to deliver all that was specified in the treaty by three installments at intervals of a month. The Sultan then sent an envoy to Tyre with rich presents, quantities of perfumes, and fine raiment—all of which were for the king of the French.

...Ibn Barîc and his comrades returned to the king of England while the Sultan went off with his bodyguard and his closest friends to the hill that abuts on Shefa'Amr...Envoys did not cease to pass from one side to the other in the hope of laying the foundation of a firm peace. These negotiations continued till our men had procured the money and the tale of the prisoners that they were to deliver to the French at the end of the first period in accordance with the treaty. The first installment was to consist of the Holy Cross, 100,000 dinars and 1,600 prisoners. Trustworthy men sent by the Franks [French, or Europeans] to conduct the examination found it all complete saving only the prisoners who had been demanded by name, all of whom had not yet been gathered together. And thus the negotiations continued to drag on till the end of the first term...

This proposition the Sultan rejected, knowing full well that if he were to deliver the money, the cross, and the prisoners, while our men were still kept captive by the Franks, he would have no security against treachery on the part of the enemy, and this would be a great disaster to Islam.

Then the king of England, seeing all the delays interposed by the Sultan to the execution of the treaty, acted perfidiously as regards his Muslims prisoners. On their yielding the town he had engaged to grant them life, adding that if the Sultan carried out the bargain he would give them freedom and suffer them to carry off their children and wives; if the Sultan did not fulfil his engagements they were to be made slaves. Now the king broke his promises to them and made open display of what he had till now kept hidden in his heart, by carrying out what he had intended to do after he had received the money and the Frank prisoners. It is thus that people of his nation ultimately admitted.

In the afternoon of Tuesday...about four o'clock, he came out on horseback with all the Frankish army; knights, footmen, Turcoples, and advanced to the pits at the foot of the hill of Al 'Ayâdîyeh, to which place he had already sent on his tents. The Franks, on reaching the middle of the plain that stretches between this hill and that of Keisân, close to which place the sultan's advanced guard had drawn back, ordered all the Muslims prisoners, whose martyrdom God had decreed for this day, to be brought before him. They numbered more than three thousand and were all bound with ropes. The Franks then flung themselves upon them all at once and massacred them with sword and lance in cold blood. Our advanced guard had already told the Sultan of the enemy's movements and he sent it some reinforcements, but only after the massacre. The Muslims, seeing what was being done to the prisoners, rushed against the Franks and in the combat, which lasted till nightfall, several were slain and wounded on either side. On the morrow morning our people gathered at the spot and found the Muslims stretched out upon the ground as martyrs for the faith. They even recognised some of the dead, and the sight was a great affliction to them. The enemy had only spared the prisoners of note and such as were strong enough to work.

The motives of this massacre are differently told; according to some, the captives were slain by way of reprisal for the death of those Christians whom the Muslims had slain. Others again say that the king of England, on deciding to attempt the conquest of Ascalon, thought it unwise to leave so many prisoners in the town after his departure. God alone knows what the real reason was.

The Book of Dede Korkut, "The Story of Bugach Khan"

The collection of songs and stories that form the Dede Korkut *is now considered the national foundational epic for Turkey. Originally of oral tradition, they were increasingly written down beginning in the tenth century CE. The stories tell of the movement of the Turkic peoples westward across the steppe and their struggles against powerful foes. After conversion to Islam, the stories developed an Islamic overlay.*

Source: *from* The Book of Dede Korkut, *ed. by G. Lewis (Hammondsworth, 1974).*

Focus Questions:
1. What items are most valued and why?
2. What behaviors are most valued?
3. What is important about the phrase, "feed all the hungry, give clothes to the naked, and pay off the debts to the poor"? How does that contrast the wife to the khan?

THE STORY OF BUGACH KHAN, SON OF DIRSE KHAN

One day Bayindir Khan, son of Kam Gan, arose and ordered that his large Damascus tent be erected. His brown parasol rose high up in the sky. Thousands of silk carpets were spread all around. It was customary for Bayindir Khan, Khan of Khans, to invite all the Oghuz princes to a feast once a year. As usual he gave a feast this year, too, and had many stallions, young male camels, and rams slaughtered for the occasion. He had three tents set up at three different places: one was white, one was red, and the third was black. He ordered that whoever was without children be accommodated in the black tent, with a black felt rug spread under him, and that be served the stew of the black sheep. He said, "Let him eat if he wants to eat; if he does not, let him go." He then said: "Put the man with a son in the white tent, and the man with a daughter in the red tent. The man without any children is cursed by Allah, and we curse him, too. Let this [be] clear to all."

The Oghuz princes began to gather one by one. It happened that a prince among them by the name of Dirse Khan had neither a son nor a daughter. He spoke to his men as follows. Let us see, my khan, what he said:

> "When the cooling breeze of morning blows,
> And the bearded gray lark sings his song,
> And the long-bearded Persian chants the ezan
> When the Bedouin horses nicker on seeing their master;
> At the time of the twilight,
> When the beautiful-breasted mountains are touched by the sun
> At such a time, the warriors and gallant princes prepare for action."

At the break of the dawn Dirse Khan, accompanied by forty warriors, set out for the feast of Bayindir Khan.

Bayindir Khan's warriors welcomed Dirse Khan and asked him to go into the black tent, the floor of which was covered with a black felt rug. They placed the stew of black sheep before him and said, "My khan, this is the order of Bayindir Khan."

Dirse Khan asked: "What fault has Bayindir Khan found in me? Is it because of my sword or my table? He has men of lower status accommodated in the white and red tents. What is my fault that I am being put in a black tent?"

They said, "My khan, today Bayindir Khan's order is as follows:

"Whoever is without a son or a daughter is cursed by Allah; we curse him, too."

Standing up, Dirse Khan said to his men: "Rise and let us be off, my young men. The fault is either in me or in my lady."

Dirse Khan returned home, called his lady, and said to her:

> "Will you come here, my love, the crown of my home?
> Walking along so tall, like a cypress tree,
> With long back hair that falls to her feet,
> With brows like a tigthened bow;
> With a mouth too small for two almods;
> Her red cheeks like the apples of autumn.
> My melon, my lady, my love!
> Do you know what happened to me?

Bayindir Khan had three tents to put up: one white, one red, and one black. He had guests with sons put in the white tent; those with daughters in the red tent; and those with neither in the black tent with black felt carpet spread on its floor. He ordered that the stewed meat of the black sheep be served them, saying, 'If they eat, let them eat; if they do not, let them go away. Since Almighty Allah cursed them, we curse them too.' When I reached there they met me and led me to the black tent, laid back felt carpet under me, and served me the stewed meat of the black sheep, saying, 'The man without a son or a daughter is cursed by Allah; therefore, he is cursed by us, too. Let this be so known to you.' My wife, which of us is sterile, you or I? Why does Almighty Allah not give us a healthy son?"

Dirse Khan then continued in song.

> "O child of a khan, shall I now get up
> And grasp you by the throat,
> And crush you beneath my hard boots?
> Shall I draw my sword of black steel
> And remove your head from your body,
> And show you how sweet life can be?
> Shall I spill your red blood on the ground?
> O child of a khan, tell the reason to me,
> Or I shall inflict something dreadful on you."

The wife of Dirse Khan replied:

> "Oh, Dirse Khan, be not cruel to me.
> Be not angry and speak so harshly to me.
> But come now and have your red tent set up.
> Have some stallions, some rams, and some male camels slaughtered.
> Invite then the princes of Inner and Outher Oghuz.
> Feed all the hungry, give clothes to the naked, and pay off the debts of the poor.
> Heap up meat like a hill;
> Make a lakeful of koumiss; and give a magnificent feast.
> Then speak your wish. Maybe Allah will give us a healthy son,
> An answer to prayers of a worthy man."

Following his lady's advice, Dirse Khan gave a large feast and then made his wish. He had stallions, young male camels, and rams slaughtered. He invited all the princes of the Inner and the Outer Oghuz to this feast. He fed the hungry, dressed the naked, and paid off the debts of the debtor; he had meat heaped up like a hill, and a lakeful of kousmiss made. The princes raised their hands to the heavens and prayed.

Consequently, the wish of Dirse Khan was fulfilled, and his lady became pregnant. In due time she bore a male child. She had her child brought up in the care of nurses. As the horse is quick foot, so the minstrel is quick of tongue. As vertebrated [sic] and ribbed creatures grow fast, in the same way the son of Dirse Khan was soon fifteen years old.

One day Dirse Khan and his son went to the camp of Bayindir Khan. Bayindir Khan had a bull and a young male camel. The bull could powder harsh stones like flour with the impact of his horns. The bull and the camel were set to fight one another twice a year, once in summer and once in autumn. Bayindir Khan and the strong Oghuz princes used to enjoy themselves watching these fights.

This bull was let out of the palace one summer day. Three men on each side were holding it with iron chains. The bull was released in the middle of a playing field, where the son of Dirse Khan was playing at knuckle bones with three other boys from the camp. When the bull was released, the boys were told to run away. The other three boys ran away, but the son of Dirse Khan stood where he was. The bull ran toward the boy with the intent to kill him. The boy dealt the bull a terrific blow on the forehead. Then he pushed the bull to the edge of the playing field, with his fist pressing on its forehead. There they struggled to and fro. The bull stood pressing its forelegs against the ground, while the boy kept his fist on its forehead. It was impossible to say which was the winner. The boy thought to himself: "The pole holds the tent straight. Why am I supporting this bull?" Saying so, he pulled away his fist and ran to one side, while the bull, unable to stand on its feet, crashed on the ground head downward. Then the boy cut the throat of the bull with his knife.

The Oghuz princes gathered around the boy and said: "Well done, boy! Let Dede Korkut come and name him, then take him to his father and request a principality and a throne for him."

When they called for Dede Korkut, he came. He took the young man to his father and said to him:

> "O Dirse Khan!
> Give this young man a principality now.
> Give him a throne for the sake of his virtue.
> Give him also a tall Bedouin horse
> He can ride—such a capable man.
> Give him ten thousand sheep
> To make shish kebab for himself; he has virtue.
> Give him next a red camel from out of your herd.
> Let it carry his goods; he has virtue.
> Give a large lavish tent with a golden pole
> To provide him with shade.
> Give a suit to this man and a coat that has birds on its shoulders
> Let him wear both of these; he has skill.
>
> This young man fought and killed a bull on the playing field of Bayindir Khan," continued Dede Korkut. "Therefore, let your son's name be *Bugach*. I give him his name, and may Allah give him his years of life."

Upon this, Dirse Khan gave his son a principality and a throne. After the son had sat upon his throne for a while, he began to despise the forty young warriors of his father. As a result of this, they bore him a grudge and plotted among themselves: "Let us turn his father against him, so that he may put the son to death, and thus our esteem with the khan may continue and grow."

Twenty of these warriors went to Dirse Khan and said to him: "Do you know what has happened Dirse Khan? Your son (may he never prosper) has become a very bad-tempered man. Taking his forty warriors, he attacked the mighty Oghuz people. When he saw a pretty girl, he kidnapped her. He insulted old men with white beards and squeezed the breasts of white-haired old women. The news of these evil deeds of your son will reach the ears of Bayindir Khan—through the clear waters of streams and over Ala Mountain lying back there—and people will be saying, 'How could the son of Dirse Khan do such terrible things?'" The warriors then continued: "You would rather die than live. Bayindir Khan will call you his presence and will give you a serious punishment. Such a son is not worthy of you. It is better not to have such a son. Why do you not put him to death?"

"Bring him over here. I shall kill him," said Dirse Khan.

While he was speaking in this manner, the other twenty treacherous young men came and gave Dirse Khan the following unfounded information. "Your son went hunting in the beautiful mountains where he killed wild animals and birds without your permission. He brought the game to his mother. He drank strong red wine and had a good time in her company and there made up his mind to kill his father. Your son has become an evil person. The news of these deeds will reach Bayindir Khan, Khan of Khans, over Ala Mountain and people will begin to say, 'How could Dirse Khan's son do such terrible things?' They will call you before Bayindir Khan and punish you there. Such a son is not worthy of you. Why do you not kill him?"

"Bring him over here. I shall kill him. I do not want a son like him," said Dirse Khan.

His warriors said: "How can we bring your son here? He will not listen to us. Get up; take your warriors with you, call on your son, and ask him to go hunting with you. Then kill him with an arrow during the hunt. If you cannot kill him in this way, you will never be able to kill him."

> When the cooling breeze of morning blows,
> And the bearded gray lark sings his song,
> When Bedouin horses nicker on seeing their master,
> And the long-bearded Persian chants the *ezan*,
> At the time of the twilight, when girls
> And brides of the mighty Oghuz wear their gorgeous gowns,
> When the beautiful-breasted mountains are touched by the sun
> At such a time, the warriors and gallant princes prepare for action.

At the break of dawn, Dirse Khan arose and set out for the hunt, taking his son and forty warriors with him. They hunted wild animals and birds for a while. Then some of the treacherous warriors approached Dirse Khan's son and said to him: "Your father said, 'I want my son to chase the deer and kill them in front of me; I also want to see how he rides, and how he uses his sword and shoots his arrow. This will make me happy and proud and will give me confidence.'"

Not knowing his father's real intention, Bugach chased the deer and drove them toward his father and killed them before him. While doing this, Bugach said to himself, "Let my father see me ride and be proud; let him see me shoot my arrow and have confidence; let him see how I use my sword and rejoice."

The forty treacherous warriors then said to Dirse Khan; "Dirse Khan, do you see how he is driving the deer toward you? He means to shoot his arrow at you and kill you. Kill him before he kills you."

After the young man had driven the deer past his father several times, Dirse Khan took out his strong bow strung with the tendon of a wolf. Standing in his stirrups, he pulled his bowstring hard and let his arrow go. He shot his son between the shoulder blades. When the arrow pierced his chest, red blood poured out, filling his shirt. He clasped his horse's neck and slipped to the earth. Dirse Khan wanted to fall upon the body of his son, but his men did not allow him to do so. He then turned the head of his horse in the opposite direction and rode to his camp.

Dirse Khan's lady had decided to celebrate her son's first hunt by giving a feast to the mighty Oghuz princes, and for this purpose she had stallions, young male camels, and rams killed. She now arose and taking with her the forty narrow-waisted girls of her household went to welcome Dirse Khan. Lifting her head, she looked first at Dirse Kahn, then gazed around, but nowhere could she see her dear son. She was shocked, and her heart began to beat fast. Her black eyes were filled with blood and tears. Let us hear what she said to her husband.

> "Come to me here,
> The crown of my head, the throne of my house,
> My khan father's son-in-law,
> My lady mother's favorite,
> You, who were given me by my parents,
> You, whom I saw when I opened my eyes,
> The one whom I loved at first sight.
> O Dirse Khan, you arose from your place;
> You mounted the back of your stallion strong,
> And hunted the mountains with beautiful breasts.
> You rode off as two, but return now alone.
> Where is my son whom I found in the dark of the night?
> My searching eye—may it be confounded—twitches badly, Dirse Khan.
> My child-nursing breast—may it go quite dry—is sore.
> My white skin is swollen, though bitten by no yellow snake.
> My one son is lost! My poor heart is burning!
> Water I poured into beds of dry rivers.
> Alms I have given to black-suited dervishes.
> The hungry I saw I have fed.
> I had meat heaped up like a hill;
> I hade lakefuls of koumiss fermented,
> And I managed, with great travail, to bear a son.
> Tell me, Dirse Khan, what befell my only son!
> Say if you let our son fall down Ala Mountain out there.
> Say if you let our son be carried down the fast-flowing river.
> Say if you let our son be eaten by lions and tigers.
> Say if you let black-dressed infidels, they of a savage faith,
> Capture our son. To strike at the infidels, they with the savage religion.
> Let me never return from the search for my son
> Before I am wounded, fall off my strong horse,
> Wiping away my red blood with my sleeve,
> And sprawl on the road with broken limbs.
> Tell me, O Dirse Khan, what befell my only son.
> Let my luckless head be a sacrifice for you this day."

So speaking, she wept and gave voice to her sorrow. But Dirse Khan did not answer her.

Meanwhile, those forty treacherous men came along. They said to her: "Your son is safe and well. He has been hunting. He will be back today or tomorrow. Do not worry about him. He cannot speak now, because he is a bit drunk."

Dirse Khan's lady turned back, but she could not rest. With her forty slim girls, she mounted and rode in search of her son. She climbed Kazilik Mountain from which snow and ice never melt all the year around. She drove her horse up steep hills. When she looked down, she saw that crows were descending on a river and flying in and out of it. She spurred her horse and rode in that direction.

This was the place where the young man had collapsed. When the crows had seen blood, they wanted to come down upon him, but his two dogs kept the crows from his body. When the young man had fallen there, the gray-horsed Hizir had appeared to him, and stroking his wounds three times, had said: "Do not be afraid of these wounds. You will not die of them. Mountain flowers mixed with your mother's milk will be balm to them." Having said this, he disappeared.

Then the young man's mother came upon him. Seeing her son lying there covered with blood, she addressed him with the following song. Let us see, my khan, what she said.

> Your slit back eyes now taken by sleep—let them open.
> Your strong healthy bones have been broken,
> Your soul all but flown from your frame.
> If your body retains any life, let me know.
> Let my poor luckless head be a sacrifice to you.
> Kazilik Mountain, your waters still flow;
> Let them, I pray, cease their growing.
> Kazilik Mountain, your deer still run fast;
> Let them cease running and turn into stone.
> How can I know, my son, if it was lion
> Or tiger? How can I know, my son?
> How did this accident happen to you?
> If your life is still in your body, my son, let me know.
> Let my poor luckless head be a sacrifice to you.
> Speak a few words to me now."

As she said these things, her words entered his mind. He lifted his head, opened his eyes, and looked at his mother's face. He spoke to her. Let us see, my khan, what he said.

> "Come closer, my mother,
> Whose milk I once drank,
> White-haired, beloved, and honorable mother.
> Curse not the running streams;
> Kazilik Mountain has done no wrong.
> Curse not its growing grass;
> Kazilik Mountain has no sins.
> Curse not its swift-running deer;
> Kazilik Mountain has no fault.
> Curse not the lions and tigers;
> Kazilik Mountain has no guilt.
> The evil and guilt all belong to my father."

The young man then went on, "Do not cry, Mother. Do not worry. This wound will not kill me. The gray-horsed Hizir came to me and stroked my wound three times, saying, 'You will not die of this wound. Mountain flowers mixed with your mother's milk will be your balm.'"

When he said this, the forty slim girls went to gather mountain flowers. The young man's mother squeezed her breasts once, but no milk came out. She squeezed once more, but still no milk came out. The third time she struck herself and squeezed her breasts even harder, and finally some milk stained with blood appeared. Mixing the milk with the mountain flowers, they applied this balm to the young man's wound. Then they put him on a horse and took him to his camp. There he was delivered into the care of a physician and concealed from the sight of Dirse Khan.

As the horse is quick of foot, so the poet is quick of tongue. My khan, the young man's wounds were healed in forty days and he recovered completely. He was once again able to ride and wear his sword, to hunt and shoot birds. Dirse Khan knew nothing of all this. He thought that his son was dead.

But his forty threacherous men soon heard of this and discussed among themselves what they should do. They said: "If Dirse Khan sees his son, he will kill us all. Let us catch Dirse Khan, tie his white hands at his back, put a rope around his white neck, and take him to the land of the infidels." They did as they had decided. They tied his white hands behind him, and they put a rope around his white neck. Then they beat him until blood oozed from his white flesh. Dirse Khan was made to walk while they accompanied him on horseback. They led him to the land of the bloody infidels. While Dirse Kahn was thus a captive, the Oghuz boys knew nothing of his plight.

Dirse Khan's lady, however, learned of this. She went to her son and spoke to him. Let us see, my khan, what she said.

"Do you know what has happened, my son? Not only the steep rocks but the very earth should have shaken, for although there were no enemies in our lands, your father was attacked. Those forty treacherous companions of his captured him, tied his white hands behind him, put a rope around his neck, and forced him to walk while they rode on horseback. They took him toward infidel territory. Come, now, my son. Take your forty warriors with you and save our father from those forty faithless men. Go now and spare your father, even if he did not spare you."

The young man followed his mother's advice. He arose, strapped on his big steel sword, took his tight bow in one hand, and held his golden spear under his other arm. Then, as his strong horse was held, he mounted and, accompanied by his forty young men, went in pursuit of his father.

The treacherous retainers of Dirse Khan had stopped along the way and were drinking red wine. As Bugach Khan rode along, the forty treacherous men saw him approaching. They said "Let us go and capture that young man and take both him and Dirse Khan to the infidels."

Dirse Khan said: "Oh, my forty companions, there is no doubt about the oneness of Allah. Untie my hands, give me a lute, and I shall persuade that young man to go back. Let me loose or kill me." They untied his hands and gave him his lute.

Dirse Khan did not know that the young man was his own son. He went to him and sang.

> "If tall stallions have gone, let me count them my loss.
> Tell me if any of yours were among them, young man,
> So that I may restore them without any fight. Turn back!
> If a full thousand sheep have gone from the fold, let me count them my loss.
> Tell me if any of yours were among them,
> So that I may restore them without any fight. Turn back!
> If red camels have gone from the herd, let me count them my loss.
> Tell me if any of yours were among them,
> So that I may restore them without any fight. Turn back!
> If brides with brown eyes and white faces have gone, let me count them my loss.
> And if your betrothed was among them, tell me,
> So that I may restore them without any fight. Turn back!
> If white-bearded elders have gone, let me count them my loss.

If your white-bearded father was with them, tell me,
So that I may restore them without any fight. Turn back!
If you came after me, I have killed my own son.
Young man, it is not any sin that is yours. Turn back!"

The young man replied to the song of his father. Let us see, my khan, what he said.

"Tall stallions may count as your loss,
But one of the lost is mine;
I shall not give him up to the forty base men.
From the herds the red camels are mine;
I shall not give him up to the forty base men.
Thousands of sheep may be counted your loss,
But among them are some that are mine;
I shall not give him up to the forty base men.
The brides with brown eyes and white faces may count as your loss,
But among them is my betrothed;
I shall not give him up to the forty base men.
If the golden-topped tents may be counted as your loss,
Mine too is among them;
I shall not give him up to the forty base men.
If white-bearded elders are counted your loss,
My foolish old father is also among them;
I shall not give him up to the forty base men."

He waved a handkerchief to his own forty young men, and they came and gathered around him. With their aid, he fought with the enemy. Some of these he killed and some he captured. When he had saved his father in this manner, he returned home.

Dirse Khan thus discovered that his son was alive. Bayindri Khan, Khan of Khans, gave the young man a principality and a throne. Dede Korkut sang songs on the occasion and composed this legend of the Oghuz. Following this, he sang:

"Even they passed away from this world.
They stayed for a while and then moved along, Just as the caravan does.
Even they were removed by death
While this mortal world remained behind, The world where men come and go,
The world which is rounded off by death."

Then he said: "When black Death comes, may Allah keep you safe. May He let you rule in good health. May Almighty Allah whom I praise be your friend and keeper.";

This I pray, my khan. May your tall, stately mountains never fall. May your big shade tree never be cut down, and may your clear running waters never run dry. May your wings never be broken. May your gray horse never slip while running. May your big steel sword never be notched and may your spear never be broken in battle. May your white-haired mother's and white-bearded father's place be paradise. May Allah keep your household fire burning. May our merciful Allah never abandon you to the guile of the treacherous.

Al-Tha'alibi, *Recollections of Bukhara*

Originally, Persia and much of Central Asia were ruled as provinces under the Caliphate, but as the empire fragmented in the tenth-century CE, much of the area fell under the rule of the Saminid dynasty, ruling from Bukhara. This wealthy state controlled the important and lucrative boundary between the steppe and the Middle East. While it lasted, the Saminid kingdom provided a stable and rich environment to support a revival of Persian traditions and learning.

Source: The Book of Curious and Entertaining Information, *trans. by C. E. Bosworth (London, 1899).*

Focus Questions:
1. Why is a rhetorical style used in this selection?
2. How does Bukhara compare with tenth-century Europe?
3. What are the learned men most likely discussing?

Bukhara was, under the Samanid rule, the Focus of Splendour, the Shrine of Empire, the Meeting place of the most unique intellects of the Age, the Horizon of the literary stars of the world, and the Fair of the greatest scholars of the Period. Abu Ja'far Muhammad b. Musa al-Musawi related to me as follows: "My father Abu'l-Hasan received an invitation to Bukhara in the days of the Amir-i-Sa'id [Nasr II b. Ahmad, reigned A. D. 913–942], and there were gathered together the most remarkable of its men of letters...And when these were settled in familiar conversation one would engage with another in plucking the fringes of some discussion, each offering to the other fragrant flowers of dialectic, and pursuing the perfumes of Culture, and letting fall in succession necklaces of pearls, and blowing on magical knots. And my father said to me, 'O my son, this is a notable and red-letter day: make it an epoch as regards the assembling of the standards of talent and the most incomparable scholars of the age, and remember it, when I am gone, amongst the great occasions of the period and the notable moments of thy life. For I scarcely think that in the lapse of the years thou wilt see the like of these met together,' And so it was, for never again was my eye brightened with the sight of such a gathering."

Liutprand of Cremona, Excerpt from *Report of his Mission to Constantinople*

Liutprand (d. 970 CE) was a highly educated bishop at Pavia, Italy, who became active in the Lombard king's court. In 949 he was sent as an ambassador by this minor king to Constantinople, the ancient seat of the Byzantine Empire. Later Liutprand entered service in the court of the powerful Otto I, Holy Roman Emperor, who sent him on a similar mission in 968. This latter trip was designed to obtain the hand of the Byzantine emperor's daughter to marry Otto, and was ultimately successful, forming a calculated political match between two powerful kingdoms.

Source: The Works of Liutprand of Cremona, *trans. by F. A. Wright (London, 1930).*

Focus Questions:
1. In what ways are the two empires compared?
2. What is going on with Liutpand's description of the procession?
3. Look at the various peoples and places mentioned. What can we discover about the two empires from these specific places?

On the seventh day before the Ides (June 7), moreover, on the sacred day—of Pentecost itself, in the palace which is called the crown hall, I was led before Nicephorus—a monstrosity of a man, a pygmy, fat-headed and like a mole as to the smallness of his eyes; disgusting with his short, broad, thick, and half hoary beard; disgraced by a neck an inch long; very bristly through the length and thickness of his hair; in color an Ethiopian; one whom it would not be pleasant to meet in the middle of the night; with extensive belly, lean of loin, very long of hip considering his short stature, small of shank, proportionate as to his heels and feet; clad in a garment costly but too old, and foul-smelling and faded through age; shod with Sicyonian shoes; bold of tongue, a fox by nature, in perjury, and lying a Ulysses. Always my lords and august emperors you seemed to me shapely, how much more shapely after this! Always magnificent, how much more magnificent after this! Always powerful, how much more powerful after this! Always gentle, how much more gentle henceforth! Always full of virtues, how much fuller henceforth. At his left, not in a line but far below, sat two whatever corn there was anywhere; giving a minimum price to the despairing owners. And when he had done this on the side towards Mesopotamia, where the supply of grain on account of the absence of the mice was greater: the amount of corn that he had equaled the amount of the sands of the sea. When, therefore, on account of this vile transaction, famine was everywhere shamefully raging, he brought together eighty thousand men under pretext of a military expedition; and he sold to them, during one whole mouth [sic], for two gold pieces what he had bought for one. These, my master, are the reasons which compelled Nicephorus now to lead his forces against the Assyrians. But what sort of forces? I ask. Truly, I answer, not men, but only images of men; whose tongue only is bold, but whose right hand is frigid in war. Nicephorus did not look for quality in them, but only for quantity. How perilous this is for him he will learn to his sorrow, when the multitude of unwarlike ones, brave only on account of numbers, shall be put to rout by a handful of our men who are skilled in war—nay, thirsting for it.

When you were besieging Bari only three hundred Hungarians seized five hundred Greeks near Thessalonica and led them into Hungary. Which attempt, inasmuch as it succeeded, induced two hundred Hungarians in Macedonia, not far from Constantinople, to do the like; of whom forty, when they were retreating incautiously through a narrow pass, were captured. These Nicephorus, freeing them from custody and adorning them with most costly garments, has made his body guard and defenders—taking them with him against the Assyrians. But what kind of an army he a [sic] has you can conjecture from this—that those who are in command over the others are Venetians and Amalfians!

But no more of this! Learn now what happened to me. On the sixth day before the Calends of August (July 27), I received at Umbria, outside of Constantinople, permission from Nicephorus to return to you, And when I came to Constantinople, the patrician Christophorus, the eunuch who was the representative of Nicephorus there, sent word to me that I could not then start to return because the Saracens at that time were holding the sea and the Hungarians the land—I should have to wait until they retired. Both of which facts, oh woe is me, were false! Then wardens were placed over us to prevent myself, and my companions from going out of our habitation. They seized and slew or put in prison the poor of Latin race who came to me to beg alms. They did not permit my Greek interpreter to go out even to buy supplies—but only my cook, who was ignorant of the Greek tongue and who could speak to the vendor, when he bought of him, not with words but by signs of his fingers or nods of his head. He bought for four pieces of money only as much as the interpreter for one. And when some of my friends sent spices, bread, wine and apples—pouring theta [sic] all on the ground, they sent the bearers away overwhelmed with blows of the fist. And had not the divine pity prepared before me a table against my, adversaries, I should have had to accept the death they arranged for me. But He who permitted that I should be tempted, mercifully granted then that I should endure. And these perils tried my soul at Constantinople from the second day before the Nones of June (June 4), until the sixth day before the Nones of October (Oct. 2)—one hundred and twenty days.

But, to increase my calamities, on the day of the Assumption of the Virgin Mary the holy mother of God (August 15), there came an evil augury for me—envoys of the apostolic and universal pope John, through whom he asked Nicephorus, the emperor of the Greeks "to close an alliance and firm friendship with his beloved and spiritual son Otto "august emperor of the Romans." Before the question as to why—this word, this manner of address, sinful and bold in the eyes of the Greeks, did not cost its bearer his life—why he was not annihilated before it was read, I, who, in other respects, have often shown myself enough of a preacher and with words enough at my command, seem dumb as a fish! The Greeks inveighed against the sea, cursed the waves, and wondered exceedingly how they had been able to transport such an iniquity and why the yawning deep had not swallowed up the ship. "Was it not unpardonable," they said, "to have called the universal emperor of the Romans, the august, great, only Nicephorus: 'of the Greeks;' 'a barbarian, a pauper: of the Romans'? Oh sky! Oh earth! Oh sea! But what," they said, "shall we do to those scoundrels, those criminals?" They are paupers, and if we kill them we pollute our hands with vile blood; they are ragged, they are slaves, they are peasants; if we beat them we disgrace not them, but ourselves; for they are not worthy of the gilded Roman flail and of such punishments. Oh would that one were a bishop, another a margrave! For sewing them in sacks, after stinging blows with whips, after plucking out their beards or their hair, they would be thrown into the sea. But these," they said, "may continue to live; and, until the holy emperor of the Romans, Nicephorus, learns of this atrocity, they may languish in narrow confinement."

When I learned this I considered them happy because poor, myself unhappy because rich. When I was at home, my desire was to excuse my poverty; but placed in Constantinople, fear itself taught me that I bad the wealth of a Croesus. Poverty had always seemed burdensome to me—then it seemed welcome, acceptable, desirable; yes, desirable, since it keeps its votaries from perishing, its followers from being flayed. And since at Constantinople alone this poverty thus defends its votaries, may it there alone be considered worth striving after!

The papal messengers, therefore, being thrown into prison, that offending epistle was sent to Nicephorus in Mesopotamia; whence no one returned to bring an answer until the second day before the Ides of September (Sept. 12). On that day it came, but its import was concealed from me. And after two days— on the eighteenth day namely, before the Calends of October (Sept. 14)—I brought it about by prayers and gifts that I might adore the life-giving and salvation-bringing cross. And there in the great crowd, unnoticed by the guards, certain persons approached me, and rendered my saddened heart joyful through stolen words.

Benjamin of Tudela, Selection from *Book of Travels*

Benjamin of Tudela (1127–1174 CE) was a Rabbi from Spain who made an extended journey to Jerusalem (1160–1172). On his journey he traveled via Byzantium, Syria, Persia, Mesopotamia, and Palestine before returning home twelve years later. Back home, Benjamin wrote a very descriptive travelogue that provides an excellent source on the condition of medieval Jewish communities and the local Christian or Islamic cultures.

Source: Adler, Marcus Nathan, trans., The Itinerary of Benjamin of Tudela *(New York: Philipp Feldheim, Inc., 1907).*

Focus Questions:
1. How do Benjamin's descriptions compare with those of Liutprand?
2. Trace the origins of people and goods to find the reach of Constantinople.
3. Why are the Jews treated badly by the Greeks?

A three days' voyage brings one to Abydos, which is upon an arm of the sea which flows between the mountains, and after a five days' journey the great town of Constantinople is reached. It is the capital of the whole land of Javan, which is called Greece. Here is the residence of the King Emanuel the Emperor. Twelve ministers

12 BENJAMIN OF TUDELA

are under him, each of whom has a palace in Constantinople and possesses castles and cities; they rule all the land. At their head is the King Hipparchus, the second in command is the Megas

(p. 20) Domesticus, the third Dominus, and the fourth is Megas Ducas, and the fifth is Oeconomus Megalus; the others bear names like these. The circumference of the city of Constantinople is eighteen miles; half of it is surrounded by the sea, and half by land, and it is situated upon two arms of the sea, one coming from the sea of Russia, and one from the sea of Sepharad.

All sorts of merchants come here from the land of Babylon, from the land of Shinar, from Persia, Media, and all the sovereignty of the land of Egypt, from the land of Canaan, and the empire of Russia, from Hungaria, Patzinakia, Khazaria, and the land of Lombardy and Sepharad. It is a busy city, and merchants come to it from every country by sea or land, and there is none like it in the world except Bagdad, the great city of Islam. In Constantinople is the church of Santa Sophia, and the seat of the Pope of the Greeks, since the Greeks do not obey the Pope of Rome. There are also churches according to the number of the days of the year. A quantity of wealth beyond telling is brought hither year by year as tribute from the two islands and the castles and villages which are there.

(p. 21) And the like of this wealth is not to be found in any other church in the world. And in this church there are pillars of gold and silver, and lamps of silver and gold more than a man can count. Close to the walls of the palace is also a place of amusement belonging to the king, which is called the Hippodrome, and every year on the anniversary of the birth of Jesus the king gives a great entertainment there. And in that place men from all the races of the world come before the king and queen with jugglery and without jugglery,

13 CONSTANTINOPLE

and they introduce lions, leopards, bears, and wild asses, and they engage them in combat with one another; and the same thing is done with birds. No entertainment like this is to be found in any other land.

This King Emanuel built a great palace for the seat of his government upon the sea-coast, in addition to the palaces which his fathers built, and he called its name Blachernae. He overlaid its columns and walls with gold and silver, and engraved thereon representations of the battles before his day and of his own combats. He also set up a throne of gold and of precious stones,

(p. 22) and a golden crown was suspended by a gold chain over the throne, so arranged that he might sit thereunder. It was inlaid with jewels of priceless value, and at night time no lights were required, for every one could see by the light which the stones gave forth. Countless other buildings are to be met with in the city. From every part of the empire of Greece tribute is brought here every year, and they fill strongholds with garments of silk, purple, and gold. Like unto these storehouses and this wealth, there is nothing in the whole world to be found. It is said that the tribute of the city amounts every year to 20,000 gold pieces, derived both from the rents of shops and markets, and from the tribute of merchants who enter by sea or land.

The Greek inhabitants are very rich in gold and precious stones, and they go clothed in garments of silk with gold embroidery, and they ride horses, and look like princes. Indeed, the land is very rich

(**p. 23**) in all cloth stuffs, and in bread, meat, and wine.

Wealth like that of Constantinople is not to be found in the whole world. Here also are men learned in all the books of the Greeks, and they eat and drink every man under his vine and his fig tree.

They hire from amongst all nations warriors called Loazim (Barbarians) to fight with the Sultan Masud, King of the Togarmim (Seljuks), who are called Turks; for the natives are not warlike, but are as women who have no strength to fight.

14 BENJAMIN OF TUDELA

No Jews live in the city, for they have been placed behind an inlet of the sea. An arm of the sea of Marmora shuts them in on the one side, and they are unable to go out except by way of the sea, when they want to do business with the inhabitants. In the Jewish quarter are about 2,000 Rabbanite Jews and about 500 Karaites, and a fence divides them. Amongst the scholars are several wise men, at their head being the chief rabbi R. Abtalion, R. Obadiah, R. Aaron Bechor Shoro, R. Joseph Shir-Guru, and R. Eliakim, the warden. And amongst them there are artificers in silk and many rich merchants. No Jew

(**p. 24**) there is allowed to ride on horseback. The one exception is R. Solomon Hamitari, who is the king's physician, and through whom the Jews enjoy considerable alleviation of their oppression. For their condition is very low, and there is much hatred against them, which is fostered by the tanners, who throw out their dirty water in the streets before the doors of the Jewish houses and defile the Jews' quarter (the Ghetto). So the Greeks hate the Jews, good and bad alike, and subject them to great oppression, and beat them in the streets, and in every way treat them with rigour. Yet the Jews are rich and good, kindly and charitable, and bear their lot with cheerfulness. The district inhabited by the Jews is called Pera.

From Constantinople it is two days' voyage to Rhaedestus, with a community of Israelites of about 400, at their head being R. Moses, R. Abijah, and R. Jacob. From there it is two days to Callipolis (Gallipoli), where there are about 200 Jews, at their bead being R. Elijah Kapur, R. Shabbattai Zutro, and R. Isaac Megas, which

(**p. 25**) means "great" in Greek. And from here it is two days to Kales. Here there are about fifty Jews, at their head being R. Jacob and R. Judah. From here it is two days' journey to the island of Mytilene, and there are Jewish congregations in ten localities on the island. Thence it is three days' voyage to the island of Chios, where there are about 400 Jews, including R. Elijah Heman and R. Shabtha. Here grow the trees from which mastic is obtained. Two days' voyage takes one to the island of Samos, where there are 300 Jews, at their head being R. Shemaria, R. Obadiah, and R. Joel. The islands have many congregations of Jews. From Samos it is three days to Rhodes, where there are about 400 Jews, at their head being R. Abba, R. Hannanel, and R. Elijah. It is four days' voyage from here to Cyprus, where there are Rabbanite Jews and Karaites; there

15 THE GREEK ISLANDS—ANTIOCH

are also some heretical Jews called Epikursin, whom the Israelites have excommunicated in all places. They profane the eve of the sabbath, and observe the first night of the week, which is the termination of the Sabbath.

Lu You, excerpt from *Diary of a Journey to Sichuan*

Lu You (1125–1210 CE) was a middle-level administrator in the Chinese civil service. As was typical for the classically educated bureaucrats of the time, he also wrote and published poetry. Lu You argued for a policy of expelling the Jurchen from northern China, but the lack of success in its achievement condemned him to lesser posts. One such provincial assignment is mentioned in his diary which describes his journey through southern China.

Source: *Chun-Shu Chang and Joan Sanytle, trans., Lu Yu, "Diary of a Journey to Sichuan,"* South China in the Twelfth Century *(Hong Kong: The Chinese University Press) pp. 168–171.*

> **Focus Questions:**
> 1. What are Lu You's thoughts about province? How does he compare with modern tourists?
> 2. What are his comments on the calligraphy of the stele?
> 3. Why do you think the sub-prefect post is often left vacant?

SOUTH CHINA IN THE TWELFTH C.

17th day, I attended a staff party given by the local authorities at the Wan-fang Pavilion of the Wang-yang Hall. It is a sandy and rocky place. According to Prefectural Administrator Chia, the prefectural granary takes in tax revenue at the two harvests yearly, fall and summer; the wheat, millet, and non-glutinous rice are altogether 5,000 or so *shih*; this is barely comparable, to (the production of) one poor household in the Wu area (in Kiahsu).

18th day, For the first time we obtained a ch'an boat. It is quite small, but its wide bottom and light weight made it convenient for going up the rapids.

19th day, I attended a staff party given by the local authorities at the Kuei-hsiang Hall. We wanted to leave this evening, but did not succeed. I visited Sung Yu's (290?–222? B.C.) residence. It is east of (the seat of) Tzu-kuei Hsien. It has been made into a wineshop. Formerly there was a stone inscribed with the three characters, "Sung Yu chai," but recently it has been discarded, on account of the local people avoiding a taboo of the Prefectural Administrator's family. Perhaps it will be lost through this action. It is too bad.

20th day, We left Kuei-chou by the Shaman-Peak Gate. We visited the Monastery of Rejoicing Heaven's Blessing and stayed there a while. I read the stele dating from the first Year of Tien-pao (742) in the T'ang; it records the dream of Emperor Ming-huang (T'ang Hsuan-tsung, r. 712–756) about Lao-tzu. It was erected by the Prefect of Pa-tung (i.e., Kuei-chou), Liu T'ao. The calligraphy is quite dear and free. On the side of the stele are written the names of the prefectural officials of that time. These characters are also excellent. There was also a stele erected during the Hsien-te period (954–959) of Shih-tsung of the (Later) Chou (951–960) by the Military Governor's Administrator of Ching-nan, Sun Kuang-hsien (d. 968), in honor of the Prefect of Kuei-chou, Kao Ts'ung-jang. Ts'ung-jang was a son of the royal family of the King of Nan-p'ing (i.e., Kao Chi-hsing, r. 925–928). Sun Kuang-hsien is also a well-known person. There is a biography of him in the dynastic history, During the Five Dynasties, Kuei(-chou) and Hsia(-chou) both were under the jurisdiction of Ching-chu. In front of the hall are cedars several hundred years old. Below the monastery are the Cha Rapids, strewn with countless rocks. We ate at the Ling-ch'uan Temple and afterwards boarded the boat. We passed the Yeh Rapids. These are famous rapids. The water being low and the boat light, in an instant we had passed them.

21st day, From the boat we looked up at Stone Gate Pass. It was barely (wide enough) for one person to pass. It is the most dangerous place in the empire. In the evening we moored at Pa-tung Hsien (modern Pa-tung Hsien, Hupeh). The river and mountains were beautiful and imposing, far surpassing Tzu-kuei. But the town was extremely desolate. In the town there were only a hundred-odd households. From the subprefectural offices on down, the houses were all thatched and there wasn't a single tile. Sheriff of Tzu-kuei and Provisionally in Charge of Subprefectural Affairs (of Pa-tung) *Yu ti-kuang-lang* Wang K'ang-nien and Sheriff and Concurrent Subprefectural Registrar *Yu ti-kung-lang* Tu Te-hsien came to call. They are both natives of Shu. I paid homage to the Shrine of Duke K'ou of Lai (K'ou Chun 961–1023), and climbed the Autumn Wind Pavilion. It looks down on the river and hills. Today it was heavily overcast and snowing lightly, and the wind was whistling by. Again I looked at the pavilion's name and it filled me with a mournful mood. For the first time I sighed over being drifted away from home. Next I climbed the Twin Cedars Hall and the White Cloud Pavilion. Below the hall there used to be cedars planted by K'ou, the Duke of Lai. Now they have withered and died. Nevertheless, the southern mountains rising one above the other are elegant and lovely. The White Cloud Pavilion, on the other hand, has the most secluded and marvelous surroundings in the empire. Ranges of mountains rising layer after layer surround it. In their midst one can see ancient trees in great numbers, often two or three hundred years old. A pair of waterfalls outside the pavilion railing flow over a rocky gully, like leaping pearls and splashing jade. Their cold penetrates to the bone. Below the falls is Mercy Creek which flows swiftly to meet the river. In traveling from Wu to Ch'u I have come over 5,000 *li* and passed through fifteen prefectures. As to the scenic beauty of pavilions and towers, none can compare to the White Cloud Pavilion. And it is just behind the subprefectural office buildings. Pa-tung, after all, has hardly any (official) business and whoever is acting as its Subprefect could sleep and eat in the pavilion, and his pleasure would be boundless. Nevertheless, the post of subprefect is apt to lie vacant for two or three years at a stretch. Why is it that no one is willing to fill it?

22nd day. We left Pa-tung, and the mountains became increasingly marvelous. There was the Grotto of the Master, a single cave at the highest point on a steep cliff, which no man could reach. Yet it seemed to have a railing. I don't know who the "Master" was. We passed the Three Branch Spring. It came out of a hole in the mountain. There were only two branches. A local saying goes, "If [the spring flows in] three branches, it will be a good year. In two branches, then there will be medium harvest. Should there be only one or if it ceases to flow at all, [it means] a year of famine."

We moored at P'i-shih. It rained in the night.

23rd day, We visited the Monastery of Congealed Truth on Wushan (Shaman Mountain), and I paid my respects at the Shrine of the Immortal of Wonderful Functions. The immortal is what people popularly call the Shen Nu (Goddess) of Shaman Mountain. The summits of the peaks enter the heavens and their feet are planted in the river. Authorities on such matters hold that none of the mountains T'ai, Hua, Heng, or Lu, are as marvelous as this one, However, we could not see all of the Twelve Peaks. Of the eight or nine peaks which we could see, the Shen Nu peak has the most subtle beauty and marvelous steepness. It is a fitting abode for an immortal. The sacrificial priest (at the shrine) said, "Each year on the fifteenth day of the eighth moon, at night when the moon is bright, there is the sound, of string and bamboo instruments [i.e., flutes and strings] coming from the peak's summit. The mountain monkeys all sing. Not until dawn does the music gradually fade away. Behind the shrine and halfway up the mountain is a stone altar which is flat and wide. According to a legend, the Hsia Emperor Yu saw Shen Nu and deceived magic charms here. From the top of the altar we had a view of the Twelve Peaks. They resembled a folding screen. Today the sky was clear and in all directions there was not the slightest cloudiness or haze. Only over the Shen Nu Peak were there a few white clouds, like phoenixes and cranes dancing to and fro. For a long time they did not disperse. It was a strange sight. The shrine used to have several hundred crows, which sent off and welcomed travelers' boats." Already in the T'ang a poem by the Prefect of K'uei-chou, Li I, said, "The flock of crows delighted in the left-over sacrificial meat." Recently, in the first year of the Ch'ien-tao period (1165) the crows suddenly stopped coming. Now there is not a single crow. I don't know the reason for it.

We moored at the Clearwater Grotto. The cave is extremely deep and its rear entrance comes out at the back of the mountain. But it is dark and murky and a stream runs through it, so one can rarely enter. In dry years when they pray for rain, it is quite effective. The Acting Subprefectural Administrator of Wu-shan Tso wen-lin-Iang Jan Hui- chih Sheriff *Yu ti-kung-lang* Wen Shu-chi came to call.

24th day, Early in the morning we reached Wushan Hsien (modern Wushan Hsien, Hupeh). It is in the (Wu) Gorge and is also a large subprefecture, The town surpasses both Kuei-chou and Hsia-chou. Across the river is Nan-ling Mountain, which is very high. There is a road like a thread, winding up to the summit, called the Hundred and Eight Coils. It is the main road to Shih-chou (modern En-shih Hsien, Hupeh). Huang Lu-chih's poem, "Holding hands we ascended the Hundred and Eight Coils; Even now I return in my dreams to that winding 'sheep's intestines'," refers to this place. In the subprefectural offices is an ancient iron basin. Its base is pointed, it is shaped like a half vase, sturdy and thick. The inscription is inside; it dates from the Yung-p'ing period (58–75) [of Emperor Ming-ti] of the (Later) Han. Where it is broken, the iron is a lustrous black, like fine lacquer. The calligraphy is simple, unadorned, and appealing. There is a stone inscription of a "Description" of the basin by Huang Lu-chih. In brief, it says that in the first year of the Chien-chung ching-kuo period (1101) [of Emperor Hui-tsung], Huang's younger brother Shu-hsiang (whose courtesy name was) Ssu-chih was transferring from (the post of) Sheriff of Fu-ling Hsien (modern Fu-ling Hsien, Szechwan) to, be the Acting Subprefect of this *hsien*. Huang Luchih came from Jung-thou (modern I-pin Hsien, Szechwan) and lodged at the sub-prefectural offices. This basin was formerly used to grow lotus. Huang rinsed it out and then could see the writing in it.

I visited the former Detached Palace of Ch'u. It is popularly called the Palace of Slender Waists. There is a pond which was the scene of court banquets arid entertainment in those times. Today it has been almost completely filled in. In three directions there are bare mountains; only looking to the south are the river and mountains wonderfully beautiful. There is also a general's tomb; the general was a man of the Eastern Chin (317–420). There is also one stele behind the tomb. Its feet have sunk into the ground, so that the stele leans forward as if about to fall over. Only half the inscription still remains.

Marco Polo, excerpt from *Travels*

One of the most famous medieval European travelers was the Italian merchant, Marco Polo (1254–1324 CE). He wrote a very detailed and accurate description of his travels to and around Asia that in many ways remains unsurpassed. His father and uncle had made an earlier trip through the Mongol lands, meeting Kublai Khan, the Mongol ruler of China, who gave them a lavish reception. Marco accompanied his uncle on the long second trip (1271–1295) in which Marco also met Kublai Khan. Marco remained in the khan's service for seventeen years as an administrator in many parts of China, before he and his uncle finally returned home with their accumulated wealth.

Source: *Marco Polo,* Travels, *ed. by Henry Yule (London, 1870).*

Focus Questions:
1. What are the dangers of the trip?
2. What might the "spirit voices" be?
3. Consider who and what makes up a caravan.

"When a man is riding through this desert by night and for some reason—falling asleep or anything else—he gets separated from his companions and wants to rejoin them, he hears spirit voices talking to him as if they were his companions, sometimes even calling him by name. Often these voices lure him away from the path and he never finds it again, and many travelers have got lost and died because of this. Sometimes in the night travelers hear a noise like the clatter of a great company of riders away from the road; if they believe that these are some of their own company and head for the noise, they find themselves in deep trouble when daylight comes and they realize their mistake. There were some who, in crossing the desert, have seen a host of men coming towards them and, suspecting that they were robbers, returning, they have gone hopelessly astray…Even by daylight men hear these spirit voices, and often you fancy you are listening to the strains of many instruments, especially drums, and the clash of arms. For this reason bands of travelers make a point of keeping very close together. Before they go to sleep they set up a sign pointing in the direction in which they have to travel, and round the necks of all their beasts they fasten little bells, so that by listening to the sound they may prevent them from straying off the path."

A Fourteenth-century Italian Guide for Merchants

After the Mongol conquests, missionaries and merchants traveled with increasing regularity to China via the Silk Road. The journeys peaked in the thirteenth and fourteenth centuries CE until the route became too treacherous. As a result of this, the focus shifted to finding a sea route to Asia. Some travelers (such as Marco Polo) wrote travelogues, while others, as our example shows here, wrote practical advice for those leaving for far-off places.

Source: *A fourteenth-century Italian guide for merchants, from Henry Yule,* Cathay and the Way Thither *(London, 1866).*

Focus Questions:
1. What is needed for the journey?
2. What are the hazards, great and small?
3. Note the lists of goods. What are their various origins?

CATHEY AND THE WAY THITHER—VOL. 2

CHAPTER II
Things needful for merchants who desire to make the journey to Cathay above described.

In the first place, you must let your beard grow long and not shave. And at Tana you should furnish yourself with a dragoman. And you must not try to save money in the matter of dragomen by taking a bad one instead of a good one. For the additional wages of the good one will not cost you so much as you will save by having him.[1] And besides the dragoman it will be well to take at least two good men servants, who are acquainted with the Cumanian tongue. And if the merchant likes to take a woman with him from Tana, he can do so; if he does not like to take one there is no obligation, only if he does take one he will be kept much more comfortably that if he does not take one. Howbeit, if he do take one, it will be well that she be acquainted with the Cumanian tongue as well as the men.[2]

And from Tana travelling to Gittarchan you should take with you twenty-five days provisions, that is to say, flour and salt fish, for as to meat you will find enough of it at all the places along the road. And so

---

[1] The Italian here is very obscure and probably defective, but this seems the general sense; or perhaps, "so much as the greed of the other will cause you loss."
[2] The Cumanian was apparently a Turkish dialect.

also at all the chief stations noted in going from one country to another in the route, according to the number of days set down above, you should furnish yourself with flour and salt fish; other things you will find in sufficiency, and especially meat.

The road you travel from Tana to Cathay is perfectly safe, whether by day or by night, according to what the merchants say who have used it. Only if the merchant, in going or coming, should die upon the road, everything belonging to him will become the perquisite of the lord of the country in which he dies, and the officers of the lord will take possession of all.[3] And in like manner if he die in Cathay. But if his brother be with him, or an intimate friend and comrade calling himself his brother, then to such an one they will surrender the property of the deceased, and so it will be rescued.

And there is another danger: this is when the lord of the country dies, and before the new lord who is to have the lordship is proclaimed; during such intervals there have sometimes been irregularities practiced [sic] on the Franks, and other foreigners. (They call *Franks* all the Christians of these parts from Romania westward).[4] And neither will the roads be safe to travel until the other lord be proclaimed who is to reign in room of him who is deceased.

Cathay is a province which contained a multitude of cities and towns. Among others there is one in particular, that is to say the capital *city*, to which is great resort of merchants, and in which there is a vast amount of trade; and this city is called Cambalec. And the said city Path a circuit of one hundred miles, and is all full of people and houses and of dwellers in the said city.

You may calculate that a merchant with a dragoman, and with two menservants, and with goods to the value of twenty-five thousand golden florins, should spend on his way to Cathay from sixty to eighty *sommi* of silver, and not more if he manage well; and for all the road back again from Cathay to Tana, including the expenses of living and the pay of servants, and all other charges, the cost will be about five *sommi* per head of pack animals, or something less. And you may reckon the *sommo* to be worth five golden florins.[5] You may reckon also that each ox-waggon will require one ox, and will carry ten cantars Genoese weight; and the camel-waggon will require three camels, and will carry thirty cantars Genoese weight; and the horse-waggon will require one horse, and will commonly carry six and half cantars of silk, at 250 Genoese pounds to the cantar. And a bale[6] of silk may be reckoned at between 110 and 115 Genoese pounds.

You may reckon also that from Tana to Sara the road is less safe than on any other part of the journey; and yet even when this part of the road is at its worst, if you are some sixty men in the company you will go as safely as if you were in your own house.

Anyone from Genoa or from Venice, wishing to go to the places above-named, and to make the journey to Cathay, should carry linens[7] with him, and if he visit Organci he will dispose of these well. In Organci he should purchase *sommi* of silver, and with these he should proceed without making any further invest-

---

[3] This custom seems to have prevailed very generally (see *Sto. Stephano in India in the Fifteenth Century*, p. 7). It was also the law of Lesser Armenia unless a subject of the kingdom was left heir (*J. As.*, ser. v, tom. xviii, 346).

[4] Romania means Greece, or nearly so. By Giov. da Uzzano the Morea and the isle of Scio are both spoken of as belonging to Romania (pp. 89 and 160). And the expression in the text (*tutti i Christian delle parti di Romania innanzi in verso it ponente*) seems to *include* Romania. Yet I do not think the Greeks were or are regarded as Franks.

[5] Taking the gold florin or ducat at 9s. 6d., the value of the goods will be nearly £12,000 and the cost of the merchants journey from £140 to £190 going, and nearly £12 a head on his beasts coming back.

[6] *Scibetto.* I cannot trace this word in any dictionary, but it looks like Arabic. The nearest thing I can find is sibt—hides of ox leather (*Frey-tag*). It is possible that the silk may have been packed in such. From India and China now it is generally packed in mats. Pegolotti writes it in another place in the plural *iscibetti*, with *far delli* as synonymous (p. 131). The Genoese pound of twelve ounces was equal to about; of the London pound (Ng), as we learn from Pegolotti in another part of his book.

[7] *Tele*

ment, unless it be some bales of the very finest stuffs which go in small bulk, and cost no more for carriage than coarser stuffs would do.

Merchants who travel this road can ride on horseback or on asses, or mounted in *any way* that they list to be mounted.

Whatever silver the merchants may carry with them as far as Cathay the lord of Cathay will take from them and put into his treasury. And to merchants who thus bring silver they give that paper money of theirs in exchange. This is of yellow paper, stamped with the seal of the lord aforesaid. And this money is called *balishi*;[8] and with this money you can readily buy silk and all other merchandize that you have a desire to buy. And all the people of the country are bound to receive it. And yet you shall not pay a higher price for your goods because your money is of paper. And of the said paper money there are three kinds, one being worth more than another, according to the value which has been established for each by that lord.[9]

And you may reckon that you can buy for one *sommo* of silver nineteen or twenty pounds of Cathay silk, when reduced to Genoese weight, and that the sommo should weigh eight and a half ounces of Genoa, and should be of the alloy of eleven ounces and seventeen deniers to the pound.[10]

You may reckon also that in Cathay you should get three or three and a half pieces of damasked silk[11] for a *sommo*; and from three and a half to five pieces of *nacchetti*[12] of silk and gold, likewise for a *sommo* of silver.

CHAPTER III
Comparison of the weights and measures of Cathay and of Tana. lbs. oz.

The maund[13] of Sara = in Genoa weight
Organci
Oltrarre Armalec Camexu

---

[8] The Riccardian MS. has here palisci, as in the previous chapter *babisci*. No doubt in both places the original had balisci.

[9] This seems to allude to three classes of notes, as in Kublai's issue of 12G0 mentioned above.
You may reckon also that in Cathay you should get three or three and a half pieces of damasked silk for a *sommo* ; and from three and a half to five pieces of *nacchetti* of silk and gold, likewise for a *sommo* of silver.

[10] *i.e.*, 7 pennyweights of alloy to 11 oz. 17 dwts. of pure silver. Giov. da Uzzano in the next century speaks of the *sommi* from Caff a as being of both gold and silver, the alloy of the latter being 11 oz. 13 to 15 dwt. (p. 188).

[11] The word is *cammocca*. This the dictionaries generally are good enough to tell us means "a kind of cloth." Mr. Wright on Mandeville says it is "a rich cloth of silk mentioned not unfrequently in medieval writers," but this is still very unprecise. I had arrived at the conclusion that it must be *damasked silk*, and I now find this confirmed by Ducange (Gloss. *Grcecitatis*, etc.): "Iccgwu as, *Pannus sericus more damasceno confectus*." Moreover the word is almost certainly the Arabic *kimkhwd*,
Vestis scutulata Damascena" (Freytag). I suppose that the *kinkhwdb* of Hindustan, now applied to a gold brocade, is the same word or a derivative.

[12] In a later chapter describing the trade at Constantinople, our author details "silk velvets, *cammucca*, maramati, gold cloth of every kind, *nacchetti* and *nacchi* of every kind, and likewise all cloths of gold and silk except *zendadi* (gauzes)." The *nacchi* and *nacchetti* appear to have been cloths of silk and gold. The former (*nakh*) is so explained by Ibn Batuta, who names it several times. It was made, he tells us, at Nisabur in Khorassan, and in describing the dress of the princess of Constantinople he says she had on "a mantle of the stuff called *nakh*, and also *nasy*." These two, however, were apparently not identical, but corresponded probably to the *nacchi* and *nacchetti* of Pegolotti. For Polo in the Ramusian version has "panni d'oro *nasiti* (*nasici* ?) fin, e nach, e panni di seta." And in the old version printed in Baldelli Boni's first volume this runs "*nasicci*, drappi dorati ;" whilst Rubruquis mentions *nasic* as a present given him by Mangu Khan. I know not what *maramati* is, unless it should rather be *maramali* for *makhmal*, velvet. (*Ibn Batuta, ii, 309, 388, 422; iii, 81; Polo in Ramus*., pt. i, c. 53; *Il IJiilione, i, 57; Pub.*, *p. 317*.)

[13] This should be equal to thirty, not twenty, Genoese pounds, as is shown by passages at pp. 31, 37, of Pegolotti: Is this *great pound* the origin of the Russian *good*.

TANA ON THE BLACK SEA

At Tana, as shall next be shown, they use a variety of weights and measures, viz.:

The *cantar*, which is that of Genoa.
The *great poun*[14] = 20 lbs. Genoese.
The *ruotolo*,[15] of which 20 = 1 great pound.
The *little pound*, which is the Genoese pound.
The *tochetto*, of which 12 = 1 great pound.
The *saggio*, of which 45 = 1 sommo.
The *picco*.[16]

Wax, ladanum,[17] iron, tin, copper, pepper, ginger, all coarser spices, cotton, madder, and suet, cheese, flax, and oil, honey, and the like, sell by the great pound.

Silk, saffron, amber wrought in rosaries and the like, and all small spices sell by the little pound.

Vair-skins by the 1000; and 1020 go to the 1000. Ermines by the 1000; 1000 to the 1000.

Foxes, sables, fitches and martens, wolfskins, deerskins, and all cloths of silk or gold, by the piece.

Common stuffs, and canvasses of every kind sell by the *picco*.

Tails are sold by the bundle at twenty to the bundle. Oxhides by the hundred in tale, giving a hundred and no more.

Horse and pony hides by the piece.

Gold and pearls are sold by the *saggio*.[18] Wheat and all other corn and pulse is sold at Tana by a measure which they call *cascito*.[19] Greek wine and all Latin wines are sold by the cask as they come. Malmsey and wines of Triglia and Candia are sold by the measure.

Caviar is sold by the *fusco*, and a *fusco* is the tail-half of the fish's skin, full of fish's roe.[20]

---

[14] *Mena*, representing the Arabic man, I suppose from Greek and Lat. mina, diffused over all the East with an infinite variety of values from below two pounds up to one hundred pounds. We have Anglicized it in India into maund. The man of Ghazan Khan, which may be meant here, was of 260 drachms.

[15] The *can taro* and *ruotolo* both survive in Southern Italy and Sicily, the former derived from the *kantdr* and the latter from the *rithl* of the Arabs, though the first of these words, and perhaps both, must have come to the Arabic from the Latin.

[16] The *pik* is still the common cloth measure in the Levant. It seems generally to be about twenty-eight inches.

[17] *Ladanum* or *labdanum* (the *lc%din* of the Arabs), is a gum resin derived from the *Cistus creticus*, which grows in the Islands of the Levant. It is exported in solid pieces of cylindrical and other forms. A long description of the mode of collecting it, etc., will be found in *Tournefort, Voyage du Levant, i,* 84, *et seq.* According to Herodotus, ladanum was derived "from a most inodorous place," viz., the beards of he-goats, which collected it from the bushes in browsing (*Rawlinson's Herod., bk. iii,* 113).

[18] The *saggio* in Italy was $^7A^z$ of a pound, i.e., of an ounce (*Pegol,* p. 31). Here it was a little more, as may be deduced from its relation to the sommo opposite.

[19] *Cascito* must have been miswritten for *cafico*. There is a measure called *kafiz* in Arabic, and specified as *cafizium* in some of the treaties (*Not. et Ext., xi,* 30). Hammer-Purgstall mentions *kofeiz* as a standard measure at Tabriz, which is doubtless the same (*Gesch. der Golden Horde,* etc., p. 225). And Pegolotti himself has *cafisso* as a Moorish measure. Indeed, I need not have sought this word so far away. It is still used in Sicily as *Cafisu* for an oil-measure, the fifth part of a *Cantaro*. It also exists in Spanish as *Cahiz,* and will be found in Ducange in a variety of forms, *Cafflum, Caficium, Cafisa, Cappitius,* etc.

[20] Caviare is now exported in small kegs. *Fusco* is perhaps just *fish*. In the dialect of the Goths of the Crimea, that word was *fisct* according to Busbeck. The sturgeon of the Borysthenes are already mentioned by Herodotus as large fish without prickly bones, called *antaccei*, good for pickling, and according to Professor Rawlinson caviare also was known to the Greeks as *Taptxoc Avxa, caiov.*

CHAPTER IV

Charges on merchandize which are paid at Tana on things entering the city, nothing being paid on going forth thereof.

Gold, silver, and pearls at Tana pay neither *eomerehio* nor *tamufga*, nor any other duties.

On wine, and ox-hides, and tails, and horse-hides, the Genoese and Venetians pay four percent, and all other people five per cent.

What is paid for the transit of merchandize at Tana

Silk—15 aspers per pound.

All other things—at...aspers for 3 cantars.

CHAPTER V

gives details as to the relation of the Tana weights

At Tana the money current is of *sommi* and aspers of silver. The *sommo* weighs 45 *saggi* of Tana, and is of the alloy of 11 oz. 17 dwt. of fine silver to the pound. And if silver be sent to the Tana mint, they coin 202 aspers from the *sommo*,[21] but they pay you only 190, retaining the rest for the work of the mint and its profit. So a sommo at Tana is reckoned to be 190 aspers. And the sommi are ingots of silver of the alloy before mentioned, which are paid away by weight. But they do not all weigh the same, so the ingots are weighed at the time of payment, and if the weight is less than it ought to be the balance is paid in aspers, to make up every sommo to the value of 45 saggi of Tana weight.

And there are also current at Tana copper coins called *folleri*, of which sixteen go to the asper. But the *folleri* are not used in mercantile transactions, but only in the purchase of vegetables and such small matters for town use.[22]

CHAPTER VI

On the expenses which usually attend the transport of merchandize from Ajazzo of Erminia to Torissi, by land.

In the first place from ALALLO as far as COLIDARA,[23] i.e., as far as the King of Armenia's territory extends, you pay altogether 41 taccolini and 31 deniers (at the rate of 10 deniers to the taccolino) on every load, whether of camels or of other beasts. Now taking the taccolino to be about an asper, the amount will be about 41 aspers of Tauris per load. And 6 aspers of Tauris are equal to one Tauris bezant.

At GANDON, where you enter upon the lands of Bonsaet,
    i.e. of the lord of the Tartars,[24] on every load. 20 aspers.
At the same place, for watching, ditto
At CASENA
    At the CARAVANSERAI of the ADMIRAL[25]

---

[21] The *asper* must therefore have contained silver to the amount of about 0s. 2.8d.

[22] *Follero* is the Byzantine copper *Follis*, and perhaps Persian pal.

[23] Respecting Aiazzo see note, p. 278 *supra*. *Colidara* should perhaps be Gobidar, the name of an Armenian fortress and barony in Taurus, which is mentioned in *Journ. As., ser. v, vol. xviii, 314.*

[24] *Bonsaet* is Abu Said Bahadar Khan, the last effective sovereign of the Mongol dynasty in Persia, who died 1335. He is called Busaid by some Arabic writers, and on some Mongol coins. The Pope in addressing him calls him *Boyssethan,* i.e. Busaid Khan (*D'Ohsson, iv, 716; ifosheim, 144*).

[25] *Gavazera del Ammiraglio,* I suppose *Karwdnsarai-ul-Amir.* The same word is used at each place rendered caravanserai.

At GADUE
At the CARAVANSERAI of CASA JACODII
At the entrance to SALVASTRO[26] from Aiazzo
    Inside the city
Leaving the city on the road to Tauris
    At DUDRIAGA,[27]

than is perfectly' o what the merit erchant, in gip rything belongit?t lord of the conntli rd will take pos. in Cathay. Betifl e friend and ova suchanonetheya -ed, and so it i

and measures to those of Venice, etc.; as to the weights and measures of Caffa; and as to those of Tabriz (*Torissi di Persia*). The duties at Tabriz are called *Camunoca*.

Excerpts from The History of the Life and Travels of Rabban Bar Sawma

Bar Rabban Sawma (1260–1313 CE) was a Christian monk from northern China. He was a member of a group of Turks who, like a number of steppe peoples, had been converted to Nestorian Christianity by missionaries from the Middle East. Rabban Sawma traveled with a companion, Markus, on pilgrimage to Jerusalem but was sidetracked on a diplomatic mission for the Mongol khan. He went to Byzantium and Western Europe seeking allies for a combined attack intended to push the Mamluk Egyptians out of Jerusalem. Rabban Sawma died after returning to Baghdad, having never reached Jerusalem.

Source: *Sir E. A. Wallis Budge, trans.,* The Monks of Kublai Kahn Emperor of China. *(London: The Religious Tract Society, 1928)*

Focus Questions:
1. Why was Rabban Sawma's theology questioned so closely in Rome?
2. How did the Nestorians and Europeans react to one another?
3. Compare Sawma'a experiences with those of European travelers going east.

THE MONKS OF KUBLAI KAHN EMPEROR OF CHINA

CHAPTER VII.

(47) ON THE DEPARTURE OF RABBAN SAWMA TO THE COUNTRY OF THE ROMANS IN THE NAME OF KING ARGHON AND OF THE CATHOLICUS MAR YAHBH-ALLAHA.

Now MAR YAHBH-ALLAHA, the Catholicus, increased in power, and his honour before the King and Queens grew greater daily. He pulled down the church of MAR SHALITA which was in MARAGHAH, and he rebuilt it at very great expense. And instead of using [the old] beams [and making a single roof] he made [the new church] with two naves (*haikili*); and by the side of it he built a cell in which to live. For his affection for the house of King ARGHON was very warm, because ARGHON loved the Christians with his whole heart. And ARGHON intended to go into the countries of Palestine and Syria and to subjugate them and take possession of them, but he said to himself, "If the Western Kings, who

---

[26] Sebaste, now Siwas.
[27] The proper reading is probably *Duvriaga*, viz., Divrik or Teceptio a place still existing between Sivas and Erzingan.

are Christians, will not help me I shall not be able to fulfill my desire." Thereupon he asked the Catholicus to give him a wise man (48), "one who is suitable and is capable of undertaking an embassy, that we may send him to those kings." And when the Catholicus saw that there was no man who knew (166) the language except Rabban Sawma, and knowing that he was fully capable of this, he commanded him to go [on the embassy].

THE JOURNEY OF RABBAN SAWMA; TO THE COUNTRY OF THE ROMANS IN THE NAME OF KING ARGHON AND OF THE CATHOLICUS MAR YAHBHALLAHA.

Then RABBAN SAWMA said, "I desire this embassy greatly, and I long to go." Then straightway King ARGHON wrote for him "Authorities" (*pukdana*) to the king of the Greeks, and the king of the PEROGAYE (Franks?) that is to say Romans, and Yarlike [i.e. the "Ordinances" of the Mongolian kings], and letters, and gave him gifts for each of the kings [addressed by him]. And to RABBAN SAWMA he gave two thousand *mathkale* (£1,000?) of gold, and thirty good riding animals, and a Paiza (see above, pp. 62, 63). And RABBAN SAWMA came to the cell of the Catholicus to obtain letter from MAR YAHBH-ALLAHA, and to say farewell to him. The Catholicus gave his permission to depart (49), but when the time for his departure arrived, it did not please the Catholicus to permit him to go. For he said [unto Rabban Sawma], "How can this possibly take place? Thou hast been the governor of my cell, and thou knowest that through thy departure my affairs will fall into a state of utter confusion." And having said such words as (167) these they said farewell to each other, weeping as they did so. And the Catholicus sent with him letters, and gifts which were suitable for presentation to Mar Papa (the Pope), and gifts [i.e. offerings] according to his ability.

RABBAN SAWMA IN ITALY AND IN GREAT ROME.

And he departed from Constantinople and went down to the sea. And he saw on the sea-shore a monastery of the Romans, and there were laid up in its treasure-house two funerary coffers of silver; in the one was the head of MAR JOHN CHRYSOSTOM, and in the other that of MAR PAPA who baptized CONSTANTINE. And he went down to the sea [i.e. embarked on a ship] and came to the middle thereof, where he saw a mountain from which smoke ascended all the day long and in the night time fire showed itself on it. And no man is able to approach the neighbourhood of it because of the stench of sulphur [proceeding therefrom]. Some people say that there is a great serpent there. This sea is called the "Sea of Italy." Now it is a terrible sea, and very many thousands of (54) people have perished therein. And after two months of toil, and weariness, and exhaustion, RABBAN SAWMA (171) arrived at the sea-shore, and he landed at the name of which was NAPOLI (Naples); the name of its king was IRID SHARDALO [= IL RE SHARL DU or, the King Charles II?]. And he went to the king and showed him the reason why they had come; and the king welcomed him and paid him honour. Now it happened that there was war between him and another king, whose name was IRID ARKON [= the King of Aragon, JAMES II?]. And the troops of the one had come in many ships, and the troops of the other were ready, and they began to fight each other, and the King of ARAGON (?) conquered King CHARLES II, and slew twelve thousand [of] his men, and sunk their ships in the sea. [According to Chabot this naval engagement took place in the Bay of Sorrento on St. John's Day, June 24, 1287, and the great eruption of Mount Etna on June 18.] Meanwhile RABBAN SAWMA and his companions sat upon the roof the mansion in which they lived, and they admired the way in which the Franks waged war for they attacked none of the people except those who were actually combatants (55). And from that place they travelled inland on horses, and they passed through towns and villages and marvelled because they found no land which was destitute of buildings. On the road they heard that MAR PAPA [Honorius IV who died in 1287] was dead. (172) And the Cardinals said unto him, "For the present rest thyself, and we will discuss the matter together later"; and they assigned to him a mansion and caused him to be taken down thereto.

Three days later the Cardinals sent and summoned RABBAN SAWMA to their presence. And when he went to them they began to ask him questions, saying, "What is thy quarter of the world, and why hast thou come?" And he replied in the selfsame words he had already spoken to them (57). And they said unto him, "Where doth the Catholicus live? And the Cardinals. And thus they did, and [their act] was pleasing to those Cardinals. And when RABBAN SAWMA went into their presence no man stood up before him, for by reason of the honourable nature of the Throne, the twelve Cardinals were not in the habit of doing this. And they made RABBAN SAWMA sit down with them, and one of them asked him, "How art thou after all the fatigue of the road?" And he made answer to him, "Through you prayers I am well and rested." And the Cardinal said unto him, "For what purpose hast thou (173) come hither?" And RABBAN SAWMA said unto him, "The Mongols and the Catholicus of the East have sent me to Mar Papa concerning the matter of Jerusalem; and they have sent letters with me." And the Cardinals said unto him, "For the present rest thyself, and we will discuss the matter together later"; and they assigned to him a mansion and caused him to be taken down thereto.

Three days later the Cardinals sent and summoned RABBAN SAWMA to their presence. And when he went to them they began to ask him questions, saying, "What is thy quarter of the world, and why has thou come?" And he replied in the selfsame words he had already spoden to them (57). And they said unto him, "Where doth the Catholicus live? And which of the Apostles taught the Gospel in thy quarter of the world?" And he answered them, saying, "MAR THOMAS, and MAR ADDAI, and MAR MARI taught the Gospel in our quarter of the world, and we hold at the present time the canons [or statutes] which they delivered unto us." The Cardinals said unto him, "Where is the Throne of the Catholicus?" He said to them, "In BAGHDAD." They answered, What position hast thou there?" And he replied, "I am a deacon in the Cell of the Catholicus, and the director of the disciples, and the Visitor-General." The Cardinals said, "It is a marvellous thing (174) that thou who art a Christian, and a deacon of the Throne of the Patriarch of the East has come upon an embassy from the king of the Mongols." And RABBAN SAWMA said unto them, "Know ye, O our Fathers, that many of our Fathers have gone into the countries of the Mongols, and Turks, and Chinese and have taught them the Gospel, and at the present time there are many Mongols who are Christians. For many of the sons of the Mongol kings and queens (58) have been baptized and confess Christ. And they have established churches in their military camps, and they pay honour to the Christians, and there are among them many who are believers. Now the king [of the Mongols], who is joined in the bond of friendship with the Catholicus, hath the desire to take PALESTINE, and the countries of SYRIA, and he demandeth from you help in order to take JERUSALEM. He hath chosen me and hath sent me to you because, being a Christian, my word will be believed by you." And the Cardinals said unto him, "What is thy confession of faith? To what 'way' art thou attached? Is it that which Mar Papa holdeth to-day or some other one?" RABBAN SAWMA replied, "No man hath come to us Orientals from the Pope. The holy Apostle whose names I have mentioned taught us the Gospel, and to what they delivered unto us we have clung to the present day." The Cardinals (175) said unto him, "How dost thou believe? Recite thy belief, article by article." RABBAN SAWMA replied to them, saying:

THE BELIEF OF RABBAN SAWMA, WHICH THE CARDINALS DEMANDED FROM HIM.
"I believe in One God, hidden, everlasting, without beginning and without (59) end, Father, and Son, and Holy Spirit: Three Persons, coequal and indivisible; among Whom there is none who is first, or last, or young, or old: in Nature they are One, in Persons they are three: the Father is the Begetter, the Son is the Begotten, the Spirit proceedeth.

"In the last time one of the Persons of the Royal Trinity, namely the Son, put on the perfect man, Jesus Christ, from MARY the holy virgin; and was united to Him Personally (*parsopaith*), and in him saved (or redeemed) the world. In His Divinity He is eternally of the Father; in His humanity He was born [a Being] in time of MARY; the union is inseparable and indivisible for ever; the union is without mingling, and without mixture, and without compaction. The Son of this union is perfect God (60) and perfect man, two Natures (*keyanin*), and two Persons (*kenomin*)—one parsopa (...)

The Cardinals said unto him, "Doth the Holy Spirit proceed from the Father or from the Son, or is it separate?" RABBAN SAWMA replied, (176) "Are the Father, and the Son, and the Spirit associated in the things which appertain to the Nature (*keyana*) or separate?" The Cardinals answered, "They are associated in the things which concern the Nature (*keyana*) but are separate in respect of individual qualities." RABBAN SAWMA said, "What are their individual qualities?" The Cardinals replied, "Of the Father, the act of begetting: of the Son the being begotten: of the Spirit the going forth (proceeding)." RABBAN SAWMA said, "Which of Them is the cause of that Other?" And the Cardinals replied, "The Father is the cause of the Son, and the Son is the cause of the Spirit." RABBAN SAWMA said, "If they are coequal in Nature (*keyana*), and in operation, and in power, and in authority (or dominion), and the Three Persons (*kenome*) are One, how is it possible for one of Them to be the cause of the Other? For of necessity (**61**) the Spirit also must be the cause of some other thing; but the discussion is extraneous to the Confession of faith of wise men. We cannot find a demonstration resembling this statement of yours.

"For behold, the soul is the cause both of the reasoning power and the act of living, but the reasoning power is not the cause of the act of living. The sphere of the sun is the cause of light and heat, and heat is not the cause of light. Thus we think that which is correct, (**177**) namely, that the Father is the cause of the Son and the Spirit, and that both the Son and the Spirit are causation of His. Adam begot Seth, and made Eve to proceed [from him], and they are three; because in respect there is absolutely no difference between begetting and making to go forth (or proceed)."

Then the Cardinals said unto him, "We confess that the Spirit proceedeth from the Father and the Son, but not as we said, for we were only putting thy modesty [or, religious belief?] to the test." And RABBAN SAWMA said, "It is not right that to something which is one, two, three, or four causes should be [assigned]; on the contrary I do not think that this resembleth our Confession of Faith." Now though the Cardinals restrained (**62**) his speech by means of very many demonstrations, they held him in high esteem because of his power of argument.

Then RABBAN SAWMA said unto them, "I have come from remote countries neither to discuss, nor to instruct [men] in matter of the Faith, but I came that I might receive a blessing from MAR PAPA, and from the shrines of the saints and to make known the words of King [ARGHON] and the Catholicus. If it be pleasing in your eyes, let us set aside discussion, and do ye give attention and direct someone to show us the churches here and the shrines of the saints; [if ye will (**178**) do this] ye will confer a very great favour on your servant and disciple."

Then the Cardinals summoned the Amir of the city and certain monks and commanded them to show him the churches and the holy places that were there; and they went forth straightway and saw the places which we will now mention. First of all they went into the church of PETER and PAUL. Beneath the Throne is a naos, and in this is laid (**63**) the body of SAINT PETER, and above the throne is an altar. The altar which is in the middle of that are [sic], temple has four doorways, and in each of these two folding doors worked with designs in fro [sic]; MAR PAPA celebrates the Mass at this altar, and no person besides himself may stand on the bench of that altar. Afterwards they saw the Throne of MAR PETER whereon they make MAR PAPA to sit when they appoint him. And the also saw the strip of fine [or thin] linen on which our Lord impressed His image and sent to King ABHGAR of URHAI (Edessa). Now the extent of that temple and its splendour cannot be described; it stands on one hundred and eight pillars. In it is another altar at which the King of their Kings receives the laying on of hands [i.e. is consecrated and crowned], and is proclaimed "Ampror (Emperor) King of Kings," by the Pope. And they say that after the prayer Mar Papa takes up the Crown with his feet (**179**) and clothes the Emperor with it (**64**), that is to say, places it upon his own head [to show], as they say, that priesthood reigneth over sovereignty[or kingship].

And when they had seen all the churches and monasteries that were in Great Rome, they went outside the city to the church of MAR PAUL the Apostle, where under the altar is his tomb. And there, too, is the chain wherewith Paul was bound when he was dragged to that place. And in that altar there are also a reliquary of gold herein is the head of MAR STEPHEN the Martyr, and the hand of MAR

KHANANYA (ANANIAS) who baptized PAUL. And the staff of PAUL the Apostle is also there. And from that place they went to the spot where PAUL the Apostle, was crowned [with martyrdom]. They say that when his head was cut off it leaped up thrice into the air, and at each time cried out CHRIST! CHRIST! And that from each of the three places on which his head fell there came forth waters which were useful for healing purposes, and for giving help to all those who were afflicted. And in that place there is a great shrine (65) wherein are the bones of martyrs and famous Fathers, and they were blessed by them.

And they went also to the Church of my Lady MARYAM, and of MAR JOHN the Baptist, and saw therein the seamless tunic of our Lord. And there is also in that church the tablet [or (180) slab] on which our Lord consecrated the Offering and gave it to His disciples. And each year Mar Papa consecrates on that tablet the Paschal Mysteries. There are in that church four pillars of copper [or brass], each of which is six cubits in thickness; these, they say, the kings brought from Jerusalem. They saw also there the vessel in which CONSTANTINE, the victorious king, was baptized; it is made of black stone [basalt?] polished. Now that church is very large and broad, and there are in the nave (*haikla*) one hundred and forty white marble pillars. They saw also the place where SIMON KIPA [i.e. Simon the Rock] disputed with SIMON [Magus], and where the latter fell down and his bones were broken.

From that place they went into the church of MART MARYAM, and [the priests] brought out for them reliquaries made of beryl (crystal?), wherein was (66) the apparel of MART MARYAM, and a piece of wood on which our Lord had lain when a child. They saw also the head of MATTHEH the Apostle, in a reliquary of silver. And they saw the foot of PHILIP, the Apostle, and the arm of JAMES, the son of ZABHDA! (ZEBEDEE}, in the Church of the Apostles, which was there. And after these [sights] they saw buildings which it is impossible to describe in words, and as the histories of those buildings would make any description of them very long I abandon [the attempt]. (181) After this RABBAN SAWMA and his companions returned to the Cardinals, and thanked them for having held him to be worthy to see these shrines and to receive blessings from them. And RABBAN SAWMA asked from them permission to go to the king who dwelleth in Rome; and they permitted him to go, and said, "We cannot give thee an answer until the [new] Pope is elected."

And they went from that place to the country of TUSZKAN (TUSCANY), and were honourably entreated, and thence they (67) went to GINOH (GENOA). Now the latter country has no king, but the people thereof set up to rule over it some great man with whom they are pleased.

And when the people of GENOA heard that an ambassador of King ARGHON had arrived, their Chief went forth with a great crowd of people, and they brought him into the city.

And there was there a great church with the name of SAINT SINALORNIA (SAN LORENZO), in which was the holy body of MAR JOHN the Baptist, in a coffer of pure silver. And RABBAN SAWMA and his companions saw also a six-sided paten, made of emerald, and the people there told them that it was off this paten from which our Lord ate the Passover with His disciples, and that it was brought there when Jerusalem was captured. And from that place they went to the country of ONBAR, [according to Bedjan, Lombardy] and they saw that the people there (182) did not fast during the first Sabbath of Lent. And when they asked them, "Wherefore do ye do thus, and separate yourselves from all [other] Christians" (68), they replied, "This is our custom. When we were first taught the Gospel our fathers in the Faith were weakly and were unable to fast. Those who taught them the Gospel commanded them to fast forty days only."

Marchione di Coppo Stefani, *The Florentine Chronicle*, "Concerning a Mortality in the City of Florence in Which Many People Died"

Florence was one of the great Mediterranean trading cities of the Middle Ages. As such, exposure to the plague was almost guaranteed. The plague in Florence has been brilliantly described by Boccaccio in his Decameron, though his was a fictional account. In contrast, Marchione di Coppo Stefani (1327–1383 CE), a minor Florentine official, wrote a first hand chronicle of events in Florence at the time of the plague. The chronicle provides a rich description of the plague's effects, the city's reactions, and of the aftermath.

Source: *Marchione di Coppo Stefani,* The Florentine Chronicle *(c. 1380).*

Focus Questions:
1. What is the response of the physicians?
2. How do families respond?
3. After the plague has ended, how do the survivors act socially and economically?

RUBRIC 643: CONCERNING A MORALITY IN THE CITY OF FLORENCE IN WHICH MANY PEOPLE DIED.

In the year of the Lord 1348 there was a very great pestilence in the city and district of Florence. It was of such a fury and so tempestuous that in houses in which it took hold previously healthy servants who took care of the ill died of the same illness. Almost none of the ill survived past the fourth day. Neither physicians nor medicines were effective. Whether because these illnesses were previously unknown or because physicians had not previously studied them, there seemed to be no cure. There was such a fear that no one seemed to know what to do. When it took hold in a house it often happened that no one remained who had not died. And it was not just that men and women died, but even sentient animals died. Dogs, cats, chickens, oxen, donkeys and sheep showed the same symptoms and died of the same disease. And almost none, or very few, who showed these symptoms, were cured. The symptoms were the following: a bubo in the groin, where the thigh meets the trunk; or a small swelling under the armpit; sudden fever; spitting blood and saliva (and no one who spit blood survived it). It was such a frightful thing that when it got into a house, as was said, no one remained. Frightened people abandoned the house and fled to another. Those in town fled to villages. Physicians could not be found because they had died like the others. And those who could be found wanted vast sums in hand before they entered the house. And when they did enter, they checked the pulse with face turned away. They inspected the urine from a distance and with something odoriferous under their nose. Child abandoned the father, husband the wife, wife the husband, one brother the other, one sister the other. In all the city there was nothing to do but to carry the dead to a burial. And those who died had neither confessor nor other sacraments. And many died with no one looking after them. And many died of hunger because when someone took to bed sick, another in the house, terrified, said to him: "I'm going for the doctor." Calmly walking out the door, the other left and did not return again. Abandoned by people, without food, but accompanied by fever, they weakened. There were many who pleaded with their relatives not to abandon them when night fell. But [the relatives] said to the sick person, "So that during the night you did not have to awaken those who serve you and who work hard day and night, take some sweetmeats, wine or water. They are here on the bedstead by your head; here are some blankets." And when the sick person had fallen asleep, they left and did not return. If it happened that he was strengthened by the food during the night he might be alive and strong enough to get to the window. If the street was not a major one, he might stand there a half hour before anyone came by. And if someone did pass by, and if he was strong enough that he could be heard when he called out to them, sometimes there might be a response and sometimes not, but there was no help. No one, or few, wished to enter a house where anyone was sick, nor did they even want to deal with those healthy people who came out of a sick person's house. And they said to them: "He is stupefied, do not speak to him!" saying further: "He has it because there is a bubo in his house." They call the swelling a bubo. Many died unseen. So they remained in their beds until they stank. And the neighbors, if there were any, having smelled the stench, placed them in a shroud and sent them for burial. The house remained open and yet there was no one daring enough to touch anything because it seemed that things remained poisoned and that whoever used them picked up the illness.

At every church, or at most of them, they dug deep trenches, down to the waterline, wide and deep, depending on how large the parish was. And those who were responsible for the dead carried them on their backs in the night in which they died and threw them into the ditch, or else they paid a high price to those who would do it for them. The next morning, if there were many [bodies] in the trench, they covered them over with dirt. And then more bodies were put on top of them, with a little more dirt over those; they put layer on layer just like one puts layers of cheese in a lasagna. The beccamorti [literally vultures] who provided their service, were paid such a high price that many were enriched by it. Many died from [carrying away the dead], some rich, some after earning just a little, but high prices continued. Servants, or those who took care of the ill, charged from one to three florins per day and the cost of things grew. The things that the sick ate, sweetmeats and sugar, seemed priceless. Sugar cost from three to eight florins per pound. And other confections cost similarly. Capons and other poultry were very expensive and eggs cost between twelve and twenty-four pence each; and he was blessed who could find three per day even if he searched the entire city. Finding wax was miraculous. A pound of wax would have gone up more than a florin if there had not been a stop put [by the communal government] to the vain ostentation that the Florentines always make [over funerals]. Thus it was ordered that no more than two large candles could be carried [in any funeral]. Churches had no more than a single bier which usually was not sufficient. Spice dealers and beccamorti sold biers, burial palls, and cushions at very high prices. Dressing in expensive woolen cloth as is customary in [mourning] the dead, that is in a long cloak, with mantle and veil that used to cost women three florins climbed in price to thirty florins and would have climbed to 100 florins had the custom of dressing in expensive cloth not been changed. The rich dressed in modest woolens, those not rich sewed [clothes] in linen. Benches on which the dead were placed cost like the heavens and still the benches were only a hundredth of those needed. Priests were not able to ring bells as they would have liked. Concerning that [the government] issued ordinances discouraging the sounding of bells, sale of burial benches, and limiting expenses. They could not sound bells, sell benches, nor cry out announcements because the sick hated to hear of this and it discouraged the healthy as well. Priests and friars went [to serve] the rich in great multitudes and they were paid such high prices that they all got rich. And therefore [the authorities] ordered that one could not have more than a prescribed number [of clerics] of the local parish church. And the prescribed number of friars was six. All fruits with a nut at the center, like unripe plums and unhusked almonds, fresh broadbeans, figs and every useless and unhealthy fruit, were forbidden entrance into the city. Many processions, including those with relics and the painted tablet of Santa Maria Inpruneta, went through the city crying our "Mercy" and praying and then they came to a stop in the piazza of the Priors. There they made peace concerning important controversies, injuries and deaths. This [pestilence] was a matter of such great discouragement and fear that men gathered together in order to take some comfort in dining together. And each evening one of them provided dinner to ten companions and the next evening they planned to eat with one of the others. And sometimes if they planned to eat with a certain one he had no meal prepared because he was sick. Or if the host had made dinner for the ten, two or three were missing. Some fled to villas, others to villages in order to get a change of air. Where there had been no [pestilence], there they carried it; if it was already there, they caused it to increase. None of the guilds in Florence was working. All the shops were shut, taverns closed; only the apothecaries and the churches remained open. If you went outside, you found almost no one. And many good and rich men were carried from home to church on a pall by four beccamorti and one tonsured clerk who carried the cross. Each of them wanted a florin. This mortality enriched apothecaries, doctors, poultry vendors, beccamorti, and greengrocers who sold of poultices of mallow, nettles, mercury and other herbs necessary to draw off the infirmity. And it was those who made these poultices who made alot of money. Woolworkers and vendors of remnants of cloth who found themselves in possession of cloths [after the death of the entrepreneur for whom they were working] sold it to whoever asked for it. When the mortality ended, those who found themselves with cloth of any kind or with raw materials for making cloth was enriched. But many found [who actually owned cloths being processed by workers] found it to be moth-eaten, ruined or lost by the weavers. Large quantities of raw and processed wool were lost throughout the city and countryside.

This pestilence began in March, as was said, and ended in September 1348. And people began to return to look after their houses and possessions. And there were so many houses full of goods without a master that it was stupefying. Then those who would inherit these goods began to appear. And such it was that those who had nothing found themselves rich with what did not seem to be theirs and they were unseemly because of it. Women and men began to dress ostentatiously.

RUBRIC 635: HOW MANY OF THE DEAD DIED BEAUSE OF THE MORTALITY OF THE YEAR OF CHRIST 1348.

Now it was ordered by the bishop and the Lords [of the city government] that they should formally inquire as to how many died in Florence. When it was seen at the beginning of October that no more persons were dying of the pestilence, they found that among males, females, children and adults, 96,000 died between March and October.

RUBRIC 636: HOW THEY PASSED ORDINANACE CONCERNING MANY THINGS IN FLORENCE.

In the said year, when the mortality stopped, women and men in Florence were unmindful of [traditional modesty concerning] their dress. And ordinances were passed concerning this giving authority to the Judge of the Grascia to enforce these ordinances. The tailors made such boundless demands for payment that they could not be satisfied. Authority was granted [to the judge] that he should handle all matters himself. Servants were so unhappy about the very high prices [they paid] that it was necessary to make great efforts to restrain [the price rises]. The workers on the land in the countryside wanted rent contracts such that you could say that all they harvested would be theirs. And they learned to demand oxen from the landlord but at the landlord's risk [and liability for any harm done to the animal]. And then they helped others for pay by the job or by the day. And they also learned to deny [liability for] loans and [rental] payments. Concerning this serious ordinances were instituted; and [hiring] laborers became much more expensive. You could say that the farms were theirs; and they wanted the oxen, seed, loans quickly and on good terms. It was necessary to put a brake on weddings as well because when they gathered for the betrothal each party brought too many people in order to increase the pomp. And thus the wedding was made up of so many trappings. How many days were necessary and how many women took part in a woman's wedding. And they passed many other ordinances concerning [these issues].

Ibn Battuta, *The Travels of Ibn Battuta*, "Ibn Battuta in Mali"

The traditional trade centers of the Indian Ocean and Mediterranean Sea slowly accumulated more areas into their economic spheres. East Africa readily participated in the Indian Ocean trade, its coastal cites booming. West Africa also benefited with connections to the wealthy Islamic areas along the Mediterranean. Rich kingdoms like Mali grew rich from acting as intermediaries in the trans-Saharan trade. Ibn Battuta's account is a reminder of the centrality of Arabic traders to many of these trade routes.

Source: *Ibn Battuta*, Ibn Battuta in Mali, *trans. from the Arabic by C. Defrémery and B. R. Sanguinétti (Paris, 1958).*

Focus Questions:
1. What are the modes of transport?
2. What goods are in demand?
3. What is Ibn Battuta's attitude towards the inhabitants?

(pp. 309, 310)

...I set out on the 1st Muharram of the year seven hundred and fifty-three (18 February, 1352 C.E.) with a caravan including amongst others a number of the merchants of Sijilmasa [*present day Morocco/Algerian frontier region*]. After twenty-five days we reached Taghaza, an unattractive village, with the curious feature that its houses and mosques are built of blocks of salt, roofed with camel skins. There are no trees there, nothing but sand. In the sand is a salt mine; they dig for the salt, and find it in thick slabs, lying one on top of the other, as though they had been tool-squared and laid under the surface of the earth. A camel will carry two of these slabs. No one lives at Taghaza except the slaves of the Masufa tribe, who dig for the salt; they subsist on dates imported from Dara and Sijilmasa [*Morocco*], camel's flesh, and millet imported from the Negrolands. The Negroes come up from their country and take away the salt from there. At Walata a load of salt brings eight to ten mithqals; in the town of Mali it sells for twenty to thirty, and sometimes as much as forty. The Negroes use salt as a medium of exchange, just as gold and silver is used elsewhere; they cut it up into pieces and buy and sell with it. The business done at Taghaza, for all its meanness, amounts to an enormous figure in terms of hundred-weights of gold dust...

Thus we reached the town of Walata after a journey of two months to a day. Walata is the northernmost province of the Negroes, and the Sultan's representative there was one Farba Husayn, Farba meaning deputy (in their language)...

... It was an excessively hot place, and boasts a few small date-palms, in the shade of which they sow watermelons. Its water comes from underground water beds at that point, and there is plenty of mutton to be had. The garments of the inhabitants, most of whom belong to the Masufa tribe, are of fine Egyptian fabrics. Their women are of surpassing beauty, and are shown more respect than the men. The state of affairs amongst these people is indeed extraordinary. Their men show no sign of jealousy whatever; no one claims descent from his father, but on the contrary from his mother's brother. A person's heirs are his sister's sons, not his own sons. This is a thing which I have seen nowhere in the world except among the Indians of Malabar. But those are heathens; these people are Muslims, punctilious in observing the hours of prayer, studying books of law, and memorizing the Koran. Yet their women show no bashfulness before men and do not veil themselves, though they are assiduous in attending prayers. Any man who wishes to marry one of them may do so, they do not travel with their husbands...

The women have their "friends" and "companions" amongst the men outside their own families, and the men in the same way have "companions" amongst the women of other families. A man may go into his house and find his wife entertaining her "companion," but he takes not objection to it. One day at Walata I went into the *qadi's* [*Muslim judge*] house, after asking his permission to enter, and found with a young woman of remarkable beauty. When I saw her I was shocked and turned to go out, but she laughed at me, instead of being overcome by shame, and the quadi said to me, "Why are you going out? She is my companion." I was amazed at their conduct, for he was a theologian and a pilgrim to boot. I was told that he had asked the sultan's permission to make the pilgrimage that year with his "companion" (whether this one or not I cannot say) but the sultan would not grant it.

(pp. 313, 314)

...On feast-days, after Dugha [*the interpreter*] has finished his display, the poets come in. Each of them is inside a figure resembling a thrush, made of feathers, and provided with a wooden head with a red beak, to look like a thrush's head. They stand in front of the sultan in this ridiculous make-up and recite their poems. I was told that their poetry is a kind of sermonizing in which they say to the sultan: "This *pempi* [*throne*] which you occupy was that whereon sat this king and that king, and such were this one's noble actions and such and such the other's. So do you too do good deeds whose memory will outlive you." After that the chief of the poets mounts the steps of the *pempi* and lays hid head on the sultan's lap, then climbs to the top of the *pempi* and lays his head on first on the sultan's right shoulder and then on his left, speaking all the while in their tongue, and finally he comes down again. I was told that this practice is a very old custom amongst them prior to the introduction of Islam, and they have kept it up.

...The Negroes possess some admirable qualities. They are seldom unjust, and have a greater abhorrence of injustice than any other people. The sultan shows no mercy to anyone who is guilty of the least act of it. There is a complete security in their country. Neither traveler nor inhabitant in it has anything to fear from robbers or men of violence. They do not confiscate the property of any white man [*Arab trader*] who dies in their country, even if it be accounted wealth. On the contrary, they give it into the charge of some trustworthy person among the whites, until the rightful heir takes possession of it. They are careful to observe the hours of prayer, and assiduous in attending them in congregations, and in bringing up their children to them. On Fridays, if a man does not go early to the mosque, he cannot find a corner to pray in, on account of the crowd. It is a custom of theirs to send each man his boy (to the mosque) with his prayer-mat; the boy spreads it out for his master in a place befitting him and remains on it (until his master comes to the mosque). The pray-mats are made of the leaves of a tree resembling a date-palm, but without fruit.

Another of their good qualities is their habit of wearing clean white garments on Fridays. Even if a man has nothing but an old worn shirt, he washes it and cleans it, and wears it at the Friday service. Yet another is their zeal for learning the Koran by heart. They put their children in chains if they show any backwardness in memorizing it, and they are not set free until they have it by heart. I visited the quadi in his house on the day of the festival. His children were chained up, so I said to him, "Will you not let them loose?" He replied, "I shall not do so until they learn the Koran by heart." Among their bad qualities are the following. The women servants, slave-girls, and young girls go about in front of everyone naked, without a stitch of clothing on them. Women go into the sultan's presence naked and without coverings, and his daughters also go about naked. Then there is the custom of their putting dust and ashes on their heads as a mark of respect, and the grotesque ceremonies we have described when the poets recite their verses.

Selection from *Narrative of the Journey of Abd-er Razzak*

About all we know of Abdur Razzaq is he was the Persian ambassador to Calicut, India, traveling there from 1442 to 1444. Calicut was a leading trading city for the spice trade from east to west, much of which traveled via the Malabar Coast of India during monsoon seasons. The spice trade was of sufficient import for the Persians to send ambassadors to ensure good relations and to monitor the trade.

Source: *Major, K.H.* India in the Fifteenth Century *(London: Hakluyt Society, 1857), pp. 3–49.*

Focus Questions:
1. What were the consequences of delay at Daralaman?
2. What were the outcomes of delay for merchants?
3. How much do you think the storm description is literary and how much factual? Why would the difference be important?

NARRATIVE OF MY VOYAGE INTO HINDOOSTAN, AND DESCRIPTION OF THE WONDERS AND REMARKABLE PECULIARITIES WHICH THIS COUNTRY PRESENTS.

Every man, the eyes of whose intelligence are illuminated by the light of truth, and whose soul, like a bird soars with fixedness of vision into the regions of knowledge, observes with certainty, and brings home to his recognition the fact, that the revolution of the great bodies which people the heavens, as well as the progress of the smaller bodies which canopy the earth, are subject to the wisdom and the will of a Creator, Who is alike holy and powerful; that the intellegence of his omniscience, and characteristic of His omniscience, are manifested alike in the nature of those beings, which resemble the atoms contained in creation, as well as in the movements and actions of them; that the bridle which guides created beings is held by the hand of a power, by that of Providence; that the proudest existences are forced; bow the head beneath the commands of a God who does everything according to His pleasure.

"If Providence were not the mover of all the events of the world, how is it that the progress of those events is so frequently in opposition to our own will?"

"In every occurrence, whether fortunate or unfortunate, it is Providence who holds the reins, and guides His creatures; the proof of this is found in the fact that the measures adopted by men are all fallacious."

The events, the perils, which accompany a voyage by sea (and which in themselves constitute a shoreless and a boundless ocean), present the most marked indication of the Divine omnipotence, the grandest evidence of a wisdom which is sublime. Hence it is that the utility of such a voyage as this has been shown in the most perfect manner in the marvelous language of the king, who is the author of all knowledge, and also that the execution of so important an undertaking cannot be either accomplished or related, but by the help of that living and powerful Being, who makes easy that which is most difficult.

In pursuance of the orders of Providence, and of the decrees of that Divine prescience, the comprehension of which escapes all the calculations and reflections of Man, I received orders to take my departure for India; and how shall I be able to set forth the events of my journey with clearness, seeing that I have wandered at hap-hazard into that country devoted to darkness. His majesty, the happy Khakan, condescended to allot to me any provisions and post horses. His humble slave, after having made the necessary preparations, started on his journey on the first day of the month of Ramazan (January 13th), by the route of Kohistan. In the middle of the desert of Kerman, he arrived at the ruins of a city, the wall of which wild four bazaars could still be distinguished; but no inhabitant was to be found in all the country round.

(I passed in the desert near ancient dwellings, none of which presented signs of anything but ruin and decay.)

This desert extends to the frontier of Mekran and Seistan, as far as the environs of the city of Damghan, and all this space presents formidable dangers to travellers.

On the eighteenth day of Ramazan (Jan. 30th) I reached the city of Kerman; it is a pleasant place, as well as one of great importance. The darogah (governor), the Emir Hadji Mohamed-Kaiaschirin, being then absent, I was compelled to sojourn in this city until the day of the feast. The illustrious Emir Borhan-Eddin-Seid-Khalil-Allah, son of the Emir Naim-Eddin-Seid-Nimet-Allah, who was the most distinguished personage of the city of Kerman, and even of the whole world, returned at this time from the countries of Hindoostan. He loaded me with attentions and proofs of his kindness. On the fifth day of Schewal (February 16th) I quitted the city of Kerman. On my road I met the Emir Hadji-Mohammed, on his return from an expedition which he had made into the province of Benboul. Continuing my journey, I arrived towards the middle of the month at the shore of the Sea of Oman, and at Bender-Ormuz. The prince of Ormuz, Melik-Fakhr-Eddin-Touranschah, having placed a vessel at my disposal, I went on board of it, and made my entry into the city of Ormuz. I had had assigned to me a house, with everything that I could require, and I was admitted to an audience of the prince.

Ormuz, which is also called Djerrun, is a port situated in the middle of the sea, and which has not its equal on the surface of the globe. The merchants of seven climates, from Egypt, Syria, the country of Roum, Azerbijan, Irak Arabi, and Irak-Adjemi, the provinces of Fars, Khorassan, Ma-wara-amahar, Turkistan, the kingdom of Deschti-Kaptchack, the countries inhabited by the Kalmucks, the whole of the kingdoms of Tchin and Matchin, and the city of Khanbalik, all make their way to this port; the inhabitants of the sea coasts arrive here from the countries of Tchin; Java, Bengal, the cities of Zirbad, Tenasserim, Sokotora, Schahrinou, the islands of Diwah-Mahall, the countries of Malabar, Abyssinia, Zanguebar, the ports of Bidjanagar, Kalbergah, Gudjarat, Kanbait, the coasts of Arabia, which extend as far as Aden, Jiddah, and Yembo; they bring hither those rare and precious articles which the sun, the moons and the rains have combined to bring to perfection; and which are capable of being transported by sea. Travellers from all countries resort hither, arid, in exchange for the commodities which they bring; they can without trouble or difficulty obtain all that they desire. Bargains are made either by Money or by exchange.

For all objects, with the exception of gold and silver; a tenth of their value is paid by way of duty.

Persons of all religions, and even idolaters, are found in great numbers in this city, and no injustice is permitted towards any person whatever. This city is also named Daralaman (the abode of security). The inhabitants unite the flattering character of the people of Irak with the profound cunning of the Indians.

I sojourned in this place for the space of two months and the governors sought all kinds of pretexts to detain me; so that the favorable time for departing by sea, that is to say the beginning or middle of the monsoon, was allowed to pass, and we came to the end of the monsoon, which is the season when tempests and attacks from pirates are to be dreaded. Then they gave me permission to depart. As the men and horses could not all be contained in the Caine vessel; they were distributed among several ships. The sails were hoisted, and we commenced our voyage.

As soon as I caught the smell of the vessel, and all the terrors of the sea presented themselves before me, I fell into so deep a swoon, that for three days respiration alone indicated that life remained within me. When I came a little to myself, the merchants, who were my intimate friends, cried with one voice that the time for navigation was passed, and that every one who put to sea at this season was alone responsible for his death, since he voluntarily placed himself in peril. All, with one accord, having sacrificed the sums which they had paid for freight in the ships, abandoned their project, and some difficulties disembarked at the port of Muscat. For myself, I quitted this city, escorted by the principal companions of my voyage, and went to a place called Kariat, where I established myself and fixed my tents, with the intention of there remaining. The merchants of the coasts designate by the word *telahi* (loss) the condition in which they find themselves: when, having undertaken a sea voyage, they cannot accomplish it, and are obliged to stop in some other place. In consequence of the severity of pitiless weather and the adverse manifestations of a treacherous fate, my heart was crushed like glass and my soul became weary of life, and my season of relaxation became excessively trying.

At the moment when, through the effect of so many vicissitudes, the mirror of my understanding had become covered with rust, and the hurricane of so many painful circumstances had extinguished the lamp of my mind, so that I might say in one word I had fallen into a condition of apathetic stupidity, on a sudden in evening met a merchant who was on his return from the shores of Hindoostan. I asked him whither he was going. He replied: "My only object is to reach the city of Herat." When I heard him utter the name of that august city I went very nearly distracted. The merchant having consented at my request to tarry awhile, I threw off the following verses upon paper.

> When in the midst of strangers, at the hour of the evening prayer I set me down to weep,
> I recall my adventures, the recital of which is accompanied with unusual sighs.
> At the remembrance of my mistress and of my country I weep so bitterly,
> That I should deprive the whole world of the taste and habit of travelling.
> I am a native of the country of the Arabs, and not of a strange region.
> O mighty God, whom I invoke! Vouchsafe to bring me back to the companionship of my friends.

Everything which relates to my condition, and to the tediousness and dangers against which I have had to contend, has been set forth in fair detail in this narrative. As far as regards a certain number of men and horses, which were embarked at Ormuz upon a separate vessel, I have been unable hitherto to ascertain what has been their fate. It may be that some day I shall be able to put their adventures into writing.

DESCRIPTION OF WHAT OCCURRED DURING THE TIME THAT I WAS INVOLUNTARILY DETAINED UPON THE SEA SHORE, AND OF WHAT HAPPENED TO ME IN THE ENCAMPMENT OF KARIAT, AND IN THE CITY OF KALAHAT.

At then that I was perforce sojourning in the place called Kariat, and upon the shores of the ocean, the new moon, of the month of Moharrem of the year 846 [May 1442], showed me in this abode of weariness the beauty of her disk. Although it was at that time spring; in the season in which the nights and days are of equal length, the heat of the sun was so intense that it burned the ruby in the mine and the marrow in the bones; the sword in its scabbard melted like wax, and the gems which adorned the handle of the khandjar were reduced to coal.

> Soon as the sun shone forth from the height of heaven,
> The heart of stone grew hot beneath its orb
> The horizon was so much scorched up by its rays,
> That the heart of stone became soft like wax;
> The bodies of the fishes, at the bottom of the fish-ponds.
> Burned like the silk which is exposed to the fire
> Both the water and the air gave out so burning a heat,
> That the fish went away to seek refuge in the fire;

Sons, Kojah-Masood and Kojah Mohammed, both natives of Khorassan, who had fixed their abode in the kingdom of Bidjanagar, were appointed to undertake the duties of ambassadors, and various presents and stuffs were accordingly sent to them. Fatah-Khakan, the one of the descendants of the Sultan Firouz-Schah, who had filled the throne of Delhi, also dispatched a delegate named Kojah-Djemaleddin, charged with a present and a letter.

On the day of the audience of dismissal, the king said to the humble author of this work: "It has been asserted that thou wast not really sent by his majesty Mirza-Schah-Rokh, otherwise we should have shown thee greater attentions; if thou comest back on a future occasion into my territories, thou shalt meet with a reception worthy of a king such as we are." But the author said to himself mentally: "If, when once I have escaped from the desert of thy love, I reach my own country, I will never again set out on another voyage, not even in the company of a king."

In a letter addressed to his majesty, the monarch inserted those statements so full of malignity which had been invented by the inhabitants of Ormuz, and expressed himself in the following terms: "We had had the intention of seeking the good will of the emperor by some gifts and presents worthy of a sovereign. Certain persons, however, have assured us that Abd-er-Razzak was not in any way attached to the court of your majesty." In detailing the titles which are assumed by the august Khakan, he said: "This prince unites in his person the qualities of a king, and that which constitutes the glory of a sovereign, with the purity of the prophets, and the virtues of the saints." So that the tongue of great and small, the writing of every able man, and the pen of every secretary ought to express (with respect to this monarch) the following sentiment.

Thou art a Noah, who, like Abraham, possesses the love of God; a Khidr, who holds the rank of Moses.

Thou art Ahmed, who encircles the majesty of the throne of God; thou art Jesus, whose aspect expresses the Divine Spirit, Henceforth the habitable globe shall be regarded as forming part of thine empire; it is therefore that thou holdest the equinoctial line under the line of thy authority.

As, according to the Ideas of these people, the country of Bidjanagar is placed under the equinoctial line, the expression to "hold the equinoctial line under the line of his authority," is perfectly correct.

The humble author of this work, after having completed his negociations, set forth on his journey, and directed his homeward course towards the shores of the sea of Oman.

ACCOUNT OF THE AUTHOR'S VOYAGE ON HIS RETURN FROM THE COUNTRIES OF HINDOOSTAN. DESCRIPTION OF A STORM. HISTORY OF THE DELUGE.

The sun of the Divine Mercy displayed itself above the horizon of happiness. The star of fortune arose to the east of my hopes. The bright glimmer of joy and satisfaction showed itself in the midst of the darkness of night, in conformity to this maxim:

"God is the friend of those who hold the true faith: He will bring them forth from the darkness, and will lead them forth into the light."

Those nights of affliction and weariness, passed in the sad abode of idolatry and error, were succeeded by the breaking of the dawn of happiness, and the brilliant out-shining of the sun of prosperity; and the evening, which was full of the anxieties of weakness, became changed into days of gladness and confidence.

The duration of the night was longer than that of the day, but now the face of everything is changed. The latter has been constantly on the increase, and the former on the decrease.

As the city from which I was returning was situated at the extremity of the regions of Hindoostan, and as the whole country which I had traversed was inhabited by idolators, my travelling resources had been entirely absorbed by the troubles I had undergone. But why speak of what does not deserve to be recalled? At all events in spite of my grievous position, in place of hope I have but this maxim, as my sole provision for my voyage:

"Despair not of the mercy of God."

With a heart full of energy, and with vast hopes, I set out on my journey, or rather, I committed myself to the goodness and compassion of God. On the twelfth day of the month of Schaban [Nov. 5th, 1443], accompanied by the ambassadors, I left the city of Bidjanagar to commence my journey. After travelling eighteen days, on the first day of the month of Ramazan [Nov. 23rd, 1443], I reached the shores of the sea of Oman and the port of Maganor. There I had the honour of being admitted to the society of the Sheriff-Emir Seid-Ala-eddin-Meskhedi, who was a hundred and twenty years old. For many years he had been an object of veneration both to Mussulmans and idolators. Throughout the country his words were regarded as oracles, and no one ventured to object to his decisions.

One of the ambassadors of Bidjanagar, Kojah-Masud, had just died in this city.

Under this vault, the dwelling of evil, who knows in what spot our head will rest beneath the brink of the tomb!

After having celebrated in the port of Maganor the festival which follows the fast, I made my way to the port of Manor [Honawer] to procure a vessel, and I laid in all the provisions necessary for twenty persons during a voyage of forty days. One day, at the moment that I was on the point of embarking, I opened the Book of Fates, the author of which was the Iman Djafar-Sadek, and which is composed from verses of the Alcoran. There I found a presage of joy and happiness, for I lighted upon this verse:

"Fear nothing, for thou hast been preserved from the hand of unjust men."

Struck with the coincidence of this passage with my situation, I felt all those anxieties disappear from my heart, which had caused me alarm in the prospect of encountering the sea. Abandoning myself entirely to the hope of a happy deliverance, I embarked on the eighth day of the month of Zu'lkadah [Jan. 28th, 1444] and put to sea. While the vision of those ships, which float over the mountain-like waves of the sea, presented to my thoughts the traces of the Divine power, at the same time, in the conversation of the companions of my voyage, I collected observations respecting remarkable names and facts worthy of note, and throughout our little company peace and contentment prevailed.

The eye of sad events and of misfortunes was gone to sleep, Fortune appeared to have given herself up to indolence, and we were surrounded with happiness.

The ship, after a million of shocks, reached the open sea.

On a sudden there arose a violent wind on the surface of the sea, and on all sides were heard groaning and cries.

The night, the vessel, the wind, and the gulf, presented to our minds all the forebodings of a catastrophe. On a sudden, through the effect of the contrary winds, which resembled men in their drink, the wine which produced this change penetrated even to the vessel. The planks of which it was composed, and which by their conformation seemed to form a continuous line, were on the point of becoming divided like the separate letters of the alphabet. To our thoughts was strikingly presented the truth of that passage:

"The waves cover it, the billow rises beneath it, and above it is the cloud."

The sailor who, with respect to his skill in swimming, might be compared to a fish, was anxious to throw himself into the water like an anchor. The captain, although familiarized with the navigation of all the seas, shed bitter tears, and had forgotten all his science. The sails were torn, the mast was entirely bent by the shock of the wind. The different grades of passengers who inhabited this floating house threw out upon the waves riches of great value, and, after the manner of the Sofis, voluntarily stripped themselves of their worldly goods. Who could give a thought to the jeopardy in which their money and their stuffs were placed, when life itself, which is so dear to man, was in danger? For myself, in this situation, which brought before my eyes all the threatening terrors which the ocean had in its power to present, with tears in my eyes I gave myself up for lost. Through the effect of the stupor, and of the profound sadness to which I became a prey, I remained, like the sea, with my lips dry and my eyes moist, and resigned myself entirely to the Divine Will. At one time, through the driving of the waves, which resembled mountains, the vessel was lifted up to the skies; at another, under the impulse of the violent winds, it descended like divers to the bottom of the waters.

The agitation of the waters of the sea caused my body to melt like salt which is dissolved in water, the violence of the deluge annihilated and utterly dispersed the firmness which sustained me, and my mind, hitherto so strong, was like the ice which is suddenly exposed to the heat of the month of Tamouz; even now my heart is troubled and agitated, as is the fish which is taken out of fresh water.

May the torrent of destruction overturn the edifice of fate, which thus brings in successive waves the waters of misfortune tune upon my head.

Many times I said to myself, and it was in language dictated by my situation that I repeated, this verse.

"A dismal night! The fear of the waves, and so frightful an abyss! What judgment can they who are so peaceful on shore form of our situation?"

The pure water of my life was troubled by the agitation of the sea; and the brilliant mirror of my ideas, in consequence of the dampness of the water, and the putrefaction of the air, was covered with rust. Each moment that the pupils of my eyes contemplated that muddy water, it resembled, through the effect of my extreme alarm, a flaming sword. At the sight of the agitated sea, overset by the tempestuous winds, I drew from my breast an icy sigh; it was a sharp weapon, which tore my very soul.

Overwhelmed at every point, and seeing the gate of hope shut on every side against me, with an eye full of tears and a heart full of burning chagrin, I addressed myself to God with the expression of this verse.

"Oh, our Lord, place not upon us a burden which is too heavy for our strength to bear!"

I prayed to the Being, who is supremely merciful, and who never upbraideth with his benefits, to be pleased, from the immense sea of His goodness, to bedew and to bestow fresh verdure upon the little shrub of my existence and to deign, in the distribution of the water of His kindness, to wash completely and disperse from the face of my situation the dust which rendered my life a grievance to me. In the midst of this sad position, I reflected and put the question to myself: "What, then, is this catastrophe, which has made fortune in her revolution fall so heavily upon me?"

What, then, is this shame, which, through the hostility of a perfidious fate, of a base and contemptible destiny, has caused the serenity of my face to disappear? On the one side, I have been unable to snatch my precious life from the fury of the waves of death, nor have I been able, in carrying out the business of my sovereign, to bring to the surface of the water the pearl of my exertions. For a generous soul neglects nothing which can tend to the fulfillment of the obligations which it has contracted towards its benefactor, and when it becomes a question of executing the business of its master, it regards life itself, which is ordinarily so precious, as utterly valueless. If the man of sincerity casts [his loyalty to] his king into the fire of events, his nature, like that of a gem, must show no alteration in the smallest atom; or rather the gold of his loyalty, after the manner of pure gold, becomes still more refined.

I was in the midst of these reflections, and everything about me spoke of dejection and trouble, when at length, by virtue of that Divine promise: *"Who is He who hears the prayers of the afficted, and drives away his misery?"*, on a sudden, the zephyr of God's infinite mercy began to blow upon me from that point which is indicated by these words: *"Despair not of the mercy of the Most High."* The morning of joy began, to dawn from the East of happiness, and the messenger of a propitious fate brought to the ears of my soul these consolatory words: "Since on your behalf we have divided the sea, we have saved you." The impetuous hurricane was changed to a favourable wind, the tossing of the waves ceased, and the sea, in conformity with my desires, became completely calm. My fellow-passengers, after having celebrated at sea the feast of victims, gained sight, at the close of the month of Zu'lhidjah [middle of March, 1444] of the mountain of Kalahat, and found themselves at length in safety from all the perils of the deep. At this period, the new moon of the month of Moharrem, of the year 848 [middle of March 1444], like a beneficent spirit looked, on us with a friendly eye.

THE CLOSING EVENTS OF THE AUTHOR'S VOYAGE BY SEA. HIS ARRIVAL AT ORMUZ, UNDER THE PROTECTION OF GOD MOST HIGH.

In retracing the story of my voyage, I had reached the point at which the new moon of Moharrem showed us her shining face on the sea. The vessel still remained at sea for several days. On our arrival at the port of Muscat we cast anchor.

After having repaired the damages which the vessel had suffered through the effect of the storms, we re-embarked, and continued our voyage.

After leaving Muscat, the vessel arrived at the port of Jurufgan, where it put in for a day or two. On this occasion we felt during one night such excessive heat, that at day break one would have said that the heavens had set the earth on fire. So intense was the heat which scorched up the atmosphere, that even the bird of rapid flight was burnt up in the heights of heaven, as well as the fish in the depths of the sea. I re-embarked and set sail from the port of Jurufgan, and reached Ormuz on the forenoon of Friday, the eighth day of the month of Safar [April 22nd, 1444]. Our voyage from the port of Honawer to Ormuz had lasted sixty-five days.

Ma Huan, Excerpt from *The Overall Survey of the Ocean's Shores*

Ma Huan was one of the officials who accompanied Zheng He on his great voyages of 1405–1433 CE. Upon his return he wrote a travelogue which gives an account of Indian Ocean region geography, including routes and distances, and on the various products of the region. The spirit of curiosity and inquiry points to a learned man seeking knowledge.

Source: *Ma Huan.* The Overall Survey of the Ocean's Shores *(London: Hakluyt Society, 1970).*

Focus Questions:
1. What is Ma Huan's attitude towards other cultures?
2. Why compile knowledge of Indian Ocean cultures?
3. What exactly does Ma Haun seek to compile, and why?

MA CHING'S FOREWORD OF 1444[28]

FOREWORD[29]

In olden times, when Hsiao Ho entered the frontier-gate, he acquired only maps and records;[30] [and] when Hsuan-ling conquered the city, he merely gathered men.[31] The historians wrote of them—and with ample justification.

It is magnificent to reflect how The Grand Exemplar The Cultured Emperor[32] and The Subtle Exemplar The Elegant Emperor[33] of our own dynasty both commanded the grand eunuch Cheng Ho to lead heroes and cross over the seas[34]...and trade with the various foreign peoples. [Such] splendid men, [such] strong ships and oars, [such] proficiency in technical skill—none [of such things] existed in former times.

But [surely] in their hearts their two Majesties did not really desire boastfully to provoke numerous conflicts far and wide in distant regions? Because their fame [already] extended to the barbarians of the south and north,[35] causing every person with a soul throughout the world, whether stupid or alert, to be imbued with their virtue and civilizing-influence, so that all would know their Emperor and respect their parents.

Of those who received the command and went, I do not know how many million men there were; but those who performed their duty and proclaimed the imperial commands—who would they be except Master Tsung-tao Ma of Shan yin?[36] This exceedingly capable gentleman, after receiving his first appointment, crossed the ocean three times;[37] he travelled through every foreign country; [and] he seized gold, silk, and valuables without any benefit to himself.

And on his return he compiled a single volume [entitled] *The Overall Survey of the Ocean's Shores*. It records the distances to the lands of the island barbarians,[38] the changes in the countries, the places which adjoin the boundaries, and the arrangement of cities and suburbs, with the differences of costume, the varieties of diet, the punishments and prohibitions, laws and regulations, customs and products.[39] Nothing is left unrecorded[40]; because it was this gentleman's intention, [and] his whole wish, to make

---

[28] This title does not appear in Feng's book.

[29] Literally, 'Notice'. This Foreword does not appear in C, in S, or in the Peking National Library example of K; but it is to be found in the Columbia University Library copy of K and in the copy used by Feng. Apparently the Foreword has not previously been translated into English.

[30] Hsiao Ho was an intimate friend and adviser of Liu Pang (later the first Han emperor Kao Ti), a leading commander of the forces belonging to the state of Ch'u; when these forces in 207 B.C. occupied Hsien yang, capital of the state of Ch'in, Hsiao Ho was overwhelmed with offerings of money, silks, and other valuables, but he would accept nothing except the charts, the registers, the documents, and the writings (K. S. Latourette, *The Chinese* (3rd ed., revised, New York, 1957); Tsui Chi, p. 78; Needham, vol. p. 535; H. A. Giles, *A Chinese Biographical Dictionary* (London and Shanghai, 1898); H. H. Dubs, *The History of the Former Han Dynasty*, vol. 1 (Baltimore, 1908), p. 58.

[31] Fang Hsuan-ling assisted Li Shih-min (later the second T'ang emperor T'ai-tsung) to consolidate the newly won empire of Li Yuan (later the first T'ang emperor Kao-tsu) in 618 and the following years (Giles, *Biography*, pp, ass, 461; Latourette, *Chinese*, pp. 180–1). Consulting the *T'ang shu*, T'ang History, we learn that the present allusion refers to the campaigns of pacification north of the Wei river; while others wrangled over 'pearls and trinkets' in captured cities, Fang at once collected men and placed them in positions of authority where they could help the cause (*Erh-shih-wu shih*, vol. iv, *T'ang shu*, p. 3311).

[32] The temple-name of the emperor Ch'eng-tsu.

[33] The temple-name of the emperor Hsuan-tsung, whose 'reign-title' was Hsuan-te.

[34] Feng thought that some characters had fallen out here.

[35] Literally, 'Man mai' (Giles, nos. 7644; 7611), the wild tribes of the south and north, respectively.

[36] 'Tsung-tao' constituted Ma Huan's 'courtesy name' (tzu). Shan yin was a hsien forming with Kuei chi hsien the prefectural city of Shao hsing in Chekiang province (Playfair, no. 5462).

[37] On Cheng Ho's fourth, sixth, and seventh expeditions.

[38] Literally, 'I' (Giles, no. 5397), barbarous tribes, especially those of the east.

[39] This list indicates the topics which were expected to be introduced in contemporary accounts of foreign travels.

[40] This is an overstatement; there are a number of omissions; for instance, Ma Huan fails to mention the system of weights and measures used in Aden, Bengal, Hormuz, or Mecca.

the people of the future, for a thousand years hereafter, realize that the way of our country is in harmony with nature and that we have achieved this measure of success in civilizing the barbarians of the south and east.

The great books [written by] the historians of other days, in manifesting [this] gentleman's wishes, will hand down his name with that of Hsiao and Fang as imperishable.[41] Is he not indeed a remarkable man?

The day before the chrysanthemum moon [in the cyclic year] *chia-tzu* of the Cheng-t'ung [period].[42]

Written by Ma Ching[43] of Ch'ien t' ang.[44]

POEM COMMEMORATING THE JOURNEY[45]

The Emperor's glorious envoy[46] received the divine commands,
proclaim abroad the silken sounds,[47] and go to the barbarous lands'.
His giant ship on the roaring waves of the boundless ocean rode;
afar, o'er the rolling billows vast and limitless, it strode.
The vast sea's rolling billows in lovely breakers sweep;
clusters of mounts, green floating shells,[48] in mystery fade and peep.
Within Chan city's havens halts awhile, repose he takes;

Raise the sails! they scud along; She-p'o[49] he quickly makes.
From the Central Glorious Country[50] She-p'o is distant far,
a noisome steam is heaven's breath, and strange the people are.
With unkempt heads and naked feet, a barbarous tongue they speak;
dresses and hats they use not, nor rites[51] nor virtue seek.
Here when the heavenly writing[52] came, a happy clamour meeting,
chieftains and heads of the barbarous tribes all vied to give it greeting.
Tribute of southern gold, rare gems, from distant parts appear;

---

[41] History has not fulfilled Ma Ching's prognostication, for Ma Huan's book was never widely known.

[42] The 'chrysanthemum moon' is the ninth moon, when this dower (chit) blooms (Giles, no. 2964); in the chia tut year the ninth moon began in October 8444. Thus the date of this Foreword is to October 5444.

[43] Otherwise unknown; Pelliot thought that he knew Ma Huan and was probably a Muslim (Pelliot, 'Encore', p. 2,3).

[44] A hsien forming with Jen ho (Jin-ho) hsien the prefectural city of Hang-chou in Chekiang province (*Playfair*, no. 936).

[45] The Poem appears only in C and in the copy of K. It may also be found in I Mou-teng's novel called Hsi yangchi, *Records of the Western Ocean*, written 1597; this gives a fabulous account of Cheng Ho's voyages (Pelliot, 'Voyages', p. 34 n. 3; A. Wylie, *Notes on Chinese Literature* (Shanghai, 1867, re-issued, Peking, 1939 p. 163). The novel contains many such poems; this particular poem appears in ch. f. 52; it has a few variations of reading, none of which Feng adopts. Pelliot thought that Ma Huan wrote the poem in 1416, and that it reports observations made during the expedition of 1413–15 (Pelliot, 'Voyages', pp. 261–2, 294, and 303, n. 2). Apparently the poem has not been previously translated into English.

[46] Cheng Ho.

[47] The emperor's words.

[48] A picturesque image.

[49] Champa, the territory now comprised in Central Vietnam. By Central Vietnam is meant the part of Vietnam lying between 17° 59' N (Hoanh-son) in the north at 10° 30' N (Cape Ba Kb) in the south. The port was Qui Nhon, called 'New Department', Hsin chou, by the Chinese.

[50] An old Chinese name for Java.

[51] China.

[52] Li (Giles, no, 6949); defined as 'Rules, partly defined and partly undefined, for correct conduct and good manners' (Cheng T'ien-hsi, *China Moulded by Confucius* (London, 1946), p. 37); described as 'the body of ancient custom, usage and ceremonial...which unnumbered generations of the Chinese people had instinctively felt to be right'; 'we may equate it with natural law' (Needham, vol. II, p. 544).

Whereupon he selected an interpreter and others, seven men in all, and sent them with a load of musk, porcelain articles, and other such things; [and] they joined a ship of this country and went there.[53] It took them one year to go and return.[54]

They bought all kinds of unusual commodities, and rare valuables, *ch'i-lin*, lions, 'camel-fowls', and other such things; in addition they painted an accurate representation of the 'Heavenly Hall'[55]; [and] they returned to the capital.[56]

The king of the country of Mo-ch'ieh also sent envoys[57] who brought some local articles, accompanied the seven men—the interpreter [and others]—who had originally gone there, and presented the articles to the court.

The 'facing day' of the autumn moon in [the cyclic year] hsin-wei of the Ching-t'ai [period][58].

Written by Ma Huan, the mountain-woodcutter of Kuei chi.

KU P'O'S AFTERWORD OF 1451 (?)[59]

AFTERWORD[60]

TO THE OVERALL SURVEY OF THE OCEAN'S SHORES

When I was young, I looked at [a book called] *A Record of Foreign Places*,[61] and I learnt about the extent of the earth's surface, about the difference in customs, about the appearance of human beings, and about the different varieties of products—astounding, pleasant, attractive, striking [things].

Yet I suspected that the book was written by a novelty-seeker, and I ventured to think that such things did not exist in reality.

Now I see the actual facts in the record made by Master Ma Tsung-tao[62] and Master Kuo Ch'ung-li[63] of their experiences in the various foreign countries, and I see for the first time that the statements in *A Record of Foreign Places* are credible and not false.

---

[53] Ma Huan uses ambiguous language; the editor follows Pelliot in interpreting it to mean that Hung Pao's emissaries joined Calicut men in a Calicut ship (Pelliot, 'Voyages', pp. 303-4); it might almost equally well mean that they joined Meccan men in a Meccan ship (Duyvendak, *Ma Huan*, p.74) or joined Chinese men in a Chinese ship. Pelliot ('Voyages', p. 304) thought that Ma Huan was one of, the seven emissaries and visited Mecca.

[54] Ma Huan is again ambiguous; he means, the editor is advised, that the emissaries arrived back in China a year after they left Calicut; compare Pelliot, 'Voyages', pp. 303-4; 'Notes', p. 298.

[55] The Ka'ba.

[56] Peking.

[57] A note in Huang Sheng-tseng (ch. f. 53) says that the king sent a minister named Sha Wan (Giles, nos. 9624; 12,489) and others. Duyvendak (*Ma Huan*, p. 74, n. 3) noted that this envoy, as in many other cases, will have been an ordinary merchant, assuming an official guise.

[58] The 'facing day' was the fifteenth day of the moon, because on that day the moon faces the sun. The 'autumn moon' was probably the second moon of autumn; in which case the date will be 9 September, 1451 (Pelliot, 'Voyages', p. 257, n.)

[59] This heading does not appear in Feng's book.

[60] Literally, 'After Notice'. This Afterword, called Postface by Duyvendak and Pelliot, appears only in C. Feng has taken some readings from the Afterword of a MS book called 'San Pao cheng-i chi', 'Collected [Accounts] of San Pao's Conquests of the Barbarians', a work which is known only from a notice (Pelliot, 'Voyages', pp. 257-8; 'Encore', p. 211). The present Afterword has been translated by Duyvendak, *Ma Huan*, pp. 10-13.

[61] I yu chili (Giles, nos. 5505; 53,662; 1922); see Pelliot, Voyages', pp. 260-1.

[62] Tsung-tao (Giles, nos. 51,9 76; 50,780) was the 'style' or 'courtesy name' of Ma Huan.

[63] Giles, nos. 6617; 2930; 6949; nothing is known about him or his contribution to Ma Huan's book. Ch'ung-li' is his 'style'; we do not know his 'personal name'; see Duyvendak, *Ma Huan*, p. 52.

Ch'ung-li is a man from Jen ho in Hang,[64] and Tsung-tao is a man from Kuei chi in Yueh.[65] Both profess the religion of the Heavenly Square[66] in the Western Regions, and are truly excellent gentlemen.

Some time ago The Grand Exemplar The Emperor[67] issued an imperial order that the grand eunuch Cheng Ho should take general command of the treasure-ships and go to the various foreign countries in the Western Ocean to read out the imperial commands and bestow rewards for meritorious service; and these two gentlemen, being skilled interpreters of foreign languages, received appointments in this [capacity].

Three times they accompanied [Cheng Ho's] train, travelling ten thousand *li*. They started out from Wu hu[68] in Min;[69] first they put in to Chan city,[70] then Chao-wa[71] and Hsien Lo,[72] then again Old Haven,[73] Su-men,[74] Nan-p'o,[75] Hsi-lan,[76] and Ko-chih;[77] most distant of all, A-tan[78] and the Heavenly Square[79] were visited—in all more than twenty countries. In each country they stayed and travelled for many a day.

As to the extent of the earth's surface, they noted the difference in distances. As to the diversity of customs, they noted the difference in morals. As to the appearance of the people, they noted the difference in their attractiveness. As to the products of the land, they noted the difference in their importance. All these things they recorded in writing. Their record completed, they made a book. They certainly expended care and industry.

Their task completed, the two gentlemen returned to their native villages, and constantly went out to enlighten other people, to enable everybody to acquire knowledge about conditions in foreign regions, and to see how far the majestic virtue of our imperial dynasty extended—far-flung as in this [book].[80]

Ch'ung-li, still concerned at his inability to make people fully acquainted with the facts, wishes to avail himself of the printed word[81] in order to spread his message. Through his friend Lu-T'ing-yung[82] he has asked me for a notice; accordingly I have recorded this summary after [his work].[83]

Written by Ku P'o, Chi-hung, Supervising and Inspecting Imperial Clerk in this year.[84]

---

[64] Jen ho was a district (*hsien*) forming with Ch'ien t'ang hsien the prefectural city of Hang chou in Chekiang province.

[65] Kuei chi was a district (*hsien*) forming with Shan yin hsien the prefectural city of Shao hsing, about 26 miles south-east of Hang chou. Yueh was the name of an area comprising parts of modern Kiangsi and Chekiang provinces.

[66] Mecca. This statement is the source of our knowledge that Ma Huan was a Muslim.

[67] The emperor Hsuan-tsung whose 'reign-title' was Hsuan-te.

[68] Five Tigers strait in the Min estuary.

[69] Min was the name of an area comprising the greater part of the modern Fukien province.

[70] Champa, Central Vietnam.

[71] Java.

[72] Thailand.

[73] Palembang.

[74] Aru, Deli district in eastern Sumatra.

[75] That is, Su-men-to-la, Semudera, Lho Seumawe in northern Sumatra.

[76] Ceylon.

[77] Cochin.

[78] Aden.

[79] Mecca.

[80] The last sentence represents a translation of 15 characters added by Feng to C.

[81] Literally, 'wishes to engrave the catalpa' (tzu); the classical *tzu* (Giles, no. 12,356) has been identified with ch'iu (Giles, no. 2503), *Catalpa kaempferi*, a wood much used for cutting blocks for printing. Thus it was Kuo Ch'ung-li who pressed for the book to be printed.

[82] Otherwise unknown.

[83] The editor translates this last sentence in accordance with Pelliot's understanding of the passage; Duyvendak had previously expressed the opinion that this Afterword had originally been a Preface; see Duyvendak, *Ma Huan*, p. 13 and Pelliot, 'Voyages', pp. 261–2.

[84] This sentence represents a translation of it characters added by Feng to C on the authority of the 'San Pao cheng-i chi'. Ku P'o is otherwise unknown. The date was probably 141r. See Pelliot, 'Encore', p. 211.

Al'Umari describes Mansa Musa of Mali

Control of the Trans-Saharan trade from the cities of the Sahel to the North African ports was a certain guarantee to enormous wealth. During the medieval period, three great empires: Ghana, Mali, and Songhay, dominated this traffic in gold, salt, slaves, and ivory. The most fabulous of the West African emperors was Mansa Musa of Mall (1312–1337 CE), whose lavish display and largess while on his pilgrimage to Mecca drew international attention. The following description is from Al' Umari, an Arab traveler.

Source: *N. Levtzion & J. F. P. Hopkins, eds.,* Corpus of Early Arabic Sources for West African History *(Cambridge, England: Cambridge University Press, 1981), pp. 267–272.*

Focus Questions:
1. What light does Al'Umari's account shed on the Malian army? On the treatment of the corpses of the dead?
2. In what way was Musa's conduct found to be contrary to Muslim law, and how did the Emperor react upon being informed of this?
3. According to Musa, what happened to his predecessor, and under what circumstances did Musa himself come to the throne?
4. What economic and/or other effects did Musa's pilgrimage have in Egypt?

The king of this country imports Arab horses and pays high prices for them. His army numbers about 100,000, of whom about 10,000 are cavalry mounted on horses and the remainder infantry without horses or other mounts. They have camels but do not know how to ride them with saddles.

Barley is quite lacking; it does not grow there at all.

The emirs and soldiers of this king have fiefs (iqta-'at) and benefices (in'a-ma-t). Among their chiefs are some whose wealth derived from the king reaches 50,000 mithqa-ls of gold every year, besides which he keeps them in horses and clothes. His whole ambition is to give them fine clothes and to make his towns into cities. Nobody may enter the abode of this king save barefooted, whoever he may be. Anyone who does not remove his shoes, inadvertently or purposely, is put to death without mercy. Whenever one of the emirs or another comes into the presence of this king he keeps him standing before him for a time. Then the newcomer makes a gesture with his right hand like one who beats the drum of honour (ju-k) in the lands of Tu-ra-n and Ira-n. If the king bestows a favour upon a person or makes him a fair promise or thanks him for some deed the person who has received the favour grovels before him from one end of the room to the other. When he reaches there the slaves of the recipient of the favour or some of his friends take some of the ashes which are always kept ready at the far end of the king's audience chamber for the purpose and scatter it over the head of the favoured one, who then returns grovelling until he arrives before the king. Then he makes the drumming gesture as before and rises.

As for this gesture likened to beating the ju-k, it is like this. The man raises his right hand to near his ear. There he places it, it being held up straight, and places it in contact with his left hand upon his thigh. The left hand has the palm extended so as to receive the right elbow. The right hand too has the palm extended with the fingers held close beside each other like a comb and touching the lobe of the ear.

The people of this kingdom ride with Arab saddles and in respect of most features of their horsemanship resemble the Arabs, but they mount their horses with the right foot, contrary to everybody else.

It is their custom not to bury their dead unless they be people of rank and status. Otherwise those without rank and the poor and strangers are thrown into the bush like other dead creatures.

It is a country where provisions go bad quickly, especially [clarified] butter (samn), which is rotten and stinks after two days. This is not to be wondered at, for their sheep go scavenging over the garbage heaps and the country is very hot, which hastens decomposition.

When the king of this kingdom comes in from a journey a parasol (jitr) and a standard are held over his head as he rides, and drums are beaten and guitars (tunbu-r) and trumpets well made of horn are played in front of him. And it is a custom of theirs that when one whom the king has charged with a task or assignment returns to him he questions him in detail about everything which has happened to him from the moment of his departure until his return. Complaints and appeals against administrative oppression (maza-lim) are placed before this king and he delivers judgment on them himself. As a rule nothing is written down; his commands are given verbally. He has judges, scribes, and government offices (di-wa-n). This is what al-Dukka-li- related to me.

The emir Abu-'l-Hasan 'Ali- b. Ami-r Ha-jib told me that he was often in the company of sultan Mu-sa- the king of this country when he came to Egypt on the Pilgrimage. He was staying in [the] Qara-fa [district of Cairo] and Ibn Ami-r Ha-jib was governor of Old Cairo and Qara-ta at that time. A friendship grew up between them and this sultan Mu-sa- told him a great deal about himself and his country and the people of the Su-da-n who were his neighbours. One of the things which he told him was that his country was very extensive and contiguous with the Ocean. By his sword and his armies he had conquered 24 cities each with its surrounding district with villages and estates. It is a country rich in livestock—cattle, sheep, goats, horses, mules—and different kinds of poultry—geese, doves, chickens. The inhabitants of his country are numerous, a vast concourse, but compared with the peoples of the Su-da-n who are their neighbours and penetrate far to the south they are like a white birthmark on a black cow. He has a truce with the gold-plant people, who pay him tribute.

Ibn Ami-r Ha-jib said that he asked him about the gold-plant, and he said: "It is found in two forms. One is found in the spring and blossoms after the rains in open country (sahara-). It has leaves like the naji-l grass and its roots are gold (tibr). The other kind is found all the year round at known sites on the banks of the Ni-l and is dug up. There are holes there and roots of gold are found like stones or gravel and gathered up. Both kinds are known as tibr but the first is of superior fineness (afhal fi- 'l-'iya-r) and worth more." Sultan Mu-sa- told i-bn a-mi-r Ha-jib that gold was his prerogative and he collected the crop as a tribute except for what the people of that country took by theft.

But what al-Dukka-II says is that in fact he is given only a part of it as a present by way of gaining his favour, and he makes a profit on the sale of it, for they have none in their country; and what Dukka-li-says is more reliable.

Ibn Ami-r Ha-jib said also that the blazon (shi'a-r) of this king is yellow on a red ground. Standards ('alam) are unfurled over him wherever he rides on horseback; they are very big flags (liwa-'). The ceremonial for him who presents himself to the king or who receives a favour is that he bares the front of his head and makes the ju-k-beating gesture towards the ground with his right hand as the Tatars do; if a more profound obeisance is required he grovels before the king. "I have seen this (says Ibn Ami-r Ha-jib) with my own eyes." A custom of this sultan is that he does not eat in the presence of anybody, be he who he may, but eats always alone. And it is a custom of his people that if one of them should have reared a beautiful daughter he offers her to the king as a concubine (ama mawtu-'a) and he possesses her without a marriage ceremony as slaves are possessed, and this in spite of the fact that Islam has triumphed among them and that they follow the Malikite school and that this sultan Mu-sa- was pious and assiduous in prayer, Koran reading, and mentioning God [dhikr].

"I said to him (said Ibn Ami-r Ha-jib) that this was not permissible for a Muslim, whether in law (shar') or reason ('aql), and he said: 'Not even for kings?' and I replied: 'No! not even for kings! Ask the scholars!' He said: 'By God, I did not know that. I hereby leave it and abandon it utterly!'

"I saw that this sultan Mu-sa- loved virtue and people of virtue. He left his kingdom and appointed as his deputy there his son Muhammad and emigrated to God and His Messenger. He accomplished the obligations of the Pilgrimage, visited [the tomb of] the Prophet [at Medina] (God's blessing and peace be upon him!) and returned to his country with the intention of handing over his sovereignty to his son and abandoning it entirely to him and returning to Mecca the Venerated to remain there as a dweller near the sanctuary (muja-wir); but death overtook him, may God (who is great) have mercy upon him.

"I asked him if he had enemies with whom he fought wars and he said: 'Yes, we have a violent enemy who is to the Su-da-n as the Tatars are to you. They have an analogy with the Tatars in various respects. They are wide in the face and flat-nosed. They shoot well with [bow and] arrows (nushsha-b). Their horses are cross-bred (kadi-sh) with slit noses. Battles take place between us and they are formidable because of their accurate shooting. War between us has its ups and downs.'"

(Ibn Sa'i-d, in the Mughrib, mentions the Dama-dim tribe who burst upon various peoples of the Su-da-n and destroyed their countries and who resemble the Tatars. The two groups appeared upon the scene at the same moment.)

Ibn Ami-r Ha-jib continued: "I asked sultan Mu-sa- how the kingdom fell to him, and he said: 'We belong to a house which hands on the kingship by inheritance. The king who was my predecessor—did not believe that it was impossible to discover the furthest limit of the Atlantic Ocean and wished vehemently to do so. So he equipped 200 ships filled with men and the same number equipped with gold, water, and provisions enough to last them for years, and said to the man deputed to lead them: "Do not return until you reach the end of it or your provisions and water give out." They departed and a long time passed before anyone came back. Then one ship returned and we asked the captain what news they brought. He said: "Yes, O Sultan, we travelled for a long time until there appeared in the open sea [as it were] a river with a powerful current. Mine was the last of those ships. The [other] ships went on ahead but when they reached that place they did not return and no more was seen of them and we do not know what became of them. As for me, I went about at once and did not enter that river." But the sultan disbelieved him.

"'Then that sultan got ready 2,000 ships, 1,000 for himself and the men whom he took with him and 1,000 for water and provisions. He left me to deputize for him and embarked on the Atlantic Ocean with his men. That was the last we saw of him and all those who were with him, and so I became king in my own right.'

"This sultan Mu-sa-, during his stay in Egypt both before and after his journey to the Noble Hija-z, maintained a uniform attitude of worship and turning towards God. It was as though he were standing before Him because of His continual presence in his mind. He and all those with him behaved in the same manner and were well-dressed, grave, and dignified. He was noble and generous and performed many acts of charity and kindness. He had left his country with 100 loads of gold which he spent during his Pilgrimage on the tribes who lay along his route from his country to Egypt, while he was in Egypt, and again from Egypt to the Noble Hija-z and back. As a consequence he needed to borrow money in Egypt and pledged his credit with the merchants at a very high rate of gain so that they made 700 dinars profit on 300. Later he paid them back amply (?: bi-'l-ra-jih). He sent to me 500 mithqals of gold by way of honorarium.

"The currency in the land of Takru-r consists of cowries and the merchants, whose principal import these are, make big profits on them." Here ends what Ibn Ami-r Ha-jib said.

From the beginning of my coming to stay in Egypt I heard talk of the arrival of this sultan Mu-sa- on his Pilgrimage and found the Cairenes eager to recount what they had seen of the Africans' prodigal spending. I asked the emir Abu- 'l-'Abba-s Ahmad b. al-Ha-k the mihmandar and he told me of the opulence, manly virtues, and piety of this sultan. "When I went out to meet him (he said), that is, on behalf of the mighty sultan al-Malik al-Na-sir, he did me extreme honour and treated me with the greatest courtesy. He addressed me, however, only through an interpreter despite his perfect ability to speak in the Arabic tongue. Then he forwarded to the royal treasury many loads of unworked native gold and other valuables. I tried to persuade him to go up to the Citadel to meet the sultan, but he refused persistently, saying: 'I came for the Pilgrimage and nothing else. I do not wish to mix anything else with my Pilgrimage.' He had begun to use this argument but I realized that the audience was repugnant to him because he would be obliged to kiss the ground and the sultan's hand. I continued to cajole him and he continued to make excuses but the sultan's protocol demanded that I should bring him into the royal presence, so I kept on at him till he agreed.

"When we came in the sultan's presence we said to him: 'Kiss the ground!' but he refused outright saying: 'How may this be?' Then an intelligent man who was with him whispered to him something we could not understand and he said: 'I make obeisance to God who created me!' then he prostrated himself and went forward to the sultan. The sultan half rose to greet him and sat him by his side. They conversed together for a long time, then sultan Mu-sa- went out. The sultan sent to him several complete suits of honour for himself, his courtiers, and all those who had come with him, and saddled and bridled horses for himself and his chief courtiers. His robe of honour consisted of an Alexandrian open-fronted cloak (muftaraj) embellished with tard wahsh cloth containing much gold thread and miniver fur, bordered with beaver fur and embroidered with metallic thread, along with golden fastenings, a silken skull-cap with caliphal emblems, a gold-inlaid belt, a damascened sword, a kerchief [embroidered] with pure gold, standards, and two horses saddled and bridled and equipped with decorated mule[-type] saddles. He also furnished him with accommodation and abundant supplies during his stay.

"When the time to leave for the Pilgrimage came round the sultan sent to him a large sum of money with ordinary and thoroughbred camels complete with saddles and equipment to serve as mounts for him, and purchased abundant supplies for his entourage and others who had come with him. He arranged for deposits of fodder to be placed along the road and ordered the caravan commanders to treat him with honour and respect.

"On his return I received him and supervised his accommodation. The sultan continued to supply him with provisions and lodgings and he sent gifts from the Noble Hija-z to the sultan as a blessing. The sultan accepted them and sent in exchange complete suits of honour for him and his courtiers together with other gifts, various kinds of Alexandrian cloth, and other precious objects. Then he returned to his country.

"This man flooded Cairo with his benefactions. He left no court amIr (amir muqarrab) nor holder of a royal office without the gift of a load of gold. The Cairenes made incalculable profits out of him and his suite in buying and selling and giving and taking. They exchanged gold until they depressed its value in Egypt and caused its price to fall."

The mihmanda-r spoke the truth, for more than one has told this story. When the mihmanda-r died the tax office (di-wa-n) found among the property which he left thousands of dinars' worth of native gold (al-dhahab al-ma'dini) which he had given to him, still just as it had been in the earth (fi- tura-bih), never having been worked.

Merchants of Misr and Cairo have told me of the profits which they made from the Africans, saying that one of them might buy a shirt or cloak (thawb) or robe (iza-r) or other garment for five dinars when it was not worth one. Such was their simplicity and trustfulness that it was possible to practice any deception on them. They greeted anything that was said to them with credulous acceptance. But later they formed the very poorest opinion of the Egyptians because of the obvious falseness of everything they said to them and their outrageous behaviour in fixing the prices of the provisions and other goods which were sold to them, so much so that were they to encounter today the most learned doctor of religious science and he were to say that he was Egyptian they would be rude to him and view him with disfavour because of the ill treatment which they had experienced at their hands.

Muhanna' b. 'Abd al-Ba-qi- al-'Ujrumi- the guide informed me that he accompanied sultan Mu-sa- when he made the Pilgrimage and that the sultan was very open-handed towards the pilgrims and the inhabitants of the Holy Places. He and his companions maintained great pomp and dressed magnificently during the journey. He gave away much wealth in alms. "About 200 mithqals of gold fell to me" said Muhanna' "and he gave other sums to my companions.'" Muhanna' waxed eloquent in describing the sultan's generosity, magnanimity, and opulence.

Gold was at a high price in Egypt until they came in that year. The mithqal did not go below 25 dirharns and was generally above, but from that time its value fell and it cheapened in price and has remained cheap till now. The mithqal does not exceed 22 dirhams or less. This has been the state of affairs for about twelve years until this day, by reason of the large amount of gold which they brought into Egypt and spent there.

A letter came from this sultan to the court of the sultan in Cairo. It was written in the MaghribI style of handwriting on paper with wide lines. In it he follows his own rules of composition although observing the demands of propriety (yumsik fi-h na-mu-san li-nafsih ma'a mura-'a-t qawa-ni-n al-adab). It was written by the hand of one of his courtiers who had come on the Pilgrimage. Its contents comprised greetings and a recommendation for the bearer. With it he sent 5,000 mithqals of gold by way of a gift.

The countries of Ma-li- and Gha-na and their neighbours are reached from the west side of Upper Egypt. The route passes by way of the Oases (Wa-ha-t) through desert country inhabited by Arab and then Berber communities (tawa-'if) until cultivated country is reached by way of which the traveller arrives at Ma-li- and Gha-na. These are on the same meridian as the mountains of the Berbers to the south of Marrakech and are joined to them by long stretches of wilderness and extensive desolate deserts.

The learned faqih Abi 'l-Ru-b 'lsa- al-Zawa-wi- informed me that sultan Mu-sa- Mansa- told him that the length of his kingdom was about a year's journey, and Ibn Ami-r Ha-jib told me the same. Ai-Dukka-li-'s version, already mentioned, is that it is four months' journey long by the same in breadth. What al-Dukka-li- says is more to be relied on, for Mu-sa- Mansa- possibly exaggerated the importance of his realm.

Al-Za-wa-wi- also said: "This sultan Mu-sa- told me that at a town called ZKRY he has a copper mine from which ingots are brought to BYTY. "There is nothing in my kingdom (he said) on which a duty is levied (shay' mumakkas) except this crude copper which is brought in. Duty is collected on this and on nothing else. We send it to the land of the pagan Su-da-n and sell it for two-thirds of its weight in gold, so that we sell 100 mithqals of this copper for 66 2/3 mithqals of gold." He also stated that there are pagan nations (umam) in his kingdom from whom he does not collect the tribute (jizya) but whom he simply employs in extracting the gold from its deposits. The gold is extracted by digging pits about a man's height in depth and the gold is found embedded in the sides of the pits or sometimes collected at the bottom of them.

The king of this country wages a permanently Holy War on the pagans of the Su-da-n who are his neighhours. They are more numerous than could ever be counted.

Anonymous Descriptions of the Cities of Zanj

The Indian Ocean was, long before the Atlantic was opened by European navigators, one of the world's major maritime commercial arteries. The east coast of Africa was a prime component of this trade, and ships from Egypt, Arabia, India, and as far afield as China plied their way to the Swahili Cities of the Zanj (Africans). These cities, chief among them: Kilwa, Mogadishu, Mombasa, Tanga, Malindi, Sofala, and Zanzibar, developed the language from whose name they are collectively known (Swahili was originally conceived as a commercial language). The cities were known to travelers of varied backgrounds, as evidenced in the following selections.

Source: *G. S. P. Freeman-Grenvillem,* The East African Coast: Selected Documents from the 1st to the 19th Century *(London: Rex Collins, 1975), pp. 19–24.*

Focus Questions:
1. Do the three accounts agree on any one (or more) points? Explain.
2. How do the three accounts shed light on the religious life of the Eastern Africans?
3. What are the chief products for trade and consumption?

AL-IDRISI: THE FIRST WESTERN NOTICE OF EAST AFRICA

The Zanj of the East African coast have no ships to voyage in, but use vessels from Oman and other countries which sail to the islands of Zanj which depend on the Indies. These foreigners sell their goods there, and buy the produce of the country. The people of the Djawaga islands go to Zanzibar in large and small ships, and use them for trading their goods, for they understand each other's language. Opposite the Zanj coasts are the Djawaga islands; they are numerous and vast; their inhabitants are very dark in colour, and everything that is cultivated there, fruit, sorghum, sugar-cane and camphor trees, is black in colour. Among the number of the islands is Sribuza, which is said to be 1,200 miles round; and pearl fisheries and various kinds of aromatic plants and perfumes are to be found there, which attract the merchants.

Among the islands of Djawaga included in the present section is Andjuba [Anjouan-Johanna], whose principal town is called Unguja in the language of Zanzibar, and whose people, although mixed, are actually mostly Muslims. The distance from it to Banas on the Zanj coast is 100 miles. The island is 400 miles round; bananas are the chief food. There are five kinds, as follows: the bananas called kundi; fill whose weight is sometimes twelve ounces; omani, muriani, sukari. It is a healthy, sweet, and pleasant food. The island is traversed by a mountain called Wabra. The vagabonds who are expelled from the town flee there, and form a brave and numerous company which frequently infests the surroundings of the town, and which lives at the top of the mountain in a state of defence against the ruler of the island. They are courageous, and feared for their arms and their number. The island is very populous; there are many villages and cattle. They grow rice. There is a great trade in it, and each year various products and goods are brought for exchange and consumption.

From Medouna [on the Somali coast] to Malindi, a town of the Zanj, one follows the coast for three days and three nights by sea. Malindi lies on the shore, at the mouth of a river of sweet water. It is a large town, whose people engage in hunting and fishing. On land they hunt the tiger [sic] and other wild beasts. They obtain various kinds of fish from the sea, which they cure and sell.

They own and exploit iron mines; for them iron is an article of trade and the source of their largest profits. They pretend to know how to bewitch the most poisonous snakes so as to make them harmless to everyone except those for whom they wish evil, or on whom they wish to take vengeance. They also pretend that by means of these enchantments the tigers and lions cannot hurt them. These wizards are called al-Musnafu in the language of the people.

It is two days' journey along the coast to Mombasa. This is a small place and a dependency of the Zanj. Its inhabitants work in the iron mines and hunt tigers. They have red coloured dogs which fight every kind of wild beast and even lions. This town lies on the sea shore near a large gulf up which ships travel two days' journey; its banks are uninhabited because of the wild beasts that live in the forests where the Zanj go and hunt, as we have already said. In this town lives the King of Zanzibar. His guards go on foot because they have no mounts: horses cannot live there.

CHAO JU-KUA: ZANZIBAR AND SOMALIA IN THE THIRTEENTH CENTURY

Zanguebar (Ts'ong-Pa)

The Ts'ong-pa country is an island of the sea south of Hu-ch'a-la. To the west it reaches a great mountain. The inhabitants are of Ta-shi [Arab] stock and follow the Ta-shi religion. They wrap themselves in blue foreign cotton stuffs and wear red leather shoes. Their daily food consists of meal, baked cakes and mutton.

There are many villages, and a succession of wooded hills and terraced rocks. The climate is warm, and there is no cold season. The products of the country consist of elephants' tusks, native gold, ambergris and yellow sandal-wood.

Every year Hu-ch'a-la and the Ta-shi localities along the sea-coast send ships to this country with white cotton cloth, porcelain, copper and red cotton to trade.

Berbera Coast (Pi-p'a-lo)

The country of Pi-p'a-lo contains four cities; the other places are all villages which are constantly at feud and fighting with each other. The inhabitants pray to Heaven and not to the Buddha. The land produces many camels and sheep, and the people feed themselves with the flesh and milk of camels and with baked cakes.

The other products are ambergris, big elephants' tusks and big rhinoceros' horns. There are elephants' tusks which weigh over 100 carries and rhinoceros' horns of over ten catties weight. The land is also rich in putchuk, liquid storax gum, myrrh, and tortoise-shell of extraordinary thickness, for which there is great demand in other countries. The country also brings forth the so-called 'camel-crane' [ostrich], which measures from the ground to its crown from six to seven feet. It has wings and can fly, but not to any great height.

There is also in this country a wild animal called tsu-la [giraffe]; it resembles a camel in shape, an ox in size, and is of a yellow colour. Its fore legs are five feet long, its hind legs only three feet. Its head is high up and turned upwards. Its skin is an inch thick.

There is also in this country a kind of mule [zebra] with brown, white, and black stripes around its body. These animals wander about in mountain wilds; they are a variety of camel. The inhabitants of this country, who are great huntsman, hunt these animals with poisoned arrows.

ABU-AL-FIDA: MALINDI, MOMBASA, AND SOFALA

Malindi is a town of the land of the Zanj, 81 1/2° long., 2° 50' lat. West of the town is a great gulf into which flows a river which comes down from the mountain of Komr. On the banks of this gulf are very large dwellings belonging to the Zanj; the houses of the people of Komr are on the south side. East of Malindi is al-Kerany, the name of a mountain very famous among travellers; this mountain runs out into the sea for a distance of about 100 miles in a north-east direction; at the same time it extends along the continent in a straight line north for a distance of about fifty miles. Among other things which we might say about this mountain are the iron mine which is on the continental side and the lodestone in the part which is in the sea, which attracts iron.

At Malindi is the tree of zendj (the ginger tree) (or at Mallndi there are many Zanjian sorcerers). The King of the Zanj lives at Malindi. Between Mombasa and Mnllndi is about a degree. Mombasa is on the coast. On the west is a gulf along which buildings stand as far as 300 miles. Nearby to the east is the desert which separates the land of the Zanj from Sofaia.

Among the towns of the country of Sofala is Batyna (or Banyna). It is situated at the end of a great gulf, away from the equinoctial line, under 2 1/2° lat., 87° long. According to Ibn Said, on the West of Batyna is Adjued, the name of a mountain which projects into the sea towards the north-east for a distance of 100 miles. The waves of the sea make a great noise here. The people of Sofala live to the east of this mountain: their capital is Seruna, under 99° long., 2 1/2 lat. [south]. The town is built on a large estuary where a river, which rises in the mountain of Komr, flows out. There the King of Sofala resides.

Then one arrives at the town of Leirana. Ibn Fathuma, who visited the town, said that it was a seaport where ships put in and whence they set out. The inhabitants profess Islam. Leirana is on long. 102°, lat. 0° 30' [south]. It is on a great gulf.

The town of Daghuta is the last one of the country of Sofala and the furthest of the inhabited part of the continent towards the south. It is on long. 109°, lat. 12°, south of the equator.

Sofala. According to the Canon it is on 50° 3' long., 2° lat., south of the equator. Sofala is in the land of the Zanj. According to the author of the Canon, the inhabitants are Muslims. Ibn Said says that their chief means of existence are mining gold and iron, and that they dress in leopard skins. According to Masudi, horses do not reproduce in the land of the Zanj, so that the warriors go on foot or fight from the backs of oxen.

Ibn Wahab: An Arab Merchant Visits Tang China

Ibn Wahab was an Arab merchant from Basra who sailed to China via the Indian Ocean c. 872 CE. His travel account includes a description of his interview with the emperor. Wahab's visit occurred at the height of the T'ang dynasty (618–907 CE) with its flourishing arts and trade, and efficient civil service. The Chinese had connections and influence throughout Eurasia as can be seen by the presence of Ibn Wahab, an Arab merchant trading all the way in China.

Source: *Fitzgerald, C.P. China: A Short Cultural History (London: Cresse Press, 1950), pp. 339–340.*

Focus Questions:
1. According to the religious material gathered, with whom does China maintain cultural contacts?
2. What is the emperor's attitude towards the various religions? Why?
3. What religions do you think are so casually mentioned in the last sentences?

"When I was received by the Emperor," Ibn Wahab relates, "he told the interpreter to ask me, 'can you recognize your Master, if you see him?'" The Emperor referred to Mahomet, upon whom be God's

Blessing. I replied: 'How can I see him, since he is in Heaven with the Most High God?' 'I am talking of his likeness,' said the Emperor. 'I would know that,' I replied. Then the Emperor called for a box containing rolls which he put in front of him, and passed them to his interpreter, saying: 'Let him see his Master.' I recognized the portraits of the Prophets, and I said a blessing. 'Why are you moving your lips?' asked the Emperor. 'Because I am blessing the Prophets,' I answered. 'How did you know them?' he asked. 'By their attributes; for instance, here is Noah with his Ark, which saved him and his family when at the command of God all the earth was drowned in the Flood.' At these words the Emperor laughed, and said, 'You have certainly recognized Noah. As for the Flood, we do not believe it. The Flood did not submerge the whole world. It did not reach China or India.' 'That is Moses with his staff,' I said. 'Yes,' said the Emperor, 'but he was not important and his people were few.' 'There,' I said, 'is Jesus on his ass, surrounded by his apostles.' 'Yes,' said the Emperor: 'He lived only a short time. His mission lasted only thirty months.' Then I saw the Prophet on a camel, and his companions, also on camels, around him. I wept, being much moved. 'Why do you weep?' asked the Emperor. 'Because I see our Prophet, my ancestor.' [Ibn Wahab was of the Koreish.] 'Yes, it is he,' said the Emperor. 'He and his people founded a glorious empire. He did not see it completed, but his successors have.' Above each picture was an inscription [in Chinese], which I supposed to contain an account of their history. I saw also other pictures, which I did not recognize. The interpreter told me that they were the prophets of China and India."

Chapter 13

Medieval and Early Modern Thought

Jean Bodin, *Six Books of the Commonwealth*, "The True Attributes of Sovereignty"

Jean Bodin (ca. 1530–1596 CE) was a French political theorist and lawyer. Bodin studied civil law at the University of Toulouse, taught and practiced law, and in 1571 served in the household of the king's brother. The events and turmoil of sixteenth-century France heavily influenced his thought, which was devoted to the maintenance of order. He is most well known for identifying and recognizing the importance of the state's sovereignty. In Six Books of the Commonwealth (1576), Bodin contended that the state, preferably in the form of a monarch, held supreme power. He favored religious toleration and also wrote about the state's role in finance and trade.

Source: *Jean Bodin, "The True Attributes of Sovereignty," Six Livres de la Republique (Six Books of the Commonwealth).*

Focus Questions:
1. According to Bodin, what kind of rights of sovereignty does a sovereign possess?
2. To Bodin, what is the difference between custom and law?

SIX BOOKS OF THE COMMONWEALTH BOOK I, CHAPTER X: THE TRUE ATTRIBUTES OF SOVEREIGNTY

The first attribute of the sovereign prince therefore is the power to make law binding on all his subjects in general and on each in particular. But to avoid any ambiguity one must add that he does so without the consent of any superior, equal, or inferior being necessary. If the prince can only make law with the consent of a superior he is a subject; if of an equal he shares his sovereignty; if of an inferior, whether it be a council of magnates or the people, it is not he who is sovereign. The names of the magnates that one finds appended to a royal edict are not there to give force to the law, but as witnesses, and to make it more acceptable...When I say that the first attribute of sovereignty is to give law to all in general and each in particular, I mean by this last phrase the grant of privileges. I mean by a privilege a concession to one or a small group of individuals which concerns the profit or loss of those persons only...

It may be objected however that not only have magistrates the power of issuing edicts and ordinances, each according to his competence and within his own sphere of jurisdiction, but private citizens can make law in the form of general or local custom. It is agreed that customary law is as binding as statute law. But if the sovereign prince is author of the law, his subjects are the authors of custom. But there is a difference between law and custom. Custom establishes itself gradually over a long period of years, and by common consent, or at any rate the consent of the greater part. Law is made on the instant and draws its force from him who has the right to bind all the rest. Custom is established imperceptibly and without any exercise of compulsion. Law is promulgated and imposed by authority, and often against the wishes of the subject. For this reason Dion Chrysostom compared custom to the king and law to the tyrant. Moreover law can break custom, but custom cannot derogate from the law, nor can the magistrate, or any other responsible for the administration of law, use his discretion about the enforcement of law as he can about custom. Law, unless it is permissive and relaxes the severity of another law, always carries penalties for its breach. Custom only has binding force by the sufferance and during the good pleasure of the sovereign prince, and so far as he is willing to authorize it. Thus the force of both statutes and customary law derives from the authorization of the prince...Included in the power of making and unmaking law is that of promulgating it and amending it when it is obscure, or when the magistrates find contradictions and absurdities...

All the other attributes and rights of sovereignty are included in this power of making and unmaking law, so that strictly speaking this is the unique attribute of sovereign power. It includes all other rights of sovereignty, that is to say of making peace and war, of hearing appeals from the sentences of all courts whatsoever, of appointing and dismissing the great officers of state; of taxing, or granting privileges of exemption to all subjects, of appreciating or depreciating the value and weight of the coinage, of receiving oaths of fidelity from subjects and liege-vassals alike, without exception of any other to whom faith is due...

But because law is an imprecise and general term, it is as well to specify the other attributes of sovereignty comprised in it, such as the making of war and peace. This is one of the most important rights of sovereignty, since it brings in its train either the ruin or the salvation of the state. This was a right of sovereignty not only among the ancient Romans, but has always been so among all other peoples...Sovereign princes are therefore accustomed to keep themselves informed of the smallest accidents and undertakings connected with warfare. Whatever latitude they may give to their representatives to negotiate peace or an alliance, they never grant the authority to conclude without their own express consent. This was illustrated in the negotiations leading up to the recent treaty of Cateaux-Cambresis, when the king's envoys kept him almost hourly informed of all proposals and counter-proposals...In popular states and aristocracies the difficulty of assembling the people, and the danger of making public all the secrets of diplomacy has meant that the people have generally handed responsibility over to the council. Nevertheless it remains true that the commissions and the orders that it issues in discharge of this function proceed from the authority of the people, and are despatched by the council in the name of the people...

The third attribute of sovereignty is the power to institute the great officers of state. It has never been questioned that the right is an attribute of sovereignty, at any rate as far as the great officers are concerned. I confine it however to high officials, for there is no commonwealth in which these officers, and many guilds and corporate bodies besides, have not some power of appointing their subordinate officials. They do this in virtue of their office, which carries with it the power to delegate. For instance, those who hold feudal rights of jurisdiction of their sovereign prince in faith and homage have the power to appoint the judges in their courts, and their assistants. But this power is devolved upon them by the prince...It is therefore not the mere appointment of officials that implies sovereign right, but the authorization and confirmation of such appointments. It is true however that in so far as the exercise of this right is delegated, the sovereignty of the prince is to that extent qualified, unless his concurrence and express consent is required.

The fourth attribute of sovereignty, and one which has always been among its principal rights, is that the prince should be the final resort of appeal from all other courts...Even though the prince may have published a law, as did Caligula, forbidding any appeal or petition against the sentences of his officers, nevertheless the subject cannot be deprived of the right to make an appeal, or present a petition, to the prince in person. For the prince cannot tie his own hands in this respect, nor take from his subjects the means of redress, supplication, and petition, notwithstanding the fact that all rules governing appeals and jurisdictions are matters of positive law, which we have shown does not bind the prince. This is why the Privy Council, including the Chancellor de l'Hopital, considered the action of the commissioners deputed to hold an enquiry into the conduct of the President l'Alemant irregular and unprecedented. They had forbidden him to approach within twenty leagues of the court, with the intention of denying him any opportunity of appeal. The king himself could not deny this right to the subject, though he is free to make whatsoever reply to the appeal, favourable or unfavourable, that he pleases...Were it otherwise, and the prince could acquit his subjects or his vassals from the obligation to submit their causes to him in the last instance, he would make of them sovereigns equal with himself...But if he would preserve his authority, the surest way of doing so is to avoid ever devolving any of the attributes of sovereignty upon a subject...

With this right is coupled the right of pardoning convicted persons, and so of overruling the sentences of his own courts, in mitigation of the severity of the law, whether touching life, property, honour, or domicile. It is not in the power of any magistrate, whatever his station, to do any of these things, or to make any revision of the judgement he has once given...In a well-ordered commonwealth the right should never be delegated either to a special commission, or to any high officer of state, save in those circumstances where it is necessary to establish a regency, either because the king is abroad in some distant place, or in captivity, or incapable, or under age. For instance, during the minority of Louis IX, the authority of the Crown was vested in his mother Blanche of Castile as his guardian...Princes however tend to abuse this right, thinking that to pardon is pleasing to God, whereas to exact the utmost punishment is displeasing to Him. But I hold, subject to correction, that the sovereign prince cannot remit any penalty imposed by the law of God, any more than he can dispense any one from the operation of the law of God, to which he himself is subject. If the magistrate who dispenses anyone from obedience to the ordinance of his king merits death, how much more unwarrantable is it for the prince to acquit a man of the punishment ordained by God's law? If a sovereign prince cannot deny a subject his civil rights, how can he acquit him of the penalties imposed by God, such as the death penalty exacted by divine law for treacherous murder?

Kino Tsurayaki, Excerpt from *The Tosa Diary*

The Tosa Diary is a literary work presented in the voice of a woman. It was written in 936 by Kino Tsurayaki (872–945 CE), a courtier and poet at the Imperial court. He was quite successful both in administration and in publishing several literary works—achievements expected of the highly cultured court of the time. Eventually in 930 Tsurayaki was appointed governor of Kochi province in Shikoku, southeast Japan. He wrote the diary as a very stylistic literary account of the journey home in 935.

Source: *Ki no Tsurayuki,* The Tosa Diary *(936), trans. by William Porter, 2005.*

Focus Questions:
1. What are the challenges on the voyage?
2. What civilization lies between Kochi and Kyoto?
3. What is the attitude of the writer to the pilot and ship's crew?

The "Tosa Diary" describing the return to Kyoto of a governor of Tosa Province, was probably written in the year 936, from notes taken on the voyage. Although the fiction is maintained throughout that the diary is being written by one of the ladies in the party, it is reasonably certain that the author is the governor himself, the celebrated poet Ki no Tsurayuki.

Tosa province is the ancient name for the present Kochi Prefecture, in the south of Shikoku island.

Diaries are things written by men, I am told. Never the less I am writing one, to see what a woman can do.

Twenty-first day, Twelfth moon (the year does not matter):
Late at night we made our departure from the house. But I must set things down in a little more detail. A certain gentleman, after four or five years in the province, had finished his term of office as governor, and now, with all the usual round of concluded and papers of release duly received, he set out from the official residence and moved to a place near to the point of embarktion [sic]. Before he went, however, various people, acquaintances and strangers alike, come to take their leave. The farewells were particularily [sic] distressing for those who had been closely associated with him over these years. There was an endless coming and going all day long, and the communion lasted well into the night.

Twenty-second day:
We offered up prayers for a calm and peaceful voyage—"all the way to Izumi Province." Fujiwara no Tokizane arranged a farewell celebration "for the road" (not very appropriate for a ship, perhaps) at which every one, from master to servant became disgustingly drunk.

Twenty-fourth day:
The Provincial overseer of religion arrived to give us a farewell party. Everyone, high and low, old and young was fuddled with drink. Even people who have never learnt to write the figure for one were dancing figures of eight.

Twenty-fifth day:
A messenger arrived from the official residence, it seems with an invitation for the ex-governor. The ex-governor accepted. The various entertainments lasted all day and night, and well into the next morning.

Twenty-sixth day:
Today they were still at the new governor's residence, feasting and making merry. Even the servants have received presents, I am told. Chinese verses were declaimed, and the new governor, his guest, and others joined in an exchange of extempore Japanese poems. I cannot write Chinese verse in this diary, but one of the Japanese poems, composed by the new governor went like this:

For your sake I left Kyoto, and journeyed here to meet you—I journeyed in vain if I came to lose you.

Before taking his leave the former governor replied:

Over the white-crested waves I came, and following came another.

Where I return, he shall return—and who is that other but you?

There were more poems, by others, but apparently none of them was particularly well constructed. After exchanging a few more words the former governor and the present governor descended together into the garden. Present and former masters of the house grasped hands, wished each other good fortune—in accents unsteadied by wine—and went their respective ways.

Twenty-seventh day:

Our boats left Otsu, rowing a course for Urado. As they cast off, I thought sadly of my master's young daughter—born in Kyoto, and suddenly taken from us in this remote province. While recording, in these last days, the busy preparations for our departure, I have said nothing on this matter; but now that we are at last under way on the return voyage to Kyoto, my only sensations are of grief and longing for a young girl who is not coming with us. There are others, too, who could not bear the sadness of it.

Someone wrote this poem

> Kyoto bound, our thoughts are heavy yet
> With grief for one who never shall return.
> Later another poem was composed:
> Forgetful, "Wherever is that child?" I cry
> And, oh, the sadness of the truth!

Meanwhile we reached a place called Kako Point, where we were overtaken by the brothers of the new governor and other friends, who brought us presents of sake and food. The whole company disembarked onto the beach, and we talked to each other of the sorrows of parting. Of all the people at the governor's residence, these who have now come are said to have shown themselves the most kind and considerate on that occasion...While we were exchanging poems the chief pilot—a man of no sensibility—having taken his fill of sake and thinking it high time to be off, announced:

"The tide is full. There should be a wind soon"; and we made ready to re-embark...This evening we anchored at Urado, where we were later overtaken by Fujiwara no Tokizane, Tachibana no Suehira, and others.

Proceeding eastward from Urado along the Pacific coast of Shikoku, they reach a harbour called Ominato the following night. Here they are detained for nine days, waiting for clear weather. After a disappointing New Year's day, which only serves to increase their general yearning for Kyoto, they occupy themselves in receiving visitors and composing poems.

Ninth day, Second moon:

Early in the morning we left Ominato and made for the anchorage of Naha. A large number of people gathered to see us off, determined not to leave us so long as we remain within the confines of the provincial district...

From now on we row farther and farther out to sea. It is for this reason that all these people gathered here to see us off. Little by little, at every stroke of the oars, the watchers standing by the shore slip away in the distance, just as we on the boats too, grow more and more indistant [sic] to them. On the shore, perhaps, there are thing they would like to say to us. On the boats there are thoughts we wish to convey to them—but to no avail. Even so, though we can expect no reply, we compose this last poem:

> No courier have we, and though with heavy hearts
> We leave—perhaps they'll never know we grieved.

Soon we pass the pine-covered beaches of Uta. Pines beyond number! How many tens of centuries have they stood there? Waves wash the roots of each tree, and from each topmost branch a crane soars into the air. We watched in tireless fascination. Someone on the boat recited this poem:

As far as the eye can see, on each pine top there rests a crane
Each crane to each pine, perhaps a faithful companion these thousand years!

The poem, however, cannot compare with the sight itself. As we proceed in this manner, absorbed in the scenery, night gradually draws on. The mountains and sea grow dark. Soon it becomes impossible to distinguish east from west, and for warning of a change in the weather we must rely completely on the pilot's judgement. Even the men, unaccustomed to such a situation, show signs of anxiety. With the women it is much worse—we hide our heads in the bottom of the boat and sob. But while we are in this sad condition, the pilot and the boatmen, sing songs completely unconcerned:

In the spring fields lonely I cry
My hands I have cut, I have cut,
Gathering herbs in the sharp pampas grass.
And will my parents eat these herbs,
Or are they for my husband's mother?
Oh I wish I never got married!

or:

Where is that lad who came last night?
I'll ask him for money.
"I'll pay tomorrow," he said—but he lied.
He's brought no money, of course, but worse–
He hasn't come himself!

There are many others besides, but I shall not write them down. The sea grows rougher, but listening to these songs and to the boatman's laughter we feel more easy at heart, at last, after a long days voyage, we reach harbor. An old gentleman and an old lady have meanwhile fallen sick, and they retire to bed without supper.

Tenth day:
Today we remain at this harbour of Naha.

The following day they proceed to Muroto, their last stoping place within the province of Tosa. Here they are detained by bad weather for five days.

Seventeenth day:
The clouds have cleared, and in the early hours before dawn there is a fine clear moon. We set out in our boats. A perfect image of the clouds above is reflected in the bottom of the sea—it must have been on a night like this that the ancient poet wrote of "ours piercing the moon on the waves, the boat traversing skies in the sea's depths." At least, those are his words so far as I remember. Someone composed this poem on a similar theme:

As we row over the moon in the sea bottom,
Will our oars be entangled in a Katsura tree.
Hearing this another said:
Gazing down, we row across a firmament
Beneath the water—how small we feel!

As we proceed it grows gradually lighter. "Dark clouds have suddenly appeared!" shouts the pilot. "It will storm I think. I'm turning the boat back!" We return to the harbour amid rain, feeling miserable.

They wait for several more days at Muroto, for a chance to round Muroto cape.

Twenty-first day:

At about the hour of the Hare we set out once again. All the other boats move out at the same time, so that, as we look around us, it seems as if early spring seas are already dotted with fallen autumn leaves. Perhaps in answer to our constant prayer, the wind no longer blows, and we row along in bright sunshine...

As we continue on our way, talking of this and that, the master of the boat anxiously scans the seas. It seems that, now we are leaving the bounds of the province, there is danger that pirates may seek vengeance on the ex-governor. As we think of this, the sea once more becomes a place of terror. All of us have grown white-haired these last weeks. Truly an age of seventy or eighty years is soon to be reached at sea!

> Tell us, Lord of the Islands, which is the whitest
> The surf on the rocks or the snow on our heads
>
> Ask him Pilot

Twenty-second day:

We set out from last night's harbour. Mountains are visible in the far distance. A boy of eight—looking even less than his years—was amazed to discover that, as our boats move, the mountains appear to move with us. He composed this poem:

> Viewed from a moving boat, even mountains move
> But do the mountain pines know this.

It is a fitting poem for a child. Today the sea is rough. Around the rocks the foam is like driving snow, and the waves themselves are flowers in bloom:

> A wave is but a single thing we're told but from its hue
> You'd think it was a mixture—flowers and snow

Twenty-third day:

The sun appears, but is soon obscured by a cloud. Since we have been told that this particular area is infested by pirates, we pray for the protection of the gods and Buddhas.

Twenty-sixth day:

Being told again (with what truth, I do not know) that pirates are on our tracks, we started out about midnight, and on our way made offerings to the gods. The pilot cast our paper charms into the sea, and they drifted off to the east he cried: "In the same direction in which these offerings drift, vouchsafe that this vessel may speed!" Hearing this, a young girl made a poem:

> Blow steadily, wind, behind our boat, even as you blow
> These charms offered to the sea gods.

At about this time the wind was good, and the pilot—with an air of self-importance, and with evident relief—ordered the sails to be raised. Hearing his words of command we women, young and old alike, were overjoyed, feeling that Kyoto is not far off now...

The next two days are stormy, and the boats remain in harbour—the place is not specified, but it is presumably somewhere in the region of the present city of Tokushima. On the twenty-ninth day of the second moon they move on to Naruto, and the following day they make for Awaji Island and the mainland.

Thirtieth day

The wind and rain have stopped. Having heard that pirates operate only by day, we started at midnight, rowing past the Awa whirlpool. It was pitch black and we could see to neither the left or right. As we passed the whirlpool men and women alike prayed fervently to the gods and buddhas. Near dawn we passed a place called Nushima, and then Tanagawa. Pressing on in great haste, we arrived at Nada in Izumi Province, there is no need to worry about pirates.

High seas detain them for three days at Nada.

Fourth day, Third moon:

"Today, judging by the wind and the clouds, we shall have very bad weather," said the pilot, and we did not venture from this harbour. But all day long there had not been a sign of wind or waves. Even as a judge of the weather, this pilot is useless. Along the beach of the harbour were innumerable shells and pebbles of great beauty, and someone in the boat, still unable to think of anything except the child who is no longer with us, composed this poem:

> Wash your shells to my ship, o waves!
> I'll gather forgetting-shells for one I loved.
> Another, equally unable to bear his grief, and sick in the spirit after the trials of the voyage replies:
> I'll gather no forgetting-shells but jewels,
> Mementos of the jewel-like one I loved.

I grief [sic] even a father grows childlike. It might be said, I suppose, that this particular child could hardly be likened to a jewel—but "a departed child has a beautiful face," goes the proverb...

Fifth day

Today we haste out of Nada, and steered for the harbour of Ozu. Pines stretch endlessly along the beaches...As we were rowed along, admiring the view and talking of this and that, a sudden wind rose and no matter how desperately the boatmen rowed, we were driven slowly backwards. The boat was in danger of foundering on the waves, "The god of Sumiyoshi is the same as other gods. There is something on board the ship he wants," said the pilot. "Make an offering of paper symbols," he urged. The master complied, but the wind did not abate—it blew all the harder, and the waves rose higher. "Paper symbols are not to the god's taste. The ship makes no headway!" shouted the pilot. "Have you nothing which will please him better?" "There's nothing but this," said the master. "I have two eyes but only one mirror. I shall give this mirror to the god." He threw it into the waves, and as it sank the sea suddenly became as smooth as the face of the mirror. Someone composed this poem:

> Seeking to fathom the mind of the raging god we cast
> A mirror into the stormy sea. In that his image is revealed.

An amazing experience! Surely this cannot be the god whom we commonly associate with such gentle things as "Limpid Waters," "The Balm of Forgetfulness," and "pines along the shore"? We have all seen with our own eyes—and with the help of the mirror—what sort of god he is.

On the following day, to the great joy of al the passengers, Naniwa (Osaka) is reached, and the ship commences its voyage up the river Yodo towards Kyoto. Progress is slow, owing to the shallowness of the channel, but after five days the bridge at Yamazaki—the terminus for river traffic was sighted.

Eleventh day:

After a little rain the skies cleared. Continuing up river, we noticed a line of hills converging on the eastern bank. When we learned that this is the Yawata Hachiman Shrine, there was great rejoicing and we humbly abased ourselves in thanks. The bridge of Yamazaki came in sight at last, and our feelings of joy could no longer be restrained. Here, close by the Ooji Temple, our boat came to anchor; and here we waited, while various matters were negotiated for the remainder of the journey. By the riverside, near the temple, there were many willow trees, and one of our company, admiring their reflection in the water, made the poem:

> A pattern of wave ripples, woven—it seems—
> On a loom of green willows reflected in the stream.

They waited several days at Yamazaki for carriages to arrive from Kyoto. Kyoto is reached late at night, on the sixteenth of the second moon.

Sixteenth day

As we reached the house and passed through the gate, everything stood briefly out brightly under the clear moon. Things were even worse than we had heard—there was a wilderness of decay and dilapidation. The heart of the neighbour to whose care we entrusted the house has proved a wilderness, too. Seeing that his house and ours were like one, divided only by fence, we left everything to his care and good hopes. Whenever we sent him news or instructions, we sent small presents as well. However, tonight we have no intention of showing any displeasure. Wretched though the place looks, we shall thank him for his trouble.

In a marshy spot in the garden we had excavated a pit, forming a pond, around which stood a groove of pine trees. It looks as if, in five or six years, a thousand years have left their mark here—one bank of the pond has collapsed, new trees have sprung up among the old, and such is the general air of neglect that all who look are afflicted with a sense of sadness. Old memories come flooding back, and the saddest of all are those of a child who born in this house and who has not returned. To see others from the ship surrounded by excited happy children, only makes our grief more difficult to bear. One who shares our inmost thoughts composed this poem:

> When one, whose home is near, has not returned,
> How sad to see these new young pines!
> Still unconsoled, perhaps, he wrote another:
> The one I knew—if only she had been an ageless pine!
> What need then of these grievous farewells?

There are many things which we cannot forget, and which gives us pain, but I cannot write them all down. Whatever they may be, let us say no more.

Speculum Principi, "The Animal Life of Greenland and the Character of the Land in Those Regions"

The "mirror of the prince" was a popular medieval format for providing a manual of information and advice for rulers. The Norwegian version, written about 1250 CE, follows the process of other European mirrors. However, it not only describes Norwegian law and kingship but also geographical information on matters as diverse of the Northern Lights and the Norwegian settlements in Greenland.

Source: *Marcellus Larson, trans.,* The King's Mirror *(1917).*

Focus Questions:
1. What are the resources in Greenland? What is not available?
2. How do the geography and climate affect the settlement?
3. Where might Greenlanders go for timber and other materials?

XVII

The Animal Life Of Greenland And The Character of The Land In Those Regions

Son. These things must seem wonderful to all who may hear of them, both what is told about the fishes and that about the monsters which are said to exist in those waters. Now I understand that this ocean must be more tempestuous than all other seas; and therefore I think it strange that it is covered with ice both in winter and in summer, more than all other seas are. I am also curious to know why men should be so eager to fare thither, where there are such great perils to beware of, and what one can look for in that country which can be turned to use or pleasure. With your permission I also wish to ask what the people who inhabit those lands live upon; what the character of the country is, whether it is ice-clad like the ocean or free from ice even though the sea be frozen; and whether corn grows in that country as in other lands. I should also like to know whether you regard it as mainland or as an island, and whether there are any beasts or such other things in that country as there are in other lands.

Father. The answer to your query as to what people go to seek in that country and why they fare thither through such great perils is to be sought in man's three-fold nature. One motive is fame and rivalry, for it is in the nature of man to seek places where great dangers may be met, and thus to win fame. A second motive is curiosity, for it is also in man's nature to wish to see and experience the things that he has heard about, and thus to learn whether the facts are as told or not. The third is desire for gain; for men seek wealth wherever they have heard that gain is to be gotten, though, on the other hand, there may be great dangers too. But in Greenland it is this way, as you probably know, that whatever comes from other lands is high in price, for this land lies so distant from other countries that men seldom visit it. And everything that is needed to improve the land must be purchased abroad, both iron and all the timber used in building houses. In return for their wares the merchants bring back the following products: buckskin, or hides, sealskins, and rope of the kind that we talked about earlier which is called "leather rope" and is cut from the fish called walrus, and also the teeth of the walrus.

As to whether any sort of grain can grow there, my belief is that the country draws but little profit from that source. And yet there are men among those who are counted the wealthiest and most prominent who have tried to sow grain as an experiment; but the great majority in that country do not know what bread is, having never seen it. You have also asked about the extent of the land and whether it is mainland or an island; but I believe that few know the size of the land, though all believe that it is continental and connected with some mainland, inasmuch as it evidently contains a number of such animals as are known to live on the mainland but rarely on islands. Hares and wolves are very plentiful and there are multitudes of reindeer. It seems to be generally held, however, that these animals do not inhabit islands, except where men have brought them in; and everybody seems to feel sure that no one has brought them to Greenland, but that they must have run thither from other main lands. There are bears, too, in that region; they are white, and people think they are native to the country, for they differ very much in their habits from the black bears that roam the forests. These kill horses, cattle, and other beasts to feed upon; but the white bear of Greenland wanders most of the time about on the ice in the sea, hunting seals and whales and feeding upon them. It is also as skillful a swimmer as any seal or whale.

In reply to your question whether the land thaws out or remains icebound like the sea, I can state definitely that only a small part of the land thaws out, while all the rest remains under the ice. But nobody knows whether the land is large or small, because all the mountain ranges and all the valleys are covered with ice, and no opening has been found anywhere. But it is quite evident that there are such openings, either along the shore or in the valleys that lie between the mountains, through which beasts can find a way; for they could not run thither from other lands, unless they should find open roads through the ice and the soil thawed out. Men have often tried to go up into the country and climb the highest mountains in various places to look about and learn whether any land could be found that was free from ice and habitable. But nowhere have they found such a place, except what is now occupied, which is a little strip along the water's edge.

There is much marble in those parts that are inhabited; it is variously colored, both red and blue and streaked with green. There are also many large hawks in the land, which in other countries would be counted very precious—white falcons, and they are more numerous there than in any other country; but the natives do not know how to make any use of them.

Murasaki Shikibu, Selections from *The Tale of Genji*

Genji is generally considered the first book written in novel form. It was produced in the early eleventh century by Murasaki Shikibu (976–1031 CE), a noble woman in Kyoto. She most likely wrote the book for her fellow female nobles. As such it is replete with courtly politics and love affairs, all acted out with highly stylized courtly behavior. The period in which the book was written was one of continued refinement in Buddhism, and in literature and art. This period also saw the development of feudal nobles and the samurai class.

Source: *Murasaki Shikibu.* The Tale of Genji *(1011).*

> **Focus Questions:**
> 1. What are the attitudes of Japanese society by class and gender?
> 2. Why is it best to choose a girl from a middling family?
> 3. What does having a "ministry of rites" tell us?

THE PAULOWNIA COURT

The autumn tempests blew and suddenly the evenings were chilly. Lost in his grief, the emperor sent off a note to the grandmother. His messenger was a woman of middle rank called Myo-bu. It was on a beautiful moonlit night when he dispatched her.

Myo-bu reached the grandmother's house. Her carriage was drawn through the gate and made its way through the tangles.

The weeds grew ever higher and the autumn winds tore threateningly at the garden.

The grandmother was unable to control her tears. After a pause she read the message from the emperor.

He said that he was in a deep grief over losing the lady and could not bear to think of the child languishing in the house of tears.

Myo-bu was much moved to find the emperor waiting up for her. Making it seem that his attention was on the small and beautifully planted garden before him, now in full autumn bloom, he was talking quietly with some women, among the most sensitive of his attendants. He had become addicted to the illustrations by the emperor Uda for "The Song of Everlasting Sorrow" and to poems on that subject, and to Chinese poems as well which reminded him of his relation with Koi.

He listened attentively as Myo-bu described the scene she had found. He took up the letter she had brought from the grandmother telling of his worry about the future of the child.

Looking at the keepsakes Myo-bu had brought back, he reviewed his memories over and over again, from his very earliest days with the dead lady.

The months passed and the young prince returned to the palace. At the age of seven, an embassy came from Korea. Hearing that among the emissaries was a skilled physiognomist, the emperor would have liked to summon him for consultation.

He decided, however, to send Genji to the Koro mansion, where the party was lodged.

The boy was disguised as the son of the grand moderator, his guardian at court. Korean cocked his head in astonishment.

"It is the face of one who should ascend to the highest place and be father to the nation," he said quietly, as if to himself. "But to take it for such would no doubt be to predict trouble. Yet it is not the face of the minister, the deputy, who sets about ordering public affairs."

The moderator was a man of considerable learning. There was much of interest in his exchanges with the Korean. There were also exchanges of Chinese poetry among the three of them. The boy offered a verse that was received with high praise. The emperor summoned the new lady, Fujitsubo who resembled the dead lady. Gradually his affections shifted to this new lady who consoled him a lot. People began calling Genji "the shining one" and the lady "the lady of the radiant sun." The emperor wanted the two of them to be close to each other.

When he reached the age of twelve, he went through his initiation ceremonies and received the cap of an adult. It was held in the Grand Seiryouden Hall.

The throne faced east on the east porch, and before it was Genji's seat and that of the minister who was to bestow on him the official cap. The freshness of his face and his boyish coiffure were again such as to make the emperor regret that the change must take place. The secretary of the treasury performed the ritual cutting of the boy's hair.

As the beautiful locks fell the emperor was seized with a hopeless longing for his dead lady. The ceremony over, the boy withdrew to change into adult trousers and descended into the courtyard for ceremonial thanksgiving.

The emperor was stirred by the deepest of emotions. He had on brief occasions been able to forget the past, and now it all came back again. Vaguely apprehensive lest the initiation of so young a boy bring a sudden aging, he was astonished to see that his son delighted him even more. Genji married Aoi-no-Ue, the daughter of the Minister of Left. The bride was older, and ill at ease with young husband. Fujitsubo was for him a sublime beauty.

THE BROOM TREE

(This is the story when Genji is 17 years old. He spent little time with his bride. He stayed most of the time in the court and seldom visited her. But with his brother-in-law, To-no-Chujo, he was on particularly good terms.)

The summer rains came, the court was in retreat. It had been raining all day. Genji was back in his own palace quarters. To-no-Chujo was also there. Genji pulled a lamp near and sought to while away the time with his books. Numerous pieces of colored paper, obviously letters, lay on a shelf. To-no-Chujo made no attempt to hide his curiosity.

It was not likely that very sensitive letters would be left scattered on a shelf, and it may be assumed that the papers treated so carelessly were the less important ones.

To-no-Chujo was reading the correspondence through piece by piece. This will be from her, and this will be from her, he would say. Sometimes he guessed correctly and sometimes he was far afield.

(Two young courtiers, a guard officer and a functionary in the Ministry of Rites, appeared on the scene. They talked on of the varieties of women.) The guard officer once had a woman who was a model of devotion; but she was violently jealous.

One day I said to her: "If you go on doubting me as you have, I will not see you again."

She answered: "Maybe this is the time," and then, suddenly, she took my hand and bit my finger.

After parting, he never visited her again, and the woman passed away in sorrow.

The guard officer talked on. "There was another one besides jealous woman. I was seeing her at about the same time. She was more amiable than the one I have just described to you. Everything about her told of refinement. Her poems, her handwriting when she dashed off a letter, the koto (long Japanese zither) she plucked a note on—everything seemed right. She was clever with her hands and clever with words.

And I learned that I was not her only secret visitor.

One bright moonlit autumn night I chanced to leave court with a friend. He got in the same carriage and got off in the front of the woman's house. The chrysanthemums were at their best and the red leaves were beautiful in the autumn wind. He took out a flute and played a tune on it. Blending nicely with the flute, there came the mellow tones of a Japanese koto." After that he stopped seeing her.

"Let me tell you a story about a shy woman I once knew," said To-no-Chujo. "I was seeing her in secret. She was an orphan and had borne a child. I sensed that she had come to depend on me. I went on seeing her, but only infrequently. She did not seem to feel any resentment though I visited so seldom. My affection grew.

Later, my wife found a roundabout way to be objectionable, and when I looked in on her again the woman had disappeared." (That woman and child will appear in the later chapter as Yugao and Tamakazura.)

"When I was still a student I knew a remarkably wise woman. She was most attentive to my needs. I learned many estimable things from her, to add to my store of erudition and help me with my work. Her letters were lucidity itself, in the purest Chinese."

(But unfortunately, she was the sort of woman who lacked gentleness.)

One day when he visited her, she insisted on talking to me through a very obtrusive screen. She said she had been indisposed with a malady known as coryza. "I have been imbibing of a steeped potion made from garlic," she said, and continued that when she had disencumbered herself of this aroma, they could meet once more.

But he thought that he had had enough and left her then.

(One day, Genji could not return to his mansion, since his mansion laid in a forbidden direction according to Buddhism.) He decided to visit the governor of Kii in Kyoto. The governor's mansion had been cleaned and made presentable. The shallow rivers were created pleasingly in the garden. A fence of wattles, of a deliberately rustic appearance, enclosed the garden, and much care had gone into the plantings. Insects were humming, one scarcely knew where, fireflies drew innumerable lines of light. Genji sat in the east room of the mansion facing the south side of the garden. His men were already tippling, out where they could admire a brook flowing under a gallery. The governor seemed busy and hurried off for viands. (That night he saw Utusemi and her stubbornness was what interested him.)

(He was attracted by her thoughtful character.)

All was quiet. Genji could make his way through to Utusemi. She was so small that he lifted her up easily.

She stood in confusion. She spoke with great firmness, but her thoughts were far from as firm. How happy she might have been if she had not made this unfortunate marriage with the old governor, the father of the Kii governor.

The first cock was crowing and Genji's men were awake. Genji parted, attracted to her extraordinary coldness.

She trembled to think that a dream might have told him of the night's happenings.

(Genji's longing was undiminished. He could not forget how touchingly fragile and confused Utsusemi had seemed.)

Genji asked the governor of Kii to introduce him to Kokimi, the young brother of Utusemi. He gave the boy a letter for his sister. But Utsusemi gave no reply to her brother, telling "You are a child, and it is quite improper for you to be carrying such messages." The hand was splendid, but she should not wait for this kind of letter. She belonged to another man, whom she must abandon if she would follow Genji.

THE SHELL OF THE LOCUST

Genji could not forget Utsusemi. With Kokimi as guide, he returned to the governor's mansion. It was a hot summer night. Genji made his way through the door and blinds. Utsusemi had been playing Go with another lady. One panel of a screen just inside had been folded back, and the curtains thrown over their frames, because of the heat. The view was unobstructed. Utsusemi was a small and rather ordinary woman. But the other was very handsome and tall.

Her Go partner stayed overnight with Utsusemi. When everyone went to sleep Genji entered into the room. Detecting an unusual perfume, Utsusemi got up and slipped out of the room leaving her summer robe. Genji was delighted to see that there was only one lady asleep. He guessed what had happened and felt ridiculous. His heart was resentfully on the other. But the girl beside him had a certain young charm of her own, and presently he was deep in vows of love.

EVENING FACES

In the summer evening, Genji stopped to inquire after his old nurse, Koremitsu's mother, on his way from court to pay one of his calls at Rokujo mansion. His carriage was simple and unadorned and he had no servants. Beside the nurse's house was a new fence of plaited cypress. The four or five narrow shutters above had been raised, and new blinds, white and clean, hung in the aperture. The white flowers of Yugao, which meant "evening faces," were in bloom on the board wall. Genji sent his man to ask the name of the flower. That was the beginning of the encounter between Genji and Yugao.

Koremitsu passed the flower to Genji on a white fan. A little girl of the house handed it to him. As he finished his visit to the nurse, he asked for a torch, and shone its light on the fan on which the evening face had rested. It was permeated with a lady's perfume, elegant and alluring. On it was a poem, "I think I need not ask whose face it is, so bright, this evening face, in the shining dew." Genji ordered Koremitsu to make inquiries about the woman.

Autumn came. Genji visited the lady of Rokujo. He had cooled toward her, which made her sleepless. She feared the rumor of their difference in age. On a morning of heavy mist, she lifted her head from her pillow to see him off. He paused to admire the profusion of flowers below the veranda and sent a little girl to cut them. Chujo, the servant of the lady Rokujo, followed him down the gallery. She was a pretty and graceful woman. He asked her to sit her with him for a time at the corner of the railing.

The bright full moon of the Eight Month came. Genji stayed over at Yugao's house. Towards dawn he was awakened by the plebeian voices coming from the shabby house down the street, the sound of mill-stone and singing of wild geese. There was a tasteful clump of black bamboo just outside and the dew-drops on the leaves in the front of the garden beamed reflecting the morning sunshine. Autumn insects sang busily. It was all clamorous, and also rather wonderful. She was so delicately beautiful, which struck him deeply. Viewing the outside together, they promised their never-ending love.

One day Genji took Yugao out by carriage and they spent some happy hours. Afterward, it was about midnight and he had been asleep for a while when an exceedingly beautiful woman appeared by his pillow. He awoke, feeling as if he were in the power of a malign[ant] being. The light had gone out. He ordered his men to bring the light. He reached for the girl. She was not breathing. Ukon, her servant lay face down at her side. A devil had seized Yugao and killed her.

Koremitsu wrapped the body and took it to a temple on mount Higashi. He happened to know the nun over there. Barely conscious, Genji made his way back to Nijo. In the evening, he went to the temple. The girl's face was unchanged and very pretty. The grand tone in which the worthy monk, the son of a nun, was reading a sutra brought on what Genji thought must be the full flood tide of his tears. Ukon, lying behind a screen, wept too.

Now genuinely ill, Genji took to his bed for one month after Yugao's death. He had lost weight, but this only made him more handsome. He summoned Ukon one quiet evening. The autumn tints were coming over the maples. Looking out upon the garden, he asked about Yugao. Ukon told him that her father was a guard captain. After his death, To-no-Chujo was very attentive and bore a very pretty little girl. When To-no-Chujo's wife discovered her, she ran off and hid herself. (This story was told previously in the 9th graphic of chapter 2.)

LAVENDER

Genji was suffering from malaria. He took four or five attendants along to visit a sage in the northern hills. He was a most accomplished worker of cures. Genji had once sent off a messenger to him, but the holy man replied that he was too old and unable to leave his place. The old man lived in a cave surrounded by rocks, high in the hill. The cherry blossoms had already fallen in the city, as it was late in the Third Month. But in the mountain, the cherry blossoms were at their best, which delighted Genji deeply.

Between the cures and incantations during the daytime, Genji walked a few blocks in the nearby villages. He saw a wattle fence in front of a temple, which was of better workmanship than similar fences nearby. In the evening Genji took Koremitsu and went to see the place again. Behind the fence, he could see the nun reading a text spread out on an armrest. She was in her forties and looked cultivated. Then a pretty girl of perhaps ten ran in and complained to the nun in a weeping voice that Inuki had let her baby sparrows loose. That was the first time Genji saw the Murasaki-no-Ue.

When Genji was invited into the temple, he asked the bishop about the little girl. She was a daughter of the Prince Hyobu. Her mother was the sister of Fujitsubo. She was dead and the grandmother, the nun, looked after the child. Genji proposed to the bishop that he would take care of her but the bishop refused. While the bishop went out to conduct services, Genji visited the nun and asked her to take the child with him. But she hesitated because of the difference in age and background.

When Genji improved, the bishop prepared a breakfast of unfamiliar fruits and wine. Genji, the bishop and the sage composed some poems regretting his departure. The bishop gave farewell presents: a rosary of carved ebony which Prince Shotoku had obtained in Korea, still in the original Chinese box, wrapped and attached to a branch of cinquefoil pine; and several medical bottles of indigo decorated with spray of cherry and wisteria. The sage offered him a sacred mace that had special protective powers. As a large party from Kyoto, including To-no-Chujo, arrived, they had another party.

Fujitsubo was ill and had gone home to her family. As Genji wanted to see her, he pressed Omyobu to be his intermediary. It was a short night in summer and the meeting appeared to be as a dream. He sighed and regretted that he could not fully express his feeling. Since when she had met him before, Fujitsubo had determined that there would not be another night, Fujitsubo was shocked to see him and felt shame that she could not turn him away. Soon she became pregnant and was tormented with the agony of guilt.

Returning to Kyoto, he visited his wife, but she, as always, showed no suggestion of warmth, which made him uncomfortable. After her memorial service in the autumn, Genji visited the house of the girl, Murasaki. The house was badly kept and almost deserted. Shonagon, the girl's nurse, was worried about her future. Genji promised her that he would take care of the girl. The girl came running in; she was a bright lovely child. It was a stormy night. Genji slept beside her protecting her from the trembling thunder.

It was still dark when Genji made his departure, giving his word that he would come back. There was a heavy mist and the ground was white. Passing the house of a woman he had been seeing in secret, he had someone knock on the gate. There was no answer, and so he had someone else from his retinue, a man of very good voice, chant a poem of his. Though there was a poem given in response, no one came out.

Before Prince Hyobu, the father of the girl, came, Genji took the girl away to his Nijo residence in the middle of night. Only the nurse Shonagon accompanied her. Genji prepared a room for her in the west wing where no one was living. At first, Murasaki and the nurse feared what would happen to them, but gradually they became accustomed to the new life. Genji worked hard to make them feel at home. He wrote down poems and drew pictures for her to copy.

THE SAFFLOWER

Tayu, the nun of his old nurse, told Genji that the Princess Hitachi was living alone and consoling herself by playing the koto, a Japanese lute. The prince was touched by the story and visited her in spring. The moon was beautiful and nearly full. The Princess was regarding the garden and enjoying the delicate fragrance of plum blossoms. Tayu did not mention to her that Genji was near and asked her to play the koto. Though her touch was not particularly distinguished, he found it very pleasing.

Listening to the music of the kote, Genji approached the main hall. When he leaned to the bamboo fence to see her closer, there was someone before him. He thought that it must be a young man who had come to see the Princess Hitachi and fell back in the shadows. Then the man talked to him: it was his friend To-no-Chujo. They left the palace together that evening. To-no-Chujo was puzzled when they parted, because Genji had gone neither to his Sanjo mansion where his wife lived or his own at Nijo. He followed Genji to find out where he would go. Genji regretted being thoughtless.

The preparation for the outing in October had started more than a month before. The Emperor Kiritsubo was set to visit Sujakuin Palace. Young sons passed their time practicing at dance and music. Not only the flute was loud, but also the big drums brought out onto the veranda pounded. Genji also participated in the rehearsals. He was busy and forgot about the Princess Hitachi.

On a snowy night, Genji visited the Princess Hitachi after a long interval. When the daylight came, he was surprised to see her. She was not at all beautiful, and was wearing an old-style dress, which was wrong for the young princess. The gate was ruined and leaning in the snow. The aged gatekeeper and his daughter tried to open the gate, but it took a long time to open it until his men pushed. He was extremely sorry for her and resolved to support her.

After the meeting of the New Year, Genji visited the Princes Hitachi feeling sorry for her. But her red nose emerged in profile, which discouraged him again. Back at Nijo, his Murasaki was pretty indeed. He asked himself why he sought other woman when he had lovely Murasaki at home. She was drawing sketches. Genji also drew a lady with a red nose and painted his nose red as well.

AN AUTUMN EXCURSION

In the Middle of the Tenth Month, there was a royal excursion to the Suzaku Palace.

It was the 50th birthday celebration for Ichi-in, who was the Emperor's father. Music came from boats decorated as various sized dragons, which were rowed out over the lake. People danced to a variety of Chinese and Korean songs. Most admirable flutists were selected when Genji and To-no-Chujo danced the "Wave of the Blue Ocean" together. The dancing was held among the falling leaves, whose beauty frightened the people.

On New Year's Day, on his way to the morning festivities at court, Genji went to the west wing to see Murasaki. She had already taken out her dolls.

When Genji asked, "As New Year comes, do you feel grown up?" she answered, "Inuki has broken this, I am repairing it." Inuki was the girl who had let the sparrow out. The nurse, Shonagon, told her, "This year you must try to be more grown up. You should not play with dolls after the age of ten." Murasaki still looked childish.

The Emperor showed off his new born baby saying that he resembled Genji very much. Genji had a mixed feeling of fear, awe and pleasure. He returned to Nijo and calmed down in his room. It was early summer and the garden was full of wild carnations in full bloom. He broke off a few of them and sent them to Fujitsubo with a poem saying that the paper was weighted with his tears as with the dew of wild carnations.

The emperor enjoyed the company of pretty women in his court. All the court ladies around him were talented and charming. There was a rather old lady called Naishi. She was wellborn and cultivated, but at the same time very indiscriminate towards love. When Genji had made a joke about her, she became serious.

One day when she had finished dressing the emperor's hair she found herself alone with Genji. He tugged on her apron. She gave him a sidelong glance that was hidden behind a gaudy fan.

One evening in the cool after a shower, Genji was strolling past the Ummeiden Pavilion. Naishi was playing attractively on her lute. Genji passed a joyful time with her. Taking a little bit of rest, Genji suspected someone was entering. Gathering his clothes, he hid behind a screen. A man roared in wielding a sword. It was To-no-Chujo. Though Naishi was trembling, it appeared to be pretence. As Naishi was a woman of the world, she must have had a similar experience before.

THE FESTIVAL OF THE CHERRY BLOSSOMS

At the end of the Second Month, the festival of cherry blossoms took place in the Grand Hall. Late in the night, Genji went quietly went up towards Fujitsubo's residence, but the door was tightly closed. He made his way to the gallery by Kokiden's pavilion, where he found the door was open. The sixth daughter of the Minister of the Right appeared. She recognized his voice and did not refuse him. The dawn soon approached. She did not tell him her name. They exchanged their fans and he was on his way in a hurry. The misty moon of the twentieth day hung over the sky.

The lady of that misty moon, remembering the encounter, was sunk in distress. She had to marry with the crown prince in the Fourth Month. Late in the Third Month, the Ministry of the Right held a wisteria banquet. He invited Genji to the festivities. His elegant dress dominated the other guests and his beauty outshone the blossoms. After playing the instruments, he went to a corner where the princess of the ministry stood pretending to be drunk. He tried to find out the owner of the fan. The voice who had replied to his poem was the lady's.

HEARTVINE

The Kamo festival was held on the birthday in the Forth Month. The older emperor's third daughter, whose mother was Kokiden, replaced the high priestess. Because of this alteration, the processions taking place were grander than usual. Genji was among the attendants. The roads were full of people and vehicles. The Rokujo lady had also come quietly to see the procession. But a latecomer took her place: it was Aoi's carriage. Aoi's servants had broken the stools for her carriage shafts. She was filled with tears at that insult.

On the following day, Genji decided to set out to view the festival with Murasaki. He went to her room in the west wing. Ladies were also preparing for the outing. He found that her hair was too long, so he summoned a doctor to check the Buddhist calendar to confirm whether the day was suitable for a haircut. Then he trimmed her hair himself. She stood on the Go plate to check the length of her hair.

Since the quarrel over the carriage, the Rokujo lady spent the time restlessly. Rumors spread that her spirit or that of her father clung to Aoi-no-Ue. That was the malign spirit. She herself dreamed that her soul had indeed gone to Aoi and tortured her. She believed that your soul left your body when you one hated someone strongly. The odor of poppy seeds never vanished.

Aoi died too soon. This was only after she gave birth to a baby boy safely, which was a great relief to all the people. But she was again seized with the malign spirit and died. Even the old emperor sent a personal message. He received condolences from the crown prince and Fujitsubo. The crowds of mourners overwhelmed the wide crematory of Torinobe. It was late in the Eight Month and a quarter moon still hung. Returning to Sanjo, Genji lamented over the death of Aoi while contemplating the moon of the dawn.

Genji passed his days at Sanjo mourning for his wife. He prayed earnestly, recalling over the past years they had spent together. He missed Murasaki. He went to bed alone and spent sleepless nights. In a late autumn misty dawn, a letter of sympathy was brought in, written on dark blue gray paper attached to a half opened bud of chrysanthemum. The hand was that of the Rokujo lady. As he had a horrible experience of facing her spirit at the death of Aoi, the letter appeared to him empty.

After forty-nine days, he left the minister's place and returned to his Nijo mansion. He found Murasaki had grown to be nearest to his ideal. Soon he married with Murasaki at the beginning of winter. The ceremony was not held, but only the nuptial seats were prepared on the third night of the wedding. No grand banquet followed, but the event was limited to just the two of them, which was extraordinary. Koremitus himself prepared the sweets, which were delivered to the pillow of Genji by Shonagon and her daughter Ben.

SACRED TREE

Since the death of Aoi, Genji had stopped his visits to the Rokujo lady. She decided to go to Ise with her daughter. It was the beginning of September, and the departure date approached. Genji visited her at the temporary shrine at Sagano. The autumn flowers were gone and insects hummed weakly. A wind blew lonesome through the pine trees. The low wattle fence surrounded the shrines and the gate made of black wood gave an awesome dignity. The prince proffered a branch of the sacred tree, and told her in a poem: "With heart unchanging as this evergreen sacred tree, I entered." After talking through the night, her bitterness was erased.

In the middle of September, the Rokujo lady went down to Ise to escort her daughter. The family expected that she should be the empress in the future, so she had become the late crown prince's wife at sixteen. But at twenty he had left her behind. Now at thirty she left for Ise, filled with all these memories.

As the carriages of the ladies were lined up before the mansion of Genji, he sent a poem to be attached to a sacred tree. Then he spent the day alone, sunk in a sad reverie.

The illness of the emperor became worse. Inquiring after his son, the emperor asked Genji to be good to his son and continue the guardianship of his son just as until now. He left his estate to the crown prince and Genji. At the beginning of November, the emperor died peacefully. For Fujitsubo and Genji, it was a greater pain than anybody else. Ladies assembled at the deceased sovereign's palace and performed the service of the forty-ninth day.

As the old emperor had died, Fujitsubo returned to her palace in Sanjo. She commissioned religious services in hopes of freeing herself from Genji's attention. She was very careful not to be approached by him. Genji could manage to find a way to enter her room secretly. She fainted with pain and fell down. But Genji stayed there even the daybreak came. Omyobu and Ben hid Genji in the closet and looked after Fujitsubo. Her brother, Prince Hyobu and her chamberlain came and sent for priests excitedly.

Sulking with the severe refusal of Fujitsubo, Genji went to Unnlinnin Temple where either an older brother or her mother, Koi, presided. Borrowing the uncle's cell for fasting and meditation, he stayed for several days. He gathered erudite monks and listened to their discussions. The color of falling leaves was beautiful. He read the sixty Tendai sutras and reflected on what Fujitsubo thought and on himself. When he returned from the temple, even the lowest people came to see him off.

Fujitsubo performed the memorial services on the anniversary of the old emperor in November. In the Twelfth Month, she organized the reading of eight scrolls. The reading on the first day was dedicated to her father, the late emperor, on the second to her mother, the empress, and on the third to her husband. The third day was a special day, and the monks read the climactic fifth scroll. Prince Hyobu and Genji made a procession with offerings. On the last day, Fujitusbo announced her intention of becoming a nun, which surprised all of them because of the suddenness.

The arbitration of Kokiden became stronger. The minister of the Left resigned to show his protest. Genji and To-no-Chujo were also in obscurity. They seldom went to court. They spent their time reading and playing instruments. On a mild rainy day in summer, To-no-Chujo brought many collections of Chinese poetry. Genji also opened some cases and took out several unusual collections. Inviting court people and doctors, he enjoyed rhyme-guessing games with them.

Oborozukiyo, the lady of the misty moon, was spending some time with her family. Genji met her secretly. One night during a great thunderstorm, the minister of the Right happened to enter her room. Oborozukiyo slipped through the curtains in a hurry with a flushed face. He caught the sash of Genji entwined in her skirt. Puzzling, he found a paper of Genji's writings. Enraged by them, he made a report to Kokiden, which became a scandal.

THE ORANGE BLOSSOMS

Reikeiden had been one of the old emperor's ladies. Taking advantage of a rare break in the early summer rains, he visited her. Her residence was lonely and quiet, as he had expected. He talked over the memories of his lifetime with her during the night. The tall trees in the garden became darker in the light of the past twentieth day's moon. The scent of orange blossoms from the neighboring house drifted in, to call back the past. He heard the call of a cuckoo that was similar to the one he had heard at the Inner River on his way here. He met the sister of the lady Hanachirusato, with whom he had had a chance encounter at court before.

SUMA

The scandal of his love affair with Oborozukiyo caused a worse situation for Genji. There was a possibility that he would be exiled. To avoid the worst punishment, he decided go to the Suma coast on his own initiative in the late Third Month.

Before his departure, he visited his father-in-law at night. His carriage was a humble one covered with cypress basketwork, so as not to attract the notice of Kokiden side. He talked of old times with the Minister and To-no-Chujo and lamented the uncertainty of life. His little son Yugiri also aroused his tears. He summoned and spent the night with Chunagon. When the moon in its first suggestion of daylight was most beautiful, he got up to leave. He sat against the railing a corner of the veranda and contemplated the falling cherry blossoms. Chunagon came out to see him off at the door.

To-no-Chujo and Prince Hotaru, Genji's brother, came calling. Since he was now without rank and office, he changed to informal, plain colored dress of silk. As he combed his hair he could not help noticing that loss of weight had made him even handsomer. Murasaki sat behind the pillar gazing at him with tears. Unable to see her sadness, he told her: "I must go into exile; in this mirror, an image of me will remain yet beside you."

Prince Hotaru went back in the evening.

On the night before his departure he visited his father's grave in the northern hills. He went first to take leave of Fujitsubo to ask her message for him. The moon had risen and he set out. He was on horseback and had only five or six attendants. He stooped to bow at the Lower Kamo Shrine. Grasses overgrew the path to the grave. The forest was thick. Genji complained to him that his last will and testament was destroyed, and about other things. When the moon had gone behind a cloud, he seemed to his father as he once had been.

The departure was still dark in the night. Genji wore a rough travel dress for hunting. Until Fushimi, they took a land route and then by boat to Naniwa, descending the Yodo river. In those days it took one day from Kyoto to Naniwa. On the following day, they set out to Suma. He missed Murasaki a lot. As he had never been on such a journey, he felt helpless. All the sad, exotic things along the way were new to him. The favorable wind brought them to Suma at four p.m. on the second day.

His new house was not far away from the place where Ariwara Narihira had lived before. It was some distance from the coast, in lonely mountains. The fence, grass-roofed cottages, reed-roofed galleries and everything else about the place were interesting. The confidential steward, Yoshikiyo assigned the regional people to necessary tasks. The governor of the province discreetly performed numerous services for Genji.

At Suma, the melancholy wind was blowing. There was an appealing profusion of flowers in the garden. Genji came out to the gallery from where he had a good view of the coast. Wearing a dark robe loosely tied, he announced himself as a disciple of the Buddha; he slowly intoned a sutra, which was inauspiciously beautiful. From off shore came voices of fishermen raised in song. The barely visible boas were like little seafowl on an utterly lonely sea. He brushed away a tear induced by the calls of wild geese overhead, almost like the sound of splashing oars. His hand against his black rosary was beautiful enough to bring comfort to men who had left their families behind. When he listened to the roar of the wind and the waves at his pillow, he could not stop his tears. In those nights, he woke up still in the dark and plucked a few notes on his koto. During the day, he spent time writing and painting to forget his sorrow.

Having been forbidden from writing to Genji by Kokiden at Kyoto, letters stopped coming. Genji spent unbearable days. The smoke near at hand must, he supposed, be the smoke of the salt. In fact, someone was burning brushwood. He felt ashamed of himself living among plebeian people.

The day of the serpent in the Third Month is a good day to wash away one's worries. He summoned a soothsayer to perform the purification. When he pushed the large doll bearing sins into the river, he could see himself in it. He prayed to heaven proclaiming why a blameless person like me had to be punished. Suddenly the sky turned black and the lightning and a thunderstorm came and would not stop.

AKASHI

The days went by and the thunder and rain continued. Genji was intimidated.

A messenger did come from Murasaki. He arrived soaked to the skin, appearing less than human. Genji would not normally have invited in such a shabbily dressed man. Yet the man brought him affection. He thought himself become weak and vulnerable. The letter of Murasaki and his story about city made him even lonelier.

On the following morning, when the storm had subsided, an old monk came from Akashi to see Genji. Genji was puzzled how the monk could have reached the shore in the severe storm. He sent Yoshiyuki to see the old man. Then he said that he had come here to take Genji to his own place, as he had been instructed in a dream. Genji also had a dream of the old emperor who had come through the skies to help him. After deliberation, he decided to go the Akashi coast. Taking along only four or five attendants, he boarded a boat. Then a strange wind came up and they arrived at Akashi as if they had flown.

On a quiet moonlit night in the Fourth Month, he could see the Awaji Island in front of his new residence. The sea was like the familiar water of his garden in the city. He took the seven-stringed koto, long neglected. The monk, who was conducting his practice in the temple and his daughter, Akashi Princes who lived in the hills, were moved by the sound. Casting aside his beads, he came running to the main house. Sending to the house on the hill for a lute and a thirteen-stringed koto, he played with Genji together. Until late at night they played the instruments. The old man told the story of his past and asked Genji to marry his daughter.

In the city, on the night of a storm, the emperor Sujaku had a dream. His father stood at the stairs of the east garden of the Seiryo chamber and had a great deal to say about Genji. Perhaps because his eyes had met the angry eyes of his father, he came down with a very painful eye ailment (In the graphic, the old emperor stands in the gallery.) On the very same night, Genji also had a dream about the old emperor at Suma. He encouraged Genji and told him to leave the Suma shore.

Accepting the demand of the old monk, Genji invited his daughter to come to his house. But she refused to be summoned like a servant. Yielding to her resistance, Genji went on horseback to the hill with Koremitsu on the night of the near full moon. The coast lay full in sight below. He would like to show it to Murasaki. The temptation was strong to turn his horse's head and gallop on to the city. On seeing the monk's daughter, Princess Akashi, Genji was strongly impressed with her nobleness.

Late in the Seventh Month, the emperor issued an order to summon Genji who had become twenty-eight years old. The Akashi lady was pregnant. As he could not take her along, he comforted her with promises that he would choose an opportune time to bring her to the city. The lady was sunk in the deepest gloom fearing to be left alone and longing for the love of Genji. The monk became senile, lamenting that his daughter could not go with Genji. On a moonlit night, while conducting his practice, the monk fell into the brook and bruised his hip on one of the garden stones.

CHANNEL BUOYS

From about the beginning of the Third Month, Genji thought about the Akashi lady, for her time was approaching. He sent off a messenger who returned with good news that a girl was safely delivered on the sixteenth. He was reminded of what a fortune-teller had once told him. Genji would have three children who would be certain to become emperor, empress and chancellor. Genji badly regretted letting his daughter not be born in Kyoto.

When the long rains of early summer came, he paid a visit to Hanachirusato, the lady of orange blossoms. She was totally dependent on Genji. Through she saw little of him, she never showed her resentment like a modern girl. He knew that she would not make him uncomfortable. He was himself very beautiful in the misty moonlight. She was waiting for him out near the veranda, in contemplation of the night. From nearby there came the metallic cry of a water rail. Her soft and modest character pleased Genji.

In the autumn Genji made a pilgrimage to Sumiyoshi shrine. It was a brilliant progress, thanks to his prayers. A huge number of attendants participated. Men who had in earlier days led bitter lives like Koremitsu and Yoshikiyo were among them. For the Akashi lady it was tormenting to see the entire splendor but not see Genji himself. Even a small child like Yugiri had his own servants. The lady felt the difference between Genji and her own family. It seemed that her daughter was utterly significant. As she thought that the god would scarcely notice her little offering, she directed her boat to Naniwa.

Returning to Kyoto, the Rokujo lady fell ill and died. In his retreat, holding a religious service, Genji sent frequently to inquire after her daughter to console her. It was a day of high wind, driving snow and sleet. He thought how much more miserable the weather must seem to her. Genji sent a poem saying that the spirit of her mother would watch over her. He wrote it with a dazzling brush on a paper of cloudy azure.

THE WORMWOOD

While Genji had descended to Suma, no one took care for Suetsumuhana, the Princess Hitachi.

Her house was deteriorating. The owls hooted in the forest. The strange phantoms called Kodama appeared. The rushes were thick and wormwood touched the eaves; bindweed had firmly barred the gates. The boys deliberately drove their cows and horses around in the spring and summer. A typhoon blew down the galleries of her house. Even robbers passed, finding there nothing to see.

Princess Hitachi had an aunt who had a grudge against her sister, the mother of the princess. Now that her sister's house was in ruins she would have liked to hire her niece as governess. The aunt was proud of her husband who was presently appointed assistant viceroy of Kyushu. Parking her luxurious cart in front of the mansion, she pleaded with her lady to go with her. When the princess refused to go, she got so angry that she took all the reliable women. The princess was in such despair she wept.

Wisteria blossoms, trailing from a giant pine, waved gently. The branches of a willow dropped to the ground in a great disordered forest, which Genji remembered. He had his carriage stopped, and sent

Koremitsu to see the interior. He knew Suetsumuhana still lived there. Koremitsu beat at the grass with a horsewhip and led Genji, whose feet and ankles were soaking. The Princess Hitachi, who had not changed, impressed him.

PATCH

It happened that the party of Utsusemi, the wife of the vice-governor of Hitachi, who was on the way to return to Kyoto, and Genji's party, who was on a journey to Ishiyama shrine came across each other at the Osaka barrier. The vice-governor pulled his ten carriages to a stop under the cedars at the top of the barrier rise. Their coachman knelt respectfully for Genji to pass. Genji gave Uemonsa (formerly Kogimi) a message for his sister. He remembered their old days, which she too was unable to forget.

THE PICTURE CONTEST

Genji and Fujitsubo had made every effort to send Akikonomu, the former high priestess of Ise to the court to strengthen the position of Genji in the government. Therefore, Suzaku, the former emperor, was disappointed as he had been in love with her for long time. They would be a perfect couple as they were the same age. Imagining the feeling of Suzaku, Genji gave careful instructions to the superintendent for her marriage. He did not wish the Suzaku emperor to think that he was managing the girl's affairs.

The present emperor Reizei loved paintings. To amuse him, a contest of paintings was held between two parties in the court. On the left, the Plum Pavilion and Akikonomu faction had seated themselves wearing red robes and put all paintings in red boxes. On the right, the Kokiden faction in blue robes had lined up with their paintings in blue boxes. Genji and To-no-Chujo were present. Prince Hotaru acted as umpire. Although many famous paintings of the four seasons and Tsukinami were brought in, Prince Hotaru had not reached a final decision. Finally, the Suma scroll was offered by Genji, and that brought the victory to the left faction. (The graphic of this scene was created after a model of the contest held at court in the fourth Tentoku era.)

THE WIND IN THE PINES

In autumn, the Akashi lady and her mother with a little girl took the boat to go to Kyoto, escorted by Genji's servants. But they were sad thinking of the old man who had to stay alone. He believed in the bond between his daughter and Genji and that the little one would bring pleasure to the people of the country. So he determined to stay alone and continued his prayers for the future. But his face was twisted with sorrow.

Genji prepared a residence for Akashi lady at Oi villa whose scenery had the same taste of the seashore of Akashi. The garden water was pleasant and interesting. But Genji did not visit her soon. With little to occupy her, the lady felt sorrow and missed her home. Taking out the seven-stringed Chinese koto that Genji had left with her, she played a brief strain to the wind in the pine trees. As her mother resting beside her made a poem of Akashi, the lady replied with a poem.

On the third day of his visit to Akshi, Genji moved to Katsura, because many court people had come over to Oi in search of him. An impromptu banquet was held. The voices of fishermen made him think of the sea women in Akashi. The young falconers offered a sampling of their take, tied to autumn reeds. Wine cups were tossed back and forth. People enjoyed poems and music. At the end, even the emperor delivered his personal message.

A RACK OF CLOUD

When the snow had melted in the Twelfth Month, Genji paid his next visit to take the little princess to Kyoto. The Akashi lady resumed the struggle to control herself, which was not entirely successful. As the little girl tried to jump innocently into the carriage, the lady approached as far as the veranda to which it had been drawn up. Only the nurse and a young woman called Shosho got into the carriage, taking with them the sword and a sacred guardian doll. Genji could imagine the lady's anguish at sending her child off to a distant foster mother. She wrote a poem asking when she could see her daughter next.

Taking more than usual care, Genji chose robes for the visit to the Akashi lady in Oi. His trousers were beautifully dyed and scented, and over them he had thrown an informal court robe of white lined with red. Looking after him as he came to say goodbye, his radiance competed with the evening sunlight. The little girl clung to his trousers and begged to go with him. Looking fondly down at her, Genji sad "I'll be back tomorrow." Murasaki felt vaguely apprehensive.

Fujitsubo had passed away in the Third Month at the age of thirty-six. As she had offered her faith and devotion to everybody, grief descended on the court. Not wanting to be seen weeping, Genji withdrew to the chapel, and spent the day there in tears. Wisps of cloud at the crest of the mountains in the clear evening light were colored in gray, which resembled his mourning weeds.

THE MORNING GLORY

He paid a visit to Princess Asagao, whose name meant "the morning glory." Her attitude was very stiff and formal. He came back and lay awake with disappointment. He had the shutters raised early and stood looking out at the morning mist. He broke off a morning glory in the garden and sent it to Asagao with a poem saying, "I wonder if the flower has been taken past its bloom."

In the Eleventh Month, the festival was canceled. Genji set off for Momozono mansion again. The traffic seemed to be going through the north gate. It would have been undignified for Genji to join the stream, and so he sent one of his men in through the great western gate. A chilly-looking porter rushed out to open it. But the gate was rusty, which gave him great trouble. Genji murmured, "When did wormwood overwhelm this gate? The hedge is now under snow, so going to ruin."

There was a heavy fall of snow. In the evening there were new flurries. The moon turned the deepest recesses of the garden into a gleaming white. The contrast between the snow on the bamboo and the snow on the pines was very beautiful. The flowerbeds were wasted, the brook seemed to send up a strangled cry, and the lake was frozen and somehow terrible. Genji sent little maidservants into the garden, telling them that they must make snowmen. They seemed to enjoy themselves, which was all very charming. At night, Genji confessed to Murasaki his love affairs with various women.

THE MAIDEN

Genji thought that Yugiri should go to the university to become a minister of state. So he put him in the sixth rank of the university, which surprised people who had expected that Yugiri would be promoted rapidly. Genji had a strong intention to promote the solid education of knowledge. Genji conducted mock examinations the day before the exam, inviting tutors to attend. Yugiri studied hard and passed the test for formal commencement of studies within six months. Genji was satisfied with Yugiri's result.

Genji was this year to provide a dancer for the Gosechi dances at the harvest festival, in the Eleventh month. The prettiest and talented girls were selected for the Lord's inspection. Genji ordered a final rehearsal for the presentation at court. He had chosen one of Koremitsu's daughters among them. The glimpse of Koremitsu's daughter had excited Yugiri. He delivered her a love letter, which amused Koremitsu. (Koremitsu is one of Genji's closest servants.)

The new grand Rokujo mansion was finished. Lady Murasaki, Akikonomu, the lady of orange blossoms and Lady Akashi moved in. Genji lived with Murasaki in the southeast quarter, where spring blossoming trees and bushed were planted in large number. The hills were high and the lake was most ingeniously designed. Planted in the forward parts of the garden were cinquefoil pines, maples, cherries, wisteria, yamabuki and rock azalea, most of them spring season trees and shrubs. Touches of autumn too were scattered through the grove.

The southwest quarter was assigned to Akikonomu. For her mother, Lady Rokujo had once lived there. The hills, preserved from the old garden, were chosen for their rich autumn colors. Clear spring water went singing off into the distance, over rocks designed to enhance the music. There was a waterfall, and the whole expanse was a wild profusion of autumn flowers and leaves. The beauty of falling leaves exceeded that of the mountains of Sagano, a reputed place for autumn sight seeing.

The lady of orange blossoms lived in the northeast quarter. A cool natural spring and shadow of trees were designed to give the image of a summer town. In the forward parts of the garden the wind blowing through thickets of Chinese bamboo would be cool in the summer, and the trees were as deep as mountain groves. There was a hedge of mayflower as well as oranges, wild carnations, roses and gentians to remind of days long ago, and a few spring and autumn flowers too. Here, the lady of orange blossom took care of Yugiri and Tamakazura.

A part of the northeast quarter was fenced off for equestrian grounds. Because the Fifth Month would be its liveliest time, there were irises along the lake, from where people could enjoy horse races and equestrian archery. On the far side were stables where the finest horses would be kept.

A Lady Akashi lived in the northwest quarter. Beyond artificial hillocks to the north were rows of warehouses, screened off by pines, which would be beautiful in new falls of snow.

THE JEWELED CHAPLET

The year passed. Genji did not forget Yugao of the evening faces, who had died suddenly a long time ago. Her daughter went down to Dazaifu at the age of four, because the nurse's husband had been appointed deputy viceroy of Kyushu and the family had gone off with him to his post. Not knowing of her death, they prayed for information of any sort about the mother. They could not find any way to seek her father, To-no-Chujo. The nurse finally decided that she would keep the child to remember the mother by. When they set off, the child asked "Are we going to mother's?" The nurse and her daughter wept.

Years passed. The girl was even prettier than her mother. The young gallant of the region called Taifunogen heard about her and sent letters. Then Taifunogen decided the date of marriage one-sidedly. The nurse and her family set for Kyoto to escape from him. Although they had provided themselves with a fast boat and the winds did good service, and their speed was almost frightening, a pilot found them and almost reached them at Echo Bay. But the pursuit of the gallant was more threatening than that of the pilot. Fortunately, they had escaped from the pilot and Taifunogen and were relieved when they reached the Yodo River.

Returning to Kyoto more than fifteen or sixteen years later, the family of the nurse found difficulties in living. They prayed for god to save them. In autumn, they made pilgrimages to Hatsuse on foot. The walk was exhausting for the girl. When they lodged at the Tsubaki Market, Ukon happened to be staying in the same place. Looking through an opening in the curtains, she was surprised to find the old familiar faces. Ukon paid visit to the temple every year to pray for the gods to find the girl of the evening faces.

The nurse and Ukon were in tears. The nurse's party and Ukon arrived in time for the evening services. The temple swarmed with pilgrims. As the seat of the party was far from the front in the temple, Ukon invited them to her place almost under the Buddha. She could make this kind of arrangement owing to the special privilege of her master Genji, the chancellor. They stayed there for three days. Ukon prayed for good luck for Tamakazura.

Ukon told Genji what had happened. He decided to adopt Tamakazura as his daughter and assigned the lady of the orange blossoms to take care of her. On the night when Tamakazura moved into the west wing of the summer quarter, Genji saw her for the first time. When he pushed away the curtain of the porch, she was confused and looked away. But he had seen her enough to be very pleased. He was moved, and brushed away a tear telling that there had been no time through all years when she was out of his mind.

Genji went to the little princess of Akashi on New Year's Day. Her page girls and young servants were out on the hill busying themselves with seeding pine to learn the fortune of that year. The Akashi lady had sent over some New Year delicacies in bearded baskets and with them a warbler on a very cleverly fabricated cinquefoil pine branch. A poem was attached saying that she was waiting for the first warbler.

THE FIRST WARBLER

When the busy day of the New Year ceremonies finished, Genji went calling on Suetsumuhana, the safflower princess. Her hair had been her only charm when she was young, but now the flow was a white trickle. Her nose was red on her white face as before. He arranged the curtain not to see her profile. As she looked cold, he sent to the Nijo warehouses for figured silks. Yet the plantings were fine. He spoke very softly that it seemed a pity that there was no one to appreciate the rose plum, just coming into bloom.

BUTTERFLIES

To reply to the Empress Akikonomu, who had sent an ornamental box of arranged autumn leaves and flowers in the last autumn, Murasaki would have liked to answer properly by showing off her spring garden. Genji agreed, but casual visits were out of question for one in her position. Numbers of her young women were rowed out over the south lake, which ran from her southwest quarter to Murasaki's southeast, with a hillock separating the two. Genji's entourage was deliciously exotic. The dragon and phoenix boats were brilliantly decorated in the Chinese fashion. The professional flutists struck up a melody. The little pages and helmsmen, their hair still bound up, wore Chinese dress. A willow trailed its branches in the deepening green, the cherry blossoms were at their best, the wisteria was rich, and yellow yamabuki reflected on the lakes as if about to join its own image. Waterfowls swam holding twigs in their bills. Genji and some young women watched from the angling pavilion.

There was to be a reading of the Prajnaparamita Sutra commissioned by Empress Akikonomu. Murasaki had prepared the floral offerings. She chose eight of her prettiest girls to deliver them, dressing four as birds and four as butterflies. The birds brought cherry blossoms in silver vases, the butterflies brought yamabuki, the yellow flowers, in gold vases. After they handed over the flowers to the monks, the girls started dancing. The music for the dance of the birds rang forth to the singing of warblers, to which the waterfowls on the lake added their clucks and chirps. The butterflies seemed to fly higher than the birds as they disappeared behind a low fence of yamabuki. It was with great regret that the audience saw the dances come to an end.

FIREFLIES

Unaware that Genji had arranged it, Prince Hotaru was delighted to receive a positive invitation from Tamakazura. The seat for the prince was prepared in front of her, just separated by curtains. Genji had earlier put a large number of fireflies in a cloth bag. Now he released them. Prince Hotaru was certain to look in Tamakazura's direction. Genji wanted him to suspect her. The prince was excited to feel that she sat so close to him.

On the fifth day of the Fifth Month, Yugiri brought some friends to Rokujo after a ceremony of equestrian archery at court. They enjoyed some more equestrianism, which was again more varied than that at the palace. The lady of orange blossoms, Tamakazura, and her servants watched from the galleries of the northeast quarter. The women on the southeast quarter were watching from the distance. Genji went out to look at the equestrian ground. Genji often held similar events at his residence, as a demonstration of his power.

WILD CARNATIONS

It was a very hot day. Genji was cooling himself with his son Yugiri in the angling pavilion of the southeast quarter. Several of To-no-Chujo's sons came over. "You came at a very good time," said Genji. "I was feeling bored and sleepy." Fresh fishes from the West River and Kamo River were brought in and cooked in front of Genji. He was amused with the gossip of their father who recently had found his stray daughter, called Omi-no-kimi. As the sons thought that it did not bring honor to their father or to the family, they seemed uncomfortable. Genji was angry that To-no-Chujo had prevented the love of his son Yugiri for his daughter Kumoinokari. Offering wine, ice water and rice, he made fun of Chujo.

To-no-Chujo went to Kumoinokari's room unannounced. She was napping, very small and pretty, and managing to look cool in her single gossamer robe. Her head was cradled on one arm. The hair that flowed behind her in natural tresses was neither too long nor too thick, but was neatly cut. She looked up at him as he tapped with his fan, her eyes round, and the flush that came over her face delighted him. He lectured her to be vigilant even in her room and forbade her to see Yugiri.

Later he passed the room of Omi-no-kimi who was at a backgammon contest. Rubbing her hands, she was tattling off her prayer at a most wondrous speed. Omi was pretty and had beautiful hair. But a narrow forehead and a torrential way of speaking canceled out her good points. To-no-Chujo reprimanded her to slow down her speech. Replying that the speed was in her nature, she showed no sign of shame. It made Chujo uncomfortable to realize that he might have been looking at his own mirror image.

FLARES

In the Seventh Month, Genji stayed very late in the Tamakazura's room. Leaving his heart behind, he was about to leave, when he noticed that the lamps in the garden were low. Saying that an unlighted garden on a moonless summer night could almost be frightening, he sent a guard officer to stir and refuel them under a spindle tree far enough from the house so that the interior remained cool. In the soft light of the moderate flare, the lady was more beautiful than ever. The koto, Japanese zither, is seen against the spot where they had pillowed side by side a moment ago. Genji regards Tamakazura reluctantly.

THE TYPHOON

In Empress Akikonomu's autumn garden, the plantings were more beautiful than usual. All the autumn colors were gathered together, and emphasized by low fences of black and red. Though the flowers were familiar, they looked different in shape. The morning and evening dews were like gem-studded carpets. She returned to her residence in Rokujo. They forgot the spring's garden, which had been so pleasing a few months before.

As the Empress Akikonomu was ill, Genji sent Yugiri to the palace with a message. He could see from the south veranda of the east wind in the southwest quarter that two shutters and several blinds had been raised at the main hall. Women were visible in the dim light. Some young women had come forward and were leaning against the balustrades. Little girls were pouring water into the insect cages and picking wild carnations. When Yugiri stepped forward, the women withdrew calmly. He felt the elegance maintained by Akikonomu.

THE ROYAL OUTING

In the Twelfth Month there was a royal outing to Oharano. All the ministers and councilors and whole court had turned out for the occasion. The princes and high officials were beautifully fitted out. Their guards and grooms, very good-looking, had put on special dresses. The princes and high courtiers in charge of falcons were in fine hunting dress. The falconers from the royal guards were even more interesting, all in printed robes of most fanciful design. Even the skies seemed intent on favoring the occasion, for there were flurries of snow. The procession left the palace at six in the morning and proceeded south along Suzaku Avenue and west on Gojo. Carriages of viewers lined the streets all the way to the river Katsura. The princes of Rokujo and Tamakazura were among the spectators. Tamakazura paid special attention to the Emperor Reizei, her own father, To-no-Chujo, Prince Hotaru and General Higeguro. The emperor in his red robe, who resembled Genji, attracted Tamakazura. It was her opinion that no one compared with him.

At the beginning of the Second Month, Genji set out for Sanjo to inquire about Princess Omiya, who had been ill. At that moment, he told her everything: that the father of his adopted daughter Tamakazura was To-no-Chujo, the Minister of the Interior at present. Surprised with this news, she called the minister who came over with his many children to see Genji. Genji told him about Tamakazura's past and asked him to do the honor of tying the ceremonial apron for her. They laughed and wept and the earlier stiffness disappeared. It was very late when they went their separate ways.

PURPLE TROUSERS

Genji sent Yugiri to Tamakazura with a message from the emperor to summon her to the court. She had been friendly enough in the days when he had thought her his sister, and it did not seem right to be suddenly cool and distant. She received him at her curtains as before. He had not forgotten the glimpse he had of her the morning after the typhoon. Now the situation had changed, and he had come provided with a fine bouquet of purple pantaloon to attract her attention. But her answer was careful. The ribbons of his cap were tied up in a sign of mourning for his grandmother.

The Ninth Month came. The time approached for Tamakazura to start her service at court. Her women brought messages to her from various suitors. She had them read to her. General Higeguro wrote that he would do everything to get her during the Ninth Month. Prince Hotaru wrote her not to forget him even in the court. The royal guard Sahyoenokami wrote that it was difficult to forget her. Although Higeguro showed his strong intention to marry her, Tamakazura only replied to Prince Hotaru.

THE CYPRESS PILLAR

Unexpectedly, Tamakazura married the black bearded General Higeguro whose wife was a daughter of Shikibukyo, a royal prince. Higeguro had no experience with other women for a long time. Now he had to visit Tamakazura at Rokujo, which made him uncomfortable. Therefore, he decided to redecorate the east wing of his house. The house was ruined for he did not maintain it well.

The wife of Higeguro had been beautiful when she was young. But a malign power had made her behavior eccentric and violent for many years. There was no affection between them. One evening, it was snowing outside. Higeguro tried to persuade his wife to accept his new marriage with Tamakazura. As she seemed to be calmed down, he began to prepare for an outing. Suddenly she stood up, swept the cover from a large censer, stepped behind her husband and poured the ashes over his head. A malign spirit had captured her.

The Prince Shikibukyo got angry because his stepson stayed with Tamakazura. So he made his daughter and his granddaughter return to his residence. Divorce in those days was no different from today. She came back her to her home with furniture that she brought in when she married. Women who lost their jobs went away separately. Higeguro's favorite daughter Makibashira was reluctant to go with her mother. She set down a poem on a sheet of paper and thrust it into a crack in the cypress pillar, writing not to forget her.

Tamakazura was assigned apartments on the east side of the palace. Higeguro continued to stay in the guard's quarter. He wanted her to withdraw from the court immediately. When she was wondering how to reply to a poem from Prince Hotaru, the emperor came calling. He was unbelievably handsome and the very image of Genji. He reproved her for having gone against his wishes. She did not wish to seem coy. Higeguro was restless knowing that the emperor had called on Tamakazura.

A BRANCH OF PLUM

Prince Hotaru came calling on the tenth of the Second Month. A gentle rain was falling and the rose plum near the veranda was in full and fragrant bloom. The brothers were admiring the blossoms when a note came attached to a plum branch. It was from Princess Asagao. She had also sent a box containing large balls of perfume. In the letter, she said she would like him to deliver this present to the princess of Akashi. Prince Hotaru admired the beauty of the decoration and Genji wrote a poem of appreciation.

It was now decided that Genji's daughter would go to court. Genji collected books and scrolls for her library. He invited the finest calligraphers to create masterpieces. Selecting poems from these admired anthologies, Genji tried several styles with fine results, formal and cursive Chinese and the more radically cursive Japanese "ladies hand." He secluded himself as before in the main hall for concentration. He had with him only two or three women whom he could count on for comments. He seems to be enjoying his job, taking a brush between his teeth.

WISTERIA LEAVES

Early in the Fourth Month, the Minister of the Interior (To-no-Chujo) arranged a banquet of wisteria, which was full in bloom. He invited Yugiri. The Minister had begun to grow restless when finally Yugiri arrived. When the moon came out, the wine was served. Pretending to be very drunk, the Minister admired Yugiri who had waited long and well to obtain permission to marry his daughter, Kumoinokari. The long-standing ill feeling between them disappeared. Kashiwagi broke off an unusually long and rich spray of wisteria and presented it to Yugiri with a cup of wine. That was a romantic happy ending for Yugiri and Kumoinokari who had been separated for six years.

Yugiri was promoted to middle counselor. He moved into his grandmother's Sanjo house, which was filled with many good memories. One beautiful evening sitting near the veranda, Yugiri and Kumoinokari exchanged poems recalling the grandmother who had always protected them. Having heard that the garden was in its autumn glory, To-no-Chujo stopped by on his way from court. As the house was where he had lived in his young days, the Minister of the Interior was moved finding that the couple now lived there happily.

The present emperor Reizei and former emperor Suzaku paid a state visit to Rokujo, which was an extraordinary event. Genji s preparations were brilliant. The royal party went first to the equestrian ring where the ritual of review was performed in finery. Then the party moved to the southeast quarter for the banquet. The lieutenants of the inner guards of east and west advanced and knelt before the royal seats, one presenting the take from the pond and the other a brace of fowl caught by the royal falcons in the northern hills. The emperor ordered Genji to move up to sit at the same level, which showed Genji off in utmost glory.

The Suzaku emperor had been ill since his visit to Rokujo. It had been his wish to take holy orders and retire from the world. But he worried about whom his daughter, the Third Princess could look to for support when he finally withdrew from the world. Her mother, a sister of Fujitsubo, had died in disappointment. Yugiri came to see him. Intending to marry Kumoinokari soon, he was in the full bloom of youth. The emperor looked at him wondering whether he might not offer a solution to the problem of the Third Princess. The emperor asked Yugiri to take his message that he would like to see his father Genji ardently.

Peter Abelard, "Sic et Non"

Peter Abelard (1079–1142 CE) was a scholar at the new universities that were sprouting up all over Europe in order to digest the massive influx of Islamic and Greco-Roman knowledge. Abelard was famous for his skills in rhetoric and logic and for his dramatic love affair with Heloise. His most referenced work, Sic et Non, *was an attempt to face the various contradictions in the Bible. While not solving the problems, Abelard did create a logical and rational means to analyze the pros and cons of an argument.*

Source: *Brian Tierney, ed.,* Great Issues in Western Civilization, vol. 1 *(New York: Random House, 1972), pp. 412–414.*

Focus Questions:
1. What is truth and how is it found?
2. What are the errors in scripture? How does Abelard deal with them?
3. What do you conclude from the phrase, "For by doubting we come to inquiry; through inquiring we perceive the truth"?

Among the multitudinous words of the Holy Fathers, some sayings seem not only to differ from one another, but even to contradict one another. Hence it is not presumptuous to judge concerning those by whom the world itself will be judged, as it is written, "They shall judge nations" (Wisdom 3:8) and, again, "You shall sit and judge" (Luke 22:30). We do not presume to rebuke as untruthful or to denounce as erroneous those to whom the Lord said, "He who hears you hears me; he who despises you despises me" (Luke 10:26). Bearing in mind our foolishness we believe that our understanding is defective rather than the writing of those to whom the Truth Himself said, "It is not you who speak but the spirit of your Father who speaks in you" (Matthew 10:20). Why should it seem surprising if we, lacking the guidance of the Holy Spirit through whom those things were written and spoken, the Spirit impressing them on the writers, fail to understand them? Our achievement of full understanding is impeded especially by unusual modes of expression and by the different significances that can be attached to one and the same word, as a word is used now in one sense, now in another. Just as there are many meanings so there are many words. Tully says that sameness is the mother of satiety in all things, that is to say it gives rise to fastidious distaste, and so it is appropriate to use a variety of words in discussing the same thing and not to express everything in common and vulgar words...

We must also take special care that we are not deceived by corruptions of the text or by false attributions when sayings of the Fathers are quoted that seem to differ from the truth or to be contrary to it; for many apocryphal writings are set down under names of saints to enhance their authority, and even the texts of divine Scripture are corrupted by the errors of scribes. That most faithful writer and true interpreter, Jerome, accordingly warned us, "Beware of apocryphal writings..." Again, on the title of Psalm 77 which is "An Instruction of Asaph," he commented, "It is written according to Matthew that when the Lord had spoken in parables and they did not understand, he said, 'These things are done that it might be fulfilled which was written by the prophet Isaias, I will open my mouth in parables.' The Gospels still have it so. Yet it is not Isaias who says this but Asaph." Again, let us explain simply why in Matthew and John it is written that the Lord was crucified at the third hour but in Mark at the sixth hour. There was a scribal error, and in Mark too the sixth hour was mentioned, but many read the Greek *epismo* as gamma. So too there was a scribal error where "Isaias" was set down for "Asaph." We know that many churches were gathered together from among ignorant gentiles. When they read in the Gospel, "That it might be fulfilled which was written by the prophet Asaph," the one who first wrote down the Gospel began to say, "Who is this prophet Asaph?" for he was not known among the people. And what did he do? In seeking to amend an error he made an error. We would say the same of another text in Matthew. "He took," it says, "the thirty pieces of silver, the price of him that was prized, as was written by the prophet Jeremias." But we do not find this in Jeremias at all. Rather it is in Zacharias. You see then that here, as before, there was an error. If in the Gospels themselves some things are corrupted by the ignorance of scribes, we should not be surprised that the same thing has sometimes happened in the writings of later Fathers who are of much less authority...

It is no less important in my opinion to ascertain whether texts quoted from the Fathers may be ones that they themselves have retracted and corrected after they came to a better understanding of the truth as the blessed Augustine did on many occasions; or whether they are giving the opinion of another rather than their own opinion...or whether, in inquiring into certain matters, they left them open to question rather than settled them with a definitive solution...

In order that the way be not blocked and posterity deprived of the healthy labor of treating and debating difficult questions of language and style, a distinction must be drawn between the work of later authors and the supreme canonical authority of the Old and New Testaments. If, in Scripture, anything seems absurd you are not permitted to say, "The author of this book did not hold to the truth"—but rather that the codex is defective or that the interpreter erred or that you do not understand. But if anything seems contrary to truth in the works of later authors, which are contained in innumerable books, the reader or auditor is free to judge, so that he may approve what is pleasing and reject what gives offense, unless the matter is established by certain reason or by canonical authority (of the Scriptures)...

In view of these considerations we have undertaken to collect various sayings of the Fathers that give rise to questioning because of their apparent contradictions as they occur to our memory. This questioning excites young readers to the maximum of effort in inquiring into the truth, and such inquiry sharpens their minds. Assiduous and frequent questioning is indeed the first key to wisdom. Aristotle, that most perspicacious of all philosophers, exhorted the studious to practice it eagerly, saying, "Perhaps it is difficult to express oneself with confidence on such matters if they have not been much discussed. To entertain doubts on particular points will not be unprofitable." For by doubting we come to inquiry; through inquiring we perceive the truth, according to the Truth Himself. "Seek and you shall find," He says, "Knock and it shall be opened to you." In order to teach us by His example He chose to be found when He was about twelve years old sitting in the midst of the doctors and questioning them, presenting the appearance of a disciple by questioning rather than of a master by teaching, although there was in Him the complete and perfect wisdom of God. Where we have quoted texts of Scripture, the greater the authority attributed to Scripture, the more they should stimulate the reader and attract him to the search for truth. Hence I have prefixed to this my book, compiled in one volume from the saying of the saints, the decree of Pope Gelasius concerning authentic books, from which it may be known that I have cited nothing from apocryphal books. I have also added excerpts from the Retractions of St. Augustine, from which it will be clear that nothing is included which he later retracted and corrected.

Al Ghazali, Excerpt from *Confessions*

Al Ghazali (1058–1111 CE) was an educated Iranian scholar in Baghdad in one of the most reputable institutions of learning. He changed course, however, and took up the sufi mystic path of contemplation and writing. Al Ghazali's scholarly background helped him reconcile orthodox Islam with the individualism of Sufism. His influence helped develop arguments on the separateness of reason and faith.

Source: *Al Ghazali,* Confessions *(1100), trans. by Claude Field (E. P. Dutton, 1909).*

> **Focus Questions:**
> 1. What is truth to Al Ghazali?
> 2. How is truth found?
> 3. What is meant by "broken the fetters of tradition and freed myself from hereditary beliefs"?

QUOTH THE IMAM GHAZALI:

Glory be to God, whose praise should precede every writing and every speech! May the blessings of God rest on Mohammed, his Prophet and his Apostle, on his family and companions, by whose guidance error is escaped!

You have asked me, O brother in the faith, to expound the aim and the mysteries of religious sciences, the boundaries and depths of theological doctrines. You wish to know my experiences while disentangling truth lost in the medley of sects and divergencies of thought, and how I have dared to climb from the low levels of traditional belief to the topmost summit of assurance. You desire to learn what I have borrowed, first of all from scholastic theology; and secondly from the method of the Ta'limites, who, in seeking truth, rest upon the authority of a leader; and why, thirdly, I have been led to reject philosophic systems; and finally, what I have accepted of the doctrine of the Sufis, and the sum total of truth which I have gathered in studying every variety of opinion. You ask me why, after resigning at Baghdad a teaching post, which attracted a number of hearers, I have, long afterward, accepted a similar one at Nishapur. Convinced as I am of the sincerity, which prompts your inquiries, I proceed to answer them, invoking the help and protection of God.

Know then, my brothers (may God direct you in the right way), that the diversity in beliefs and religions, and the variety of doctrines and sects which divide men, are like a deep ocean strewn with shipwrecks, from which very few escape safe and sound. Each sect, it is true, believes itself in possession of the truth and of salvation, "each party," as the Qur'an saith, "rejoices in its own creed"; but as the chief of the apostles, whose word is always truthful, has told us, "My people will be divided into more than seventy sects, of whom only one will be saved." This prediction, like all others of the Prophet, must be fulfilled.

From the period of adolescence, that is to say, previous to reaching my twentieth year to the present time when I have passed my fiftieth, I have ventured into this vast ocean; I have fearlessly sounded its depths, and like a resolute diver, I have penetrated its darkness and dared its dangers and abysses. I have interrogated the beliefs of each sect and scrutinized the mysteries of each doctrine, in order to disentangle truth from error and orthodoxy from heresy. I have never met one who maintained the hidden meaning of the Qur'an without investigating the nature of his belief. nor a partisan of its exterior sense without inquiring into the results of his doctrine. There is no philosopher whose system I have not fathomed, nor theologian the intricacies of whose doctrine I have not followed out.

Sufism has no secrets into which I have not penetrated; the devout adorer of Deity has revealed to me the aim of his austerities; the atheist has not been able to conceal from me the real reason of his unbelief. The thirst for knowledge was innate in me from an early age; it was like a second nature implanted by God, without any will on my part. No sooner had I emerged from boyhood than I had already broken the fetters of tradition and freed myself from hereditary beliefs.

Having noticed how easily the children of Christians become Christians, and the children of Muslims embrace Islam, and remembering also the traditional saying ascribed to the Prophet, "Every child has in him the germ of Islam, then his parents make him Jew, Christian, or Zarathustrian," I was moved by a keen desire to learn what was this innate disposition in the child, the nature of the accidental beliefs imposed on him by the authority of his parents and his masters, and finally the unreasoned convictions which he derives from their instructions.

Struck with the contradictions which I encountered in endeavoring to disentangle the truth and falsehood of these opinions, I was led to make the following reflection: "The search after truth being the aim which I propose to myself, I ought in the first place to ascertain what are the bases of certitude." In the next place I recognized that certitude is the clear and complete knowledge of things, such knowledge as leaves no room for doubt nor possibility of error and conjecture, so that there remains no room in the mind for error to find an entrance. In such a case it is necessary that the mind, fortified against all possibility of going astray, should embrace such a strong conviction that, if, for example, any one possessing the power of changing a stone into gold, or a stick into a serpent, should seek to shake the bases of this certitude, it would remain firm and immovable. Suppose, for instance, a man should come and say to me, who am firmly convinced that ten is more than three, "No; on the contrary, three is more than ten, and, to prove it, I change this rod into a serpent," and supposing that he actually did so, I should remain none the less convinced of the falsity of his assertion, and although his miracle might arouse my astonishment, it would not instill any doubt into my belief.

I then understood that all forms of knowledge which do not unite these conditions (imperviousness to doubt, etc.) do not deserve any confidence, because they are not beyond the reach of doubt, and what is not impregnable to doubt can not constitute certitude.

Roger Bacon on Experimental Science, 1268

Roger Bacon (c. 1214–1294 CE) was a scholastic philosopher and theologian who was a friend of Robert Grosseteste and other founding members of the burgeoning tradition of mathematics and empiricism. Bacon's works address theological matters as well as ways of understanding God's world, that include reason, mathematics, experience, and even experiment.

Source: *Oliver J. Thatcher, ed., "The Early Medieval World,"* The Library of Original Sources, Vol. V, *(Milwaukee: University Research Extension Co., 1901), pp. 369–376.*

Focus Questions:
1. What, in this text, is actually meant by experiment?
2. What is the role of mathematics?
3. How does divine intervention help?

ON EXPERIMENTAL SCIENCE

Having laid down the main points of the wisdom of the Latins as regards language, mathematics and optics, I wish now to review the principles of wisdom from the point of view of experimental science, because without experiment it is impossible to know anything thoroughly.

There are two ways of acquiring knowledge, one through reason, the other by experiment. Argument reaches a conclusion and compels us to admit it, but it neither makes us certain nor so annihilates doubt that the mind rests calm in the intuition of truth, unless it finds this certitude by way of experience. Thus many have arguments toward attainable facts, but because they have not experienced them, they overlook them and neither avoid a harmful nor follow a beneficial course. Even if a man that has never seen fire, proves by good reasoning that fire burns, and devours and destroys things, nevertheless the mind of one hearing his arguments would never be convinced, nor would he avoid fire until he puts his hand or some combustible thing into it in order to prove by experiment what the argument taught. But after the fact of combustion is experienced, the mind is satisfied and lies calm in the certainty of truth. Hence argument is not enough, but experience is.

This is evident even in mathematics, where demonstration is the surest. The mind of a man that receives that clearest of demonstrations concerning the equilateral triangle without experiment will never stick to the conclusion nor act upon it till confirmed by experiment by means of the intersection of two circles from either section of which two lines are drawn to the ends of a given line. Then one receives the conclusion without doubt. What Aristotle says of the demonstration by the syllogism being able to give knowledge, can be understood if it is accompanied by experience, but not of the bare demonstration. What he says in the first book of the Metaphysics, that those knowing the reason and cause are wiser than the experienced, he speaks concerning the experienced who know the bare fact only without the cause. But I speak here of the experienced that know the reason and cause through their experience. And such are perfect in their knowledge, as Aristotle wishes to be in the sixth book of the Ethics, whose simple statements are to be believed as if they carried demonstration, as he says in that very place.

Whoever wishes without proof to revel in the truths of things need only know how to neglect experience. This is evident from examples. Authors write many things and the people cling to them through arguments which they make without experiment, that are utterly false. It is commonly believed among all classes that one can break adamant only with the blood of a goat, and philosophers and theologians strengthen this myth. But it is not yet proved by adamant being broken by blood of this kind, as much as it is argued to this conclusion. And yet, even without the blood it can be broken with ease. I have seen this with my eyes; and this must needs be because gems cannot be cut out save by the breaking of the stone. Similarly it is commonly believed that the secretions of the beaver that the doctors use are the testicles of the male, but this is not so, as the beaver has this secretion beneath its breast and even the male as well as the female produces a secretion of this kind. In addition also to this secretion the male has its testicles in the natural place and thus again it is a horrible lie that, since hunters chase the beaver for this secretion, the beaver knowing what they are after, tears out his testicles with his teeth and throws them away. Again it is popularly said that cold water in a vase freezes more quickly than hot; and the argument for this is that contrary is excited by the contrary, like enemies running together. They even impute this to Aristotle in the second book of *Meteorology*, but he certainly did not say this, but says something like it by which they have been deceived, that if both cold and hot water are poured into a cold place as on ice, the cold freezes quicker (which is true), but if they are placed in two vases, the hot will freeze quicker. It is necessary, then, to prove everything by experience.

Experience is of two kinds. One is through the external senses: such are the experiments that are made upon the heaven through instruments in regard to facts there, and the facts on earth that we prove in various ways to be certain in our own sight. And facts that are not true in places where we are, we know through other wise men that have experienced them. Thus Aristotle with the authority of Alexander, sent 2,000 men throughout various parts of the earth in order to learn at first hand everything on the surface of the world, as Pliny says in his *Natural History*. And this experience is human and philosophical just as far as a man is able to make use of the beneficent grace given to him, but such experience is not enough for man, because it does not give full certainty as regards corporeal things because of their complexity and touches the spiritual not at all. Hence man's intellect must be aided in another way, and thus the patriarchs and prophets who first gave science to the world secured inner light and did not rest entirely on the senses. So also many of the faithful since Christ. For grace makes many things clear to the faithful, and there is divine inspiration not alone concerning spiritual but even about corporeal things. In accordance with which Ptolemy says in the *Centilogium* that there is a double way of coming to the knowledge of things, one through the experiments of science, the other through divine inspiration, which latter is far the better as he says.

Of this inner experience there are seven degrees, one through spiritual illumination in regard to scientific things. The second grade consists of virtue, for evil is ignorance as Aristotle says in the second book of the *Ethics*. And Algazel says in the logic that the mind is disturbed by faults, just as a rusty mirror in which the images of things cannot be clearly seen, but the mind is prepared by virtue like a well polished mirror in which the images of things show clearly. On account of this, true philosophers have accomplished more in ethics in proportion to the soundness of their virtue, denying to one another that they can discover the cause of things unless they have minds free from faults. Augustine relates this fact concerning Socrates in Book VIII, chapter III, of the *City of God*: to the same purpose Scripture says, to an evil mind, etc., for it is impossible that the mind should lie calm in the sunlight of truth while it is spotted with evil, but like a parrot or magpie it will repeat words foreign to it which it has learned through long practice. And this is our experience, because a known truth draws men into its light for love of it, but the proof of this love is the sight of the result. And indeed he that is busy against truth must necessarily ignore this, that it is permitted him to know how to fashion many high sounding words and to write sentences not his own, just as the brute that imitates the human voice or an ape that attempts to carry out the works of men, although he does not understand their purpose. Virtue, then, clears the mind so that one can better understand not only ethical, but even scientific things. I have carefully proved this in the case of many pure youths who, on account of their innocent minds, have gone further in knowledge than I dare to say, because they have had correct teaching in religious doctrine, to which class the bearer of this treatise belongs, to whose knowledge of principles but few of the Latins rise. Since he is so young (about twenty years old) and poor besides, not able to have masters nor the length of any one year to learn all the great things he knows, and since he neither has great genius or a wonderful memory, there can be no other cause, save the grace of God, which, on account of the clearness of his mind, has granted to him these things which it has refused to almost all students, for a pure man, he has received pure things from me. Nor have I been able to find in him any kind of a mortal fault, although I have searched diligently, and he has a mind so clear and far seeing that he receives less from instruction than can be supposed. And I have tried to lend my aid to the purpose that these two youths may be useful implements for the Church of God, inasmuch as they have with the Grace of God examined the whole learning of the Latins.

The third degree of spiritual experience is the gift of the Holy Spirit, which Isaiah describes. The fourth lies in the beatitudes which our Lord enumerates in the Gospels. The fifth is the spiritual sensibility. The sixth is in such fruits as the peace of God, which passes all understanding. The seventh lies in states of rapture and in the methods of those also, various ones of whom receive it in various ways, that they may see many things which it is not permitted to speak of to man. And whoever is thoroughly practiced in these experiences or in many of them, is able to assure himself and others, not only concerning spiritual things, but all human knowledge. And indeed, since all speculative thought proceeds through arguments which either proceed through a proposition by authority or through other propositions of argument, in accordance with this which I am now investigating, there is a science that is necessary to us, which is called experimental. I wish to explain this, not only as useful to philosophy, but to the knowledge of God and the understanding of the whole world: as in a former book I followed language and science to their end, which is the Divine wisdom by which all things are ordered.

And because this experimental science is a study entirely unknown by the common people, I cannot convince them of its utility, unless its virtue and characteristics are shown. This alone enables us to find out surely what can be done through nature, what through the application of art, what through fraud, what is the purport and what is mere dream in chance, conjuration, invocations, imprecations, magical sacrifices and what there is in them; so that all falsity may be lifted and the truths we alone of the art retained. This alone teaches us to examine all the insane ideas of the magicians in order not to confirm but to avoid them, just as logic criticizes the art of sophistry. This science has three great purposes in regard to the other sciences: the first is that one may criticize by experiment the noble conclusions of all the other sciences, for the other sciences know that their principles come from experiment, but the conclusions through arguments drawn from the principles discovered, if they care to have the result of their conclusions precise and complete. It is necessary that they have this through the aid of this noble science. It is true that mathematics reaches conclusions in accordance with universal experience about figures and numbers, which indeed apply to all sciences and to this experience, because no science can be known without mathematics. If we would attain to experiments precise, complete and made certain in accordance with the proper method, it is necessary to undertake an examination of the science itself, which is called experimental on our authority. I find an example in the rainbow and in like phenomena, of which nature are the circles about the sun and stars, also the halo beginning from the side of the sun or of a star which seems to be visible in straight lines and is called by Aristotle in the third book of the *Meteorology* a perpendicular, but by Seneca a halo, and is also called a circular corona, which have many of the colors of the rainbow. Now the natural philosopher discusses these things, and in regard to perspective has many facts to add which are concerned with the operation of seeing which is pertinent in this place. But neither Aristotle or Avicenna have given us knowledge of these things in their books upon Nature, nor Seneca, who wrote a special book concerning them. But experimental science analyzes such things.

The experimenter considers whether among visible things, he can find colors formed and arranged as given in the rainbow. He finds that there are hexagonal crystals from Ireland or India which are called rainbow-hued in Solinus Concerning the Wonders of the World and he holds these in a ray of sunlight falling through the window, and finds all the colors of the rainbow, arranged as in it in the shaded part next the ray. Moreover, the same experimenter places himself in a somewhat shady place and puts the stone up to his eye when it is almost closed, and beholds the colors of the rainbow clearly arranged, as in the bow. And because many persons making use of these stones think that it is on account of some special property of the stones and because of their hexagonal shape the investigator proceeds further and finds this in a crystal, properly shaped, and in other transparent stones. And not only are these Irish crystals in white, but also black, so that the phenomenon occurs in smoky crystal and also in all stones of similar transparency. Moreover, in stones not shaped hexagonally, provided the surfaces are rough, the same as those of the Irish crystals, not entirely smooth and yet not rougher than those—the surfaces have the same quality as nature has given the Irish crystals, for the difference of roughness makes the difference of color. He watches, also, rowers and in the drops falling from the raised oars he finds the same colors, whenever the rays of the sun penetrate the drops.

The case is the same with water falling from the paddles of a water-wheel. And when the investigator looks in a summer morning at the drops of dew clinging to the grass in the field or plane, he sees the same colors. And, likewise, when it rains, if he stands in a shady place and the sun's rays beyond him shine through the falling drops, then in some rather dark place the same colors appear, and they can often be seen at night about a candle. In the summer time, as soon as he rises from sleep while his eyes are not yet fully opened, if he suddenly looks at a window through which the light of the sun is streaming, he will see the colors. Again, sitting outside of the sunlight, if he holds his head covering beyond his eyes, or, likewise, if he closes his eyes, the same thing happens in the shade at the edges, and it also takes place through a glass vase filled with water, sitting in the sunlight. Similarly, if any one holding water in his mouth suddenly sprinkles the water in jets and stands at the side of them; or if through a lamp of oil hanging in the air the rays shine in the proper way, or the light shines upon the surface of the oil, the colors again appear. Thus, in an infinite number of ways, natural as well as artificial, colors of this kind are to be seen, if only the diligent investigator knows how to find them.

Experimental science is also that which alone, as the mistress of the speculative sciences, can discover magnificent truths in the fields of the other sciences, to which these other sciences can in no way attain. And these truths are not of the nature of former truths, but they may be even outside of them, in the fields of things where there are neither as yet conclusions or principles, and good examples may be given of this, but in everything which follows it is not necessary for the inexperienced to seek a reason in order to understand at the beginning, but rather he will never have a reason before he has tried the experiment. Whence in the first place there should be credulity until experiment follows, in order that the reason may be found. If one who has never seen that a magnet draws iron nor heard from others that it attracts, seeks the reason before experimenting, he will never find it. Indeed, in the first place, he ought to believe those who have experimented or who have it from investigators, nor ought he to doubt the truth of it because he himself is ignorant of it and because he has no reason for it.

The third value of this science is this—it is on account of the prerogatives through which it looks, not only to the other sciences, but by its own power investigates the secrets of nature, and this takes place in two ways—in the knowledge of future and present events, and in those wonderful works by which it surpasses astronomy commonly so-called in the power of its conclusions. For Ptolemy in the introduction of the Almagest, says that there is another and surer way than the ordinary astronomy; that is, the experimental method which follows after the course of nature, to which many faithful philosophers, such as Aristotle and a vast crowd of the authors of predictions from the stars, are favorable, as he himself says, and we ourselves know through our own experience, which cannot be denied. This wisdom has been found as a natural remedy for human ignorance or imprudence; for it is difficult to have astronomical implements sufficiently exact and more difficult to have tables absolutely verified, especially when the motion of the planets is involved in them. The use of these tables is difficult, but the use of the instruments more so.

This science has found definitions and ways through which it quickly comes to the answer of a whole question, as far as the nature of a single science can do so, and through which it shows us the outlines of the virtues of the skies and the influence of the sky upon this earth, without the difficulty of astronomy. This part so-called has four principal laws as the secret of the science, and some bear witness that a use of this science, which illustrates its nature, is in the change of a region in order that the customs of the people may be changed. In connection with which Aristotle, the most learned of philosophers, when Alexander asked of him concerning some tribes that he had found, whether he should kill them on account of their barbarity or let them live, responded in the Book of Secrets if you can change their air let them live; if not, kill them. He wished that their air could be altered usefully, so that the complexion of their bodies could be changed, and finally the mind aroused through the complexion should absorb good customs from the liberty of their environment; this is one use of this science.

Saint Francis of Assisi, Selection from His *Admonitions*

Francis of Assisi (1182–1226 CE) was born of a wealthy Italian merchant family, but gave it all up to live a life of simplicity and poverty. He was participating in the great church-reform movement of his time that sought a return to the early church—living supposedly like the early apostles. Francis wore rags, begged for food, and spent time helping the poor and sick. He attracted followers, which were eventually accepted by the Pope as the Franciscan order. To help guide his new supporters, Francis wrote a series of Admonitions regarding good religious behavior.

Source: *Fr. Kajetan Esser, trans., Saint Francis of Assisi,* Admonitions, *from the Critical Latin Edition (Rome: Editiones Collegii S. Bonaventurae ad Claras aquas, Grottaferrata, 1976).*

Focus Questions:
1. How do the *Admonitions* compare to the Rule of St. Benedict?
2. What sins are condemned?
3. What is the best demeanor for a Christian?

Chapter I: On the Body of the Lord

The Lord Jesus said to His disciples: "I am the Way, the Truth and the Life; no one comes to the Father except through Me." • "If" you know "Me," you would know "My Father as well; and from now on you shall know Him and have seen Him." • "Philip said to Him: Lord, show us the Father, and that suffices for us." • "Jesus said to him: So much time I have been with you, and you do not known Me? Philip, he who sees Me, sees even" My "Father" (Jn 14:6-9). • The Father dwells "in inaccessible light" (cf. 1 Tm 6:16), and "God is spirit" (Jn 4:24), and "no one ever sees God" (Jn 1:18). • For this reason He cannot be seen except in spirit, "since it is the spirit which vivifies, the flesh is good for nothing" (in 6:64). • But neither does the Son in that, which He is equal to the Father, seem to anyone to be otherwise than the Father, otherwise than the Holy Spirit. • Whence all who saw the Lord Jesus according to the Humanity and both did not see and believe according to the spirit and the Divinity, that He Himself is the true Son of God, have been damned; • so even now all who see the Sacrament, which is sanctified by the words of the Lord upon the altar by the hand of the priest in the form of bread and wine, and do not see and believe according to the spirit and the Divinity, that this is truly the Most Holy Body and Blood of Our Lord Jesus Christ, have been damned, since the Most High Himself testifies, who said: • "This is My Body and" My "Blood of the New Testament [which is poured forth on behalf of the many]" (Mt 14:22,24); • and "He who eats" My Flesh "and drinks" My Blood, "has life eternal" (cf. in 6:55). • Whence of the Spirit of the Lord, who dwells in His faithful, is he who receives the Most Holy Body and Blood of the Lord. • All others, who do not share this same Spirit and presume to receive Him, eat "and" drink "judgement upon themselves" (cf. 1 Cor. 11:29).

Whence: "Sons of men, how long with a heavy heart?" (Ps 4:3) • Why is it that do you not know the truth and believe "in the Son of God?" (cf. Jn 9:35) • Behold, every day He humbles Himself (cf. Phil 2:8), just as when "from royal thrones" (Wis 18:15) He came into the womb of the Virgin; • every day He comes to us Himself humbly appearing; • everyday He descends from the bosom of the Father upon the altar in the hands of the priest. • And just as to the holy Apostles in true flesh, so even now He shows Himself to us in the Sacred Bread. • And just as when they gazed at His very own flesh they saw only His flesh, but contemplating with spiritual eyes believed Him to be God, • so we too seeing bread and wine with bodily eyes, are to see and firmly believe, that they are His Most Holy Body and Blood, living and true. • And in such a manner the Lord is always with His faithful, just as He Himself says: "Behold I am with you even to the consummation of the age" (cf. Mt 28:20).

Chapter II: On the wickedness of one's own willfulness

The Lord said to Adam: From "every tree eat, however, from the tree of good and evil you may not eat" (cf. Gen 2:16.17). • From every tree of paradise he could eat, because while he did not go against obedience, he did not sin. • For one eats of the tree of the knowledge of good, who appropriates his own will to himself and exalts himself because of the good things, which the Lord says and works in him; • and so through the suggestion of the devil and the transgression of the mandate it has become the fruit of the knowledge of evil. • Whence it is proper, that he endure punishment.

Chapter III: On perfect obedience

The Lord says in the Gospel: "He who" will "not" have renounced "all that he possesses, cannot be My disciple" (Lk 14:33); • and: "He who will have wanted to save his soul, shall lose it" (Lk 9:24). • That man abandons all that he possesses, and loses his own body, who offers himself whole to obedience in the hands of his prelate. • And whatever he does and says, that he himself knows, which is not contrary to his will, as long as what he does is good, is true obedience. • And if at any time the subject sees better and more useful things for his own soul than those which the prelate precepts him, let him sacrifice these willingly to God; but those which are the prelate's, let him strive to fulfill. • For this is charitable obedience (cf. 1 Pet 1:22), since it satisfies God and neighbor.

If indeed the prelate precepts anything against his soul, though he is not to obey him, nevertheless let him not give him up. • And if he has endured persecution by others for that reason, let him love (dilectio) them more for God's sake. • For he who will endure persecution rather than wanting to be separated from his brothers, in truth remains continually in perfect obedience, since he lays down "his own life" (cf. Jn 15:13) on behalf of his brothers. • For there are many religious, who under the appearance of seeing better things than those which their prelates precept, look back (cf. Lk 9:62) and return "to the vomit" of their own willfulness (cf. Prov. 26:11; 2 Pet 2:22); • these are murderers and on account of their bad examples cause many souls to perish.

Chapter IV: That no one should appropriate to himself the office of superior

I did not come "to be ministered unto, but to minister" (cf. Mt 20:28), says the Lord. • Let those, who are set up over others, glory as much because of that office of superior, as if they had been appointed to the office of washing the feet of the brothers. • And in as much as they are more disturbed because of having lost their office of superior than because of (having lost) the office regarding feet, so much more do they assemble purses for themselves to the danger of their souls (cf. John 12:6).

Chapter V: That no one should be proud, but rather glory in the Cross of the Lord

Be attentive, oh man, to how many excellent things the Lord God has placed in you, since He created and formed you "to the image" of His own Beloved Son according to the body "and to (His) likeness" according to the spirit (cf. Gen 1:26). • And all the creatures, which are under heaven, after you serve, know and obey their Creator better than you. • And even the demons did not crucify Him, but you with them have crucified Him and even now you crucify (Him) by delighting in vices and sins. • Whence therefore can you glory? • For if you were so subtle and wise that you had "all knowledge" (cf. 1 Cor 13:2) and knew how to interpret every "kind of tongue" (cf. 1 Cor 12:28) and to search subtly after celestial things, in all these things you cannot glory; • since one demon knew of celestial things and now knows of earthly things more than all men, (even) granted that there has been someone, who received from the Lord a special understanding of the highest wisdom. • Similarly even if you were more handsome and wealthy than all and even if you were working miracles, as would put demons to flight, all those things are injurious to you and nothing (about them) pertains to you and you can glory in them not at all. • But in this we can glory, "in" our "infirmities" (cf. 2 Cor 12:5) and bearing each day the Holy Cross of Our Lord Jesus Christ (Lk 14:27).

University of Paris Medical Faculty, Writings on the Plague

Attempts were made to explain the plague including attributing it to divine wrath or even to a plot by Jews. Church scholars sought rational explanations based on the understanding that disease was caused by bad air which in turn may have been brought about by a planetary conjunction or by earthquakes and volcanoes. However rational, all explanations and cures were complete failures (though the idea of quarantine did somewhat succeed).

Source: *R. Hoeniger, ed.,* Der Schwarze Tod *(Berlin: 1882), appendix iii, pp. 152–6.*

Focus Questions:
1. What are the scholars trying to do and why?
2. What are the universal and particular causes of the plague?
3. Who is most likely to catch the pestilence?
4. What might be people's attitude to scholars and science after the plague?

CHAPTER 1 OF THE FIRST PART: CONCERNING THE UNIVERSAL AND DISTANT CAUSE

We say that the distant and first cause of this pestilence was and is the configuration of the heavens. In 1345, at one hour after noon on 20 March, there was a major conjunction of three planets in Aquarius. This conjunction, along with other earlier conjunctions and eclipses, by causing a deadly corruption of the air around us, signifies mortality and famine—and also other things about which we will not speak here because they are not relevant. Aristotle testifies that this is the case in his book *Concerning the Causes of the Properties of the Elements*, in which he says that mortality of races and the depopulation of kingdoms occur at the conjunction of Saturn and Jupiter, for great events then arise, their nature depending on the trigon in which the conjunction occurs. And this is found in ancient philosophers, and Albertus Magnus in his book, *Concerning the Causes of the Properties of the Elements* (treatise 2, chapter 1) says that the conjunction of Mars and Jupiter causes a great pestilence in the air, especially when they come together in a hot, wet sign, as was the case in 1345. For Jupiter, being wet and hot, draws up evil vapours from the earth and Mars, because it is immoderately hot and dry, then ignites the vapours, and as a result there were lightning, sparks, noxious vapours and fires throughout the air.

These effects were intensified because Mars—a malevolent planet, breeding anger and wars—was in the sign of Leo from 6 October, 1347 until the end of May this year, along with the head of the dragon, and because all these things are hot they attracted many vapours; which is why the winter was not as cold as it should have been. And Mars was also retrograde and therefore attracted many vapours from the earth and the sea which, when mixed with the air, corrupted its substance. Mars was also looking upon Jupiter with a hostile aspect, that is to say quartile, and that caused an evil disposition or quality in the air, harmful and hateful to our nature. This state of affairs generated strong winds (for according to Albertus in the first book of his *Meteora*, Jupiter has the property of raising powerful winds, particularly from the south), which gave rise to excess heat and moisture on the earth; although in fact it was the dampness which was most marked in our part of the world. And this is enough about the distant or universal cause for the moment.

CHAPTER 2 OF THE FIRST PART: CONCERNING THE PARTICULAR AND NEAR CAUSE

Although major pestilential illnesses can be caused by the corruption of water or food, as happens at times of famine and infertility, yet we still regard illnesses proceeding from the corruption of the air as much more dangerous. This is because bad air is more noxious than food or drink in that it can penetrate quickly to the heart and lungs to do its damage. We believe that the present epidemic or plague has arisen from corrupt air in its substance, and has not changed in its attributes. By which we wish it be understood that air, being pure and clear by nature, can only become putrid or corrupt by being mixed with something else, that is to say, with evil vapours. What happened was that the many vapours which had been corrupted at the time of the conjunction were drawn up from the earth and water, and were then mixed with the air and spread abroad by frequent gusts of wind in the wild southerly, gales, and because of these alien vapours which they carried the winds corrupted the air in its substance, and are still doing so. And this corrupted air, when breathed in, necessarily penetrates to the heart and corrupts the substance of the spirit there and rots the surrounding moisture, and the heat thus caused destroys the life force, and this is the immediate cause of the present epidemic.

And moreover these winds, which have become so common here, have carried among us (and may perhaps continue to do so in future) bad, rotten and poisonous vapours from elsewhere: from swamps, lakes and chasms, for instance, and also (which is even more dangerous) from unburied or unburnt corpses—which might well have been a cause of the epidemic. Another possible cause of corruption, which needs to be borne in mind, is the escape of the rottenness trapped in the centre of the earth as a result of earthquakes—something which has indeed recently occurred. But the conjunctions could have been the universal and distant cause of all these harmful things, by which air and water have been corrupted.

CHAPTER 3: CONCERNING PROGNOSTICATION AND SIGNS

Unseasonable weather is a particular cause of illness. For the ancients, notably Hippocrates, are agreed that if the four seasons run awry, and do not keep their proper course, then plagues and mortal passions are engendered that year. Experience tells us that for some time the seasons have not succeeded each other in the proper way. Last winter was not as cold as it should have been, with a great deal of rain; the spring windy and latterly wet. Summer was late, not as hot as it should have been, and extremely wet—the weather very changeable from day to day, and hour to hour; the air often troubled, and then still again, looking as if it was going to rain but then not doing so. Autumn too was very rainy and misty. It is because the whole year here—or most of it—was warm and wet that the air is pestilential. For it is a sign of pestilence for the air to be wain and wet at unseasonable times.

Wherefore we may fear a future pestilence here, which is particularly from the root beneath, because it is subject to the evil impress of the heavens, especially since that conjunction was in a western sign. Therefore if next winter is very rainy and less cold than it ought to be, we should expect an epidemic round about late winter and spring—and if it occurs it will be long and dangerous, for usually unseasonable weather is of only brief duration, but when it lasts over many seasons, as has obviously been the case here, it stands to reason that its effects will be longer-lasting and more dangerous, unless ensuing seasons change their nature in the opposite way. Thus if the winter in the north turns out to be cold and dry, the plagues might be arrested.

We have not said that the future pestilence will be exceptionally dangerous, for we do not wish to give the impression that it will be as dangerous here as in southern or eastern regions. For the conjunctions and the other causes discussed above had a more immediate impact on those regions than on ours. However, in the judgement of astrologers (who follow Ptolemy on this), plagues are likely, although not inevitable, because so many exhalations and inflammations have been observed, such as a comet and shooting stars. Also the sky has looked yellow and the air reddish because of the burnt vapours. There has also been much lightning and flashes and frequent thunder, and winds of such violence and strength that they have carried dust storms from the south. These things, and in particular the powerful earthquakes, have done universal harm and left a trail of corruption. There have been masses of dead fish, animals and other things along the sea shore, and in many places trees covered in dust, and some people claim to have seen a multitude of frogs and reptiles generated from the corrupt matter; and all these things seem to have come from the great corruption of the air and earth. All these things have been noted before as signs of plague by numerous wise men who are still remembered with respect and who experienced them themselves.

No wonder, therefore, that we fear that we are in for an epidemic. But it should be noted that in saying this we do not intend to exclude the possibility of illnesses arising from the character of the present year—for as the aphorism of Hippocrates has it: a year of many fogs and damps is a year of many illnesses. On the other hand, the susceptibility of the body of the patient is the most immediate cause in the breeding of illnesses, and therefore no cause is likely to have an effect unless the patient is susceptible to its effects. We must therefore emphasize that although, because everyone has to breathe, everyone will be at risk from the corrupted air, not everyone will be made ill by it but only those, who will no doubt be numerous, who have a susceptibility to it; and very few indeed of those who do succumb will escape.

The bodies most likely to take the stamp of this pestilence are those which are hot and moist, for they are the most susceptible to putrefaction. The following are also more at risk: bodies bunged up with evil humours, because the unconsumed waste matter is not being expelled as it should; those following a bad life style, with too much exercise, sex and bathing; the thin and weak, and persistent worriers; babies, women and young people; and corpulent people with a ruddy complexion. However those with dry bodies, purged of waste matter, who adopt a sensible and suitable regimen, will succumb to the pestilence more slowly.

We must not overlook the fact that any pestilence proceeds from the divine will, and our advice can therefore only be to return humbly to God. But this does not mean forsaking doctors. For the Most High created earthly medicine, and although God alone cures the sick, he does so through the medicine which in his generosity he provided. Blessed be the glorious and high God, who does not refuse his help, but has clearly set out a way of being cured for those who fear him. And this is enough of the third chapter, and of the whole first part.

68. THE ASTROLOGICAL CAUSES OF THE PLAGUE, GEOFFREY DE MEAUX

Geoffrey de Meaux was an astrologer who had been associated with the French Court earlier in the fourteenth century. The astrological measurements given in this treatise, however, relate to Oxford, which suggests that it was composed (or at least rewritten) there. Unlike the three astrologers mentioned in 57, de Meaux wrote this commentary on the 1345 conjunction after the outbreak of plague, and accordingly stresses the malign role of Saturn and Mars rather than the possible contribution of Jupiter.

Bodleian Library, Oxford, MS Digby 176 fos. 26–29.

I have been asked by some of my friends to write something about the cause of this general pestilence, showing its natural cause, and why it affected so many countries, and why it affected some countries more than others, and why within those countries it affected some cities and towns more than others, and why in one town it affected one street, and even one house, more than another, and why it affected nobles and gentry less than other people, and how long it will last. And they asked that after explaining the cause I should discuss appropriate remedies, drawing on my own opinions and medical advice. In order to demonstrate the cause of all these things I shall begin with the basics, as set forth by the wise authors, philosophers and astrologers who have had things to say on such matters.

Ptolemy in chapter 4 of the third book of his *Quadripartitum* cites Plato and Aristotle in support of the contention that God first created the heavens and the stars, and endowed them with the power to rule all earthly matters, and because of this it can be said that everything which befalls us happens at the will of God; for it is God himself who moves the heavens and whatever is within them, and it is through this motion that there come all the chances of generation and corruption, and all the other chances which lie outside our free will. Haly also cites Ptolemy as saying in the prologue to the first book of the *Quadripartitum* that the heavenly bodies confer on the inferior bodies below them similar powers, if they are naturally disposed to receive them. He also says in the *Quadripartitum* that heavenly bodies can bring about changes and events when they are turned towards us, and that this is a natural power, like the power of adamant to attract iron or scammony to purge yellow bile. Friar Roger Bacon in his treatise on the significance of places says that every point on the earth is at the apex of a pyramid formed by the converging lines of various heavenly powers; and this explains why you get plants of various species within one tiny piece of ground, or find twins who differ in character and behaviour, and in their aptitude for scholarship, languages or business.

Ptolemy divided the twelve signs of the Zodiac, through which all the planets move, into four groups of three, which he called trigons or triplicities, each of which is identified with one element. Thus the trigon of Aries, Leo and Sagittarius is identified with fire, which is hot and dry; the trigon of Taurus, Virgo and Capricorn with earth, which is cold and dry; the trigon of Gemini, Libra and Aquarius with air, which is hot and wet; and the trigon of Cancer, Scorpio and Pisces with water, which is cold and wet. Ptolemy also divided the whole inhabited world into four principal parts, each of which he identifies with one of the trigons. Ptolemy also says that the conjunctions of the two highest planets, that is Saturn and Jupiter, are of three types: major, minor and mean. A major conjunction is one in which these two planets begin their conjunction in the trigon of fire and remain in conjunction in the other trigons in turn until they return to the trigon of fire, but another sign from that in which they started, and this happens every 960 years. A mean conjunction is when these two highest planets begin their conjunction in one of the four triplicities and it lasts until they enter another, and this happens every 240 years. A minor conjunction is when they come together in any one trigon and this happens about every 20 years.

Now that the basics have been discussed, you can consider the reasons for such a great mortality in so many countries, and how the illness came through the influence of the stars. Ptolemy in chapter 4 of the second part of the *Quadripartitum* says: the important things are the strengths and powers of the hour, the conjunctions and oppositions, eclipses of the sun and moon, and the places the planets cross at that hour. Wherefore it has been, and is, known by all astrologers that in the year 1345 (taking the year to begin in January) there was a total eclipse of the moon, of long duration, on 18 March. At the longitude of Oxford it began an hour after the moon rose, and at the time the two planets were in conjunction in Aquarius, and Mars was with them in the same sign, within the light of Jupiter.

The sun is the lord, the director of all events, both general and specific, and the moon is second to him in dominion and power, and their effect is to intensify the effects of the planets acting with them. It is therefore in the natural course of events, and not to be wondered at, that such a great configuration should bring about major events on the earth, from the nature of the planets which drew to themselves the natures of the sun and moon. For when the sun is directly opposite the moon, as occurs in a total eclipse, then the power of each of them reaches the earth in a straight line, and the mingling of the influence of sun and moon with that of the superior planets creates a single celestial force which operates in conformity with the nature of the superior planets, which have drawn to themselves the powers of the sun and moon. The same thing happens in compound medicines: turbith naturally expels phlegm from the stomach and veins, and if it is mixed with ginger the mixture expels phlegm, and since ginger is not in itself an expellant it has taken on the nature of turbith. It is the same with the planets. On their own they cannot achieve anything great or universal, but when compounded with the sun and moon (at a time when these are aligned with each other and with the earth) they bend the nature of the two luminaries to their own nature, and thus with the power of the two luminaries are able to achieve great things which have a general and universal impact.

These natural causes affect the whole inhabited world between east and north. According to Ptolemy, Saturn, which was one of the partners in the conjunction, governs the whole eastern part of the inhabited world; Mars the whole western part; and Jupiter, besieged by both of them in the conjunction, rules the whole northern part. Thus the greater part of the earth was influenced, because of the place of the conjunction and because the planets involved rule parts of the world, as I have just described, and also because all the parts of the world where the eclipse was visible above the horizon shared in the effect of the configuration. Therefore this is why it affected so many provinces. And the reason why some were affected more than others is that a planet has no effect in a place over which it exerts no influence, as Ptolemy testifies in his *Centilogium*, and the superior planets in this conjunction had an influence over the places they rule and not elsewhere. And the reason why some towns and cities were affected more than others in the same provinces is as follows. Each city, town and home has fixed stars and planets ruling it, as Ptolemy testifies in the *Centilogium*. Therefore wherever the rulers of these places agree in power and effect with the planets and stars bringing the general mortality, those subject to them will have been made ready to receive that celestial influence upon their bodies.

It now remains to assign a reason why in one town it affected one street more than another, and also one house more than another. The answer is the same in both cases. Not all streets were affected in the same way, or both sides of one street, or neighbouring houses, because they do not have the same influences or rulers, and therefore the impact of the heavens cannot affect them all equally—for that action of which I speak is natural and operates according to the rules of nature. It cannot act in the same way in every case, but only has an effect insofar as the ground has been prepared for it.

It now remains to say why nobles and gentry were less affected than the rest of the population. It was and is known to all astrologers that at the time of this eclipse the three superior planets were in the sign of Aquarius, where the fixed stars are not of the first magnitude and, save for one which is in the south, far distant from us, are lesser stars which signify the common people, and therefore the effect of the illness which they brought touched those people more...

It now remains to say how long the effects of that configuration on 18 March, 1345 will last. It is known to all astrologers that the duration of obscurity of the lunar eclipse when there was the conjunction of the three superior planets was three hours, 29 minutes and 54 seconds. That three hours and a half (roughly) when multiplied by 20, which is the number of years between these minor conjunctions of Saturn and Jupiter, make 70, which, divided by the 13 lunar months which make up the solar year, give 5 years and 5 lunar months, denoting the duration of the universal effect of that configuration of the two superior planets together with the lunar eclipse, as Ptolemy witnesses in the second book of the *Quadripartitum* where he says: the impact of a solar eclipse will last for as many years as there were hours of darkness, and in the case of a lunar eclipse for as many months as there were hours of darkness. And the commentator adds at that point that this calculation relates just to the eclipse; when it occurs with something else, such as a conjunction of Saturn and Jupiter, the duration of its effect will be proportionately lengthened.

You should understand, however, that I do not wish to imply that the mortality comes only from Saturn and Jupiter but rather through Mars, which was mixed with them at the time of the eclipse. And the condition which resulted from all of these will last according to the nature of the dominant planets in that configuration...

Now it remains to write about the best remedy to be taken against this celestial influence, and you should know, as Ptolemy says in the third chapter of the first book of the *Quadripartitum*, that not all the things which befall men through the heavenly bodies are inevitable—that is, cannot be avoided. Some of the works of the stars are inevitable in this sense, and cannot in the nature of things be avoided, but others are things which it is possible to avoid, so that one part of the events befalling men arose through the general and universal pestilence, and did not befall them because of their individual nature. For in that mortality the greater and stronger force throws down the weaker and lesser. And you ought to know that should someone's nativity be the opposite of the configuration bringing the mortality, the mortality would not touch him; but should his nativity be broadly similar to the configuration, it would be clear that he lacks the contrary forces by which he could resist it. For as doctors and students of natural science know, transmutation is easy between bodies which have matching qualities. And where a person's nativity does not fully correspond to the configuration and yet is not totally contrary to it either, the body can, (given a good regimen and certain medicines which I will describe later), be preserved from this pestilence, but if he adopts a bad regimen then he can easily contract it.

Now the nature of the sun and moon is drawn, as I said earlier, to the nature of the dominant planets in the configuration, and those were Saturn and Mars; not Jupiter, although at the time of the eclipse he was exalted above Mars both in the eccentric and epicycle. For Jupiter is of a temperate power, and the more easily overcome as a result; just as temperate medicines are easily overwhelmed when mixed with intemperate medicines, and become intemperate themselves. Thus at the time of the eclipse, Jupiter was besieged by both the infortunes and, mixed with them, took the nature of both of them, but rather more of Saturn than of Mars; because Saturn was stronger than Mars in that place, because he had more dignities in that place, and because he was exalted above them in both the eccentric and epicycle. Saturn thus obtained dominion, and Mars was his second, as Ptolemy testifies.

Because Saturn was dominant, he brings cold, (greater than the sun could counter), to each country under his rule, and because of the sign in which the conjunction occurred men will experience the onset of lingering illnesses such as tuberculosis, catarrh, paralysis and gout; passions of the heart arising from unhappiness; and the deaths of those who have endured long weakness. And since the conjunction was in the air sign of Aquarius it signified great cold, heavy frosts, and thick clouds corrupting the air; and since this is a sign which represents the pouring out of water, the configuration signifies that rivers will burst their banks and the sea flood. And because of the persistently cold atmosphere bitter humours cannot be expelled from the sea as usual, and because of the persistent cold there will be few fish in the sea and those that there are will rot because of the cold, which traps vapours and humours in their bodies. For his part, Mars in that sign denotes strife among men, and sudden death which comes among all sorts of men, especially among children and adolescents, and illnesses entailing fevers and the spitting of blood, and also violent death and ulcers.

59. THE DANGERS OF CORRUPTED AIR, BENGT KNUTSSON

This account is taken from the treatise of Bengt Knutsson, a mid-fifteenth-century bishop of Vasteras, near Stockholm. Knutsson took over wholesale one of the most popular plague tracts of the fourteenth century, that of John Jacobus (Jean Jacme), written c. 1364. Jacobus was a royal and papal physician and Chancellor of Montpellier, and the various autobiographical references later in the work refer to him, not to Knutsson.

This extract represents a little over half the treatise; the last two sections (on the comforts of the heart and blood letting) have been omitted. The text is taken from a fifteenth-century English translation of Knutsson. I have modernized the spelling and made a few grammatical changes for the sake of clarity, but have not attempted a complete modern 'translation'.

A Little Book for the Pestilence, Manchester, 1911, a facsimile of a printed English translation of Knutsson in the John Rylands Library, Manchester.

Here begins a little book which treats and rehearses many good things necessary for the infirmity and great sickness called the Pestilence, the which often infects us, made by the most expert doctor in physic the Bishop of Arusiens in the realm of Denmark.

At the reverence and worship of the blessed Trinity and of the glorious Virgin St. Mary and for the conservation of the common weal, as well for them that be whole as for remedy of them that be sick, I the Bishop of Arusiens in the realm of Denmark, doctor of physic, will write by the most expert and famous doctors, authorities in physic, some things about the infirmity of pestilence which daily infects us and soon suffers us to depart out of this life.

First I will write the tokens of this infirmity.
Secondly the causes whereof it comes.
Thirdly the remedies for the same.
Fourthly comfort for the heart and the principal members of the body.
Fifthly when it shall be the season to let blood.

First as I said the tokens of this infirmity. Seven things ought to be noted here:

The first is when on a summer's day the weather often changes, so in the morning the weather appears rainy, afterwards it appears cloudy and finally windy from the south.

The second token is when in summer the days appear all dark and look like rain, and yet it does not rain. And if many days continue thus, great pestilence is to be dreaded.

The third token is when there is a great multitude of flies upon the earth, then it is sign that the air is venomous and infected.

The fourth token is when stars often seem to fall, then it is a token that the air is infected with much venomous vapour.

The fifth token is when a blazing star is seen in the sky, then it should fortune that soon after there will be great manslaughter in battle.

The sixth token is when there is great lightning and thunder, namely out of the south.

The seventh token is when great winds blow out of the south for they be foul and unclean.

Therefore when these tokens appear great pestilence is to be dreaded, unless God of his mercy will remove it.

The pestilence comes of three things. Sometimes it comes from the root beneath, at other times from the root above, so that we may feel sensibly how the change of air appears to us, and sometimes it comes of both together: from the root above as well as from the root beneath—as when we see a siege or privy next to a chamber or any other particular thing which corrupts the air in substance and quality, which is a thing which may happen every day. And thereof comes the ague of pestilence. And many physicians are deceived about this, not suspecting this ague to be a pestilence. Sometimes it comes of dead carrion or the corruption of standing waters in ditches or sloughs or other corrupt places, and these things are sometimes universal and sometimes particular. By the root above is meant the heavenly bodies, by whom the spirit of life is corrupted in man or beast. In like wise, as Avicenna says in his fourth book, by the form of the air above the bodies beneath may be infected.

For the inspissation above corrupts the air and so the spirits of man are corrupted. This infirmity comes also from the root above or beneath: when the inspissation above corrupts the air or when the putrefaction or rotten carrion of the vile places beneath cause an infirmity in man. And such an infirmity is sometimes an ague, sometimes an apostume or a swelling and that is in many things. Also the inspissated air is sometimes venomous and corrupt, hurting the heart so that nature is grieved in many ways, but so that he does not perceive his harm. For the urine appears fair and shows good digestion, yet nevertheless the patient is likely to die. Wherefore many physicians, seeing the urine of their patients, speak superficially and are deceived. Therefore it is necessary that every patient provide himself with a good and expert physician.

These things before written are the causes of pestilence; but about these things two questions are asked. The first is why, within one town, one man dies and another does not. Where men are dead in one house, in another house no one dies. The other question is whether pestilence sores are contagious. To the first question I say that it may happen for two causes: that is to say because of the thing that does or the thing that suffers. An example of that thing that does: the influence of the bodies above affects that place or that place more than this place or this place. And one patient is more disposed to die than another. Therefore it is to be noted that bodies inclined to be hot have open pores, whereas infected bodies have the pores stopped with many humours. Where bodies have open pores, as in the case of men who abuse themselves with women or often have baths, or men who are hot with labour or great anger, they are the more disposed to this great sickness.

To the second question I say that pestilence sores are contagious because of infectious humours, and the reek or smoke of such sores is venomous and corrupts the air. And therefore one should flee such persons as are infected. In pestilence time nobody should stand in a great press of people because some man among them may be infected. Therefore wise physicians visiting sick folk stand far from the patient, holding their face towards the door or window, and so should the servants of sick folk stand. Also it is good for a patient to change his chamber every day and often to have the windows open against the north and east and to spar the windows against the south. For the south wind has two causes of putrefaction. The first is it that makes a man, whether whole or sick, feeble in his body. The second cause is as it is written in *Aphorisms* chapter 3, the south wind grieves the body and hurts the heart because it opens man's pores and enters into the heart. Wherefore it is good for a whole man in time of pestilence when the wind is in the south to stay within the house all day, and if it shall be necessary for a man go out, yet let him abide in his house until the sun be up in the east and passing southward.

Here after follow the remedies for the pestilence.

Now it is to be known by what remedies a man may preserve himself from the pestilence. First see the writings of Jeremiah the prophet that a man ought to forsake evil things and do good deeds and meekly confess his sins, for it is the highest remedy in time of pestilence: penance and confession to be preferred to all other medicines. Nevertheless I promise you verily it is a good remedy to void and change the infected place. But some may not profitably change their places. Therefore as much as they can they should eschew every cause of putrefaction and stinking, and namely every fleshly lust with women is to be eschewed. Also the southern wind, which is naturally infective. Therefore spar the windows against the south in like wise as it is said before, until the first hour after the middle of the day then open the windows against the north. Of the same cause every foul stench is to be eschewed, of stable, stinking fields, ways or streets, and namely of stinking dead carrion and most of stinking waters where in many places water is kept two days or two nights. Or else there be gutters of water cast under the earth which cause great stink and corruption. And of this cause some die in that house where such things happen, and in another house die none as is said afore. Likewise in that place where worts and cabbages putrefy it makes a noisome savour and stinking. For in likewise as by the sweet odour of balsam the heart and the spirits have recreation, so of evil savours they be made feeble. Wherefore keep your house that an infected air enter not in, for an infected air most causes putrefaction in places and houses where folk sleep. Therefore let your house be clean and make clear fire of wood flaming. Let your house be made with fumigation of herbs, that is to say with leaves of bay tree, juniper, *uberiorgani* [unidentified] it is in the apothecary shops, wormwood, rue, mugwort and of the wood of aloes which is best but it is dear. Such a fume taken by the mouth and ears opens the inward parts of the body. Also all great repletion is to be eschewed because full bodies be easily infected as Avicenna says in the fourth canon: they that charge their bodies to repletion shorten their life.

Also common baths are to be eschewed, for a little crust corrupts all the body. Therefore the people as much as is possible is to be eschewed, lest of infectious breath some man be infected. But when the multitude of people may not be eschewed, then use the remedies following. In the morning when you rise wash a little rue and one or two filbert nuts clean and eat them, and if that cannot be had then eat bread or toast sopped in vinegar, namely in troublous and cloudy weather. Also in the time of pestilence it is better to abide within the house for it is not wholesome to go into the city or town. Also let your house be sprinkled especially in summer with vinegar and roses and with the leaves of the vine. Also it is good to wash your hands oft times in the day with water and vinegar and wipe your face with your hands and smell to them. Also it is good always to savour sour things. In Montpellier I might not eschew the company of people for I went from house to house because of my poverty to cure sick folks, therefore bread or a sponge sopped in vinegar I took with me holding it in my mouth and nose because all sour things stop the way of humours and suffer no venomous things to enter into a man's body and so I escaped the pestilence, my fellows supposing that I should not live. These forsaid things I have proved by my self:

60. EARTHQUAKES AS THE CAUSE OF PLAGUE

This is the final section of a treatise usually known, from its opening words, as Is it from divine wrath that the mortality of these years proceeds. It was probably produced in Germany in the generation after the 1348–49 outbreak. In the first part of the treatise, not printed here, the author considers various explanations of the plague, including the astrological one—which he rejects on the grounds that similar conjunctions occur frequently without being followed by plague, and that the configuration of the heavens should have an equal impact on all mankind, which the plague did not. He then turns to his preferred explanation: that the earthquakes of 1347 released poisonous fumes into the atmosphere.

Karl Sudhof; Festschriften aus den ersten 150 Jahren nach der Epidemic des 'schwarzen Todes' 1348: XI, Archiv fur Geschichte der Medizin XI, 1918–19.

There is a fourth opinion, which I consider more likely than the others, which is that insofar as the mortality arose from natural causes its immediate cause was a corrupt and poisonous earthy exhalation, which infected the air in various parts of the world and, when breathed in by people, suffocated them and suddenly snuffed them out. I can bring two pieces of evidence in support of my proposition, both securely grounded in natural science. The first is that when air which is full of vapours and earthy fumes is enclosed and shut up for a long time in the prison of the earth it becomes so corrupted that it constitutes a potent poison to men. This is especially marked in caverns or deep inside the earth, where there is no fresh air supply, as is often seen in the case of wells which have been unused for a long time and have remained sealed up for many years. For when such wells are opened in order to be cleaned out it often happens that the first man to enter is suffocated, and sometimes in turn those who follow him. And the common people are so ignorant that they blame this on a basilisk lurking inside.

John Ball Sermon

The long-term results of the plague created a shortage of labor, which created higher wages, better conditions, and even the end of the serfdom. Attempts to control and regulate prices and wages were defeated by stark reality. Therefore, for those who survived the plagues, the Late Middle Ages were a time of relative plenty with more land, more wealth, more demand for luxuries. Higher expectations could lead to peasants showing active resentment against attempts to restrict them or limit their newfound prosperity—one large-scale rebellion occurred in England in 1381.

Source: *Jean Froissart,* Chronicles *(Penguin, 1963).*

Focus Questions:
1. To whom are the peasants taking their complaints, and about whom are they complaining?
2. What is the basis for their complaints?
3. What do the peasants seek?

THE PEASANT REVOLT IN ENGLAND (1381)

While these negotiations and discussions were going on, there occurred in England great disasters and uprisings of the common people, on account of which the country was almost ruined beyond recovery. Never was any land or realm in such great danger as England at that time. It was because of the abundance and prosperity in which the common people then lived that this rebellion broke out, just as in earlier days the Jack Goodmans rose in France and committed many excesses, by which the noble land of France suffered grave injury.

These terrible troubles originated in England from a strange circumstance and a trivial cause. That it may serve as a lesson to all good men and true, I will describe that circumstance and its effects as I was informed of them at the time.

It is the custom in England, as in several other countries, for the nobles to have strong powers over their men and to hold them in serfdom: that is, that by right and custom they have to till the lands of the gentry, reap the corn and bring it to the big house, put it in the barn, thresh and winnow it; mow the hay and carry it to the house, cut logs and bring them up, and all such forced tasks; all this the men must do by way of serfage to the masters. In England there is a much greater number than elsewhere of such men who are obliged to serve the prelates and the nobles. And in the counties of Kent, Essex, Sussex and Bedford in particular, there are more than in the whole of the rest of England.

These bad people in the counties just mentioned began to rebel because, they said, they were held too much in subjection, and when the world began there had been no serfs and could not be, unless they had rebelled against their lord, as Lucifer did against God; but they were not of that stature, being neither angels nor spirits, but men formed in the image of their masters, and they were treated as animals. This was a thing they could no longer endure, wishing rather to be all one and the same, and, if they worked for their masters, they wanted to have wages for it. In these machinations they had been greatly encouraged originally by a crack-brained priest of Kent called John Ball, who had been imprisoned several times for his reckless words by the Archbishop of Canterbury. This John Ball had the habit on Sundays after mass when everyone was coming out of church, of going to the cloisters or the graveyard, assembling the people round him and preaching thus:

"Good people, things cannot go right in England and never will, until goods are held in common and there are no more villeins and gentlefolk, but we are all one and the same. In what way are those whom we call lords greater masters than ourselves? How have they deserved it? Why do they hold us in bondage? If we all spring from a single father and mother, Adam and Eve, how can they claim or prove that they are lords more than us, except by making us produce and grow the wealth which they spend? They are clad in velvet and camlet lined with squirrel and ermine, while we go dressed in coarse cloth. They have the wines, the spices and the good bread: we have the rye, the husks and the straw, and we drink water. They have shelter and ease in their fine manors, and we have hardship and toil, the wind and the rain in the fields. And from us must come, from our labour, the things which keep them in luxury. We are called serfs and beaten if we are slow in our service to them, yet we have no sovereign lord we can complain to, none to hear us and do us justice. Let us go to the King—he is young—and show him how we are oppressed, and tell him that we want things to be changed, of else we will change them ourselves. If we go in good earnest and all together, very many people who are called serfs and are held in subjection will follow us to get their freedom. And when the King sees and hears us, he will remedy the evil, either willingly or otherwise."

These were the kind of things which John Ball usually preached in the villages on Sundays when the congregations came out from mass, and many of the common people agreed with him. Some, who were up to no good, said: "He's right!" and out in the fields, or walking together from one village to another, or in their homes, they whispered and repeated among themselves: "That's what John Ball says, and he's right."

Ibn Battuta, Selections from the *Rihla*

Ibn Battuta (1304–1369 CE) was a scholar and judge from Morocco. It is estimated that he traveled some 75,000 miles during an extensive 30-year journey around the Islamic world, from Africa to Asia and back. His book, Rihla *(translated as "Journey"), places Ibn Battuta in the tradition of great Arabic medieval geographers, providing a detailed account of the places and cultures he witnessed in his travels.*

Source: *Ibn Battuta,* Travels in Asia and Africa, 1325–1354, *trans. and ed. by H. A. R. Gibb (London, 1929).*

Focus Questions:
1. Compare the description of Cairo with the plague description, how would Cairo appear afterwards?
2. What groups receive the most attention in his descriptions?
3. Who is left out? Why?

ARRIVAL IN CAIRO (PP. 50–55)

I arrived at length at Cairo, mother of cities and seat of Pharaoh the tyrant, mistress of broad regions and fruitful lands, boundless in multitude of buildings, peerless in beauty and splendour, the meeting-place of comer and goer, the halting-place of feeble and mighty, whose throngs surge as the waves of the sea, and can scarce be contained in her for all her size and capacity. It is said that in Cairo there are twelve thousand water-carriers who transport water on camels, and thirty thousand hirers of mules and donkeys, and that on the Nile there are thirty-six thousand boats belonging to the Sultan and his subjects which sail upstream to Upper Egypt and downstream to Alexandria and Damietta, laden with goods and profitable merchandise of all kinds.

A pleasure garden
On the bank of the Nile opposite Old Cairo is the place known as The Garden, which is a pleasure park and promenade, containing many beautiful gardens, for the people of Cairo are given to pleasure and amusements. I witnessed a fete once in Cairo for the sultan's recovery from a fractured hand; all the merchants decorated their bazaars and had rich stuffs, ornaments and silken fabrics hanging in their shops for several days.

Religious institutions
The mosque of 'Amr is highly venerated and widely celebrated. The Friday service is held in it and the road runs through it from east to west. The madrasas [college mosques] of Cairo cannot be counted for multitude. As for the Maristan [hospital], which lies "between the two castles" near the mausoleum of Sultan Qala'un, no description is adequate to its beauties. It contains an innumerable quantity of appliances and medicaments, and its daily revenue is put as high as a thousand dinars.

There are a large number of religious establishments ["convents"] which they call khanqahs, and the nobles vie with one another in building them. Each of these is set apart for a separate school of darwishes, mostly Persians, who are men of good education and adept in the mystical doctrines. Each has a superior and a doorkeeper and their affairs are admirably organized. They have many special customs one of which has to do with their food. The steward of the house comes in the morning to the darwishes, each of whom indicates what food he desires, and when they assemble for meals, each person is given his bread and soup in a separate dish, none sharing with another. They eat twice a day. They are each given winter clothes and summer clothes, and a monthly allowance of from twenty to thirty dirhams. Every Thursday night they receive sugar cakes, soap to wash their clothes, the price of a bath, and oil for their lamps. These men are celibate; the married men have separate convents.

At Cairo too is the great cemetery of al-Qarafa, which is a place of peculiar sanctity and contains the graves of innumerable scholars and pious believers. In the Qarafa the people build beautiful pavilions surrounded by walls, so that they look like houses. They also build chambers and hire Koran-readers who recite night and day in agreeable voices. Some of them build religious houses and madrasas beside the mausoleums and on Thursday nights they go out to spend the night there with their children and women-folk, and make a circuit of the famous tombs. They go out to spend the night there also on the "Night of midSha'ban," and the market-people take out all kinds of eatables. Among the many celebrated sanctuaries [in the city] is the holy shrine where there reposes the head of alHusayn. Beside it is a vast monastery of striking construction, on the doors of which there are silver rings and plates of the same metal.

The great river Nile
The Egyptian Nile surpasses all rivers of the earth in sweetness of taste, length of course, and utility. No other river in the world can show such a continuous series of towns and villages along its banks, or a basin so intensely cultivated. Its course is from South to North, contrary to all the other great rivers. One extraordinary thing about it is that it begins to rise in the extreme hot weather at the time when rivers generally diminish and dry up, and begins to subside just when rivers begin to increase and overflow. The river Indus resembles it in this feature. The Nile is one of the five great rivers of the world, which are the Nile, Euphrates, Tigris, Syr Darya and Amu Darya; five other rivers resemble these, the Indus, which is called Panj Ab [i.e. Five Rivers], the river of India which is called Gang [Ganges]—it is to it that the Hindus go on pilgrimage, and when they burn their dead they throw the ashes into it, and they say that it comes from Paradise—the river Jun [Jumna or perhaps Brahmaputra] in India, the river Itil [Volga] in the Qipchaq steppes, on the banks of which is the city of Sara, and the river Saru [Hoang-Ho] in the land of Cathay. All these will be mentioned in their proper places, if God will. Some distance below Cairo the Nile divides into three streams, none of which can be crossed except by boat, winter or summer. The inhabitants of every township have canals led off the Nile; these are filled when the river is in flood and carry the water over the fields.

Upriver
From Cairo I travelled into Upper Egypt, with the intention of crossing to the Hijaz. On the first night I stayed at the monastery of Dayr at-Tin, which was built to house certain illustrious relics—a fragment of the Prophet's wooden basin and the pencil with which he used to apply kohl, the awl he used for sewing his sandals, and the Koran belonging to the Caliph Ali written in his own hand. These were bought, it is said, for a hundred thousand dirhams by the builder of the monastery, who also established funds to supply food to all comers and to maintain the guardians of the sacred relics.

Thence my way lay through a number of towns and villages to Munyat Ibn Khasib [Minia], a large town which is built on the bank of the Nile, and most emphatically excels all the other towns of Upper Egypt. I went on through Manfalut, Asyut, Ikhmim, where there is a berba with sculptures and inscriptions which no one can now read-another of these berbas there was pulled down and its stones used to build a madrasa—Qina, Qus, where the governor of Upper Egypt resides, Luxor, a pretty little town containing the tomb of the pious ascetic Abu'l-Hajjaj, Esna, and thence a day and a night's journey through desert country to Edfu.

Camels, hyenas, and bejas
Here we crossed the Nile and, hiring camels, journeyed with a party of Arabs through a desert, totally devoid of settlements but quite safe for travelling. One of our halts was at Humaythira, a place infested with hyenas. All night long we kept driving them away, and indeed one got at my baggage, tore open one of the sacks, pulled out a bag of dates, and made off with it. We found the bag next morning, torn to pieces and with most of the contents eaten. After fifteen days' travelling we reached the town of Aydhab, a large town, well supplied with milk and fish; dates and grain are imported from Upper Egypt.

Its inhabitants are Bejas. These people are black-skinned; they wrap themselves in yellow blankets and tie headbands about a fingerbreadth wide round their heads. They do not give their daughters any share in their inheritance. They live on camels' milk and they ride on Meharis [dromedaries]. One-third of the city belongs to the Sultan of Egypt and two-thirds to the King of the Bejas, who is called al-Hudrubi. On reaching Aydhab we found that al-Hudrubi was engaged in warfare with the Turks [i.e. the troops of the Sultan of Egypt], that he had sunk the ships and that the Turks had fled before him. It was impossible for us to attempt the sea-crossing [across the Red Sea], so we sold the provisions that we had made ready for it, and returned to Qus with the Arabs from whom we had hired the camels.

Back downriver to Cairo; from Cairo to Syria and Jerusalem

We sailed thence down the Nile (it was at the flood time) and after an eight days' journey reached Cairo, where I stayed only one night, and immediately set out for Syria. This was in the middle of July 1326. My route lay through Bilbays and as-Salihiya, after which we entered the sands and halted at a number of stations. At each of these there was a hostelry which they call a khan, where travellers alight with their beasts. Each khan has a water wheel supplying a fountain and a shop at which the traveller buys what he requires for himself and his beast.

Crossing the border into Syria

At the station of Qatya customs-dues are collected from the merchants, and their goods and baggage are thoroughly examined and searched. There are offices here, with officers, clerks, and notaries, and the daily revenue is a thousand gold dinars. No one is allowed to pass into Syria without a passport from Egypt, nor into Egypt without a passport from Syria, for the protection of the property of the subjects and as a measure of precaution against spies from Iraq. The responsibility of guarding this road has been entrusted to the Badawin [Bedouin]. At nightfall they smooth down the sand so that no track is left on it, then in the morning the governor comes and looks at the sand. If he finds any track on it he commands the Arabs to bring the person who made it, and they set out in pursuit and never fail to catch him. He is then brought to the governor, who punishes him as he sees fit. The governor at the time of my passage treated me as a guest and showed me great kindness, and allowed all those who were with me to pass. From here we went on to Gaza, which is the first city of Syria on the side next the Egyptian frontier.

ON THE ROAD TO JERUSALEM: HEBRON AND BETHLEHEM (PP. 55–57)

From Gaza I travelled to the city of Abraham [Hebron], the mosque of which is of elegant, but substantial construction, imposing and lofty, and built of squared stones. At one angle of it there is a stone, one of whose faces measures twenty-seven spans. It is said that Solomon commanded the jinn to build it. Inside it is the sacred cave containing the graves of Abraham, Isaac, and Jacob, opposite which are three graves, which are those of their wives. I questioned the imam, a man of great piety and learning, on the authenticity of these graves, and he replied: "All the scholars whom I have met hold these graves to be the very graves of Abraham, Isaac, Jacob and their wives. No one questions this except introducers of false doctrines; it is a tradition which has passed from father to son for generations and admits of no doubt." This mosque contains also the grave of Joseph, and somewhat to the east of it lies the tomb of Lot, which is surmounted by an elegant building. In the neighbourhood is Lot's lake [the Dead Sea], which is brackish and is said to cover the site of the settlements of Lot's people.

On the way from Hebron to Jerusalem, I visited Bethlehem, the birthplace of Jesus. The site is covered by a large building; the Christians regard it with intense veneration and hospitably entertain all who alight at it.

Jerusalem and its holy sites

We then reached Jerusalem (may God ennoble her!), third in excellence after the two holy shrines of Mecca and Medina and the place whence the Prophet was caught up into heaven. Its walls were destroyed by the illustrious King Saladin and his Successors, for fear lest the Christians should seize it and fortify themselves in it. The sacred mosque is a most beautiful building, and is said to be the largest mosque in the world. Its length from east to west is put at 752 "royal" cubits and its breadth at 435. On three sides it has many entrances, but on the south side I know of one only, which is that by which the imam enters. The entire mosque is an open court and unroofed, except the mosque al-Aqsa, which has a roof of most excellent workmanship, embellished with gold and brilliant colours. Some other parts of the mosque are roofed as well. The Dome of the Rock is a building of extraordinary beauty, solidity, elegance, and singularity of shape. It stands on an elevation in the centre of the mosque and is reached by a flight of marble steps. It has four doors. The space round it is also paved with marble, excellently done, and the interior likewise. Both outside and inside the decoration is so magnificent and the workmanship so surpassing as to defy description. The greater part is covered with gold so that the eyes of one who gazes on its beauties are dazzled by its brilliance, now glowing like a mass of light, now flashing like lightning. In the centre of the Dome is the blessed rock from which the Prophet ascended to heaven, a great rock projecting about a man's height, and underneath it there is a cave the size of a small room, also of a man's height, with steps leading down to it. Encircling the rock are two railings of excellent workmanship, the one nearer the rock being artistically constructed in iron and the other of wood.

The Christian holy places

Among the grace-bestowing sanctuaries of Jerusalem is a building, situated on the farther side of the valley called the valley of Jahannam [Gehenna] to the east of the town, on a high hill. This building is said to mark the place whence Jesus ascended to heaven. In the bottom of the same valley is a church venerated by the Christians, who say that it contains the grave of Mary. In the same place there is another church which the Christians venerate and to which they come on pilgrimage. This is the church of which they are falsely persuaded to believe that it contains the grave of Jesus [Church of the Holy Sepulcher]. All who come on pilgrimage to visit it pay a stipulated tax to the Muslims, and suffer very unwillingly various humiliations. Thereabouts also is the place of the cradle of Jesus which is visited in order to obtain blessing.

IBN BATTUTA ARRIVES AT DAMASCUS (PP. 65–73)

I entered Damascus on Thursday 9th Ramadan 726 [9th August, 1326], and lodged at the Malikite college called ash-Sharabishiya. Damascus surpasses all other cities in beauty, and no description, however full, can do justice to its charms.

The Ummayad Mosque

The Cathedral Mosque, known as the Umayyad Mosque, is the most magnificent mosque in the world, the finest in construction and noblest in beauty, grace and perfection; it is matchless and unequalled. The person who undertook its construction was the Caliph Walid I [AD 705–715]. He applied to the Roman Emperor at Constantinople, ordering him to send craftsmen to him, and the Emperor sent him twelve thousand of them. The site of the mosque was a church, and when the Muslims captured Damascus, one of their commanders entered from one side by the sword and reached as far as the middle of the church, while the other entered peaceably from the eastern side and reached the middle also. So the Muslims made the half of the church which they had entered by force into a mosque and the half which they had entered by peaceful agreement remained as a church. When Walid decided to extend the mosque over the entire church he asked the Greeks to sell him their church for whatsoever equivalent they desired, but they refused, so he seized it. The Christians used to say that whoever destroyed the church would be stricken with madness and they told that to Walid. But he replied "I shall be the first to be stricken by madness in the service of God," and seizing an axe, he set to work to knock it down with his own hands. The Muslims on seeing that followed his example, and God proved false the assertion of the Christians.

This mosque has four doors. The southern door, called the "Door of Increase," is approached by a spacious passage where the dealers in second-hand goods and other commodities have their shops. Through it lies the way to the [former] Cavalry House, and on the left as one emerges from it is the coppersmiths' gallery, a large bazaar, one of the finest in Damascus, extending along the south wall of the mosque. This bazaar occupies the site of the palace of the Caliph Mu'awiya I, which was called al Khadri [The Green Palace]; the Abbasids pulled it down and a bazaar took its place.

The eastern door, called the Jayrun door, is the largest of the doors of the mosque. It also has a large passage, leading out to a large and extensive colonnade which is entered through a quintuple gateway between six tall columns. Along both sides of this passage are pillars, supporting circular galleries, where the cloth merchants amongst others have their shops; above these again are long galleries in which are the shops of the jewellers and booksellers and makers of admirable glass-ware. In the square adjoining the first door are the stalls of the principal notaries, in each of which there may be five or six witnesses in attendance and a person authorized by the qadi to perform marriage-ceremonies. The other notaries are scattered throughout the city. Near these stalls is the bazaar of the stationers who sell paper, pens, and ink. In the middle of the passage there is a large round marble basin, surrounded by a pavilion supported on marble columns but lacking a roof. In the centre of the basin is a copper pipe which forces out water under pressure so that it rises into the air more than a man's height. They call it "The Waterspout" and it is a fine sight. To the right as one comes out of the Jayrun door, which is called also the "Door of the Hours," is an upper gallery shaped like a large arch, within which there are small open arches furnished with doors, to the number of the hours of the day. These doors are painted green on the inside and yellow on the outside, and as each hour of the day passes the green inner side of the door is turned to the outside, and vice versa. They say that inside the gallery there is a person in the room who is responsible for turning them by hand as the hours pass.

The western door is called the "Door of the Post"; the passage outside it contains the shops of the candlemakers and a gallery for the sale of fruit.

The northern door is called the "Door of the Confectioners"; it too has a large passageway, and on the right as one leaves it is a khanqah, which has a large basin of water in the centre and lavatories supplied with running water. At each of the four doors of the mosque is a building for ritual ablutions, containing about a hundred rooms abundantly supplied with running water.

A controversial theologian
One of the principal Hanbalite doctors at Damascus was Taqi ad-Din Ibn Taymiya, a man of great ability and wide learning, but with some kink in his brain. The people of Damascus idolized him. He used to preach to them from the pulpit, and one day he made some statement that the other theologians disapproved; they carried the case to the sultan and in consequence Ibn Taymiya was imprisoned for some years. While he was in prison he wrote a commentary on the Koran, which he called "The Ocean," in about forty volumes. Later on his mother presented herself before the sultan and interceded for him, so he was set at liberty, until he did the same thing again. I was in Damascus at the time and attended the service which he was conducting one Friday, as he was addressing and admonishing the people from the pulpit. In the midst of his discourse he said "Verily God descends to the sky over our world [from Heaven] in the same bodily fashion that I make this descent," and stepped down one step of the pulpit. A Malikite doctor present contradicted him and objected to his statement, but the common people rose up against this doctor and beat him with their hands and their shoes so severely that his turban fell off and disclosed a silken skull-cap on his head. Inveighing against him for wearing this, they haled him before the qadi of the Hanbalites, who ordered him to be imprisoned and afterwards had him beaten.

The other doctors objected to this treatment and carried the matter before the principal amir, who wrote to the sultan about the matter and at the same time drew up a legal attestation against Ibn Taymiya for various heretical pronouncements. This deed was sent on to the sultan, who gave orders that Ibn Taymiya should be imprisoned in the citadel, and there he remained until his death.

The Plague of 1348

One of the celebrated sanctuaries at Damascus is the Mosque of the Footprints (al-Aqdam), which lies two miles south of the city, alongside the main highway which leads to the Hijaz, Jerusalem, and Egypt. It is a large mosque, very blessed, richly endowed, and very highly venerated by the Damascenes. The footprints from which it derives its name are certain footprints impressed upon a rock there, which are said to be the mark of Moses' foot. In this mosque there is a small chamber containing a stone with the following inscription "A certain pious man saw in his sleep the Chosen One [Muhammad], who said to him 'Here is the grave of my brother Moses.'"

I saw a remarkable instance of the veneration in which the Damascenes hold this mosque during the great pestilence on my return journey through Damascus, in the latter part of July 1348. The viceroy Arghun Shah ordered a crier to proclaim through Damascus that all the people should fast for three days and that no one should cook anything eatable in the market during the daytime. For most of the people there eat no food but what has been prepared in the market. So the people fasted for three successive days, the last of which was a Thursday, then they assembled in the Great Mosque, amirs, sharifs, qadis, theologians, and all the other classes of the people, until the place was filled to overflowing, and there they spent the Thursday night in prayers and litanies. After the dawn prayer next morning they all went out together on foot, holding Korans in their hands, and the amirs barefooted. The procession was joined by the entire population of the town, men and women, small and large; the Jews came with their Book of the Law and the Christians with their Gospel, all of them with their women and children. The whole concourse, weeping and supplicating and seeking the favour of God through His Books and His Prophets, made their way to the Mosque of the Footprints, and there they remained in supplication and invocation until near midday. They then returned to the city and held the Friday service, and God lightened their affliction; for the number of deaths in a single day at Damascus did not attain two thousand, while in Cairo and Old Cairo it reached the figure of twenty-four thousand a day.

Hugo Grotius, selections from *On the Law of War and Peace*

Hugo Grotius (1583–1645 CE) was a Dutch jurist and legal scholar. Grotius's 1625 treatise, On the Law of War and Peace, *is considered to be the founding and most comprehensive early work on modern international law. In it, Grotius surveyed classical history and the Bible and argued that natural law established rules of conduct for nations and individuals, thereby constituting a legal foundation for international cooperation. Grotius studied law at the University of Leiden and wrote numerous theological and legal works, such as* The Free Seas (1604), *which advocated the unrestricted navigation of the seas for free trade.*

Source: *Hugo Grotius,* On the Law of War and Peace *(1625).*

Focus Questions:
1. According to Grotius, does the principle of natural right depend on God and religion?
2. What does Grotius contend about natural law when he observes Aristotle's statement "that some things are no sooner named, than we discover their evil nature"?

BOOK I

Chapter 1: ON WAR AND RIGHT

X. Natural right is the dictate of right reason, shewing the moral turpitude, or moral necessity, of any act from its agreement or disagreement with a rational nature, and consequently that such an act is either forbidden or commanded by God, the author of nature. The actions, upon which such a dictate is given, are either binding or unlawful in themselves, and therefore necessarily understood to be commanded or forbidden by God. This mark distinguishes natural right, not only from human law, but from the law, which God himself has been pleased to reveal, called, by some, the voluntary divine right, which does not command or forbid things in themselves either binding or unlawful, but makes them unlawful by its prohibition, and binding by its command. But, to understand natural right, we must observe that some things are said to belong to that right, not properly, but, as the schoolmen say, by way of accommodation. These are not repugnant to natural right, as we have already observed that those things are called JUST, in which there is no injustice. Some times also, by a wrong use of the word, those things which reason shews to be proper, or better than things of an opposite kind, although not binding, are said to belong to natural right.

We must farther remark, that natural right relates not only to those things that exist independent of the human will, but to many things, which necessarily follow the exercise of that will. Thus property, as now in use, was at first a creature of the human will. But, after it was established, one man was prohibited by the law of nature from seizing the property of another against his will. Wherefore, Paulus the Lawyer said, that theft is expressly forbidden by the law of nature. Ulpian condemns it as infamous in its own nature; to whose authority that of Euripides may be added, as may be seen in the verse of Helena:

"For God himself hates violence, and will not have us to grow rich by rapine, but by lawful gains. That abundance, which is the fruit of unrighteousness, is an abomination. The air is common to men, the earth also where every man, in the ample enjoyment of his possession, must refrain from doing violence or injury to that of another."

Now the Law of Nature is so unalterable, that it cannot be changed even by God himself. For although the power of God is infinite, yet there are some things, to which it does not extend. Because the things so expressed would have no true meaning, but imply a contradiction. Thus two and two must make four, nor is it possible to be otherwise; nor, again, can what is really evil not be evil. And this is Aristotle's meaning, when he says, that some things are no sooner named, than we discover their evil nature. For as the substance of things in their nature and existence depends upon nothing but themselves; so there are qualities inseparably connected with their being and essence. Of this kind is the evil of certain actions, compared with the nature of a reasonable being. Therefore God himself suffers his actions to be judged by this rule, as may be seen in the xviiith chap. of Gen. 25. Isa. v. 3. Ezek. xviii. 25. Jer. ii. 9. Mich. vi. 2. From. ii. 6., iii. 6. Yet it sometimes happens that, in those cases, which are decided by the law of nature, the undiscerning are imposed upon by an appearance of change. Whereas in reality there is no change in the unalterable law of nature, but only in the things appointed by it, and which are liable to variation. For example, if a creditor forgive me the debt, which I owe him, I am no longer bound to pay it, not because the law of nature has ceased to command the payment of a just debt, but because my debt, by a release, has ceased to be a debt. On this topic, Arrian in Epictetus argues rightly, that the borrowing of money is not the only requisite to make a debt, but there must be the additional circumstance of the loan remaining undischarged. Thus if God should command the life, or property of any one to be taken away, the act would not authorise murder or robbery, words which always include a crime. But that cannot be murder or robbery, which is done by the express command of Him, who is the sovereign Lord of our lives and of all things. There are also some things allowed by the law of nature, not absolutely, but according to a certain state of affairs. Thus, by the law of nature, before property was introduced, every one had a right to the use of whatever he found unoccupied; and, before laws were enacted, to avenge his personal injuries by force.

XI. The distinction found in the books of the Roman Law, assigning one unchangeable right to brutes in common with man, which in a more limited sense they call the law of nature, and appropriating another to men, which they frequently call the Law of Nations, is scarcely of any real use. For no beings, except those that can form general maxims, are capable of possessing a right, which Hesiod has placed in a clear point of view, observing "that the supreme Being has appointed laws for men; but permitted wild beasts, fishes, and birds to devour each other for food." For they have nothing like justice, the best gift, bestowed upon men.

Cicero, in his first book of offices, says, we do not talk of the justice of horses or lions. In conformity to which, Plutarch, in the life of Cato the elder, observes, that we are formed by nature to use law and justice towards men only. In addition to the above, Lactantius may be cited, who, in his fifth book, says that in all animals devoid of reason we see a natural bias of self-love. For they hurt others to benefit themselves; because they do not know the evil of doing willful hurt. But it is not so with man, who, possessing the knowledge of good and evil, refrains, even with inconvenience to himself, from doing hurt. Polybius, relating the manner in which men first entered into society, concludes, that the injuries done to parents or benefactors inevitably provoke the indignation of mankind, giving an additional reason, that as understanding and reflection form the great difference between men and other animals, it is evident they cannot transgress the bounds of that difference like other animals, without exciting universal abhorrence of their conduct. But if ever justice is attributed to brutes, it is done improperly, from some shadow and trace of reason they may possess. But it is not material to the nature of right, whether the actions appointed by the law of nature, such as the care of our offspring, are common to us with other animals or not, or, like the worship of God, are peculiar to man.

XII. The existence of the Law of Nature is proved by two kinds of argument, a priori, and a posteriori, the former a more abstruse, and the latter a more popular method of proof. We are said to reason a priori, when we show the agreement or disagreement of any thing with a reasonable and social nature; but a posteriori, when without absolute proof, but only upon probability, any thing is inferred to accord with the law of nature, because it is received as such among all, or at least the more civilized nations. For a general effect can only arise from a general cause. Now scarce any other cause can be assigned for so general an opinion, but the common sense, as it is called, of mankind. There is a sentence of Hesiod that has been much praised, that opinions which have prevailed amongst many nations, must have some foundation. Heraclitus, establishing common reason as the best criterion of truth, says, those things are certain which generally appear so. Among other authorities, we may quote Aristotle, who says it is a strong proof in our favour, when all appear to agree with what we say, and Cicero maintains that the consent of all nations in any case is to be admitted for the law of nature. Seneca is of the same opinion, any thing, says he, appearing the same to all men is a proof of its truth. Quintilian says, we hold those things to be true, in which all men agree. We have called them the more civilized nations, and not without reason. For, as Porphyry well observes, some nations are so strange that no fair judgment of human nature can be formed from them, for it would be erroneous. Andronicus, the Rhodian says, that with men of a right and sound understanding, natural justice is unchangeable. Nor does it alter the case, though men of disordered and perverted minds think otherwise. For he who should deny that honey is sweet, because it appears not so to men of a distempered taste, would be wrong. Plutarch too agrees entirely with what has been said, as appears from a passage in his life of Pompey, affirming that man neither was, nor is, by nature, a wild unsociable creature. But it is the corruption of his nature which makes him so: yet by acquiring new habits, by changing his place, and way of living, he may be reclaimed to his original gentleness. Aristotle, taking a description of man from his peculiar qualities, makes him an animal of a gentle nature, and in another part of his works, he observes, that in considering the nature of man, we are to take our likeness from nature in its pure, and not in its corrupt state.

Niccolo Machiavelli, Excerpts from *The Prince*

Niccolo Machiavelli (1469–1527 CE) was a Florentine political thinker, historian, and statesman. Machiavelli served as a state official and diplomat and wrote several works on politics and history. He is best known for his 1513 work The Prince. *First published posthumously in 1532,* The Prince *provides advice on how to maintain political power, and stands out for advocating behavior without regard to moral principles. Machiavelli's work is famous—or infamous—for promoting the idea that the ends justify the means. The cunning, shrewd advice in* The Prince *was written against the backdrop of intense political intrigue and conflict.*

Source: *Niccolo Machiavelli,* The Prince *(1532), trans. by W. K. Marriott, 1905.*

Focus Questions:
1. In Chapter V, does Machiavelli consider a state that has known liberty to have any special value to be respected?
2. In Chapter XVIII, what is the most important goal that a ruler should have, and how does Machiavelli justify craftiness and deceit?

CHAPTER V

Concerning the Way to Govern Cities or Principalities Which Lived Under Their Own Laws Before They Were Annexed

Whenever those states which have been acquired as stated have been accustomed to live under their own laws and in freedom, there are three courses for those who wish to hold them: the first is to ruin them, the next is to reside there in person, the third is to permit them to live under their own laws, drawing a tribute, and establishing within it an oligarchy which will keep it friendly to you. Because such a government, being created by the prince, knows that it cannot stand without his friendship and interest, and does its utmost to support him; and therefore he who would keep a city accustomed to freedom will hold it more easily by the means of its own citizens than in any other way.

There are, for example, the Spartans and the Romans. The Spartans held Athens and Thebes, establishing there an oligarchy, nevertheless they lost them. The Romans, in order to hold Capua, Carthage, and Numantia, dismantled them, and did not lose them. They wished to hold Greece as the Spartans held it, making it free and permitting its laws, and did not succeed. So to hold it they were compelled to dismantle many cities in the country, for in truth there is no safe way to retain them otherwise than by ruining them. And he who becomes master of a city accustomed to freedom and does not destroy it, may expect to be destroyed by it, for in rebellion it has always the watch-word of liberty and its ancient privileges as a rallying point, which neither time nor benefits will ever cause it to forget. And what ever you may do or provide against, they never forget that name or their privileges unless they are disunited or dispersed but at every chance they immediately rally to them, as Pisa after the hundred years she had been held in bondage by the Florentines.

But when cities or countries are accustomed to live under a prince, and his family is exterminated, they, being on the one hand accustomed to obey and on the other hand not having the old prince, cannot agree in making one from amongst themselves, and they do not know how to govern themselves. For this reason they are very slow to take up arms, and a prince can gain them to himself and secure them much more easily. But in republics there is more vitality, greater hatred, and more desire for vengeance, which will never permit them to allow the memory of their former liberty to rest; so that the safest way is to destroy them or to reside there.

CHAPTER XVIII

Concerning the Way in Which Princes Should Keep Faith

Every one admits how praiseworthy it is in a prince to keep faith, and to live with integrity and not with craft. Nevertheless our experience has been that those princes who have done great things have held good faith of little account, and have known how to circumvent the intellect of men by craft, and in the end have overcome those who have relied on their word. You must know there are two ways of contesting, the one by the law, the other by force; the first method is proper to men, the second to beasts; but because the first is frequently not sufficient, it is necessary to have recourse to the second. Therefore it is necessary for a prince to understand how to avail himself of the beast and the man. This has been figuratively taught to princes by ancient writers, who describe how Achilles and many other princes of old were given to the Centaur Chiron to nurse, who brought them up in his discipline; which means solely that, as they had for a teacher one who was half beast and half man, so it is necessary for a prince to know how to make use of both natures, and that one without the other is not durable. A prince, therefore, being compelled knowingly to adopt the beast, ought to choose the fox and the lion; because the lion cannot defend himself against snares and the fox cannot defend himself against wolves. Therefore, it is necessary to be a fox to discover the snares and a lion to terrify the wolves. Those who rely simply on the lion do not understand what they are about. Therefore a wise lord cannot, nor ought he to, keep faith when such observance may be turned against him, and when the reasons that caused him to pledge it exist no longer. If men were entirely good this precept would not hold, but because they are bad, and will not keep faith with you, you too are not bound to observe it with them. Nor will there ever be wanting to a prince legitimate reasons to excuse this nonobservance. Of this endless modern examples could be given, showing how many treaties and engagements have been made void and of no effect through the faithlessness of princes; and he who has known best how to employ the fox has succeeded best.

But it is necessary to know well how to disguise this characteristic, and to be a great pretender and dissembler; and men are so simple, and so subject to present necessities, that he who seeks to deceive will always find someone who will allow himself to be deceived. One recent example I cannot pass over in silence. Alexander VI did nothing else but deceive men, nor ever thought of doing otherwise, and he always found victims; for there never was a man who had greater power in asserting, or who with greater oaths would affirm a thing, yet would observe it less; nevertheless his deceits always succeeded according to his wishes, because he well understood this side of mankind.

Therefore it is unnecessary for a prince to have all the good qualities I have enumerated, but it is very necessary to appear to have them. And I shall dare to say this also, that to have them and always to observe them is injurious, and that to appear to have them is useful; to appear merciful, faithful, humane, religious, upright, and to be so, but with a mind so framed that should you require not to be so, you may be able and know how to change to the opposite.

And you have to understand this, that a prince, especially a new one, cannot observe all those things for which men are esteemed, being often forced, in order to maintain the state, to act contrary to faith, friendship, humanity, and religion. Therefore it is necessary for him to have a mind ready to turn itself accordingly as the winds and variations of fortune force it, yet, as I have said above, not to diverge from the good if he can avoid doing so, but, if compelled, then to know how to set about it.

For this reason a prince ought to take care that he never lets anything slip from his lips that is not replete with the above-named five qualities, that he may appear to him who sees and hears him altogether merciful, faithful, humane, upright, and religious. There is nothing more necessary to appear to have than this last quality, inasmuch as men judge generally more by the eye than by the hand, because it belongs to everybody to see you, to few to come in touch with you. Every one sees what you appear to be, few really know what you are, and those few dare not oppose themselves to the opinion of the many, who have the majesty of the state to defend them; and in the actions of all men, and especially of princes, which it is not prudent to challenge, one judges by the result.

For that reason, let a prince have the credit of conquering and holding his state, the means will always be considered honest, and he will be praised by everybody because the vulgar are always taken by what a thing seems to be and by what comes of it; and in the world there are only the vulgar, for the few find a place there only when the many have no ground to rest on.

One prince[1] of the present time, whom it is not well to name, never preaches anything else but peace and good faith, and to both he is most hostile, and either, if he had kept it, would have deprived him of reputation and kingdom many a time.

Thomas Aquinas, *Summa Theologica*, "Of Human Law"

Thomas Aquinas (1225–1274 CE) was a Catholic theologian and philosopher. Born to a noble family, Aquinas excelled in his studies in Italy and Paris. Though his family resisted his decision to enter the Dominican monastic order, Aquinas's writings marked the pinnacle of Medieval Scholastic thought. His most famous work, Summa Theologica *(Summary of Theology), though unfinished, covered a range of topics—such as natural law and the nature and existence of God—and aimed to reconcile reason with faith, and the ideas of Aristotle with Christian Scriptures. Pope John XXII canonized Aquinas in 1323, and in the sixteenth century the Catholic Church declared Aquinas's ideas to be official doctrine.*

Source: *Fathers of the English Dominican Province, trans., Thomas Aquinas,* Summa Theologica *(New York Benziger Bros. 1947–48).*

Focus Questions:
1. Would you describe Aquinas' Scholastic form of writing as "theoretical" or "applied"?
2. What is Aquinas's purpose in discussing natural law?

QUESTION #95: OF HUMAN LAW

Article 4:

Whether Isidore's division of human laws is appropriate?

Objection 1. It would seem that Isidore wrongly divided human statutes or human law (Etym. v, 4, seqq.). For under this law he includes the "law of nations," so called, because, as he says, "nearly all nations use it." But as he says, "natural law is that which is common to all nations." Therefore the law of nations is not contained under positive human law, but rather under natural law.

Objection 2. Further, those laws which have the same force, seem to differ not formally but only materially. But "statutes, decrees of the commonalty, senatorial decrees," and the like which he mentions (Etym. v, 9), all have the same force. Therefore they do not differ, except materially. But art takes no notice of such a distinction: since it may go on to infinity. Therefore this division of human laws is not appropriate.

---

[1] Maximilian I, Holy Roman Emperor.

Objection 3. Further, just as, in the state, there are princes, priests and soldiers, so are there other human offices. Therefore it seems that, as this division includes "military law," and "public law," referring to priests and magistrates; so also it should include other laws pertaining to other offices of the state.

Objection 4. Further, those things that are accidental should be passed over. But it is accidental to law that it be framed by this or that man. Therefore it is unreasonable to divide laws according to the names of lawgivers, so that one be called the "Cornelian" law, another the "Falcidian" law, etc.

On the contrary, The authority of Isidore (Objection 1) suffices.

I answer that, A thing can of itself be divided in respect of something contained in the notion of that thing. Thus a soul either rational or irrational is contained in the notion of animal: and therefore animal is divided properly and of itself in respect of its being rational or irrational; but not in the point of its being white or black, which are entirely beside the notion of animal. Now, in the notion of human law, many things are contained, in respect of any of which human law can be divided properly and of itself. For in the first place it belongs to the notion of human law, to be derived from the law of nature, as explained above (2). In this respect positive law is divided into the "law of nations" and "civil law," according to the two ways in which something may be derived from the law of nature, as stated above (2). Because, to the law of nations belong those things which are derived from the law of nature, as conclusions from premises, e.g., just buyings and sellings, and the like, without which men cannot live together, which is a point of the law of nature, since man is by nature a social animal, as is proved in Polit. i, 2. But those things which are derived from the law of nature by way of particular determination, belong to the civil law, according as each state decides on what is best for itself.

Secondly, it belongs to the notion of human law, to be ordained to the common good of the state. In this respect human law may be divided according to the different kinds of men who work in a special way for the common good: e.g., priests, by praying to God for the people; princes, by governing the people; soldiers, by fighting for the safety of the people. Wherefore certain special kinds of law are adapted to these men.

Thirdly, it belongs to the notion of human law, to be framed by that one who governs the community of the state, as shown above (90, 3). In this respect, there are various human laws according to the various forms of government. Of these, according to the Philosopher (Polit. iii, 10) one is "monarchy," i.e., when the state is governed by one; and then we have "Royal Ordinances." Another form is "aristocracy," i.e., government by the best men or men of highest rank; and then we have the "Authoritative legal opinions" [Responsa Prudentum] and "Decrees of the Senate" [Senatus consulta]. Another form is "oligarchy," i.e., government by a few rich and powerful men; and then we have "Praetorian," also called "Honorary," law. Another form of government is that of the people, which is called "democracy," and there we have "Decrees of the commonalty" [Plebiscita]. There is also tyrannical government, which is altogether corrupt, which, therefore, has no corresponding law. Finally, there is a form of government made up of all these, and which is the best: and in this respect we have law sanctioned by the "Lords and Commons," as stated by Isidore (Etym. v, 4, seqq.).

Fourthly, it belongs to the notion of human law to direct human actions. In this respect, according to the various matters of which the law treats, there are various kinds of laws, which are sometimes named after their authors: thus we have the "Lex Julia" about adultery, the "Lex Cornelia" concerning assassins, and so on, differentiated in this way, not on account of the authors, but on account of the matters to which they refer.

Reply to Objection 1. The law of nations is indeed, in some way, natural to man, in so far as he is a reasonable being, because it is derived from the natural law by way of a conclusion that is not very remote from its premises. Wherefore men easily agreed thereto. Nevertheless it is distinct from the natural law, especially it is distinct from the natural law which is common to all animals.

The Replies to the other Objections are evident from what has been said.

Chapter 14

Islamic Empires

Excerpts from the Biography of Emperor Akbar of India

Jalaluddin Muhammad Akbar, also known as Akbar the Great (1542–1605), was the greatest of the Moghul Emperors of India. Not only was he a successful military leader, defeating both the Aghans who had temporarily unseated his father from his throne and, at the Battle of Panipat, a coalition of Hindu princes, but he initiated the collection and compilation of art and literature from many regions of the world. Above all, he was a religious moderate who respected Hindu temples, married a Rajput princess, and attempted to found his own syncretic religion, as well as holding debates between holy men of many different religions. He commissioned a biography, from which the following excerpts are taken.

Source: *Biography of Emperor Akbar*, A'in Akbari, *trans. by H. Blochmann, 1927.*

Focus Questions:
1. What aspects of the harem and the kitchen are emphasized in the documents? How might a critic of Akbar's have interpreted these passages? (Note that he had a reputation for loving women and alcohol.)
2. What do the excerpts tell us about Akbar's daily life? How easy was the job of running a large empire as an absolute monarch?
3. What key elements of Akbar's religious beliefs do the passages reveal? How might these have been received by devout Muslims? Hindus? Why was an image of holiness important to Akbar? Can we tell if it is more than just an image?

THE IMPERIAL HAREM

His Majesty is a great friend of good order and propriety in business. Through order, the world becomes a meadow of truth and reality; and that which is but external, receives through it a spiritual meaning. For this reason, the large number of women—a vexatious question even for great statesmen—furnished his Majesty with an opportunity to display his wisdom, and to rise from the low level of worldly dependence to the eminence of perfect freedom. The imperial palace and household are therefore in the best order.

His majesty forms matrimonial alliances with princes of Hindustan, and of other countries; and secures by these ties of harmony the peace of the world.

As the sovereign, by the light of his Wisdom, has raised fit persons from the dust of obscurity, and appointed them to various offices, so does he also elevate faithful persons to the several ranks in the service of the seraglio. Short-sighted men think of impure gold, which will gradually turn into pure gold; but the farsighted know that his Majesty understands how to use elixirs and chemical processes. Any kind of growth will alter the constitution of a body; copper and iron will turn to gold, and tin and lead to silver; hence it is no matter of astonishment if an excellent being changes the worthless into men. "The saying of the wise is true that the eye of the exalted is the elixir for producing goodness." Such also are the results flowing from the love of order of his Majesty, from his wisdom, insight, regard to rank, his respect for others, his activity, his patience. Even when he is angry, he does not deviate from the right path; he looks at everything with kindly feelings, weighs rumours well, and is free from all prejudice; he considers it a great blessing to have the good wishes of the people, and does not allow the intoxicating pleasures of this world to overpower his calm judgment.

His Majesty has made a large enclosure with fine buildings inside, where he reposes. Though there are more than five thousand women, he has given to each a separate apartment. He has also divided them into sections, and keeps them attentive to their duties. Several chaste women have been appointed as daroghas, and superintendents over each section, and one has been selected for the duties of writer. Thus, as in the imperial offices, everything is here also in proper order. The salaries are sufficiently liberal. Not counting the presents, which his Majesty most generously bestows, the women of the highest rank receive from 1610 to 1028 Rs. per mensem. Some of the servants have from 51 to 20, others from 40 to 2 Rs. Attached to the private audience hall of the palace is a clever and zealous writer, who superintends the expenditure of the Harem, and keeps an account of the cash and the stores. If a woman wants anything, within the limit of her salary, she applies to one of the Tahwi-lda-rs (cash-keepers) of the seraglio. The Tahwi-lda-r then sends a memorandum to the writer, who checks it, when the General Treasurer makes the payment in cash, as for claims of this nature no cheques are given.

The writer also makes out an estimate of the annual expenditure, writes out summarily a receipt, which is countersigned by the ministers of the state. It is then stamped with a peculiar imperial seal, which is only used in grants connected with the Harem, when the receipt becomes payable. The money itself is paid by the cash-keeper of the General Treasury to the General Tahwi-lda-r, who on the order of the writer of the Harem, hands it over to the several Sub-Tahwi-lda-rs for distribution among the servants of the seraglio. All moneys are reckoned in their salaries at the current rate.

The inside of the Harem im guarded by sober and active women; the most trustworthy of them are placed about the apartments of his Majesty. Outside the enclosure the eunuchs are placed; and at a proper distance, there is a guard of faithful RAjpUts, beyond whom are the porters of the gates. Besides, on all four sides, there are guards of Nobles, Ahadi-s, and other troops, according to their ranks.

Whenever Begams, or the wives of nobles, or other women of chaste character, desire to be presented, they first notify their wish to the servants of the seraglio, and wait for a reply. From thence they send their request to the officers of the palace, after which those who are eligible are permitted to enter the Harem. Some women of rank, obtain permission to remain there for a whole month.

Notwithstanding the great number of faithful guards, his Majesty does not dispense with his own vigilance, but keeps the whole in proper order.

THE IMPERIAL KITCHEN

His Majesty even extends his attention to this department, and has given many wise regulations for it; nor can a reason be given why he should not do so, as the equilibrium of man's nature, the strength of the body, the capability of receiving external and internal blessings, and the acquisition of Worldly and religious advantages, depend ultimately on proper care being shown for appropriate food. This knowledge distinguishes man from beasts, with whom, as far as mere eating is concerned, he stands upon the same level. If his Majesty did not possess so lofty a mind, so comprehensive an understanding, so universal a kindness, he would have chosen the path of solitude, and given up sleep and food altogether; and even now, when he has taken upon himself the temporal and spiritual leadership of the people, the question, "What dinner has been prepared to-day?" never passes over his tongue. In the course of twenty-four hours his Majesty eats but Once, and leaves off before he is fully satisfied; neither is there any fixed time for this meal, but the servants have always things so far ready, that in the space of an hour, after the order has been given, a hundred dishes are served up. The food allowed to the women of the seraglio commences to be taken from the kitchen in the morning, and goes on till night.

Trustworthy and experienced people are appointed to this department; and all good servants attached to the court, are resolved to perform well whatever service they have undertaken. Their head is assisted by the Prime Minister himself. His Majesty has entrusted to the latter the affairs of the state, but especially this important department. Notwithstanding all this, his Majesty is not unmindful of the conduct of the servants. He appoints a zealous and sincere man as Mi-r Baka-wal, or Master of the Kitchen, upon whose insight the success of the department depends, and gives him several upright persons as assistants. There are also treasurers for the cash and the stores, several tasters, and a clever writer. Cooks from all countries prepare a great variety of dishes of all kinds of grains, greens, meats; also oily, sweet, and spicy dishes. Every day such dishes are prepared as the nobles can scarcely command at their feasts, from which you may infer how exquisite the dishes are which are prepared for his Majesty.

In the beginning of the year the Sub-treasurers make out an animal estimate, and receive the amount; the money bags and the door of the store-house being sealed with the seals of the Mi-r Baka-wal and the writer; and every month a correct statement of the daily expenditure is drawn up, the receipt for which is sealed by the same two officers, when it is entered under the head of the expenditure. At the beginning of every quarter, the Di-wa-n-i buyu-ta-t and the Mi-r Baka-wal, collect whatever they think will be necessary; e.g. Sukhda-s rice from Bhara-ji, Dewzi-ra rice from Gwa-lia-r, Jinjin rice from Ra-jóri- and Ni-mlah, ghi- from Hisa-r Fi-ru-za; ducks, water-fowls, and certain vegetables from Kashmi-r. Patterns are always kept. The sheep, goats, berberies, fowls, ducks, etc., are fattened by the cooks; fowls are never kept less than a month. The slaughter-house is without the city or the camp, in the neighbourhood of rivers and tanks, where the meat is washed, when it is sent to the kitchen in sacks sealed by the cooks. There it is again washed, and thrown into the pots. The water-carriers pour the water out of their leather bags into earthen vessels, the mouths of which are covered with pieces of cloth, and sealed up; and the water is left to settle before it is used. A place is also told off as a kitchen garden, that there may be a continual supply of fresh greens. The Mi-r Baka-wal and the writer determine the price of every eatable, which becomes a fixed rule; and they sign the day-book, the estimates, the receipts for transfers, the list of wages of the servants, etc., and watch every transaction. Bad characters, idle talkers, unknown persons are never employed; no one is entertained without a personal security, nor is personal acquaintance sufficient.

The victuals are served up in dishes of gold and silver, stone and earthenware; some of the dishes being in charge of each of the Sub-Baka-wals. During the time of cooking, and when the victuals are taken out, an awning is spread, and lookers-on kept away. The cooks tuck up their sleeves, and the hems of their garments, and hold their hands before their mouths and noses when the food is taken out; the cook and the Baka-wal taste it, after which it is tasted by the Mi-r Baka-wal, and then put into the dishes. The gold and silver dishes are tied up in red cloths, and those of copper and china in white ones. The Mi-r Baka-wal attaches his seal, and writes on it the names of the contents, whilst the clerk of the pantry writes out on a sheet of paper a list of all vessels and dishes, which he sends inside, with the seal of the Mi-r Baka-wal, that none of the dishes may be changed. The dishes are carried by the Baka-wals, the cooks, and the other servants, and macebearers precede and follow, to prevent people from approaching them. The servants of the pantry send at the same time, in bags containing the seal of the Baka-wal, various kinds of bread, saucers of curds piled up, and small stands containing plates of pickles, fresh ginger, limes, and various greens. The servants of the palace again taste the food, spread the table cloth on the ground, and arrange the dishes; and when after some time his Majesty commences to dine, the table servants sit opposite him in attendance; first, the share of the derwishes is put apart, when his Majesty commences with milk or curds. After he has dined, he prostrates himself in prayer. The Mi-r Baka-wal is always in attendance. The dishes are taken away according to the above list. Some victuals are also kept half ready, should they be called for.

The copper utensils are tinned twice a month; those of the princes, etc., once; whatever is broken is given to the braziers, who make new ones.

THE MANNER IN WHICH HIS MAJESTY SPENDS HIS TIME

The success of the three branches of the government, and the fulfilment of the wishes of the subjects, whether great or small, depend upon the manner in which a king spends his time. The care with which His Majesty guards over his motives, and watches over his emotions, bears on its face the sign of the Infinite, and the stamp of immortality; and though thousands of important matters occupy, at one and the same time, his attention, they do not stir up the rubbish of confusion in the temple of his mind, nor do they allow the dust of dismay to settle on the vigour of his mental powers, or the habitual earnestness with which His Majesty contemplates the charms of God's world. His anxiety to do the will of the Creator is ever increasing; and thus his insight and wisdom are ever deepening. From his practical knowledge, and capacity for everything excellent, he can sound men of experience, though rarely casting a glance on his own ever extending excellence. He listens to great and small, expecting that a good thought, or the relation of a noble deed, may kindle in his mind a new lamp of wisdom, though ages have passed without his having found a really great man. Impartial statesmen, on seeing the sagacity of His Majesty, blotted out the book of their own wisdom, and commenced a new leaf. But with the magnanimity which distinguishes him, and with his wonted zeal, he continues his search for superior men, and finds a reward in the care with which he selects such as are fit for his society.

Although surrounded by every external pomp and display, and by every inducement to lead a life of luxury and ease, he does not allow his desires, or his wrath, to renounce allegiance to Wisdom, his sovereign—how much less would he permit them to lead him to a bad deed! Even the telling of stories, which ordinary people use as a means of lulling themselves into sleep, serves to keep His Majesty awake.

Ardently feeling after God, and searching for truth, His Majesty exercises upon himself both inward and outward austerities, though he occasionally joins public worship, in order to hush the slandering tongues of the bigots of the present age. But the great object of his life is the acquisition of that sound morality, the sublime loftiness of which captivates the hearts of thinking sages, and silences the taunts of zealots and sectarians.

Knowing the value of a lifetime, he never wastes his time, nor does he omit any necessary duty, so that in the light of his upright intentions, every action of his life may be considered as an adoration of God.

It is beyond my power to describe in adequate terms His Majesty's devotions. He passes every moment of his life in self-examination or in adoration of God. He especially does so at the time, when morning spreads her azure silk, and scatters abroad her young, golden beams; and at noon, when the light of the world-illuminating sun embraces the universe, and thus becomes a source of joy for all men; in the evening when that fountain of light withdraws from the eyes of mortal man, to the bewildering grief of all who are friends of light; and lastly at midnight, when that great cause of life turns again to ascend, and to bring the news of renewed cheerfulness to all who, in the melancholy of the night, are stricken with sorrow. All these grand mysteries are in honor of God, and in adoration of the Creator of the world; and if dark-minded, ignorant men cannot comprehend their signification, who is to be blamed, and whose loss is it? Indeed, every man acknowledges that we owe gratitude and reverence to our benefactors; and hence it is incumbent on us, though our strength may fail, to show gratitude for the blessings we receive from the sun, the light of all lights, and to enumerate the benefits which he bestows. This is essentially the duty of kings, upon whom, according to the opinion of the wise, this sovereign of the heavens sheds an immediate light. And this is the very motive which actuates His Majesty to venerate fire and reverence lamps.

But why should I speak of the mysterious blessings of the sun, or of the transfer of his greater light to lamps? Should I not rather dwell on the perverseness of those weak-minded zealots, who, with much concern, talk of His Majesty's religion as of a deification of the Sun, and the introduction of fire-worship? But I shall dismiss them with a smile.

The compassionate heart of His Majesty finds no pleasure in cruelties, or in causing sorrow to others; he is ever sparing of the lives of his subjects, wishing to bestow happiness upon all.

His Majesty abstains much from flesh, so that whole months pass away without his touching any animal food, which, though prized by most, is nothing thought of by the sage. His august nature cares but little for the pleasures of the world. In the Course of twenty-four hours he never makes more than one meal. He takes a delight in spending his time in performing whatever is neceseary and proper. He takes a little repose in the evening, and again for a short time in the morning; but his sleep looks more like waking.

His Majesty is accustomed to spend the hours of the night profitably; to the private audience hall are then admitted eloquent philosophers and virtuous SUfIs, who are seated according to their rank and entertain His Majesty with wise discourses. On such occasions His Majesty fathoms them, and tries them on the touch-stone of knowledge. Or the object of an ancient institution is disclosed, or new thoughts are hailed with delight. Here young men of talent learn to revere and adore His Majesty, and experience the happiness of having their wishes fulffilled, whilst old men of impartial judgment see themselves on the expanse of sorrow, finding that they have to pass through a new course of instruction.

Abu'l-Fazl Allami's Ain-i-Akbari

Abu'l-Fazl Allami's Ain-i-Akbari is a chronicle of the Mughal Emperor Akbar's Court (1556–1605). Originally written in Persian, the work provides much insight into the emperor's reign and the author presents the reader with an ideal of royalty embodied by his patron, the Emperor Akbar.

Source: *H. Blochmann, trans., Abu'l-Fazl 'Allami, A'in Akbari (3 vols.), (Calcutta, 1927).*

> **Focus Questions:**
> 1. What portrait of Akbar emerges from this account?
> 2. What does the description of the imperial household say about the Mughal state?

BOOK ONE, CHAPTER ONE

The Imperial Household

He [Akbar] is a man of high understanding and noble aspirations who, without the help of others, recognizes a ray of the Divine power in the smallest things of the world; who shapes his inward and outward character accordingly, and shows due respect to himself and to others. He who does not possess these qualifications, ought not to engage in the struggle of the world, but observe a peaceable conduct. If the former be given to retirement, he will cultivate noble virtues; and if his position be a dependent one, he will put his whole heart in the management of his affairs, and lead a life free from distressing cares.

True greatness, in spiritual and in worldly matters, does not shrink from the minutiae of business, but regards their performance as an act of Divine worship.

If he cannot perform every thing himself, he ought to select, guided by insight and practical wisdom, one or two men of sagacity and understanding, of liberal views in religious matters, possessing diligence and a knowledge of the human heart, and be guided by their advice.

The wise esteem him not a king who confines his attention to great matters only, although some impartial judges excuse a king that does so, because avaricious sycophants who endeavor by cunning to obtain the position of the virtuous, often remind him of the difference of ranks, and succeed in lulling asleep such kings as are fond of external greatness, their only object being to make a trade of the revenues of the country, and to promote their own interests. But good princes make no difference between great and small matters; they take, with the assistance of God, the burden of this world and the responsibility of the world to come on the shoulder of resolution, and are yet free and independent, as is the case with the king of our time. In his wisdom, he makes himself acquainted with the successful working of every department, which, although former monarchs have thought it derogatory to their greatness, is yet the first step towards the establishment of a good government. For every branch he has made proper regulations, and he sees in the performance of his duty a means of obtaining God's favor.

The success of this vast undertaking depends upon two things; first, wisdom and insight, to call into existence suitable regulations; secondly, a watchful eye, to see them carried out by men of integrity and diligence.

Although many servants of the household receive their salaries on the list of the army, there was paid for the household in the thirty-ninth year of the Divine era, the sum of 309,186,795 dams [Mughal currency]. The expenses on this account, as also the revenues, are daily increasing. There are more than one hundred offices and workshops, each resembling a city, or rather a little kingdom; and by the unremitting attention of his Majesty, they are all conducted with regularity, and are constantly increasing, their improvement being accompanied by additional care and supervision on the part of his Majesty.

Some of the regulations I shall transmit, as a present, to future enquirers, and thus kindle in others the lamp of wisdom and energy.

As regards those regulations which are of a general nature, and which from their subject matter, belong to each of the three divisions of the work, I have put them among the regulations of the Household.

Sunni versus Shi'ite: Letter from Selim I to Ismail I

This selection is a letter from the Ottoman ruler, Selim I to his Persian rival, Isma'il I, leader of the Shi'ite Safavid state. Ismail had entered Ottoman territory and had demanded that Ottoman subjects accept Shi'ism. This response by Selim I, a committed Sunni, reveals the divisive competition among Islamic religious sects and political leaders. Selim I won the battle of Chaldiran in 1514 and protected his territory from Shi'ite encroachment.

Source: C. T. Foster and F. H. Blackburne Daniell, "Sunni versus Shi'ite," in The Life and Letters of Ogier Ghiselin de Busbecq, vol. 1 (London: Hakluyt Society, 1881), pp. 152–156; 219–221.

Focus Questions:
1. What is the purpose of this warning to Amir Isma'il from Sultan Selim I?
2. How does Selim use the Qur'an to justify his actions?
3. Aren't Sunnis and Shi'ites both Muslims? What was the reason for this confrontation?
4. Why was Selim I so sure that he embodied the "true religion" and that this justified his military threat?
5. What is the purpose of this warning to Amir Isma'il from Sultan Selim I?
6. How does Selim use the Qur'an to justify his actions?

The Supreme Being who is at once the sovereign arbiter of the destinies of men and the source of all light and knowledge, declares in the *Qur'an* that the true faith is that of the Muslims, and that whoever professes another religion, far from being hearkened to and saved, will on the contrary be cast out among the rejected on the great day of the Last Judgment; He says further, this God of truth, that His designs and decrees are unalterable, that all human acts are perforce reported to Him, and that he who abandons the good way will be condemned to hell-fire and eternal torments. Place yourself, O Prince, among the true believers, those who walk in the path of salvation, and who turn aside with care from vice and infidelity. May the purest and holiest blessings be upon Muhammad, the master of the two worlds, the prince of prophets, as well as upon his descendants and all who follow his Law!

I, sovereign chief of the Ottomans, master of the heroes of the age...I, the exterminator of idolaters, destroyer of the enemies of the true faith, the terror of the tyrants and pharaohs of the age; I, before whom proud and unjust kings have humbled themselves...and whose hand breaks the strongest scepters;...I address myself graciously to you, Amir Isma'il, chief of the troops of Persia...and predestined to perish...in order to make known to you that the works emanating from the Almighty are not the fragile products of caprice or folly, but make up an infinity of mysteries impenetrable to the human mind. The Lord Himself says in His holy book: "We have not created the heavens and the earth in order to play a game" [*Qur'an*, 21:16]. Man, who is the noblest of the creatures and the summary of the marvels of God, is in consequence on earth the living image of the Creator. It is He who has set up Caliphs on earth, because, joining faculties of soul with perfection of body, man is the only being who can comprehend the attributes of the divinity and adore its sublime beauties; but because he possesses this rare intelligence, he attains this divine knowledge only in our religion, and by observing the precepts of the prince of prophets, the Caliph of Caliphs, the right are of the God of Mercy; it is then only by practicing the true religion that man will prosper in this world and merit eternal life in the other. As to you, Amir Isma'il, such a recompense will not be your lot; because you have denied the sanctity of the divine laws; because you have deserted the path of salvation and the sacred commandments; because you have impaired the purity of the dogmas of Islam; because you have dishonored, soiled, and destroyed the altars of the Lord, usurped the scepter of the East by unlawful and tyrannical means; because coming forth from the dust, you have raised yourself by odious devices to a place shining with splendor and magnificence; because you have opened to Muslims the gates of tyranny and oppression; because you have joined iniquity, perjury, and blasphemy to your sectarian impiety; because under the cloak of the hypocrite, you have sowed everywhere trouble and sedition; because you have raised the standard of irreligion and heresy; because yielding to the impulse of your evil passions, and giving yourself up without rein to the most infamous disorders, you have dared to throw off the control of Muslim laws and to permit lust and rape, the massacre of the most virtuous and respectable men, the destruction of pulpits and temples...the repudiation of the *Qur'an*, the cursing of the legitimate Caliphs. Now as the first duty of a Muslim and above all of a pious prince is to obey the commandment, "O, you faithful who believe, be the executors of the decrees of God!" the ulama [religious leadership] and our doctors have pronounced sentence of death against you, perjurer and blasphemer, and have imposed on every Muslim the sacred obligation to arm in defense of religion and destroy heresy and impiety in your person and that of all your partisans.

Animated by this [religious decree], conforming to the *Qur'an*, the code of divine laws, and wishing on one side to strengthen Islam, on the other to liberate the lands and peoples who writhe under your yoke, we have resolved to lay aside our imperial robes in order to put on the shelf and coat of mail, to raise our ever victorious banner, to assemble our invincible armies, to take up the gauntlet of the avenger, to march with our soldiers, whose sword strikes mortal blows...In pursuit of this noble resolution, we have entered upon the campaign, and guided by the hand of the Almighty, we hope soon to strike down your tyrannous arm, blow away the clouds of glory and grandeur which trouble your head and cause your fatal blindness, release from your despotism your trembling subjects, smother you in the end in the very mass of flames which your infernal [spirit] raises everywhere along your passage, accomplishing in this way on you the maxim which says: "He who sows discord can only reap evils and afflictions." However, anxious to conform to the spirit of the law of the Prophet, we come, before commencing war, to set out before you the words of the *Qur'an*, in place of the sword, and to exhort you to embrace the true faith; this is why we address this letter to you...

But if, to your misfortune, you persist in your past conduct; if, puffed up with the idea of your power and your foolish bravado, you wish to pursue the course of your iniquities, you will see in a few days your plains covered with our tents and inundated with our battalions. Then prodigies of valor will be done, and we shall see the decrees of the Almighty, Who is the God of Armies, and sovereign judge of the actions of men, accomplished. For the rest, victory to him who follows the path of salvation!

Ogier Ghiselin de Busbecq, "Süleyman the Lawgiver"

The energy of the Ottoman Empire perhaps reached its zenith under the direction of Sultan Süleyman "the Lawgiver" (r. 1520–1566 CE). One of the most important assessments of Süleyman's influence came from Ogier Ghiselin de Busbecq, the ambassador from Austria to Süleyman's court at Istanbul from 1554–1562. Busbecq had been dispatched in the recent wake of the unsuccessful Ottoman siege of Vienna in 1529, and his mission was to use his diplomatic skills to prevent another possible attack on the city. Busbecq's letters reveal much about Süleyman, his court, capital, Islamic traditions, and treatment of women.

Source: *C. T. Foster and F. H. Blackburne Daniell, "Süleyman the Lawgiver," in* The Life and Letters of Ogier Ghiselin de Busbecq, vol. 1 *(London: Hakluyt Society, 1881), pp. 152–156.*

Focus Questions:
1. What are the most important qualities for success and advancement in the Ottoman empire?
2. Busbecq maintained that between Christians and Muslims, "one of us must prevail and the other be destroyed." Why did he think Christian nations were at a disadvantage?
3. By painting such a picture, was Busbecq hoping to frighten European nations into reform?
4. What are the most important qualities for success and advancement in the Ottoman Empire?

The Sultan [Süleyman "The Lawgiver"] was seated on a very low ottoman, not more than a foot from the ground, which was covered with a quantity of costly rugs and cushions of exquisite workmanship; near him lay his bow and arrows...The Sultan then listened to what I had to say; but the language I used was not at all to his taste, for the demands of his Majesty breathed a spirit of independence and dignity, which was by no means acceptable to one who deemed that his wish was law; and so he made no answer beyond saying in an impatient way, "Giusel, giusel," that is, "well, well." After this we were dismissed to our quarters.

The Sultan's hall was crowded with people, among whom were several officers of high rank. Besides these, there were all the troopers of the Imperial guard, and a large force of Janissaries [the elite infantry corps], but there was not in all that great assembly a single man who owed his position to anything save his valor and his merit. No distinction is attached to birth among the Turks; the respect to be paid to a man is measured by the position he holds in the public service. There is no fighting for precedence; a man's place is marked out by the duties he discharge...It is by merit that men rise in the service, a system which ensures that posts should only be assigned to the competent. Each man in Turkey carries in his own hand his ancestry and his position in life, which he may make or mar as he will. Those who receive the highest offices from the Sultan are for the most part the sons of shepherds or herdsmen, and so far from being ashamed of their parentage, they actually glory in it, and consider it a matter of boasting that they owe nothing to the accident of birth; for they do not believe that high qualities are either natural or hereditary, nor do they think that they can be handed down from father to son, but that they are partly the gift of God, and partly the result of good training, great industry, and unwearied zeal; arguing that high qualities do not descend from a father to his son or heir, any more than a talent for music, mathematics, or the like...Among the Turks, therefore, honors, high posts, and judgeships are the rewards of great ability and good service. If a man is dishonest, or lazy, or careless, he remains at the bottom of the ladder, an object of contempt; for such qualities there are no honors in Turkey!

This is the reason that they are successful in their undertakings, that they lord it over others, and are daily extending the bounds of their empire. These are not our ideas, with us there is no opening left for merit; birth is the standard for everything; the prestige of birth is the sole key to advancement in the public service.

The Turkish monarch going to war takes with him over 40,000 camels and nearly as many baggage mules, of which a great part, when he is invading Persia, are loaded with rice and other kinds of grain. These mules and camels also serve to carry tents and armor, and likewise tools and munitions for the campaign...The invading army carefully abstains from encroaching on its supplies at the outset, as they are well aware that, when the season for campaigning draws to a close, they will have to retreat over districts wasted by the enemy, or scraped as bare by countless hordes of men and droves of baggage animals, as if they had been devastated by locusts; accordingly they reserve their stores as much as possible for this emergency...

From this you will see that it is the patience, self denial, and thrift of the Turkish soldier that enable him to face the most trying circumstances, and come safely out of the dangers that surround him. What a contrast to our men!...

For each man is his own worst enemy, and has no foe more deadly than his own intemperance, which is sure to kill him, if the enemy be not quick. It makes me shudder to think of what the result of a struggle between such different systems must be; one of us must prevail and the other be destroyed, at any rate we cannot both exist in safety. On their side is the vast wealth of their empire, unimpaired resources, experience and practice in arms, a veteran soldiery, an uninterrupted series of victories, readiness to endure hardships, union, order, discipline, thrift, and watchfulness. On ours are found an empty exchequer, luxurious habits, exhausted resources, broken spirits, a raw and insubordinate soldiery, and greedy generals; there is no regard for discipline, license runs riot, the men indulge in drunkenness and debauchery, and, worst of all, the enemy are accustomed to victory, we, to defeat. Can we doubt what the result must be?

Ogier Ghiselin de Busbecq, Excerpt from "Women in Ottoman Society"

The energy of the Ottoman Empire perhaps reached its zenith under the direction of Sultan Süleyman "The Lawgiver" (r. 1520–1566 CE). One of the most important assessments of Süleyman's influence came from Ogier Ghiselin de Busbecq, the ambassador from Austria to Süleyman's court at Istanbul from 1554–1562. Busbecq had been dispatched in the recent wake of the unsuccessful Ottoman siege of Vienna in 1529, and his mission was to use his diplomatic skills to prevent another possible attack on the city. Busbecq's letters reveal much about Süleyman, his court, capital, Islamic traditions, and treatment of women.

Source: *C. T. Foster and F. H. Blackburne Daniell, "Women in Ottoman Society," in* The Life and Letters of Ogier Ghiselin de Busbecq, vol. 1, *(London: Hakluyt Society, 1881) pp. 219–221.*

Focus Questions:
1. What is the role of women in Ottoman society?
2. Why are women completely covered in Ottoman society? What were the expectations for women at this time and what distinctions were made between wives and concubines?

The Turks are the most careful people in the world of the modesty of their wives, and therefore keep them shut up at home and hide them away, so that they scarce see the light of day. But if they have to go into the streets, they are sent out so covered and wrapped up in veils that they seem to those who meet them mere gliding ghosts. They have the means of seeing men through their linen or silken veils, while no part of their own body is exposed to men's view. For it is a received opinion among them, that no woman who is distinguished in the very smallest degree by her figure or youth, can be seen by a man without his desiring her, and therefore without her receiving some contamination; and so it is the universal practice to confine the women to the harem. Their brothers are allowed to see them, but not their brothers-in-law. Men of the richer classes, or of higher rank, make it a condition when they marry, that their wives shall never set foot outside the threshold, and that no man or woman shall be admitted to see them for any reason whatever, not even their nearest relations, except their fathers and mothers, who are allowed to pay a visit to their daughters at the [festival of Bairam].

On the other hand, if the wife has a rather high rank, or has brought a larger dowry than usual, the husband promises on his part that he will take no concubine, but will keep to her alone. Otherwise, the Turks are not forbidden by any law to have as many concubines as they please in addition to their lawful wives. Between the children of wives and those of concubines there is no distinction, and they are considered to have equal rights. As for concubines, they either buy them for themselves or win them in war; when they are tired of them there is nothing to prevent their bringing them to market and selling them; but they are entitled to their freedom if they have borne children to their master...The only distinction between the lawful wife and the concubine, is that the former has a dowry, while the slaves have none. A wife who has a portion settled on her [a dowry] is mistress of her husband's house, and all the other women have to obey her orders. The husband, however, may choose which of them shall spend the night with him. He makes known his wishes to the wife, and she sends to him the slave he has selected...Only Friday night...is supposed to belong to the wife; and she grumbles if her husband deprives her of it. On all the other nights he may do so as he pleases.

Divorces are granted among them for many reasons which it is easy for the husbands to invent. The divorced wife receives back her dowry, unless the divorce has been caused by some fault on her part. There is more difficulty in a woman's getting a divorce from her husband.

Paul Rycaut on the State of the Ottoman Empire, 1668

Militarily speaking, the strongest force in the West during the 16th and 17th centuries CE was that of the Ottoman Turks. From being an obscure Muslim nation, the Ottomans emerged with a vengeance in the 15th century, capturing Constantinople in 1453, and ultimately establishing hegemony over the Balkans, North Africa, the Arabian peninsula, and the western portion of the Near East. Ottoman armies kept European powers under constant pressure, besieging Vienna in 1527 and 1683. Few Westerners were permitted to observe conditions within the mysterious Ottoman state; the following observations date from 1668.

Source: *Harry Schwartz, ed., Paul Rycaut,* The Present State of the Ottoman Empire *(N.Y.: Arno Press & New York Times, 1971), pp. 3–5, 167, 190–191.*

Focus Questions:
1. What conclusions does Rycaut reach as to the tyrannical slant of Ottoman government? Does he envision the possibility or desirability of reform?
2. What attitude do the Turks assume towards dogs and camels?
3. Who are the Jannisaries and how are they recruited?

In this Government, severity, violence, and cruelty are natural to it; and it were as great an errour [sic] to begin to loose the reigns, and ease the people of that oppression to which they and their fore-fathers have since their first original have been accustomed, as it would be in a nation free-born, and used to live under the protection of good laws, and the clemency of a virtuous and Christian Prince, to exercise a Tyrannical power over their estates and lives, and change their liberty into servitude and slavery. The *Turks* had the original of their Civil Government founded in the time of war: for when they first came out of *Scythia*, and took arms in their hands, and submitted unto one General, it is to be supposed, that they had no Laws but what were Arbitrary and Martial, and most agreeable to the enterprise and design they had then in hand, when *Tangrolipix* overthrew the *Persian Sultan*; possessed himself of his Dominions and Power, and called and opened the way for his companions out of *Armenia*; when *Cutlumuses* revolted from him, and made a distinct kingdom in *Arabia*: when other Princes of the *Selcuccian* family in the infancy of Turkish power had by wars among themselves, or by Testament made division of their possessions; when *(Anno 1300) Ottoman*, by strange fortunes, and from small beginnings swallowed up all the other Governments into the *Ogusian* Tribe, and united them under one head, until at last it arrived to that greatness and power it now enjoys. The whole condition of this people was but a continued state of war; wherefore it is not strange, if their laws are severe, and in most things arbitrary; that the Emperor should be absolute and above law, and that most of their customs should run in a certain channel and course not answerable to the height and unlimited power of the Governour, and consequently to the oppression and subjection of the people: and that they should thrive most by servitude, be most happy, prosperous and contented under Tyranny, is as natural to them, as to a body to be nourished with that diet, which it had from its infancy or birth been acquainted with. But not only is Tyranny requisite for this people, and a stiff rein to curb them, left by an unknown liberty, they grow mutinous and unruly, but likewise the large territories and remote parts of the Empire require speedy preventions, without processes of law, or formal indictment: jealousie and suspition [sic] of mis-government being license and authority enough for the Emperour to inflict his severest punishments: all which depends on the absoluteness of the Prince; which because it is that whereby the *Turks* are principally supported in their greatness, and is the prime Maxim and Foundation of their State, we shall make it the discourse and subject of the following Chapter.

...

The *Turks* having (as is before declared) laid the first foundation of their Government with the principles most agreeable to Military Discipline, their Generals or Princes, whose will and lusts they served, became absolute Masters of their Lives and Estates; so that what they gained and acquired by the Sword with labours, perils, and sufferings, was appropriated to the use and benefit of their Great Master. All the delightful fields of *Asia*, the pleasant plains of *Tempe* and *Thrace*, all the plenty of Egypt and fruitfulness of the Nile, the luxury of Corinth, the substance of *Peleponesus*, *Athens*, *Lemnos*, *Scio*, and *Mitylen*, with other Isles of the *Ægean* Sea, the Spices of *Arabia*, and the riches of a great part of *Persia*, all *Armenia*, the Provinces of *Pontus*, *Galatia*, *Bythinia*, *Phrygia*, *Lycia*, *Pamphylia*, **Palestine**, *Cœlostria*, and *Phœnicia*, *Colchis*, and a great part of *Georgia*, the tributary principalities of *Moldavia* and *Valachia*, *Romania*, *Bulgaria* and *Servia*, and the best part of *Hungary*, concur all together to satisfise the appetite of one single person; all the extent of this vast territory, the Lands and Houses, as well as the Castles and Arms, are the proper goods of the Grand Signior, in his sole disposal and gift they remain, whose possession and right they are; only to lands dedicated to religious use...

...

Those who would appear of a compassionate and tender nature, hold it a pious work to buy a Bird from a cage to give him his liberty; and hold it a merciful action to buy bread and feed the Dogs, of which there is a great number of diseased Curs in all streets appropriate to no Master, but are mangy and foul, and no small causes of breeding the Plague, so frequent in all the Cities of the *Turks*. And this care of Dogs is accounted so charitable, that there are certain laws made for the protection and maintenance of them: and it is a lighter offense to deny bread to a poor Christian who is famished in his chains, then to the Dogs of their street, which are fit for nothing but to breed Infection; and some bind themselves by a vow to give such a quantity of bread a day to the Dogs of such a street, others bequeath it by Testament; for they maintain their quarters from other wandering Curs, and joyn [sic] together in a strange manner to preserve certain limits free from others that are not whelped and bred amongst them.

The Camel is another sort of Beast to which the *Turks* bear not only a love, but a Religious reverence, accounting it a greater sin to over-burthen and tyre them with too much labour than the Horse, because it is the Beast most contmon [sic] to the Holy parts of *Arabia*, and carries the *Alchoran* in Pilgrimage; so that I have observed those who have the government of the *Camels*, when they have given water to them in a Bason, to take of the foam or froth that comes from the mouth of the Beast, and with that, as if it were some rare Balsome, with a singular devotion to anoint their Beards...

...

The next main sinew of the *Ottoman* Power is the order of the *Janizaries*, which is as much as to say, the new Militia; and yet their Antiquity may be deduced from *Ottoman* the first King of the Turks; but because they received honours and priviledges [sic] from *Amurath* their third King; our Turkish History accounts that to be the time of the first original: it is certain that in his time they were modelized [sic], and certain Laws prescribed both for their education and maintenance; when by the counsel of *Catradin*, otherwise called *Kara Rustbenes*, *Amurath's* prime Vizier, it was ordained that for the augmentation of this Militia, every fifth Captive taken from the Christians, above the age of 15 years, should be the dues of the *Sultan* who at first were to be distributed amongst the Turkish Husbandmen in *Asia*, to learn and be instructed in the Turkish Language and Religion.

Their number at first was not accounted above 6 or 7000, now with time they are encreased [sic] to the number of twenty thousand effective men; but were there a list taken of all those who assume this title of *Janizary*, and enjoy their priviledges though not their pay, there would be found above a hundred thousand; six or seven go under the name of one *Janizary*, for gaining by this means a priviledge of being free from all Duties and Taxes, they bestow a certain summe of money or annual presents on the Officers, in consideration of which they are owned and countenanced as *Janizaries*. Their Habit is as the Picture represents, wearing alwaies the beard of their Chin and underlip shaven, which some say they learned from the *Italians*; but certain it is, that this Custom is more ancient, than since the time of their Neighbourhood unto *Italy*: this manner of their shaving being generally used as a token of their subjection, and so all the Pages and Officers in the *Seraglio* of great men, orders of the Gardeners, *Baltagees* or Hatchetmen and others are distinguished by this mark to be in service and obliged to the attendance of a Master: But when they are either licensed from the War, or promoted to Office, or freed to their own disposal, they immediately suffer their Beards to grow as a signe of their liberty and gravity.

In former times this Militia consisted only of the Sons of Christians, educated in the Mahometan Rights; but of late that politick Custom hath been disused, the reason of which some attribute to the abundance of people the *Turks* having of their own to supply all their occasions: but I am rather induced to another opinion, having not observed the multitude which Histories and Travellers tell us, that the Turks swarm with; and rather assigne the neglect of this practice, so prejudicial to Christian Interest in these parts, to the corruption of the Officers, and the carelessness in their Discipline.

Fathers Simon and Vincent Report on Shah Abbas I, the Safavid Ruler of Persia

The Safavid state in Persia had been built upon a fervent commitment to the Shi'ite sect of Islam. The greatest Safavid ruler, Shah Abbas I (r. 1588–1629 CE) had inherited his throne at a difficult time. His father had been forced to abdicate and much of his empire was on the brink of disintegration. Ottoman invaders from the west and Uzbecs from the east had placed tremendous pressure on the new monarch. But within fifteen years, Abbas I had defeated both groups and the Mughals in India as well by 1621, securing more territory and trading posts in the Persian Gulf. He then focused on international trade and manufacturing and on protecting his territories through diplomatic contacts.

In executing this strategy, Shah Abbas I cultivated relations with several European countries whose skills in war and technology were of the highest importance. Abbas was more interested in European gunsmiths than in the vagaries of Muslim doctrine. As a result, he allowed European missionaries to visit his realm and openly seek converts among his Muslim population. The following accounts are from Fathers Simon and Vincent, Carmelite friars dispatched to Abbas's capital at Isfahan in 1605. They spent six months gathering information and then made their report to Pope Paul V.

Source: *Robert Simon, "Shah Abbas I," A Chronicle of the Carmelites in Persia and the Papal Mission of the Seventeenth and Eighteenth Centuries (London: Eyre and Spottiswoode, 1939), pp. 158–161.*

Focus Questions:
1. What qualities made Shah Abbas I an effective leader?
2. According to Father Simon, why was Shah Abbas I both loved and feared?
3. Father Simon noted that "no one knows what [Shah Abbas I] believes." Was the Shah a devout Muslim? Why did he provide Christian churchmen with such flexibility in trying to convert Muslims in his realm? What does this say about Shah Abbas I as a political and religious leader?
4. What was Father Vincent's argument in rejecting the charge that Catholics were idolators?
5. Father Vincent stated that, "the English are heretics and false Christians and that Roman Catholics are the true Christians." Compare this with Sultan Selim I's argument in rejecting the Shi'ite sect that Sunni Muslims were the "true religion." What does this tell you about sectarian disputes within a religion? Which is the "true religion"?

SHAH ABBAS I

FATHER SIMON

The king, Shah Abbas...is [43] years old...of medium height, rather thin than fat, his face round and small, tanned by the sun, with hardly any beard; very vivacious and alert, so that he is always doing something or other. He is sturdy and healthy, accustomed to much exercise and toil: many times he goes about on foot, and recently he had been forty days on pilgrimage, which he made on foot the whole time. He has extraordinary strength, and with his scimitar can cut a man in two and a sheep with its wool on at a single blow—and the Persian sheep are of large size. He has done many other feats and has found no one to come up to him in them. In his food he is frugal, as also in his dress, and this to set an example to his subjects; and so in public he eats little else than rice, and that cooked in water only. His usual dress is of linen, and very plain: similarly the nobles and others in his realm follow suit, whereas formerly they used to go out dressed in brocade with jewels and other fopperies: and if he sees anyone who is overdressed, he takes him to task, especially if it be a soldier. But in private, he eats what he likes.

He is sagacious in mind, likes fame and to be esteemed: he is courteous in dealing with everyone and at the same time very serious. For he will go through the public streets, eat from what they are selling there and other things, speak at ease freely with the lower classes, cause his subjects to remain sitting while he himself is standing, or will sit down beside this man and that. He says that is how to be a king, and that the king of Spain and other Christians do not get any pleasure out of ruling, because they are obliged to comport themselves with so much pomp and majesty.

He causes foreigners to sit down beside him and to eat at his table. With that and accompanying all such informality he requires that people shall not [lack] respect toward him and, should anyone fail in this regard, he will punish the individual severely. So the more he demonstrates kindliness to his subjects and the more familiarly he talks with them, they tremble before him, even the greatest among them, for, while joking, he will have their heads cut off. He is very strict in executing justice and pays no regard to his own favorites in this respect; but rather is the stricter with them in order to serve an example to others. So he has no private friends, nor anyone who has influence with him...While we were at Court, he caused the bellies of two of his favorites to be ripped open, because they behaved improperly to an ordinary woman. From this it comes about that there are so very few murderers and robbers. In all the time I was at Isfahan, there was never a case of homicide.

He is very speedy in dispatching business: when he gives audience, which he does at the gate of his palace...he finishes off all the cases that are brought to him. The parties stand present before him, the officers of justice, and his own council, with whom he consults when it pleases him. The sentence which he gives is final and is immediately executed. If the guilty party deserves death, they kill him at once...

Because of the great obedience [the nobles] pay the Shah, when he wills to have one of the nobles killed, he dispatches one of his men to fetch the noble's head: the man goes off to the grandee, and says to him: "The Shah wants your head." The noble replies: "Very well," and lets himself be decapitated—otherwise he would lose it and with it, all his family would become extinct. But, when [the nobles] allow themselves to be decapitated, [the Shah] aggrandizes the children...

Regarding the religion of the king, I think that no one knows what he believes: he does not observe the Muslim law in many things, nor is he a Christian. Six or seven years ago he displayed many signs of not being averse to our Faith: God knows whether they were feigned, or came from his heart. In his [harem] he has many Christian Armenian, Georgian, and Circassian women. I think that he lets them live as they wish, because when I enquired what the Shah did with so many [holy] pictures that were presented to him as gifts and some relics of the Saints, for which he asked, the answer was made to me that he used to give them to the women in his harem. Besides that he is well informed regarding the mysteries of our holy Faith and discourses on the mystery of the most holy Trinity: he knows many examples and allusions which the Saints give in order to prove it, and discourses about the other mysteries—which we know from a man who had the opportunity of hearing him—if he does not talk about the women in his harem or about some demon or other. On account of the many disappointments which he asserts the Christians have caused him all this fervor has cooled. With all that he does not detest them. For he converses and eats with them, he suffers us to say frankly what we believe about our Faith and his own: sometimes he asks us about this. To us he has given a house: he knows that we say Mass publicly, he allows whoever may wish among the Persians to come to it, and we can teach them freely regarding our holy Faith, whenever they make inquiries about it...I believe that the king realizes the objective with which our friars go out there. Till now none of them has been converted: I think they are waiting for one of the nobles or of their [religious leaders] to break the ice...

THE WORSHIP OF IDOLS

FATHER VINCENT

Two days previously the English had been with the king and discoursed at great length on the matter of religion and spoken ill of the Catholics saying that they were idolaters, who adored pictures and images, and made the sign of the cross, etc. The Shah had said that he would bring the Fathers together with them, so that they might hold a disputation on these matters.

This was the motive why the king of Persia asked the Fathers about the difference there is between Catholics and English. The Father Visitor answered that the English are heretics and false Christians and that Roman Catholics are the true Christians...

In order to convince him, the Fathers put the question to the king: "Because your Highness and your people prostrate yourselves and worship seals and beads made of earth, would it be right for us to call your Highness and your people idolaters? Certainly not, because we know that, when you perform that act of adoration, you do not mean by it that the seal and stone are God, but do it out of piety and reverence for that soil, as it comes from the places of sepulture of your ancestors and that great men whom you consider saints." The Shah answered: "That is not the chief reason and intention we have for worshiping on earthen seals and beads, but rather in that act of veneration we make an act of recognizing that we are clay, and that from earth God created us, and we adore the Creator of this: and the reason why in the mosques and in our houses while we say our prayers on matting and carpets, our prayers would not be lawful and acceptable, unless we said them [touching] the earth. With this in view, for more convenience and cleanliness we use the earthen medallions [to touch with our foreheads during prayer] and beads: and that they are of this or that soil is an accidental matter: it suffices that it be earth. And so, when we have any other sort of stone, even if it be a piece of rock, we have no need of a seal. It is also true that we venerate it (the seal) as a memorial and a pious object, as you say, but not mainly for that reason."

To this the Fathers replied: "Very good! And thus our Christian religion does not adore nor serve images, as if they were gods, nor does it expect from them the future judgment (God preserve us from such a thing!), but it venerates images for the things they represent. They serve us also as memorials to remind us of the virtues of those saints they represent, in order that we may imitate them and beg them to intercede by their prayers with our Lord God, that He will grant us what we ask and that we may be good and his servants, as they have been, so that we may attain the glory which they now enjoy. So that, just as your Highness and your people do not say that the earthen medallion is God, no more do we say that the statues of the saints are gods, nor do we adore them as such." With these reasonings the Shah and his courtiers remained content.

Excerpts from the Biography of Shah Abbas I

Persia, under the remarkable Safavid Dynasty, was the sole Middle Eastern power able to meet the Ottomans on equal terms—and the two great Islamic states were often in conflict. Persia was Shiite in its religious orientation while the Ottomans adhered to the Sunni variety of Islam. The most outstanding Safavid Emperor was Shah Abbas the Great (1588–1629 CE), whose capital at Isfahan was fabled to be one of the wealthiest and most beautiful cities of the East. A portrait of Shah Abbas has been bequeathed to us through the biography written by his secretary, Eskander Bey Monshi (1560–1632?).

Source: *Roger M. Savory, trans.,* Eskander Bey Monshi: History of Shah Abbas the Great, Vol. 1 *(Boulder, CO: Westview Press, 1978), pp. 523, 527–529, 531, 533.*

Focus Questions:
1. To what extent was clemency a part of Shah Abbas' policy? To what degree was severity employed? Which predominated?
2. What novelties in policy does Eskander seem to indicate derived their inspiration from the Shah?
3. What does Eskander indicate about the Shah's personality?
4. Reading between the lines of Eskander's biography of the Shah, what would it be like to live in the state administered by Shah Abbas? Do the positives outweigh the negatives, or vice-versa? Explain.

DISCOURSE 5

On Shah 'Abbas's Justice, Concern for the Security of the Roads, and Concern for the Welfare of His Subjects

The greater part of governing is the preservation of stability within the kingdom and security on the roads. Prior to the accession of Shah 'Abbas, this peace and security had disappeared in Iran, and it had become extremely difficult for people to travel about the country. As soon as he came to the throne, Shah 'Abbas turned his attention to this problem. He called for the principal highway robbers in each province to be identified, and he then set about eliminating this class of people. Within a short space of time, most of their leaders had been arrested. Some of them, who had been driven by misfortune to adopt this way of life, were pardoned by Shah 'Abbas and their troubles solved by various forms of royal favor. Overwhelmed by this display of royal clemency, these men swore to serve the king and to behave as law-abiding citizens. Others, however, were handed over to the *sahna* (a police official) for punishment, and society was rid of this scourge. With security restored to the roads, merchants and tradesmen traveled to and from the Safavid empire.

The welfare of his people was always a prime concern of the Shah, and he was at pains to see that the people enjoyed peace and security, and that oppression by officialdom, the major cause of anxiety on the part of the common man, was totally stamped out in his kingdom. Substantial reductions were made in the taxes due to the *di van*: first, the tax on flocks in Iraq, amounting to nearly fifteen thousand Iraqi *toman*, was remitted to the people of that province, and the population of Iraq, which is the flourishing heart of Iran and the seat of government, by this gift was preferred above the other provinces. Second, all *di van* levies were waived for all Shi'ites throughout the empire during the month of Ramazan. The total revenues for one month, which according to the computation of the *di van* officials amounted to some twenty thousand *toman*, were given to the people as alms. The object was that they should be free from demands for taxes during this blessed month, which is a time to be devoted to the service and worship of God.

DISCOURSE 7

On Shah 'Abbas's Policy-making and Administration

If scholars consider Sha 'Abbas to be the founder of the laws of the realm and an example in this regard to the princes of the world, they have justification for this opinion, for he has been responsible for some weighty legislation in the field of administration.

One of his principal pieces of legislation has been his reform of the army. Because the rivalries of the *qezelbas* tribes had led them to commit all sorts of enormities, and because their devotion to the Safavid royal house had been weakened by dissension, Shah 'Abbas decided (as the result of divine inspiration, which is vouchsafed to kings but not to ordinary mortals), to admit into the armed forces groups other than the *qezelbas*. He enrolled in the armed forces large numbers of Georgian, Circassian, and other *golams*, and created the office of *qollar-aqasi* commander-in-chief of the *golam* regiments), which had not previously existed under the Safavid regime. Several thousand men were drafted into regiments of musketeers from the Cagatay tribe, and from various Arab and Persian tribes in Khorasan, Azerbaijan, and Tabarestan. Into the regiments of musketeers, too, were drafted all the riff-fall from every province—sturdy, serviceable men who were unemployed and preyed on the lower classes of society. By this means the lower classes were given relief from their lawless activities, and the recruits made amends for their past sins by performing useful service in the army. All these men were placed on the golam muster rolls. Without question, they were an essential element in 'Abbas' conquests, and their employment had many advantages.

Shah 'Abbas tightened up provincial administration. Any emir or noble who was awarded a provincial governorship, or who was charged with the security of the highways, received his office on the understanding that he discharge his duties in a proper manner. If any merchant or traveler or resident were robbed, it was the duty of the governor to recover his money for him or replace it out of his own funds. This rule was enforced throughout the Safavid empire. As a result, property was secure, and people could travel without hindrance to and from Iran.

Another of Shah 'Abbas' policies has been to demand a truthful reply whenever he asked anyone for information. Lying, he said, is forbidden and considered a sin by God, so why should it not be a sin to lie to him who is one's king, one's spiritual director, and one's benefactor? Is not falsehood to such a one ingratitude? In the opinion of Shah 'Abbas, lying to one's benefactor constituted the rankest ingratitude. If he detected anyone in a lie, he visited punishment upon him. The effects of this policy have been felt at all levels of society. For example, if someone has committed various acts that merit the death penalty and the king questions him on his conduct, the poor wretch has no option but to tell the truth. In fact, the opinion is commonly held that, if a person tells a lie to the Shah, the latter intuitively knows he is lying. The result is that the biggest scoundrel alive hesitates to allow even a small element of falsehood to creep into any story he is telling the Shah. The beneficial effects of this on government and the administration of justice need no elaboration.

DISCOURSE 8

On His Simplicity of Life, Lack of Ceremony, and Some Contrary Qualities

The character of the Shah contains some contradictions; for instance, his fiery temper, his imperiousness, his majesty, and regal splendor are matched by his mildness, leniency, his ascetic way of life, and his immortality. His is equally at home on the dervish's mat and the royal throne. When he is in good temper, he mixes with the greatest informality with the members of his household, his close friends and retainers with others, and treats them like brothers. In contrast, when he is in a towering rage, his aspect is so terrifying that the same man who, shortly before, was his boon companion and was treated with all the informality of a close friend, dares not to speak a word out of turn for fear of being accused of insolence or discourtesy. At such times, the emirs, sultans, and even the court wits and his boon companions keep silent, for fear of the consequences. The Shah, then, possesses these two contrasting natures, each of which is developed to the last degree.

DISCOURSE 9

On Shah 'Abbas's Concern for the Rights of His Servants and His Avoiding Laying Hands on Their Possessions

One of the most agreeable qualities of this monarch is his compassionate treatment of his servants, which is coupled with a concern that faithful service should receive its just reward. His record in this regard is so outstanding that it is not matched by that of any other chivalrous prince. As long as his servants are constant in their loyalty, the royal favor is lavished upon them, nor is it withdrawn for any trifling offense committed out of ignorance or from negligence. If any of his servants dies from natural causes, or gives his life in battle in the defense of the faith and the state, the Shah is generous in his treatment of their dependents. In the case of officeholders, even if their sons are too young at the time of their father's death to be fit for office, nevertheless, in order to resuscitate their families, he confers the same office on the sons out of his natural generosity and magnanimity.

Moreover, since the Shah considers the possessions and treasures of this world of little value, even if the deceased has left substantial sums of money, such is the Shah's magnanimity and concern to follow the prescripts of canon law that he (unlike the majority of princes) does not lay covetous eyes on the inheritance, but divides it among the heirs in the proportions ordained by God. This is regarded by some as his most praiseworthy characteristic, for most of the princes of the world consider it impossible for them to show greater appreciation for their servants than by following this practice, which brings with it heavenly rewards.

DISCOURSE 10

On Shah 'Abbas's Breadth of Vision, and His Knowledge of World Affairs and of the Classes of Society

After he has dealt with the affairs of state, Shah 'Abbas habitually relaxes. He has always been fond of conviviality and, since he is still a young man, he enjoys wine and the company of women. But this does not affect the scrupulous discharge of his duties, and he knows in minute detail what is going on in Iran and also in the world outside. He has a well-developed intelligence system, with the result that no one, even if he is sitting at home with his family, can express opinions which should not be expressed without running the risk of their being reported to the Shah. This has actually happened on numerous occasions.

As regards his knowledge of the outside world, he possesses information about the rulers (both Muslim and non-Muslim) of other countries, about the size and composition of their armies, about their religious faith and the organization of their kingdoms, about their highway systems, and about the prosperity or otherwise of their realms. He has cultivated diplomatic relations with most of the princes of the world, and the rulers of the most distant parts of Europe, Russia, and India are on friendly terms with him. Foreign ambassadors bearing gifts are never absent from his court, and the Shah's achievements in the field of foreign relations exceed those of his predecessors.

Shah 'Abbas mixes freely with all classes of society, and in most cases is able to converse with people in their own particular idiom. He is well versed in Persian poetry; he understands it well, indulges in poetic license, and sometimes utters verses himself. He is a skilled musician, an outstanding composer of rounds, rhapsodies, and part-songs; some of his compositions are famous. As a conversationalist, he is capable of elegant and witty speech.